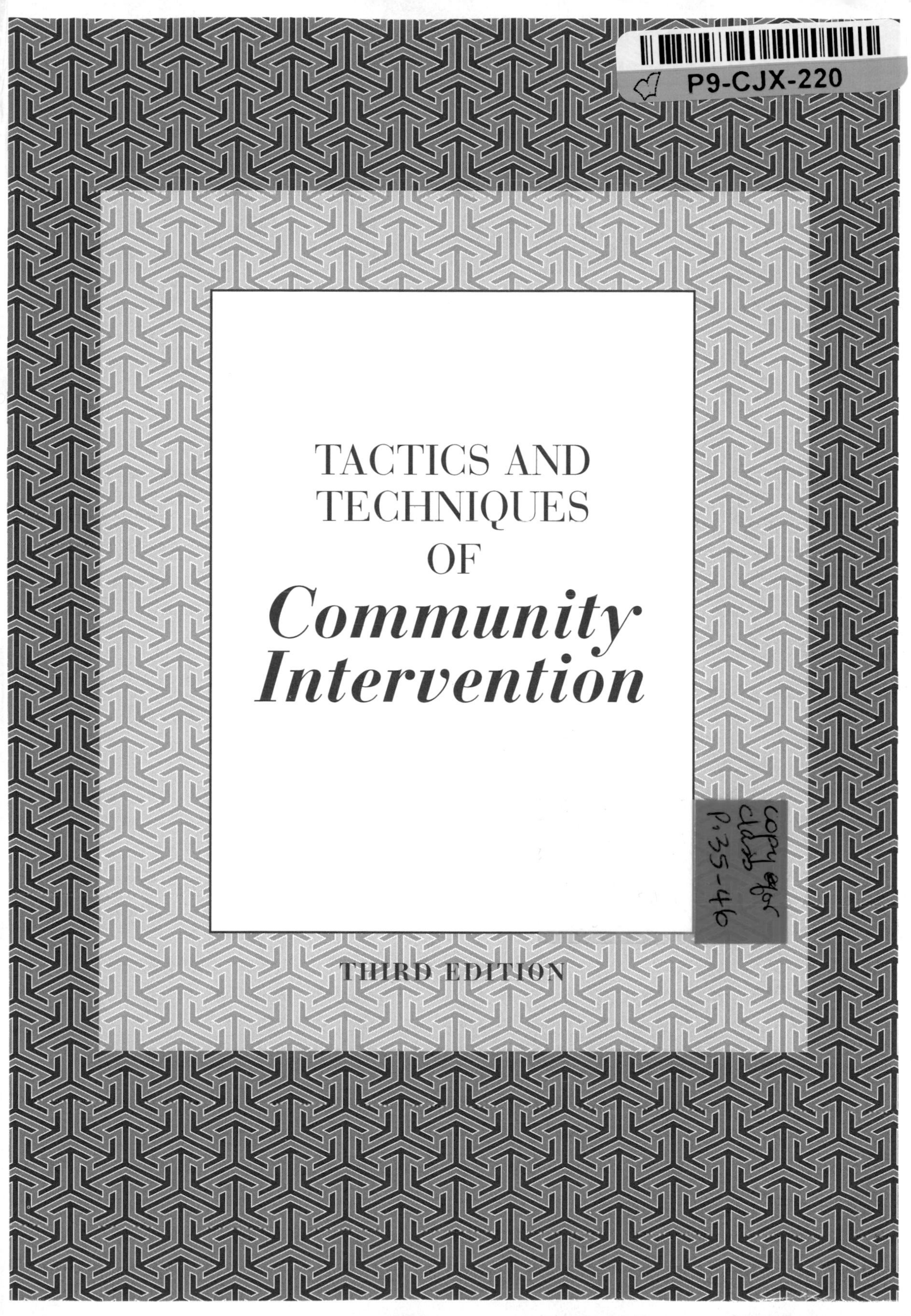
P9-CJX-220
TACTICS AND
TECHNIQUES
OF
Community
Intervention
THIRD EDITION

Ruth White
4/20/99

# TACTICS AND TECHNIQUES OF *Community Intervention*


*Editors*

**John E. Tropman**
University of Michigan

**John L. Erlich**
California State University, Sacramento

**Jack Rothman**
University of California, Los Angeles


THIRD EDITION

F.E. PEACOCK PUBLISHERS, INC.
ITASCA, ILLINOIS

*Library of Congress Catalog Card No. 94-66870*
*ISBN 0-87581-391-7*
*Printed in the United States of America*
*Printing: 10 9 8 7 6 5 4 3*
*Year: 00 99 98 97*

# Contents

**THANKS TO THE FOLLOWING AUTHORS AND PUBLISHERS**

"Need Identification and Program Planning in the Community Context" by Larry M. Siegel, C. Clifford Attkisson, and Linda G. Carson. Reprinted with the permission of the authors and Academic Press, Inc. from EVALUATION OF HUMAN SERVICE PROGRAMS edited by C. C. Attkisson, W. A. Hargreaves, M. J. Horowitz, and J. E. Sorensen. Copyright ©1978 by Academic Press, Inc.

"Analyzing the Human Service Agency" by Yeheskel Hasenfeld. Reprinted with the permission of the author and F. E. Peacock Publishers, Inc. Copyright ©1984 by F. E. Peacock Publishers, Inc.

"Ethnic-Sensitive Practice with Families" by Wynetta Devore and Elfreide Schlesinger. Reprinted with the permission of Macmillan Publishing Company from ETHNIC-SENSITIVE PRACTICE WITH FAMILIES by Wynetta Devore and Elfreide Schlesinger. Copyright ©1987 by Merrill Publishing Company an imprint of Macmillan Publishing Company, Inc.

"Know Yourself" by Stephen Burghardt. Reprinted with the permission of Sage Publications from ORGANIZING FOR COMMUNITY ACTION. Copyright ©1982 by Sage Publications, Inc.

"Value Conflicts and Decision Making: Analysis and Resolution" by John E. Tropman. Reprinted with the Permission of F. E. Peacock Publishers, Inc., from TACTICS AND TECHNIQUES OF COMMUNITY PRACTICE (Second Edition). Copyright ©1984 by F. E. Peacock Publishers, Inc.

"Introduction to Feminist Visions for Social Work" by Nan Van Den Bergh and Lynn B. Cooper. Reprinted with the permission of NASW Press from FEMINIST VISIONS FOR SOCIAL WORK. Copyright ©1986, National Association of Social Workers, Inc.

"Organizing with People of Color: A Perspective" by Felix G. Rivera and John L. Erlich. Reprinted with the permission of the authors from COMMUNITY ORGANIZING A DIVERSE SOCIETY edited by Felix G. Rivera and John L. Erlich, Allyn & Bacon, 1992.

"Leading and Managing Community Organizations in the '90s" by Jean M. Kruzich and Michael J. Austin. Reprinted with the permission of the authors.

"Women's Ways and Effective Management" by Roslyn H. Chernesky and Marcia J. Bombyk. Revised for this edition by Roslyn H. Chernesky. Reprinted with the permission of the authors and Sage Publications, Inc., from AFFILIA. Copyright ©1988 Women and Social Work, Inc.

"Innovative Management in Turbulent Times" by Karen Wolk Feinstein. Reprinted with the permission of The Haworth Press, Inc., 10 Alice St., Binghamton, N.Y. 13904, from ADMINISTRATION IN SOCIAL WORK, Vol. 9(3) pages 35–46. Copyright ©1985 by The Haworth Press, Inc.

"The Human Service Executive" by David M. Austin. Reprinted with the permission of The Haworth Press, Inc., 10 Alice St., Binghamton, N.Y. 13904, from ADMINISTRATION IN SOCIAL WORK, Vol. 13(3/4) pages 13–36. Copyright ©1989 by The Haworth Press, Inc.

"On-Site Analysis: A Practical Approach to Organizational Change" by Robert J. Myers, Peter Ufford, and Mary-Scot Magill. Reprinted with the permission of the authors and OSCA Publishing from INTRODUCTION TO ON-SITE ANALYSIS. Copyright ©1989 by OSCA Publishing.

"Desired Job Skills for Human Service Administrators" by Richard Hoefer. Reprinted with the permission of the author.

"Effective Second-Story Bureaucrats: Mastering the Paradox of Diversity" by Henry M. Havassy. Reprinted with the permission of NASW Press from SOCIAL WORK. Copyright ©1990 National Association of Social Workers, Inc.

"Policy Management in the Social Agency" by John E. Tropman. Reprinted with the permission of the author.

"Alternative Frameworks for Program Evaluation" by Robert O. Washington. Reprinted with the permission of the author.

"Effectiveness of Family Reunification Services: An Innovative Evaluative Model" by Peg McCartt Hess, G. Folaron, and A. B. Jefferson. Reprinted with the permission of NASW Press from SOCIAL WORK, Vol. 37 (4) (July 1992). Copyright © 1992 National Association of Social Workers, Inc.

"The Nitty Gritty of Program Evaluation: A Practical Guide" by William C. Birdsall and Roger W. Manela. Reprinted with the permission of the authors.

"The Politics of Program Evaluation" by Eleanor Chelimsky. Reprinted with the permission of Transaction from SOCIETY. Copyright ©1987 by Transaction.

"Code of Ethics of the National Association of Social Workers," and "Commentary" by Robert Cohen. Reprinted with the permission of NASW Press from NASW NEWS. Copyright ©1980 National Association of Social Workers, Inc., NASW NEWS, Vol. 25(4,5,6).

"Framework for Ethical Decision Making in Philanthropy: A Matrix of Relationships." Reprinted with the permission of the author. ©1992 by Lewis C. Rudolph.

"Guides to Making Ethical Decisions," found in *Ethical Decisions for Social Work Practice* by Frank Loewenberg and Ralph Dolgoff. Reprinted with the permission of F. E. Peacock Publishers, Inc. Copyright ©1984 by F. E. Peacock Publishers, Inc.

"Black Public Administrators and Opposing Expectations" by Mylon Winn. Reprinted by permission of Greenwood Publishing Group, Inc., Westport, CT, from CONTEMPORARY PUBLIC POLICY PERSPECTIVES AND BLACK AMERICANS, by Mylon Winn/edited by Mitchell F. Rice and Woodrow Jones, Jr. Copyright ©1984 by Mitchell F. Rice and Woodrow Jones, Jr., and published in 1984 by Greenwood Press.

"Experiences of Women Activists: Implications for Community Organizing Theory and Practice" by Cheryl Hyde. Reprinted with the permission of the School of Social Work at Western Michigan University from the JOURNAL OF SOCIOLOGY AND SOCIAL WELFARE. Copyright ©1986 by the School of Social Work at Western Michigan University.

"The Bare Bones of Personnel Management: The Job Description" by John Martin. Reprinted with the permission of the author.

"The Effective Meeting: How to Achieve High-Quality Decisions" by John E. Tropman and Gersh Morningstar. Reprinted with the permission of the authors.

"How to Use and Present Community Data" by Richard L. Douglass. Reprinted with the permission of the author.

"Troubleshooting Guide for Research and Evaluation" by John Gottman and Robert Clasen. Reprinted with the permission of F. E. Peacock Publishers, Inc. Copyright ©1984 by F. E. Peacock Publishers, Inc.

"Budgeting in Community Organizations: Principles for the '90s" by Marilyn L. Flynn. Reprinted with the permission of the author.

"Index of Dissimilarity and the Professional Unit Method of Analysis" by John E. Tropman and Elmer J. Tropman. Reprinted with the permission of the authors.

# Preface to the Third Edition

This edition of *Tactics* involves substantial changes over the last one, in both organization and content. The basic goal remains, however, to provide a "hands on," more "recipe-oriented" book for community practitioners, specifically, and for macro practitioners, generally. The aim is to offer some "how to do it" pieces that professionals can use as they get into the practicalities of social change implementation.

Perhaps the most obvious change is the title. The earlier version, *Tactics and Techniques of Community Practice*, was designed to be a companion title to *Strategies Of Community Organization*, as is this version. While the concept of pairing "Tactics" to "Strategy" remains solid, the definition of community organization has changed a bit, and we are seeking to take that into account.

In its early days, the term community organization was broadly inclusive, involving policy interests, administrative interests, and a broad range of styles of community intervention. Over the years, the phrases "community organization" and "community practice" have come to evoke more neighborhood-based kinds of community activities. And while "community organization" was becoming more focused, training programs in universities were becoming broader. Developments in nonprofit management, policy analysis, fund-raising, and public policy all represent parts of what once was "community organization." Thus, the new title, *Tactics And Techniques Of Community Intervention*, is designed to appeal to the broadest possible range of practitioners in a community setting, including administrators, policy makers, nurses, teachers, clinicians, and so on. Similarly, community has a broad definition, referring as it does to communities defined by geography (urban, suburban, and rural, as well as neighborhoods), identification (the African-American community, the community of scholars, the Jewish community, etc.) and loci of activity—the university community (all people who work for a particular university), the manufacturing community, the shipping community, and so on. This book focuses on providing, then, specific tools for assisting practitioners who are trying to build community, and change community, whether that community is one of workplace, geography, or common identification (race, gender, or membership). Based upon the word itself, "community" means bonds (unity) that are generated by things people have in common.

What does "build or change" mean in this context? At least four steps are involved: One is community-creating, which involves developing an awareness of the unity—from commonality that is present, but not, perhaps, recognized; a second step is the development of community capacity, which here refers to the ability of the community to take action on its own behalf; third is the development of capability, meaning movement to the actuality of community activity (just having the capacity does not mean one does anything with it); and step number four involves community competence, which means not only taking steps (capability) but also doing them well (being competent at those steps). This volume provides practitioners with tools to assist communities in each of these areas.

The revisions for this edition are especially focused on this end. Two new sections have been added—one on "implementation" and a section on "work guides." Both changes provide more specific, more detailed material for students and practitioners. Fewer than half of the pieces in the second edition have been retained, and of those, several have been completely rewritten or contain updated commentary. New pieces and emphases reflect a feminist perspective, coalition-building, organizational change, program evaluation, and budgeting, among other issues.

Community is, perhaps, the greatest challenge facing developed countries today. While there are encouraging signs of long-standing enmities and differences falling away, new ones seem to be developing almost on a daily basis. Practitioners need to work within communities to assist them in formulating and moving toward their goals while at the same time working between communities to try to ensure that "my goal achievement" does not come at "your expense." Good intentions are not enough. Larger strategies have to be bonded with specific tactics. Community organization professionals need to do more than "good"—they need to do it right, and do it well. This volume assists materially in that direction.

I would like to thank my colleague editors, John Erlich and Jack Rothman, for their constant support and encouragement throughout this process. To our colleague and former editor Fred Cox, now retired, we express thanks and appreciation for his outstanding contributions in laying such a successful foundation. Finally, I would like to express a special note of recognition of and fondness for my father, the late Elmer J. Tropman. His work has appeared in a previous edition of *Tactics*, and he was excited to be working on another contribution. Though he was ill, we collaborated on one of the articles, but he died before he could see its fruition. His influence suffuses all of my contributions.

—John E. Tropman
—John L. Erlich
—Jack Rothman

# Introduction

The final decade of the twentieth century has not begun well. For the world, as for Americans, this is an unsettled, troubling, and critical time in history. The lessons of two world wars and countless smaller—but often equally tragic—wars appear to have taught us little about sharing resources and sharing power.

Production has moved from the comparatively crude industrialization of the turn of the nineteenth century to the highly sophisticated, computer-driven technology that directs our lives, but from which many are excluded. Urbanization and suburbanization (in many so-called "advanced" countries) are essential parts of a process that has occurred over the same time period.

Massive changes in social conditions have also characterized this century. The welfare state was born, developed, and, according to many observers, has gone into a state of decline. From the pioneering work of Bismark's Germany to the Royal Commission Report of 1909 in Britain to the Social Security Act of 1935 in the United States and the War on Poverty of the mid-1960s, governments have moved from limited involvement in the social welfare of the citizenry to extensive efforts (with certain Scandinavian countries often cited as the "best" examples) to maintain basic standards of decency of the past 30 years. By the end of the 1980s, about 800 billion dollars were being pumped into social welfare in the United States under public auspices. At the same time, there has been an enormous expansion in the not-for-profit sector. In the mid-1980s, that sector included over 700 thousand agencies with one or more paid staff and an annual expenditure of some 200 billion dollars. And, major advances in the human condition have clearly taken place. Among the most significant are the break-up of the Soviet Union, a decline in threat of nuclear holocaust, the end of apartheid in South Africa, and a general recognition of our global interdependence. The factor of smoking (both first- and secondhand) in disease, along with the significance of early childhood education, has come to be much more commonly accepted.

At times, however, it feels as if for every problem that shows significant improvement, another has taken its place. AIDS, drugs and youth gangs, domestic violence, and the deterioration of our public schools have dominated our consciousness in recent years. Whole generations of young people—especially urban males of color—have found their life options severely limited.

As this third edition goes to press, the political will of the country seems sorely tested. The federal government, the Congress, the states, and local city and metropolitan authorities seem unable to act in a concerted and forthright fashion. The spirit of compromise and commonweal is strangely absent. It is almost as if we are being called upon to reinvent civil society.

The social welfare profession, much as we might prefer it otherwise, is right in the middle of these situations. Dependent as we are on public funds, we have been less than anxious to ask the hard questions about achieving the maximum efficiencies with fewer dollars. Struggling for survival, we look like we are being dragged (often kicking and screaming in our frustration) toward the next century. Indeed, it truly is the best of times and the worst of times. But how to put the new technology and knowledge to the task of improving the human condition?

From a macro practice perspective, accomplishment requires both strategy and tactics. We distinguish between them as follows:

> Strategy we see as "an orchestrated attempt to influence a person or system in relation to some specific goal which the actor desires." Tactics and techniques may be viewed as specific intervention devices or means that contribute to the operationalization of a strategy. Thus the key differences between strategy and tactics and techniques involve scope and duration. Tactics generally are more modest in these respects.[1]

While the range and variety of current problems clearly demand action at the level of strategy, the opportunities available to most human service professionals in the macro arena are often quite limited. This volume focuses on what might be done with what the practitioner has obtained or can obtain relatively easily. At the same time, the increasing complexity and size of organizations, institutions, and communities suggest that macro practice—planning, program development, organizing, administration, and policy making—is perhaps more important now than it ever was before. Management of clients, groups of employees, and organizations represents an especially urgent challenge.

The notion of an organization as a community—suggested in an earlier edition of this book—both reflected and anticipated much that we see today. Increasingly, in organizations of all kinds, it has been recognized that workers contribute more easily and effectively if they have the opportunity to participate in the decisions that affect them. Alternatively, alienation in the workplace (and alienation elsewhere reflected in the workplace) surely contributes to such problems as substance abuse

---

[1]Fred Cox, John Erlich, Jack Rothman, John Tropman, eds., *Tactics and Techniques of Community Practice,* 2nd ed. (Itasca, Ill., F.E. Peacock, 1984), p. v.

and domestic violence. A study at General Motors found that 20 percent of GM workers have *on-the-job* substance abuse problems.[2] The tactics and techniques of macro practice—organizing, planning, and administration—suggest a variety of ways to establish leverage in this situation. New human resources departments in many corporations and organizations have taken on individual, family, and small-group counseling roles previously handled by social agencies. While some of these services are delivered in house by social workers or contracted out to social agencies, institutional and organizational issues are just beginning to be addressed by human resources departments.

In 1939, the Lane Report defined community organization as "organizing community resources to meet community needs." The community was much more identifiable then, largely a geographic entity disorganized by the dislocations of the Great Depression and the vast ethnic immigrations to the cities (as well as the internal migration to urban areas), as well as increasing differentiation by race and class. "Organizing" focused on matching resources with the needs of those at the bottom of the economic ladder—the disadvantaged, the underclass, the poor. While this traditional focus must not be neglected, especially in light of worsening conditions of racism, the nature of current social problems suggests that most of us are part of one or more human service targets—for example, as people of color, as gays and lesbians, as women, as the physically challenged, and as single parents. Indeed, many middle-class people are included in targeted geographical areas, ethnic subgroups, employment classifications, and organizations.

Fresh ideas and visions about what needs to be done, and how to do it, are very much in order. Perhaps the concepts of "inspiriting" and "crystalizing" offer us guidance in this regard. Inspiriting refers to providing assistance and creating a positive emotional climate, in specific cultural and geographical communities, that enhances and uplifts individuals rather than divesting them of their energies. In our own personal lives, we can all remember those unique moments when, in an effort as part of a team, a group, or a religious community, we felt both transported and empowered beyond ourselves. To be sure, our needs continued to be present; but we were also willing, if not eager, to advance the common goal. Crystalizing, in this context, means providing the locus and means through which the energy of inspiriting becomes effectual. Bellah and his colleagues discuss the commitment of the "establishment" as present in the earlier part of this century. They refer to it as the "establishment vision."

> It was primarily associated with those segments of the industrial and financial elite who at the end of the nineteenth century created and endowed a network of private institutions such as: universities, hospitals, museums, symphony orchestras, schools, churches, clubs, and associations alongside with their new corporations...The creators of these institutions sought to spread a cosmopolitan ethic of noblesse oblige and public service to give local magnets a sense of national responsibility.[3]

---

[2]Detroit Free Press, February 2, 1991.

[3]Robert Bellah et al., *Habits of the Hearts* (New York: Harper & Row, 1985), p. 258.

Such guidance and support can no longer be expected from the economic and/or political elite. Indeed, human services professionals are increasingly called upon to provide aspects of this leadership and creative energy. Humorists, however, offer a context in which to view the limits that may be imposed on our individual and collective efforts. One notes that American society is a Good Samaritan, but not a great Samaritan. Another points out tellingly for human services practitioners: One not only has to do good, "One has to do it well."

This book, then, is designed particularly to provide guidance in addressing the detailed steps that will help implement the strategies that one employs. It begins with *Assessment,* Part One, which focuses primarily on the sources of information about problems and how one might approach the diagnostic task.

Part Two deals with *Option Selection.* In almost all cases assessment directs one to a variety of possible courses of action. How do we judge which might be best, and what factors ought to be taken into account in making this judgment? Complete and easy answers are often elusive, but this section provides concrete suggestions as to how one might proceed.

*Implementation, Mobilization,* and *Development* comprise Part Three, which focuses on putting ideas into action. Implementation is an initial stage that translates the option(s) into program(s). During this process, mobilization of resources is required, and the development of new or different resources is often needed. These resources may invoke material goods, such as money and people, as well as values, like commitments and self-esteem.

As programs get underway, issues of *Administration, Management,* and *Policy* often become important. Part Four gives attention to these typically neglected practice dimensions. Programs must run reasonably efficiently and effectively, and the human resource needs of workers, as well as of clients, must be attended to. *Evaluation* (Part Five) requires, indeed insists, that the human service professions measure what they do: "Are we really helping?" This aspect of macro practice has suffered in recent years—especially in light of tightening budgets. Despite the difficulty of doing evaluations, and the admitted "softness" of many of our measures of success (or failure), there is no avoiding the hard questions about whether we are doing any good, and whether the good we are doing might be achieved more effectively, more efficiently, and with less expense. Clearly, too, from a macro-analytic point of view, considering all the money spent and all the problems that remain, very legitimate questions about efficacy and targeting may be asked.

The social work business—the craft of helping—is beset by many value dilemmas, or *Dilemmas of Practice,* Part Six. These dilemmas have been identified by a range of authors and are summarized in a book by one of the editors.[4]

For example, how does one balance the demands of adequacy (providing for those most in need) with the demand for equity (providing for people in relation to what they have contributed to the system)? Often there are no easy or simple an-

[4]John E. Tropman, *American Values and Social Welfare* (Englewood Cliffs, N.J.: Prentice Hall, 1987).

swers. In some cases, the best we may be able to do is to determine the most effective way of asking the necessary questions about competing values.

Finally, Part Seven, called *Work Guides,* is designed to give specific, brief, and concrete directions that workers can follow. The most frequent concerns of practitioners and students, as mentioned to the editors, are addressed—personnel policies, running an effective meeting, presenting community data, troubleshooting an evaluation, and personal professional conflict.

As we move professionally, personally, and nationally toward the twenty-first century, we face enormous challenges. Despite great progress in some areas, the prospects for fully utilizing the knowledge and skills, the tactics and techniques, of macro practice seem rather bleak. In no sense have we come close to the old philosophical goal of working ourselves out of a job. The problems that have troubled us over the past 20 years—including racism, sexism, homophobia, and desperate poverty—remain very much with us. Indeed, solutions to old problems seem to breed new difficulties.

Our mission is to be as effective and efficient as we can be. The material in this book is designed to motivate us toward that end and inform and support us in the effort.

—John E. Tropman
John L. Erlich

PART ONE

# Assessment

Leroy ("Satchel") Paige, one of the greatest pitchers in the history of baseball, offered this assessment of the best way to promote a long healthy life:

1. Avoid fried meats, which angry up the blood.
2. If your stomach disputes you, lie down and pacify it with cool thoughts.
3. Keep the juices flowing by jangling around gently as you move.
4. Go very light on the vices, such as carrying on in society.
5. Avoid running at all times.
6. Don't look back. Something may be gaining on you.

Unfortunately, no such short, concrete, and clear list exists of guidelines for assessment in macro practice—especially not from a single, highly qualified, and experienced source. However, assessment is an essential step in helping the practitioner decide how to get from where he or she is to where he or she wants to go.

The 1939 Lane Report, in which macro practice (then "community organization") was first systematically defined, noted that a primary function was "the discovery and definition of needs" and balancing needs and resources "in order to better meet changing needs." Thus the assessment of needs was acknowledged as a central role of community practice. It also seems clear that assessment must be multidimensional if it is going to take into account the variety of factors that come into play in any given problem situation. Indeed, this ecological perspective is shared by micro practice. As Hepworth and Larson point out:

To access the problems of a client system (individual, couple, or family) thus requires extensive knowledge about that system as well as consideration of the multifarious systems (e.g., economic, legal, educational, medical, religious, social, interpersonal) that impinge upon the client system.[1]

What service needs do we want to address? In the first selection, this initial question is addressed by Siegel, Attkisson, and Carson. A strong case is made for identification and assessment of needs at the local, community, and regional level. Also stressed is a requirement for citizen and consumer participation with professional personnel in the planning process.

Thoroughly explored are key variables that merit careful consideration when an assessment of human service needs is being planned, including information, resources available, the current state of program development, and the range of community attitudes toward various approaches to assessment.

A second vital and often neglected component of assessment is the agency or organization that employs the practitioner. The analysis of this agency is the subject of the second article, by Hasenfeld. It should be noted that his comprehensive framework may also be equally valuable in sizing up both organizational allies and organizational targets of change. The complexity and internal conflicts that characterize the modern organization suggest the importance of a step-by-step exploration (even if it may seem tedious and unnecessarily detailed in retrospect).

To maximize their effectiveness, Hasenfeld argues for practitioners to be aware of everything from agency environment—the agency's market relations, and regulatory groups to which the agency is accountable—to organizational structures, domain and goals, and client and resource inputs.

Paradoxically, issues of racial and ethnic sensitivity, while part of the "politically correct" assessment process, are often reduced to a "given" that receives scant attention. Who defines these issues, based on what authority or mandate? What complexities and nuances—especially as they vary from group to group—are to be taken into account? In the third article in this section, Devore and Schlesinger address these and other dimensions that must not be discounted if practice with people of color is to be successful. Also highlighted are some of the areas where micro and macro considerations are overlapping or interwoven.

Burghardt, in the final selection, cautions practitioners to consider their personal characteristics as part of the assessment process. From an individual standpoint, this may be one of the most difficult parts of assessment for macro practice practitioners. While micro practice people are often given to introspection by the nature of much of what they do, it is often argued that the reverse is true of macro practitioners. That is, because of the level at which macro practice people operate—community, organizational, representative group, and the like—the last thing taken into account is who and what the practitioner brings to the situation. As the editors are well aware from their own experiences, this personal awareness is neglected at great peril—to both the change effort and the practitioner himself or herself.

---

[1]Dean H. Hepworth and JoAnn Larson, *Direct Social Work Practice*, 3rd ed. (Belmont, Calif.: Wadsworth, 1990), p. 201.

Austin's piece on human service executives in Part Four also draws attention to self-analysis as a key component of practitioner effectiveness.

As in any ecological approach, the full range of variables must be taken into account. The cross-pressures, constraints, and limitations on current community practice suggest that adequate assessment may be absolutely vital if the majority of such efforts are not to be doomed before they ever really get started.

—John L. Erlich

1.

Larry M. Siegel, C. Clifford Attkisson, and Linda G. Carson

# NEED IDENTIFICATION AND PROGRAM PLANNING IN THE COMMUNITY CONTEXT

Assessment of service needs is a neglected and misunderstood aspect of human service program planning. Optimally, legislative blueprints for national social and health programs should emerge from systematic, scientific need assessment efforts that are designed to identify the extent and degree of need for specific services in the general population. In practice, however, national programs emerge from a political context of confrontation between special and general interests, social service ideologies, demands for service, and the competition for access to resources. As a result, our communities are peppered with uncoordinated and loosely integrated programs that overlap and compete for sparse resources. Without adequate assessment of human service needs, this poorly monitored and uncoordinated situation will persist and worsen.

This article describes the central issues of need identification and assessment. Following the initial discussion, several basic need assessment methodologies are described and illustrated. The basic assumptions on which the article is based are that identification and assessment of service needs (a) must be undertaken at the local community and regional level in a fashion that stimulates coordination and integration of human services at the community level; (b) must be a rationalizing force in the regional health and human service planning process; and (c) must carefully blend citizen and consumer participation with professional personnel in a planning process designed to stimulate program relevance to human service needs.

## A DEFINITION OF NEED IDENTIFICATION AND ASSESSMENT

*Need identification* describes health and social service requirements in a geographic or social area, whereas *need assessment* is aimed at estimating the relative importance of these needs. The process of need identification and assessment involves two distinct steps: (a) the application of a measuring tool or an assortment of tools to a defined social area; and, following this attempt at measurement, (b) the application of judgment to assess the significance of the information gathered in order to determine priorities for program planning and service development (Blum, 1974). Assessment is a research and planning activity that is focused on a specific social area. Within social areas, need assessment strategies are designed to provide data that will enable planners to determine the extent and kinds of needs there are in a community; to evaluate existing service resources systematically; and to provide information for planning new service programs in the light of the community's needs and human service patterns.

---

C. Clifford Attkisson is with the Department of Psychology, University of California.

Basically, the various known assessment techniques produce information that describes or defines social conditions or situations. These conditions are not necessarily predetermined to be positive or negative. The interpretation of social situations depends on the values and expectations of those individuals doing the interpreting. As Blum (1974) states, "The identical situation may be seen as good by those whose value expectations are met, and as bad by those whose values are not; those whose values are unrelated, or who do not connect the condition to values, may not perceive the condition at all, or view it as a natural state of affairs [pp. 219–220]."

The same rationale may be applied when considering the term "need" in situations where assessment activities are characterized as "need identification." Need in this context might usefully be defined as the gap between what is viewed as a necessary level or condition by those responsible for this determination and what actually exists. Need is at best a relative concept and the definition of need depends primarily upon those who undertake the identification and assessment effort.

## JUSTIFICATION AND GOALS FOR NEED STUDIES

The concepts of need identification and assessment are such that there is no set of generally agreed upon steps which, when carefully followed, lead one to a comprehensive assessment of needs. The reality is that planners and program administrators must decide what information will generate the most comprehensive identification and assessment of needs in a specific geographic service area, and what proportion of program resources should reasonably be allocated for this effort. Some of the relevant variables that merit careful consideration when planning an assessment of human service needs include:

### 1. Information

What assessment data are most relevant for the local program? How easily can the desired data be obtained? What is the potential accuracy and usefulness of the data?

### 2. Resources Available

What staff and fiscal resources are available to the assessment effort? What is the cost estimate of collecting (purchasing) these data? Will the expected benefits from the data outweigh their cost? Are these resources sufficient to obtain the desired information?

### 3. State of Program Development

Is the service system new or in early program planning stages? How wide is the range of services currently available? Is there a service system organizational network?

### 4. Community Attitudes

What is the community tolerance for surveys, community forums, and other approaches to assessment?

Planning human service programs for the future will require an approach to need identification that has clear sanctions and sufficient resources. Collaborative networks must be formed to act as regional information-gathering systems. These regional systems, probably organized at the multicounty level, should perform intensive field surveys and serve as a conduit through which appropriate information will be channeled to the community level.

## CONVERGENT ANALYSIS

In a comprehensive need assessment effort *convergent analysis* may be conceptualized as the second of the two operational stages, the first one being need *identification.*

Convergent analysis is a methodological framework in which information relative to human service needs may be identified, defined, evaluated, and given priority in a progressive manner. The tasks to be completed in this final analytical stage are synthesis and integration of all collected information from a variety of data collection methods.

Convergent analysis usually begins with data internal to the service system, such as legal and fundor mandates, historical trends relevant to service delivery, and client utilization information. Other forces feeding into the initial phase of convergent analysis are the orientation, training and interests of administrators and providers, and the perspectives of advisory and policy board members. The process then integrates information assembled about a specified social area or target community via a network of techniques designed to capture a wide range of perceptions about conditions in the community.

Convergent analysis is used here in the sense that the information gathered from a range of need assessment methods, deployed both systematically and sequentially, will yield a reasonably accurate identification of community needs and an assessment of the relative priorities among the needs identified. "Convergent" in this context has several meanings. First, there is a convergence of different information coming from divergent sources (e.g., citizens, consumers, service providers, and political leaders). Second, there is a convergence of different assessment strategies, each with some overlapping, yet unique, bits of information. Third, convergent also describes the cumulative nature of an ideal assessment procedure viewed across time. Information obtained at different (though sequential) points in time (information from a wide range of data collection method and perspectives) is convergent to the extent that it can be pooled in an ongoing fashion to yield an accurate depiction of human service needs of a particular social area. All three of the above concepts of convergence analysis imply that, with each stepwise increment of information, one more clearly approximates a valid description of the social area under study. In other words, convergent analysis provides a dynamic process for reaching a convergent and discriminant validation of the needs in a social area (Campbell & Fiske, 1959). Finally, the last meaning of convergence in our formulation is to be found in the range of organizational levels through which assessment information must be channeled. Information from both state and national perspectives "converges" on service program networks at the community level. When integrated with regionally and locally generated "need" data, this information allows for more systematic program planning and development.

## BASIC PURPOSES OF NEED IDENTIFICATION AND ASSESSMENT

Assessment provides one important informational input to a much broader *planning process* that leads to (a) the selection of and priority setting among problems and target populations to be addressed; (b) the selection and operationalization of specific community program activities; and (c) the evaluation of these program activities. Assessment information helps to assure that there will be additional inputs to prevent sole reliance on professional formulations of service needs and/or to prevent overriding influence by the most vocal or powerful community groups in program planning.

Assessment also has an inportant role in established community programs. In such agencies, assessment can provide a continuing examination of the relevance of existing service activities to changing human service needs and priorities.

Assessment strategies are varied, and selection of a particular strategy is dependent upon the type of information sought. Assessment efforts may study the distribution of social problems in a population and the factors that influence the distribution. In the mental health field, for example, some assessment studies attempt to relate certain social or health characteristics of a population to various rates of mental disorder; or, studies may focus upon the relation between ecological characteristics of a social area and the rates of mental disorder (Bloom, 1975). Other studies employ field survey strategies in order to identify mental health problems and service needs more specifically (Warheit, Bell, & Schwab, 1974).

Most field survey efforts are designed to assess the prevalence and incidence of those who already suffer from particular disorders and to identify those subpopulations having the highest risk of experiencing specific mental health problems within a social area. When it is possible to identify populations at risk, such findings are very important in planning for services, especially preventive ones. In addition to collecting information about the range of social and health problems in a community and specification of populations at risk, program planners must also identify cultural and linguistic barriers or other features of the service system that impede effective delivery of services—such as awareness, acceptability, accessibility, and availability of services.

Beyond describing needs, assessment is also useful in identifying those factors within the human service network which aid or impede attempts to meet those needs. First, assessment may be used to specify current and/or potential resources that can be channeled or reallocated to respond to unmet needs. Second, an assessment effort is useful in gaining an understanding of the political and social value system underlying a particular social area. These values often determine what needs are identified and also tend to determine which needs receive priority in the program planning process. Finally, analysis of assessment data may suggest new interventions and may ultimately be helpful in uncovering the etiology of certain conditions. Knowledge about social, environmental, and biologic etiology will eventually lead to more effective preventive programs (Blum, 1974; Broskowski & Baker, 1974).

## ASSESSMENT CONTRASTED WITH PROGRAM EVALUATION

Care must be taken not to confuse community need assessment with evaluation. Both program evaluation and need assessment are parts of a larger program planning–implementation–development cycle, but need assessment is an environmental monitoring system. As an environmental monitoring system, it is a conceptually separate and operationally different process when compared to and contrasted with program evaluation.

## WHEN TO DO A NEED IDENTIFICATION

Considerable attention must be given by human service programs to clarification and specification of the purposes and potential uses of a proposed assessment effort. Since the process requires a substantial expenditure of resources, it should primarily be considered when there is both an opportunity and a commitment either for planning new services or for restructuring existing ones on the basis of needs that may be identified. If there is no commitment to planning or restructuring programs in accordance with those needs identified, no useful purpose is served by an assessment effort. At best, failure to use need assessment information in planning represents a waste of resources and, at worst, certain assessment procedures (such as the "community forum") may serve to heighten community expectations that needs identified will be addressed in actual service or preventive operations.

## AN OVERVIEW OF NEED IDENTIFICATION AND ASSESSMENT METHODOLOGIES

A comprehensive, convergent analysis of human service needs requires utilization of information resources that exist in (or can be obtained from) national, regional, state, and community depositories. At the local level each human service agency has unique informational needs that logically can be identified through local effort. Beyond this, however, there is a large body of information held in common by, and/or is mutually relevant to, a number of agencies comprising the human services network within a given social area. Where informational requirements overlap, a cost-efficient and effective need assessment effort can only be undertaken and/or coordinated at the regional planning level.

The various approaches to need assessment presented in this article may be undertaken at any planning level: community, regional, state, and more rarely, national. The auspices for any particular need assessment will vary accordingly. Nevertheless, mounting effective need assessment programs will require each planning body to develop a master strategy which will coordinate assessment and dissemination of assessment information throughout an area.

A need assessment program that is organized at the regional planning level affords a number of advantages. First, a single regional assessment effort instead of numerous community efforts could guarantee a substantial conservation of financial and human resources. Tremendous duplication of effort and greatly exaggerated cost could ensue if each social agency in a given area were to undertake a unilateral assessment of community needs. Second, an ongoing regional assessment effort could also share successful models that are practical to employ on a smaller scale and that would be more appropriately undertaken at the community agency level. Third, the regional assessment activity could provide readily available, decision-relevant data to community-based programs on a regular, planned basis. And fourth, need assessment conducted under regional auspices would be less influenced by local political pressure, and in that way, could serve as a vehicle for more "objective" data than that which could be obtained at the agency level.

Without the integrative capacity, production capacity, and economic advantages of this regional approach to need assessment, it is doubtful that individual community-based programs will be able to conduct assessment programs that can adequately provide the necessary information. This state of affairs would not only be a serious blow to the development of flexible, responsive human service networks but also would seriously affect the relevance of specific agencies and services.

Several constraints limit the depth and scope of need assessment efforts undertaken by community-based agencies. First, the financial base for program planning and development may be too sparse to support an extensive assessment effort. Second, the time frame in which an assessment activity is performed may limit the scope of its findings. Many, if not most, need assessments undertaken by community-based agencies are carried out in a relatively short period of time to meet, for example, governmental grant deadlines. These efforts tend to monopolize agency assessment lines. Third, internal pressure from highly vocal consumer groups often requires that immediate action be taken on a human service problem. In such circumstances, a comprehensive, time-consuming assessment effort is neither feasible nor appropriate. In these instances, where accessibility to time and/or money is limited, need assessment plans at the agency level may still be implemented to provide useful information. Excellent examples of such an effort are provided by Beigel, Hunter, Tamerin, Chapin, and Lowery (1974) and Beigel, McCabe, Tamerin, Lowery, Chapin, and Hunter (1974).

Regardless of the level at which need assessment is undertaken (local, regional, or state) there are eight need identification and assessment approaches that can provide the basis for a convergent analysis of human service needs. Each approach can be described as serving one or more information gathering functions: (a) *compilation* of information which is available but not yet disseminated within the boundaries of the social system, (b) *development* of new information, and (c) *integration* of all relevant identification that is developed from within the system or gathered from outside the system's boundaries. One of the eight approaches performs all three informational functions, three serve two functions, and four represent only one function. The various approaches to need assessment, where the information may be obtained, how the data are formulated, and where "need" information is best utilized in the planning and development process, are summarized in Table 1.1. Table 1.1 is developed from the perspective of the community-based human service program, and assumes that regional planning bodies will soon join the local community agency in the need assessment data collection, analysis, and dissemination process.

A need assessment approach that collects information from already existing sources and subsequently organizes it in some coherent fashion illustrates a data *compilation* function. Frequently the required information exists outside the boundaries of the community-based program, for example, the National Clearinghouses of Drug Abuse Information, Mental Health Information, and Alcohol Information. Assessment approaches may also *develop* or collect new information. Here, original information bearing on the needs of a particular community is generated. Finally, a technique is classified as an *integrator* of information when data from two or more sources are organized to effect a more valid description of human service needs than is possible when information is drawn from a single source. It is in the combination of all three informational functions (compilation, development, and integration) that a convergent analysis of human service needs is achieved.

There are several important methods that can be employed to obtain information about human service needs. This section provides an outline of the various approaches including (a) a brief definition for each strategy, (b) the time at which utilization of a particular technique is appropriate,

TABLE 1.1
Need Identification and Assessment Methods

| Methods and Method Families | | Characteristics and Technical Considerations Regarding the Use of Each Method | | | | | |
|---|---|---|---|---|---|---|---|
| | | Perspective Being Represented | Optimal Sponsor | Source of Information | Information Processing Function | Measurement Expertise Needed | Time and Resources Needed |
| Indicator approaches | 1. Social and health indicator analyses | Government and private agencies | Local, state, regional, or federal planners | Public archives, planning agencies | Compilation of existing data | Moderate to high | Moderate to extensive |
| Social area survey approaches | 2. Demands for services | Service agencies and consumers | Community agencies along with above | Information systems | Compilation | Moderate | Moderate |
| | 3. Analysis of service providers and resources | Planners | Local and regional planners | Local records and surveys | Compilation and development of new data | Low | Moderate |
| | 4. Citizen surveys | Private citizens | Regional, state, or federal planners | Face-to-face, telephone, or mailed surveys | Development of new data | High | Extensive |
| Community group approaches | 5. Community forums | Private citizens and consumers | Community agencies | Public meetings | Integration of existing and new data | Low | Moderate |
| | 6. Nominal group techniques | Planners, service providers, citizens | All levels | Specific projects | Development of new data | Moderate | Minimal |
| | 7. Delphi technique | Planners, service providers, experts | All levels | Specific projects | Development and integration | Moderate | Moderate |
| | 8. Community impressions | Citizens, key informants, consumers, providers | Community agencies, regional planners | Specific projects | Development, compilation, and integration | Moderate | Minimal |

and (c) the source(s) from which data can be obtained. Each method provides a different perspective on needs. A more lengthy discussion of each technique follows in the final major sections of this article.

## Social and Health Indicator Analysis

The social and health indicator approach to need identification consists of compiling and making inferences of need from descriptive statistics found in public records and reports. It is based on the assumption that particular descriptors, such as proximity to the urban core and socioeconomic status, are viable indicators of human service needs (Bloom, 1975; Siegel, Attkisson, & Cohn, 1977). The viability of particular indicators depends upon three factors: (a) the validity and reliability of the descriptive information, (b) the logical and statistical appropriateness of procedures used to derive the social and health indicators for the community (Schulberg & Wechsler, 1967), and (c) the subjective sense or feel for the given community which is developed through these sources of information about the community.

The Social and Health Indicator approach is invaluable as an initial descriptive approach to understanding a given social area (Sheldon & Parke, 1975). Social indicator approaches range from the very simplistic designs using one or two indicators, such as census data on income, housing or a population density index, to very complex designs that consist of many variables requiring the use of complex statistical procedures such as cluster or factor analysis (Bloom, 1975).

## Social Area Surveys

*1. Demands for Services.* This approach to need identification includes compilation of existing information and integration of those sources of information. Here the aim is to review the various human service providers' (both individual and agency) past and current services-rendered patterns and requests for service by citizens in an attempt to understand the number and types of human services demanded in a particular community. These data may be secured through structured interviews with appropriate staff and board members, extrapolations from past and current clinical records and management information systems, or analysis of agency charters, licenses, funding applications, contracts, and grants. Analysis can also identify current commitments, mandates, policies, and goal statements within the human service system. Appropriate target groups include agency management, agency staff and board members, funding organizations, and citizen advocacy groups.

*2. Analysis of Service Resources.* This need assessment device involves a descriptive enumeration of the human service agencies and individual providers within a community. It can best be classified as a compilation and integration of information that exists at the agency level. This integration may take the form of a human services directory for a particular community. Important to the process of identifying existing service resources is the assessment of whether current efforts are efficiently and effectively focused on known needs.

*3. Citizen Surveys.* Here the assessment effort is concerned with eliciting differing perspectives on the nature and magnitude of human service needs from community residents. The main function of this technique is the development of new information through stratified random sampling of the community residents. This technique is most appropriately used to supplement generalized and indirect assessments, such as social and health indicator analyses, with the more personal perspective of community residents.

### Ascertaining Community Views Through Community Group Approaches

*1. Community Forum.* This approach consists of an open meeting to which all members of a community are invited and at which all participants are urged to present their views regarding the human service needs of a particular social area. Although this information is often used to validate previously existing data, the technique itself is concerned with generating new information only; that is, obtaining community residents' input on a particular issue or issues.

*2. Nominal Group Approach.* The nominal group approach is principally a noninteractive workshop designed to maximize creativity and productivity and to minimize the argumentative style of problem-solving and competitive discussion. Within this format, a *selected group of community residents* is invited to share group subject views regarding community needs or to identify barriers to relevant, effective human service delivery in a social area. The nominal group approach is most appropriately used as a method for obtaining citizen and consumer input into the need assessment and program planning process.

*3. Delphi Approach.* This approach to need identification includes the development of a questionnaire, which is distributed to a panel of resource persons and/or a select group of community residents whose opinions on a particular issue or issues are highly valued. From their responses, a perspective can be derived regarding human service needs. This technique is quite useful and most appropriate when respondents have a minimal amount of time available for an identification effort. The Delphi process of obtaining individual opinions on a particular issue is best classified as development of new information.

*4. Community Impressions Approach.* There are three steps to this assessment procedure. First, a small but representative group of individuals is interviewed about their views of human service needs. Second, this information is then integrated with existing data taken from public records and other assessment efforts to yield a richer understanding of the community needs. Third, the resulting community portrait is then validated and/or revised according to information gained from various groups in the community through the community forum process.

This approach serves as an information integrator and validator. It employs data from three different assessment efforts, and at the same time provides new information in the form of community impressions. The community impressions approach is an economical and necessary step on the path to a creative convergence of need assessment information gained from the various other need assessment approaches.

## SOCIAL AND HEALTH INDICATOR ANALYSIS

This approach consumes preexisting, publicly available information (census data, public health data, and criminal justice data, for example) and integrates this information in an attempt to gain a clear and parsimonious description of a social area. It does not produce new information. Rather, it analyzes, integrates, and disseminates already existing information. Although the task sounds simple, most social and health indicator analyses are complex, expensive and time-consuming.

Social and health indicator analysis cannot be treated in a detailed and systematic manner here. For more details, see Attkisson, et al., Chapters 9 and 10.

## SOCIAL AREA SURVEY APPROACHES TO NEED IDENTIFICATION

One of the first steps in a convergent analysis of human service needs is to survey existing community service resources. Surveys of social and health agencies provide information about major problems existing in a community, about help-seeking behaviors in a community, about service resources and gaps in these resources, and about existing outreach and preventive efforts in a community.

There are three main types of information that a survey of practitioners and agencies can provide. They are (a) the analysis of *demands* for service placed upon agencies and private practitioners; (b) the specification, by type, of the various human services resources in a designated social area and their corresponding capacity to respond to human service problems; and (c) a description of the pattern and the extent of interrelationships among human service resources in the community.

In analyzing demands for service, the objective is to understand the magnitude and types of requests for human services. When assessing human service resources, however, planners are concerned with comprehending the capacity of the service systems to respond to those requests and with the quality of such responses. In delineating the interagency relationships in a particular community, we hope to clarify the extent and kind of collaborative efforts that characterize the human service network.

### Need Identification Through Analysis of Demands for Service

This approach requires a survey of the entire human services network within a community. The typical survey seeks information not only from the primary health service agencies, for example, or institutions within a community but also from other community agencies which interface with and provide a range of supporting and interlocking services to the primary health care network. Many agencies can potentially be included: mental health clinics and centers, hospitals (including psychiatric and general hospitals), drug and alcohol treatment and related service programs, private practitioners, family service programs, public health departments, churches, probation and family courts, and other social and health organizations or service providers.

Although analysis of demand for services is an important element of a broader assessment strategy, there are a few caveats related to using this approach exclusively in assessing service needs (Feldstein, 1973; Schaefer, 1975). Even though a service is well utilized, it does not necessarily follow that this service is addressing a high-priority need in the community. A high utilization rate may possibly be due to any of the following: (a) the service is well publicized; (b) it is inexpensive; (c) it is one of the only services available in the community; (d) the various professionals in the community are unaware of alternative services; and/or (e) more pejoratively, high utilization may reflect professional preferences for particular service modalities. Reciprocally, services addressing high-priority problems may be underutilized because they are unpublicized, because client referral procedures are too cumbersome, or because they have marginal relevance to professional investments. In addition, high service utilization rates may signal the need for the development of preventive programs in a particular service area. And, finally, there are likely to be important differences between those who seek or receive care and those who do not. Many "needers" are not utilizers and some utilizers are, relatively speaking, "non-needers." These caveats should be carefully considered as indicators of the hazards involved in extrapolating from populations receiving services to the population at large.

In analyzing demands for services it may be possible to secure satisfactory response from a fairly brief, well-designed, mailed questionnaire. A followup letter or phone call to nonrespondents is usually necessary to increase the response rate. A method for substantially increasing the number of returns from mailed questionnaires has been described by Robin (1965). It involves a minimum of two and a maximum of five contacts with the potential respondent. The first contact is a prequestionnaire letter which, if possible, should be written on letterhead and cosigned by someone who represents broadly recognized authority and who is able to validate the importance of the survey and the appropriateness of the respondent's participation. Optimally, the letter must (a) request individual participation; (b) explain the assessment methodology, its importance, and possible applications; (c) inform the respondent that he or she will soon receive an assessment questionnaire; and finally (d) describe procedures for safeguarding confidentiality in handling all information. The second contact consists of a cover letter and the questionnaire. Contacts three to five consist of a series of followup strategies, should these be necessary. The reader is referred to Robin's article for further explanation of this survey strategy (Robin, 1965).

When possible, utilization surveys should be conducted in a systematic site visit format. Personal interviews with through-the-mail followups almost always produce greater reliability and validity of survey results.

### Analysis of Existing Service Resources

Beyond assessing demands for human services it is also important for every community to identify and assess its human service resources. A count of resources by type and capacity allows human service program planners to identify gaps and duplications among existing services. This knowledge of existing resources may then be contrasted with information derived from other assessment strategies relative to estimates of met and unmet needs. Usually a single survey can produce information about both (a) demands for services in the community, and (b) existing service resources.

The specific content and format of social and health agency surveys must vary from community to community to the extent that agencies in a given social area differ in structure and service objectives. Nevertheless there are a number of general interest areas that are applicable to most agencies when conducting this type of survey:

1. Range of human services provided
2. Client entry policies, conditions of eligibility for service, including age, sex, financial criteria, geographic restrictions, and particular focal or target population groups
3. Personnel characteristics and personnel development efforts

   a. Service providers by training and credentials
   b. Provider training and continuing education opportunities
   c. Treatment modalities provided
   d. Number of individuals providing various services
   e. Average client load per staff member
4. Financial characteristics
   a. Charge for services—fee schedule, eligibility for third party reimbursement, sliding scale provisions
   b. Agency support—public or private, fees and other sources of funding categorized as percentage of total support budget
5. Accessibility, availability, and awareness of services
   a. Location of facility—proximity to target populations and proximity to public transportation
   b. Intake procedure—amount of information required, publicity for the available services, hours when services are provided, comfort and acceptability of the facility to clients, and availability of child-care when necessary
6. Referrals (demand)
   a. Number within a standardized time frame
   b. Source categorized by service type or status of referring agent
   c. Reasons (symptoms, problem areas)
   d. Other characteristics such as geographic locale of referring agents, geographic origin of clients who are referred, and temporal patterns of referrals
7. Accepted for service
   a. Number over a specified time period
   b. Diagnosis or other nomenclature for designated problems
   c. Sociodemographic characteristics of clients—age, race, sex, census tract, socioeconomic status
   d. Those refused service and reasons for refusal
8. Waiting list
   a. Number of persons on waiting list
   b. Reasons for waiting list
   c. Symptoms or problem areas of individuals placed on waiting lists
   d. Other characteristics, such as average time on waiting list and proportion of those placed on waiting list who do not eventually receive service
9. Services provided
   a. Human service problem areas thought to be of highest priority as well as services that are in increasing demand
   b. Range of actual services provided categorized by units of service
   c. List of referral resources that interface the agency
10. Referrals initiated
   a. Frequency of referrals made (listed across the range of agencies within the social area)
   b. Problems in making referrals—including such factors as transportation, financial, language, and cultural barriers.

### Identification of Need Through Analysis of Interagency Relationships—Some Further Thoughts

An analysis of the interagency relationships including the extent of collaboration among human service resources in a community is thought to be important in a comprehensive approach to need assessment. Such exploration will (a) uncover underutilized resources; (b) give an indication of how these resources are perceived and utilized by peer agencies; (c) determine the extent to which community exists, the degree of service duplication, and the extent to which there is inadequate integration within the human service network; and (d) identify those agencies or providers who maintain collaborative ties and who might work well in a collective effort. Suggestions for restructuring or in other ways improving services may result. This type of inquiry is probably best accomplished by site visits conducted by skilled interviewers with appropriate credentials.

The main advantages of assessing need through analysis of interagency relationships are the relatively low cost of collecting and analyzing the information and the ready availability of such information. In addition, this type of survey, which tends to increase communication between human service agencies and providers, often leads to a greater sensitivity to the needs of community residents and as a result to a more adequate integration of human services. This strategy also allows for a general inventory of community resources—information that is useful when integrating need assessment information into program planning. One particularly useful subsidiary benefit of human services resource identification is the publication and distribution of a human services information directory complete with referral procedures applicable to the network of human service providers.

The two main disadvantages to this type of need identification involve, first, the difficulty in obtaining reliable data and second, drawing conclusions about a population solely on the basis of service utilization. One must proceed with caution when attempting to estimate the needs of an entire community on the basis of information obtained from an analysis of information about a sample of persons receiving services from the community's public and private care providers. In the mental health field, for example, there is a great deal of research which suggests that there is a wide gulf between the mental health needs of a community as determined by field prevalence surveys and the number of persons receiving mental health care in the same community. Other research has shown that many residents of a community may not require new or additional mental health services, because they are receiving services from agencies or providers outside of the community. A systematic need identification and assessment program must always include data concerning (a) the extent to which identified needs are being met by resources within or outside the social area being studied, and (b) the appropriateness of reliance on external resources to meet social area needs.

## Citizen Surveys: Community Residents' Perspectives on Human Service Needs

In this section, we describe three survey techniques that allow broader citizen and community participation in the identification of needs and the establishment of service priorities than those discussed to this point. Such surveys provide citizen perspectives on the nature and magnitude of service needs in the community. Either anonymous, through-the-mail, stratified random sampling or direct interview-based methods can be employed to assemble this type of information.

Through-the-mail surveys should include a random sample of people living within a geographically defined service area. The sample may be stratified by such variables as census tract, age, race, or economic status. Almost always, respondents in such surveys are anonymous.

The following types of information that were viewed as particularly relevant to mental health planning were included by

Meier (1973) in a survey of residents in Contra Costa County, California: (a) community problems in order of perceived importance; (b) sources of help perceived as available for particular problems; (c) mental health problems thought most important; (d) attitudes toward utilization of a public mental health program; (e) mental health services thought most important; (f) mental health problems experienced in their own families; (g) help received for these problems; (h) satisfaction obtained from mental health services received; and (i) nomination of providers from whom one would seek help for problems of drug abuse in children and adolescents.

In some social areas face-to-face interviews with citizens have produced a better response rate and more useful information than anonymous mailed surveys. Since most surveys of this type are not particularly complex, it may be possible, without undue difficulty, to train community volunteers as interviewers (Warheit, et al., 1974). This use of community interviewers may have several secondary benefits, which include (a) involving a cadre of community people in the actual planning phase of a program; (b) educating both the interviewers and interviewees about existing or potential services; and (c) conducting the survey in an atmosphere of familiarity, which decreases interviewee's reluctance to provide survey information. Since any survey of community residents requires considerable energy and a significant amount of financial resources, a human service program should carefully contrast the advantages and disadvantages of community surveys with those of community forums as described in this article. An approach that combines some survey features with the methodology of a community forum will be described in a later section of this article.

Still another option worth consideration when planning a resident survey is the telephone approach, which yields a much higher rate of response than a mailed questionnaire. This may be a more viable technique for programs serving middle-income areas where more people have telephones than in low-income areas, although the bias of an increasing number of unlisted telephone numbers should not be overlooked. One study comparing advantages and disadvantages of mailing or telephoning a followup questionnaire on discharged hospital patients showed that approximately 85% of the patients and relatives completed the telephone interviews as compared with a 35% return of the mailed questionnaires. It was found that certain questions provoked markedly different responses when the type of interview was by mail rather than phone (Schwartz, 1973). We would expect that the differences in response to questions would not be as great when contrasting telephone with personal interviews as they would be when comparing telephone and mail techniques. Nevertheless, design characteristics of any type of survey determine to a great extent the response rate achieved with a survey strategy. Meier (1973), for example, employed a mailed questionnaire survey format that was unusually successful—both in terms of response rate and results.

There are three primary advantages in using the survey approach to need identification. According to Warheit et al. (1974), carefully designed and conducted surveys provide the most scientifically valid and reliable information obtainable regarding citizen views of their service needs and utilization patterns. It is also the most direct method of obtaining data about the needs of persons in a community. Finally it is very flexible and can be designed in an extremely wide variety of ways to answer questions related to human service needs. The value of selective use of surveys to assess in depth the specific needs of known high-risk populations cannot be overemphasized.

Disadvantages of the survey method of need identification include the following: In comparison to other methods, it tends to be more expensive. Some respondents are reluctant to offer information about themselves or other family members. Finally, the data obtained are based on self-report and are not independently verified in the typical case. A more thorough description of community survey methodology is presented in Attkisson et al., Chapter 10 [not reprinted here].

## ASCERTAINING COMMUNITY VIEWS THROUGH GROUP APPROACHES

In addition to surveys, there are many different ways in which citizen and consumer views of human service needs can be ascertained. In this section, we describe four methods that are useful in undertaking a relatively quick and inexpensive assessment from the perspective of the community: (a) community forums, (b) workshops using the nominal group technique, (c) the Delphi technique, and (d) the community impressions approach.

When a human services network must conduct a community assessment rapidly, any one of the community group methods may be used independently; however, they are most usefully employed in conjunction with approaches described in previous sections of this article. Once surveys have been undertaken and social and health indicator analyses have been conducted, community group methods can be used to gain an additional perspective on the reliability or the interpretation of the previously collected information. The more formal data collection procedures do not capture all relevant information and the data that are collected by formal data collection approaches may not provide an up-to-date portrait of the human service system in a community.

The community group methods can also be invaluable in determining which need areas among those detected during the formal data gathering have highest priority in the community. Because of disparate values and perspectives, different interest groups in a community will view certain conditions as more important than others: they will also hold varying notions as to the distribution of needs and the most appropriate approaches to interventions.

Linking survey with community group approaches is the only reliable mechanism for achieving a convergent analysis of needs and priorities—an analysis on which planning decisions can be based.

### Community Forums as a Means of Needs Assessment

Any person living or working in a community is potentially an information resource on the sociological and psychological aspects of that community. Community residents either directly, through personal experience, or indirectly, through observation or study, form impressions about the human service needs in a social area. The perspectives of residents concerning the accessibility, availability, acceptability, and organization of services comprise indispensable clues about the human service needs of the community as a whole. It is unlikely that any one person has a comprehensive view of human service needs or that two people have the same view. Yet, each person's view portrays some potentially important aspect of the existing reality. In the process of integrating these various viewpoints, a useful, although impressionistic, picture of the human service needs in a community begins to emerge. The community forum represents a quick and effective method of eliciting this desired information.

A community forum is an open meeting for all members of a designated community. Its purpose is to provide a setting for members of a community to express their opinions about a particular issue—in this case the human service needs of the community. Forums resemble an old fashioned "town meeting," but can be more open and flexible. Any person attending is considered an important information resource and is encouraged to express his or her views. In general, forums last 3–4 hours and may include a wide range of activities: information exchange, communication of details about new programs or projects, introduction of various community members, and more general social interaction. The major function of the forum, however, is to elicit views from as many people as possible on a single issue. Although it is possible, the forum itself rarely involves decision making on the basis of views presented. At heart it is a means of problem identification and of obtaining citizen reaction to service efforts.

For further details on planning and carrying out community forums, see Attkisson, et al. (1978), pp. 240–241 and Cox, et al. (1984).

There are four advantages in using the community forum approach. First, community forums are, without question, quite economical in relation to other methods of need assessment. Planning for the meeting, including publicity, can be accomplished in a matter of weeks, and the forum itself may only last a few hours. The costs include the publicity, the time of any paid personnel in planning and implementing the forum and in analyzing the forum results, the time of a recording secretary, the provision of necessary transportation and child-care services to facilitate attendance of certain community members, and perhaps the rental of a meeting place. Many of these tasks may be accomplished by community volunteers.

Second, forums allow a wide range of individuals from the community to express their opinions about human service needs. Since the forum is open to all members of the community, a presentation of all important views can potentially be heard. Of particular importance is the fact that the views of those individuals who fall into the underserved or nonserved category in the community can be heard.

Third, the forum may serve as a catalyst for the initiation of plans and actions about the human service needs in the community. During the forum, those who have not previously considered the question of service needs may be stimulated to do so. As a result of interest generated by the forum, one could well expect the initiation of certain activities related to meeting human service needs.

Fourth, the forum provides those responsible for the need assessment with an opportunity not only to hear from many different elements of the community about unmet needs, but also to identify those participants and agencies most interested in doing something about them. These individuals can be invaluable in the convergent analysis phase of assessment and in developing plans to meet the needs identified.

There are also four main disadvantages to community forums. First, given a sizable forum attendance, it is unlikely that everyone who wishes to speak will have a chance to do so. Thus, certain information that could be quite relevant to the assessment of needs may never be presented.

Second, not all members of the community can or will attend a forum. Certain viewpoints about unmet human service needs may not be represented at the forum. The results of the forum provide an impressionistic and probably incomplete picture of needs.

Third, although the forum does provide an opportunity for expressing many valuable perspectives, particularly concerning need identification, it is usually the case that the discussion does not go beyond this point.

Fourth, the forum may mobilize certain elements of the community, or at least heighten the awareness of existing human service needs in the community. As a result, the expectations of community members may be raised in ways that cannot or will not be met. Organizers of the forum have a responsibility to inform attendees of realistic outcomes that may be expected from the forum and to advise participants that the process of problem identification is only the first phase of a problem-solving process.

From the advantages and disadvantages of the community forum approach it can be concluded that forums are most appropriate if there is interest in (a) uncovering citizen feelings and impressions about human service needs—particularly citizens who represent those groups that are underrepresented in census data and utilization rates; and (b) identifying directly in a public arena the concerns of citizens as well as enlisting stimulating support for planning efforts directed at those needs.

## The Nominal Group Technique

A second community group approach to need identification in human services is the nominal group technique (Delbecq & Van de Ven, 1971) that is used extensively in industrial, governmental, educational, and health organizations. The nominal group technique was developed through a series of experiments over a period of 10 years by Delbecq and his colleagues, and is a model approach to problem identification and program planning (Delbecq, Van de Ven, & Gustafson, 1975). This group process method was designed for the identification of organizational problems and formulation of appropriate and innovative tactics to solve them. Following an initial problem identification and ranking process, the nominal group is a methodology for involving critical reference groups in successive phases of program planning and development: (a) clients (consumers) and first-line staff, in the problem exploration stage; (b) external resource people and internal specialists, in solution and resource exploration; (c) key administrators and resource controllers, in priority development; (d) organizational staff in program proposal inception and development; and (e) all constituencies, in final approval and designs for evaluation.

The usefulness of the nominal group technique is based on Delbecq and Van de Ven's research, which indicated that a nominal group—one in which individuals work in the presence of one another but initially do not interact—allows production of a greater number of problem dimensions, more high-quality suggestions, and a larger number of more highly differentiated kinds of solutions than groups in which members are encouraged or allowed to interact during the generation of critical problem variables (Delbecq & Van de Ven, 1971).

The nominal group process initially involves silent, individual effort in a group setting, with working groups limited to eight to ten individuals. Basically, the process includes posing a question or a series of questions to a group and inviting each group member to list brief responses or answers to the question during a silent period of 10–15 minutes. These questions may seek possible solutions to a particular problem or may merely seek opinions about a particular human service problem in a community. When used in human service need assessment, participants may be asked to identify their own human service needs, to list the needs they perceive for other groups in the community, or to identify important factors or issues to be considered in a community program planning process. This initial silent time spent in idea generation is followed by an interval in which all ideas generated by individuals are shared with the total group. The group leader, in round-robin fashion, asks each participant to offer one idea from his or her list. Each idea is then recorded on large sheets of paper, which are then displayed for continued review by the total group. Every effort is made to record the ideas exactly as they are offered from the participants. The leader continues the round-robin until all ideas on each participant's list are exhausted. This procedure may take 1–2 hours, depending upon the type of questions posed and the number of ideas generated. During this phase, participants are asked to refrain from making comments or discussing any of the ideas, as the round-robin is for enumeration of ideas only.

Once the round-robin is completed, a discussion period follows in which participants are free to clarify, elaborate, or defend any of the ideas presented. During this discussion, participants may add new ideas to the list; they may eliminate certain ideas; they may combine ideas that seem to overlap substantially; or they may condense ideas that appear similar. One means of facilitating this process is for the leader to read one idea at a time from the list generated, to ask for discussion, comments, or questions in reference to that idea, and then to move on to the next. Participants are not required to defend or otherwise substantiate an idea.

Once the leader feels that sufficient clarification has been achieved, each participant is then asked to select those ideas (from the total list) that are considered most important. Each person selects five or more (as desired) ideas judged personally to be most important, and ranks them accordingly. These "votes" are then tallied, and the result is the group's rank ordering of those ideas generated in order of importance. In a human services need assessment, for example, individuals may be asked to rank those identified needs which are the most critical for program planning and intervention. All selection and ranking is done individually and anonymously.

The nominal group technique allows for group decision making or idea sharing without the typical competitive problems of the interacting group. Also, each participant privately expresses his or her perception of the relative importance of the many different problem areas or need areas generated by the group as a whole. The silent period in the nominal group process is critical to the production of ideas. It allows each member time for reflection and thought. It encourages the generation of minority ideas; it avoids hidden agendas; it imposes a burden on all present to work and contribute and to have a sense of responsibility for the group's success; it facilitates creativity; it allows for the airing of personal concerns; and it is especially useful in a heterogeneous group as it does not allow any one person or point of view to dominate.

By following the silent period with round-robin sharing, all ideas are shared with the group before they are discussed and each member has assurance that all of his or her ideas will be heard. In the discussion that follows, the feedback and information-sharing benefits of the interacting group are gained. The group has a chance to question and to clarify each idea presented. Other advantages accruing to the nominal group technique include social modeling of disclosure by more secure group members, which facilitates disclosure on the part of less secure members; a setting in which the pooling of resources from a heterogeneous, potentially noncollaborative group may occur; and finally, the potential for new perspectives on or cognitive remapping of "old" or existing problems.

The main disadvantage of the nominal group technique is that it lacks precision. Votes or rankings are made without thorough or careful sorting out of all of the ideas generated into appropriate categories. Another disadvantage, and quite an important one in our experience, is that although most participants enjoy the process and feel satisfied with the results, some participants may feel manipulated because they are not used to participating in a highly structured process. These disadvantages are minor and can be handled by careful planning, preparation of participants, and followup feedback to participants.

## The Delphi Technique

An additional community groups approach to human service need identification is the Delphi technique (Dalkey, 1967; Dalkey & Helmer, 1963). The Delphi is a procedure for the systematic solicitation and collation of informed judgments on a particular topic (Delbecq et al., 1975). The Delphi is usually composed of a set of carefully designed sequential questionnaires. With each subsequent questionnaire, summarized information and opinion feedback derived from earlier questionnaires are provided. This summarized information is carefully organized to provide a common reference point against which the Delphi judges base their responses. The sequential questionnaires take the form of a structured dialogue between persons who do not meet, but whose opinions are valuable to the issue at hand.

This method for systematically eliciting and refining group judgments has three defining characteristics (Dalkey, 1969; Delbecq et al., 1975): (a) anonymous response to question or questions, (b) iteration or controlled feedback of various stages of the information collection process, and (c) statistical analysis and formulation of group responses.

First, anonymity may be ensured by the use of questionnaires or, where resources permit, on-line computer communication. Second, the Delphi exercise is conducted in a series of rounds between which a summary of the results of the previous round is distributed to each participant. Third, the form in which this controlled feedback is given is statistical, and usually consists of the group medium (Dalkey, 1967, 1969; Delbecq et al., 1975), although other less directive forms of iteration are being considered (e.g., the quantity of the individual's score).

The Delphi technique consists of five basic steps:

1. A questionnaire is developed relative to a key issue or set of issues.
2. Questionnaires are distributed to a panel of experts or key individuals. Since it is not necessary and often not desirable to have these experts meet, the questionnaire can be mailed to the participants serving on the panel.
3. When the questionnaires are returned, the results are tallied to determine areas of agreement and disagreement.
4. When disagreement occurs, a second questionnaire containing the various reasons given by the experts for their initial judgments is distributed to the panel.

5. The above steps are repeated, hopefully until an agreement can be reached.

The Delphi has typically gained widest use in areas of broad- or long-range policy formulation in, for example, the U.S. Air Force and in industry for technological forecasting and evaluation of corporate planning (Helmer, 1967). Various public agencies are beginning to use the Delphi for planning exercises related to education, health, and urban growth. Although the original experiments relating to the Delphi centered around questions having definitive factual answers, the originators believe this method is appropriate in areas of "value judgment" where preset "answers" are not available.

This method of assessment has a number of possible human service applications: to determine or develop a typology of human service needs; to explore or expose underlying assumptions or information leading to different judgments as to human service needs; to correlate informed judgments on a topic spanning a wide range of social roles and/or disciplines; and to educate the respondent group as to the diverse and interrelated aspects of human services needs (Turoff, 1971).

The Delphi involves at least two separate groups of individuals. First, the user body is composed of the individual or individuals expecting some product from the exercise which is useful to their purposes. Next there is a design and monitor team, which constructs the initial questionnaire, summarizes the returns, and designs the followup questionnaires. The final group of individuals involved in a Delphi effort are the respondents. It is important to note that this latter group of persons who are chosen to respond to the questionnaires may in some cases also be the user body.

There are four advantages to the Delphi technique. First, because participation can be anonymous, the inhibiting influences of dominant and more verbal participants are minimized. Second, due to the fact that feedback is controlled in a systematic manner, the negative influences of individual vested interests are reduced to a minimum. Third, because responses are anonymous, group pressure to conform is significantly decreased. Fourth, the Delphi is an efficient user of the respondents' time. Efficiency in the use of time allows the involvement of individuals who cannot otherwise become involved in other more time-consuming procedures.

The main disadvantage of the Delphi technique is the lack of certainty in guidelines on its use or design. For example, there are a number of important questions for which general agreement does not exist among practitioners, users, and critics: (a) Is the respondent group completely anonymous among its own members, to the design team, or to the user body? (b) Should the Delphi be used in conjunction with a committee or ongoing study effort? (c) Should the iterations (controlled feedback) be cycled to the same respondent group, or is there a series of separate respondent groups interacting independently or parallel with one another? (d) How many iterations are needed? and (e) What form should the feedback take? A further disadvantage is that extreme positions may be dropped in order to obtain agreement and consequently many divergent, yet creative ideas may be lost. This latter disadvantage is also shared by the nominal group and other similar approaches.

A use of the Delphi at the national planning level illustrates this technique (National Institute of Drug Abuse, 1975). The Prevention Branch of the National Institute of Drug Abuse employed the Delphi process as a part of an attempt to develop "a National Strategy for Primary Drug

Abuse Prevention." The project involved 420 prevention planners, administrators, and programmers from community programs, state agencies, and federal departments. The main objective was to promote the evolution of a national strategy for primary prevention that would be conceptually sound and capable of implementation. Furthermore, the effort was designed (a) to involve in the strategy development those federal, state and community-based practitioners who would be directly affected by it, and (b) to facilitate collaboration and resource sharing among the scattered advocates of primary prevention.

In order to attain these objectives, the following three tasks were proposed:

1. Development of a sound, supportable definition of primary drug abuse prevention
2. Clarification of what is being done now in prevention, as well as recommendations on the kinds of new strategies that should be implemented
3. Descriptions of the training and technical assistance resources needed at state and local levels.

The project was divided into two phases. In Phase I, a total of 70 participants were convened at three sites to address the objectives. The information generated at these sessions was then refined by 30 of the participants before and during a fourth meeting.

In Phase II, the Phase I recommendations were presented to an additional 340 prevention workers at five regional conferences. The results of the entire process were then tabulated and incorporated into a final report that included:

1. A working definition of primary drug abuse prevention
2. An exhaustive list of those activities that are now being done or should be done by preventors
3. A section devoted to training and technical assistance. This latter section describes the information and program support needs that were identified at all nine conferences.

## The Community Impressions Approach

The community impressions approach was developed by Cohn and her colleagues at the School of Public Health at the University of California, Berkeley (1972). It allows for direct focus on those groups in the population that have been identified as having the greatest human service needs and is a procedure for involving those groups in subsequent planning and evaluation activities directed at establishing programs to reduce their needs. A comprehensive view of needs combines hard data with impressions and feelings about need. In this process it is very important to identify and involve those groups with the greatest human service needs in both the assessment and subsequent planning and program development activities.

The community impressions approach integrates existing data about human service needs with community impressions about such needs. First, community impressions are obtained from key individuals living or working in the community. Then, on the basis of all available sources of data (social indicator, survey and community group data) groups identified as having the greatest human service needs are approached in order to verify findings and/or to explore human service needs further. The approach has three major steps:

*1. Key Informant Interviews.* In this approach, interviews are conducted with 10 or 15 individuals who have extensive first-hand knowledge of the community and who either live or work in the community. Interviewees are selected on the basis of the longevity of their involvement in the community and/or the nature of their involvement with the community. These informants are asked to provide their perspectives on the human service needs of different groups in the community. Thus, a public health nurse, members of any community action agencies, long-time residents, a policeman or fireman, the local health officer, and others are interviewed in order to elicit their impressions. The interviews are conducted from a list of questions about the existing human services in the community and about certain demographic characteristics of the population with the aid of a map of the community under study. Answers to questions such as "Where do the elderly live?" and "What public transportation exists between different parts of the community and the local community mental health center?" are recorded on the map. Slowly, a picture of the community, from service and demographic viewpoints, begins to emerge. Typically, the interview will result in some fairly concrete statements of need. Once 10 to 15 key community members have been interviewed, their impressions are collapsed onto one map. It is highly probable that there will be some discrepancies in both information and impressions. In analyzing the discrepancies in impressions about need, the need assessor should settle the discrepancies by erring "in favor" of identifying groups as having unmet needs (i.e., if one interviewee identified a group as having many human service problems, and another interviewee identified that same group as having few, the group should be recorded at this time as having many—this will be verified with the group under question at a later date).

*2. Integration of Existing Information.* Existing data from the widest possible range of needs assessment methods are then integrated with the community impressions. Emphasis here should be on balancing efforts to integrate as much available, existing data as possible in order to move toward a convergent analysis of needs. Once enough information has been collected to satisfy the assessor's need for factual information about the community, this "hard data" should be added to the map of impressions from interviewees, thus yielding a richer understanding of the needs of the community. This combined picture should not be taken as complete, however. It should ideally be validated with relevant groups in the community.

*3. The Community Forum.* A community forum is planned and held for each group or section of the community identified as having significant unmet human service needs (see the section on community forums). One purpose of the forum is to allow those groups identified as having unmet needs to validate or invalidate those needs. In addition to validation, however, the forum serves as an opportunity to explore in greater depth the nature and perceived etiology of these needs. Moreover, the forum serves as an opportunity to involve those persons with the greatest need in the process of defining and placing priorities on those needs. In this manner, the forum helps to complete the need assessment process while initiating the process of responding to the needs identified.

The community impressions approach has a number of advantages and disadvantages. First, it can be carried out with minimal expenditure of time and resources.

Second, it allows for consideration and convergence of a variety of informational sources, both those that represent what might be regarded as "factual clues" about human service needs and those that might be regarded as "impressionistic clues" about human service needs.

Third, it relies on more than information generated by "outsiders." Those identified as having unmet human service needs have an opportunity to determine whether or not they think and feel that they do in fact have unmet needs. Additionally, these groups have an opportunity to voice opinions about better procedures for meeting their needs and to become involved in activities that may lead to reduction of those needs.

Fourth, through the discussion and interaction that characterizes this approach, channels of communication among different human service agencies in the community may be strengthened or in some cases established. As a result, a more effective, broad-based, community approach to need assessment, to the establishment of priorities, and the allocation of resources may take place.

As fruitful as the community impressions approach may be, the results insofar as possible must be subjected to the same tests of reliability and validity that are applied to the results from the various types of need assessment surveys. Typically it is found that reasonable standards of reliability and validity cannot be confirmed, and the results must be generally considered as impressionistic. Due to this problem, there is no way to ensure that every group with human service needs will be identified or that all of the needs of those identified will have been recorded. Community impressions must be considered as one perspective about needs among many others, and divergencies in perspectives must be resolved in the subsequent program planning process.

The community impressions approach is most useful when one is interested in undertaking quickly and at little cost an assessment of the unmet human service needs in different groups within the community. The approach takes into consideration the content of data from other approaches *and* also the thoughts and feelings of various community members. The approach is particularly useful if one is committed to involving those with greatest needs in processes which will help reduce their needs.

## SUMMARY

Need identification and assessment are integral aspects of human service planning and development. *Need identification* is the process of describing the health and social service needs of a geographic area. In the *need assessment* process, planners set priorities on identified needs with reference to relative importance, available resources, and available service technology.

The area of need assessment-identification is in its nascence, and no universally accepted methodology exists that will yield a comprehensive assessment of need. Moreover, the evaluation and interpretation of human service need is influenced by (a) the vested interests and values of those formulating program goals; (b) the diffuse and interrelated nature of social and health needs; (c) the rapidly changing character of human service needs; and (d) the capabilities and interests of staff as well as the availability of appropriate service technology and adequate financing.

Within the limits of current assessment methodologies, information about needs is useful in (a) describing demands for services; (b) assessing service resources; (c) developing detailed community descriptions; (d) delineating groups likely "to be at risk"; (e) examining the relevance of existing services; (f) clarifying those factors that influence the occurrence of social and health problems; and (g) enumerating factors that aid or impede effective service delivery.

The most comprehensive picture of human service need can be obtained through a convergent analysis of need. Convergent analysis assumes that useful information about need emerges out of a process that receives input (a) at different, although sequential points in time; (b) from a number of different organizational levels; (c) from a variety of informational sources (community members, public records, service agency data, professional staff); and (d) through a family of assessment strategies. Further assumptions basic to a convergent analysis are that no single stakeholder, no one informational source, no single organizational level, no specific technique, and no single point in time will provide a comprehensive human service need assessment. It is only through the systematic, progressive convergence of multiple perspectives filtered through multiple assessment methods that the most useful information for planning is obtained. A convergent analysis identifies the widest range of need information that is relevant for program planning and service development by assessing need at all community and organizational levels.

The variety of assessment strategies used in a convergent analysis provides three different informational functions: (a) *compiling* existing information; (b) *developing* new information; and (c) *integrating* existing and newly developed information. There are advantages and disadvantages of each need assessment strategy when viewed in isolation. However, when seen as part of a total convergence of information, deployment of a range of methods provides the basis for an integrated perspective on need.

There are three basic orientations to assessing human service need: (a) the social and health indicators approach; (b) social area surveys; and (c) the community groups approaches. The *social and health indicator approach* to need assessment compiles publicly available information, and, on the basis of these data, needs are inferred. *Social area surveys* compile and integrate information about demands for service; provide information about resources that are currently available to meet the needs of the community; and provide citizens' views about needs and need priorities. In addition, new information can be generated on a personal self-report level from community members through direct interview surveys. Finally, the community group approaches to assessment are quick and inexpensive methods to use in conjunction with other assessment techniques. The group methods provide perspectives from community members by developing new information, compiling already existing information, and integrating existing information with the perspectives of persons living in the community.

## REFERENCES


Attkisson, C. C., Hargreaves, W. A., Horowitz, M. J., & Sorenson, J. E. (Eds.). *Evaluation of human service programs.* New York: Academic Press, Inc., 1978.

Beigel, A., Hunter, E. J., Tamerin, J. S., Chapin, E. H., & Lowery, M. J. Planning for the development of comprehensive community alcoholism services: I. The prevalence survey. *American Journal of Psychiatry,* 1974, *131,* 1112–1115.

Beigel, A., McCabe, T. R., Tamerin, J. S., Lowery, M. J., Chapin, E. H., & Hunter, E. J. Planning for the development of comprehensive community alcoholism services: II. Assessing community awareness and attitudes. *American Journal of Psychiatry,* 1974, *131,* 1116–1120.

Bloom, B. L. *Changing patterns of psychiatric care.* New York: Human Sciences Press, 1975.

Blum, H. L. *Planning for health.* New York: Human Sciences Press, 1974.

Broskowski, A., & Baker, F. Professional, organizational, and social barriers to primary prevention. *American Journal of Orthopsychiatry,* 1974, *44,* 707–719.

Campbell, D. T., & Fiske, D. W. Convergent and discriminant validation by the multitrait-multimethod matrix. *Psychological Bulletin, 1959, 56,* 81–105.

Cohn, A. H. *Solutions to unique problems encountered in identifying the medically underserved and involving them in the planning process.* Unpublished manuscript, School of Public Health, University of California, Berkeley, California, 1972.

Cox, F. M., Erlich, J. L., Rothman, J., & Tropman, J. E. (Eds.). *Tactics and techniques of community practice.* 2nd ed. Itasca, Illinois: F. E. Peacock Publishers, Inc., 1984.

Dalkey, N. C. *Delphi.* Santa Monica, California: Rand Corporation, 1967.

Dalkey, N. C. *The Delphi method: An experimental study of group opinion.* Santa Monica, California: Rand Corporation, 1969.

Dalkey, N. C., & Helmer, O. An experimental application of the Delphi method to the use of experts. *Management Science,* 1963, *9,* 458–467.

Delbecq, A. L., & Van de Ven, A. H. A group process model for problem identification and program planning. *Journal of Applied Behavioral Science,* 1971, *7,* 466–492.

Delbecq, A. L., Van de Ven, A. H., & Gustafson, D. H. *Group techniques for program planning: A guide to nominal group and Delphi processes.* Glenview, Illinois: Scott Foresman & Company, 1975.

Demone, H. W., & Harshbarger, D. (Eds.). *A handbook of human service organizations.* New York: Behavioral Publications, 1974.

Feldstein, P. J. Research on the demand for health services. In J. B. McKinlay (Ed.), *Economic aspects of health care.* New York: Prodist, Milbank Memorial Fund, 1973.

Goldsmith, H. F., Unger, E. L., Rosen. B. M., Shambaugh, J. P., & Windle, C. D. *A typological approach to doing social area analysis.* (DHEW Publication No. ADM 76-262.) Washington, D.C.: U.S. Government Printing Office, 1975.

Helmer, O. *Analysis of the future: The Delphi method.* Santa Monica, California: Rand Corporation, 1967.

Meier, R. *Contra Costa mental health needs.* Unpublished manuscript. Contra Costa County Mental Health Services. Martinez, California. 1973.

National Institute of Drug Abuse, Prevention Branch, Division of Resource Development. *Pyramid.* 1975, *1,* 1–2. (Available from: NIDA, 1526 18th Street, N.W., Washington, D.C. 20036.)

Robin, S. A procedure for securing returns to mail questionnaires. *Sociology and Social Research,* 1965, *50,* 24–35.

Schaefer, M. E. Demand versus need for medical services in a general cost-benefit setting. *American Journal of Public Health,* 1975, *65,* 293–295.

Schulberg, H. C., & Wechsler, H. The uses and misuses of data in assessing mental health needs. *Community Mental Health Journal,* 1967, *3,* 389–395.

Schwartz, R. Follow-up by phone or by mail. *Evaluation.* 1973, *1(2),* 25–26.

Sheldon, E. B., & Parke, R. Social indicators. *Science,* 1975, *188,* 693–699.

Siegel, L. M., Attkisson, C. C., & Cohn, A. H. Mental health needs assessment: Strategies and techniques. In W. A. Hargreaves, C. C. Attkisson, & J. E. Sorensen (Eds.). *Resource materials for community mental health program evaluation* (2nd ed.). (DHEW Publication No. ADM 77-328.) Washington, D.C.: U.S. Government Printing Office, 1977.

Turoff, M. Delphi and its potential impact on information systems. *AFIPS Conference Proceedings,* 1971, *39,* 317–326.

Warheit, G. J., Bell, R. A., & Schwab, J. J. *Planning for change: Needs assessment approaches.* Rockville, Maryland: National Institute of Mental Health, 1974.

2.

**Yeheskel Hasenfeld**

# ANALYZING THE HUMAN SERVICE AGENCY

Social work practice is embedded in an organizational context. The characteristics of the organization—mandate and domain, interorganizational relations, service technology, and structure of work—determine to a significant extent how social workers discharge their professional responsibilities, and particularly the structure and content of their relations and transactions with client systems. To wit: organizational mandate and domain define the type of clients the worker will encounter; interorganizational relations influence the resources the worker will have to respond to client needs; and the service technology will prescribe the range of service techniques and procedures the worker can use. Most importantly, the degree of professional discretion available to the worker is organizationally determined.

To enhance their effectiveness, social workers must understand the organizational parameters and dynamics which shape their role performance and responses to client systems. Too readily, workers tend to blame the client, themselves, or their immediate superiors for perceived failures and difficulties in responding to client needs. Less often do they realize and recognize that factors inherent in the political economy of the organization constrain their behavior and professional effectiveness (Hasenfeld, 1983). Such misplaced "diagnosis" renders the workers impotent in attempting to change and improve their performance. It is, therefore, incumbent on the social workers to understand the political economy of their organization, namely the determinants and processes by which power and resources are mobilized from the environment and allocated internally (Wamsley and Zald, 1976). Only with such knowledge can the workers hope to undertake organizational change strategies to enhance the effectiveness of their service delivery system (Hasenfeld, 1980).

Community practitioners must understand not only the organizational context of their own practice, but also the organizations that directly affect the welfare of the client systems on whose behalf they advocate. Effective advocacy, brokerage, and mediation—key roles for community practitioners—require a thorough understanding of the political economy of the targeted organizations. Similarly, community planning, and specifically mobilization of resources on behalf of community groups, requires careful analysis of the interorganizational relations among the key human service organizations in the community. In both instances, the organizational analysis is a prerequisite for the selection of appropriate community intervention tactics.

The purpose of the following "organizational map" is to direct the worker in gathering systematic information about the organization. The aim is to give the worker a basic knowledge of the organization and to identify those elements requiring further inquiry. The first part of the mapping process focuses on the agency's interorganizational relations and includes sec-

---

Yeheskel Hasenfeld is on the faculty of the School of Social Work, UCLA.

tions on the agency environment, market relations, and regulatory groups. The second part directs attention to the internal features of the organization: its structure, technology, domain and goals, clients, and resources. Technical terms are defined at the point in the text where they are introduced.

## THE AGENCY AND INTERORGANIZATIONAL RELATIONSHIPS

### I. Agency Environment

To understand the behavior of any agency, it is necessary to be knowledgeable about the community in which it functions. A wide array of factors may influence agency behavior, but it is expected that these will vary among agencies and communities.

A. Locate, study, and summarize demographic data relevant to understanding the environment in which this agency exists. Included would be data about population composition and mobility, economic base, tax policy and situation, governmental, welfare, business and industrial structures, housing, medical facilities, and so forth. (Sources for the above data include: U.S. Census and Department of Labor reports, courts, city planning commissions, school census and planning reports, Chamber of Commerce, university library, etc.)

B. As far as possible, map the "organization set" for the agency being studied. Indicate differential types of relationships such as formal authority, regulatory, complementary, informal, etc.
   1. Of these relationships, which ones are perceived by the agency as most important in the transactions? Why? Which ones the least? Why?
   2. With which additional groups, organizations, institutions, etc., would the agency like to develop relationships? Why?
   3. Identify any major problems the agency has encountered in developing linkages with other groups.

C. What is the nature of the communication system between the agency and its "organizational set"?
   1. What mechanisms has the agency used or developed to secure and process information from its organizational set and the general environment?
   2. Identify formal and informal channels of communication.
   3. What is the quality of the information exchanged?
   4. What barriers and gaps to communication can be identified?

D. What planning, coordinating, or governing bodies exist between the agency and its organizational set?
   1. Does the agency have delegated representatives to such bodies? If so, to which groups? How are representatives selected?
   2. Is content from these activities considered in agency meetings or is the representation only a pro forma type?

E. Identify the principal sources of material resources for the agency (e.g., taxes, fees, contributions, endowments).
   1. What strategies has the agency developed to secure and maintain resources?
   2. What problems has the agency encountered in this area?

F. Identify any major areas of conflict between the agency and members of the "organizational set." How has the agency handled such conflict?

G. As far as possible assess the relative power position of the agency to other groups in the organizational set.

1. How much influence does the agency seem to have?
2. What coalitions, if any, has the agency joined? Why?

H. Identify the principal sources of legitimation for the agency (e.g., political groups, governmental units, public at large, professional organizations, special interest groups).

In all of the above, indicate the impact of the various environmental characteristics upon the activities of the agency. For example, do certain characteristics of the "organization set" facilitate or constrain agency decision making?

From the perspective of the organization, what type of external pressures and forces have interfered most in the organization accomplishing its goals? What modes of influence and adaptation has the organization used to minimize such pressures?

## II. Market Relations

Market relations are: (1) the complex of arrangements, exchanges, and contingencies the target agency (i.e., the agency under study) encounters in disposing of its output. The units which receive the agency's outputs are "receiving units" (questions A–J). (2) Its relations with other agencies offering complementary and similar (competing) services (questions K–T). Complementary services are those services provided by external units which assist the target agency in achieving its tasks with the clients, services given to clients concomitantly with those of the target agency, and services given to clients upon referral by the target agency.

A. Identify the major external units (families, communities, agencies, etc.) which import, purchase, or use the agency's outputs; in so doing, indicate the nature and proportion of the agency's output marketed to each of these units.

B. How does the target agency identify external units as actual or potential "receiving units"?
   1. Is information about the receiving units (e.g., their address, contact personnel, input criteria) readily available in codified form for appropriate staff in the target agency?
      a. If "no," how do staff know about potential receiving units?
      b. If "yes," provide illustrative examples and indicate how such information is maintained "current."

C. Where possible, for each of the units receiving the outputs of the agency, identify:
   1. The amount of freedom they have in accepting or rejecting the output.
   2. The nature of the preconditions, if any, they set up for accepting certain outputs.

D. Can you discern how these preconditions were set up and by whom?

E. What type of information, if any, is requested by each of these units about the output and in what form is it furnished to them? (For example, what information is given to a halfway house that accepts a client from a state hospital?)

F. Who in the agency is in charge of marketing the agency's outputs to these units? What is their training and status in the agency?

G. From interviews with these staff and analyzing clients' characteristics upon exit from the agency, estimate the extent to which the agency takes into account the preconditions and specifications made by the units receiving the outputs.

H. Are there any indications of difficulties, strains, and problems on the part of the agency in meeting these preconditions? Describe them.

I. What are the possible and actual reactions of the receiving units if some preconditions are not met?

J. Summarize the patterns of the relations between the target agency and each of its receiving units.

K. Identify the units which provide *complementary* services to the target agency. In so doing, describe:
   1. The nature of the service given.
   2. The kinds of clients (or staff) receiving it.
   3. The frequency with which these services are provided.

L. Identify the preconditions, if any, that the target agency must meet to secure these services.

M. How do staff evaluate the importance of securing each of these services in terms of accomplishing their tasks?

N. What services, payments, or other resources does the target agency provide, if any, to each of these units?

O. Identify those agencies in the community which provide services *similar* to the target agency. Indicate the extent of the similarity in terms of services given and clients served.

P. How does the executive core of the target agency compare the agency vis-à-vis these agencies in terms of:
   1. Tasks performed by staff?
   2. Desired goals to be achieved?
   3. Characteristics of clients?
   4. Staff-client relations?

   Indicate in the comparison what is perceived to be unique to the target agency by the executive core.

Q. Rank these agencies and the target agency in terms of budget size, number of clients served per year, and number of line personnel. (In the case of multifunction agencies, compare the subunits engaged in the same kinds of services.)

R. Does the target agency have any form of contact, arrangement, etc., with these agencies? If so, describe their content.

S. Is there competition for clients among these agencies? If so, how is it manifested?

T. Are there efforts underway to move toward complementarity, combines, or other forms of organization where the target agency and one or more other agencies provide similar services for clients?

## III. Regulatory Groups

Regulatory groups are all the major organizations, legislative or legal bodies, associations, boards, etc., toward which the target agency must be *accountable* and from which it must receive approval, formal and informal, for its domain and the legitimacy of its activities. Such units may certify the agency, review operations of the agency as a whole or subunits of it, enact rules the agency must adopt, etc.

A. Identify the major units and organizations that periodically inspect, review, and evaluate various aspects of the agency's activities. In so doing classify the various units according to:
   1. The regulatory function that each unit performs (e.g., certifies, accredits, makes recommendations, legislative review, etc.)
   2. The aspect of the agency's activities of concern to each of these units.
   3. The kinds of mechanisms each unit uses to maintain relations with the agency and vice versa (e.g., representative from an agency's board, periodic meetings. etc.).

B. What criteria, if any, are being used by each unit to evaluate the agency's activities?

C. Were these criteria agreed upon mutually by the agency and the unit, imposed on the agency, suggested by the agency, or established in other ways? What is the agency's view of the legitimacy and utility of the regulatory unit's regulatory efforts?
D. What specific kinds of information are requested by these units and in what form is information furnished to them? Analyze the nature of the information given in terms of:
   1. Is it intrinsic to the nature of the activities reviewed; that is, does the information directly describe the nature of the activities reviewed, or provide some indirect assessment of them?
   2. Does each unit requesting the information specify the kind of questions, data, and analysis it wants, or are these left to agency personnel to decide?
   3. Is the information provided on a continuous or discontinuous basis?
   4. Does the information provided lend itself to further analysis beyond that done by the agency? If so, does the agency receive any feedback from the regulatory units about comparative performance, etc., vis-à-vis other similar agencies?
E. Who in the agency is in charge of maintaining relations and working with these units? In each of the regulatory units who is in charge of maintaining contact with the target agency, and how is it done?
F. What are the possible sanctions that each of these units can impose on the agency? Rank the units in terms of severity of sanctions each can potentially impose. Can the unit freely impose the sanctions?
G. By interviewing the agency's executive core, find out which of these units they consider the agency is most dependent upon in terms of continuation of services and what reasons they give for their assertions.
H. Based on your observations, review of reports, etc., estimate the amount of effort, resources, and personnel time spent by the agency to meet the requirements of each unit.
I. For each of these units, what do the agency's staff conceive to be the regulatory group's expectations re:
   1. The characteristics of the clients?
   2. The desired changes to be achieved?
   3. The appropriate intervention techniques that need to be utilized?
J. What is the nature of any discrepancies between each unit's expectations and those of other units or the staff's expectations?
K. Assess the impact of the regulatory functions of each of these units upon the effectiveness and efficiency of the provision of services to clients by the agency.
L. Identify any civic groups which, though they do not carry regulatory functions, have been involved in supporting, challenging, or expressing concern about the mandate of the agency.
   1. Estimate the resources (financial, personnel, prestige, connections with other organizations, etc.) that each of these groups has or can mobilize.
   2. What types of pressures or support have they brought on the agency?
   3. Identify any conflicting expectations these groups may have in relation to the agency's operations.
   4. How does the agency handle its relations with each of these groups?

## ORGANIZATIONAL ANALYSIS

### I. Organizational Structures, Technologies, and Processes

A. Structure
   1. Outline the organizational chart of

the agency, identifying the major formal structural components which can be used to characterize the organization.

2. What various informal structures can be identified in the organization, and what effects, if any, have these structures had on organizational technologies and processes?

B. Technology
   1. Describe the various types of technologies in the organization.
      a. The organization's standards governing the performance, control, and specification of that technology.
      b. The kind of feedback mechanisms that exist or have been established to assess the technology.
      c. The manner in which that technology is linked with other components of the organization.
      d. The method of evaluating the output.

C. Decision making. Identify issues that have significant consequences for the service delivery of the agency.
   1. Describe the factors that have led to the emergence of each issue.
   2. Identify the roles and positions of the key participants in the decision-making process.
   3. Evaluate the relative influences or power of each participant.
   4. What position toward the issue did each participant take? What assumptions and ideologies underlay them?
   5. Identify the processes and procedures through which decisions were reached or attempted.
   6. What relations (i.e., locations, bargaining, competition) were formed among the participants in arriving at each decision?
   7. Assess the degree of participation in the decision process of various staff groups and clients.
   8. What organizational constraints played a role in affecting the nature of the issue and the resulting decision?
   9. What mechanisms were developed to implement the decisions?
   10. How will the decisions affect services?

D. Control-coordinating. Describe the formal and informal process of socialization and control of individual staff members, divisions or departments, and clients in the organization.

E. Conflict-communication
   1. Identify and describe major areas of internal and external conflict.
   2. What strategies and tactics have been used by the organization to resolve these conflicts?
   3. What type of conflict has been viewed by the organization as functional? Why? What type as dysfunctional? Why?
   4. What systems have been developed for transmitting information within and outside of the organization?
   5. How does the agency evaluate the effectiveness of the received and transmitted information, both within and outside of the organization?

## II. Organizational Domain and Goals

A. Organizational domain means the claims which the organization stakes out for itself in terms of: (1) the range of human problems, issues, and concerns it purports to handle. (These may include concerns about problems of malfunctioning as well as concerns about enhancement and improvement of individual and social functioning); (2)

the services offered; and (3) the population entitled to use the service.

1. Identify and list the specific human problems and concerns that this agency is set up to handle. In so doing, classify these by (a) the unit to which the problem or concern is related (e.g., individual, family, community, etc.), and (b) what in the unit is the target of concern (e.g., occupational role of the individual, parent-child relations, organization of community health services, etc).
2. Identify and list the services that the agency offers vis-à-vis the problems and issues it attempts to handle.
3. Identify those units which are eligible for the services offered by the agency. In so doing enumerate the conditions and qualifications they have to meet in order to be officially eligible for services.

B. Organizational goals. The concept of organizational goals generates different meanings and different guides for action in various parts of the organization, varying with the frames of reference and objectives of those who define or interpret organizational goals. Yet, they should be distinguished from organizational domain. The domain defines the areas in which the organization will function, but not the desired ends and outcomes its members aim at achieving in these areas and the corresponding services. Such definitions are the function of goals.

1. Cite the official statements, if any, which describe the mission and goals of the agency. Have there been major changes in the content of such statements in the agency's recent past?
2. As a result of interviewing the executive core of the agency, how would you describe their perspectives on the organization's goals?
   a. What do they see as the agency's objectives in relation to the clients? What priorities do they establish among the several goals?
   b. What perceptions do they have about the relevant characteristics of their clients as they define them?
   c. What roles do they see the agency playing in the larger community?
   d. What aspects of the agency's programs do they see as best reflecting their objectives?
   e. What do they identify as the major problems or tasks that require prompt solutions?
3. Summarize the ideological commitments of the executive core, that is, their belief systems about the characteristics of the clients; the nature and purpose of the intervention technologies; the desired changes to be achieved in the clients and the role of line personnel vis-à-vis clients.
4. From interviews with line personnel answer the following:
   a. What do they perceive as their major objectives in relation to clients?
   b. Can you discern a priority ranking among the various objectives mentioned?
   c. What perceptions do they hold about the relevant characteristics of their clients?
   d. What perceptions do they hold about the proper staff-client relations?
   e. What role do they see the agency playing in the larger community?
5. From interviews with clients, answer the following:

a. What do they see as the major objectives of the agency?
b. What expectations do they have of staff?
c. What would they like the agency to do which it does not do currently?

6. Summarize the similarities and discrepancies among the perspectives of the executive core, line staff, and clients about agency's goals.
7. From observations of staff-clients relations, what are your conclusions as to actual tasks that staff perform?
8. From reviewing the agency's allocation of personnel, budget, and other resources to various work units, which tasks and objectives receive more priority?
9. Compare the existing priority given to various tasks based on allocation of resources to that purported by the executive core and other staff.

### III. Client Inputs

A. Present a profile of the clients served by this agency.
   1. If the clients are individuals or families describe:
      a. Age, sex, and race
      b. Socioeconomic status
      c. Place of residence
      d. Most frequent presenting problems or concern
   2. If the clients are other organizations or associations, describe:
      a. The stated goals and functions of these organizations
      b. The major services they provide to achieve their goals
      c. The characteristics of their constituent population (see 1)
      d. The amount of resources (financial, personnel) these organizations have

B. What is the rate or extent of the problem in the community which the agency is designed to serve? What proportion of this possible case load is served by the agency?

C. What admission criteria do clients have to meet in order to benefit from the services of the agency?

D. How were these criteria established (e.g., were they externally imposed, based on individual staff decision, etc.); and how much control did the agency's staff have in setting them?

E. Observing staff, analyzing data on the clients' characteristics, and comparing those accepted for services versus those rejected, identify the *actual* mechanisms staff use to select and screen clients.

F. How do these compare to the formally stated admission criteria?

G. Identify and chart the different routes that clients can take in the agency, and indicate some of the major criteria used to route clients at each juncture (e.g., initial routing to major divisions in the agency, further routing to specific services, movement from one work unit to another, etc.). Develop a flow chart of initial client case processing.

H. In assigning clients to services, can you differentiate subcohorts of clients, each of whom is characterized by a common client profile and a common service (e.g., all clients of a certain age, race, income, and problem receive a certain kind of service)?

I. By interviewing and observing staff and clients, analyze the extent to which clients can actively negotiate their admission for services and be actively involved in decisions about the kinds of services that will be provided for them.

J. Can you identify what types of clients have better chances of negotiating successfully with staff as compared to those who have little chances of doing so?

K. What alternatives do clients have in seeking the needed services?

L. To what extent is the agency dependent on clients for financial support?

M. To what extent is cooperation on the part of the client essential for staff to perform their tasks?

N. Are clients referred to the agency by other organizations (or individual professionals)? If so,
   1. Describe the organizations engaged in referral and the extent of their referral.
   2. Analyze the extent to which the target agency is dependent upon each of these organizations for receiving clients, financial support, professional services (e.g., testing, diagnosis, supporting services, etc.) and personnel.
   3. To what extent is the target agency free to accept or reject referrals?
   4. What kinds of services, if any, does the target agency reciprocate for referrals?

O. Identify any pressures exerted on the agency to accept and reject certain client cohorts:
   1. What are the agency's responses to these demands?
   2. What do you consider to be the organizational reasons for such responses?

P. Identify the people in the agency in charge of client intake, their professional status, and their position in the agency.

Q. What is the ratio of clients per line staff (e.g., average case load)?

R. Can you infer from observations and other information what types of clients the agency seems to prefer?

S. In some agencies clients are given some form of representation (e.g., P.T.A. membership, advisory board, etc.). Do clients in the target agency have any form of representation? If so, describe:
   1. The criteria used and the ways clients are recruited to such roles
   2. The formal tasks assigned to such a body
   3. The nature of the decisions made by this body
   4. The role of staff vis-à-vis this representation
   5. The amount of influence such a body has on the agency's policies and the amount of control staff have on the decisional processes of this group

T. Are there any segments of the agency's clients who are organized in some formal pattern, yet not represented in the agency governance structure (e.g., welfare recipients' associations)? If so,
   1. Describe the characteristics of the clients belonging to that association
   2. How did it come into being?
   3. What are its major objectives?
   4. What strategies are being utilized to achieve these objectives?
   5. How does the executive core react and respond to this association?
   6. Can you discern any influence such association has over the agency's policies?

U. What are the various methods used by the agency to assess clients' needs?

V. From the perspectives of the executive, various other staff, client community residents, or others outside the organization, what are the areas of conflicts and gaps in client services and types of service delivery patterns in the organization? What steps have been taken to resolve conflicts and close such gaps?

### IV. Resources Inputs

By resources inputs we refer mainly to those external units which provide the target agency with its financial basis and those units which provide its personnel. You should note that many units will assume a number of functions in relation to the target agency, such as combining regulatory and funding functions. Hence there may be considerable overlap in your analysis of these units.

A. Financial

1. Identify the major units which provide the agency with its financial resources.
   a. What proportion of the total agency's budget is contributed by each of these units?
   b. To what extent does each supporting unit specify the activities for which the funds are to be allocated?
2. What criteria are being used by each of these units in determining their allocation of resources to the agency?
3. Can you discern whether these criteria have been determined by the unit exclusively, by negotiation with the target agency, or what?
4. What types of information are requested by these units, and in what forms are they furnished to them? Provide examples.
5. Who in the agency is in charge of maintaining relations and working with the target agency?
6. In each of the funding units, who is in charge of maintaining contact with the target agency?
   a. What forms do such contacts take?
   b. Does such a person participate in the policy decision-making processes in the agency?
7. Through interviewing agency's staff in charge of contact with each unit, what do they perceive to be the specific preconditions and requirements that the agency has to meet in order to secure funds from each unit?
8. Based on your observations, review of reports, etc., estimate the amount of efforts, resources, and personnel time spent by the agency to meet the requirements of each unit.
9. Are there any indications of difficulties or strains on the part of the agency to meet the preconditions set by the funding units?
10. How do these external units check whether their requirements have been met by the agency?
11. Can agency's staff identify any expectations or beliefs on the part of each funding unit regarding:
    a. The characteristics of the clients?
    b. The desired changes to be achieved?
    c. The appropriate intervention techniques?
    d. The role of staff vis-à-vis clients?
12. How do these beliefs compare with those of the agency's staff?
13. Assess the impact that each funding unit has on the ways in which the agency renders its services (e.g., type of service given, nature of personnel agency can afford to hire, number of clients served, etc.), through the requirements each makes, the amount of resources given, restrictions on their use, and the like.
14. What external units are considered to be the agency's immediate competitors for resources vis-à-vis each of the fund providing units?
15. Does the target agency provide any services to each of the funding units?

Are there other agencies which provide similar services to these units?

16. Describe the budgetary process in the agency in relation to such factors as planning programs, determining cost, securing funds, allocating funds, etc.
17. Describe the method(s) the agency has used in an attempt to measure benefits (outcome). To what extent is the planned program congruent with the organization's outputs? What problems have been encountered internally and externally in justifying its program and budget?

B. Personnel

1. Identify the units from which the agency's personnel are recruited.
2. What criteria are used by the agency for hiring personnel for each major work unit (excluding building maintenance staff)?
3. Analyze staff characteristics in terms of their formal education, training for current task, and prior experience.
4. What methods are used by the agency to recruit its staff? What problems does the executive core encounter in recruitment efforts?
5. In the eyes of the executive core what kinds of demands, questions, and contingencies are expressed by potential staff as conditions for employment?
6. How are these met and handled by the agency?
7. Are there any direct relations between the agency and the units which provide staff?
   a. Describe the nature of these relations.
   b. Does the agency provide any services (e.g., training, research, etc.) to these units?
8. Identify the major professional and occupational associations with which staff affiliate. Does their affiliation serve a regulatory function? If so, how?
9. Are there conflicts among staff groups with different professional and organizational affiliations in relation to their beliefs? How are these expressed in the agency?
10. From the perspectives of the executive core, which of these associations has had the greatest influence on the agency's ideologies in working with clients?
11. What formal and informal criteria are used for evaluating the performance of staff?
12. What is the agency's orientation to the use of paraprofessionals?
13. If there are paraprofessionals in the agency, what mechanisms, if any, are or have been used to integrate professional and paraprofessional staff?
14. Has the agency experienced any particular positive and negative consequences as a result of employing paraprofessionals?

## CONCLUSION

The mapping of the agency's critical elements should provide you with a beginning understanding of its structure and operations. Morever, it should sensitize you to those aspects of the agency which are most relevant to the community organization issue you are addressing. For example, should your concern be the increased access to agency services by clients from oppressed social groups, the mapping may indicate the magnitude of the problem by studying the client input patterns and point to potential barriers that may exist because of personnel characteristics and training, interorganizational relations, or the operationalization of agency domain and goals. Hence, the mapping process serves as a diagnostic tool in identifying organizational factors affecting community practice.

**REFERENCES**

Hasenfeld, Y., "Implementation of Change in Human Service Organizations: A Political Economy Perspective," *Social Service Review* 54(1980): 508–520.

______, *Human Service Organizations* (Englewood Cliffs, N.J.: Prentice-Hall, 1983).

Wamsley, G.L., and M. H. Zald, *The Political Economy of Public Organizations* (Bloomington, Ind.: Indiana University Press, 1976).

## 3.

**Wynetta Devore and Elfreide Schlesinger**

## ETHNIC-SENSITIVE PRACTICE WITH FAMILIES

While social work is practiced in many different settings, most practice involves work with families, whether work is carried out in the voluntary family service agency, the juvenile justice system, the schools, the health care system, and many others. Whether a marriage is tottering or a child is ill or in trouble with the law or at school, the family as a system is or should be involved. Problems are frequently traced to the family at the same time as the family is sought as source of support and solution. It is within the family that many life cycle tasks are carried out.

Understanding of family dynamics, of intergenerational struggles, and of how the ethnic reality impinges on the family's capacity to play its varying roles is crucial for the ethnic-sensitive social worker.

Wynetta Devore is a professor at the School of Social Work, University of Syracuse. Elfreide Schlesinger is a professor at the School of Social Work, Rutgers.

In this chapter, prevailing views of family functioning are reviewed. These are related to the model of ethnic-sensitive practice developed.

Case examples serve as the vehicle for illustrating how the perspectives of ethnic-sensitive practice are brought to bear on work with troubled families.

The family is a major primary group; its tasks, though universal, are interpreted in diverse ways by each ethnic group and at each social class level.

Family functions have been and continue to be discussed in the literature. Analysts continue to concern themselves with the changes that have come about as America has moved from an agricultural to a technological society. In earlier days the family performed economic, status-giving, educational, religious, recreational, protective, and affectional functions. Other institutions such as the school and the church have assumed greater responsibility for education and religious development of family members. Much family-centered recreation has been replaced by sports events in which individuals may be participants or spectators; and by social clubs, movies, and concerts. Many activities are related to life cycle stage (Cub Scouts, Pop Warner Football, business womens' clubs, senior citizens' clubs).

The family continues to have major economic and affectional functions—generally known as the *instrumental* and *expressive* functions.

An alternative interpretation of the functions of the family has been presented by Ackerman (1958). It is a more contemporary view of the major social purposes served by the family that focuses on the development of the expressive function. Ackerman stresses (1) the provision of opportunity for "social togetherness," the matrix for the affectional bond of family relationships; (2) the opportunity to evolve a personal identity, tied to family identity; (3) the patterning of sexual roles; (4) the training for integration into social roles and the acceptance of social responsibility; as well as (5) the cultivation of learning and support for individual creativity and initiative. Ogburn's perspective (1938) in relation to the economic and affectional function and Ackerman's expansion of the latter form a base from which to consider the family in relation to the ethnic reality.

The definitions of family are as varied as are the delineation of its functions. The one selected here is particularly useful for our purposes since it encompasses the varied family constellations which are encountered in the course of social work practice. Papajohn and Spiegel (1975) developed a framework for family analysis intended to detect family states or conditions conducive to "good" or "bad" mental health. Their framework is universal, in that it imposes no boundaries, except those determined by families themselves. Among their reference points for defining family are two that are useful for our purposes:

1. The family is a major unit of the social system. Its structural and functional characteristics extend into other subsystems such as the occupational and educational system.
2. The family is an agency for the transmission of cultural values.

In its form and function the family is connected with the values of a given ethnic group (Papajohn and Spiegel, 1975). These ethnic values are the core of ethnicity which has survived through many generations in various forms.

In presenting our model of ethnic-sensitive practice we called attention to the importance of relating the past history of ethnic groups to the contemporary situations which they confront. The exploration of that history will reveal that the values held by various groups are a product of that history, and that these cannot easily be separated from sociopolitical events. For example, the interrelatedness between the "Polish character" and its past history is clarified by this statement made by Edmund Muskie, a prominent Polish American (1966). "There is much of glory in Poland's past—glory which was the product of the love of liberty, fierce independence, intense patriotism, and courage so characteristic of the Polish people." The past to which Muskie referred included guarantees of religious freedom laid down in 1573, and the development of a constitution in 1791 which considered individual freedom as essential to the well-being of the nation. The Polish family of the present is a product of that history and may be expected to hold many of the values that Muskie identifies. Fiery independence continues to characterize many Poles. As we have noted over and over again, such values seep into the dispositions to work, to child-rearing, and to the role of women. As Polish and other ethnic families encounter mainstream America, struggles may ensue as values begin to shift or take on a different shape. Social workers must be aware of the delicate balance which sometimes ensues. The third-generation Italian father is less distrusting of the outsider than was his grandfather and may allow his daughter to date outside of the immediate ethnic circle; but at the same time he may maintain a traditional view on premarital sex (Kephart, 1977). This shift accommodates to the realities of present-day society but maintains a position in which women are held in high regard and effort is made to protect them from the outside world, which is "not to be trusted." The consequence of this evolution of values is often intergenerational conflict. Daughters in Italian families cannot appreciate the effort it may have taken for their fathers to permit them to date non-Italian men; their fathers cannot understand a changing code of sexual morality which does not condemn a bride who is not a virgin.

Each ethnic family, as a major unit of the social system, is influenced by the various aspects of the larger society. These influences serve to throw into question values which have been treasured for generations and have sustained the family for several generations in America. The resulting tension between resistance and accommodation may cause family turmoil, some of which may eventually come to the attention of a social worker.

These are but some of the kinds of family issues of which the ethnic-sensitive social worker must be particularly aware. The model for ethnic-sensitive practice presented elsewhere in this work presents a basis for attention to these aspects of family tensions.

In order to highlight how the various components of the model are brought to bear in practice, a variety of cases are presented here. Each case is distinctive in relation to the ethnic reality and how it influences the ways in which families and workers respond to the problems presented. In all cases social workers are expected to draw on the various layers of understanding and to adapt the various skills and techniques used to the ethnic reality.

To achieve the goal of ethnic-sensitive practice, social workers must be continually aware of the second layer of understanding, which relates to awareness of their own ethnicity, recognizing that such awareness is incorporated as part of the "professional self." Social workers are not immune to the feelings of ambivalence about the fact of ethnic diversity and their own location in the ethnic geography. Greeley (1974) suggests that we are all torn between pride in our heritage and resentment at being trapped in that heritage. He speculates that the ambivalence is probably the result of the immigrant experience of shame, and defensive pride in an unappreciative society. No matter what the origin or nature, social workers must be aware of their own feelings about their ethnic identity.

### The Case of Clyde Turner

When Clyde Turner saw the social worker at the Mental Health Unit of the hospital he said that he had come because he needed "a rest to get himself together." He was self-referred, but had been in mental health treatment centers before. The diagnosis made was schizophrenia. The tension and anxiety that he felt were evident in his behavior. Problems seemed to be generated by internal and external stresses.

Clyde is black; he is 20 years old and a sophomore at a university near his home. His father, Roland, is on the faculty of another university in the area; he is working on his doctoral dissertation. Eleanor, his mother, is not employed outside of their home. His sister Jeanette, age 17, is a high school student who gets excellent grades.

Clyde said that family pressure is a part of his problem. He feels that he has not had a chance to become an independent person. The family upsets him and he becomes very argumentative.

His father has urged him to take five "profitable" courses in the next semester. Clyde had planned to take three such courses and two in the humanities, which would lessen the burden of school.

In an effort to "move away" from his family Clyde joined a fraternity but when the "brothers" learned of his problems they began to ridicule him and became patronizing.

School, family, friends all became "hassles" and Clyde sought refuge in the mental health unit for a rest.

Clyde's tensions and anxieties are in the present. The diagnosis of schizophrenia is not in question. There is sufficient evidence from previous admissions to other mental health centers to confirm the schizophrenic assessment. Relief of his tension and anxiety are of primary concern.

As the model for ethnic-sensitive practice is applied, consideration must be given to the first layer of understanding, knowledge of human behavior. This knowledge provides the data that begin to explain Clyde's disease. His natural struggle for independence at the emerging adult stage is hampered by the nature of his illness. The symptoms confound him and his parents, who at middle age, have begun to look forward to a life without child care responsibilities. One of their children, however, continues to need care, which they seem unable to provide.

The Turners are a middle-class black family; that is their ethnic reality. Mr. Turner's thrust for advanced education for himself and his son are among the dispositions that often flow from that position. Unlike many black middle-class families, that status is achieved with the employment of only one adult; Mr. Turner's salary as an educator provides sufficient income to maintain their middle-class position in appropriate style.

In other ways, however, the Turners are characteristic of the black middle class as delineated by Willie (1974); (1) one family member has completed college and attends graduate school on a part-time basis after adulthood; (2) they want their children to go to college immediately after high school so that they will not need to struggle as long to attain their goals as did the parents; (3) there is little time for recreation because of intense involvement in work. Mr. Turner teaches at the college and works on his dissertation; Mrs. Turner works hard at housekeeping activities. They are socially accepted and respected in their own community. There are many adults who pursue graduate degrees in their adulthood, but for blacks there has been the continual resistance by racist institutions which were reluctant to admit them. This is part of the experience of blacks in America of which Clyde's social worker must be aware.

As Clyde and his father disagree about his selection of courses for the coming term they respond to an unconscious, unspoken, value of the black middle class. Education will enable black people to change their position in society; it will move them upward. There is no discussion about *whether* Clyde will return to school; the discussion is about *what* he will study when he returns.

In the struggle for independence Clyde sought out peers and as a result became a member of a black fraternity. It is in peer groups such as this, whose membership is comprised of one ethnic group, that one often finds comfort. These groups affirm identity through special social projects and recreational activities undertaken. For Clyde, however, they intensified stress because of their inability to respond in comforting ways to his incapacities. But, like Clyde, they too are emerging young black men seeking a place for themselves in the larger society. They may, however, be enlisted by the social worker to serve as a support group for Clyde. Efforts to provide them with a clearer picture of Clyde's difficulties may well enable them to refrain from ridicule and include Clyde more completely in the group activities.

Although there is no mention of extended family, further inquiry may uncover a kinship network that is available to give emotional support to the entire family. Although middle-class blacks may sever connection with family members as they move upward, there is significant evidence that many retain a family support system mainly because of the vulnerability of their middle-class position (McAdoo, 1978).

As a young college student Clyde is subject to the stress of academic life, even without the extreme stress of his illness. How many other students at the university suffer? What resources in counseling are available? How adequate are those that exist? How may the services of the mental health unit be expanded or adapted to meet the needs of students from any college who reside in this suburban community? How does the stress of Clyde's illness disrupt the family as they struggle to maintain middle-class status?

These are among the questions that may be raised by social workers as they work with college students of any ethnic or social class group. Attention is focused on practice which moves from dealing with individual client need to modifying those larger systems which influence, positively or negatively, the client's day-to-day activities.

It is not the intention of this discussion to suggest a specific course of action which Clyde's social worker might take—that will depend upon many aspects of this case not presented. The activity will, however, be related to the route Clyde took to the social worker. It was totally voluntary and based upon previous successful experiences in mental health settings. The mental health unit is one of the services provided in a suburban general hospital. A majority of patients, of all ethnic groups, hold middle-class status. In such a setting there is often little involvement with larger systems. Yet evidence of systematic failure as it relates to the Turner family may be seen in the pervasiveness of racism. The energy invested in overcoming the obstacles required to attain a middle-class position may have some relationship to Clyde's problems; the specifics have to be determined by the worker and family.

The ethnic-sensitive worker, having applied the perspective of the model, now has more data available that will give a wider view of the Turner family as it struggles to cope with their schizophrenic son.

## The Case of Michael Bobrowski

It was Jean Bobrowski who took her husband Michael to the Family Counseling Association. It seemed the only way to help him. Since he lost his job he sat around the house or wandered aimlessly. She was very worried and went to see Father Paul, who suggested that she take her husband to the association. The priest spoke to him also and encouraged his cooperation.

Mr. and Mrs. Bobrowski are Polish. When he was employed Mr. Bobrowski was a truck driver. His work record was poor. When he backed a truck over a gasoline pump and failed to report it to his employers, he was fired. Because he was a member of the union, Mr. Bobrowski had expected that the union would help him find other employment but this did not materialize. He is ineligible for unemployment due to the circumstances of his dismissal. Mrs. Bobrowski now takes care of other people's children; his job had been the sole source of their income. They have lost their home due to nonpayment of the mortgage.

The Bobrowskis have been married for 30 years. He is presently 55, she is 50. Their son Michael, Jr., is 28 and lives in California with his wife and young son. Debbie, their daughter, is 24, married, and lives nearby. She has two children.

Both of the Bobrowskis are members of the Polish American Home, a social club, and the American Legion. They get a great deal of pleasure from the activities of each group, but they are less active since Mr. Bobrowski lost his job.

A major problem for this family is financial; the strain is becoming evident in this couple's relationship. The lack of employment is devastating to this Polish working-class family. While difficult for most people, this particular kind of devastation is to be expected in the case of a Polish family. To the Slavic work is the reason for living; if one cannot work then one is useless.

The work of Stein (1976, 1978) suggests that this attitude cuts across all social classes. In addition, essential goals of life are to own one's own home and to amass cash wealth as a cushion for security. Mr. Bobrowski has failed in all areas. His behavior has deprived him of work and, although he wishes to work, his union has not supplied employment as he expected. He has lost his home due to his failure to pay the mortgage. There are no cash reserves set aside. His application for unemployment insurance has been denied. The independence of character referred to by Muskie cannot be exemplified when there is no work, no home, no reserve. He is unable to protect his wife, who must now take care of other people's children in order to support the family. In their later adulthood, when there is the universal expectation of less responsibility because the children are emancipated, the Bobrowskis find themselves dependent and may need to seek resources from public agencies. The task of coping with a diminishing work role usually executed at old age must be accomplished earlier than expected. Although Mr. Bobrowski resists, it is unlikely that he will ever have steady employment again due to his poor work history.

Despite the emphasis on hard work and building up a cash reserve, the chances of attaining the security envisioned are fairly slim for Polish and other working-class families. Their income may appear to be substantial; the hard work that they do pays well. But they, as do many working-class families, have attempted to find the "good life" through the acquisition of consumer items. Many of these items are purchased "on time" and so the family income that appears to be "good" is spread out to make payments on the car, appliances, mortgage or perhaps a truck, camper, or small boat—before the purchase of food or medical care. Rubin (1976) has identified this precarious position on the edge of financial disaster as one contributor to the "worlds of pain" of the white working class.

An understanding of the realities of Michael Bobrowski's ethclass position, in which he suffers from the pain of a working-class position and failure to meet ethnic group expectation, enables the ethnic-sensitive worker to go beyond the problems of finance and depression.

An awareness of community resources will provide a direction as the worker seeks to help the family. Other resources must be enlisted by the ethnic-sensitive worker committed to simultaneous activity at micro and macro levels.

The couple is active in two secondary groups: the American Legion and the Polish American Home. Both are sources of strength in their lives. In each there is a sense of patriotism, which has been identified as a distinctive Polish characteristic. They are able to affirm their "Polishness" among other Poles at Polish American Home gatherings. Their present problems in living have caused them to become less active. They feel the stigma of unemployment and the depression which followed. Yet, this group may be able to help to diminish the sense of stigma. Mr. Bobrowski is not the only member who has problems leading to tensions and anxieties. Others may have marital conflict and problems with their children or parents. The nature of interpersonal relationships are such that similar problems may surface in many families. Is it possible for the Polish American Home to become an outreach center for the Family Counseling Association?

The Polish association could, with joint effort by the social worker and community leaders, become a part of the effort to minimize the stigma attached to mental health problems and to seeking service, which often plagues white ethnic communities (Giordano, 1973). Programs and services may be encouraged that span the life cycle, from day care services to senior citizens' activities, centered about the home and located in community-based institutions.

Mr. Bobrowski's route to the social worker was highly voluntary. He followed the suggestion of his priest, a significant person in his life. At the family association he may expect to be active in the plans for the solution of his problems. If he chooses not to continue services, he may be encouraged to continue until the work is completed but he will not be "punished" for this decision.

As social workers consider the route to services as well as the other aspects of the model for ethnic-sensitive practice, many components of Mr. Bobrowski's life are revealed that may have been overlooked in the past.

### The Case of Bobby Ramirez

Bobby is 15 years old, the fourth of five sons in the family of Luis and Berta Ramirez. He was referred to the child welfare agency by the family court after episodes of delinquent behavior. The charges included truancy and automobile theft. On one occasion he stole a truck and demolished it. He is believed to be incorrigible at home, having little regard for the expectations set forth by his father. It is the expectation of the court that the child welfare agency will find a place for him outside the community: a foster home or, as a last resort, a residential treatment center.

The Ramirez family is Mexican American. Mr. Ramirez was born in Mexico but came to the United States as an infant; his wife Berta was born here but her parents were born in Mexico. Their eldest son, age 23, is self-supporting and lives outside of their home. The second son lives at home but is partially dependent upon his parents. The work that he finds is of an unskilled nature and does not provide him with an income essential for living. The other sons at home besides Bobby are 17 and 13; both attend school.

Mr. and Mrs. Ramirez have completed high school and are employed. Luis is a sanitation worker for the city; Berta is a domestic worker. They live with their sons in a two-bedroom house, which they rent. At one time they owned a house but lost it when they were unable to keep up the payments. There is never enough money to save for the down payment on another house, even though that is their wish.

They have barely enough money for clothing. In order to stretch the food budget, their diet often includes rice and beans prepared in the Mexican way. There is no money for recreation and so leisure time is spent with friends and family. Parties are often spontaneous. Friends, whose circumstances are similar, bring food and beer. There is dancing, drinking, eating, and a great deal of happiness in just being together.

Bobby Ramirez's route to the social worker was totally coercive; it is the decree of the court, which has also suggested a solution. In addition, he is in a state of dual marginality, that involving his ethnic minority status on the one hand and adolescence on the other (Long and Virgil, 1980): the universal tasks of coping with puberty and a growing sexual awareness, seeking for independence from parents, and developing the skills for that independence...are compounded by his ethnicity. Exposure to the Mexican American and Anglo worlds may well have produced pressures which force him to make a choice rather than make a decision; internal ambivalence develops. Garcia (1971) suggests the kinds of questions which confront Bobby and many other Mexican American youth and which may generate ambivalence: Should I reject my parents and accept the culture, ideals, and aspirations of the Anglos? If I do, will my family reject me? But, if I claim my cultural identity will I eliminate the possibility of admission to the Anglo world that offers success and escape from poverty? The temptation is to choose the Anglo way.

This beginning knowledge of Bobby's adolescent dilemma comes from the layers of understanding focused on a (1) general knowledge of human behavior and (2) an awareness of the ethnicity of others. The problem identified by the court is juvenile delinquency—a place must be found for him. As the worker begins this task, the model for ethnic-sensitive practice aids in developing insights that may make this transition less painful for all involved. Although the parents seem to concur with the decision of the court there is pain, for Bobby has brought the honor of the family into question.

Although Bobby has ignored the authority of his father by breaking the family rules (a major transgression among Mexican Americans), Luis as the head of his household will nevertheless take part in the planning for Bobby's future. Some Mexican American fathers feel so shamed by this kind of behavior on the part of their sons that they will offer no support (Murillo, 1976). Failure in the adult policing roles does not deny him the role of representing the family in the community and in association with other systems, in this instance the child welfare department. The roles of policing and representing the family are among the activities associated with *machismo.*

In his analysis of *macho,* the masculine role, Paz (1961) sees it as one which incorporates superiority, aggressiveness, insensitivity, and invulnerability subsumed under one word—*power*. The history of this position of honor, strength, and masculinity lies in associations which lead back to a history of the "warring, sacrificing Aztecs and their medieval Spanish conquerors" (Queen and Haberstein, 1970). In the present, *machismo* calls for an aloof authoritarian head of the family who directs its activities, arbitrates disputes, polices behavior, and represents the family in the community and society.

The social worker may expect Mrs. Ramirez to be devoted to her husband and children, including the eldest son who has moved away. Children, family, and a few friends are the core of life for Mexican American women (Murillo, 1976). Even though she works as a domestic, she does not do this every day; she must leave some time for her family responsibilities.

Her employment, along with that of her husband, provides barely enough income for the family to survive. Domestics and sanitation workers clean up after others. They carry out the most menial of tasks. The completion of high school has not provided access to higher positions; racism and discrimination have limited their opportunities. Although all family members speak English fluently, their surname and physical appearance provoke attitudes which diminish them in stature and attack their self-esteem.

A smaller family would require fewer resources but a smaller family would deny a tradition which supports large families.

This tradition, however, serves to diminish the opportunity to attain the ordinary material rewards of American life. Mexican Americans are much more marginal in this respect than most other populations (Moore, 1970); they have few new clothes, a limited diet, and little recreation. The ethnic reality involves a life of near poverty, but at the same time there is much pride in their ethnic heritage; this is certainly true for the adults. Support comes from ethnic associates, who in an informal way share resources. This activity is not limited to the parties mentioned earlier but may be a regular occurrence, in respect to daily needs.

The decree of the court gives the social worker and the Ramirez family little choice; Bobby must be placed outside of the home. The court, however, is representative of those macro systems which appear to be blind to the needs of those most vulnerable: the poor, ethnic minority families. To remove Bobby from the community protects automobile owners from his larceny; it does nothing to address his adolescent conflict as he is trapped between two cultures of almost equal force.

The ethnic-sensitive worker has a heightened awareness of the need to promote change in the judicial system which will recognize the larger world of Bobby Ramirez and others like him. Perhaps efforts may be made to seek out *compadres* (godparents) of offenders, as a matter of policy, to assess their ability to lend support to their godchildren and become part of the process in planning for their care. The community in which the Ramirez family lives has few recreational resources for children and teenagers, a complaint that has often been expressed by the Ramirez boys and their friends. A study of the community will determine the accuracy of their statement. If their claim is indeed true, what efforts may be made to organize the various kinship groups in the area so that together they may press for funds from the city recreation budget to provide the supervised recreation needed by all of the children in this poor ethnic neighborhood?

The model for ethnic-sensitive practice focuses the social worker's attention on how ethnicity and social class impact on the daily life of families. Bobby's acting out behavior has led him to a social worker, who with patience and greater awareness may begin to change his life and the lives of other young Mexican Americans with similar problems. In so doing the worker also takes into account the unique family dynamics involved.

## SUMMARY

Each of the families presented in this chapter (the Turners, the Bobrowskis, and the Ramirezes) is attempting to carry out the functions of family presented early in the chapter. Sometimes they succeed, sometimes they fail. The potential for success or failure is related to their social class position and their ethnicity. Willie (1974) concludes (1) that all families in America share a common value system and (2) that they adapt to the society and its values in different ways, largely because of racial discrimination. Discrimination has intensified Mr. Turner's efforts to gain more education in order to maintain and enhance his middle-class position; on the other hand, it has kept Luis Ramirez in a near poverty position, denying him power over the destiny of his family. The Bobrowskis' expectations of working-class prosperity are denied as income is used to "pay the bills" for minor luxuries.

In each family, however, there are the joys of ethnicity that come from association with others who are like them—this is a source of comfort and power of peoplehood. These relationships will continue as will the family; as a collection of individuals; as a group; as a major unit of the social system; and as an agency for the transmission of cultural values (Papajohn and Spiegel, 1975). It is in the family that the stresses and strains of daily life are played out; children are born and reach adulthood; men and women love and hate; interpersonal and intrapersonal conflicts develop and subside as men, women, and children struggle with the demands of the larger society and with their own needs for sexual and emotional fulfillment. This is the base from which the ethnic-sensitive worker involved with families begins. The particular approaches to practice may vary.

Some may choose a broad-ranging psychosocial approach with the Turners, Bobrowskis, Ramirezes, and others like them. Others may find task-centered, structural approaches useful as a way of helping them to struggle with the problems presented. Others may help them to focus primarily on the external, structurally induced sources of their problems. Whichever approach they choose, ethnic-sensitive workers will be aware of how the route to the social worker constrains problem definition and work to bring those definitions into line with social work values. Essential also is simultaneous attention to how micro and macro systems impinge on family functioning, and attention to those macro tasks which will enhance such functioning. Always crucial is awareness of the layers of understanding and a recognition that techniques and skills may need to be adapted in order to respond to the families' ethnic reality.

## REFERENCES


Ackerman, Nathan A. 1958. *The psychodynamics of family life: diagnosis and treatment of family relationships.* New York: Basic Books, Inc.

Garcia, Alejandro. 1971. "The Chicano and social work." *Social Casework, 52*(5), May.

Giordano, Joseph. 1973. *Ethnicity and mental health—research and recommendations.* New York: American Jewish Committee.

Gordon, Milton M. 1964. *Assimilation in American life: the role of race, religion and national origins.* New York: Oxford University Press.

Greeley, Andrew M. 1974. *Ethnicity in the United States: a preliminary reconnaissance.* New York: John Wiley & Sons, Inc.

Kephart, William M. 1977. *The family, society and the individual* (4th Ed.). Boston: Houghton-Mifflin Co.

Long, John M., and Vigil, Diego. 1980. "Cultural styles and adolescent sex role perceptions." In Melville, Margarita B. (Ed.). *Twice a minority: Mexican American women.* St. Louis: The C. V. Mosby Co.

McAdoo, Harriet Pipes. 1978. "Factors related to stability of upwardly mobile black families." *Journal of Marriage and Family, 40,* November.

Moore, Joan. 1970. In Queen, Stuart, A. and Haberstein, Robert W. (Eds.). *The family in various cultures.* New York: J. B. Lippincott, Co.

Murillo, Nathan. 1976. "The Mexican-American family." In Hernandez, Carrol, Haug, Marsha J., and Wagner, Nathaniel N. (Eds.). *Chicanos: social and psychological perspectives* (2nd Ed.). St. Louis: The C. V. Mosby Co.

Muskie, Edmund. 1966. "This is our heritage." In Renkiewicz, Frank (Ed.). *The Poles in American 1608–1972: a chronology and fact book.* Dobbs Ferry, N.J.: Oceana Publications, Inc.

Ogburn, William. 1938. "The changing functions of the family." In Winch, Robert F. and Goodman, Louis Wolf (Eds.). 1968. *Selected studies in marriage and the family* (3rd Ed.). New York: Holt, Rinehart and Winston, Inc.

Papajohn, John, and Spiegel, John. 1975. *Transactions in families.* San Francisco: Jossey-Bass Publishers.

Paz, Octavio. 1961. Quoted in Queen, Stuart, A. and Haberstein, Robert W. (Eds.). 1970. *The family in various cultures.* New York: J. B. Lippincott Co.

Queen, Stuart A., and Haberstein, Robert W. 1970. *The family in various cultures* (4th Ed.). New York: J.B. Lippincott Co.

Rubin, Lillian Breslow. 1976. *Worlds of pain: life in the working-class family.* New York: Basic Books, Inc.

Stein, Howard F. 1976. "A dialectical model of health and illness—attitudes and behavior among Slovac-Americans." *International Journal of Mental Health, 5*(3).

Stein, Howard F. 1978. "The Slovac-American 'swaddling ethos': homeostat for family dynamics and cultural continuity." *Family Process, 17,* March.

Willie, Charles V. 1974. "The black family and social class." *American Journal of Orthopsychiatry, 44*(1), January.

## 4.

**Stephen Burghardt**

## KNOW YOURSELF: A KEY TO BETTER ORGANIZING

As organizers we often fear we will not be as good as we need to be—that in fact we are not personally able to do the work well enough (or are not knowledgeable enough) to perform well. Holding on to this fear has been the undoing of many organizers, for the simple reality of organizing life is that good organizers are *always* making mistakes and being a little less effective than they ought to be. Furthermore, our slim grass-roots resource base always makes these errors appear more glaring: You forget to find a meeting place and the leaflet cannot be done; outreach stops; plans for publicity grind to a halt. People in larger institutions make the same errors, but no one notices as quickly, for other tasks can be carried out regardless of the occasional foul-up. Knowing this helps the grass-roots organizer a little bit, but just a little. In fact, our slim resource base necessitates some personal awareness of how we best work, the type of awareness many organizers too often would prefer ignoring.

Stephen Burghardt is on the faculty of Hunter College.

While perhaps preferring to ignore personal issues, organizers work in situations too complex for such a unilaterally cool attitude toward personal dynamics. The following two examples give some indication of that complexity.

(1) A few years ago, a young organizer had spent the week working on a tutorial program proposal—meeting with teachers and students, getting their ideas, finding out about previous programs' successes and failures. He had been relatively efficient, and the overall report seemed a good synthesis. A meeting had been called for the potential board of directors to review progress. After a decent introduction, the organizer's response to questions grew more and more irritable. Interaction with others seemed hostile; he seemed to want to "move the agenda," even when the discussion was on the agenda. As time wore on, people were pleased with the outline of his work, but a little perplexed at his method of handling it during the meeting. Likewise, the organizer felt frustrated and drained at the end of the meeting, angry with people's "slowness" but puzzled at why he felt so "antsy" over issues he knew needed to be discussed.

(2) A number of experienced organizers were reviewing their work in the South Bronx over the previous three months. As a group of

politically conscious, primarily white activists working in an all black-Latin neighborhood, they had been trying to develop a political approach to neighborhood revitalization. Some things had gone well—a few people were attending meetings and getting interested in sweat equity programs—but progress were slow. One member was singled out for particular criticism, as his functioning on the street with residents seemed awkward and defensive. The widespread opinion, *including his own,* was that his failure to communicate well on the street was a function of his "poor political understanding of racism." He was expected to read various books and articles and report on his progress at a later date. No attention was ever said to the obvious fact that he was never comfortable in informal settings; all that was sufficient would be for him to learn and change. He never did. Indeed, his tendency toward withdrawn formality seemed to increase.

Both these examples illustrate some important personal questions every organizer needs to answer regarding particular personal strengths and limitations in our work. In the first instance, why was such a nuts-and-bolts meeting so difficult for the organizer to handle? What had really created the defensiveness and irritability? In the second, why did experienced people so easily ignore problems that had little to do with a person's political beliefs? Why did they seek to correct them through a "better political line"? Furthermore, what can be done for any organizer to minimize these problems?

These problems—one common to new organizers, the other to more experienced activists—speak to the heart of the personal side of organizing. Every organizer is quite good in certain areas of work, less effective in others. However, as these two examples suggest, many organizers are unwilling or unable to admit this, not for political reasons, but for personal ones. While we design strategies to be flexible and base our tactical choices on varying levels of available resources, we rarely apply the same standards to *ourselves,* inflexibly and unrealistically expecting ourselves to do whatever needs to be done, even if the results are potentially harmful to the group and, in the long run, taxing to our mental health.

There are two reasons that this happens. One is the often unconscious but nevertheless powerful acceptance of a "great man/woman theory of organizing" that expects us to be all things to all people in all kinds of organizing situations.[1] This is exemplified by Saul Alinsky's criteria for a good organizer in "The Education of An Organizer," which lists everything from political skill to good humor to high levels of intuitive insight as "musts" for your effective work.[2] Such a list is more than a little intimidating, for it leaves the new or inexperienced organizer with a sense of failure, even when her or his skills are quite adequate in many situations. Likewise, experienced organizers come to assume they *should* meet such criteria; if unable to do so, one can "correct" the problem through content-related tasks like reading and political study.

Second, these personality problems are compounded by the basic personality type of most grass-roots organizers. An informal survey of mine conducted over the years has revealed again and again that most organizers (about 70 percent) tend to be much more task- than process-oriented.[3] This means that most organizers prefer outer-directed, content-oriented issues over inner-directed, process-oriented interactions that may involve feelings, emotions, and interpersonal processes rather than mere abstract material. When this content- and outer-directed personal tendency is coupled with the above great man/woman theory of organizing, organizers often foster a blanket attempt to force ourselves through work areas of less personal effectiveness "because we should be able to do them." Indeed, for all our concern with tactics, we often give little thought to the *personal realities of tactical implementation.* "Develop your political perspective, choose your strategy and tactics, and then do it" seems to be a sufficient way to function, saving adroitness for strategic discussion and not one's actual ability to implement desired tactics.

The outcome for these twin issues, as the two painful examples underscore, is that many organizers end up being either less effective or more emotionally drained than they need to be, and thus more likely to leave organizing because of "burnout." Instead of following a few personal guidelines, these activists "push on," even when they are highly irritated with group process, disinterested in fact-finding, uncomfortable with street-smart spontaneity, or whatever. Imagine if you applied these same pressures to others. What kind of an open, democratic organizing approach would that be? It is far more freeing to respect and recognize that you begin this work with certain skills *and* limitations that are heightened or lessened in different organizing situations. You then can learn to use your abilities with greater tactical flexibility. The irony in this kind of humbling self-respect is that it will carry over into greater respect for the people with whom we work, too—by not berating ourselves for limitations that are actually beyond our control, it is less likely we would do the same to others.

There are a number of important procedures to follow in understanding yourself in different situations that can improve tactical effectiveness. (I call this "tactical self-awareness."[4]) First, identify whether or not you are more task-oriented or process-oriented. Don't cop out by saying you are both; everyone should be both, but each of us tends to be more comfortable with one orientation than the other, especially when we are new to this work. I have spent fifteen years of learning how to deal with my task-oriented tendencies, and now can blend process and task *some* of the time, but hardly always. You won't be any different.

Second, review the organizing situations you are involved in and determine whether they emphasize process or task activities. For example, new group situations stress much discussion and group facilitation, which means a process-oriented person will be most effective here. Likewise, specific planning meetings with a high degree of content-focused work and few interpersonal demands means that the situation will be most comfortable for a task-oriented person. Apply this approach to all the activities of the week—street work, meetings, planning sessions, and so on.

Once you go through the situations for their degree of *personal fit* with your own makeup, see if it is possible for you to take greater responsibility for the ones most comfortable for you, getting others to take tasks you find more personally problematic. If this is not possible, build supports for yourself along the way. For example, at longer, process-oriented meetings, I always write a reminder in my organizing notes (or copy of the agenda notice) to "stay calm—people need to talk." This note may seem silly, but it has become a sufficient cue to remind me that the problem in the slow discussion is *with me,* not with others. Likewise, those resistant to fact-finding can allot themselves five specific days in which to do the work instead of the imagined three, allowing for the reality that their tendency to procrastinate will lengthen its completion time. You should provide similar helpful cues in situations that are troublesome for you.

You cannot run away from your limitations, of course, especially in grass-roots organizing, where resources—and personnel—are rarely to be found in abundance. However, when you take on personally more difficult tasks, try not to take on too much at once. You are not too good in informal settings but have to attend that fund-raising party? Try to tend bar or serve food, rather than serving as the official greeter. You dislike office routine but have to help maintain one? Be responsible for keeping the office clean and not keeping the books; whatever mess you make will be quickly visible and easily correctable. Over time you can note improvement and move on to more demanding tasks, but try to start with realistic, modest objectives that are attainable.

Finally, you should consistently work to undermine "great organizer" theories *by judging your progress in personal performance by relative, not absolute, standards.* The group needs to succeed, of course, but here I am talking about your own improvement in the different situations of organizing: from writing to public speaking, from being relaxed in newly formed groups to handling responsibilities for office routine. Real self-respect allows you to be less than perfect, taking pride from improvement that is real improvement for *you,* while perhaps less so for someone else. For example, I am proud that I have an almost-neat and up-to-date filing system. I have known I should have had one for fifteen years; my present filing system has been in place for two. At the same time, I have always worked well in the formation of groups. My desk, unfortunately, is a mess, and I still need to improve daily routines. You should find yourself able to note areas of accomplishment in all parts or organizing, letting progress, however slow, be cause for quiet satisfaction.

There are other levels where tactical self-awareness is important. Perhaps the two most important relate to (1) often unconsciously derived but quite real difficulties one has with particular individuals, and (2) vestiges of racism, sexism, and class bias that are within all of us.

Tactical self-awareness deals with your awareness of how personally comfortable you are in getting certain tasks done in certain situations. Those situations almost always involve people but at times include certain individuals with whom, for some reason, you do not get along. As grass-roots organizing has few institutional barriers to help minimize interpersonal conflict, it is important to notice when these interpersonal tensions exist for no apparent reason.

For example, I knew someone who always got into arguments with a fellow steering committee member over almost every issue—until she went home to a family picnic and saw the strong physical similarity between her antagonist and a second cousin she disliked. As remarkable as this story is, we all come up against individuals who, for no discernible reason, irritate us. When this happens a little too often and you cannot identify political differences, you find that his or her work is equal to others', and so on, the chances are the problem lies within you. Try to understand its origin, looking over your personal history to identify previous events or individuals who triggered the discomfort.[5]

After you have reflected on this and are sufficiently certain that the problem has little to do with the person's actual behavior, try to get up enough courage to speak with the person about *your* problem. That person will hardly be thrilled by what you have to say (by now you may rub him or her the wrong way, too), but your honesty and willingness to share the personal issue will at least clarify the problem and might lead to a mutually rewarding discussion.

If this fails or you are just not comfortable enough to initiate such an encounter yet, plan in the future to minimize your interactions so that the work is unimpaired. If that is not possible, *work* to lessen your antagonism. For example, make certain you do not comment on their remarks or even raise your hand immediately after he or she has spoken; try not to work on the same subcommittee, especially if they call for a lot of interpersonal interaction.

The other issue, one that infiltrates all organizing, is the unresolved problem of racism, sexism, and class bias lying within us. This topic is too important to leave to the end of one chapter,...But here it is important to look at the issue in terms of how we can begin undoing problems we want to have but nevertheless find ourselves succumbing to: the sexist joke here, the racist fear or condescending class bias there. Fight as we may to eradicate societal problems, we cannot simply eradicate these feelings by wishing them away. It is far more important—and a lot more effective—to admit they exist and work from there.

In fact, these problems are so universal, *plaguing everyone,* that some of the personal techniques used on racism, sexism, and class bias are quite similar to what has been discussed above. (This realization itself is liberating, for I believe one of the reasons people so rarely admit to these problems is the fear of being singularly identified.) To review, those techniques are:

(1) Identify which areas or issues are most problematic for you. (Don't say "all" and be too guiltily global or "none" and too politically perfect; choose fairly and realistically.)

(2) Once you know them—say, racism and sexism—do not expect to be as effective as you would be under like situations with different people. You won't be.

(3) Bring in supports and other people to make certain the tasks are done well. (I'm not talking about running away from the problem, either, but of realistically dealing with it in the context that other organizing demands need to be met. The only way to run away from these issues in grass-roots organizing is to stop being an organizer.)

(4) Measure your progress in relative, not absolute, terms.

This last is painfully hard to do, for it is hard to admit to racism, sexism, or class bias. No one *should* have any of these problems. But since we do—*and will spend a lifetime in dealing with these issues*—allow yourself to take comfort from the progress you make in confronting your bias, seeing its roots, and learning how to free yourself from that prejudice.[6] It will not be easy, but there is no alternative. Over time, as you relax and learn from others, progress can be made that opens you up to the genuine friendships, trust, and good comradeship that are so much a part of the joys of grass-roots organizing. Just allow yourself time to improve, set out and use techniques to aid in your quest, and the chances are you will achieve your goals with far deeper personal fulfillment and meaning than you ever expected.

This said, let me stress that I am *not* suggesting that relative standards of personal growth as an organizer are a substitute for meeting the absolute needs of people which are the reasons we organizers organize in the first place. At the same time, it is equally important to be less absolute about ourselves and the pace at which we ourselves can change. Indeed, if we can learn to live with and apply these standards where they need to be applied (and not reverse them) our work will undoubtedly be a much richer experience for us all.

## EXERCISES: TASK VERSUS PROCESS ORIENTATION

Before trying to determine your basic orientation, it is important to begin by identifying certain situations that are either more process- or more task-oriented in their content and demands on the activist.

**Higher process-content organizing situations:**

- new group meetings
- the introductory agenda items at most meetings
- individual follow-up
- informal parties and get-togethers
- the "action" part of demonstrations, marches, and so on
- education and communication events, speak-outs, and so on

**Higher task-oriented situations:**

- subcommittee meetings
- controversial, "politically loaded" agenda items
- office routine
- planning meetings
- the running of marches, demonstrations, and so on
- grant writing

**Check which of the following task-oriented skills that you are good at:**

- running tight-knit meetings
- giving factual reports
- performing subcommittee tasks
- writing
- emphasizing political/economic dynamics in strategy formation
- planning
- organizational maintenance: office routines

**Check which of the following process-oriented skills that you are good at:**

- running newly formed groups
- preparing social events
- facilitating discussion
- speaking informally
- emphasizing personal/subjective dynamics in strategy formation
- individual follow-up
- organizational maintenance: interpersonal relations

Once you have checked off what you do best and in which situations, look back at a recent meeting in which you were involved. Note the items on the agenda, and divide them into either task- or process-oriented sections. Which items left you feeling most comfortable and most effective? Which ones caused the most problems?

Since any one meeting has other dynamics operating that need to be considered, do this task and process itemization at a few meetings to see what orientation you are personally more comfortable with. Then, as you plan your group's actions over the next month, examine them not only for their political content and strategic considerations but for which of these two orientations seem to dominate, and which items. Try to make assignments accordingly with other members (assuming other considerations are met).

**NOTES**

1. This "theory" and many of the issues discussed here are more fully developed in Steve Burghardt, *The Other Side of Organizing* (Cambridge, Mass.: Schenkman, 1981), especially Chapters 3 and 4.
2. Saul Alinsky, "The Education of an Organizer," in *Rules for Radicals* (Boston: Beacon Press, 1967).
3. Burghardt, *Other Side,* Chapter 3.
4. See also Steve Burghardt, "Expanding the Use of Self: Steps Toward Tactical Self-Awareness," *Journal of Applied Social Science,* Summer 1981.

5. I am not advocating therapy here, unless one wants to explore these issues in greater emotional depth. One undertakes therapy only if one wants it, not as some prescription to be swallowed whole before one is ready.

6. This is especially hard for people when they first recognize how prevalent racism, sexism, or class bias is. As one organizer put it, "It's horrible. Once I saw how racism works here on the job, I saw it *everywhere*—how people don't look blacks in the eye, their fears, my hangups, the new TV stereotypes. All I feel is this remorse and anger at myself and everyone else, and I'm feeling like I'll never get off this track—I feel obsessed." This initial "crisis of conscience" phase, if one lets oneself go through it, does pass. You can then go on to use the above techniques effectively. The reason for the first phase's apparently immobilizing power is that it is dealing with material that is objectively obvious and emotionally powerful at the same time. You suffer from "overload" in ways that *do* slow you down. However, this new integration of powerful perceptions and new material is the work to be done here. Accept this, and the process itself will become that much faster.

PART TWO

# Option Selection

"Rule the Pool" announces the back of the sweatshirt worn by members of a middle-school swimming team. A quick reading of this motto might suggest that domination is the only criterion by which this team will judge how to approach its competitive endeavors. Actually, the message is probably intended much more for its effect on the opponents than as a statement of this team's philosophy. In the parlance of modern professional sports, the goal is pretty clearly intimidation.

While there is a certain appeal to the simplistic nature of a set of criteria by which one might select a single tactical option rather than another, the real world usually brings us up short. As in the example above, even if a single criterion comes easily to mind, it may well represent a misinterpretation of the facts. It would be easier if there were not such a range of possibilities open to the macro practitioner—or if the possibilities would submit themselves more rationally to a set of dimensions by which their potential effectiveness might be judged.

For most practitioners, the question is more likely, "What are the basic things that must be taken into account if a reasonable preference for one option over others is to be clarified?" Of late, it often appears that one key issue evolves around, "Is it cheap?" This may be followed by "Who is going to pay for it?" and "Who is going to take responsibility if things do not go as well as expected?"

Personalistic areas also seem more prominent than they once were. Such matters as "How am I going to look doing this," and "What's my agency going to get out of this?" seem part of the undercurrent, even if they are not expressed. Despite strong continuing rhetoric to the contrary, the needs of clients appear to have been pushed further back. From another perspective, there seems to have been a general decline in risk-taking behavior. In fact, many practitioners report that their colleagues who have taken on bureaucracies or been out front in advocating for the rights of clients have quietly been let go when cost savings have been required.

The option selection tangle is certainly complex and fraught with peril, especially in the difficult human services environment of the 1990s. From their own experiences, the editors propose a focus on what they believe to be particularly urgent and critical issues that confront practitioners in almost all macro practice situations.

In our current era, it sometimes seems as if we are in constant battles over values—in areas ranging as widely as from pro-life and pro-choice, to giving or denying birth-control devices to teens, to providing or withholding support for endangered people across the globe. Tropman's article confronts the centrality of these dilemmas. Such issues as individual and family, self-reliance and interdependency, fairness, and helping those most in need are addressed. Because much of the work of planners and program developers (to say nothing of administrators and managers) impinges on matters of policy, it is frequently impossible to avoid these dilemmas. Indeed, the attempt to avoid such questions often automatically labels the practitioner as a perpetuator of the status quo—however noble the actual reason for such avoidance. To aid in the planning process as it goes forward, Tropman also offers a worksheet for taking value dilemmas directly into account.

No less important, and much more frequently neglected, are feminist perspectives. The feminist vision, Van Den Bergh and Cooper argue, not only includes the demand for gender equality but also addresses how our private and public lives are conducted. The allocation of power and privilege in American society is directly involved. The analysis by Van Den Bergh and Cooper proposes viewing reality in a fashion that is "holistic, integrated, and ecological." Among the issues carefully considered are false dichotomies, the need to reconceptualize power, valuing process equally with product, and the political aspect of the personal. The interweaving and overlapping of direct and indirect practice dimensions are also explored in the second article.

In the third selection, Rivera and Erlich make a strong argument for key dimensions to be addressed if efforts in ethnic minority communities are to be successful. In part, option alternatives need consideration in light of the stage of development of each community. For example, newer Southeast Asian communities cannot be regarded as virtually the same as older, much more established Japanese and Chinese communities. Moreover, Rivera and Erlich propose a set of structural variables by which to judge the degree to which a target community may be more "gesellschaft" (a system in which relationships are impersonal, contractual, and utilitarian) as compared with more "gemeinschaft" (a system in which relations are personal, informal, and traditional). This appraisal, then, may be a vital guide to choosing the best possible available option in a given situation. The consequences of such a choice for community practitioners are also considered.

The final article in this section focuses on the ethical dilemmas that arise as new information technology is applied to practice. Because of the increasing dependence of many macro level practitioners on computerized information, Cwikel and Cnaan's piece is particularly timely. Among the issues addressed are (1) Who ought to have access to personal information about individuals and families? (as well, by implication, as sensitive data such as rates of teen pregnancy by race in certain neighborhoods?), and (2) How best to make useful information available to those who need it? A recent break-in at a community-based agency, with which one of the editors works, that resulted in the "mysterious disappearance" of a set of computer disks is a grim reminder of some of these issues.

While the lip-service offered in honor of all these considerations may seem both strong and clear, as a practical matter they are often caught up in the political quagmire that surrounds most substantial community practice efforts in the 1990s. The blessings of political correctness in matters as diverse as value conflicts, feminist perspectives, ethnic minority community considerations, and ethical dilemmas related to information technology are not easily come by. However, if we are to be honest with ourselves, the essential humanism of the profession demands consideration of these diverse elements of option selection.

—John L. Erlich

5.

**John E. Tropman**

# VALUE CONFLICTS AND DECISION MAKING: ANALYSIS AND RESOLUTION*

In complex urban society the community organizer and planner is required to make, or become involved with, complex decisions of great importance. Problems that were once considered the domain of the family—such as sex education—are more and more becoming elements of the public domain. Educational planning, health planning, social services planning, planning for children and the aged, for women going back to work and men leaving work—these and others are becoming the subject of intensive social work activity.

Essential to these planning activities is the assessment process. Many kinds of assessments, and ones we talk about in other articles, involve demographic counts, community surveys, and even personalistic assessments of the worker's own orientations and involvements. One kind of assessment that is frequently left out, however, is what might be called a values assessment. Such an assessment differs from the process of "values clarification," which often involves a recognition of the individual worker's personalistic involvements in a situation. Rather, what is important is a sense of the structure of the values involved in the different groups. Planners often have no precedents to guide them. They frequently must rely on their subjective appraisal of the situation. Included in their appraisal are values of the community, values of the society, values of the client groups involved, and professional values, among others. This piece can provide a framework for making such an assessment, so that it is no longer necessary for the planner to "fly by the seat of her or his pants." While this piece provides no magic formula for making hard decisions, it does offer a new approach to analyzing the values involved in the planning process.

## WHAT ARE VALUES?

Values are those gut-level feelings people have about fundamental aspects of life, which give it meaning and direction. Some of the more familiar values are family values, religious values, and work values. Values are ideas to which commitments are attached. There is no rule that they must be well-ordered, complete, consistent, or unambiguous. Indeed, as planners know, the reverse is the most likely situation.

Values have many complex, changing, and often conflicting meanings. People's values vary depending on their age, race, sex, income, education, and much more. To understand our own values, as well as those of others, we must realize that values intrude in subtle and unexpected ways. Values are so much a part of us that we are often not even aware of their influence. As

---

*Portions of this article were supported by the American Values and the Elderly Project, sponsored by the Administration on Aging, Grant # 90-1-1325. Special thanks are given to Beverly LaLonde, Jane McClure, Sue Sweeny, and Terrence Tice for comments on an earlier draft.

John E. Tropman is with the School of Social Work, The University of Michigan.

a result, we often do not have the perspective we need to make appropriate decisions or to understand the actions of others.

Planners may be in the crucial position of making precedent-setting decisions involving fundamental values. It is therefore very important that they understand the complexities of values.

Values:

- vary among different people
- shift and change
- often go unrecognized
- often conflict with one another

The purpose of this paper is to aid practitioners in exploring their own and others' values and the ways they influence many different kinds of decisions affecting the planning process.

## Value Conflicts

Our perspective on American values suggests that the values we hold often come in pairs, or sets of opposing beliefs. Part of the complex nature of values is our tendency to believe in values which compete with one another. For example, belief in family responsibility as well as individual fulfillment is one example. Americans tend to be committed to both parts of this pair of values: to the family as a central American institution, and to the importance of fulfilling our individual needs. When faced with a plan about responsibility to one's family or to one's goals, citizens are often placed in a value dilemma. Though both parts of the values pair may not carry equal weight, when we make a decision, we try to strike a balance between two desirable choices.

For example, more and more women are choosing to work while their families are growing. Though the public in general might be more accepting of this choice now than in the past, each woman still must find her own balance between independence, work, and responsibility to family. Social planners and community organizers need to be continually aware of the value tensions that are inherent in the system and make an assessment of these dilemmas and tensions a part of their ongoing "sensing" of the community or field of practice. Seven value dilemmas seem most critical.

individual —— family
self-reliance —— interdependency
secular —— religious
equity —— adequacy
struggle —— entitlements
private —— public
work —— leisure

## VALUES DILEMMAS IN COMMUNITY PRACTICE

Social planners and community organizers are continually involved in issues of assessment. These assessments involve, typically, money and personnel, issues and answers to the problems that beset the local community, the organization, or the subgroup. Planners and organizers continually struggle with finding solutions to community problems. What is often not so clear, however, is the fact that these problems involve value conflicts characterized by high ambivalence. As suggested, values upon which decisions are based are values which all of us hold. It is not "us" versus "them" but "us" versus "us" as well.

A second point involves us and our clients. The list of value conflicts suggests that the kinds of values our profession supports, on balance, tend to be on the right-hand side of the list—family, interdependency, religious, adequacy, entitlements, public, leisure—tend to be subdominant ones, not, overall, as strongly held as those values on the left—individual, self-reliance, secular, equity, struggle, private, and work values. Thus our profession, our field, and to some extent, we ourselves, are in the position of advocating subdominant values. In fact, the very concept of "community" smacks of a subdominant value, linked more to interdependency than to self-reliance. Our client groups, too, often seem more linked to subdominant values than to dominant ones. Thus, to a certain extent, as we push the more subdominant values, we threaten the major value orientations in the society, in the community, and even within ourselves.

## POLICY PLANNING AND PLANNERS

Under new guidelines, children of dependent elderly parents can be paid by the state for providing home care for their parents. Many people feel that children should do this as part of their family responsibilities without pay. Others feel that older people who need or want to work should be paid to provide home health care for other elderly people.

As a planner in the Department of Social Services, you have the option to propose payments to family members or to several elderly people who have been home care providers for many years. What do you recommend?

### Planners as Policymakers

As a practitioner, you may not consider yourself a policy maker. But you are. Policy can be defined as a decision or series of decisions that apply to a group of people or to many situations. Policy that is made in legislatures is only one level of policy. It is then up to the practitioner to interpret the laws passed in legislative bodies.

Policy is a matter of making choices. Furthermore, the most difficult policy choices involve making a decision *not* between good and evil or right and wrong, but between two or more good choices or two or more unsatisfactory choices. Policy decisions often involve a serious conflict between two strongly held beliefs, so that it is very difficult for us to know which way to compromise.

The social planner is frequently involved in assessing situations where there is a turbulent environment, where feelings run high. Should a program be in a religious institution or a nonreligious one? Should a program be run under private auspices, or should public funds be found to support it? While the planners do not make policy, they are often involved in making the crucial recommendations that become policy.

Though these values may seem foreign and rather academic, some questions based on these values are familiar:

- How much should the government do for people?
- Does the government owe everyone an adequate income?
- Should people be allowed to work as long as they want?
- How much responsibility should the family take in caring for its older members?

These seven pairs in Table 5.1 are not the only values involved in decision making. Yet they seem to be involved again and again, whether in debate over the Social Security Act or in consulting with a client about retirement. Everyone has value orientations which influence the style and approach they take with policy issues.

For each pair of values, Table 5.1 suggests a statement that a person holding that value might agree with. The values on the left—private, equity, work, and so on—

TABLE 5.1
Value Dilemmas

| | |
|---|---|
| 1. individual/family | suggests the need to balance between our own needs and the needs of our family. |
| 2. self-reliance/interdependency | emphasizes the strain between the desire to "go it alone" and the need to depend on others. |
| 3. secular/religious | suggests the tension between looking for rational explanations for life's ups and downs and turning to religious sources for support. |
| 4. equity/adequacy | refers to the conflict between fairness to all and the responsibility to help those most in need. |
| 5. struggle/entitlement | suggests the tension between the importance of working for everything we get and being entitled to certain things just because we are human beings. |
| 6. private/public | describes the conflict between use of personal or corporate means, and use of government to achieve desired social goals. |
| 7. work/leisure | confronts the issue of work and its meanings. How much work should we do, and for how long? When should work stop and leisure begin? |

tend to favor individual efforts and rewards. Over the years public opinion has tended to support the view that the welfare of each person is an individual or private concern. Values on the other side—public, family, adequacy, for example—tend to emphasize collective well-being. Government intervention, labor unions, and other community and social organizations are supported by these values. Only recently has public opinion tended to support these values in major policy issues.

Thus, certain values tend to be balanced by an opposite value (Table 5.2). Yet, as our experience reflects, any value or set of values may conflict with any other. Depending on the issue, certain values will be viewed as more important than others. In other cases, several values pairs may seem equally relevant. Value conflicts arise because selecting one value as the basis for action automatically raises an alternative view, whether we want it to or not.

Value conflict and compromise take place on many levels ranging from the national policy-making level to the agency-practitioner level.

**PLANNER DECISIONS**

You are a planner with an area agency on aging. There is a small, older area of town where a community of elderly people live, and have lived for years. The city wants the property for a new library and asks your help in developing a plan to move the people there out into institutional facilities, with their families, and so on. Two or three of the older residents come to the office and ask your help in developing a plan which will let them remain where they are.

What do you do?

Planning conflicts like this one are quite common. The issue is very complex because different legitimate views are represented. Many other examples of this kind of dilemma confront the planner, such as involvement in the merger of agencies, conflicts between city hall and other types of citizen groups, conflicts between "group home" advocates and those who oppose such homes—the list goes on and on.

As a planning and community organizing professional, you must carefully think through the issue, keeping in mind the values of all concerned. Five steps will usually be involved:

TABLE 5.2
Value Conflicts

| | |
|---|---|
| "It is important that I consider my needs first." | "My family's needs are of first and foremost importance." |
| "I can get along best by myself." | "People need each other to do this." |
| "Problems can best be solved by thinking them through objectively and rationally." | "Problems become smaller if we have faith in a divine force." |
| "People should be treated the same, regardless of their needs." | "People most in need should get the most help." |
| "No one should have a good standard of living without earning it." | "Everyone deserves a decent standard of living whether he/she earns it or not." |
| "People should take care of themselves." | "The government should provide for people." |
| "Work is the most meaningful thing people do." | "Other activities are at least as important as work." |

1. *Defining the problem*
   What are the basic issues?
   What information is needed, overall, about them?
2. *Developing alternative strategies for action*
   Consider the options and the consequences.
   Seek to balance values conflicts.
3. *Decision*
   This is the point at which those in authority make the decision. Additional balancing of conflicts goes on at this point.
4. *Operational planning*
   Working with those involved to develop an operational plan to carry out the decision.
5. *Implementation*
   Carrying out the decision and evaluating it.

## Defining the Problem

Which is the more important, the need of the city for the area, or the rights of the people in the area now? What alternatives are available for both groups? Is the group of older people a "community," in the sense that they share the concern of care for each other?

## Developing Alternative Strategies

What is the range of alternatives here, including the takeover of the land and the possibility of the older people remaining in their own homes? Are there intermediate possibilities which need to be considered? What are the sets of values which need to be balanced? What may happen under these different possibilities? How can values of public and private, self-reliance and interdependence be blended?

FIGURE 5.1
Worksheet for Planning Decisions

| Problem | Values Pairs | Decision Options | Compromises | Consequences |
|---|---|---|---|---|
| | | | | |
| | | | | |
| | | | | |
| | | | | |
| | | | | |

### Decision

Which authority, or combination of authorities, is going to make the decision? What are their values? What are the values to which they are likely to be sensitive? What kinds of compromises could be possible? Could the community be relocated elsewhere even if the buildings cannot?

### Operational Planning

Once the decision has been made, there is an operational planning process, which can itself involve a host of additional decisions. How can the decision be carried out in the best interests of everyone? What about individual and family interests here? Can these be accommodated?

### Implementation

Putting the plan into effect requires an assessment of values, too. Equity and adequacy may be an issue in terms of what kinds of supports might be given to older people if they are forced to move. If the decision has gone the other way, then the city needs to find a new site that is adequate for its needs.

### Values in Decision Making

While practitioners are often required to go through a formal evaluation process, they are not required to go through a formal decision-making process. Sometimes this is because the situation demands immediate attention. At other times, decisions are almost instinctual or "gut-level." At still other times, agency or client pressures prevail, and you make a decision against your better judgment. Recognizing the part that values play in all decisions can give you real insight into decisions. As a result you have more control over the decisions you make and participate in.

The worksheet in Figure 5.1 is a decision-making exercise that focuses on values. It will help you deliberately weigh the values, options, and consequences involved in a decision.

## TACTICS FOR VALUES BALANCE

Given the fact that values come in opposing sets and we spend lots of our professional time trying to achieve a values balance within a situation of potential or actual conflict, what are some tactics we might use, some ideas to list in the "options" column of the chart? Following are a few suggestions, by no means an exhaustive list, but one intended to provide a guide for the practitioner.

### Averaging

Here the two value orientations are averaged. We have some public and some private, some secular and some religious, some individual and some family. This compromise idea is often useful, but it implies an equality of values, which is not always the case. Thus, there may need to be a *weighted average,* which takes account of the dominance/subdominance relationship.

### Sectoring

In sectoring, the two values are used in different topics or in different places, or for different groups. Federalism is an example of values sectoring, in which topic and place vary. Some affirmative action programs are of this kind. Here the planner seeks to prevent value conflict through actualizing the values in different sectors. Ethnic service agencies, each emphasizing the values of the particular group in question, are an example.

### Sequencing

In sequencing, the planner or organizer seeks to use time as the differentiating factor, rather than space, as in sectoring. One case might be a day program and a night program where different types of community needs are met at different times. Programs that are "improper" for schools in the day can be run at night, when the children are gone. Changing a program during the weekend because more men are likely to show up represents another approach to sequencing.

### Adjudicating

Sometimes the planner or community organizer needs an authoritative interpretation; sometimes a choice must be made. Here an appeal to authority can be helpful. Sometimes such an appeal is through the courts, usually when other authority has failed to be convincing. Besides the courts, however, planners and community organizers can appeal to local authorities in the form of experts, political influentials, and so on.

### Power

Sometimes the "merits" of a situation are not convincing, as in adjudicating, and community organizers seek to build coalitions of leaders and influentials to force their values (or the values for which they are advocating) to become dominant in the situation. "Political" associations are often of this type.

### Decision Rule

Sometimes there are internal decision rules to which planners can appeal or organizers can use to solve a values dilemma. Sometimes these rules refer to *roles;* certain people do this, while others do that. Older and younger people may have such different roles, for example, as have men and women and parents and children. Sometimes a condition becomes the discriminating factor—in this situation, one type of behavior is all right; in that type of situation, some other type of behavior is all right.

### Pragmatism

A popular solution is the pragmatic solution. Let's be "free" of values, it is argued, and do what seems natural and "works" in the situation. Pragmatism usually is not a rule in itself but relates to having a range of means for problem solution available—averaging, sequencing, sectoring, adjudicating, decision rule, and so on. At the means level the pragmatic person is one who has a range of ways to solve a particular values conflict and does not "value" any one over another one, in general.

## CONCLUSION

Values always conflict, because there are many of them and because they tend to come in juxtaposed pairs. Much of the work a community practitioner has to do involves working through values dilemmas and providing solutions that permit the process of community development and improvement to go forward. Assessment is a key tool here. Solutions are not likely to be forthcoming if the multiple and dual aspect of the values system is not perceived by the practitioner.

A second problem of assessment lies in the different strengths of the paired values. It seems that one set of values in which we all believe is more dominant, the other more subdominant. For the values suggested here, those which fuel the social welfare enterprise in general, and community practice in particular, seem to be more on the subdominant side. If this is so, it means that progress toward achieving social work values is likely to threaten the society in general, the community in which the practitioner is working, and the practitioner. It is important to note that community practitioners, committed especially to the improvement of the condition of those who are less well represented in the system, such as minorities, the young, the old, women in broken families, are no less interested in the dominant values than others. Community practitioners must assess their own values, as well as those within the communities they serve.

If values are multiple, or in conflict, and if some values seem to be more dominant than others, how is the practitioner to resolve the inevitable differences of view within the community and within herself or himself? There are a number of techniques that can be used for this purpose, including averaging, sequencing, sectoring, and adjudicating. This suggested list mentions only some of the techniques—there are many variations that can prove very helpful, not only in assessment, but also in crafting a solution.

## BIBLIOGRAPHY


Allison, David, *The R & D Game* (Cambridge, Mass.: MIT Press, 1969).

Baier, Kurt, and Nicholas Rescher, *Values and the Future* (New York: Praeger, 1982).

Banfield, E., and J. Q. Wilson, *City Politics* (Cambridge, Mass.: Harvard University Press, 1965).

Barbour, Ian et al., *Energy and American Values* (New York: Praeger, 1982).

Bell, Daniel, *The End of Ideology: On the Exhaustion of Political Ideas in the Fifties* (Glencoe, Ill.: Free Press, 1960).

Bengston, Vern L., and Mary C. Lovejoy, "Values, Personality and Social Structure: An Intergenerational Analysis," *American Behavioral Scientist* 16, no. 6(1963): 893.

Braybrooke, David, and Charles E. Lindblom, *A Strategy of Decision: Policy Evaluation as a Social Process* (New York: Free Press, 1963).

Degler, Carl N., *Affluence and Anxiety,* 2d ed. (Glenview, Ill.: Scott, Foresman, 1975).

Dunn, William, ed., *Values, Ethics and the Practice of Policy Analysis* (Lexington, Mass.: D. C. Heath, 1983).

Ekric, Arthur A., Jr., *Ideology and Utopias* (Chicago: Quadrangle Books, 1969).

Elder, Glenn, Jr., *Children of the Great Depression* (Chicago: University of Chicago Press, 1974).

March, James, "Theories of Choice and Making Decisions," *Transaction/Society,* Vol. 20 (November/December 1982): pp. 29–39.

Marmor, Theodore, ed., *Poverty Policy* (Chicago: Aldine-Atherton, 1971).

Piven, Frances Fox, and Richard A. Cloward, *Regulating the Poor* (New York: Vintage Books, 1971).

Rokeach, Milton, ed., *Understanding Human Values: Individual and Societal* (New York: Free Press, 1979).

Tropman, John E., "The Constant Crisis: Social Welfare and the American Cultural Structure," *California Sociologist,* Vol. 1 (Winter 1978): pp. 61–87.

______, Milan Dluhy, and Roger Lind, eds., *New Strategic Perspectives on Social Policy* (Elmsford, N.Y.: Pergamon Press, 1981).

Tropman, John E., and Jane McClure, "Policy Analysis and Older People: A Conceptual Framework," *Journal of Sociology and Social Welfare,* Vol. 5 (November 1978): pp. 822–832.

Williams, Robin, *American Society,* rev. ed. (New York: Alfred Knopf, 1961).

## 6.

**Nan Van Den Bergh and Lynn B. Cooper**

## INTRODUCTION TO FEMINIST VISIONS FOR SOCIAL WORK

In the past 25 years, social, cultural, and political institutions in the United States have experienced a tremendous upheaval. The practices and policies of these institutions have been directly challenged by large-scale, broad-based movements of people demanding changes in the existing distribution of rights, resources, and opportunities. Feminism and the feminist movement have been significant components of this process, which has actively questioned the allocation of power and privilege in American society.

The feminist vision for a different society includes the demand for gender equality as well as a commitment to altering the processes and the manner in which private and public lives are organized and conducted. This vision does not accept the existing competitive, hierarchical, and authoritarian organization of decision making and action. A feminist vision is dedicated to creating new styles and new dynamics of interaction and relationships.

Feminism is a transformational politics, a political perspective concerned with changing extant economic, social, and political structures.[1] Basically, feminism is concerned with ending domination and resisting oppression. Consequently, as a world view, it can lend perspective to any issue and is not limited to a separate ghetto called "women's issues."[2] Feminism, therefore, is infinitely broader than an "Add women and stir" perspective on social change, that is, maintaining the status quo but simply adding more women to where there used to be only or predominantly men. As a politics of transformation, feminism is relevant to more than a constituency of women. It is a vision born of women, but it addresses the future of the planet with implications accruing for males as well as females, for all ethnic groups, for the impoverished, the disadvantaged, the

---

Nan Van Den Bergh is a professor at the School of Social Work, Tulane University; Lynn Cooper is a professor at the School of Social Work, California State University at Sacramento.

handicapped, the aged, and so on.[3] Feminism is a politics for the future of the world, not just for an isolated handful of the converted.

Many areas of public and private life have been affected by feminism. This can be seen in the development of child care programs and policies, self-help and community-based health care clinics, rape crisis centers, battered women's shelters, and more. Feminism's encouragement of women to have choices in their life pursuits has also effected the influx of females into the labor market within the last two decades. In 1992, 57.8 percent of all women aged 16 and older were paid workers, and they constituted more than 46 percent of the civilian labor force.[4] It has been noted that nine out of every ten women will be in the paid labor force at some time in their lives.[5] Feminism has suggested that women can pursue careers as well as raise children. Perhaps this accounts for the fact that 75.4 percent of all mothers with children under 18 years of age were paid workers in 1992, and 59.9 percent with preschool children were also in the labor force.[6] Women can also choose not to be mothers. In general, women have accounted for 52 percent of the civilian labor force increase since 1970.[7]

Within education, feminist pedagogy has made significant inroads in challenging the traditions that have served to reinforce the existing relationships of patriarchal power and authority. This has, in part, been accomplished by the evolution of women's studies as an appropriate and important discipline within the academy. In addition, legitimacy has been provided for the study of topics such as pornography, rape, domestic violence, and incest. Also, significant attention has been directed toward the generation of nonsexist reading materials for children. Many elementary, secondary, and college texts have been critiqued in efforts to purge sex-stereotypical content as well as to make them more inclusive in subject matter pertaining to women. Within almost all academic disciplines there has been a spate of scholarship devoted to feminist issues. There are still, however, obstacles to being published that seem attributable to insidious structural sexism.

Despite the myriad outcomes of feminism generating an impact within society, it seems to have touched the field of social work only peripherally. Research has indicated that traditional and stereotypic views of women have often been prevalent among social workers.[8] Gender stereotypes continue to exist within social work texts and journal articles.[9] Moreover, studies have noted significant discrimination against women social workers in status and salary within agencies and academia. Research has also suggested that role strain and conflict frequently exist for women who choose to combine family responsibilities with a social work career or who are in an educational program preparing for an MSW.[10] It has also been suggested that a bias exists within the delivery of social services that tends to reinforce sex-stereotypical behaviors for female clients by encouraging dependency, rather than independence.[11] In summation, although the majority of social work practitioners and recipients of service are women, feminist visions seem to have had a difficult time pervading the profession.

Ironically, at its base, social work is supposed to share many of the fundamental concerns of feminism, particularly the relationship between individual and community, between individually and socially defined needs, as well as the concern with human dignity and the right to self-determination. Social work, like feminism, is theoretically committed to improving the quality of life for all people.

The codes for both social work educators (Council on Social Work Education ([CSWE]) and practitioners (National Association of Social Workers [NASW]) mirror, at many points, the feminist commitment to explain, confront, and resolve the conditions of life for oppressed people and for society in general.[12] Those professional codes underscore a feminist principle related to the need for addressing collective welfare as equivalent in importance to individual well-being. In fact, within NASW's Code of Ethics it is stated that concern for the welfare of individuals includes action for improving social conditions. Similarly, feminism has been described as "a theory of individuality that recognizes the importance of the individual within the social collectivity."[13] A social worker advocating for individual as well as societal change is intrinsically behaving in terms of feminist principles.

Feminist principles specifically relevant to social work education and practice include: eliminating false dichotomies and artificial separations, reconceptualizing power, valuing process as equally important as product, validating renaming, and believing that the personal is political. These premises, or feminist visions, can inform education and practice related to sundry populations and social problems. The task now is to define the five premises, noting how their incorporation into the profession can generate a profound impact within social work.

## ELIMINATING FALSE DICHOTOMIES AND ARTIFICIAL SEPARATIONS

Feminist analysis mandates viewing reality in a holistic, integrated, and ecological fashion. The ecological concept pertains to the interrelatedness inherent between persons and their environments.[14] This feminist concern counters the prevalent trend within Western thought of classifying knowledge and observations around principles that *separate*.[15] For example, within conventional thinking, intuition and empiricism are viewed as incompatible. Mind, spirit, and body are considered individually and not in an interrelated fashion. In addition, masculinity and femininity are not only falsely accepted as biologically ordered categories, but are also viewed as mutually exclusive entities that should be manifest for one gender but not the other. Distinctions between the sexes, rather than commonalities, are emphasized, and the isolation of individuals is reinforced.

False dichotomies, in terms of domination versus subordination politics, abound and can be thought of as "either-or" and "zero-sum" models in that someone must lose for another to gain. So pervasive is the effect of creating false dichotomies that it undergirds the infighting that occurs among oppressed groups. Trying to get a "slice of the pie," minorities tend to view each other competitively in an "us versus them" mode rather than perceive commonalities and work collaboratively against a common oppressor.

These artificial separations are particularly true for women of color, who are constantly forced to place themselves at either one end or the other of an oppression continuum. Minority women are forced to identify their discrimination as *primarily* racist or *primarily* sexist rather than as an interaction of both. Working-class people of color are dichotomized into categorizing themselves as hampered by classism or racism. Feminists of color are often chastised by ethnic men for their concern with women's rights. Such splitting tactics are an outcome of a systemic propensity to dichotomize.

The feminist concern with interrelatedness derives primarily from recognizing the inability of existing social, political, and economic arrangements to provide adequately satisfying and meaningful lives for the overwhelming number of people in this society. Feminism, committed to creating and building a new culture, utilizes a holistic, ecological, and spiritual perspective as the force behind the evolving societal paradigms.[16] Feminist political analysis has also consistently stressed the need to eliminate separating and alienating power structures. Consequently, feminist politics have focused on collective, integrative decision-making processes.[17] Equally important is the recognition that making separations out of unities and dividing a whole into conflicting components is the quintessence of patriarchal processes which isolate, separate, and divide, and is the model for hierarchical organization and order.[18]

## RECONCEPTUALIZING POWER

Power is a central concern within feminist analysis. A significant amount of discourse has related to considering ways in which patriarchy can be challenged.[19] Patriarchal processes are characterized by creating power dichotomies—in essence, generating conditions of "haves and have-nots." The concept of patriarchy has most usually been employed to describe situations of male domination and female submission. It can be generalized, however, as a paradigm describing all inequitable situations whereby many must lose so that a few can gain. Within a patriarchal mode, power is seen as a finite commodity to be controlled, particularly in determining the distribution of rights, resources, and opportunities. In most traditional models, power is viewed as property, analogous to money, involving control and domination of subordinates to make them subservient. Accordingly, those who control power manage the environment and determine goals, information is withheld, and rules are created to censure behavior.[20]

Through control of power, patriarchal modes breed subordination by promoting dependency and not providing persons with the ability to have full control over their lives. Powerlessness can be considered an inability to manage emotions, skills, knowledge, and material resources in a way leading to effective performance of valued social roles.[21] It is through performing in certain capacities, such as worker, head of household, parent, partner, and spouse, that individuals derive a sense of purpose and self. Powerlessness can prevent persons from performing optimally and can lead to isolation, anomie, and social problems.

As an alternative to the patriarchal finite notion of power, feminists have sought to reconceptualize power as infinite, a widely distributed energy of influence, strength, effectiveness, and responsibility. Power is viewed as facilitative; empowerment to action occurs rather than domination.[22] Empowerment, or claiming personal power, is a political act because it allows people control over their own lives and the ability to make decisions for themselves.

To redefine power does not mean to deny the reality of differentials that exist between persons in knowledge, influence, skills, resources, or responsibility. It is a myth to believe that persons are equally powerful or that everyone must have an equivalent amount of power. Types of power, such as knowledge power or skill power, must be recognized and acknowledged as merely being different and not more legitimate than other types of power.

From time to time, certain individuals might be more expert than others and their opinion could weigh more heavily than that of others. Structures can be created, however, that give persons more equal access to issues, resources, and information.[23] Disclosing certain data can provide the conditions by which individuals can make choices—and that is part of the process of empowering.

## VALUING PROCESS EQUALLY WITH PRODUCT

The feminist agenda of valuing process equally with product is related to both the interconnectedness and false dichotomy notions. Basically, it maintains that how one pursues a goal is as important as the accomplishment of the goal. Because of patriarchal separating processes, means and end, as well as process and product, have been dichotomized. Only what one achieves tends to be considered, rather than, with equal interest, how one arrives at goals. One consequence of this type of process is the amassing of wealth and power as an end in itself, despite the generally unethical and harmful behaviors involved in the pursuit of that end. Competition, conquest, and individualism are all reinforced when the ends are rewarded and the means to those ends are ignored.

A feminist vision of process and outcome is based on an assumption that the merit of a goal is directly related to the way in which it is achieved. Goals achieved through bad processes must always be mistrusted. How one pursues an objective becomes a goal in and of itself. Processes utilized to make decisions are as important as the final determinations.

Process can be conceptualized as an enabling and facilitative force akin to an empowering experience. Redefinition of power and attention to means are highly interrelated. For example, feminist organizational style has attempted to ensure that all participants are aware of the agenda, encouraged to speak, and comfortable in requesting clarity on issues. Moreover, being aware of process means taking time for the personal concerns of colleagues, co-workers, and supervisees, within work settings. It also means generating vehicles for feedback and critique so that persons can express both validations and dissatisfactions.

## VALIDITY OF RENAMING

Having the right to name one's own experience is a feminist agenda that has significance for all oppressed people. Inspired by the example of civil rights activists, feminists deemed early in the movement's resurgence that there was power in naming. Initially identified by Betty Friedan in 1963 as "the problem which has no name," sexism has since been defined, along with other terms denoting a new reality for women, including the term "consciousness raising" and the use of Ms.

It was through black activism that the right to name was first articulated as the cry for "Black Power" was made by Stokely Carmichael. Following this example, other ethnic minorities chose to name themselves no longer as "hyphenated" Americans but adopted terms such as Chicano, La Raza, Atzlan, and Pacific Islander, in order to describe their unique cultural identities. In addition, to emphasize the significance of being racial minorities so as to differentiate themselves from other groups also using the label "minority" (women, lesbians and gay men, the physically handicapped), some ethnic people have chosen to name themselves as "people of color" or "women of color."[24] How one names oneself is highly related to one's identity and sense of self.

Renaming includes four processes: (1) applying new labels (words) to persons, places, or things; (2) changing meanings by altering the format of language; (3) reclaiming archaic definitions; or (4) conceptually broadening the meaning of existing language. It is helpful to provide a brief indication of what each process entails.

An example of renaming would be referring to persons as black rather than Negro, Afro-American, or colored. Similarly, use of the word Ms. as an article of address for women, regardless of their marital status, exemplifies that process.

The second potential renaming action, changing meanings by altering the formats of words, can be accomplished by the utilization of hyphens or slashes. Daly, for example, refers to renaming as an "a-mazing process."[25] Hidden deceptions within language can be revealed by dividing words and employing alternative meanings for prefixes. Also, slashes and hyphens can be used to create more inclusive words, such as s/he.

Renaming via reclaiming archaic definitions entails "going back to basics" in order to purge racism and sexism in language. By searching out archaic meanings it may be possible to discern original definitions diametrically opposite to current conventional language, which may have been affected by prejudiced attitudes. For example, the word hag is typically associated with an ugly old woman. However, it emanates from the Greek word *hagios* (meaning holy), which aludes to the eminent positions women once held as spiritual leaders in society. For both feminists and ethnic activists, renaming includes reclaiming knowledge and pride in cultural, historical, and current experiences.

Finally and perhaps most important, to rename also means to expand the conceptual boundaries of words by going beyond conventional definitions. For example, the conceptual picture conjured up most frequently by the word family is a nuclear unit with a mother, father, and children. However, society is increasingly bearing witness to the burgeoning of alternative family forms, and social forecasting predicts the continuation of that phenomenon. Currently, only 16 percent of American families conform to the traditional nuclear family stereotype of an employed father, a homemaker wife-mother, and offspring.[26] Feminists have articulated the need to have a plural vision of families. In fact, it has been suggested that "families" is a more inclusive concept than "family" because it denotes the right and need of people to create a variety of loving and caring structures for their daily lives.[27] Consequently, it may be that the future will see seemingly uncontroversial words, such as family, renamed in a conceptually broadened way so as to provide a change impetus for evolving social institutions.

## THE PERSONAL IS POLITICAL

"The personal is political" was first articulated in conjunction with consciousness-raising activities during the early years of the current feminist movement. When women talked about their personal experiences in a group context, they were able to "speak bitterness" and perceive the commonalities among their lives. Consequently, it became possible to evolve beyond personal faulting and to develop an empirically based understanding of institutionalized sexism. Women learned that the problems they encountered were not individualized; they were part of a pattern generalizable to

FIGURE 6.1
Interaction Between Institutional and Individual Change

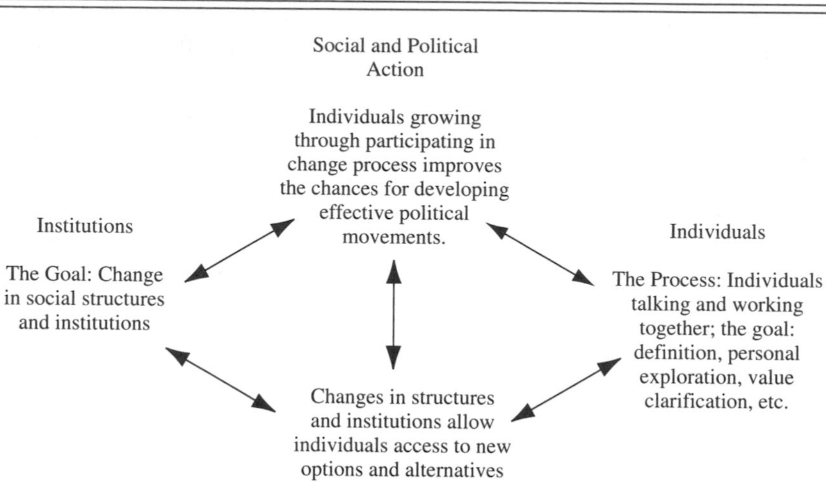


SOURCE: Adapted and reprinted with the permission of the publisher from N. B. Gluckstern, "Beyond Therapy: Personal and Institutional Change," in E. I. Rawlings and D. K. Carter, eds., *Psychotherapy for Women* (Springfield, Ill.: Charles C. Thomas, Publisher, 1977), p. 429.

sexism. This type of awareness signaled the evolution of political consciousness—a sense of individual connectedness to a system of oppression.

As a tenent of feminist analysis, this premise suggests that the values and beliefs a person harbors, the goals that one sets, and the type of life style one chooses to pursue can be considered a political statement. It demonstrates an interconnectedness between individual activities and societal structures. The social movement can influence personal behavior, just as individual activities can exert influence on society. In addition, this proposition suggests that institutional change can be effected by personal, social, and political action.

An assumption underlying the personal is political is that working to bring about changes within societal institutions can also alter the course of one's life. Challenging systems may precipitate establishing new priorities among one's personal values. Such a change could be an impetus for modifying an individual's dysfunctional patterned behaviors. Simultaneously, alterations within institutional structures can allow persons new opportunities that may facilitate individual change. This process is exemplified by Figure 6.1.

A focus on social change to bring about individual and institutional modifications is in sharp contrast to both Freudian psychology and the American ethic of "rugged individualism," which have a victim-blaming component and do not address structural inequality. The feminist agenda validates that individual experiences can be related to systemic structures and outcomes. Individual distress can be seen as having an etiology within system-based inequalities, just as institutional change can be facilitated through individual actions.

It means that women's distinctive experience as women occurs within that sphere that has been socially lived as the personal-private, emotional, interiorized, particular, individuated, intimate—so that what it is to *know* the politics of woman's situation is to know women's personal lives.[28]

## SUMMARY OF FEMINIST VISIONS

The five premises of feminist analysis—eliminating false dichotomies and artificial separations, reconceptualizing power, valuing process equally with product, renaming, and the personal is political—have the potential to alter dramatically all aspects of social work education and practice. Their incorporation into the core of social work will not be easy. These premises are intimately linked to challenging power, prestige, and the dynamics of existing practices, policies, and programs. All of these visions are relatively new; they are in the process of being developed and understood.

Feminist analysis is not static, but rather a continually evolving and expanding process. Each vision is filled with ambiguities, uncertainties, and complexities. For example, how does one utilize good processes when a crisis demands an immediate response? How does a feminist administrator convince workers accustomed to hierarchical decision making that their opinions and feelings are valid? Challenges and changes are never easy or simple, and they are often met with resistance. Feminist social work practitioners, educators, and consumers of social services must be prepared to confront and overcome resistance from others, as well as from their own insecurities and uncertainties, and to begin to make feminist visions an integral part of their lives. The implications of these visions for specific areas of social service provisions, education, and research will now be suggested.

### False Dichotomies and Artificial Separations

*Specialist vs. Generalist Practice.* Historically, social work has been composed of two primary types of services—direct and indirect. Direct practice typically refers to services provided for individuals, families, and small groups, whereas indirect practice has referred to community organization, planning, policy making, administration, and research. At different times within the history of social work, one type or the other seems to have been emphasized. At the turn of the century, an emphasis on creating settlement houses and scientifically documenting living conditions in urban areas was an important synthesis of direct and indirect service provision.

In the early 1900s, with the development and growth of monopoly capitalism, the strengthened ideological commitment to the separation of private and public lives, as well as the intensification of class and racial divisions, dramatically altered the practice of social work. Similar to medicine, and influenced by Freudianism, social work began to focus solely on the individual's personal responsibility for life's difficulties. For example, poverty was no longer primarily a problem of slum housing, poor wages, or discrimination; it began to be treated as an individual psychological difficulty.[29]

The overwhelming impact of the Great Depression beginning in 1929 sparked a renewed social work interest in societal responsibility for poverty and suffering. Many social workers, led by Bertha Reynolds, Mary Van Kleeck, and others, were actively involved in organizing unemployment councils and demonstrations and in making demands for government aid to the poor, the homeless, the unemployed, and the exploited. There was a rekindling of the commitment to understanding suffering within the context of social responsibility. Social work involvement in the development of social security and unemployment insurance during this time documents this renewed commitment.

In the 1950s, the Cold War and McCarthyism helped once again to push the social work profession away from social and political activism. There was a reemphasis on individual difficulties and responsibilities. Social workers were concerned with helping people to adjust and accept the conditions of their lives, rather than to challenge the existing order.

The 1960s civil rights dissent gave birth to the Great Society social policy, which refocused attention on the need to intervene within communities as well as with individuals. The dismantling of social programs during the 1970s, along with a trend toward engaging in private clinical practice, has swung the professional pendulum away from concern with system intervention in the 1980s.

Today, social work has bred an ethic of specialization whereby individuals are trained to practice one type of service to the exclusion of other types. This pattern can be attributed in part to an oversubscription to Taylorism and professionalism. Taylorism required that work be divided into specialized, discrete components. Professionalism demanded that only an elite group of people, specially trained and qualified, were capable of performing certain types of work. Both Taylorism and professionalism were means to increase profit through greater worker efficiency and productivity, without regard to growing worker or client alienation and ennui.

Social work practice has tended to be dichotomized so that an individual worker is a specialist, rather than a generalist. To be a generalist practitioner is to be as adept in intervening with macro systems as with individuals, families, and small groups. Because social work emphasizes the concept of "person-in-situation," it could be argued that generalist practice is the only approach true to social work's ecological foundation. In order to deal with the myriad social problems within contemporary society and the commensurate distress experienced by individuals, generalist practice appears the most tenable approach. Consequently, there needs to be reemphasis on social work embodying a dual service delivery commitment to individuals, families, and small groups intricately linked with community, organizational, administrative, and research efforts.

Conceptually, social work supports a practice that stresses concern for the welfare of individuals concomitant with action for improving social conditions. The dualism is more theoretical than actual, however, as persons tend to be dichotomized as caseworkers or administrators, clinicians or community organizers, researchers or practitioners. A social work practitioner operating on one end of the continuum or another cannot be of greatest aid to clients or systems. Implanting a feminist vision within social work education and practice is highly warranted in order to integrate components that have been artificially separated.

By eliminating false dichotomies, social work would move toward more of a generalist model. That is not to imply that practitioners would be without areas of expertise. Individuals would still have domains of particular competence. However, the overall training and practice model would be more integrated and generalist; social work practice would be more holistic, ecological, and preventive. Practitioners would be as committed to working for social change as to ameliorating individual client problems.

*Indirect Services.* The development of social planning, programs, and policies, as well as administrative responsibilities, would be reoriented from short-sighted and limited visions to the feminist theme of interconnectedness. Currently, most planning and policy generation tends to be orchestrated through a "here and now" perspective. Short-term gains are addressed and long-term implications tend not to be assessed. This reflects a finite rather than more infinite perception of reality. Industrial pollution, the environmental crisis, and nuclear proliferation are all testimonies to the pervasiveness of short-term gain planning. An inevitable outcome of this approach is perpetual crisis resolution as resources have to be invested today in order to solve problems created yesterday. Perceiving phenomena in a more interrelated fashion could generate greater integration between actions taken in the present and their future consequences. That is, policies would be implemented with a clearer sense of responsibility for their outcome in the future. A sense of social contract would undergird the planning process.

For example, consider the issue of connectedness as it applies to traditional housing planning and policy. Political, economic, and social values shape the kinds of buildings that are constructed, and buildings affect the type of social interaction that takes place within them. Views of the poor, the mentally ill, elderly people, and delinquent children influence the location and design of housing for those population groups. Housing design affects the self-image and self-esteem of those residing in the domiciles and shapes relationships among inhabitants, staff, and the surrounding community.[30] If a belief in interconnectedness were more prevalent, housing environments might be planned with greater concern for the quality of life they shape.

*Research.* Challenging false dichotomies, in conducting studies, means eliminating the separation between research and practice. Research needs to be seen as part of practice itself, a process of evaluating effort and outcome. Greater utilization of single-subject designs could bridge the existing gap between practice and research; such designs allow an evaluation of both process and outcome, do not require substantial statistical knowledge, and can be used by clients as a method for self-monitoring.

In addition, employing this agenda challenges positivism. The positivist tradition maintains that research should be objective, neutral, and value-free, with empirical knowledge separated from the pursuit of moral aims, and that all knowledge must be definable, measurable, and testable.[31] Basically, the positivist stance is antiactivist, and therefore antifeminist. Studies undertaken by feminist researchers tend to be precipitated by a strong value stance that the experiences of women and other oppressed groups may be best examined by persons of like affiliation. An extraordinary amount of social science knowledge has been formulated from studies done by and on white males and generalized to be the experience of all persons. Feminist researchers see a need to engage in research with an activist perspective in order to engender social change.

Furthermore, feminists validate the efficacy of intuitive knowing, which is derided as invalid data within the positivist tradition. To value learning gained from intuitive insights would be to eliminate a false dichotomy between left-brain analytical knowing and right-brain creative understanding. It has been postulated that scientific insights are characteristically intuitive; only later are they described and verified by linear analytical argument. Moreover, it has been suggested that the most significant creative activities of our culture have only been made possible through the collaborative work of the left and right hemispheres.[32]

*Education.* Within the educational experience, eliminating false separations means advocating for generically based core curriculum content on both the undergraduate and graduate levels. This implies providing "equal time" for course work stressing macro knowledge and practice principles as well as clinical knowledge and skills. A burgeoning of social work private practitioners within the last decade has caused curriculum to become skewed in the clinical direction. Although undergraduate preparation tends to be more generalist, it is equally important to supply indirect services information on the MSW level—and not just for nonclinical students. To practice social work, an MSW should be familiar with concepts, theories, and skills pertaining to organizational, community, and social change. Despite private career ambitions, social workers need to retain their public "roots." They must be cognizant of the clearly articulated mission of social change. Seeing clients privately does not preclude concern for pervasive societal inequities, nor the ability to engage in activism.

Eliminating false dichotomies also suggests the need to ensure that conceptual frameworks are "in contact with reality." That is, theories that are taught need to be based on people's actual experiences, not on speculative conjecture formulated by "informed observers." Too many conceptual frameworks utilized in social work point to individual rather than social pathology. Theories that blame people for their victimization or distress, or that view them out of the context of the historical period and social order in which they live, need to be replaced. Concepts need to be promulgated that indicate that people have the ability to ameliorate individual difficulties *and* that, collectively, we can solve social problems.

### Reconceptualizing Power

*Direct Services.* Applying this premise to direct services suggests that therapeutic strategies would be modeled to facilitate client empowerment. The emphasis would be on aiding clients to develop skills that could be used to influence their environment. For example, assertiveness training, improving communication abilities, and stress and time management as well as conflict resolution and negotiation and bargaining skills, would be appropriate parts of the therapeutic process. These approaches are significantly different from the examination of client intrapsychic dynamics that is the hallmark of insight-based psychoanalytic approaches. Drawing from feminist therapy, which is based upon empowerment principles, clients are encouraged to take risks in assuming personal power. Often this entails encouraging the client to express anger and to role-play ways in which that anger can be channeled toward constructive change.[33]

Feminist therapists also take the position that power between therapist and client should be either equal or continually approaching equality. This is not to negate those situations in which clients may attribute to their therapists a certain amount of power based upon the practitioners' knowledge and skills. The assumption is, however, that therapists must not exploit that difference between themselves and their clients by using professional jargon or obscure clinical terms. Clients are viewed as being experts on their own behavior, competent to understand both the impressions and the techniques of their therapists.[34]

*Indirect Services.* Reconceptualizing power on a macro level includes encouragement of planning, policy, and decision-making processes that are more collective and horizontal in structure rather than autocratic and hierarchical. In facilitating such models, it is important to recognize expertise differentials between persons; however, responsibility, as well as opportunities to exert influence, can be shared. Leadership skills can be built by offering individuals new experiences in which they are the primary facilitators of an activity.

It might also be possible to consider the incorporation of "flextime" and job-sharing options as a type of indirect services empowerment. Instead of accepting employment based solely on fixed criteria established by employers, unions representing employees could negotiate for work to take place during times and under conditions more beneficial to the workers. Working collectively in unions, employees would have more latitude and power in creating the conditions of their employment; potential "burnout" could be mediated.

Also related to the empowerment notion for indirect services might be working to decrease the number of managers and supervisors by encouraging workers to utilize peer accountability. Implementing that process could be facilitated through a team model encouraging job sharing, task rotation, and multiskill development. The use of consensus management also provides workers with the opportunity to exert more influence on decisions regarding productivity. An outcome of such processes could be the creation of close working relationships; hence, enhanced job satisfaction.[35]

Similarly, reconceptualized power might be facilitated in agencies by organizing personnel into work groups in which tasks are shifted. Such an arrangement could allow for workers to have a greater sense of integration within and connection to agency services. For example, through the process of rotating workers and job responsibilities within a public welfare department, child protective workers could gain greater experience as well as insight into the entire range of services from finding placements to doing investigations, testifying in court, and providing treatment.

Finally, reconceptualizing power for indirect services would include eliciting consumer input during the planning and policy-making process. Clearly, consumers are more likely to utilize a service if they feel that their input has been sought by decision makers. This has obvious implications for client satisfaction and is empowering because it provides consumers with the ability to exert influence on their environment.

*Research.* Research must be designed and conducted in order to facilitate client empowerment. Typically, research is viewed as an intrusive act replete with oppressive processes usually not helpful to social work recipients. It is conceptualized as something not readily integrated into practice—something that does not provide rewards to those studied, only to the researcher.

However, research can be an empowering process for clients and can assist in their growth. Single-subject designs can be easily employed with clients and can aid their empowerment by providing ongoing feedback on their movement toward achieving their goals. The process of regularly recording self-assessments on some behavioral or affective dimension can help clients understand their problems. Furthermore, there are built-in incentives to work toward change in order to see alterations in the pattern of a behavior or feeling.

Reconceptualizing power within a research context also means that the purposes of a study, as well as the findings, should not be isolated from respondents. This is to ensure that informants are not excluded from important aspects of the research process, such as determining the study questions, deciding on methodology, analyzing findings, and providing interpretation analysis. Moreover, client feedback can be elicited on the perceived appropriateness of conceptual frameworks or theoretical paradigms used to inform the study.

To employ this vision is to include clients within the research process as active rather than passive participants. It assumes that clients have knowledge, based on their personal experiences, and should be approached to ascertain their "expert" opinion on study issues. In essence, this vision suggests utilization of nonhierarchical research methods so that studies are not generated "from the top down." Rather, they will be guided by a commitment to serve those who are powerless.

*Education.* What are some potential outcomes of reconceptualizing power for social work education? Social work classes can be considered laboratories for persons experimenting in becoming empowered. Theories and issues related to power should be utilized as unifying themes in order to bridge connections between the sundry manifestations of institutionalized inequality for all oppressed groups. Rather than address the reconceptualization of power solely through a lecture or discussion context, students should experiment with becoming empowered. Role playing would allow individuals to experience being in powerless situations and then asserting influence, strength, and responsibility so as to become empowered. Students could be required to keep a journal about their experiences with powerlessness and empowerment by mandating that they attempt some risk-taking actions within their social environment. Also, students might be encouraged to role play a planning or administrative process where tasks and responsibilities are shifted among different work groups. Didactically, in fact, classroom groups could be established with learning goals that varied over the course of the semester. Students could shift responsibility in facilitating the accomplishment of certain group tasks. One benefit of using social work courses as a laboratory for experimenting with reconceptualized power is that there will be heterogeneity in the classroom population, allowing for a simulation of actual organizational and societal experience.

Students can gain a sense of empowerment by receiving validation for the knowledge they have acquired through life experience. They have information and skills to offer, and faculty can learn from student experiences. Providing reinforcement for learner knowledge establishes a model that can be replicated by the student in work with clients and within agencies.

Another vehicle for teaching empowerment through classroom experiences is utilizing contract grading. Some situations are obviously more conducive to this approach than others; but some opportunity to formulate a self-design evaluation plan should be considered by faculty as a part of the grading scheme. Relatedly, students should be encouraged to provide feedback on their experience with the course and to suggest additional directions or revisions.

### Valuing Process Equally with Product

*Direct Services.* Facilitating client independence and empowerment utilizes the principle of valuing process as equal to product. Discouraging dependency on the therapist and encouraging challenging as well as risk-taking behaviors engender a therapeutic process by which independence is learned and validated. The therapist is not envisioned as an omnipotent person who "cures" a client, but, rather, as a facilitator of individuals' innate abilities to heal themselves.

Therapy is acknowledged as a learning experience. Clients are aided in acquiring skills that can be generalized to other problems encountered in life situations, beyond the problem(s) that caused them to seek professional intervention. Direct practice approaches that fail to aid individuals in dealing with problems beyond the presenting issue(s) suggest questionable therapeutic value.

*Indirect Services.* Incorporating this feminist agenda within indirect services could ensure that the way in which programs are implemented would not contradict service provision goals. Often the ostensible merit of a service becomes contradicted through the processes generated by its implementation. For example, AFDC income maintenance programs have been theoretically created for the purpose of providing security to indigent families with dependent children. Frequently, however, programs have stipulated that in order to receive benefits, a father must not live with his family. The result has been not to provide security but rather to generate insecurity. If a program is founded on principles that generate separations, then the result can only be divisive. Programs utilizing segregating processes will likely create insecurities and alienation. Integrating processes can engender a sense of security and connectedness.

Considering process and product as equivalent in importance also has implications for administrative practice. Traditional bureaucratic management has assumed that administrators must employ a value-free, neutral style in order to expedite getting the job done. In contradiction to that model, being concerned with process includes valuing different experiences and perspectives. For example, an administrator with feminist values will validate multidimensional thinking.[36] She or he recognizes the richness of varied explanatory systems being brought to bear on any decision. This means that how one "feels" about an issue, or one's intuition about a dynamic, is given a value equivalent to concrete facts or realities.

In a related vein, relationships between co-workers are also recognized as important rather than discounted as inefficient or a waste of time. Valuing relationships, a feminist administrator tries to achieve a fit between individual and organizational needs. For example, support would be given to staff who are dealing with personal problems. Concern with process would also be exemplified by implementing flextime, job sharing, or jobs that could be partially completed at home.[37] These alternatives indicate that providing an environment sensitive to human needs is a component of concern with process.

Another example of the focus on process within a feminist administrative style would be the administrator's showing concern at the beginning of a meeting with participants sharing what is going on with them personally. This is in contrast to the traditional rap of the gavel to start a meeting on time in order to address an agenda.

Process time would be structured for critique, sharing opinions, praise, and affirmation.[38] Conflict would be dealt with as it arose rather than being tabled or dismissed. The importance of compromise, of avoiding polarities, is also recognized. Concern with process makes a feminist administrative style more focused on effectiveness than efficiency, which can be seen as the difference between long- and short-range planning.[39] Will a coercive process that engenders short-term goals be able to sustain over time? Multidimensional thinking suggests that the answer is "No."

*Education.* Teaching students empowering processes will facilitate the development of a commitment to valuing process and product. Social work pedagogy should serve as an example of participatory learning process. Educators need to be keenly aware of creating an environment that maximizes opportunities for people to make connections with each other and become empowered. For example, the beginning and end of each class can allow for personal sharing, with individuals feeling comfortable in stating "what's good and new" for them. Also, the teacher should encourage the students to express anger and pose challenges, which is a difficult and often painful task for the educator. However, by feeling that they can share their process, students may be better able to accept the instructor's process in terms of potential disappointment with student performance. Also, encouraging the articulation of conflict and providing a vehicle for its resolution can serve as a modeling experience to be applied beyond the classroom.

**Renaming**

*Direct Services.* Renaming, when applied to direct services, has implications for the support of individual client choice and life experiences. This feminist vision is particularly important for work with minorities. Encouraging clients to examine the strengths of their cultural experience validates renaming. Claiming and renaming one's heritage is an empowering process and is integral within both ethnic-sensitive and feminist practice.

Emphasizing client experience in diagnosis and treatment is a part of this renaming process. Practitioners should never assume that their ethnic clients all have the same cultural frame of reference or interpret events in the same way. Similarly, it should not be assumed that all women or all men view sex-role experiences comparably. Nor should it be assumed that all gay male and lesbian clients have had the same experience and interpret their sexuality in a similar fashion. Practitioners must constantly ask clients to define presenting problems concretely, based on the clients' own experience.

In addition, practitioners should help their clients to understand that they, the clients, have choices in how they name their experiences. In other words, to rename being a wife and mother might mean choosing to work outside the home on a part- or full-time basis, rather than being solely a homemaker. The practitioner's role is to support the idea of clients' having choices.

Another direct practice implication is facilitating group treatment for people of color. By experiencing a collective sharing and problem-solving process, oppressed persons can evolve renamed definitions of personal and collective identity. Group treatment can serve a consciousness-raising function by bringing to an individual's attention the recognition that her or his experience has been shared, to a greater or lesser degree, by others. It was through group consciousness-raising practices in the early years of feminist activism that women began to reclaim and rename what it was to be female. This same phenomenon was experienced by ethnic persons involved in civil rights activism.

*Indirect Services.* Renaming has important implications for indirect practice, including altering the perception of social workers from being "do-gooders" to being agents for social change. Most people appear to consider social workers as friendly visitors distributing alms to the poor, hoping to save souls. Social work needs to be renamed as including organizers and advocates for the elimination of institutionalized inequality and economic oppression.

Validating renaming also suggests supporting gender-centered and ethnic-centered social services, such as battered women's shelters, rape crisis centers, women's health services, and ethnic-oriented services and programs. The issue of special services for special populations is constantly debated within social work, raising such questions as the following: Should there be ethnic agencies that only serve ethnic clientele? Should ethnic foster or adoptive children only be placed within comparable ethnic homes? Should services for battered and raped women be provided by programs that are separate from existing agencies? To support renaming would seem to include validation for the need to allow special services to serve special populations.

Finally, social work must be open to accepting redefinitions of seemingly uncontroversial terms, like family. The receipt of social services is often predicated on conforming to narrowly defined criteria. Social institutions are constantly being challenged and redefined according to cultural exigencies. Consequently, a concept such as family needs redefining as more than a nuclear unit. Family should also mean single parents and children, nonbiologically affiliated persons, extended units with grandparents or other blood relatives, as well as single adults living together. There are obvious implications for adoption and foster parenting related to redefining family. Single adults, both male and female, should be allowed to adopt or act as foster parents. In addition, same-sex partners or couples who are not legally married should be considered eligible adoptive or foster parents.

*Research.* Renaming in research demands that what has been typically considered as unimportant or not scientific be reexamined as valid. This includes a premise expounded on previously, concerning the need to validate intuition and nonempirical phenomena as sources of knowledge.

Renaming also connects to the personal is political theme by underscoring the significance of individual experience. Personal issues need to be seen as politically important and scientifically valid for the generation of new knowledge and understanding. As applied to research, renaming means that clients have the right to name what is important to study and the methods that should be undertaken within research.

*Education.* Social work education must examine the experiences of oppressed groups in order to develop the potential to rename what it is to be ethnic, female, aged, gay, and so on. This includes a past, present, and future perspective. The realities of oppressed people must be explicitly studied and renamed in order to reflect the diversity of their experiences.

Although all accredited programs are mandated to cover ethnic and gender content, there seems to be no uniform pattern as to how this mandate is actualized. Unfortunately, too often that content is "ghettoized" in the curriculum and is not inclusively covered in most classes. Care must be taken not to focus solely on demographic characteristics, because this can lead to the promulgation of stereotypes.

In practice classes, students should be aided in learning techniques that allow them to define and validate client experiences. Basically, a strong need exists to ensure that students' work with clients will not be based on stereotypes. Future social workers must understand that there are continuums of experience and that good practice entails determining how clients name and define their own realities.

## The Personal Is Political

*Direct Services.* Practitioners must aid their clients in understanding that personal problems can be related to political realities. Individuals can be helped to identify both external and internal restraints. External restraints, based on political, economic, and social systems, are manifested as stereotypes, prejudices, discriminatory actions, and blocked opportunities. Internal restraints can be considered the individual's own resistances to changing her or his dysfunctional behavior patterns.[40] When a client encounters resistance in the way of a desired goal and is able to differentiate whether the restraint is internal or external, then that individual is indicating an evolving political consciousness. In essence, the client is renaming her or his experience in a more holistic and therapeutically beneficial way. The tendency to be self-blaming, guilty, and isolated is being mediated. Consequently, political education should be considered a legitimate and necessary component of the therapeutic process. It helps clients to be cognizant of how personal conflicts are connected to contradictions within society. It reinforces that the personal is political.

A second implication of incorporating this premise into direct social work is that the practitioner would be serving as an activist role model. She or he needs to break out of the constraints of the traditional counselor role. This means challenging the sexism, racism, and other prejudices within service delivery systems, as well as in the larger society. Typically, mental health workers have not taken the risks involved in initiating meaningful social action. Social workers need to serve as advocates for the individuals and groups they want to serve. If they do not play that role, then they act as agents of social control by maintaining the status quo.[41]

*Indirect Services.* The personal is political entails sharing professional skills and knowledge. In part, the power of any profession lies in its monopoly over knowledge and skills. To train or to share practice methodologies with community members is to facilitate the empowerment of others. Many human services that have evolved during the last decade as outgrowths of the feminist movement, such as rape crisis centers, battered women's shelters, and women's health services, have systematically trained community persons. This same dynamic has been true for ethnic activism. Many ethnic professionals have taken responsibility to share their knowledge and skills by training others in order to aid in the empowerment of their communities. Practitioners who participate in such training are personally making a political statement that part of their social work responsibility is to share their expertise with others.

Related to sharing knowledge and skills is personal effort undertaken in order to build competent communities. Such communities would be able to challenge existing power structures. This means aiding localities with needs assessment, resource mobilization, and program planning and implementation, as well as evaluative techniques. The practitioner does not need to act out his or her professional role when aiding in these activities but can share "how-to's" as a concerned citizen. Again, this kind of personal commitment clearly has political implications by allowing for community empowerment.

*Education.* In the classroom students need to be encouraged to share their own experiences when discussing issues of ethnicity, sex, and class. They should be helped to see how their personal experiences are indicators of systemic patterns in society. "Reaction" papers can be assigned whereby students relate how their gender, ethnicity, and class have influenced both personal and work experiences. They can be asked to reflect on the kinds of cultural messages they received concerning roles they should and should not perform.

In addition, it would be beneficial for students to read biographies and memoirs of social workers, such as Jane Addams and Bertha Reynolds, who modeled social change concern with their personal lives. Also, students could be asked to interview community activists in order to ascertain how those individuals' personal lives reflect their social change vision.

Students should be required to embark upon some kind of social change activity during their academic career. This could include distributing leaflets, participating in a march or demonstration, writing letters to the editor, acting as a spokesperson for a cause, and so on. It is essential that students be clear about the inherent linkage between social work and social change. That awareness is best facilitated by requiring that they engage in activist behaviors.

## CONCLUSION

Feminist visions for social work education and practice are much broader and more inclusive than they would be if they solely addressed "women's issues." Analysis utilizing these visions sharpens the focus on individual as well as societal change. Feminist visions aid in understanding the relationship between personal hardship and institutionalized oppression, validating the unity between public and private life. In addition to eliminating false dichotomies, such a focus also values personal experience; individuals and collectivities are encouraged to rename their realities. Empowerment of persons and communities is envisioned, which means redefining power as an energy of influence and responsibility rather than a commodity to be controlled. As much attention is focused on the process by which a goal is pursued as its accomplishment; means must justify ends.

Examining social work through feminist visions provides a focus for professional practice and education that is integrative, holistic, and ecological. As such, these perspectives can be a synergistic force allowing for accomplishment of social work's unique mission—facilitating social change in order to improve the quality of life.

## NOTES

1. Feminism has raised fundamental questions as to the underlying structure and assumptions of capital economy, professionalism, and bureaucracy. See Ann Withorn, *Serving the People: Social Services and Social Change* (New York: Columbia University Press, 1984).
2. Charlotte Bunch, *Going Public with Our Vision* (Denver, Colo.: Antelope Publications, 1983), p. 19.
3. Ibid.
4. Women's Bureau, *Time of Change: 1983 Handbook of Women Workers* (Washington,

D.C.: U.S. Department of Labor, 1983), p. 3.

5. Women's Bureau, *Twenty Facts on Women Workers* (Washington, D.C.: U.S. Department of Labor, 1980), p. 1.

6. Women's Bureau, *Time of Change.*

7. *Statistical Abstract of the U.S. 1993*, 113th ed., Washington, D.C.: U.S. Government Printing Office, 1994.

8. See Diane Kravetz, "An Overview of Content on Women for the Social Work Curriculum," *Journal of Education for Social Work,* 18 (Spring 1982), pp. 42–49; Caree Rozen Brown and Marilyn Levitt Hellinger, "Therapists' Attitudes toward Women," *Social Work,* 20 (July 1975), pp. 266–270; Dennis M. Dailey, "Are Social Workers Sexist? A Replication," *Social Work,* 25 (January 1980), pp. 46–50; Judith Davenport and Nancy Reims, "Theoretical Orientation and Attitudes toward Women," *Social Work*, 23 (July 1978), pp. 306–309; Trudy Bradley Festinger and Rebecca L. Bounds, "Sex-Role Stereotyping: A Research Note," *Social Work*, 22 (July 1977), pp. 314–315; Joel Fischer et al., "Are Social Workers Sexists?" *Social Work*, 21 (November 1976), pp. 428–433; Linda Hall Harris and Margaret Exner Lucas, "Sex Role Stereotyping," *Social Work*, 21 (September 1976), pp. 390–395; John L. Hipple and Lee Hipple, "Concepts of Ideal Woman and Ideal Man," *Social Work*, 25 (March 1980), pp. 147–149; and Ann Weick and Susan T. Vandiver, eds., *Women, Power, and Change* (Silver Spring, Md.: National Association of Social Workers, 1981).

9. See Pat Diangson, Diane Kravetz, and Judy Lipton, "Sex-Role Stereotyping and Social Work Education," *Journal of Education for Social Work,* 11 (Fall 1975), pp. 44–49; Mary S. Hanlan, "Women in Social Work Administration: Current Role Strains," *Administration in Social Work,* 1 (Fall 1977), pp. 259–265; Mary C. Schwartz, "Sexism in the Social Work Curriculum," *Journal of Education for Social Work,* 9 (Fall 1973), pp. 65–70; and Jean K. Quam and Carol D. Austin, "Coverage of Women's Issues in Eight Social Work Journals, 1970–81," *Social Work*, 29 (July–August 1984), pp. 360–364.

10. See Kravetz, "An Overview of Content on Women"; Cynthia J. Belon and Ketayun H. Gould, "Not Even Equals: Sex-Related Salary Inequities," *Social Work*, 22 (November 1977), pp. 466–471; Gould and Bok-Lim C. Kim, "Salary Inequities between Men and Women in Schools of Social Work: Myth or Reality?" *Journal of Education for Social Work,* 12 (Winter 1976), pp. 50–55; James Gripton, "Sexism in Social Work: Male Takeover of a Female Profession," *The Social Worker,* 42 (Summer 1974), pp. 78–89; Dorothy Chave Herberg, "A Study of Work Participation by Graduate Female Social Workers: Some Implications for Professional Social Work Training," *Journal of Education for Social Work,* 9 (Fall 1973), pp. 16–23; Dorothy Zietz and John L. Erlich, "Sexism in Social Agencies: Practitioners' Perspectives," *Social Work,* 21 (November 1976), pp. 434–439; and Esther Sales, Barbara K. Shore, and Floyd Bolitho, "When Mothers Return to School: A Study of Women Completing an MSW Program," *Journal of Education for Social Work,* 16 (Winter 1980), pp. 57–65.

11. See Phyllis J. Day, "Sex Role Stereotypes and Public Assistance," *Social Service Review,* 53 (March 1979), p. 114; and Miriam Dinerman, "Catch 23: Women, Work, and Welfare," *Social Work*, 22 (November 1977), pp. 472–477.

12. See *Curriculum Policy for the Master's Degree and Baccalaureate Degree Programs in Social Work Education* and *Handbook of Accreditation Standards and Procedures* (New York: Council on Social Work Education, 1982 and 1984, respectively); and *Code of Ethics* (Silver Spring, Md.: National Association of Social Workers, 1980).

13. Z. Eisenstein, *Capitalist Patriarchy and the Case for Socialist Feminism* (New York: Monthly Review Press, 1976), p. 1.

14. Carel B. Germain, *Social Work Practice: People and Environments* (New York: Columbia University Press, 1979), p. 1.

15. A. Mander, "Feminism as Therapy," in E. I. Rawlings and D. K. Carter, *Psychotherapy for Women* (Springfield, Ill.: Charles C Thomas, Publisher, 1977), p. 298.

16. See Z. Budapest, *The Feminist Book of Lights and Shadows* and *The Holy Book of Women's Mysteries* (Venice, Calif.: The Feminist Wicce, 1975 and 1976, respectively); and M. Stone, *When God Was a Woman* (New York: Harcourt Brace Jovanovich, 1976).

17. K. Millett, *Sexual Politics* (New York: Ballantine Books, 1970); S. Firestone, *The Dialectic of Sex* (New York: Bantam Books, 1971); J. Mitchell, *Women's Estate* (New York: Vintage Books, 1973); B. Deckard, *The Women's Movement* (New York: Harper & Row, 1975); A. Kuhn and A. Wolpe, *Feminism and*

*Materialism* (Boston: Routledge & Kegan Paul, 1978); and Eisenstein, *Capitalist Patriarchy.*

18. Eisenstein, *Capitalist Patriarchy,* p. 16.

19. See Millett, *Sexual Politics;* Firestone, *Dialectic of Sex;* Mitchell, *Women's Estate;* and *Feminist Revolution* (New Paltz, N.Y.: Redstockings, 1973).

20. N. Hooyman, "Toward a Feminist Administrative Style." Paper presented at the National Association of Social Workers' First National Conference on Social Work Practice in a Sexist Society, Washington, D.C., September 1980, p. 6.

21. B. Solomon, *Black Empowerment* (New York: Columbia University Press, 1976), p. 16.

22. Hooyman, "Toward a Feminist Administrative Style," p. 7.

23. Ibid., p. 8.

24. June G. Hopps, "Oppression Based on Color," Editorial, *Social Work,* 27 (January 1982), pp. 3–5.

25. M. Daly, *Gyn/Ecology: The Metaethics of Radical Feminism* (Boston: Beacon Press, 1978), p. 2.

26. B. Thorne, *Rethinking the Family: Some Feminist Questions* (New York: Longman, 1982), p. 5.

27. Bunch, *Going Public,* p. 10.

28. G. MacKinnon, "Feminism, Marxism, Method and the State: An Agenda for Theory," *Signs,* 7 (Spring 1982), p. 535.

29. For an in-depth discussion of the economic and social transformation occurring at this time, see Herman and Julia R. Schwendinger, *The Sociologists of the Chair* (New York: Basic Books, 1974); Roy Lubove, *The Professional Altruist* (Cambridge, Mass.: Harvard University Press, 1975); and Barbara Ehrenreich and Deirdre English, *For Her Own Good* (New York: Anchor Press, 1978).

30. Germain, *Social Work Practice,* p. 437.

31. L. Rosenman and R. Ruckdeschel, "Catch 1234B: Integrating Material on Women into the Social Work Research Curriculum," *Journal of Education for Social Work,* 17 (Spring 1981), p. 6.

32. R. Valet, "Creative Imagination: To Man's Advancement," *Fresno Bee,* February 13, 1983, p. G1.

33. E. Kaschak, "Feminist Psychotherapy: The First Decade," in S. Cox, ed., *Female Psychology: The Emerging Self* (New York: St. Martin's Press, 1981), pp. 393–399.

34. Ibid., p. 396.

35. Hooyman, "Toward a Feminist Administrative Style," p. 13.

36. C. Ellsworth et al., "Toward a Feminist Model of Planning for and with Women." Paper presented at the National Association of Social Workers' First National Conference on Social Work Practice in a Sexist Society, Washington, D.C., September 1980, p. 9.

37. Hooyman, "Toward a Feminist Administrative Style," p. 5.

38. M. Lapton and A. Thompson, "Living with Conflict on the Journal," *Women: A Journal of Liberation,* 2 (1980), pp. 48–50.

39. Hooyman, "Toward a Feminist Administrative Style," p. 6.

40. N. B. Gluckstern, "Beyond Therapy: Personal and Institutional Change," in Rawlings and Carter, eds., *Psychotherapy for Women,* p. 437.

41. E. I. Rawlings and D. K. Carter, "Psychotherapy for Social Change," in Rawlings and Carter, eds., *Psychotherapy for Women,* p. 47.

7.

Felix G. Rivera and John L. Erlich

# AN OPTION ASSESSMENT FRAMEWORK FOR ORGANIZING IN EMERGING MINORITY COMMUNITIES

## NEO-GEMEINSCHAFT MINORITY COMMUNITIES: IMPLICATIONS FOR COMMUNITY ORGANIZATION

Social work is running scared. As the era of "slash, cut and trim" descends upon us, the fundamental weakness of the profession becomes painfully apparent. Of course, social work has been in retreat for some time. Since the early 1970s, programs directed to the needs of the minority oppressed poor have been phased out or diminished. Program controls have largely passed from the federal government and local communities to states and municipalities. From a political standpoint, it is understandable that confrontation-stimulating community organization efforts have given way faster than most other services. However, given the demographic changes and inflation of the last decade, the profession is in the position of having to respond to rapidly expanding needs with ever-declining resources. It is not a comfortable position.

One of the most pressing issues of the decade of the 1990s will be the changing nature of ethnic minority communities as it affects community organizing. The changing and emerging communities are a result of the increase in the African-American, Latino and Chicano, Asian, Pacific Islander—especially the Indochinese refugee flow—and the Native American population, and the continued oppression of these communities. Many of the gains of the last twenty years have been eroded by a society that is threatened by education and job-related affirmative action, tired of refugee programs, and alarmed by the encroachment of minorities into previously all-white communities....

The retreat from social justice has helped to set more rigid cultural, social and economic boundaries around many minority communities. Coupled with the resurgence of such racist organizations as the Ku Klux Klan and continuing racial oppressions suffered by all ethnic minorities, a unique revitalization of cultural, social and economic survival strategies has emerged. In part, this is a special response to the needs of new arrivals. The organization and complexity of these new communities presents a serious challenge to community organization. To meet the challenge, the profession must not only be able to support community empowerment but also join the struggle for group self-determination.

This paper addresses these issues within the context of community politics and structure. We will explore a model of the new communities that we hope will sharpen the analysis of questions about leadership, economics, power, culture, and social networks and how community organization may become an integral part of the helping process in working with them.

---

Felix G. Rivera is a professor in the Department of Social Work Education, San Francisco State University; John L. Erlich is a professor of Social Work, California State University at Sacramento.

## THE NEW EMERGING COMMUNITIES

Ethnic minority communities are growing dramatically, and with this growth come attendant problems that are further exacerbated by different languages, cultures, and traditions. A cursory look at demographic data only begins to touch on the multidimensional nature of this situation.

Between 1980 and 1990, the nation's white majority decreased from 83.2 percent to 80.3 percent, while the minority population grew from 16.8 percent to 19.7 percent, or 48.8 million. All major minority groups showed a steeper rate of growth than whites, whose number increased by 6.1 percent from 188.3 million to 199.8 million, while the total population grew from 226.5 million to 248.7 million.[1] The chief of the Census Bureau's ethnic and racial division noted; "It's one of the most significant changes in the racial composition of the U.S. population in any 10-year period."[2] Any significant undercount would, of course, tend to extend these figures further in the same direction.

### Latinos and Chicanos

Among those listing themselves as "Spanish origin," there was a 50 percent increase from 1980 to 1990, from 14.6 million to 21.9 million.[3] A breakdown by subgroup was not available at the time this paper was prepared; however, there are such data for the 1990 population estimate of 48.8 million.[4] These figures break down into 13.4 million people of Mexican descent, 1,053,197 Cubans, 2.65 million Puerto Ricans, and approximately 2.4 million people from Central and South America. The Census Bureau estimates a growth rate of 50 percent from the 1980 census to 1990. Projections suggest that there will be close to 25 million Latinos and Chicanos by the year 2000 if undocumented aliens are taken into consideration.[5] With this increase in population has come a steady decline in Hispanics' relative economic position. Recent median income for Latino and Chicano families is $11,400 compared to $16,300 for the non-Latino. Puerto Ricans are the lowest on the ladder among their ethnic group with a median income of $8,000. Chicano and Latino unemployment rates hover at approximately 29 percent compared to the national average of 6 percent. Only 40 percent have completed high school compared to 46 percent for blacks and 67 percent for whites. High school dropout rates are estimated at about 85 percent for urban Latinos and Chicanos.[6] It must be pointed out that these statistics do not include the over 100,000 recently arrived refugees from Cuba nor those from El Salvador, Nicaragua, or Guatemala.

### Blacks

Blacks represented 11.7 percent of the population in 1980 and 12 percent in 1990. Their numbers increased 12.8 percent from 26.5 million to 29.9 million.[7] The black community continues to be a horrendous showcase of racism. Unemployment rates hover at about 14 percent as an overall estimate, while black male unemployment rates stood at 42 percent as of 1992, and 37.2 percent female.[8] Among blacks 67.7 percent, compared to 81 percent of whites, completed high school; and 32.7 percent of blacks compared to 11.3 percent of whites were living in poverty.[9]

Higher socioeconomic status has not been of much help to the black community. Recent research continues to verify the trends of segregation. Blacks moving into white communities in any substantial numbers have precipitated the white withdrawal from that area with continued racial segregation being the result.[10] Furthermore, blacks living in suburbs continue to find themselves living in limited areas.[11]

### Asians and Pacific Islanders

The largest proportional increase occurred among Asians and Pacific Islanders—from 3.5 million to 7.2 million, or more than double.[12] Until recently, this has been one of the most undercounted and ignored communities in the United States. The overly simplistic lumping of all Asians into one category in the census robs the community of its variety of languages, customs, and traditions that are as varied as a black Cuban's culture compared to a white Argentinian's. The community is composed of such diverse people as Pakistanis, Koreans, East Indians, Cambodians, Chinese, Filipinos, Guamanians, Japanese, Thais, Samoans, Yaps, Laotians, Vietnamese, and Hawaiians—and the list is far from complete.

The political and economic ramifications of the census miasma have been all too real for Asians and Pacific Islanders.[13] Some resaons given for a potentially serious undercount are language barriers, crowded housing conditions, fear of deportation, and non-Western cultural backgrounds of immigrants that worked to limit census takers' access to certain neighborhoods and discouraged community people from cooperating with the census takers.[14]

### Native Americans

Those listing themselves as "American Indian, Eskimo, or Aleut" increased 42 percent from 1.4 to 2 million.[15]... A strong resurgence of involvement in tribal activities and family customs among younger Indians is partially responsible for increased numbers and visibility.

While these demographic changes have proved disruptive to many communities ill-prepared to welcome larger numbers of Third World people, they have also contributed to a very important strengthening of ethnic community ties. For example, Filipinos, Vietnamese, Cubans, and Haitians are bringing not only their racial characteristics to the emerging communities but a revitalization of their culture to the many little Manilas, Saigons, and Havanas. This cultural infusion is helping to make many of these cultural enclaves more self-conscious and active when compared to the assimilationist orientation of most earlier refugee groups. Both their cultural uniqueness and identity as victims of a majority society force minorities to react in ways that are often similar as they cope and survive.

The political economy of minority communities is such that these communities continue to act as the mainstays of a dual labor market. And the difficulty these groups encounter in moving out of the peripheral or secondary sector makes for a continued (if forced) support of these communities that will not soon change.[16] Another shared experience has been the persistent theorizing about patterns of assimilation becoming almost an ideology of the more and sooner the better. Research has shown this to be a flawed perspective, thus further questioning the push toward white-determined integration of ethnic minorities into the dominant society. In fact, Cubans and Mexicans researched showed an increase in consciousness about their minority positions and the conflict associated with such roles.[17]

Another study has demonstrated that young, upwardly mobile blacks have not helped in closing the racial gap because of their consciousness and, "If anything, the progressive advance up the socioeconomic ladder by both races may result in greater disparities on certain participation-related attitudes."[18]

We need to define what we mean by an ethnic minority people within the context of the demographics presented and the new communities which we define next. The unique circumstances in which minority persons find themselves lead us to define them in several ways: (a) individuals of color different from the dominant society's, (b) individuals who belong to a community in crisis with inordinately high unmet service needs, (c) individuals who are monolingual in a language other than English, (d) individuals from Third World countries coming to the United States as refugees or emigrés, and (e) individuals who are poor.

By defining them in this way, we have set conditions that must be present for an individual or group to be so identified. Thus Native Americans or blacks, even though they are citizens of the United States, are ethnic minorities because they may have high unmet human service needs and because they belong to different cultures, different races, and are poor. A black Cuban or Puerto Rican is also included in these categories because of the language barrier—if present—and because of race and unmet service needs. An elite colonel from Cambodia or Vietnam, even while politically distant from the poor people of his country, would still come within our definition because he too has unmet service needs, is monolingual, and is racially different. The colonel's problems may be exacerbated upon entering his own ethnic community, for he may be perceived as still being the enemy. The fact is that refugees and minority citizens of the United States continue to find themselves in hostile, poor environments and that their color and culture will be used as shibboleths of exclusion rather than inclusion in the mainstream of society.

## ETHNIC MINORITY COMMUNITIES REDEFINED

In describing the current status of minority communities, the distinction made by Töennies between *gemeinschaft* and *gesellschaft* is useful. The gemeinschaft ("community") is a social system in which relationships are personal, informal, traditional, general, and sentiment-based. On the other hand, the gesellschaft ("society") is a system in which relationships are impersonal, contractual, utilitarian, specialized, and realistically based on market conditions. As Töennies noted, "In Gemeinschaft with one's family one lives from birth on, bound to it in a weal and woe.... There exists a Gemeinschaft of language, of folkways, of mores, or of beliefs."[19]

The development of minority communities with their reinvigorated support systems strongly suggests that we define them as *neo-gemeinschaft.* Our model assumes that these communities' life experiences take place within a causal, deterministic reality, based on racism and economic exploitation. We are further postulating that these systems are essentially closed once individuals enter or leave them. By closed we mean that there are definite entry and exit points in the community with definite parameters based on the respective individual cultures, sociopolitical, and economic situations.

By identifying ethnic minority communities as being *neo-gemeinschaft,* we are arguing that the primary cultural, social, political, and economic interrelationships of such communities are of fundamental importance, because these qualities are seen as major determinants of daily life in them. We also conceive of them as "new" communities because we are identifying specific groups coming together in a new country or geographical area and attempting to salvage their traditions in the face of a largely hostile existing social order. The model is based not only on empirical evidence but also on conversations with members of the various groups as well as personal experiences of the authors. *Neo-gemeinschaft* communities are an excellent example of communities becoming and evolving within an antagonistic environment. The more survival skills that are mastered by these communities, the more unique they become, thereby requiring a new and enlarged definition for their experiences.

By redefining the ethnic minority communities we get a better analytical tool for understanding how these communities are evolving. Traditional definitions of communities are like quicksilver. A summary of these definitions is presented by Effrat, who has condensed much of the literature and has arrived at three definitions: communities are categorized as institutionally distinct groups, as a solidarity of institutions, and as the arena for "primary" interaction.[20]

Cox has described communities as context, demographic characteristics, shared institutions, social system, vehicle, problems, and power relationships.[21] While the above definitions have aspects of *neo-gemeinschaft* communities, they lack the variable of race and culture within a changing context as experienced by these communities with the constant influx of new arrivals, and our additional prerequisites for being defined as a minority person. Take, for example, the immigration of more than 100,000 Cubans into the Miami area (of whom perhaps 70,000 remain). These refugees brought with them a need for redefinition of the culture beyond the established Cuban culture. Rather than putting trust in a single individual, many of these refugee groups organized along horizontal lines with no one individual recognized as the leader. Some of these communities have organized as economic collectives. Because they lack money, they employ bartering as the primary form of service sharing, putting into practice many of the craft skills learned in the home country. Indeed, many more economically secure Cubans who have been in Miami for years have partially altered their business practices to provide for barter as an alternative mode of exchange. This practice is prevalent in many minority communities.

The church has played a significant role in helping to bring groups and individuals within the community together. Churches have been required to adapt to the lifestyles of newcomers. One day they may support a fund raiser, the next they will be baptizing an infant or getting involved in organizing a housing drive. English classes and basic survival techniques (sometimes billed as "community orientations") have been offered in many churches. More established residents have been mobilized to help provide emergency food and clothing. A more personalized church has thus been thrust upon the clergy and existing practitioners.

The physical appearance of the community is also shifting. It abounds with "mom and pop" stores, stores that often serve as centers for information exchange and informal discussions. The Latino *bodega* is one example. Billboard advertising, posters, newspapers, and magazines are in the community's native language. One telltale sign is that of cooking smells, an excellent barometer. This element of phenomenological assessment is often heralded as one of the most rewarding for obvious reasons. In coping with pressures of a dominant society, these communities are forced to turn inward for almost all needed support. One of these variables of mutual support is the social network. It is defined as:

> a specific set of linkages among a defined set of persons {groups and institutions} with the...property that the characteristics of these linkages as a whole may be used to interpret the social behavior of the persons involved.[22]

The main components of social networks with which we are concerned include support, access to new and diverse information and social contacts, communication of expectations, evaluation and a shared world view, and an orientation to getting things done to improve one's lot in this country.

As Stack describes the networking process:

> The most typical way people involve each other in their daily domestic lives is by entering them into an exchange relationship. Through exchange transactions, an individual personally mobilizes others as participants in his social network.[23]

The reasons for the resurgent development of these social networks are varied. One is that the transition to new communities by ethnic minorities, some of whom may have been accustomed to leadership roles in the past, throws them into a state of powerlessness when they encounter racial and ethnic segregation. This lack of social integration and acculturation (not assimilation) into the dominant society often accounts for survival-threatening poverty, delinquency, and mental health problems.[24]

Social networks function as horizontally supportive webs throughout the community, for there are few governing elites among recently arrived individuals from the home countries or other areas. Because the communities either share the stigma of forced removal from their native countries or have left their homes because they had few options for improving their quality of life due to war, political, economic, and social turmoil, the people that arrive here may find themselves lost and anomic. And although they may be citizens, they are treated as second- or third-class citizens, still experiencing the racism and economic exploitation of their ancestors. This frustrating situation stimulates mutual support networks that have little respect for old-country leadership hierarchies. Table 7.1 illustrates some of the variables unique to *neo-gemeinschaft* communities and their implications for community organization practice when compared to gesellschaft communities. The table is not meant to be exhaustive but illustrative, and serves to introduce students of community organization and community development to some of the more significant variables and their possible application to community organization strategies.

## IMPLICATIONS FOR COMMUNITY ORGANIZATION PRACTICE

The phenomenon of new communities emerging from existing old ones is something community organizers have either not had to deal with or have little understood. One of the reasons is that organizers have assumed that the tenement buildings or housing projects or deteriorated neighborhoods have had some permanence, with the elements of community supports more or less in place. But this is not the case in the emerging communities, for although the buildings may be the same, the activities within present a unique challenge to organizers and other practitioners. For one thing, the literature has shown that evolv-

TABLE 7.1
Structural Variables in Gesellschaft and Neo-Gemeinschaft Communities and Their Implications for Community Organizing Strategies

| Variables | Gesellschaft Communities | Neo-Gemeinschaft Communities | Implications for Community Organizing Strategies |
|---|---|---|---|
| Culture (ethnicity) | The dominant society with culture and traditions not having a strong ethnic identification. English—main if only language spoken and no strong ties or identification with another country. Basically Anglo population. | Relatively homogeneous. English not spoken much, or a street variant of it. Strong tradition from the homeland making for isolated, autonomous pockets of Little Tokyos, Havanas, etc. | Knowledge of culture not enough, should be part of the culture and bilingual. Sensitive to cultural patterns and traditions. An appreciative posture a necessity. |
| Social Structure | Vertical. Limited extended family networks with no experience of oppression or racism. | Horizontal. Shared experience of racism and oppression. Many extended family networks. | Ethnic and cultural membership helps in understanding the complexities of the social structure, helps to provide access to family networks. |
| Power Structure | Mainly external elite and vertical in nature. Community gives up its power in favor of "institutional trust." | Mainly internally pluralistic, decision making usually by consensus. No trust of outside power blocks and their institutions. | Knowledge of power analysis, the formation of coalitions, "winnable" issues and knowledge of power blocks inside and outside of the community. |
| Leadership Patterns | Leadership by political culture and party system. Extended influence and authority. Charisma and personalism less important. | Charismatic leaders, *personalismo*, strong feelings of alienation and anomie. Sphere of influence limited to that community. | Knowledge and respect of the leadership patterns of the culture. An understanding of horizontal and consensual decision making, and leadership by age and wisdom. |
| Economics | All levels of economic ladder, but a strong middle class and much vertical mobility. Limited, if any, labor market segmentation. | Marginal to poor level of existence. Strong interdependence. Bartering for survival. Welfare a constant reality and reminder of their situation. Major contributors to labor market segmentation. | A thorough understanding of political economy and the need for a progressive analysis of same. The ability to identify short- and long-term issues to lessen failures. Knowledge of employment, housing, and community development strategies. |
| Physical Appearance | No unique "flavor" to the communities. A variety of housing patterns. | Strong ethnic flavor in signs, newspapers, magazines. Smells of different foods unique to the homeland. Rundown tenements and substandard housing. | Ability to understand the language and being part of the culture a necessity. |
| Social Networks | Less formal when present. Usually a "conscious" decision is made in developing them. | Strong and quite formal. Usually an integral part of the culture. | Ability to understand the language, relate to the culture, and respect network changes. |

ing minority communities require intervention strategies that go beyond many of the traditional models of community organizing.[25] As Table 7.1 very clearly suggests, the kind of organizing we are talking about cannot be done by anyone simply with the "proper motivation." A deep and sensitive cultural awareness is required. Bilinguality is clearly preferred, although supportive roles for English-speaking monolinguals may well emerge. For certain black and Native American communities bicultural experience and deep respect may take the place of specific linguistic skills. A full appreciation of a group's culture will most often require thorough knowledge of its historical experience—including traditions, political upheavals, and folkways.

The so-called mobilization style of organizing (set up shop in relation to a particular issue, mobilize around it, win what you can, and get out) will not work. Developing the trust necessary to understand, appreciate, and gain access to social networks is going to take a lot of time and patience, much of it beyond the normal workday. Some activities border on the quasi-legal and involve economic exchanges that keep money in the community rather than flowing to outsiders. One organizing key will be to figure out ways of building up existing social networks rather than generating new structures that will undermine these networks—as some of our community action agencies did during the War on Poverty. Rather than beginning with the problems, weaknesses, and inadequacies of these communities, our analysis suggests that strengths are to be noted first and foremost, and looked upon as the basis for organization building. What survival skills work best in that community? How is this shown? The thrust of organizing should be toward empowerment, which according to Solomon:

> ...enables the client to perceive his or her intrinsic and extrinsic worth. It motivates the client to use every personal resource and skill, as well as those of any other person that can be commanded, in the effort to achieve self-determined goals.[26]

The exercise of self-determination is central to the framework we have proposed. Furthermore, organizers should keep the concept of community sociotherapy in mind. Rein defines it as:

> ...the belief system which holds that such processes as organizing groups for self-help, protest, access to community facilities, or even revolution, can create a transformation of the individual personality. Participation in social action is viewed as a sociotherapeutic tool.[27]

This process of empowerment helps in giving people not only a sense of purpose, but a shared experience which will help in the development and nurturance of leadership, the identification of issues that are solvable and hopefully help to reduce the community's general feeling of malaise that may be hampering its development of self-determination and further animation.

## CONCLUSION

In responding to the needs of new and emerging minority communities, we have a choice. We may offer what modest services we can to these communities while focusing primarily on the trendy, fundable programs as we have in the recent past. Or we can take hold and establish a real priority for developing extensive community organization programs in the new communities. This will not be either easy or simple. The environment of self-determining communities is hazardous at best. However, if we are to believe in our own rhetoric, do we have any choice but to find ways to support *neo-gemeinschaft* minority communities in defining themselves, their surroundings, and their futures?

## NOTES AND REFERENCES

1. Bryce Nelson, "Percentage of Non-Whites in U.S. Rises Sharply," *Sacramento Bee,* February 24, 1981, p. A4; U.S. Census Database, 1990.
2. Ibid.
3. Ibid.
4. *Current Population Reports: Population Characteristics, Persons of Spanish Origin in the United States: March, 1978* (Washington, D.C.: U.S. Department of Commerce, Bureau of the Census, June 1979).

5. Ibid.

6. Ibid.

7. Nelson, "Percentage of Non-Whites," p. A4.

8. *Statistical Abstract of the U.S., 1993,* 113th ed. Washington, D.C.: U.S. Government Printing Office, 1994.

9. Ibid.

10. Arnold M. Denowitz, "Racial Succession in New York City, 1960–1970," *Social Forces 59,* no. 2 (December 1980): 453.

11. Wayne J. Villemez, "Race, Class and Neighborhood: Differences in the Residential Return on Individual Resources," *Social Forces* 59, no. 2 (December 1980): 428.

12. Nelson, "Percentage of Non-Whites."

13. For a detailed discussion on this issue see the papers in the "Census Issues" section of *Civil Rights of Asian and Pacific Americans: Myths and Realities* (Washington, D.C.: U.S. Commission on Civil Rights, U.S. Government Printing Office, 1980), pp. 46–49.

14. Ibid., p. 82.

15. Nelson, "Percentage of Non-Whites."

16. See, for example, R. C. Edwards, "The Social Relations of Production in the Firm and Labor Market Structure," in R. C. Edwards, M. Reich, and D. M. Gordon, eds., *Labor Market Segmentation* (Lexington, Mass.: D. C. Heath, 1975); and R. L. Bach, "Mexican Immigrants and the American State," *International Migration Review* 12 (Winter 1978): 536–558.

17. Alejandro Portes, Robert Nash Parker, and José A. Cobas, "Assimilation or Consciousness: Perceptions of U.S. Society Among Recent Latin American Immigrants to the United States," *Social Forces* 59, no. 1 (September 1980): 220–224.

18. Bruce A. Campbell, "The Interaction of Race and Socioeconomic Status in the Development of Political Attitudes," *Social Science Quarterly* 60, no. 4 (March 1980): 657.

19. Ferdinand Töennies, "Gemeinschaft and Gesellschaft," in Talcott Parsons et al., eds., *Theories of Society* (New York: Free Press, 1961) 1:191.

20. Marcia Pelly Effrat, "Approaches to Community: Conflicts and Complementaries," *Sociological Inquiry* 43, no. 3–4 (1973): 1–28.

21. Fred M. Cox, "Alternative Conceptions of Community," in Fred M. Cox, John L. Erlich, Jack Rothman, and John E. Tropman, eds., *Startegies of Community Organization,* 3d ed. (Itasca, Illinois: F. E. Peacock, Publishers, Inc., 1979), pp. 224–234.

22. J. Clyde Mitchell, ed., *Social Networks in Urban Situations* (Manchester, England: University of Manchester Press, 1969), pp. 1–50; and Roger E. Mitchell and Edison K. Trickett, "Task Force Report: Social Networks as Mediators for Social Support: Analysis of the Effects and Determinants of Social Networks," *Community Mental Health Journal,* 16, no. 1 (Spring 1980), 27–44.

23. Carol Stack, *All Our Kin: Strategies for Survival in a Black Community* (New York: Harper Colophon, 1974), p. 43. Also see Bettylou Valentine, *Hustling and Other Hard Work: Life Styles in the Ghetto* (New York: Free Press, 1978).

24. For further elaboration of this issue see Robert E. Kopsis, "Powerlessness in Racially Changing Neighborhoods," *Urban Affairs Quarterly* 14, no. 4 (June 1979): 425–442; C. S. Fischer, "On Urban Alienations and Anomie: Powerlessness and Social Isolation," *American Sociological Review,* 38, no. 3 (June 1973): 311–326, and Lee Rainwater, *Behind Ghetto Walls: Black Families in a Federal Slum* (Chicago: Aldine, 1970); and Roger E. Mitchell and Edison J. Trickett, "Task Force Report."

25. For example, see Shirley Jenkins, "The Ethnic Agency Defined," *Social Service Review,* 54 (June 1980): 250.

26. As cited in Armando Morales, "Social Work with Third World People," *Social Work* 26, 1 (January 1980): 49.

27. Martin Rein, *Social Policy: Issues of Choice and Change* (New York: Random House, 1970), p. 292.

8.

**Julie G. Cwikel and Ram A. Cnaan**

# ETHICAL DILEMMAS IN APPLYING SECOND-WAVE INFORMATION TECHNOLOGY TO SOCIAL WORK PRACTICE

The widespread use of information technology throughout society is indisputable (Naisbitt, 1982). Until recently most information technology applications in social work were in administration and research (Cnaan, 1988; Geiss & Viswanathan, 1986; Miller, 1986; Mutschler & Hasenfeld, 1986) and consisted of word processing, simple databases, spreadsheets, and statistics. Information technology has been applied to social work practice only recently and only on a very limited scale (Cnaan & Parsloe, 1990; Glastonbury, LaMendola, & Toole, 1988). The second wave of information technology applications, such as expert systems, games and therapeutic programs, electronic networks and telecommunication, and advanced (decision-supporting) databases, are increasingly being used in practice.

Whether this second wave of information technology will promote quality care and welfare of clients is not yet clear (Cnaan, 1989; Nurius, Richey, & Nicoll, 1988). It is therefore important for the profession to be aware from the outset of the ethical dilemmas that may arise when incorporating technology into social work practice (Murphy & Pardeck, 1988; Parsloe, 1990; Watson, 1990). This ethical examination is of special importance because the second wave of information technology brings even greater potential for change in social work practice, and such an examination may help the profession keep pace with the electronic information age without subjecting clients to inappropriate methods of care.

Some have envisioned that in the future of social work, the use of computers and other technologies (such as facsimile machine, electronic mail, video-telephone connection, and video-computer connection) will produce practice based on competence (Briar, 1983; Bronson & Blythe, 1987; Cnaan, 1988). Others see a bleak, if not apocalyptic, future with technology eroding humane treatment (Murphy & Pardeck, 1988; Nowotny, 1981; Parsloe, 1990). Whichever scenario prevails, it seems certain that the use of computer applications in social work practice will continue to grow rapidly. Two pertinent questions arise: (1) To what extent will social work values be incorporated into this process? (2) Will the end result promote high-quality social work practice? Answering these questions requires a balanced perspective that recognizes both the constructive potential of information technology and its conflicts with social work values. Such recognition will, it is hoped, facilitate a cautious but constructive adaptation of information technology that minimizes iatrogenic effects.

Julie G. Cwikel is a senior lecturer at the University of California, Berkeley; Ram A. Cnaan is an associate professor at the School of Social Work, University of Pennsylvania, 3701 Locust Walk, Philadelphia, PA 19104. Please direct all correspondence to Professor Cnaan.

This article identifies the major ethical dilemmas that the second wave of information technology poses for social work practice. Educators and social planners who are aware of these issues will be better prepared to use computer applications in ways that are both ethical and constructive. Ethical issues common to all disciplines, such as confidentiality of client information, length of time for preservation of client data, and the need for informed consent, are not discussed in this article, because these issues have been examined during the last two decades in the first wave of information technology applications (Parsloe, 1990; Watson, 1990).

This article discusses issues that may be raised by introducing information technology into practice. After a brief overview of the categories of second-wave software, conflicts between information technology and specific social work values, principles, and skills are examined. Suggestions for further studies and practice are presented.

## THE PROMISE OF INFORMATION TECHNOLOGY

Information technology is expected to become an integral part of social work practice. The second wave has brought new programs for diagnosis, case management, treatment planning, progress evaluation and monitoring, client education, therapy, and outcome assessment.

### Advanced Databases

Analogous to client files or patient charts, databases consist of a program or programs that allow client data to be entered, stored, and transferred or retrieved as needed. First-wave databases were used mostly for storing data and generating agencywide statistics. Most new databases also can modify or process information. For example, data for a child, although entered numerically, can be printed out as a case report that relates the client data to norms for child development. Some databases also issue periodic requests for updated information, prompting practitioners to schedule client meetings. This function is designed to facilitate quality assurance monitoring (Nurius, Berger, & Vanderweele, 1988). Other databases have preset sequences that perform standard screening or assessment tests such as those for depression, alcoholism, or personality structure (Date, 1986; Erdman & Foster, 1988). Finally, some second-wave databases, also called "decision-support systems," use a logic based on frequencies of certain data stored and provide the practitioner with practice recommendations.

### Expert Systems

Expert systems are database systems with aspects of artificial intelligence. These systems simulate the way an expert arrives at a decision by following similar steps used to synthesize information. In social work, expert systems have been able to simulate how a social worker decides to parole a young offender, place children in foster care, and evaluate the risk for suicide of psychiatric patients (Gustafson, Greist, Strauss, Erdman, & Laughren, 1977; Hedlund, Evenson, Sletten, & Cho, 1980; Schuerman, 1987).

### Games and Therapeutic Programs

Games are software programs that use enhanced graphics, sound, and interactive capacity for the purpose of entertainment, education, and therapy (Resnick & Sherer, 1990). Social workers may either use commercial games or develop their own. Games may be used to attract hard-to-reach adolescents or to educate clients and to present them with realistic options. One example is a video-computer game that simulates the problems and decisions involved in discharge from a mental health institution. Interactive programs also are used in treating phobias and depression, promoting compliance with medication regimens, providing advice on quitting smoking, and performing cognitive therapy (Hedlund, Vieweg, & Cho, 1985).

### Electronic Mail and Telecommunication

When a computer is linked by a modem to the telephone line, it can be used to relay information just as the telegraph and telephone are used. A modem makes it possible for a practitioner to access larger databases (as in an online search for references or abstracts on a certain topic) or to use electronic mail to contact other individuals connected to the electronic mail system. This enables practitioners to consult from a distance (Howell, 1987).

## ETHICAL ISSUES IN QUALITY OF CARE

The term "ethical dilemma" was defined as follows by Abramson (1984): "An ethical dilemma or moral quandary is one in which there are conflicts and tensions concerning the right and the good, when choosing one course of action will uphold one moral principle while violating another" (p. 129). Seven ethical issues regarding the practitioner-client relationship represent sources of potential conflict when information technology is introduced. The first three—(1) beneficence (autonomy vs. paternalism), (2) equity of access to scarce resources (ensuring the equality of opportunities), and (3) promotion of the common good (ensuring that the maximum number of individuals benefit from the introduction of information technology)—concern ethical values and principles. The rest—(4) preservation of individualized care, (5) maintenance of flexibility in treatment choices, (6) links with community networks, and (7) use of treatment time—concern social practice.

### Beneficence

The basis of the helping relationship is to promote the good of the client or, at least, to do no harm. This approach derives from the Hippocratic oath, *primum nolo nocere*—above all, do no harm. According to the *Code of Ethics* (National Association of Social Workers, 1990) ascribed to by social workers, promotion of self-determination is the basis by which a practitioner forms a relationship with a client. Self-determination derives from the ethical principle of autonomy, or the individual's right to decide how to expend one's resources and to control incursions into one's personal, physical, or social space. Social workers endorse the principle of autonomy because it encourages both the mutual respect of rights and, as practice has shown, client commitment and participation (Compton & Gallaway, 1987). In practice, social workers review possible decisions with competent clients, although the final decision belongs to the client. Although the therapeutic process is not necessarily egalitarian, social workers are expected to establish as democratic a relationship as possible with clients.

Abramson (1985) noted that the opposite of autonomy and self-determination is paternalism, a form of beneficence in which the concept of benefits and risks differs between practitioner and client, but the practitioner's concept prevails. Paternalism is evident when social workers believe that their professional knowledge qualifies them to decide on the client's behalf and that the result will promote the good of the client. Paternalism is most acceptable in work with young children, people who endanger themselves or others, and mentally disabled individuals. However, it is expected that the balance in these relationships also will be weighted toward the client's right to self-determination.

The introduction of information technology, especially expert systems, games, and advanced databases, poses a threat to this delicate balance of acceptable paternalism. The basic notion of advanced software is that there is a right decision and that, when known, it should be followed. When the computer specifies an intervention plan, it is the task of the social worker to market it to the client. Conflict arises when the client's preference and the computer's recommendation do not coincide. It is easy to envision situations in which supervisors and administrators would reprimand social workers who countermanded the computer because they chose to support client self-determination or because their professional discretion led them to reject the computerized recommendation. An agency that has purchased expert systems and other advanced software has a vested interest in following the computer-generated recommendations. If conflicts between computer-generated decisions and client preferences are frequent, then paternalism may reach new heights in social work practice.

One way in which clients can reassert their autonomy is through malpractice litigation. However, it will be difficult to win a legal suit when the worker and agency can argue that decisions were made on the basis of the most advanced knowledge—that is, the expert system or the management information system database. Administrators may therefore encourage social workers to follow the computer's recommendation at the expense of client's autonomy to avoid legal and financial problems.

### Equity of Access to Scarce Resources

Information is a resource that plays a major role in social work practice. Social support, for example, which has been shown to have far-reaching effects on health and well-being, is often characterized as possession of information (Cobb, 1976; House, 1981). Indeed, access to diverse networks of information has been shown to aid adjustment to life crises, such as divorce or job loss, that require major role changes (Granovetter, 1973; Hirsch, 1981). The social worker with access to information on various agencies, volunteers, philanthropies, welfare rights, and regulations has a valuable tool with which to aid clients. The concept of case management depends on the ability to link clients with a network of resources for help and support.

With the introduction of databases and telecommunication into social services, computer-literate social workers can easily access information on these resources. There are already regional databases containing information on services and their eligibility requirements and provisions (Madara, Kalafat, & Miller, 1988). In some parts of the country, teleconferences are available. In South Carolina, for example, teleconferences make adoption preparation classes readily accessible to clients throughout the state (Howell, 1987). Thus, even the novice computer-literate social worker will have access to a rich set of data in comparison to the computer-illiterate social worker. Furthermore, access to the computerized resource database also will raise issues of quality of care. Clients may miss out on available help if their social workers cannot access electronic information. Computer entrepreneurs may come into demand by private agencies to help keep social workers informed about data bases relevant to their practice.

Access to telecommunication on the agency level may be limited by cost. Because development and maintenance of a resource database is expensive, generally only one agency in a region has such a database, and access by other agencies is through telecommunication. Agencies that do not invest in information technology, usually those with small budgets such as alternative organizations, new agencies, and grass-roots organizations, are the least likely to invest in telecommunications. Because these agencies do not have the required technological resources, their clients may miss opportunities for better care, even if these agencies are the most empathic and best suited to serve their clients. More agencies without access to information technology means decreased resources, which may further accentuate the gap between the haves and the have-nots, both among agencies and among practitioners.

Inequitable access to scarce resources is not limited to databases. There also will be inequitable access to expert systems; computer-literate social workers in agencies that are computerized will be able to consult an expert system regarding their clients to validate their assessment and intervention plan. The rest will continue to rely on traditional services.

### Promotion of the Common Good

The helping relationship in social work practice includes empathy; assessment and treatment of presenting problems; access to a body of professional knowledge; and liaison with other professionals, agencies, and community services. In the age of information technology, social workers also should offer as part of their basic services to clients access to databases, electronic networks, and online libraries. These services derive from the ethical principle of the common good, which considers what goods and services in common individuals should expect from society and how these goods and services should be distributed among individuals and human service organizations. To achieve the common good, scarce goods must be distributed to promote the most good for the most people (Jonsen & Hellegers, 1974). A frequent criticism of current social work practice is that too much money and valuable resources are directed to the welfare of employees and the system and too little to those in need (Eisenstadt & Ahimeir, 1985). Reform in social services sometimes has been a vehicle to enhance the quality of working conditions for employees (Cnaan, Korazim, Meller, & Rosenfeld, 1992; Pressman & Wildavsky, 1973). Thus, an agency investing in an organizational reform must identify its intended beneficiaries.

Introducing a new information technology into any organization is a costly process (Bronson, Pelz, & Trzcinski, 1988; Schoech, 1982; Taylor, 1981). The budget must be increased, staff with new expertise must be added, new responsibilities must be created for existing staff, a new power balance will be achieved, and the organization often must wait years for meaningful results (Parsons, 1985). Most social welfare organizations operate on a limited and strict budget. Social work is computerized at the expense of other options such as continuing education, more staff positions, or innovative programs. Public services may be able to generate more funds from taxes, but such is not the case for nonprofit or for-profit agencies. Even in the case of public agencies, resources are limited, and they must compete with other units of government for these funds.

It is expected that the cost will be high when a social welfare organization introduces information technology. Initially, this cost may be at the expense of services provided to clients or of the quality of work of social workers. In the former case, services will be reduced, workers' time for clients will be cut, and the focus will shift from service delivery to system maintenance. In the latter case, workers will have to spend extra time learning the new system, but their work load will remain the same. In both cases clients may suffer in the short term, but the practitioners may have more effective and efficient methods at their disposal in the long run.

The process described above is not uniform across technologies. Introduction of word processing, statistics or graphics packages, or spreadsheets should not cause major disturbances in service delivery. On the other hand, learning to use databases, expert systems, games, and telecommunication—the second-wave information technology—will take energy and time.

### Preservation of Individualized Care

The basic tenet of differential diagnosis and care is that individuals have different needs, problems, strengths, environments, and expectations, and thus each client should be assessed and cared for as a unique person (Germain, 1973; Pincus & Minahan, 1973; Richmond, 1917). Education for social work stresses the responsibility of the professional for individualized assessment and care rather than categorization of clients into groups.

Individualized assessment and care is endangered by information technology. A key rule in forming a database or a management information system (MIS) is to select the right variables to be recorded (Cnaan, 1988; Mutschler & Cnaan, 1985; Schoech, 1982). The trade-offs are usually between the clinically relevant variables suggested by the practitioners, the management needs, the computer's memory capacity, and the length of the client record. The latter two considerations require that the client record size be manageable, which means that not all of the variables in which the practitioners are interested can be included. By way of compromise, generally those variables with relatively high frequency are included, and those with low frequency are excluded. Thus, the variables selected for the database are those perceived as most important to the agency. Workers, then, are expected to pay extra attention to the variables in the agency's database. These entries are checked both automatically (a printed request for missing data is generated after a certain period of time) and manually by the supervisor. Social workers who know that they will be evaluated on their thoroughness in recording these variables will tend to give them preference in intake and assessment processes. Thus, the database variables may indirectly guide the social workers' thinking and the supervisors' routine.

Empirical studies have shown that social workers tend to use a limited number of variables for clinical decision making, even when a large set of data is available (Kagle, 1988; Wedenoja, Nurius, & Tripodi, 1988). Similar findings are reported in the psychology of medical decision making (Moore, Aitchison, & Taylor, 1974; Wetle, Cwikel, & Levkoff, 1988). These findings suggest that those who deal with clients tend to view them as alike and to use only a few variables, rather than attempting to find their unique characteristics. This tendency to categorize clients, together with a limited database, can threaten the differential assessment and care principle.

### Maintenance of Flexibility in Treatment Choices

Social work practice is unique in its willingness to develop new models of interventions and test them out. As long as no one mode of intervention has been shown to be superior, social workers may prefer an eclectic approach to find the most effective intervention modality or combination of modalities for their clients. It is the interaction among the social worker, the client, the environment, and the mode of intervention that determines the quality of care. Thus, the personal component is significant and calls for flexibility in choice of intervention strategy.

Information technology by its nature is designed to assist social workers in deciding which mode of intervention to choose. Expert systems and MIS databases are expected to direct the decisions of social workers regarding client assessment and preferred intervention (Schoech & Schkade, 1980; Schuerman, 1987). This process is still in its earliest stages, and it is unclear whether social workers will be able to maintain their flexibility. It is likely that workers will accept a computer-generated recommendation without hesitation or further deliberation.

Ideally, however, the computer's recommendation should be an additional information source for the social worker in making decisions. For example, an expert system may recommend placing a child in foster care, but variables that are difficult to program, such as concerned neighbors or the child's effect on the family dynamics, should also be considered. The social worker should carefully consider the computerized recommendation but should not be afraid to challenge it.

It is easy to say that social workers need not conform totally to computerized practice recommendation, but it is difficult to accomplish. The computerized recommendation is ideally based on accumulated empirical experience. It will be backed by the agency's administration in anticipation that the margin of error in practice decisions will decrease. Overall there may be better-quality care for more clients, but clients with unique characteristics are likely to suffer.

### Links with Community Networks

Jordan (1987) stated that

> social work, of all the processes by which the state provides social services, is in some ways best placed to mesh with informal systems for sharing welfare. It can engage directly in the processes...within people's own language, culture and networks. (p. 208)

Social workers are able to link with networks and communities because social work has a relatively low level of professional authority, uses simple terminology, adapts to changing situations, and is flexible in its decisions. These qualities make social workers more available and open to community residents than other professionals. This ability to link with formal and informal resources, to work with indigenous networks, and to organize communities may be threatened by incorporating information technology into social work practice.

Although computers can be expected to improve the quality of care and to make allocation of resources more efficient, they may severely compromise the profession's ability to involve local residents. One reason is that computer terminology is much more precise and technical. At present, lay people can easily follow a social worker's explanation or report, but computer applications require rigid categories and technical definitions that can easily confuse those who are computer illiterate. Second, when decisions are supported by computers, social workers will be more confident, less tolerant of criticism, and less open to suggestions for alternative decisions. This in turn may lead to professional elitism and detachment from nonprofessionals. In this respect, social work and society in general stand to lose if lay people are no longer willing to assist in helping their communities.

### Use of Treatment Time

A few studies have reported that those who use computerized treatment programs do not find them impersonal (Erdman, Klein, & Greist, 1985). Still, time spent with a computer is time not spent with the client. The following report by a therapist who uses a computer-based program to assess a client's present state of symptomology (Clark, 1988) indicates that approximately one-third of the 50-minute session was spent on computer input, retrieval, and output:

> Upon arriving, the client completes a monthly Client Assessment System test program on the computer, which takes about six minutes. She types in single-keystroke answers to the 25 questions regarding the severity of her depression....I access a line graph that plots her current answers with previous ones. We discuss her progress, and I comment on points on the graph that correlate with events in her life while in therapy. This finished, the client has her weekly therapy session. (p. 15)

In evaluating the importance of significant relationships, whether in a treatment situation or otherwise, a primary parameter is the amount of time client and practitioner spend together. In evaluating the impact of treatment methods, researchers control for the amount of time spent together to eliminate bias introduced by the length of contact. Similarly, social workers who rely on computers to conduct assessments, follow-ups, and treatment sessions are not spending that time face-to-face with their clients. This may decrease the opportunity for significant interpersonal contacts, which may affect the strength of practitioner-client relationships.

## DISCUSSION

Whereas the first stage of computerizing social welfare services affected administrative functions mainly, the second stage is directed toward the practitioner. The first wave of information technology caused some ethical dilemmas such as confidentality and informed consent, which have been addressed in the literature. The second wave—the use of information technology application in social work practice—raises a new set of ethical dilemmas. At present, social work practitioners can shape and improve the computerization of social work practice by collaborating with computer experts. Case studies show that computerizing social work practice may require several developmental trials until the final product meets standards of practice and is feasible in terms of hardware and software (Benbenisty & Ben-Zaken, 1988; Cnaan, 1988; Monnickendam & Morris, 1990).

The second wave of information technology has implications for social work education, supervision, practice, and research. Ethical principles in social work have been modified over time, and they must be reexamined in light of the new developments in the field. Social work curricula should include applications of social work principles and attributes in new methodological areas, such as information technology, where dilemmas are likely to arise. Furthermore, educators should develop advanced courses in computer applications that are likely to affect social work practice. Students should become familiar with second-wave technologies as tools to be used when applicable and when not too costly. In addition, in-service training or continuing education for both supervisors and practitioners should be available.

Social work educators and supervisors will have to change the way they function. On one hand, they will have to emphasize compliance with and proper use of uniform database variables. On the other hand, they will have to promote and advocate for uniqueness and differential perspective. One solution may be to insist on using the free-format areas of client records in databases so the clients' unique characteristics can be incorporated and used. Further, computerized content analysis of these free-format sections will provide social workers with relevant clinical knowledge. Supervisors and practitioners alike must not rely solely on the predetermined variables that software requires. Because the second-wave software affects the decision-making process either directly or indirectly, attention should be given to differential assessment and care in the professional literature and scientific community to compensate for the computer's predilection for generalization at the expense of individualization.

The features that make social work unique as a profession should be enhanced, not diminished, by the introduction of information technology. It is up to the practitioners to safeguard individualized care, to demonstrate flexibility in treatment choice, to continue developing links to the lay community, and to promote autonomy and self-determination in practice even when aided by advanced technology.

Most of second-wave software can be expected to have as yet undetermined effects on practice (Binner, 1988), and new ethical dilemmas will inevitably surface as information technology is incorporated into social work practice. Some procedures, particularly those that directly affect decision making, should continue to be regarded as experimental interventions and, as in any experimental protocol, should require informed consent from clients and caution on the part of the practitioners.

The use of second-wave information technologies in social work practice must be rigorously evaluated to determine its effect. Action research is an appropriate evaluation model, because there is a need for ongoing exploration and modification. The evaluation design could use variables such as time spent with clients or computer, time spent learning the skills, practitioner and client satisfaction, and variables affecting the decision-making process.

It is too early to determine whether the introduction of second-wave information technology ultimately will improve the quality of client care. However, an examination of the ethical dilemmas may help ensure that basic social work principles and characteristics are not sacrificed in the iterative process. Technological adaptation is not a deterministic process, and the ethical dilemmas outlined here will assist the profession in harnessing the new technologies to improve client care.

## REFERENCES

Abramson, M. (1984). Ethical issues in social work practice with dying persons. In L. H. Suszychi & M. Abramson (Eds.), *Social work and terminal care* (pp. 129–135). New York: Praeger.

Abramson, M. (1985). The autonomy-paternalism dilemma in social work practice. *Social Casework, 66,* 387–393.

Benbenisty, R., & Ben-Zaken, A. (1988). Computer-aided process of monitoring task-centered family interventions. *Social Work Research & Abstracts, 24*(2), 7–9.

Binner, P. R. (1988). Mental health management decision making in the age of the computer. *Computers in Human Services, 3*(3/4), 87–100.

Briar, S. (1983). Current and future trends in clinical social work. In A. Rosenblatt & D. Waldfogel (Eds.), *Handbook of clinical social work* (pp. 1057–1058). San Francisco: Jossey-Bass.

Bronson, D. E., & Blythe, B. J. (1987). Computer support for single-case evaluation of practice. *Social Work Research & Abstracts, 23,* 10–23.

Bronson, D. E., Pelz, D. C., & Trzcinski, E. (1988). *Computerizing your agency's information system.* Beverly Hills, CA: Sage Publications.

Clark, C.F.P. (1988). Computer applications in social work. *Social Work Research & Abstracts, 24*(2), 15–19.

Cnaan, R. A. (1988). Applications of computers in clinical supervision. In B. Glastonbury, W. LaMendola, & S. Toole (Eds.), *Information technology and the human services* (pp. 128–136). New York: John Wiley & Sons.

Cnaan, R. A. (1989). Social work education and direct practice in the computer age. *Journal of Social Work Education, 25,* 235–243.

Cnaan, R. A., Korazim, Y., Meller, Y., & Rosenfeld, J. (1992). The reform of the local social services in Israel: 1984 compared with 1977. *Social Policy and Administration, 26*(2), 159–172.

Cnaan, R. A., & Parsloe, P. (1990). *The impact of information technology on social work practice.* New York: Haworth.

Cobb, S. (1976). Social support as a moderator of life stress. *Psychosomatic Medicine, 38,* 300–314.

Compton, B., & Gallaway, B. (1987). *Social work processes.* Chicago: Dorsey Press.

Date, C. J. (1986). *Database: A primer.* Reading, MA: Addison-Wesley.

Eisenstadt, S.N., & Ahimeir, O. (1985). *The welfare state and its aftermath.* London: Croom Helm.

Erdman, H. P., & Foster, S. W. (1988). Ethical issues in the use of computer-based assessment. *Computers in Human Services, 3*(1/2), 71–87.

Erdman, H. P., Klein, M. H., & Greist, J. H. (1985). Direct patient computer interviewing. *Journal of Consulting and Clinical Psychology, 53,* 760–773.

Geiss, G. R., & Viswanathan, N. (1986). *The human edge: Information technology and helping people.* New York: Haworth.

Germain, C. (1973). An ecological perspective in casework practice. *Social Casework, 54,* 323–330.

Glastonbury, B., LaMendola, W., & Toole, S. (1988). *Information technology and the human services.* New York: John Wiley & Sons.

Granovetter, M. (1973). The strength of weak ties. *American Journal of Sociology, 78,* 1360–1380.

Gustafson, D. H., Greist, J. H., Strauss, F. F., Erdman, H. P., & Laughren, T. P. (1977). A probabilistic system for identifying suicide attempters. *Computers and Biomedical Research, 10,* 83–89.

Hedlund, J. L., Evenson, R. C., Sletten, I. W., & Cho, D. W. (1980). The computer and clinical prediction. In J. B. Sidowski, J. H. Johnson, & T. A. Williams (Eds.), *Technology in mental health care delivery systems* (pp. 201–235). Norwood, NJ: Ablex.

Hedlund, J. L., Vieweg, B. W., & Cho, D. W. (1985). Mental health computing in the 1980s: I. General information systems and clinical documentation. *Computers in Human Services, 1*(1), 3–33.

Hirsch, B. J. (1981). Social networks and the coping process: Creating personal communities. In B. Gottlieb (Ed.), *Social networks and social support* (pp. 149–170). Beverly Hills, CA: Sage Publications.

House, J. S. (1981). *Work, stress, and social support.* Reading, MA: Addison-Wesley.

Howell, R. L. (1987). Teleconference technology in adoption: Utilizing educational television in adoption preparation. *Journal of Social Work & Human Sexuality, 6,* 169–179.

Jonsen, A. R., & Hellegers, A. E. (1974). Conceptual foundations from ethics of medical care. In L. R. Tancredi (Ed.), *Ethics of health care* (pp. 3–20). Washington, DC: National Academy of Sciences.

Jordan, B. (1987). *Rethinking welfare.* New York: Blackwell.

Kagle, J. D. (1988). Overcoming "personal" errors in assessment. *Arete, 13*(2), 35–40.

Madara, E., Kalafat, J., & Miller, B. N. (1988). The computerized self-help clearinghouse: Using "high tech" to promote "high touch" support networks. *Computers in Human Services, 3*(3/4), 39–54.

Miller, H. (1986). The use of computers in social work practice: An assessment. *Journal of Social Work Education, 22*(3), 52–60.

Monnickendam, M., & Morris, A. (1990). Developing an integrated computerized case management system for the Israeli Defense Forces—an evolutionary approach. *Computers in Human Services, 5*(1/2), 133–149.

Moore, M. F., Aitchison, L. S., & Taylor T. R. (1974). Use of information in thyrotoxicosis treatment allocation. *Methods in Information in Medicine, 13,* 88–92.

Murphy, J., & Pardeck, J. (1988). Introduction. *Computers in Human Services, 3*(1/2), 1–8.

Mutschler, E., & Cnaan, R. A. (1985). Success and failure of computerized information systems: Two case studies in human service agencies. *Administration in Social Work, 9,* 67–79.

Mutschler, E., & Hasenfeld, Y. (1986). Integrated information systems for social work practice. *Social Work, 31,* 345–349.

Naisbitt, J. (1982). *Megatrends: Ten new directions for transforming our lives.* New York: Warner.

National Association of Social Workers. (1990). *Code of ethics.* Silver Spring, MD: Author.

Nowotny, H. (1981). *The information society: Its impact on the home, local communities and marginal groups.* Vienna: European Centre for Social Welfare Training and Research.

Nurius, P. S., Berger, C., & Vanderweele, T. (1988). ASSIST: An alternative management information system for the social services in health care. *Social Work in Health Care, 13*(4), 99–115.

Nurius, P. S., Richey, C. A., & Nicoll, A. (1988). Preparation for computer usage in social work: Student consumer variables. *Journal of Social Work Education, 24*(1), 60–69.

Parsloe, P. (1990). An example of serendipity: The unintended impact of computers on social work practice. *Computers in Human Services, 5*(1/2), 169–185.

Parsons, H. M. (1985). Automation and the individual: Comprehensive and comparative views. *Human Factors, 27*(1), 99–112.

Pincus, A., & Minahan, A. (1973). *Social work practice: Model and method.* Itasca, IL: F. E. Peacock Publishers.

Pressman, J. L., & Wildavsky, A. (1973). *Implementation.* Berkeley: University of California.

Resnick, H., & Sherer, M. (1990). Computerized games in the human services. *Computers in Human Services, 5*(1/2), 89–111.

Richmond, V. E. (1917). *Social diagnosis.* New York: Russell Sage Foundation.

Schoech, D. (1982). *Computer use in human services.* New York: Human Sciences.

Schoech, D., & Schkade, L. L. (1980). Computers helping caseworkers: Decision support systems. *Child Welfare, 59,* 566–575.

Schuerman, J. R. (1987). Expert consulting systems in social welfare. *Social Work Research & Abstracts, 32,* 14–18.

Taylor, J. (1981). *Using microcomputers in social agencies.* Beverly Hills, CA: Sage Publications.

Watson, D. (1990). Computers, confidentiality and privation. *Computers in Human Services, 5*(1/2), 153–168.

Wedenoja, M., Nurius, P., & Tripodi, T. (1988). Enhancing mindfulness in practice perspective thinking. *Social Casework, 69,* 427–433.

Wetle, T., Cwikel, J., & Levkoff, S. E. (1988). Geriatric medical decisions: Factors influencing allocation of scarce resources and the decision to withhold treatment. *The Gerontologist, 28,* 336–343.

PART THREE

# Implementation, Mobilization, and Development: Planning and Organizing

For planners, program developers, and organizers nothing presents more of a challenge than translating the result of assessment and option selection into action. Part of the problem revolves around what might be termed the collapse of our excessive expectations. While the resource base has continued to decline, the hopes that surrounded many macro practice endeavors of the later 1960s and early 1970s continued into the beginning of the 1990s. However, the sharp economic decline of the early part of this decade has forced an almost total reevaluation of the potentials for change in social welfare.

Another dimension of the difficulty of translating agreed-upon objectives into action concerns a general decline in our civic life: Indeed, many observers suggest that there really is not much civic life left at all. A community of people generally regarded as liberals shoot down a proposal for a new emergency hospital because the sound of landing helicopters may be disturbing and lead to lower property values in the neighborhood. Providing needle exchanges for drug addicts and condoms to sexually active teenagers, despite the terrible ravages of AIDS, are both rejected on the grounds they will encourage more of the same kind of behavior that the wider community is trying to discourage. The proposal for a new homeless shelter in a new area is rejected in favor of expanding the current facilities because no one wants to accept "those kind of people" anywhere near where he or she lives.

As Kunstler notes:

> Living in a cartoon landscape of junk architecture, monotonous suburbs, ravaged countryside and trashed cities, Americans sense that something is wrong. Our discontent is expressed in phrases like "the loss of community" and "no sense of place." Yet the issue of how we live is strikingly absent from the debate about national problems, especially our economic predicament.[1]

---

[1] James Kunstler, "Zoning Ourselves Out of All Sense of Community," *The Sacramento Bee*, August 11, 1993.

Despite the widely reported and heavily documented increase in societal violence, the proposals offered to combat it—typically more prisons, more police, or better policing methods—do not inspire much confidence. Where is there a shared sense of common destiny that might serve to counteract the tendency toward violence? The yuppie greed of the 1980s, transposed into "me firstism," has lost all bounds of class, race, and gender—or at least so it often appears.

Confronting the declining sense of community with tactics and techniques that require a substantial measure of cooperation, sense of shared destiny, and commitment to compromise for the larger good puts the planner, developer or organizer in a challenging position.

The first article, by Weil, offers a set of guiding frameworks in which she notes that "a feminist framework for organizing integrates methods and strategies for action with practice principles that embody feminist values and approaches." Her article encompasses the rich women's heritage of social movement leaders and community practitioners. It also incorporates a full range of feminist approaches, and explores how feminist components inform practice models, including social planning, program development, community development, and political empowerment. A series of principles by which implementation, mobilization, and development may be guided is also part of Weil's exposition.

Basing his article on more than three decades of organizing efforts, Haggstrom emphasizes what it takes to make a success of work at the grassroots. He challenges us to confront the typical top-down style of mobilizing people for action by assisting in the gathering of people from the bottom up. In a society increasingly dominated by power, influence, and money, "solutions" to human problems tend to be based on the views of elite groups—governmental bodies and large institutions. Haggstrom would have us look toward an empowering movement for change founded in neighborhoods and the people who live in them.

Mizrahi and Rosenthal, in the third selection, argue for the importance of coalitions in effecting social change. In recent years, embattled communities have been forced to a mostly defensive position—especially given declining levels of support and expanding problems in such areas as employment, housing, education, health care, domestic violence, crime, and drugs. Coalitions may be particularly useful at this time because they preserve the integrity of individual groups while, at the same time, creating a structure strong enough to take on powerful forces such as political special-interest organizations, major institutions, and local governments. The authors lay out specific guidelines for increasing the likelihood of coalitional success.

Who should be financing low-income housing is the context of Dattalo's brief article, in which he explores key aspects of planning and program development that must take place if such an effort to stimulate and build low-income housing is to come to fruition. While the tone of the article is not optimistic, the hard-nosed approaches that Dattalo proposes have—if given a reasonable opportunity—a real chance of succeeding.

One of the most neglected of planning components—the role of the board—is the subject of the fifth selection, by Tropman. All too often the support (and/or involvement) of the board in whatever is proposed by administration and management is viewed as a sort of given. From their personal experiences, all of the editors know this to be an error—sometimes a major one. Among the things that Tropman addresses are: the potential roles of the board in policy making, boards as decision makers and overseers, internal and external board functions, and the board's responsibilities as a trainer and developer of its membership. Given the fiscal constraints under which most social agencies are currently operating, the role of the board in both maintaining current resources and developing new ones seems vital.

The selection of appropriate tactics is the subject of the sixth piece, by Netting, Kettner, and McMurty. Illuminating the processes of planning and program development, it systematically addresses the factors to be considered in light of the posture of the practitioner toward the target(s) of change—collaboration, campaign (a needed focus on education and persuasion), and contest (where important issues are in dispute). A key aspect of the authors' analysis is how tactics are interwoven with objectives, host-system roles, and client-system roles.

Using the hotly debated context of social welfare, Pawson and Russell explore a range of planning and development approaches. The focus is on operationalization of interventions, including community liaison, interorganizational coordination, and political empowerment.

In the final selection, Rivera and Erlich confront the prospects for organizing, planning, and development with communities of color. Detailed consideration is given to the skills and knowledge a practitioner must bring to such a community in order to be effective. The authors argue that there are important limits on what roles white practitioners ought to be playing in minority communities.

Macro-level practitioners are facing the most difficult situation to be experienced in the last 20 years. The combination of sharply declining resources coupled with a political environment hostile to the needs of poor and disadvantaged populations has not been equalled in recent memory. On the other hand, we are also in a time of change, and such times always present new creative opportunities. The challenge is to engage the full range of tactical means to achieve positive goals without being consumed in the process.

—John L. Erlich

9.

Marie Weil

# WOMEN, COMMUNITY, AND ORGANIZING

Organizing by women for social justice, equality, and human liberation is not a new phenomenon. Women have been powerful organizers in political and social action, union, civil rights, human rights, and peace movements, and in the development of social and community services, as well as in the women's movement. This chapter focuses on feminist issues in community organization and explores the role of women as organizers. Furthermore, it develops a framework for analyzing women's organizing work in general, as well as feminist community organization, articulating feminist principles for organizing.

A feminist framework for organizing integrates methods and strategies for action with practice principles that embody feminist values and approaches. For feminists, the framework's philosophical-theoretical foundation is critical because it shapes the questions that are posed, determines the problems that are identified as central, and sculpts the strategies for movement and change. While political-theoretical orientations may differ among feminists, there are strong commonalities related to the need for altering patriarchal structures and processes.

The entire history and development of feminism can be seen as a process of community organizing—from development of critical consciousness regarding the status of women and the oppression of minorities, to demystifying and reclaiming history,[1] through the development of social and political action movements, including the creation of specialized organizations and programs to serve the needs of women.

## PRELIMINARY DEFINITIONS AND ORIENTATIONS

Before analyzing general models of community practice and specific feminist approaches, operating definitions are needed to focus discussion on the complex issues this chapter treats.

*Women* are born female; we create ourselves as women through a social process of interaction of the self with family, peers, society, and culture; and we are feminists as we commit ourselves to the equality of women, to the elimination of oppression, to the empowerment of women and minorities, and to the creation of a nonsexist society.

*Community* can refer to any of several means of identifying connections among people. It can connote (a) the relationships among residents in a specific locale, or (b) the relationships and activities of people committed to a particular interest, concern, or problem—that is, a community of interest or a functional community. Both conceptions are grounded in the idea of community as a kind of social organism. Alternatively, it can connote (c) a particular political unit or power base.[2] Common to all three types of community is an assumption of some basis of shared concern or shared perception that can draw people together.

---

Marie Weil is a professor at the School of Social Work, University of North Carolina at Chapel Hill.

*Organizing* refers to the process of pulling together to create a functional whole.[3] It may indicate the establishment of an organization dedicated to a particular purpose or may outline and orchestrate a strategy for achieving certain goals.

*Community organization* was "formally recognized as a distinct field within social work in 1962"[4] and has increasingly been included in social work curricula. The mainstream community organization literature in social work has typically followed Rothman's typology of community organization.[5] Rothman identified three models: (a) locality development—incorporating goals of "self-help," community capacity and integration (process goals)"; (b) social planning—problem solving with regard to substantive community problems (task goals)"; and (c) social action with goals related to "shifting of power relationships and resources; basic institutional change (task or process goals)."[6] As Ecklein noted, however, all social work–based community organizers are

> ...concerned with advancing the interests of disadvantaged groups, with improving social conditions, with the delivery of needed services, with redistribution of power and influence, with enhancement of the coping mechanisms of target populations, and with strengthening community participation and integration.[7]

The most recent (1985) definition of community practice, by Taylor and Roberts, is an overarching rubric encompassing practice models and theoretical orientations in the following five areas: (1) community development; (2) political action—pluralism and participation; (3) program development and coordination; (4) planning; and (5) community liaison.[8] Each of these models can, however, still embrace Rothman's earlier definition of community organization as a strategy of "purposive community change."[9] Specific goals, strategies, target systems, and action systems will change to accord with the particular model, but all are related to process of planned change.

## WOMEN AND COMMUNITY ORGANIZATION

Many of the pioneers in social work and community organization on both local and national levels were women. Major aspects of the development of social work from the social reform movements of the late nineteenth century were led by such women as Jane Addams, Dorothea Dix, Julia Lathrop, Edith and Grace Abbott, Lillian Wald, Sophonisba Breckinridge, and Florence Kelley. Vandiver, Brandwein, and Conway documented that women played major roles in social action, as well as managing complex programs.[10]

However, the place of women within the two major traditions of community organization in social work was markedly different. Brandwein comments that men did dominate in the conservative, social maintenance tradition of the community chests and councils, which were tied to the sanctions and models of the business community. Yet women played a larger role even in this arena than they are typically credited for.[11] In contrast to the tradition of the Charity Organization Societies and councils, the social reform tradition of social work, emerging from the settlement movement, "focused on social legislation, neighborhood organizing, and advocacy for the poor and other oppressed groups"; within this tradition women were very visible and maintained many leadership positions.[12]

Social work's own drive for professionalization in the 1920s related not only to clinical aspirations but to emphasis on service and cost efficiency and adoption of business management methods. This shift brought more men into leadership positions in the planning and service coordination sector, and women in this field "tended to be confined to the smaller community councils with low budgets or in planning functions closely related to clinical services."[13] Although male administrators worked with business constituencies, women continued to lead the way in "neighborhood organizing, locality development, working with volunteers, and developing services for clients."[14] This sector of community organizing has been viewed as having less status, but it is the clear descendant of the social reform movements and can be seen to have close affinities with early and current feminist orientations.

Brandwein documented the displacement of women in community organization as beginning in the late 1950s.[15] Despite women's long history in community organization and social reform, the macro-practice field within social work has come to be dominated by men in both administrative and community practice. For a period during the late 1950s and 1960s, a fairly common point of view in social work education linked the continued life of the profession and its relative professional status to its ability to attract men into its ranks.[16] Unfortunately, the effort to develop opportunity for men coincided with the advancement of macro-practice, especially administrative and planning methods, and men quickly emerged from the ranks on a fast track to leadership in community and administrative positions considered to be more compatible with societal expectations regarding male sex-role behavior.

Another factor in this change relates to some of the patterns of male dominance that developed in the civil rights and antiwar movements of the 1960s.[17] For a variety of reasons, macro-practice came to be viewed as a male preserve in social work. Kadushin even published an article that argued for the need to maintain administration and macro-practice as a male domain so that men would not feel discomforted by their entrance into a profession preponderantly female and viewed as a "women's field."[18] The efforts to provide parity for men in professional social work education evolved into a pattern of male dominance in administration, community organization, and teaching. This pattern of male dominance has had a negative impact on the treatment of women's concerns and feminist issues in macro-practice curricula.

Feminist issues in community practice abound but have been largely ignored or underrepresented in the mainstream literature of community organization. Feminist thinking offers many positive parallels with basic social work theories of community organization, which emphasize values and methods grounded in democratic process, participatory democracy, civil and social rights, and social action. Many early leaders and workers in the development of community-based group practice and social and environmental action, as well as mental health and social justice, were women who in their lives and work embodied feminist principles. Those important women organizers and the movements with which they were involved include:

- The anti-slavery or abolitionist movement—Harriet Tubman, Sojourner Truth, Sarah and Angelina Grimké
- The mental health movement to provide care for thementally ill—Dorothea Dix, Josephine Shaw Lowell
- The suffragist movement—Susan B. Anthony, Elizabeth Cady Stanton, Lucretia Mott, Lucy Stone
- The settlement movement—Jane Addams, Lillian Wald
- The labor reform movement—Florence

Kelley and members of the National Women's Trade Union League

- The maternal and child health and child welfare movements—Lillian Wald, Julia Lathrop, Sophonisba Breckinridge
- The union movement and labor movement—Mary Van Kleeck, Emma Goldman, Rose Chernin, Frances Perkins
- Rights for blacks—National League for the Protection of Colored Women
- Legislative action and equal rights—Jane Addams, Florence Kelley, Alice Paul
- The civil rights movement and welfare rights movement—Fannie Lou Hamer, Angela Davis
- La Raza, United Farm Workers' Movement, and the Mexican American Legal Defense and Education Fund—Delores Huerta, Wilma Martinez, and Antonia Hernandez
- The older women's and men's movement—Maggie Kuhn, Gray Panthers, and OWL (Older Women's League)
- The women's movement—Theorists: Simone de Beauvoir, *The Second Sex*; Betty Friedan, *The Feminine Mystique*; Kate Millett, *Sexual Politics;* and Gloria Steinem, *Ms*. magazine. Groups: National Organization for Women, National Women's Political Caucus, Women's Action Alliance
- The peace movement—Jane Addams and Jeanette Rankin; Women Strike for Peace, Women's International League for Peace and Freedom, Women's Pentagon Action; Helen Caldicott, Physicians for Social Responsibility

Despite a rich and proud heritage of female organizers and movement leaders, the field of community organization, in both its teaching models and its major exponents, has been a male-dominated preserve, where, even though values are expressed in terms of participatory democracy, much of the focus within the dominant practice methods has been nonsupportive or antithetical to feminism. Strategies have largely been based on "macho-power" models, manipulativeness, and zero-sum gamesmanship.

This situation is reflected in the mainstream literature of community organization, where it is rare to find feminist case studies, a focus on organizing for and by women, or models employing feminist principles in organizing. Often this oversight extends even to the exclusion of the women's movement in discussions of social action. What is needed is attention to feminist ideology and action, as well as examination of how feminist practice is similar to and different from other forms of community organization. It is critical to develop and disseminate feminist models of community practice and organizing that focus on both women's issues and broader issues of social service and social justice. Continuous social action on behalf of the rights of women and other oppressed groups is needed, and feminist approaches have much to offer these efforts.

In order to develop feminist models for community organization, we need to focus on two subjects that have been largely ignored in the mainstream community organization literature: (a) women as organizers in general community practice and (b) women organizers and women's organizations focused on specific women's issues—women considered as a community of interest. The issues and problems encountered in these two practice sectors are different in several ways.

## Women and General Community Organizing

The first sector, women working as organizers in any general community organization, gives rise to a variety of issues that flow from the assumption of male dominance in political, organizational, and community structure. History indicates that even when social change is stimulated by revolution, women assume large roles in development and organizing in the early stages, but are moved back into more traditional roles as postrevolutionary society stabilizes.[19] Whether in union organizing, social agency networks, academia, or community political action, a female organizer must inevitably be conscious of the social reality pointed out by Simone de Beauvoir that she is likely to be identified as the "other."[20] She is at risk of being (a) distrusted for being female, (b) disparaged for being aggressive or not "appropriately feminine" in terms of traditional gender role expectations, or (c) treated as the token or exceptional woman—usually defined as one who looks like a woman, but thinks like a man. Any one of these positions can be damaging, not only to the organizer, but to the cause to which she is committed.

Women organizers as formal or informal leaders in a group or organization must always be conscious of and examine the reaction of others within and outside their group in terms of overt or covert sexism. They must balance attention to these issues with attention to the general strategy and social change goals.

To function effectively as a woman organizer in community practice, one needs a heightened feminist consciousness, as well as the recognition that one will continually be tested as a woman and as an organizer. When feminists are involved in general community organization or social change, they must always work to include and expand feminist agendas. They must also maintain a dual focus with regard to both process and tasks, seeking to integrate feminist goals and approaches into the general problem-solving strategy. This approach requires conscious and consistent effort to shape goals, strategies, and roles so that they approach consistency with feminist values and orientations. The woman involved in general community practice as a feminist carries the risks of the boundary spanner. She will need to maintain ties in the feminist community for support and analysis, but will need to be able to function independently in the general community practice arena, which may be either tolerant of or overtly resistant to feminist ideology.

A feminist organizing model is required, in general community issues, that acknowledges and incorporates the need to deal with sexism as well as general issues of process facilitation and task accomplishment. In addition, models or a typology of models for feminist organizing around women's issues, women's organizations, and services for women are needed.

### Women and Feminist Organizing

The central issue in feminist organizing and organizations is how to embody and carry out feminist values and principles in action strategies. The values and experiences of women form the basis for all feminist orientations and approaches to social change. Accepting that premise necessitates a heterogeneous rather than a homogeneous conception of women's realities. Differences in demographics as well as political and social points of view interact with values to shape our interpretations of social reality. Understanding differences allows for building feminist coalitions grounded in common feminist commitments, such as ending sexual harassment, rape, and physical abuse; allowing for reproductive freedom; being able to choose a partner of either sex; and having the opportunity to participate fully in public life.[21]

Feminist viewpoints extend across a continuum on which one's ideological placement is a function of one's life experiences, demographics, political involvements, and education.[22] Four theoretical models for organizing women as a community of interest are the liberal, socialist, and radical models and the feminist perspective articulated by women of color.

When feminists are engaged in organizing and in developing programs and services to meet the needs of women as a community of interest, they may operate with any (or a combination) of the orienting frameworks and action approaches grounded in a particular feminist analytical framework. These frameworks indicate the specific goals, emphases, strategies, and action systems that stem from the particular ideologies and organizing perspectives of feminists who may define themselves as liberal, socialist, radical, or women of color. Table 9.1 (pp. 124–125) illustrates the particular emphases of the major feminist frameworks and lists the common components of feminist organizing that they all share. Because tolerance and the valuing of diversity are intrinsic feminist elements, each of the frameworks for organizing women leads to common feminist goals of equality and the empowerment of women.

## MAINSTREAM AND FEMINIST PRACTICE ARENAS

Feminist organizers may practice in general community settings or in specifically feminist-oriented organizations and programs. For either mainstream or feminist practice arenas, the five basic community practice models detailed by Taylor and Roberts are relevant.[23] As noted in Table 9.2 (pp. 126–128), these include program development and coordination; social planning; community liaison; community development; and pluralism, participation, and political empowerment. To utilize and participate effectively in these models, feminists must first analyze their practice environment and then incorporate feminist issues and roles into their own and the agency's work.

The feminist perspective articulated in Table 9.2 emphasizes reconceptualizing and sharing power. It furthers the democratization of macro-practice methods by emphasizing pluralism, participation, and shared decision making. In addition, the feminist perspective stresses advocacy for women and other oppressed groups and is oriented toward human liberation.

Inclusion of feminist issues and development of roles for women in these general models can assist in ensuring the following issues are addressed in community practice models: (a) empowering women and vulnerable populations; (b) demystifying the planning process; (c) diminishing power/status differentials; (d) emphasizing process; (e) clarifying the value bases of practice models and methods; (f) acting to attain the elimination of sexism, racism, and class bias; (g) questioning power structures and redefining power; and (h) establishing belief and action systems necessary for structural and institutional change.[24] A feminist perspective strengthens these models to ensure that women, minorities, and other vulnerable populations can exercise their rights as citizens and contribute to the development of society.

These generic community practice models have been adapted and implemented by feminist practitioners and organizers to develop services and programs focused on women as a specific target population and

TABLE 9.1
Women as a Community of Interest: Frameworks and Approaches

| Model Components | Frameworks and Approaches | | | |
|---|---|---|---|---|
| | Liberal | Socialist | Radical | Women of Color |
| 1. Goals and focus in organizing | Equal rights and individual liberty. Equality of opportunity, development of egalitarian gender relations. Social reform. Consciousness raising on effects of sexism. | Elimination of sexism and class oppression. | Elimination of patriarchy—meeting common human needs—creation and celebration of women's culture. Empowerment of women. | Elimination of all human oppression. Elimination of discrimination related to race, class, and gender. Solidarity within groups and among minority and other oppressed groups. |
| 2. Assumption about causation of sexism and oppression | Sex-role socialization. | Political and economic institutions of society (capitalism and patriarchy). | Patriarchy—male power and privilege. | Racism, sexism, and class discrimination as interlocking causative factors of oppression. |
| 3. Orientation to power structure | Gain power for women in institutions and develop institutions more responsive to feminist approaches. | Need for revolutionary social and political change. | Resist patriarchy and create a women's culture. Revolution as process. | Rejection of political and social oppression. Rejection of all biological determinism. Rejection of institutionalized racism and sexism. |
| 4. Emphasis on strategy for change | Reeducation of public to eliminate sex-role stereotyping. Elimination of discrimination in employment. Legislative lobbying. Local political and social organizing. Local, regional, and national political action and policy action. | Analysis and action related to economic production, sexuality, reproduction, and socialization of children. Advocacy for women. Strategies to align with and advocate for other oppressed groups. | Redefinition of social relations and creation of a woman-centered culture. Emphasis on creative dimensions of women's lives. Emphasis on process and connections. Personal growth and empowerment through personal and political action. | Articulating feminist frameworks for women of color. Connecting feminism to racial and economic oppression. Building solidarity within oppressed groups. Supporting development and advancement of minority groups. Emphasis on common humanity and needs as well as recognition and support of the uniqueness of cultures and subcultures. |
| 5. Emphasis on tactics and techniques for social change | Political and social action primarily focused within the established political and economic system. Development of broad-based coalitions and large membership. Development of local action networks connected to regional and national associations. Development of a national presence to articulate women's issues, and lobbying for equal rights. | Analysis and praxis—analysis of common grounds for oppression, and efforts to establish collective means to solve community and individual problems. | Articulating and building on women's capacities. Reclaim women's history. Analyze and validate women's experiences and perspectives. Connection of the personal to the political. Empowerment of women. Emphasis on process and consciousness raising. | Education, reeducation. Concentration on development of political and social positions that resist all forms of oppression. Building solidarity within groups. Replacing negative stereotypes of women of color and minority groups with careful analysis of capacities, strengths, and direction. Reclaiming history. Consciousness raising. Building sisterhood among women of color and other women who recognize the triple threats of racism, sexism, and poverty. |

*Continued*

TABLE 9.1 (continued)
Women As a Community of Interest: Frameworks and Approaches

| Model Components | Frameworks and Approaches: Liberal | Socialist | Radical | Women of Color |
|---|---|---|---|---|
| 6. Major roles of change agents | Local, regional, and national level lobbying. Policy analysis and alternative policy development. Local and national political action on emerging issues. Public education and reeducation. Individual and group development through consciousness raising and mutual support. | Education, analysis, active involvement in labor activities and support of other oppressed groups. Articulation of women's issues. Development of alternative programs and services. | Analysis. Development of collectives related to services for women, support for women, women's music, arts and crafts, and literature. Definition and expansion of women's culture. | Education, analysis, consciousness raising. Redefinition of women of color. Development of political and social analysis and action frameworks. Preservation and further development of own culture. Development of groups, programs, and services to meet the needs of oppressed groups. Development of alternative programs and supports. |
| 7. Action systems—mediums of change | Local networks to respond to emerging issues. Regional and national associations to respond to issues and to support local and national action. Mutual support and consciousness-raising groups for individual and group development. | Women's study, action, and service development collectives. Alliances with other groups around common issues. | Collectives and small groups—emphasis on egalitarianism and shared power. Building enabling systems and mutual support. Building liberation through one's own actions. | Small groups or collectives focused on individual and political development of particular oppressed groups. Action within minority communities to build solidarity and promote social and economic development. Building coalitions and solidarity among oppressed groups. |

a community of interest. Feminist community practice and services may function as a specialized part of the mainstream service sector or may operate in the rapidly expanding arena of alternative services aimed specifically at women. Programs and organizations such as the Peer Consultation Project of the Southern California Rape Prevention and Study Center (SCRPSC),[25] the Family Violence Project of Jewish Family Services of Los Angeles,[26] Women Helping Women[27] in Los Angeles, the Los Angeles Commission on Assaults Against Women, the National Welfare Rights Organization, Coalition for the Medical Rights of Women, Women's Pentagon Action, National Network of Hispanic Women, and National Organization for Women all exemplify various aspects of feminist principles and commitments and community organizing.

The various roles for feminists engaged in general community practice show how women from diverse political perspectives and different ethnic and interest groups (single mothers; lesbians; older women; Asian American, black, and Hispanic women) can come together to organize around specific issues; to influence mainstream services; to develop alternative services for women; and to build unity, solidarity, and sisterhood. Unity can come from diversity when individual differences and experiences are validated and when

TABLE 9.2
Models of Community Organizing and Feminist Issues

| Current Community Practice Models* | Incorporation of Feminist Issues and Roles into Models |
|---|---|
| **Program Development and Coordination**<br>Incorporating mediative and political processes to bring about implementation of social program and plans, and developing program coordination. Focused on a specific target population, but primary constituency is professionals and agencies. Change focus is on full range of political and organizational interests related to a particular issue. Roles in identifying needs, designing programs, consensus building, public relations for functional communities, lobbying, and education of the public on specific issues (Kurzman, 1985). | Broadening program development foci to attend to special needs of women, particularly to the needs of women who are especially vulnerable because of health, mental health or disabling conditions, or racism or poverty.<br>Ensuring that women's issues are considered in the development of service networks and systems for service coordination.<br>Giving attention to sexism as it is experienced by professional women working in the service system and to the impact of sexism, racism, and poverty on women who are service consumers or potential consumers.<br>Strengthening connections and collaboration between mainstream service systems and alternative feminist and minority community programs.<br>Assisting in development of and advocacy for community-based and culturally sensitive services for women and minorities.<br>Developing women's networks and support groups for women involved in service delivery with emphasis on incorporating feminist values and principles into the operation of service systems. |
| **Social Planning**<br>Developing plans or forecasting future conditions. Research and technological focus and skills. Use of formal structure and processes to build support for outcomes intended to be logical, rational, and beneficial. Focus on application of technical skills in planning process whether role is "neutral," "transactive," or "political" in relation to sponsors' or constituencies' expectations (Rothman and Zald, 1985). | Applying technical skills and research skills in analyzing specific service needs of women, children, vulnerable populations, and oppressed populations.<br>Grounding planning approaches in target populations' experiences. Validating and giving credence to women's and other client groups' appraisal of need.<br>Working toward democratizing planning processes.<br>Strengthening consideration of and integrating cultural, ethnic, and sexual preference issues in service design.<br>Involving clients and staff in planning programs.<br>Recognizing that pure rationality is not a sufficient basis for planning, only, and incorporating cultural and value issues in planning processes.<br>Recognizing that planning is never "value-free" or "totally objective," and actively including women's values and perspectives in planning processes.<br>Intentionally using feminist ideology, values, and principles in planning. |

*Continued*

TABLE 9.2 (continued)
Models of Community Organizing and Feminist Issues

| Current Community Practice Models* | Incorporation of Feminist Issues and Roles into Models |
|---|---|
| **Community Liaison**<br>Holistic approach integrating social work roles in both environmental and interpersonal change processes. Specific community practice roles tied to goals and purpose of the agency for staff and administrators of direct service agencies. Administrative activities: interorganizational, boundary spanning, community relations, environmental reconnaissance, and support. Clinical staff activities: program development, needs identification, and client advocacy (Taylor, 1985). | Focusing on empowerment of and advocacy for oppressed groups—with particular attention to service needs of women, children, and minority populations.<br>Developing closer, functional ties to target populations; sharing information: reconceptualizing and sharing power.<br>Examining destructive and oppressive forces in the environment and personal and political lives of the target population.<br>Becoming actively involved to change oppressive and sexist forces affecting the target population.<br>Examining sexism and racism as they affect the community served and the agency and its staff.<br>Examining agency hierarchy and boundaries. Introducing feminist ideology, values, and principles in agency decision-making processes.<br>Working toward democratizing the work-place, and increasing clients' participation in decisions about service provision. |
| **Community Development**<br>Enabling approach—as both means to goals and a goal in itself. Dual emphasis on growth of individual and the group, neighborhood, or community. Practice roles encourage participation and social involvement for individual and group enhancement. Opportunity system for self-help. Developing local leadership and organizing structures to enable urban or rural people to improve social and economic conditions. Major strategies: building cooperation and collaboration and conflict resolution (Lappin, 1985). | Ensuring inclusion of women's issues in social and economic development.<br>Working to make women's culture and women's values and concerns an equal part of the development process.<br>Developing and supporting women's full participation in decision making and social and economic development.<br>Working toward empowerment of women and reconceptualization of power emphasizing inclusiveness and collective aspects.<br>Working toward further development of women's culture in social and economic production and in the arts.<br>Focusing specific attention on women's health needs, economic needs, educational interests, and opportunity structure.<br>Developing specific women's economic and social development projects.<br>Supporting self-determination of community women in developing role equity and role change. |

*Continued*

TABLE 9.2 (continued)
Models of Community Organizing and Feminist Issues

| Current Community Practice Models* | Incorporation of Feminist Issues and Roles into Models |
|---|---|
| **Pluralism, Participation, and Political Empowerment**<br>Increasing participation and power of groups who have been excluded from decision processes in order to achieve their self-determined, desired goals. Grounded in realities of struggle, conflict, and existence of conflicting interests in any community. Roles of organizers: educator, resource developer, agitator for self-determined interests of disadvantaged groups. Individual and group growth and skill development related to central focus and goal to make democracy serve the interests of groups that have lacked power. Empowerment focus through formal citizen participation or, more important, self-generated in neighborhood and minority rights associations. Groups may develop their own alternative services or programs (Grosser and Mondros, 1985). | Maximizing the participation of women and ethnic, working class, lesbian, aged, disabled, and other relevant women's groups in social systems and institutions.<br>Building process to strengthen morale and empower women in local groups and in representative groups.<br>Working for inclusion of women and women's issues in social and political decision-making processes with the goal of developing collective power.<br>Working for full representation of women in existing service, social, and political structures, and for development of separate women's organizations.<br>Working to develop alternative women-centered programs to serve unique needs of women.<br>Working to develop coalitions among women of diverse subgroups, to build, articulate, and enact common women's agenda.<br>Working to increase political and service system accountability to women's concerns and the concerns of other vulnerable populations. |

*Community Practice Model descriptions are drawn from specific chapters in *Theory and Practice of Community Social Work*, Samuel H. Taylor and Robert W. Roberts, eds. (New York: Columbia University Press, 1985). See Note 23 (p. 133) for full names of authors and titles of chapters.

common issues that transcend diversity can be understood in relation to shared values and articulated in unifying principles of feminist practice. The following community practice principles articulate feminist ideology and values as guides to action.

### Principle One—Feminist Values

Feminist organizers will act to support female values and processes. Organizers will affirm women's strengths and capacities for nurturance and caring. The values of emphasizing process, recognizing and using multidimensional thought processes, and respecting intuitive processes will be supported.

### Principle Two—Valuing Process

Feminist organizers will value and act to support both process and the products that result from process. In action, organizers will support consensus development, recognizing that diversity can be supported and polar positions avoided. The valuing of process supports being nonjudgmental. The use of process to build connections can be an educative, democratizing, and empowering force.

### Principle Three—Consciousness Raising and Praxis

Feminist organizers will recognize and support the power and impact of consciousness-raising processes. Giving women the opportunity to reflect on, reexperience, identify, and analyze the social stereotypes and environmental forces that have impeded their development and liberation can serve as a bridge to reclaiming personal history, renaming, and reconceptualizing experiences, gaining self-confidence, and building individual as well as collective strength from action.

### Principle Four—Wholeness and Unity

Feminist organizers will work to build the sisterhood and solidarity of all women. Women face many societal forces that engender separation among them and prevent them from working together. Feminist organizers will act from a position of unity that also supports individual differences as well as intra- and intergroup diversity. Separations and dichotomies are often set up between various categories of women such as lesbians and straight women; women of color and white women; poor and middle-class women; single and married mothers; and young and old women. History attests to many attempts to place different ethnic, minority, and oppressed groups in opposition to one another. In social work, dichotomies are set up separating professional from paraprofessional women, and separating both of these groups from clients. Feminist organizers will affirm the variety and diversity of women's experience and will work to synthesize and build unity that transcends diversity.

### Principle Five— Reconceptualization of Power and Empowerment

Feminist organizers will work toward the reconceptualizing of power as "transactive," limitless, and collective, and as a process that "enables the accomplishment of aspirations."[28] Feminist organizers will work toward empowerment of women through the development of nonhierarchical and democratic structures, by the sharing power, and by supporting self-determination and egalitarianism.

### Principle Six—Democratic Structuring

Feminist organizers will work to develop organizations, groups, and services that empower women—as members, staff, and consumers. Democratic decision-making processes will be developed and supported; and means to share information, resources, and power will be sought. Organizational tasks can be structured to clarify responsibilities and build autonomy.

### Principle Seven—The Personal Is Political

Feminist organizers will be cognizant of the ways in which systemic factors result in problematic personal conditions for women and will work to build unity among women to achieve collective solutions to oppressive situations. The interactive factors of personal growth and political-social action will be recognized and emphasized in approaches to problems and organizing strategies.

### Principle Eight—Orientation to Structural Change

Feminist organizers will recognize the need for and work toward fundamental change in organizational, institutional, and societal structures to eliminate sexism, racism, and other forms of oppression.

## FEMINIST RECONCEPTUALIZATION OF COMMUNITY PRACTICE

These principles in combination form an action framework for feminist community practice. They build on developing and converging feminist frameworks. Significantly, they also reflect basic values that are deeply rooted in American tradition; although not ascendent: "We have a long and enduring history of struggle to implement such values as egalitarianism, consensus democracy, nonexploitation, cooperation, collectivism, diversity, and nonjudgmental spirituality."[29] Feminism is clearly aligned with the two central social work value positions that support (1) the dignity and worth of each individual and (2) the responsibility of human beings for one another.[30] These two value positions undergird the feminist respect for diversity and concern for collective responsibility and action.

Feminists in community practice may be working with self-help groups, collectives, or organizations, as well as community or political and social action groups. They may take on roles as organizers, community researchers, advocate-planners, administrators, clinicians, trainers, or educators to empower citizens' groups and underserved or oppressed communities. In any of these roles, the feminist principles are applicable. Given the action framework of feminism, many women who are concerned with organizing and services will concentrate on developing programs that are gender-centered or ethnic-centered. The feminist perspective leads to commitment to work with women, children, aged people, the disabled, and other vulnerable populations.

The synthesis of roles and issues that women face in community practice, central issues in feminist frameworks and models for organizing, and feminist principles for community practice lead to a feminist reconceptualization of community practice. In this conception:

A. *Goals* will always relate to the elimination of oppression, such as sexism and racism; method will be integrated with vision.

B. *Power* will be conceptualized as facilitative, enabling, and shared within and among groups. Influence will be a means of expanding feminist approaches and achieving goals. In understanding power as "energy and initiative," feminists will challenge institutions that construe power as "domination."[31]

C. *Strategies* for change will stress the necessity for congruence of means and ends and will be grounded in egalitarianism, consensus building, cooperation, collectivism, power sharing, self-help, and mutual responsibility. Strategies will be personal, interpersonal, social, and political to achieve basic social change, building toward egalitarianism in personal interactions and social structures. Coalition building will be used to expand involvement in feminist agendas—among women and other groups.

D. *Action* will be based on the eight principles for organizing that were previously enumerated.

Within this reconceptualization of community practice (1) feminist theory is incorporated into the knowledge base for community practice; (2) feminist values are made explicit, and essential components for organizing and action are derived from feminist frameworks; (3) community practice models are adapted to be congruent with feminist goals, strategies, and values; and (4) feminist principles for community practice are articulated that build toward the empowerment of women. This construct constitutes a working model for feminist community practice focusing on the goal of empowering the disadvantaged, at the same time building power and competence for both clients and professionals.

This model can be applied in all community practice relating to clients, community groups, and organizations. The settings for feminist community practice are exciting and diverse. They range on a continuum from consciousness-raising groups, through food co-ops, women's health programs, and service programs, to the movement for world peace.

The feminist agenda for organizing, service development, and community action relates to women's needs through a variety of service approaches: (1) personal and group growth through life development, crises, and transitions; (2) problems of poverty and economic stability, and needs for food, clothing, and shelter; (3) needs for employment, job training, and elimination of discrimination and sexual harassment; (4) needs for health and mental health services; (5) needs for support and services for women who are victims of violence, or who are homeless; and (6) rehabilitative services for women who have problems of substance abuse or are in the prison-probation system. The needs for service development and political action are intertwined. Collective action is necessary to deal with these issues on two fronts: (1) pressuring and challenging existing service systems to re-form their view, treatment, and interaction with women and (2) development of alternative gender-focused and ethnic-focused programs that reflect feminist principles.

Feminists need to work toward humanizing and democratizing the general service delivery system so as to increase the input received from clients as well as workers' responsiveness to client needs. In alternative structures, feminist approaches building on mutuality, self-help, and reciprocity are hallmarks of client-worker interaction.

Action to build alternative feminist and ethnic-sensitive services and action to change the existing service system and social structure are both critical areas of feminist organizing *praxis*. As we move in these areas of action, those of us who teach must also enable and empower our students to carry forward feminist agendas.

## IMPLICATIONS FOR PROFESSIONAL EDUCATION

Feminist perspectives, community practice frameworks, and models need to be included in professional education. Dominant models of community organizing stress "macho" roles, tactics are often manipulative, power is construed as dominance, and democratic process and values may be sacrificed to achieve a desired end. Feminist students are bewildered at the contradiction they experience between their belief systems and action or organizing experiences; students who have no exposure to feminist approaches all too easily discount them or assume that power and dominance are the only game in town. Students interested in community and macro-practice need the opportunity to explore and engage with feminist theory and frameworks as well as to explore the differences in means and ends that feminist approaches embody.

Community and macro-practice courses need to connect students to the world of alternative services for women and minority communities and to explore ways to enlarge advocacy functions and develop positive connections between community-based, alternative services and mainstream services.[32] Students need exposure to feminist theory, frameworks, methods, and strategies. Student reports, role play, or other experiential exercises can be used to illustrate and engender reactions to different processes of decision making, different conceptions of power, and different models of group facilitation. Students need (1) cognitive exposure to feminist approaches; (2) experiential learning strategies in the classroom to examine issues of value clarification, role conflict, and leadership styles; and (3) practical exposure to community practice and social action through involvement in planning, organizing, and action tasks, such as service design, coalition development, and political action for social change through a community practice or political group. Participation in leading group discussions, canvassing, and lobbying are all activities that make community practice real.

Students need the opportunity to explore community practice roles, to explore feminist approaches, and to try out roles and experiment with styles. Such experiences can be designed for students specializing in macro-practice and those interested in clinical work. The community liaison role for clinicians can become the key to involving direct-service workers in community practice.[33]

Most important, students need an empowering model of professional education. Women students, especially those entering the macro-practice arena, need experience with a teaching-learning model that promotes feminist values and roles and that frees both women and men students from stereotypical sex-role behavior. Women students also need a learning model that is andragogical in its process. Andragogical models build on students' knowledge, values, sensitivities, and skills to promote self-directed learning.[34] Such learning models move students toward the realities, choices, values, and roles that shape professional practice and prepare them to take on responsibility. Such models are congruent with feminist approaches, can be used as a means of reconceptualizing power in the classroom as well as in the field, and can prepare students for the processes, decision making, and challenges of feminist community practice.

## CONCLUSION

The feminist vision in community practice is one of social, personal, and political transformation. Women have always been culture bearers. As we clarify and affirm the values of female consciousness and translate them into social action, these values to preserve, support, and humanize life become principles for commitment. These feminist principles connect to community practice. Community practice is both a direct form of service to client groups and communities and an indirect form of service carried out through interagency and professional actions. Community practice moves social work firmly into the arena of social action and social justice. As feminism unites the political and the personal, community practice is the means of moving social work from case to cause and from private troubles to public concerns. The vast range of areas of commitment in feminist community practice indicates the strength and flexibility of the approach. It is increasingly important to enact the feminist agenda for social change. In neighborhood organizing, consciousness-raising groups, collectives, organizations, political action, and the peace movement—the philosophy, perspective, and direction that feminism offers are healing, holistic, and nurturing. Feminism complements humanistic approaches. We must further develop our strategies and methods; nothing less than our survival—individual, collective, community, and global—is at stake.

## NOTES

1. Mary Bricker-Jenkins, "Of, By and For the People: Feminist Perspectives on Organizations and Leadership," paper presented at the Annual Program Meeting, Council on Social Work Education, Washington, D.C., February 1985.

2. Robert Fisher, *Let the People Decide: Neighborhood Organizing in America* (Boston: Twayne, 1984).

3. *American Heritage Dictionary of the English Language: New College Edition* (Boston: Houghton Mifflin, 1980).

4. Joan Ecklein, *Community Organizers* (2nd ed,; New York: John Wiley & Sons, 1984), p. 20.

5. Jack Rothman, "Three Models of Community Organization Practice, Their Mixing and Phrasing," in F.M. Cox, J.L. Erlich, J. Rothman, and J.E. Tropman, eds., *Strategies of Community Organization*, 3rd ed. (Itasca, Ill.: F.E. Peacock, 1979), pp. 25-45.

6. Ibid, p. 30.

7. Ecklein, *Community Organizers*, p. 4.

8. Samuel H. Taylor and Robert W. Roberts, "The Fluidity of Practice Theory: An Overview," in Taylor and Roberts, eds., *Theory and Practice of Community Social Work* (New York: Columbia University Press, 1985).

9. Rothman, "Three Models," p. 26.

10. Susan T. Vandiver, "A Herstory of Women in Social Work," in Elaine Norman and Arlene Mancuso, eds., *Women's Issues and Social Work Practice* (Itasca, Ill.: F.E. Peacock, 1980), pp. 21-38. See also Ruth A. Brandwein, "Toward Androgyny in Community and Organizational Practice," in Ann Weick and Susan T. Vandiver, eds., *Women, Power, and Change* (Washington, D.C.: National Association of Social Workers, 1981), pp. 158-170; and Jill Conway, "Women Reformers and American Culture, 1879-1930," *Journal of Social History*, 5 (Winter 1971-72), pp. 164-177.

11. Brandwein, "Toward Androgyny," pp. 159-160.

12. Ibid., p. 159.

13. Ibid., p. 160.

14. Ibid., p. 160

15. Ibid., pp. 161-162.

16. Diane Kravetz, "Sexism in a Woman's Profession," *Social Work*, 21 (November 1976), pp. 421-426.

17. Susan Evans, *Personal Politics: The Roots of Women's Liberation in the Civil Rights Movement and the New Left* (New York: Alfred A. Knopf, 1979).

18. Alfred Kadushin, "Men in a Woman's Profession," *Social Work*, 21 (November 1976), p. 444.

19. Margaret L. Anderson, *Thinking About Women: Sociological and Feminist Perspectives* (New York: Macmillan, 1983).

20. Simone de Beauvoir, *The Second Sex* (New York: Alfred A. Knopf, 1952).

21. Alison M. Jaggar and Paula S. Rothenberg, *Feminist Frameworks: Alternative Theoretical Accounts of the Relations Between Women and Men*, 2nd ed. (New York: McGraw-Hill, 1984). pp. xiv-xv.

22. Ibid.; and Anderson, *Thinking About Women.*

23. Taylor and Roberts, eds., *Theory and Practice of Community Social Work.* Chapters describing the five models of community practice adapted in this chapter are: Paul Kurzman, "Program Development and Service Coordination as Components of Community Practice"; Jack Rothman and Mayer N. Zald, "Planning Theory in Social Work Community Practice"; Taylor, "Community Work and Social Work: The Community Liaison Approach"; Ben Lappin, "Community Development: Beginnings in Social Work Enabling"; and Charles F. Grosser and Jacqueline Mondros, "Pluralism and Participation: The Political Action Approach."

24. Cheryl Ellsworth, Nancy Hooyman, Ruth Ann Ruff, Sue Bailey Stam, and Joan Hudyma Tucker, "Toward a Feminist Model for Planning For and With Women," in Weick and Vandiver, eds. *Women, Power, and Change*, pp. 146-157.

25. Vivian B. Brown, Barrie Levy, Marie Weil, and Linda Garnets, "Training Grass Roots Peer Consultants," *Consultation*, 1 (Summer 1982), pp. 23-29.

26. Interview with Carole Adkin, Betsy Giller, and Ellen Ledley, of the Family Violence Project, Jewish Family Service of Los Angeles, Calif., June 10, 1985.

27. Interview with Ilene Blaisch, LCSW, Director of Women Helping Women, a service sponsored by the Los Angeles, Calif., Section of the National Council of Jewish Women, July 29, 1985.

28. Mary Bricker-Jenkins and Nancy R. Hooyman, "Feminist Ideology Themes," discussion paper prepared for the Feminist Practice Project, National Association of Social Work-

ers, National Committee on Women's Issues, presented at the Annual Program Meeting, Council on Social Work Education, Detroit, Mich., March 13, 1984, p. 7. See also Bricker-Jenkins and Hooyman, "A Feminist World View: Ideological Themes from the Feminist Movement," in Bricker-Jenkins and Hooyman, eds., *Not for Women Only: Social Work Practice for a Feminist Future* (Silver Spring, Md.: National Association of Social Workers, 1986), pp. 7-22.

29. Ibid., p. 19.

30. Paula Dromi and Marie Weil, "Social Group Work Values: Their Role in a Technological Age." Paper presented at the Sixth Annual Symposium for the Advancement of Social Work with Groups, Chicago, Ill., November 1984.

31. Barbara Thorne, "Review of *Building Feminist Theory: Essays for Quest*," *Signs*, 7, No. 3 (1982), p. 711.

32. Marie Weil, "Southeast Asians and Service Delivery—Issues in Service Provision and Institutional Racism," in *Bridging Cultures: Social Work with Southeast Asian Refugees* (Los Angeles: Asian American Health Training Center and National Institute of Mental Health Asian-Pacific Social Work Curriculum Development Project, 1981), Chap. 10.

33. Marie Weil, "Community Organization Curriculum Development in Services for Families and Children: Bridging the Micro-Macro-Practice Gap," *Social Development Issues*, 6, No. 3 (December 1982), pp. 40-54.

34. Marie Weil, "Preparing Women for Administration: A Self-Directed Learning Model," *Administration in Social Work*, 7 (Fall-Winter 1983), pp. 117-131.

## 10.

**Warren C. Haggstrom**

## FOR A DEMOCRATIC REVOLUTION: THE GRASS-ROOTS PERSPECTIVE

There are two basic approaches to getting things done. The traditional way is the top-down approach: the formation of undemocratic work, military, and other organizations. In these organizations, most people who carry out the tasks of the organization don't have much say in deciding what is to be done.

The second basic approach, the grass-roots approach, is rapidly expanding, but does not yet usually involve most of the hours of the lives of those in it. When ordinary people join together on a basis of equality to accomplish something, they are taking the grass-roots approach. Currently, in the United States, the grass-roots approach includes self-help groups (about 14 million people), neighborhood organizations (about 20 million people), and the tens of millions of people involved in grass-roots co-ops, political groupings, labor unions, religious organizations, issue movements, and other voluntary organizations—a large and growing population of Americans. The grass-roots approach not only can be more efficient than is the usual way, but it can also be more beneficial educationally and psychologically for those affected.

---

I anticipate that the grass-roots approach, as it becomes perfected, will gradually replace the traditional, undemocratic top-down approach for getting things done. It is that replacement that I call a *democratic revolution.*

Will the democratic revolution be good or bad? The answer to that question depends on its outcomes, all things considered, for people. What is best for the people of the United States? Although the answer to this question involves economics, it also involves something broader: the entire human being.

We can begin by considering how to create social arrangements which will lead us to act in such a way that our actions have the best possible outcomes for people. That is a question of the effective *helping* of people.

Grass-roots organizing can be understood as a way to *help* people in need in our society. Helping is a *core* activity, *not* peripheral, and not necessarily involving altruism, in any complex society such as the United States. To evaluate and develop modes of helping, therefore, is to get at the very foundations of all aspects of American life.

## HELPING

Each person leads a unique life and more or less continues that life in such fashion as to realize best his or her potential for happiness or accomplishment. The extent to which a person realizes his or her positive potentialities is the extent to which she or he *flourishes.* To *help* a person is to enhance his or her level of flourishing or self-realization or to stave off threats to it.

Help may be

1. *unintended* (which would happen if, for example, the pursuit of economic self-interest within a capitalistic system were to enhance some aspects of self-realization throughout a society)
2. *intended* (which includes rushing to the aid of someone in distress)
3. *official* (that is, what is described as helping in an official report)

Official helping includes medicine, public health, social work, and so forth. The most important single characteristic of helping is the extent of *net effectiveness* of a helper.

*Definition 1: Given all the positive, negative, and other consequences of the helping activity, the net effectiveness of a helper is how many people are helped how much by the helper after subtracting the harmful consequences of his or her or its helping activity.*

Also, I propose the following:

*Postulate 1: The net effectiveness of helping is increased in direct relationship with the extent to which the helper is under the control of the person(s) helped.*

There are two main classifications of helping activity in the United States in which the helper is under the control of the person(s) being helped.

First, employees in top-down organizations help (a) those in charge of the organizations (executives, administrators, some board members), and also, but not necessarily, (b) those outside the organizations who are affected by them. For example, a worker in an automobile assembly plant helps the bosses and *may* also help those who buy the automobiles assembled by the plant. We can say that the employee as helper is controlled directly by the bosses and indirectly, just possibly, by automobile sales.

Workers also help themselves to the extent to which they define and control the work or its related benefits. They have very little control of work on an assembly line, but wages and fringe benefits help the worker outside the job itself.

Second, some enterprises, such as co-ops, are officially self-help in nature, and in these the helpers are usually *ipso facto* more nearly under the control of those helped than is the case in top-down organizations.

A third category in which helpers might appear to be controlled by those being helped consists of official helpers in private practice, for example, some physicians, clinical psychologists, clinical social workers, and so forth. However, efforts by the professions to be self-regulating and keep their practices autonomous through a variety of strategies usually has effectively removed much impact on this kind of helping by those ostensibly being helped. Actually, however, private practice in the helping professions can best be characterized as a kind of self-help activity.

In most official helping, there is not even the extremely limited impact on the helpers by those ostensibly being helped as patients and clients have on private practice. For example, social agencies are almost invulnerable to initiatives of their clients even though some of them have powerless "advisory" boards of clients whom they select. Institutions of formal education are similarly relatively invulnerable to initiatives of students except during rare times of crisis.

Postulate 1 thus applies to most official helping, making it possible for us to derive:

*Theorem 1: The net effectiveness of most official helping is far less than is that of helping in the two other main categories.*

Within the official helping process, it is crucial to consider the extent to which those officially helped actually are helped. Normally, these diverge widely.

For example, consider foreign aid by the United States to El Salvador. It may be publicized as help to the people of El Salvador by the generous people of the United States. But those actually helped may turn out to be almost entirely a tiny elite in El Salvador and a tiny elite in the United States.

It would be instructive to examine the efforts of the professional organizations of the helping professions. Do those organizations act effectively to reduce unmet need? Or do they act primarily on behalf of the self-interests of their members? Such an analysis may reveal that, contrary to their carefully cultivated public images, they are primarily self-help efforts by people not in need. In that case, we would propose:

*Postulate 2: The net effectiveness of most official helping is primarily an outcome of their self-help characteristics and is not related to the need of those being helped,* and

*Postulate 3: The net effectiveness of official helping is not closely related to the altruism of officially designated helpers.*

Let us next illustrate Theorem I and Postulates 2 and 3.

If you "think through" the following illustration, the reasons for supposing the validity of the three postulates and of Theorem I will become apparent.

## Official Helping (Poverty): An Illustration

Official helpers include physicians, psychiatrists, clinical psychologists, social workers, and members of many other recognized "helping" professions. Social work help is extended mostly through social agencies, nonprofit bureaucratic organizations often staffed in part by professional social workers. A child guidance clinic, a family service agency, and public welfare agencies all are social agencies. But this official social work approach to helping poor people is not effective for many reasons. Poverty is both economic and psychological. The economy of poverty has not been much affected in the United States for a long time. What help poor people have gotten by this means has come about through increases in general economic prosperity or through the allocation of public funds through the political process (like cash welfare payments, food stamps, rent supplements, medicare, public housing, and so forth). Neither prosperity nor legislation results from social work practice. The psychology of poverty has only worsened during recent decades—and social workers, in headlong retreat from their traditional preoccupation with poor people, have not even tried to affect it significantly.

The economy and the psychology of poverty can be positively altered only by some kind of social change. For example, so long as 6 to 8 percent unemployment is planned as normal, poverty on a large scale is also being planned as normal.

In American history, arguments about social policies designed to tackle social problems (poverty, crime, and so forth) have been based on the *stability assumption*: namely, that our society can remain pretty much the same as it mobilizes money and people (especially experts and professionals) to tackle such problems. The arguments have tended to be about money to be spent on dealing with the problem, and the nature and organization of the people to be mobilized. The grass-roots perspective arises in relation to the state of affairs resulting from the long reign of the stability assumption, a reign which has maintained, not diminished, most such problems.

Further, the creation of social situations in which poor people will tend to flourish, which will also benefit them psychologically, also requires planned social change. Given the extent to which business and political elites affect the expenditure of funds for helping purposes, social agencies cannot even try to work on any extent of social change which will make much difference without their funds being jeopardized. Social changes, then, do not and cannot help poor people very much.

Bureaucratic agencies are so structured that a key element in helping poor people remains unknown to the helpers. That element is the meaning of being poor, the collective psychology and subjectivity of poverty, as it exists within the communities of poor people. Without such understanding, it is impossible to enhance predictably the level of flourishing of poor clients.

Furthermore, the policies of social agencies are set by boards and administrators. But they are structurally removed by their positions from any direct acquaintance with the clientele of the agencies, or more seriously, those in greatest need, who may not be clients. Thus, the people in charge are the least able to make certain that help extended is appropriate for those who most need help. But even if boards and administrators had more knowledge, they do not have the right to decide for those needing help.

By working in bureaucratic agencies, social workers are led by their work situations to identify first with the agency or profession and only secondly with those needing help. The structured incentive system of agencies support agency maintenance and expansion, and there is no external force that requires attention to carrying out its intended goals. The result is that social agencies become self-absorbed narcissistic collectivities rather than instrumental to the determined perception and reduction of unmet need.

Traditional helping approaches separate helpers from those toward whom help is directed. As a result, it is in the interest of professional social workers to help themselves first. It is in the interest of professional social workers to reduce attention to people in need to, at best, a second priority. Official helpers act largely on the basis of their perceived self-interest. Impulses toward professionalization play a similar role, with similar consequences.

Most social workers haven't been selected for their interest in, or knowledge of, poor people, especially the invisible characteristics of communities of poor people. Social workers come mostly from two groups. One group, the largest, consists of people from nonpoor backgrounds, most of whom will remain ignorant of the experience of poverty and its meanings for their entire lives. The other group is made up of people trying to escape from their poverty backgrounds and from most poor people—they are those from among the poor who do not identify with, and who will never be of help to, persons with long-term low incomes. Furthermore, neither social work students nor the faculties of schools of social work have often been selected as people interested in, or educated for, social change efforts, and therefore, cannot even conceptualize what is needed if poor people are to be helped.

Because a broad public mistakenly believes that social work is dealing with the problems of poor people, the very existence of social work saps motivation and support for the implementation of alternative ways to meet needs and thereby diminishes the possibility that really effective help will eventually be extended to people who are poor.

There is little evidence of the effectiveness of social work intervention at any level. The research on the effectiveness of casework has produced results which can only be described as "profoundly discouraging" to caseworkers and their supporters. If social workers were concerned with helping people, they would be heavily involved in effectiveness research. They are not.

The knowledge base of contemporary social work appears to be weak. Although there are recipes for professional action, those recipes are often only distantly related to reasons or evidence. For that reason, it can be argued that social work is mostly superstition: a semiprofession based on a semimythology. Social work graduate students pay in money and time to acquire this dubious lore, oblivious to the comment of Socrates that "There is far greater peril in buying knowledge than in buying meat and drink." (Plato, Protogoras)

There is not, within social work, a language that promotes thinking and critical discourse. Nor are there arenas within which critical discourse can well occur. For example, such words as "empowerment," "problem solving," "help," and many others are used within social work imprecisely and in ways that violate their literal meanings. In the social work profession, matters of fact are supposed to be taken on faith. Crucial issues are thereby removed from analytic and critical discussion. Professional values thus make it impossible for the profession to advance except through the perfecting of whatever now exists.

The bureaucratic way of organizing helping leads to rule orientations and away from consequence orientations on the part of helpers. This not only ends in collective narcissism, but also leads to a disinclination to pay attention to, and relate to, unmet need.

Since the decisions of social agencies

and their personnel affect actual and potential clients far more than do actual and potential client decisions affect social agencies, the agency-client relationships directly increase the dependency of those seeking help. The meaning of these dependency relationships communicates the inferiority of those needing help and therefore further harms them.

The bureaucratic organization of helping tends, because of the related self-preoccupation, to maintain the status quo regardless of external social changes which always are taking place, and also regardless of the existence of unmet need.

Unintentionally, traditional social work focuses on the inadequacies and disabilities of poor people (deficiencies which need remedying) and not on their talents, capacities, intelligence, and other strengths. This focus defines poor people by their disabilities and thereby ignores other possible definitions, which would be more helpful.

The units defined by social workers have usually ignored extended families and thereby helped to undermine mutual aid resources which traditionally have been valuable supports for them. Social agencies are defining institutions.

Are most social workers or other traditional helpers to blame for this state of affairs? I think not. It is the assumptions on the basis of which traditional helping has occurred which are responsible for the deficiencies.

In February 1917 Antonio Gramsci commented with searing love and indignation: "I hate those who are indifferent." It is true that indifference is the greatest insult which can be rendered to people in need of help. But what has caused the mass indifference, even within the helping professions, to people in great need? The motives of most of them are positive (if somewhat weak). It is rather that most traditional helpers have become entangled in evil social arrangements designed to serve political, economic, military, intellectual, and social elites, and to perpetuate and expand bureaucracies, regardless of the consequences for people. As a result, the interests of most traditional helpers have worked against their extending effective help to people in great need.

The most urgent need for help in the United States is the need of the tens of millions of poor people who not only suffer greater hardships than do affluent people (there is evidence that poverty itself shortens life expectancy in a population, increases the rates of a wide variety of diseases, and assaults the personalities of those subject to it), but who also can't afford to hire helpers for themselves.

A second problem of very great consequence is nearly universal. It is the decline during past decades of the meaningfulness of life for most people, a likely outcome of the rise of bureaucracy and consumerism and a concomitant decline in the extent to which most people take charge of and define their own lives in ways that centrally matter to them, given their life histories.

## Effective Helping

On the basis of the preceding remarks, it is clear that the net effectiveness of helping has little to do with the intentions of helpers. Further, helping is a central characteristic of any society, not something restricted to a residual category.

This discussion has stressed only the effect of placing helping in the hands of those helped. But, if one does not take a second step, the effectiveness of helping remains far below what is otherwise possible. For example, if one does no more than to place helping under the control of those being helped, then helping may tend to concentrate its benefits on small elites, and the helping may deviate from the flourishing of those helped into a pandering to their tastes, wants, pleasures, satisfactions, and prejudices, or to a small sector of their lives (as with solely economic help). Thus the net effectiveness of helping will be improved by the expansion of democracy in all facets of our society and an expansion of *thinking*. Thus, we can formulate Postulate 4 considering helping as follows:

*Other things remaining the same, the net effectiveness of helping in which the helper is under the control of the person(s) helped is increased in direct relationship with the extent to which the helping process is democratic and characterized by a thinking through of how best to proceed in helping.*

It now becomes plausible to assume that an optimal institutionalization of helping can occur through the creation of an expanding, rational, self-educative, mass social movement with enough power to effectuate its major goals.

**THE GRASS-ROOTS SOLUTION**

Grass-roots organizing is a "bottom-up" process through which ordinary people join together to accomplish something. A grass-roots organizer is one who helps ordinary people to take charge of and improve their own lives through collective action directed toward accomplishing some social change. The grass-roots approach, therefore, is democratic (run by members) and is in stark contrast to the approach of accomplishing things through elites running authoritarian bureaucratic organizations (in factories, offices, social agencies, educational bureaucracies, the military, and so forth).

One basic question to ask concerning any organization called "grass roots" is "who is really in charge?" Although there are few perfect examples of a grass-roots approach, if a leader or a clique really runs things (as in political, labor union, community, or other organizations), then it is not grass roots even though it may be called "grass roots." Since words concerned with grass roots are often popular, they are frequently taken up to give a positive ring to one or another authoritarian enterprise (for example, an organization for "economic democracy," a "community development" county department). Sophisticated and authentic grass-roots organizations typically ensure that there is much honest and open critical discussion concerning what is to be done, with the right of any person vigorously protected who wants to dissent from the rest. Some co-ops, neighborhood organizations, block clubs, political organizations, labor unions, churches, towns, and so forth are grass-roots organizations.

When grass-roots organizations join together on a democratic basis, or expand greatly without losing their democratic characteristics, in order to struggle toward securing some social change, they are trying to form a *grass-roots movement*. If they are actually to become a grass-roots movement, they must make some progress toward the change they seek. As is true of grass-root organizations, a grass-roots movement may have much or little formal structure (that is, explicit and legitimated rules to guide their internal processes).

For the first centuries of its existence, Christianity was a religious grass-roots movement. The spread of the town meetings in New England early in the history of the United States was a political grass-roots movement. The spread of co-ops in many rural localities in the midwestern and southwestern United States and in parts of Canada formed a single economic grass-roots movement, which was especially prominent in the late nineteenth and early twentieth centuries. The fast spreading

ACORN (Association of Community Organizations for Reform Now), a national congery of neighborhood organizations, is a grass-roots neighborhood movement which has acquired about 34,000 dues-paying member households, mostly during the past five years.

A grass-roots movement becomes most relevant to social change by developing power. The power of such a movement usually depends upon the number of participants; the intensity of their involvement: their "staying ability"; the extent to which it is organized; the money, information, skills, and other resources available to it; its relationships to opponent vulnerabilities; and the "levels of consciousness" of its participants.

Historically, social movements have been among the most important factors in securing basic social changes. We are now seeking to combine technological innovation (another historically important source of social changes) with a scientific grass-roots movement approach with the aim of bringing about a powerful permanent process through which Americans will take charge of their society in such fashion as to flourish maximally and in so doing move toward the resolution or alleviation of all social problems, including the renewal of meaningful activity for most of the population. The progress of the grass-roots neighborhood movement during the last two decades, now involving tens of millions of people, has provided experience, sophistication, hope, and determination for the future of the grass-roots approach in our country.

## THE GENERIC GRASS-ROOTS MOVEMENT

The word "generic" refers to all aspects of people's lives: psychological, moral, social, spiritual, educational, matters of pleasure and fun, work, and so forth. The idea of the generic grass-roots movement is to create a movement that will become an effective scientific, rational, and good force for social change in our society, a movement involving most Americans that will permanently endure. We do not now know whether such a generic grass-roots movement is possible or, if it turns out to be possible, whether it can result in a major transformation of our society.

At present in our society, people with lower incomes tend to be more involved in staving off threats to their self-realization (the threat of unemployment, of being controlled by others, of being dependent, of welfare, of having to accept even worse alternative jobs, and so on), than in positive flourishing. Positive incentives are more available to those with higher incomes. It is that available incentive difference and the meanings related to it that account for much of the social class differences in vitality and activity, including intellectual activity. We may, therefore, now state:

*Postulate 5: Other things remaining the same, the grass-roots generic movement will contribute far more to the general level of personal self-realization than does the present top-down structuring of most of our society.*

## A DEMOCRATIC REVOLUTION?

Persons associated with the grass-roots movement will come to understand democratic administration (as opposed to the authoritarian approach), social change, the nature and history of social movements, power, the positives and negatives of a long-time perspective, thinking, meaning, truth, morality, relevancy, solidarity, and other topics. But, most central of all will be reality changing. Let me here briefly illustrate this essential concept. Reality consists not only of physical objects. It also consists of meanings. One meaning of a neighborhood may be that the people in it are inferior. That societally held meaning may ensure that most of the people of the neighborhood lack confidence, energy, hope, determination, much skill, and many other characteristics. That meaning of the neighborhood may have been internalized by its residents, making it difficult for them to escape it even when they leave the neighborhood.

A grass-roots organizer working in that neighborhood may begin to focus existing discontents and interests of the residents into a change process. If that organizing effort is successful, some years later the meaning of the neighborhood may become one of the adequacy, or even superiority, of its members. This new meaning, carried partly by institutionalized internal groups, will support members into greater happiness, education, constructive activity, self-esteem, a kind of self-education, and a sturdy confidence and persistence in relating to the people and institutions in the vicinity of the neighborhood. Although the physical objects (houses, streets, human bodies) of the neighborhood may have changed very little, the reality of the neighborhood would have changed a great deal. Such a process would constitute reality changing on a local scale.

The proposed generic movement can be regarded as a social invention. Like other inventions, we may know early the main outlines of what will work but still need a long struggle to perfect it, to make it practical and beneficial.

To sum up, when it comes to helping people, "realism" and careerism, given present social arrangements, are impractical and destructive even to those who engage in them. Although there is no guarantee of what will work, it is an idealism rooted in history which relates to the future through imagination, thinking, reasons, evidence, and analyses by people trying to tell the truth, which promises to work best, to be genuinely practical. But these are the qualities associated with the idealism inherent in the grass-roots perspective as it may come to be expressed in a generic grass-roots movement.

A revolution is a deliberate, basic, and sustained social transformation in a society resulting from changes in the relative power of groups within it. A revolution need not involve violence. By a "basic" transformation I mean one with substantial consequences for the general level of, and/or major varieties of, personal self-realization. We do not presuppose that a basic transformation primarily depends on something happening to the economy, the polity, the culture, technology, or any other sector or feature of society. A *democratic* revolution is one of, by, and for the people of a society. Perhaps one can now initiate in the United States a generic grass-roots movement that will eventually create an unusually desirable democratic revolution, one which will continue as a change process that will permanently work to enhance the lives of the American people.

11.

**Terry Mizrahi and Beth Rosenthal**

# MANAGING DYNAMIC TENSIONS

Coalitions, as complex organizations of organizations, inherently experience dynamic tensions. Five of these tensions and their management are described below.

## 1. THE COOPERATION-CONFLICT DYNAMIC

While shared goals and a willingness to work together are the foundation of coalition functioning, in fact coalitions are characterized by conflicts as well as cooperation. Conflict inherently occurs on several levels: (1) between the coalition and the target they wish to influence, around strategies and issues such as credibility, legitimacy and power; (2) among the coalition participants around issues such as leadership, decision making and personality/style; and (3) between the coalition and its member organizations around issues such as unshared goals, division of benefits, contributions, commitments, and representation.

Since conflict is an inevitable part of the coalition dynamic, coalition work should be approached as a conflict resolution model, where bargaining, trade-offs, negotiating, and compromise are part of all decisions, and agreements are reached by mutual consent.

Terry Mizrahi is on the faculty of Hunter College; Beth Rosenthal is a consultant with New York City.

## 2. MIXED LOYALTIES

Coalition members have a dual commitment—to the coalition and to their own organizations—producing a conflict between altruism and self-interest.

Coalitions that operate in the same service or issue areas as their member organizations may compete with members for resources, organizational time, and energy. There may also be confusion over which "hat" coalition members are wearing while participating in coalition business. Once a coalition is formed, this "mixed loyalties" tension affects the degree of commitment and the contributions that members are willing to make to the coalition, as well as what the coalition can expect from them.

Organizations frequently join coalitions for some protection, because they cannot or do not want to be visible on a particular issue. On the other hand, participating in a coalition means assuming a collective risk, presumably for a greater good or benefit. Once coalition members begin working together, an organization's autonomy may be compromised. Organizations may decide not to join or remain in a coalition because they want to control their own agenda, or are focused on their own survival.

Coalitions can minimize losses and risks for member organizations by using the following approaches:

(a) design collective efforts that do not threaten the turf or networks of the member organizations;

(b) identify and treat carefully issues or positions that could compromise members' credibility and funding;
(c) prevent direct competition between the member organizations and the coalition; and
(d) agree on actions that organizations can do in the name of the coalition versus those that they do on their own.

### 3. AUTONOMY V. ACCOUNTABILITY

A coalition must have enough autonomy to take independent action, and enough accountability to several levels within the coalition and its member organizations to retain credibility and maintain the base which is its essence. Effective coalitions decide when they can assume or need to obtain sanction from the member organizations and their constituencies.

Coalitions can balance the autonomy/accountability tension by creating a variety of ongoing communication mechanisms between the coalition and its members and their organizations. They should also clarify:

(a) how to integrate new members;
(b) who the coalition represents; and
(c) when and how different levels of participants will be involved in coalition decisions and actions.

### 4. MEANS V. MODEL

A coalition can be a means to accomplish a specific social change goal, as well as a particular model of sustained interorganizational coordination. Lack of clarity about whether the coalition is viewed primarily as a "means" or "model" can lead to differences in emphasis on process or product, degree of commitment, visions of success and failure, willingness to compromise, and time frame for accomplishment of coalition goal.

Coalitions primarily concerned about being a *model* emphasize:

(a) a goal, structure, and operating style that reinforces internal coalition development;
(b) a commitment by member organizations to the coalition as an end in itself;
(c) suspension of action toward the social change goal if necessary to build the coalition, itself.

Some coalitions approached as a *model* later transform themselves into permanent federations or organizations.

Coalitions primarily concerned about being a *means* to accomplish a specific goal:

(a) provide "just enough" structure;
(b) avoid time-consuming process issues;
(c) promote involvement only to "produce results";
(d) either tolerate or find creative ways to work with differences.

The most effective coalitions strive for consistency in process and goal, and balance skill and leadership development with coalition efficiency.

### 5. UNITY AND DIVERSITY

Coalition members share compatible, but not identical, interests, and must both utilize diversity as a strength, and find ways to act in unison. Coalitions need enough unity to act together and enough diversity to accomplish their goal and to represent a broad base. Their functioning requires a certain degree of "syncretism"—an attempt to combine or reconcile differing beliefs in all salient areas. Coalition members must reach some amount of agreement regarding goals, strategies, domain, decision making, and evaluation.

Many coalition leaders assume that unity demands uniformity and conformity. In fact, coalitions that are too unified resemble organizations and fail to achieve the essence of the coalition—the inclusion of diversity. Moreover, excess unity can lead to competition among the groups for turf, access to resources, or visibility, and can also limit the coalition's creativity. Coalitions suffer if all their members have the same perspective, expertise, and resources.

Conversely, many coalitions pursue diversity, either strategically or indiscriminately, with an open-door membership policy. Numbers are not everything—rather, it is the specific mix of diversity needed for a "winning coalition" that is essential. Because people assume that working together will be easy, they may overlook differences that may impede coalition functioning over time. Increasing a coalition's diversity will usually slow down progress toward external goals because it takes time to evolve trust, familiarity, and comfort in working together. Coalitions can become a whole that is greater than the sum of its parts, but to realize this great potential requires making creative use of the different components.

The unity/diversity tension may manifest in eight different dimensions, as described below.

### A. Goal Differences

Goal differences affect problem definition, identification of potential coalition members and choice of social change target, strategies, and solutions.

*Managing Goal Differences.* Coalitions can utilize the following approaches to resolve or minimize goal differences:

1. Select a goal that is central to everyone's interests and is seen as something that can benefit both the diverse groups and the coalition as a whole.
2. Define a goal relevant to the members' interests, but broader than any one group could address alone.
3. Identify linkages between the issues.
4. Create a superordinate goal that transcends differences among potential coalition members, and clarify how the participants' differences support the whole.
5. Compromise on goals: Create goals where all participants can get a portion of what they really want, enough to sustain their involvement.
6. Change goals over time.
7. Show how short-term goals relate to the long-term, bigger picture.

### B. Ideological Differences

People with different political or religious ideologies approach coalition work with distinct belief systems and operating principles.

*Managing Ideological Differences.* Coalitions can use the following approaches to help member groups with different ideologies work together more effectively:

1. Address a third issue unrelated to any member organization's domain.
2. Take action only on issues on which there is total agreement and allow any group to have veto power.
3. Limit joint action strictly to goals.
4. Suspend judgment on areas of difference.

5. Compromise on public position.
6. Tone down the ideologically extreme position.

### C. Differences in Expected Outcome

Organizations may agree on a common goal, but outcome expectations may differ. This tension intensifies with a coalition's success, at which time decisions about payoffs and rewards must be made.

*Managing Outcome Expectation Differences.* Coalitions can withstand divergence in the outcome expectations of their members by the following means:

1. Expand or redefine the pie rather than consider possible outcomes in zero sum terms.
2. Engage in issues which promise some tangible or intangible gains for each coalition member.
3. Enable each member organization to maintain the ability to act autonomously on issues that are not directly related to coalition activity, as long as they do not do so in the name of the coalition.
4. Select coalition issues that do not conflict with members' individual agendas.
5. Make explicit the trade-offs for everyone's involvement.
6. Discuss the consequences of winning or losing when there appears to be a zero sum outcome.

### D. Differences in Amount and Level of Power

Coalitions have to deal with the consequences of actual and perceived power differences among members and potential participants.

*Managing Power Differences.* To minimize power differences, coalitions can find ways to have the powerful group provide resources without dominating. When it is desirable to keep the powerful group(s) inside the coalition, the following mechanisms can be established:

1. a one group/one vote rule;
2. voting/not voting membership;
3. caucuses for smaller groups;
4. an agenda that gives less influential members the advantage.

Coalitions which exclude powerful groups from full participation can continue to draw upon their resources and support by:

1. making them affiliates or honorary members;
2. forming parallel/support coalitions;
3. providing technical/advisory status for the powerful group.

### E. Differences in Level and Intensity of Commitment

Organizations join and continue participating in coalitions for a variety of pragmatic and/or ideological reasons. Pragmatic reasons include some degree of self-interest—a quest for resources, power, or social contract; ideological motivations mean some shared value-based commitment to a cause or a concept of the "greater good."

*Managing Differences in Commitment.* To maximize commitment to the coalition effort and encourage a greater variety of organizations to participate, coalitions can:

1. Structure opportunities for multiple levels of commitment.
2. Develop membership agreements that

clarify what kind and level of commitment is desirable and how it should be demonstrated.
3. Plan for fluctuations in commitment over time.
4. Provide a variety of incentives to sustain participation, addressing the actual motivations of members.
5. Assure protection to members.

### F. Differences in Type and Level of Contributions

Coalitions development requires the assessment of the amount and kinds of contributions needed, and the assignment of equivalent weights to the various contributions actually provided by members. As coalitions endure, they identify whether they have the necessary contributions required both to achieve the social change goal and to maintain the coalition.

*Managing Differences in Contributions and Rewards.* Coalitions should clarify expectations about minimum contributions, how the ratio of contributions to rewards will be determined, and how differential contributions can be made to be equivalent.

1. Balance contributions with rewards. There are several ways to do this:

| | |
|---|---|
| EQUITY: | Organizations get out what they put in. |
| EQUALITY: | Regardless of what organizations put in, they get the same rewards. |
| EQUIVALENCY: | (Structured inequality) Some organizations get out more than they put in, while others get less. |

2. Determine minimum contributions according to a coalition's priorities.

### G. Differences in Color, Gender, Sexual Preference, Nationality, and Class

Longstanding differences in experiences, priorities, and problem definitions make it difficult to develop coalitions that cross color, gender, sexual preference, nationality, and class lines.

*Managing Diversity in Color, Gender, Sexual Preference, Nationality, and Class.* Coalitions consciously pursuing diversity must factor in the time and effort to make it happen. Some useful approaches include the following:

1. Include diverse groups at the coalition's inception, rather than later, which can minimize real or perceived tokenism, paternalism, and inequality.
2. Consciously give priority to increasing diversity.
3. A majority group-initiated coalition can offer some incentives ("affirmative action") to recruit minority participants, and consciously operate in new ways to share control and build trust. True diversity requires an ongoing commitment of coalition resources to issues of importance to the minority group members.
4. A minority group-initiated coalition can present its issues within a broad framework that integrates the majority perspectives, if their involvement and support is deemed necessary.

### H. Differences in Organizational and Personal Style

Organizations and individuals bring different styles of operating and interacting to their coalition work. Some style differences evolve from color, class, and gender, and some, such as personality differences, are purely idiosyncratic.

*Managing Style Differences.* Depending on their goal and the amount of time they have to act, coalitions can either accept or attempt to minimize style differences. If there is a sense of urgency about taking coalition action, differences may be tolerated. Over the long term, coalitions committed to a model of intergroup cooperation can seek ways to minimize the negative effect on style differences. To contain differences which could become destructive, spell out common rules for interaction:

1. Create and discuss ground rules for meetings and coalition operations.
2. Develop and enforce membership criteria.
3. Structure equal time to speak.
4. Conduct criticism/self-criticism of meetings which articulates and builds a common set of expectations, values, and operating methods for coalition functioning.
5. Create a policy that allows for the exclusion of deviant or disruptive personalities or organizations, if necessary.

## 12.

**Patrick Dattalo**

## MOVING BEYOND EMERGENCY SHELTER: WHO SHOULD FUND LOW-INCOME HOUSING?

During the 1980s, an unprecedented growth in the number of homeless Americans occurred (Redburn & Buss, 1986). The literature indicates that people become homeless for a variety of structural and personal reasons.

Deinstitutionalization, which has the goal of providing treatment for mentally ill people in community-based settings, is often cited as a cause of homelessness (Stern, 1984). Between 1965 and 1980, the number of patients in state institutions declined from 559,000 to 138,000 (Bassuk, 1984). Unfortunately, the number of former patients grew much faster than the ability of many communities to provide services to them. Some former mental patients are not only without needed services but also without a place to live.

Unemployment and poverty also are identified as contributing to homelessness (Shorr, 1988). During the last decade, the poorest fifth of American families became poorer while the richest fifth became wealthier. Today, the poorest 20 percent of Americans receive less than 5 percent of the nation's income; the richest 20 percent receive more than 40 percent (Reich, 1989). This trend toward greater income disparity not only reflects the growth of a single-parent underclass, but also indicates

---

Patrick Dattalo is a professor at the School of Social Work, Virginia Commonwealth University.

that full-time workers and married couples with children receive a lower share of the nation's income. Consequently, the bell curve of the distribution of national income is becoming flatter, with more people at its extreme ends.

Reduction in social welfare spending is associated with homelessness (Johnson, 1988). During the 1980s, an estimated 400,000 families became ineligible for Aid to Families with Dependent Children, and food stamp benefits were reduced or eliminated for about 1 million people.

Another cause of homelessness is the lack of affordable housing (Friedrichs, 1988). In 1987, there were about 4.2 million publicly subsidized housing units but about 8.1 million eligible households because of federal housing assistance cuts (Dreier, 1987). During the 1970s the federal government financed 200,000 new and rehabilitated low-income housing units a year; in 1986 the government financed only 27,000 units (Reamer, 1989).

Further complicating the picture is the possible loss of existing subsidized units. Within the next several years, 2 million low-income apartments built with federal assistance could lose their subsidies and be converted to market-rate apartments and condominiums. This potential loss of existing units is a result of provisions by the federal government to induce for-profit developers to build low-income housing by allowing them to buy out of federal housing programs after 20 years (Lenz, 1988).

Solutions to the problems of homeless people must be grounded in a recognition of their multiple needs and varying characteristics (Morrissey & Dennis, 1986). People without permanent shelter include increasing numbers of black people; members of other minority groups; adolescents; families; victims of family violence; and people with physical, mental health, and substance abuse problems (Ropers, 1988). Concern for the diverse needs of homeless people has prompted advocates to propose models to provide a comprehensive range of aid. Stoner (1984) described a three-tier service delivery system. The first tier consists of emergency assistance such as shelters, food, clothing, and medical care; the second tier includes transitional resources such as training, job finding, physical and mental health therapy, and assistance in locating permanent housing; and the third tier consists of stabilization services such as employment, counseling, and long-term housing.

Although some homeless people would benefit most from a series of increasingly independent living arrangements, many could move directly into long-term housing. Buttrick (1989), for example, concluded that "while little progress has been made in the provision of low-cost housing, shelters have become a growth industry and sadly are fast becoming the low-income housing of the 1980s" (p. 3).

## FUNDERS OF LOW-COST, PERMANENT HOUSING

### Federal Government

Substantial federal government funding for low-income housing began during the 1930s (Dolbeare, 1983). The Housing Act of 1937 provided financial assistance to localities for the construction of low-income housing. The Housing Act of 1949 created "urban renewal," which made additional funds available for public housing, and established new programs to meet rural housing needs. The Housing and Urban Development Act of 1968 incorporated production goals of an annual average of 600,000 new or renovated housing units for low- and moderate-income Americans during the following decade.

Between 1974 and 1983, the principal federal housing assistance program for low-income families was Section 8 of the Housing and Urban Development Act of 1968 (Reamer, 1989). Two basic types of Section 8 assistance exist: one for developing new, moderately or substantially rehabilitated units, the other for leasing existing units. The first type provides below market interest loans in exchange for agreement from the landlord to charge tenants lower rents. In the second type, tenants pay 30 percent of their adjusted income, and the federal government pays the difference between this income and the fair market rent value of the unit. However, during the last 10 years, the federal government has significantly reduced its involvement in low-income housing assistance. Consequently, the gap between supply and demand for low-income housing continues to widen, and a growing number of families are without a permanent residence.

Most new federal dollars earmarked to address the needs of homeless people have been used to provide social services and temporary shelter. The Steward B. McKinney Homeless Assistance Act of 1987 is the principal comprehensive federal initiative for helping to solve the problems of homeless people (U.S. Conference of Mayors, 1989). This act contains provisions to address emergency food and shelter, physical and mental health, housing, education, and job training needs. However, of the $388.5 million appropriated for McKinney programs in fiscal year 1989, only $45 million was for subsidized single-room occupancy housing. The balance was used for job training and education and for services to homeless people with chronic mental illness or substance abuse problems (U.S. Conference of Mayors, 1989).

The federal government also has helped to address the emergency needs of homeless people by channeling funds to states and local governments through existing programs, including the Federal Emergency Management Agency (FEMA) and the U.S. Department of Housing and Urban Development's community development block grants (U.S. Department of Health and Human Services, 1984). Passage of the federal Homeless Eligibility Clarification Act in 1986 eliminated the need for a permanent mailing address as a requirement for receiving Supplemental Security Income, Aid to Families with Dependent Children, Medicaid, and veterans' benefits. The act also allows homeless people to buy prepared food in shelters and permits Job Partnership Training Act funds to be used to support programs for homeless people.

Proponents of a stronger federal role in the funding of affordable permanent housing point to the government's ability to raise the necessary resources through income taxes (Hope & Young, 1986). The most important source of the federal government's tax revenue in 1984, income taxes have high revenue adequacy and elasticity (Aronson & Hilley, 1986). However, in any discussion of a stronger federal role in funding low-income housing, the federal budget deficit must be considered (Garner, 1988).

Excluding the social security program, the federal budget deficit increased from $40 billion in 1979 to $211 billion in 1989. Current projections are for the deficit to continue to rise to $239 billion by 1994 (Congressional Budget Office, 1989). Although Congress enacted the Gramm-Rudman-Hollings plan that calls for a balanced budget by 1993, deficit reduction has been difficult because of continued demand for government services and opposition to tax increases.

Even estimates that cuts in defense spending will save the government $100 billion by 1994 does not guarantee a reappraisal of national spending priorities (Thelwell, 1990). Policymakers who support using this "peace dividend" for low-income housing must compete with colleagues who favor deficit reduction and with supporters of increased spending on education, transportation, the environment, day care, drug prevention, and savings and loan bailouts (Beatty, 1990). It is uncertain whether a Congress caught among these countervailing demands will adopt what Beatty (1990) referred to as its "first post–Cold War budget" by reducing defense spending and beginning to address the low-income housing shortage.

**State and Local Governments**

Although state and local governments are beginning to offer housing support (more than 30 states have created housing finance authorities), few are spending money to build low-income units (National Congress for Community Economic Development, 1989). Thus far, state and local governments have focused on providing temporary housing, controlling mortgage lending practices, influencing housing-related tax policy, and providing technical assistance in interpreting federal housing program regulations. Minnesota, for instance, has developed a demonstration program for temporary housing projects, and several other states have made vacant buildings available to private shelter providers.

Most commonly, local government revenue has been used to pay the operating costs of private, nonprofit shelters (U.S. Department of Housing and Urban Development, 1984). Also, state and local governments have provided monetary support through existing programs such as FEMA, community development, community services, and social services grants, which channel funding from the federal government.

One reason that state governments are considered possible funders of permanent affordable housing is that, despite a slowing growth in their revenue levels, states took in $5.2 billion more than they spent during fiscal year 1986 (Leighland, 1988). Although 14 states reported deficits or balances of less than 1 percent at the end of fiscal year 1987, 33 states had revenue surpluses (U.S. Department of Commerce, 1988). However, states could find it difficult to generate revenue for low-income housing because of a growing disparity among state per capita incomes (Coughlin & Mandelbaum, 1988). Lower per capita incomes can reduce states' tax bases and lower revenue levels. Another potentially limiting factor is the Tax Reform Act of 1986, which removed incentives for investing in low-income housing and placed limits on the volume of tax-exempt housing bonds that can be issued by state and local housing finance agencies (Clay, 1987).

Furthermore, many states face growing constituent demands for spending on education, health care, prison construction and state employee salaries and benefits. In a recent survey, legislative staff were asked to list what they believed would be the top three priority issues for 1989 legislative sessions (Snell, 1988). The respondents identified education most often, followed by Medicare, state employee salaries, corrections, transportation, and housing. Respondents who listed housing ranked it third.

In response to growing constituent demands for public services, states increased aid to local governments by 62 percent between 1982 and 1988 (Herbers, 1990). At the same time, federal aid to local governments declined from $21 billion to $17 billion.

One factor affecting local governments' capacity to fund affordable housing is their means of generating revenue. Local governments rely heavily on property taxes (U.S. Department of Commerce, 1988). In terms of revenue adequacy and elasticity, the property tax did not keep pace with inflation, mostly because of lags in conducting assessments (Mikesell, 1986). Furthermore, although the property tax is a stable source of revenue, it has only low to moderate elasticity (Zimmerman, 1988).

Another factor is the revenue and expenditure limits states place on local governments. Restrictions on localities' revenue and expenditure levels are not new, but since the late 1970s, the movement for budgetary limitations has gained momentum. Currently, some states establish maximum property tax rates; others restrict either total tax levies or the total expenditures of localities (Zimmerman, 1988).

### Private Sector

Voluntary agencies play a significant role in assisting homeless people. However, like the public sector, the private sector's focus has been on providing social services and temporary shelter. A widely cited national survey conducted by the U.S. Department of Housing and Urban Development (1984) found that 90 percent of shelter services were supplied by private organizations and that 63 percent, or $138 million, of shelter services' total operating expenses came from private sources.

One reason for a stronger role by voluntary agencies in funding low-income housing is the Reagan administration's economic recovery program, which reduced individual tax rates by about 23 percent. Because of these reductions, individual donors could increase charitable contributions (Gronbjerg, 1990). However, other factors, such as the extent that itemized deductions are used, can influence charitable donations. In fact, although the voluntary sector has experienced increases in donations from bequests, individuals, corporations, and foundations since 1982, these increases have been slower than under the previous law, the Tax Reform Act of 1976.

Also limiting the private sector's ability to fund low-income housing is its heavy reliance on government financing. In 1987 government dollars accounted for 35 percent of private sector resources (American Association of Fund Raising Councils, 1988). So despite recent increases in total contributions, this income replaced only one-fourth of the private sector's estimated reduction in federal support (American Association of Fund Raising Councils, 1988). In summarizing the results of a survey of nonprofit organizations, Gronbjerg (1990) concluded that "the hope of recent Republican administrators that nonprofit organizations would take a more active role in caring for the poor and maintaining the social safety net ignored the extent to which they depend on government funds to operate" (p. 229). It seems unlikely that in the near future the private sector could assume a stronger role in funding low-income housing.

## RECOMMENDATIONS

In light of circumstances facing the private sector and federal, state, and local governments, a more effective use must be made of existing resources, and new funding sources must be developed. Recommendations for funding low-income housing include targeting funds to enhance the effectiveness of existing monetary support and developing additional resources.

## Targeting Existing Funds

The impact of federal support could be enhanced by targeting federal money to states and localities least able to generate adequate revenues. Formerly causing the demise of any grant program seeking broad political support, targeting can be a political selling point. The U.S. General Accounting Office (1986) has shown how the general revenue-sharing program could have been halved and still have decreased revenue-raising disparities between the poorest and richest communities through better targeting of funds. Indications are that Congress is moving away from block or discretionary funding approaches and toward targeting. For example, the alcohol, drug abuse, and mental health block grant requires half the drug abuse money to be used for services to intravenous drug users; 55 percent of mental health dollars must be used to support new or expanded programs (Arvidson, 1990).

Through targeting, the need to raise total funding can be partially offset by larger portions of a fixed amount being distributed to selected states and local governments. Targeting, then, can lead to a more effective use of limited funding. Currently, population size, which does not reflect funding capacity, is the most commonly used factor in allocation formulas (Arnold, 1981). Therefore, at a minimum targeting formulas should include measures of fiscal capacity and need.

Aronson and Hilley (1986) described an approach called the "measure of relative tax effort." This technique compares a jurisdiction's taxing effort with its fiscal capacity. Grumprecht (1983) suggested that social indicators, such as child poverty as measured by the percentage of children receiving Aid to Families with Dependent Children and the percentage of adults receiving Supplemental Security Income can be useful for fund-allocation decisions.

## Developing New Funding Sources

*Community Loan Funds.* A community loan fund offers an alternative to traditional public and private approaches to increasing the supply of low-income housing. A nonprofit, tax-exempt group matches lenders interested in community development efforts with borrowers unable to obtain financing from traditional sources (Community Economics, 1988). Lenders propose the terms of their loans, and the fund accepts loans whenever there are reasonable expectations of finding a borrower willing to accept the terms. Interest rates range from zero to levels comparable to the yield from money market accounts. Interest rates on loans are priced slightly over the lender's terms to cover the administrative costs of operating the fund. All lenders share a claim on the fund's assets and a reserve is usually kept, but funds are not insured.

These funds not only provide housing loans to those unable to obtain them from banks or mortgage companies, but also offer an alternative to socially concerned investors. Community funds can appeal to those who prefer to lend instead of donate their money and who are willing to accept a below market rate of return. Moreover, housing is insulated from speculative market forces; subsidies go directly to those in need, and deed restrictions limit rent increases or resale prices. Some loan funds concentrate on worker-owned businesses, but most focus on housing-related projects.

Community loan funds have facilitated the construction of thousands of affordable housing units (Reamer, 1989). To date, these funds have been exclusively private ventures, but they can be supported, at least in part, by public dollars. In the past several years, two dozen of these funds have been established in the United States. Because they combine social concern with investing, community loan funds are viable options to traditional fund-allocation mechanisms such as local housing authorities and direct provision by federal agencies.

*Pension Funds.* Pension funds are a rich potential source of capital for socially responsible investments in low-income housing. Public pension funds totaled more than $511 billion in 1987 and are projected to increase to more than $1 trillion by 1995. Private pension funds exceeded $1.5 trillion in 1987 and are predicted to total $3 trillion by 1995 (U.S. Department of Commerce, 1988).

Proponents of investing pension funds in low-cost housing can argue that these funds are well-suited for financing housing because of the long-term nature of pension liabilities. In addition, as unions expand their efforts to attract new members, housing finance plans by unions could become a central part of a "union as service provider" theme. Possible pension-funded housing benefits include mortgage guarantee and insurance programs, group mortgage discount plans, mortgage interest rate subsidies, down payment loans, and corporate or multi-family construction.

In contrast, opponents can argue that pursuing social goals would require investors to accept lower rates of return and greater risk than on traditional investments. Furthermore, restrictions often are placed on the type of investment public retirement systems can make (Zorn & Hanus, 1988). A common restriction is to limit the percentage of system assets in any one investment. Strict requirements have made most pension money off limits for investment in housing construction. But new investment strategies by both private and public pension funds now offer opportunities to use this major source of capital for a national housing production program.

At least five states—Connecticut, Hawaii, North Carolina, Colorado, and Michigan—have created vehicles for investing public pensions in housing programs. The most popular form is supplying mortgages to pension plan members (Roeder, 1988). There are no easy answers to the questions raised by opponents of the use of pension funds for social investment. However, by using investment strategies that balance stability, diversity, maximum yield, and social goals, pension funds can help to increase the supply of low-income housing.

## CONCLUSION

Although the emergency needs of homeless people must be met, efforts to address their longer term needs also are essential. A fundamental issue is the widening gap between supply and demand for low-income housing. The scarcity of affordable housing, accompanied by a decline in income, results in what Stern (1984) called "shelter poverty." Housing cost is the most important factor in a family's standard of living. It determines not only whether a family can secure a decent place to live, but also how much income remains for food, clothing, and transportation. Almost half of all poor renters—tenants whose income is less than $4,500 a year—pay 70 percent of their income in rent (Beatty, 1990).

Therefore, social workers should continue to promote expansion of traditional sources of funding for low-income housing and the development of new financial mechanisms. Targeting existing resources and using community loan funds and pension plan assets are viable alternatives to traditional resources. These alternatives can enable policymakers to complement a mosaic of emergency-oriented responses to homelessness with longer-term solutions.

## REFERENCES

American Association of Fund Raising Councils. (1988). *Giving USA-1988*. New York: Author.

Arnold, R. (1981). The local roots of domestic policy. In T.E. Mann & N.J. Ornstein (Eds.), *The new Congress* (pp. 250-278). Washington, DC: American Enterprise Institute for Public Policy Research.

Aronson, R.J., & Hilley, J.L. (1986). *Financing state and local government.* Washington, DC: Brookings Institution.

Arvidson, C. (1990). As the Reagan era fades, it's discretion versus earmarking in the struggle over funds. *Governing*, *3*, 21-27.

Bassuk, E.L. (1984). The homelessness problem. *Scientific American*, *251*, 40-54.

Beatty, J. (1990). A post-cold war budget. *The Atlantic, 265,* 74-82.

Buttrick, S.M. (1989). Homelessness, hunger, and hopelessness: The Reagan legacy [Editorial]. *Social Work Research & Abstracts*, *25*(4), 3.

Clay, P. (1987). *At risk of loss: The endangered future of low-income rental housing resources.* Washington, DC: Neighborhood Reinvestment.

Community Economics. (1988). *Revolving loan fund.* Greenfield, MA: Author.

Congressional Budget Office. (1989). *The economic and budget outlook: Fiscal years 1990-1994.* Washington, DC: Author.

Coughlin, C., & Mandelbaum, T.B. (1988). Why have state per capita incomes diverged recently? *Review, Federal Bank of St. Louis, 70.* 18-27.

Dolbeare, C. (1983). The low income housing crisis, In C. Hartman (Ed.), *America's housing crisis: What is to be done?* (pp. 52-84). Boston: Routledge & Kegan Paul.

Dreier, P. (1987). Community-based housing: A progressive approach to a new federal policy. *Social Policy, 18*, 18-22.

Friedrichs, J. (1988). *Affordable housing and homelessness.* New York: Walter de Gruyter.

Garner, C.A. (1988). Policy options to improve the U.S. standard of living. *Economic Review, Federal Reserve Bank Kansas City, 73*, 8-17.

Gronbjerg, K.A. (1990). Poverty and non-profit organizational behavior. *Social Service Review, 64*, 208-243.

Grumprecht, N. (1983). Block grants and funding decisions: The case for social indicators. *Social Service Review, 57*, 137-148.

Herbers, J. (1990). The growing role of the states is greater than we knew. *Governing, 3,* 11.

Homeless Eligibility Clarification Act of 1986, 7 U.S.C.A. (1985).

Hope, M., & Young, J. (1986). *The faces of homelessness.* Lexington, MA: Lexington Books.

Housing Act of 1937, 12 U.S.C.A. (1937).

Housing Act of 1949, 12 U.S.C.A. (1949).

Housing and Urban Development Act of 1968, 5 U.S.C.A. (1967).

Johnson, A.K. (1988). *Homelessness in America: A behavioral and contemporary assessment.* St. Louis: Washington University.

Leighland, J. (1988). State government finances. In W.C. Currens, J. Minton, & K. Tyson (Eds.), *The book of the states* (Vol. 27, pp. 220-248). Lexington, KY: Council on State Governments.

Lenz, T. J. (1988). Neighborhood development: Issues and models. *Social Policy, 18*, 24-30.

Mikesell, J.L. (1986). *Fiscal administration.* Chicago: Dorsey Press.

Morrissey, J., & Dennis, D. (1986). *NIMH-funded research concerning homeless mentally ill persons: Implications for policy and practice.* Rockville, MD: NIMH Public Health Service.

National Congress for Community Economic Development (1989). *Against all odds: The achievement of community-based organizations.* Washington, DC: Author.

Reamer, F.G. (1989). The affordable housing crisis and social work. *Social Work, 34,* 5-9.

Redburn, F.S., & Buss, T.F. (1986). *Responding to America's homeless.* New York: Praeger Publishers.

Reich, R.B. (1989, May 1) As the world turns. *The New Republic.* pp. 23-28.

Roeder, R.G. (1988). *Financing retirement system benefits.* Chicago: Government Finance Officers Association.

Ropers, R.H. (1988). *The invisible homeless: A new urban sociology.* New York: Human Sciences Press.

Shorr, D. (1988). *Within our reach: Breaking through the cycle of poverty.* New York: Doubleday.

Snell, R.K. (1988). *Leading fiscal issues in the 1989 legislative sessions.* Denver: National Conference of State Legislators.

Stern, M.J. (1984). The emergence of homelessness as a public problem. *Social Service Review, 58*, 291-301.

Stoner, M.R. (1984). An analysis of public and private sector provisions for homeless people. *Urban and Social Change Review, 17*, 3-26.

Tax Reform Act of 1976, 26 U.S.C.A. (1975).

Tax Reform Act of 1986, 8 U.S.C.A. (1985).

Thelwell, R. (1990). Gramm-Rudman-Hollings four years later: A dangerous fiscal illusion. *Public Administration Review, 50,* 190-198.

U.S. Conference of Mayors. (1989). *A status report on the Stewart B. McKinney Homeless Assistance Act of 1987.* Washington, DC: Author.

U.S. Department of Commerce. (1988). *County and city data book* (Table A, Items 171-187). Washington, DC: Bureau of the Census.

U.S. Department of Health and Human Services. (1984). The homeless: Background, analysis, and options. In *The federal response to the homeless crisis: Hearings before a subcommittee of the house committee on government operations* (98th Congress, Second Session). Washington, DC: U.S. Government Printing Office.

U.S. Department of Housing and Urban Development. (1984). *A report to the secretary on the homeless and emergency shelters.* Washington, DC: Office of Policy Development and Research.

U.S. General Accounting Office. (1986). *Local governments: Targeting general fiscal assistance reduces fiscal disparities.* Washington, DC: General Accounting Office.

U.S. Office of Management and Budget. (1994). *Budget of the U.S., 1994.* Washington, D.C.: U.S. Government Printing Office.

Zimmerman, J.F. (1988). Changing state-local relationships. In W.C. Currens, J. Minton, & K. Tyson (Eds.). *The book of the states* (Vol. 27, pp. 282-309). Lexington, KY: Council on State Governments.

Zorn, P., & Hanus, M. (1988). *Public pension accounting and reporting. A survey of current practices.* Chicago: Government Finance Officers Association.

13.

**John E. Tropman**

# THE ROLE OF THE BOARD IN THE PLANNING PROCESS

The planning process in community organization has historically involved citizens in decisions that affected them. Yet, we have not seriously attended to the problems of collective decision making inherent in this involvement. Sometimes the problems resulting from this neglect catch up with us. Those instances in which human service organizations have been faulted for spending inordinate amounts of money on fund raising and fund procurement represent one example. Another is lack of proper and vigorous attention on the part of the organization's board of directors to take regular responsibility for policy decisions and direction. Alternatively, one is reminded—and injunctions for maximum feasible participation of the poor are one example—of the fact that board memberships have all too frequently tilted in the direction of the corporate benefactor rather than the beneficiaries. Such a tilt was inappropriate even in the days of charitable institutions, but now, since many clients (through insurance programs indirectly) are paying part of the freight for their own service, their representation on boards becomes even more imperative.

## THREE ROLES FOR THE POLICY BOARD

Inherent in this planning process is decision making. And in human service organizations the boards represent the organization's policy center, or that place where decisions are made. A lot of organizational lore suggests that it is the executive and her or his cadre of associates who are really the "powers behind the throne" and the boards are "rubber stamps" bouncing, as it were, from issue to issue with no substantive input. Where this is the case, it represents a failure of both legal responsibility under most state charters, and of trusteeship responsibility in terms of the civic purpose that boards are charged to accomplish. Legally, for example, "directors of New York State not-for-profit corporations are required by statute to discharge their duties in good faith and with that degree of diligence, care and skill which ordinarily prudent men would exercise under similar circumstances in a like position" (Weber, 1975, p. 7). That standard of care which must be taken by the directors in the exercise of their duty means that many could be liable for various kinds of legal action if it can be shown that they were too cavalier in their attitudes. The area of legal responsibilities is too complex to detail here, but all community organizers should familiarize themselves with the state codes governing not-for-profit corporations in their state and locality.

More complex is the board's responsibility in the planning process for civic purpose. Most boards get together because, ostensibly, they are interested in improving the civic climate in the area in which they live. The individual directors (board members) share in this wish. Yet, all too often,

Special thanks to Kathryn Walter, who materially assisted in the preparation of a longer version of this piece, and to Nancy Smith, of Aurora Associates, Washington, D.C., for her helpful comments.

boards fail to accomplish the very civic purpose for which they are set up. Part of the reason lies in poor organization and poor decision-making styles. These difficulties are not unique to boards by any means, but relate to all kinds of decision-making groups. The piece later in this volume on effective meetings provides some suggestions for *meeting* structure that will be helpful in the board context as well as the planning committee context. However, there are a number of issues that deal with the board itself that need to be considered. The purpose of this paper is to suggest three of these issues in particular: the board as a decision maker and a decision overseer with some suggestions about ways in which the board can better handle those responsibilities; board responsibility for role appropriateness and internal and external functions, in particular; and the board as a trainer and developer of members and of the agency itself.

By way of introducing these topics, I suggest that the common term "board members" be changed to "director." In the corporate world people who serve on boards are called directors of the corporation. The word suggests greater power and vigor than does the more passive-sounding term "member." Under not-for-profit corporation laws, the term "directors" is used. They work jointly with the executive director to accomplish the organizational purpose from its definition to its implementation. Perhaps this change can move the perspective of many "members" from a more reactive posture to a proactive one.

The role of boards in the overall planning process is to make decisions and to see to it that those decisions are carried through. To do this, of course, boards work with the executive director and they share with the executive co-responsibility for the integrity of the organization's mission and role. The accomplishment of these purposes requires thought, organization, and structure. And to this end the remaining sections of this paper are devoted.

The target being addressed here is the formal board, one with bylaws, legal responsibilities, and a professional staff. The target is not the grass-roots association, or even some policy professional groups (local chapters of the National Association of Social Workers, for example). Those kinds of groups tend to be less formal and structured than the processes contemplated here. However, there are many times when less formal processes are appropriate and useful. Neighborhood groups may wish to use an approach that mixes task and process goals. One danger with using less formal approaches and procedures is the possible failure to accomplish the tasks through inadequate attention to the set of procedures and programs with which the group is charged. Overformalization is less likely to occur, but it also presents dangers. The key is balance.

All boards and directors groups *plan*, and to that extent they can use the suggestions outlined in this paper. They will need other procedures to meet other goals and should be aware that multiple functions require multiple procedures, not the use of one set to the exclusion of others.

## BOARDS AS DECISION MAKERS AND DECISION OVERSEERS

### Policy and Administration

The role of the board extends beyond policy making to the overseeing of policy implementation as well. The line dividing "policy" functions from "administrative" functions is always unclear. I prefer the no-

FIGURE 13.1
Functions of Boards of Directors

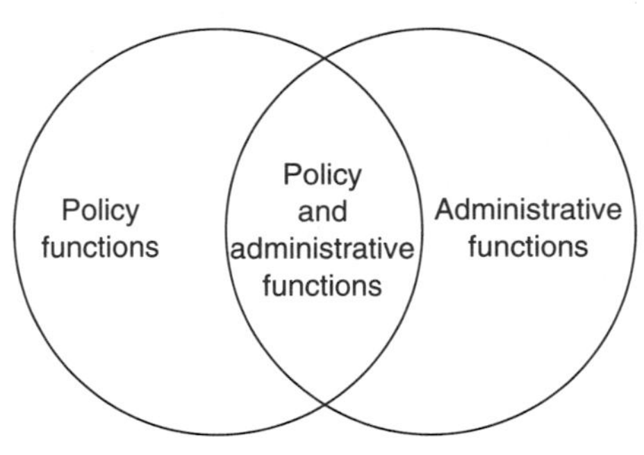


tion of intersecting sets as described in Figure 13.1.

Industrial consultants suggest, and my own information confirms the idea, that approximately one-half of board time is wasted in unnecessary agenda items, items for which there is insufficient information and so on. Therefore, board organization represents one of the most important elements of decision quality. Referring to Figure 13.1, the entire board meets on policy matters. Subcommittees, the nature of which I will suggest in a moment, meet with the executive and staff in the policy-administration intersect area, and the executive handles the administrative matters. Obviously, there is no rule for neatly allocating one item or another into the various categories, but generally speaking, the broader the scope in terms of the organization, the larger the number of people a particular proposal affects, the more a particular proposal or organizational action will cost, or the more an organization is committed based on a particular action, the more such an action is likely to be policy and to require board approval. Thus, the board itself makes decisions. The subcommittee structure both oversees decisions and develops proposals for board action. Without an appropriate subcommittee structure it is very difficult to carry out the decision-making and oversight role. I have identified nine subcommittees that are important on an ongoing basis:

1. The Executive Committee
2. The Budget and Finance Committee
3. The Resource Development Committee
4. The Personnel Committee
5. The Program Committee
6. The Public Relations Committee
7. The Community Relations Committee
8. The Nominating Committee
9. The Recruitment and Training Committee

*The Executive Committee.* The executive committee is composed of the president, officers, the executive director, and committee chairs from the board. It usually can take action in emergency situations when the board cannot meet, and it is often involved in sorting out those activities and proposals that need board approval. It coordinates the work of the other subcommittees and takes overall responsibility for the operation of the board itself.

*The Budget and Finance Committee.* The budget and finance committee deals with matters of budget generation and financial oversight, reviewing financial trajectories on a monthly basis at least and sometimes on a weekly basis. It is involved with the chief budget officer of the organization in preparing budgets and making proposals for new expenditures, handling emergencies, and so on. It is best to involve people from the financial community here so that access to banks and other kinds of financing can be facilitated when necessary. The budget and finance committee reports both overall budgetary strategy and specific budget proposals to the board.

*The Resource Development Committee.* This committee seeks to develop financial resources for the agency or organization. Its activity may involve seeking funds through public contributions, planning fund-raising events, securing grants, developing donations of property, and so on. It is important that all board members have an opportunity to serve on this committee, because raising resources is a difficult task and people "burn out." Also, the need to raise funds, as well as spend them, introduces a note of realism into the allocations process.

*The Personnel Committee.* The personnel committee develops the personnel practices guide for the organization, staying in tough with staff and their concerns, on the one hand, as well as the broader personnel community on the other. Issues involved can refer to compensation, burnout, holidays, and so on. It also typically handles grievances and selection of top agency staff.

*The Program Committee.* The program committee provides structure and purpose for the organized mission and role of the agency itself. Usually agencies have somewhat general missions and roles, which need to be given concrete programmatic manifestations. This or that activity needs to be undertaken while some other activity needs to be stopped; all activities need to be monitored and evaluated. The program committee, often composed of professionals in the area of concern, makes programmatic recommendations to the board. It generally works more closely with staff than other committees.

*The Public Relations Committee.* The public relations committee enhances and improves the agency's image with the general public. It prepares annual reports, news releases, and other pieces of public information. It seeks favorable publicity about the agency. Sometimes this committee is merged with the community relations committee, but its function tends to be focused more on media. Interviews with staff, preparing newsletters, and press releases are all tasks of the public relations committee.

*The Community Relations Committee.* The community relations committee focuses on the personal aspects of community involvement, for example, organizing tours of the agency, providing speakers for public functions, and interpreting the agency's mission and role to key people in the community. While the public relations committee tends to concentrate on involving the media, the community relations committee focuses on involving people. Often community relations links to political figures at local, state, and national levels.

*The Nominations Committee.* The nominations committee usually meets on a yearly basis, sometimes intensively for a period of time, to develop a slate of officers. At times it also reviews the appointments of top staff. It may also be merged with the recruitment and training committee, although it is preferable to keep these functions separate. While the nominations committee moves people who have already participated in organizational life into officership, the recruitment and training committee works to secure people from the outside and to bring them into the organization.

*The Recruitment and Training Committee.* The recruitment and training committee seeks to interest previously uninvolved individuals in the organization and its mission and role. This committee may develop a list of potential members in advance of any specific vacancy. In the recruitment phase, its members meet with individuals, interpret the kind of job the agency is doing, and seek to promote involvement. Its training responsibilities include preparing the board members' manual, conducting annual training sessions for the entire board, and providing additional training for individual board members if they so desire. It is important that each board member of a human service organization have one personal improvement opportunity a year made available through board membership. The reimbursement policy for this effort should be part of the recruitment and training committee task.

### How Big a Board

In general, the minimum number of members per subcommittee should be three. Thus, if three people were assigned to each of these committees, there would be a minimum board size of twenty-seven. There are usually at least three extra members for ad hoc assignments, resulting in a board of thirty. A rule of thumb for board size is the number of subcommittees plus one (for ad hoc assignments) times three.

### Subcommittee Structure

The subcommittee structure just discussed may appear to some to violate the notions of openness, spontaneity, and freedom, which should characterize the human service board. I believe just the contrary. Most boards deal with technical legal issues of great importance involving quite a bit of money. These issues cannot be approached casually or in an offhand manner; rather, they must be given sustained thought. My view is that a board operates more effectively when working from a subcommittee's recommendation. Therefore, with rare exceptions, I recommend that boards assign upcoming tasks to subcommittees, requesting that the subcommittees study the matter with appropriate staff and other members of the organization and the community to develop a proposal for action with alternative considerations and present the proposal to the board. When this groundwork is laid, the board can deal with the matter much more effectively and efficiently than it can if it is trying both to make the decision and to acquire relevant information at the same time.

### Subcommittee Functions

Basically, subcommittees have five major functions. The first is to generate decision options, the point I just made. Second, once a decision has been made in an area germane to the functioning of the subcommittee, it is the subcommittee's task to oversee the implementation of that decision. Oversight here does not mean scrutiny on a daily basis; rather it means that the subcommittee receives periodic reports on how things are going, raises questions, and gets to the executive, president, and full board if necessary. Third, subcommittees evaluate and pass recommendations to the board on activities in their area of concern and responsibility. Fourth, subcommittees become the center of the trusteeship-generating function because they seek to foresee problems. The finance committee that does not foresee difficulties is the finance committee that may find itself liable for civil action. The job and responsibility of subcommittees is to be proactive, to take leadership roles and to present suggestions based on these two orientations to the board itself. Fifth, through carrying out these four functions, the subcommittee educates the whole board and thus provides for board growth in its respective area of concern.

### From Administrative Board to Policy Board—The Problem of Transition

One particular problem that boards in the human services field have is to accomplish the transition from "administrative board" to policy board. This transition occurs in the following way. Often a human service organization has been founded by a group of interested citizens who initially get together and *are* the agency. As time passes, federal or state monies may be acquired. As more stable funding becomes available, an executive director and perhaps a secretary are hired, and the organization is beginning to move from a very informal, nonbureaucratic, personal organization to one that is more formal and bureaucratic, and includes a board of directors legally chartered under the laws of the state. This transition often leaves the agency founders feeling left out, in second place, and needing to move on. And, indeed, some organizational analysts indicate that the kinds of people who are organizational founders are very different from those who are organizational maintainers. One cannot prescribe a solution to these problems any more than one can prescribe for a safe adolescence. One can only point out the kinds of problems and difficulties that are likely to occur, to alert people to expect them, and to be sensitive to them. One such problem stems from the need for founding directors to adjust their behavior to more of a policy role and to become less involved with the actual day-to-day operation of the agency. If the member desires such day-to-day interaction, it would be better to volunteer at another agency rather than to seek to maintain old relationships and patterns in the agency that member founded. A new member, brought in to join a board which was founded in this fashion, is likely to feel irritation and then resign. One has to understand the difference between involvement of founding members as opposed to maintaining members. While this does not mean that license should be given to founding members, an understanding of their perspective often helps to locate their interests and wishes more accurately.

### Decision Accountability

One of the most important initial steps in evaluating decisions and being accountable for them is to make them in the first place. All too often when a problematic decision comes up, people ask, "When did we make that decision?" And, indeed, upon scrutiny of the records it becomes very unclear because the decision ws not made at one point, but evolved at several points. The subcommittee system permits the specific identification of areas of responsibility and the development of decisional formats in those areas of responsibility. These decision proposals then go to the full board where they are acted upon and recorded in the minutes. At the end of the year or whatever time is appropriate, one can go back and ask the question, "What decisions did we make during the particular year?" and review the collective impact on the structure and quality of those decisions overall. Because it is often difficult to assess a decision's impact immediately after it has been made, such retrospective assessment is essential to accountability. Sometimes the wisdom or foolishness of a decision emerges only after time has passed. Such accountability review also takes into consideration the extent to which the information available at the time was suficient and accurate. If an organization continually makes decisions that, as it later turns out, were ill informed, then the process of information generation needs to be studied.

The other aspect of accountability, of course, is implementation. Here the performance audit is useful. The performance audit means taking a specific look at some areas of organizational activity, assessing the speed, quality, integrity, and intelligence with which a decision was implemented. A board is not only responsible for making a decision: it is responsible for seeing to it that the decision is efficiently carried out. Generally, this responsibility falls to the executive director, and it is usually in concert with the executive that the board exercises implementive oversight and control.

## BOARD'S RESPONSIBILITY FOR ROLE APPROPRIATENESS

Board members and the board itself are responsible for acting appropriately within the context of their role. We have discussed the individual requisites of that role, particularly as they regard legal responsibilities and the avoidance of acting in self-aggrandizing and self-profiting ways. More importantly, we have mentioned the positive aspects of one's personal role, that is, acting as a trustee of civic purpose and taking a proactive, accomplishment-oriented posture.

As a means to accomplishing these ends, there are particulars of role performance that are appropriate in carrying out one's organizational responsibilities. For example, there are appropriate ways for a chair to behave and there are appropriate things for a chair to do, which a chair *must* do if organizational purposes are to be achieved. Similarly, there are appropriate member, staff and executives roles. These will not be detailed here; they are discussed at length elsewhere (Tropman, 1980). Suffice to say that there *are* role requisites for chair, member, staffer, and executive. In addition, one can violate, through inappropriate personal behavior, these requisites. I use the phrase *appropriate* to indicate the convention as social rather than legal, but it has force nonetheless.

### The Role of the Board: Internal Functions

In this section, I will discuss the role of the board itself, rather than the roles of the individual members. The board as an entity is responsible for acting appropriately. But what is "appropriate"? There appears to be a great deal of role confusion. I suggest seven functions that a board may perform and discuss them in terms of the different role behaviors that might be required when these different functions are being performed. Just as individuals may well be different at various points during the working day, depending upon the tasks they need to accomplish, so boards need to think about changing their own behavior as a group entity when tasks are different. The seven functions can be divided into two parts: internal functions and external functions. Internal functions relate to deciding policy, overseeing policy, and administering policy. External functions focus upon the interorganizational system.

*Policy Decision Functions.* These typically relate to the board as a whole and refer to those aspects of its role that involve formal legal authority as specified under articles of incorporation and under statutes of the state. Decisions made here are typically referred to as "policy decisions" although other types of decisions may have policy impact as well. Crucial to the policy-deciding function is adequate information, adequate time for review, adequate feedback from appropriate parties, and reasonably prompt action consistent with the available information. What needs to be avoided here is decisional pre- and postmaturity. Prematurity occurs when an item is brought to a policy-deciding meeting in advance of adequate available information. Typically, a great deal of time is spent on such an issue, and then it is postponed. Decisional prematurity is one of the most significant causes of decisional postmaturity. A decision delayed is, all too often, a decision denied. It is legitimate for a director to accuse a board of undue delay. The problem of what is "undue" is difficult. There is no issue on which more information cannot be garnered and on which additional perspectives would not be useful. However, there are often a series of external constraints such as grant deadlines, fiscal year deadlines, and so on, which make the very best informed decision useless if it comes too late. Therefore, within the policy-deciding function, boards need to achieve a balance between information on the one hand, and decisional needs and pressures on the other.

*Policy-Overseeing Functions.* Policy-overseeing functions—seeing that decisions are implemented—are typically accomplished through the subcommittee structure. They involve policy-generating and review components, as well as assessment and program audit elements. Policy oversight occurs once a formal decision is made by the board of directors, and not before. However, the concept of policy oversight involves a certain amount of policy proactivity—that is, the anticipation of upcoming events and the proposed adjustment of existent policies to take those new events into account. Members of policy-overseeing groups must be clear about the scope and extent of the particular policy that is being monitored and should neither overextend their role to encompass areas tangential to it nor ignore or minimize the responsibilities that they do have.

*Policy-Administering Committee.* During unique organizational situations, a policy-administering committee is set up by a board of directors. For example, in an agency crisis, power may be delegated to a small group along with appropriate financial resources, and secretarial and other logistical support to handle a particular situation. Most typically, fast-breaking type situations require the development of such a task force; the task force dissolves when those situations have been resolved.

A second situation in which the administering committee appears is during the initiation stage of an organization. That is, a group of people get together to do a task, make the decisions as they go along, and get enjoyment and gratification from accomplishment of the task itself. Soon they "turn into" an "agency." They then must begin to play more of a "director's" role.

## The Role of the Board: External Functions

Boards of directors of human service agencies play four external roles that are quite different in nature and quality from the internal roles. As agencies move into the interorganizational environment, they no longer have the imperative control given them by their charter and articles of incorporation. Rather, they move from a position based on authority to a stance based on cooperation. There are four external roles that boards may play (and sometimes they may create other community committees that play these roles, too): policy sharing, policy advisory, policy coordinating, and policy implementing.

*Policy Sharing.* Policy sharing is a role in which the board agrees to cooperate with other similar agencies, to acquaint them, and be acquainted with ongoing programs. It does not imply any adjustment in program, nor does it imply that any particular program is right, wrong, appropriate, or inappropriate. It simply reflects an agreement to get together and "show and tell" one's program. This reflects a cooperative posture only.

*The Policy-Coordinating Functions.* Sometimes policy sharing leads to a policy-coordinating function. For example, a board will be asked to perform roles with respect to other organizations in terms of program adjustment. "We'll handle young kids and you handle older kids," it might be suggested. Or "We'll handle boys and you handle girls." These types of adjustments require either prior agreement from the board or actual board agreement once the proposal is made. I suggest that policy coordination without board approval be permitted on a case basis only. Agency or organizational coordination requires conjoint planning and conjoint agreement.

*Policy Implementing.* Sometimes, within the interorganizational system, the board of directors becomes part of a team asked to implement a particular community-wide decision. Again, we are speaking of delegated functions and functions that require constant board oversight and approval. A board member joining a community-wide group for coordinating and implementing purposes does not mean that that individual carries any kind of board approval unless that approval has been specifically given. This is an important function for the board to play, and I strongly encourage boards to participate in policy-sharing, policy-coordinating, and policy-implementing activities at the community level. In such a situation, however, a special subcommittee might well be developed to handle the relationship of the particular organization to the constellation of organizations which are seeking to accomplish even larger social tasks.

*Policy Advisory.* Sometimes a board is asked for a collective opinion on a matter of community concern. The mayor, for example, may call and ask what your agency thinks about an issue. It is not sufficient to simply chew the matter around and then let the executive write up some kind of recommendation. Rather, the matter must be discussed and language must be prepared to reflect the board's perspective. It must be approved by the board and entered into the minutes. A "decision" is actually made during the policy advisory process, but the decision is a piece of advice!

There are certainly many other roles that boards as boards may play. However, these seven, divided between internal and external roles, represent the beginning of a perspective suggesting some of the differences that might be involved. I think that boards need to pay more attention to the external system than they have in the past—particularly in the human service community. Boards, as I have experienced them, tend to be more inwardly focused, playing roles as corporate citizens in the collective community less and less frequently. While it is appropriate that a balance be struck, the emphasis on the word *balance* suggests that some time, and I think more time, needs to be spent in collaborative, coordinating, implementive, and sharing types of roles. Decision-making boards often find it difficult to play these external roles because they relinquish the authority they are used to having when they deal with internal matters. This shift from authoritative posture to cooperative posture is difficult, but it must be carried out in any case.

## THE BOARD AS A TRAINER AND DEVELOPER

Boards have a responsibility for training new members and for developing ongoing members. Nowhere has this need been more seriously recognized than during the efforts to provide "maximum feasible participation of the poor" during the 1960s in the United States. During that time many individuals lacking board experience were brought on to the governing body of nonprofit charitable organizations. Rarely were they provided with any kind of orientation. Joseph Weber and Nellie Hartogs (1974) found that executives rated orientation among the lowest of priorities, while finance and personnel were among the highest. Given the perspectives in this paper, orientation becomes an absolute necessity for new members, and ongoing training is even more a requisite for all directors because they are unlikely to know what to do. Beyond the members, there needs to be some assessment of the growth of the board itself. I will consider the last point first and then suggest ways in which members can improve themselves.

### Board Growth and Development

How do we gauge whether the board is growing and moving in a more sophisticated direction and improving the quality of decisions? There is no one way, but many boards are moving to an annual program evaluation and assessment system. There are two categories of assessment generally used. One concerns itself with member meeting satisfaction, and the second is concerned with assessment of decision quality.

*Meeting Satisfaction.* To measure member meeting satisfaction, the board itself should develop an instrument to assess how well the members felt the meetings had gone during the year. There are a number of categories, such as length of time, pleasantness, adequacy of information, and so on. By developing its own instrument, the board has a greater investment and thus, it is much more likely to follow through on using it and be identified with its results. The training and recruitment committee (one of the board's subcommittees can be asked to take some responsibility here. It is important to keep in mind, however, that satisfaction with the meetings does not necessarily mean that good decisions were made, although dissatisfaction with the meetings is more likely an indicator that poor decisions were made.

*Decision Quality.* Implicit here, of course, and an assumption of any decision quality assessment, is that the minutes are so written and the board processes so structured, that it is possible to pull from the minutes a list of decisions made by the board. These must be listed in terms of their substantive content and orientation, not simply listed as "approval of the budget," but rather sentences and phrases which indicate the nature of and the direction of budgetary thrust for the year. These should be listed on a sheet and reviewed during an assessment session. People are now asked what they think of these decisions. Has any information come up that suggests that they were ill considered? The board rates its decisions on a scale of 1 to 10, A to Z, or any other appropriate scale.

The very act of sitting down and reviewing decisions is, in itself, a positive process.

*Review and Refurbishment.* In addition to reviewing decisions, there is the policy review and refurbishment function. I feel that every seven years boards need to take an in-depth look at their mission, role, and articles of incorporation to ascertain whether any adjustments are necessary. During each year of the six intermediate years, one specific area of agency board relationships is selected for review and refurbished and improved, if needed. Personnel policy might be scrutinized one year, financial policies in another year, and so on. Thus, at the end of the seventh year, all of the subparts of the organization will have been reviewed. Meeting satisfaction and decision quality assessments, when combined with policy review and refurbishment and supplemented with information from the program audits, provide a useful overview of the organizational activity. These reviews could be accomplished during a yearly one to two-day retreat, or at a special meeting in which people can look at the organization, and in doing so, reconsider their own role in it.

*Assessment of the Member.* Assessment of the member is considerably more difficult because of its personal nature. It is best, therefore, to begin on a positive side. I think that each member should have the opportunity for at least one personal growth experience per year. Typically this means attendance at a professional meeting or workshop paid for by the organization. I feel very strongly that this type of compensation (if indeed it is compensation) should represent a priority activity for agencies. Many agencies are very scrupulous about seeking staff development but completely indifferent to board development. In any event, one should assess with members whether there has been the opportunity for personal growth experience and whether that has added to the overall functioning of the board.

In addition, development programs should be run by the organization for board members (and possibly staff) once or twice a year. There are numerous training films available for board members, an outside expert could be invited to speak on board problems and activities, or a relevant article could be distributed and a board discussion organized. It is important that individual members be given the opportunity, within the context of their board membership, to think about their role. That thinking and self-reflection will undoubtedly be positively applied to the specific board in question. There are a number of personal assessment instruments available (see Figure 13.2).

Using these assessments should permit individuals to think through their own roles in a challenging but nonthreatening situation.

## Board Training

Every organized board should have a manual for directors. Again, I stress the use of the word "directors," not members, to emphasize the more vigorous and active director role.

The board manual should begin with a statement of mission, the purpose of the organization, and a brief history and "raison d'etre" of the organization. The legal responsibilities of the organization should then be detailed and should refer the reader to the articles of incorporation listed in the appendix. Following this opening section, there should be a statement of the expected responsibilities of membership, which outlines the role of the director and details the

FIGURE 13.2
Exercise: Am I a Good Board Member?

Is it possible to identify the attributes of the perfect volunteer board member? The question is academic because all human beings are a combination of strengths and of weaknesses. A good board, therefore, blends imperfect human beings into an effective working team.

There are certain attributes which help to make good board members. Some of these are listed here.

| | 0 = No ......... 10 = Yes | |
|---|---|---|
| Good Board Members: | I Am | Others Are |
| 1. Are dedicated to helping others and modest in the light of their responsibilities as board members. | | |
| 2. Approach their responsibilities in the spirit of a trustee on behalf of contributors, their intended beneficiaries, and the public at large. | | |
| 3. Stand up for their convictions, even at the cost of misunderstanding or disapproval in business or social life. | | |
| 4. Back up other board members and staff, rising to their defense when they are unjustly criticized or attacked. | | |
| 5. Treat staff as a partner in a high calling, maintaining overall supervision and control, but not interfering with day-to-day administration. | | |
| 6. Avoid being overawed by others on the board, whether they be executive staff, tycoons of business, labor or society; professionals in social work, education, medicine, etc. | | |
| 7. Welcome information and the best available advice but reserve the right to arrive at decisions on the basis of their own judgment. | | |
| 8. Respect the right of other board members and of staff to disagree with them and to have a fair hearing of their points of view. | | |
| 9. Accept as routine that decisions must be made by majority vote and will at times go against one or more members. | | |
| 10. Criticize when necessary, in a constructive way, if possible suggesting an alternative course. | | |
| 11. Recognize that time and energy are limited and that overcommitment may prove self-defeating. | | |
| 12. Endeavor to keep disagreements and controversies impersonal, and to promote unity. | | |
| 13. Maintain loyalty to their agency, within a higher loyalty to the welfare of the community and humanity as a whole. | | |

SOURCE: "Volunteer Board Member in Philanthropy," National Information Bureau, 419 South Park Avenue, New York, New York 10016. (Reprinted with permission.)

subcommittees and their functions and purposes. A third section, which can be replaced regularly, should deal with the current operating structure of the organization: names, addresses, and telephone numbers of directors; past directors; advisory committees; training program plans; retreat dates; meeting schedules—all of the specific paraphernalia of directorship. It is useful to have the names and addresses of staff on a separate sheet, which can be updated as frequently as necessary. Another section should contain a compilation of annual reports. This gives each member an opportunity to see what the agency has done over time and consider what it is likely to do in the future. Future or projected plans can also be listed here. In addition, it is useful to have a single summary sheet giving historical demographic facts about the agency, such as its annual budget, per capita expenditure on children, and the like.

Finally, if the board feels that there is any pertinent reading material essential to the board member, it can be included as well. This is only a skeletal suggestion for a board manual. Some are more simple and direct; others are more complicated and intricate. What is important is that the board develops its own manual. Following well-accepted practices of community organization, the involvement of the board in developing its own guidelines should be an important guiding principle.

### New Director Training Session

One of the most important types of board training activities is the new director training session. If the suggestion made earlier in this document is followed and the two-tier involvement process used, the new director will not begin from zero. This is too often the case, however, and it frequently takes six months to a year for the new director to become a useful participating member. In either case, whether the new director has participated in ancillary groups or is an inexperienced person in this area, there should be an orientation process. It need not be long, but it should include certain basic matters. First, the substantive thrust, purpose, mission, and commitments of the organization should be explained. While the new director may feel that his/her motives for membership are being changed or detracted by this kind of orientation, substantive contributions will come later; the board members need to know what he or she is getting into first.

A second aspect of the training should deal with the principles of good group decision making. Often this section of the new-member training program can be linked to a training program offered to other individuals on the board. Mutual education involving discussion, participation, and the acquisition of new knowledge is one very good way to establish the new member–old member bonding required for effective and efficient decision making.

## CONCLUSION

This paper has presented some systematic concerns and perspectives on the modern board. It is a much more complex, intricate, and involved process than anyone previously considered. The model board represents one of the essential vehicles through which the pluralism of American values is expressed and through which the historic striving for democratic involvement and participation for decisions which affect individual lives can be orchestrated. And yet, despite these important large-scale social functions, as well as the crucial day-to-day decision functions, board membership is casually, if not shabbily, treated. This casualness and shabbiness is a conspiracy of everyone—members who accept directorships without proper scrutiny and review, those of us who extend invitations to directorship in a thoughtless and offhand manner, executives who put board training at the bottom of the list of priority activities, and society itself, which tends to undervalue, if not devalue, group activities. Human service organizations, whether they be philanthropic or nonprofit, must receive leadership, stewardship, and trusteeship from their boards of directors if they are to survive for the future. No area of the modernization process has been as ignored as the boards of directors in terms of research, training, or suggestion. Those who are seeking to learn more about this area and improve it, hone it, and fine-tune it, are to be commended. It is not a job full of praise and thanks. Rather, one is likely to be greeted with some indifference, ambivalence, and lack of concern. It reminds one of the story of the board training session in which a man said ignorance and apathy are the two major enemies of board activities. A listening board member looked at another and said, "Do you think that is right?" The other board member replied, "I don't know and I don't care." That's the problem as it lies before us. This paper represents a small attempt to move things in the other direction, to reduce apathy and ignorance.

## REFERENCES

Tropman, John E. *Effective Meetings* (Beverly Hills, Calif.: Sage, 1980).

Weber, Joseph. *Managing Boards of Directors* (New York: The Greater New York Fund, 1975).

______ and Nellie Hartogs. *Boards of Directors* (New York: Oceana Publications, 1974).

## BIBLIOGRAPHY

Bennis, Warren G., "RX for Corporate Boards," *Technology Review* (December/January 1979).

______, "The Crisis of Corporate Boards," *Technology Review* (November 1978).

Bridges, Edwin M., Wayne J. Doyle, and David J. Mahand, "Effects of Hierarchical Differentiation on Group Productivity, Efficiency and Risk Taking," *Administrative Science Quarterly* 13 (1968).

Conrad, William R. Jr., and William E. Glenn, "The Effective Voluntary Board of Directors" (Athens, Ohio: Swallow Press Books, 1983).

Glover, E. Elizabeth, *Guide for Board Organization and Administrative Structure* (New York: Child Welfare League of America, 1972).

Greenleaf, Robert K., "1. The Servant as Leader," "2. Trustees as Servants," "3. The Institution as Servant," and "4. The Servant: Retrospect and Prospect," *The Servant Series* (Peterborough, N.H.: Windy Row Press, 43 Grove St., Peterborough, N.H. 03455, 1973).

Griggsby, C., "Separable Liabilities in Directory Trusts," *California Law Review* 60, no. 4 (1972).

Hawkins, A.J., "The Personal Liability of Charity Trustees," *The Law Quarterly Review* 95 (January 1979): 99-116.

Hone, Michael C., "Responsibilities of the Directors of Non-Profit Corporations Under the Proposed Revision of the Model Non-Profit Corporation Act." Paper presented at the American Bar Association Annual Meeting, August 1981 (unpublished paper, School of Law, University of San Francisco).

Houle, Cyril O., "Governing Boards" (San Francisco: Jossey-Bass, 1989).

Levy, Leslie, "Reforming Board Reform," *Harvard Business Review* 59 (January/February 1981): 166-172.

Mueller, Robert Kirk, "The Incomplete Board: the Unfolding of Corporate Governance." (Lexington, Mass.: D.C. Heath and Company, 1981).

National Information Bureau, "The Volunteer Board Member in Philanthropy," (New York: National Information Bureau, 1979).

Oleck, Howard L., *Non-Profit Corporations, Organizations and Associates* (Englewood Cliffs, N.J.: Prentice-Hall, 1980).

Ott, J. Steven, and Joy M. Shafritz, "The Facts on File Dictionary of Nonprofit Organization Management" (New York: Facts on File Publications, 1986).

Palmerie, Victor H., "Corporate Responsibility and the Competent Board," *Harvard Business Review* 57 (May/June 1979): 46-48.

Pascarella, Perry, "The CEO of the 80's," *Industry Week* (January 7, 1980).

Perham, John C., "Non-Profit Boards Under Fire," *Dun's Review* 114, no. 4 (October 1979): 108-113.

Prybil, Lawrence D., "Accountability Invested Trust," *Hospitals* 50 (April 1, 1976): 48-50.

Solomon, Louis D., "Restructuring the Corporate Board of Directors: Fond Hope—Faint Promise?" *Michigan Law Review* 76, no. 4 (March 1978).

Topinka, James E., Barbara H. Shilling, and Carolyn Mar, *A Guide to the California Non-*

*Profit Public Benefit Corporation Law* (San Francisco: The Management Center, 150 Post St., Suite 640, San Francisco, CA 94108).

Trecker, Harley, "Boards Can Be Better: The Productive Board Meeting" (Hartford, Conn.: Community Council of Greater Hartford, April 1980).

_______, "Boards Can Be Better: Board and Staff, The Leadership Team" (Hartford, Conn.: Community Council of Greater Hartford, May 1980).

_______, "Boards Can Be Better: Overview" (Hartford, Conn.: Community Council of Greater Hartford, February 1980).

_______, "Boards Can Be Better: An Annual Check-up for Boards" (Hartford, Conn.: Community Council of Greater Hartford, June 1980).

Tropman, John E., "A Comparative Analysis of Community Organization Agencies," in I. Speigal, ed. *Community Organization: Studies in Constraint* (Beverly Hills, Calif.: Sage, 1972).

_______, *Effective Meetings* (Beverly Hills, Calif.: Sage, 1980).

_______, Harold R. Johnson, and Elmer J. Tropman, *The Essentials of Committee Management* (Chicago: Nelson-Hall, 1979).

Waldo, Charles N., "Boards of Directors: Their Changing Roles, Structures, and Information Needs" (Westport, Conn.: Quorum Books, 1985).

_______, "A Working Guide for Directors of Not-For-Profit Organizations" (Westport, Conn.: Quorum Books, 1986).

Weber, Joseph, *Managing Boards of Directors* (New York: The Greater New York Fund, 1975).

_______, and Nellie Hartogs, *Boards of Directors* (New York: Oceana Publications, 1974).

Weihe, Vernon, "Are Your Board Members Dressed for Their Role?" *Canadian Welfare* 52 (1976).

_______, "Keeping Board Members Informed," unpublished paper, School of Social Professions, University of Kentucky, 1979.

Williams, Harold M., "Corporate Accountability," *Vital Speeches* 44, no. 15 (May 15, 1978): 558-563.

Zelman, William, "Liability for Social Agency Boards," *Social Work* 22, 4 (July 1977): 270-274.

# 14.

**F. Ellen Netting, Peter M. Kettner, and Steven L. McMurtry**

# SELECTING APPROPRIATE TACTICS

## INTRODUCTION

…[S]trategy…refers to the development of a written plan directed at bringing about the proposed change. Deciding on a strategy can be a time-consuming and detailed process. Although many may agree that a problem exists, getting agreement on just how the situation should be changed is seldom easy. Special efforts must be concentrated on tactics designed to get the change accepted.

Tactic selection tests the professional judgment of the change agent, particularly in how to approach the target system. Certain tactics can raise ethical dilemmas. Se-

F. Ellen Netting is a professor at Virginia Commonwealth University; Peter M. Kettner and Steven L. McMurtry are professors at Arizona State University.

lecting tactics calls for mature, professional judgment in community and organizational change. Social workers should be open to the possibility that practices in many of the arenas in which they operate are well entrenched and there will be a natural tendency to resist. The fact that agency missions are stated in inspiring words does not mean that all agencies carry out those missions. Practitioners must be aware that they are a part of legitimized systems that often contribute to the oppression experienced by the client group they are trying to serve. Selecting appropriate tactics requires one to think critically and to carefully analyze the target system.

## FOCUS A: SELECTING APPROPRIATE TACTICS

The choice of tactics is a critical decision point in planned change. Tactics have been defined as "any skillful method used to gain an end" (Brager et al. 1987, 288). Whereas strategy is the long-range linking of activities to achieve the desired goal, tactics are reflected in day-to-day behaviors (Brager & Holloway 1978). As the change agent engages in tactical behavior, it is important not to lose sight of the goal toward which these behaviors are directed.

Brager et al. (1987) identify four essential properties of tactics used by professional change agents: "(1) they are planned...(2) they are used to evoke specific responses...(3) they involve interaction with others...and (4) they are goal-oriented" (p. 288). In addition, it is our contention that a fifth property must be in place in professional social work change efforts: (5) the tactic will do no harm to members of the client system and, whenever possible, members of that system will be involved in tactical decision making.

Change almost always involves influencing the allocation of scarce resources—authority, status, power, goods, services, or money. Decisions about tactics, therefore, must take into consideration whether the resources are being allocated willingly or whether someone must be persuaded to make the allocation. If there is agreement on the part of the action and target systems that the proposed change is acceptable and that resources will be allocated, a collaborative approach can be adopted. If there is agreement that the proposed change is acceptable but a reluctance or refusal to allocate resources, or if there is disagreement about the need for the proposed change, then a more coercive approach may be necessary if the change effort is to proceed.

For example, a change effort may focus on the inability of physically disabled people to get around the city and travel to needed service providers. A thorough study documents the problem, and a dial-a-ride transportation service is proposed. The planning commission and city council graciously accept the report, agree on the need, and thank the Transportation for the Disabled Task Force. Three city council members favor funding, three are opposed, and one is undecided. If the undecided council member can be persuaded to favor funding, then collaborative tactics can be adopted. If, however, he or she decides to oppose funding or if a compromise would undermine the change effort, then tactics designed to coerce support must be adopted. For collaborative approaches to be adopted, there must be agreement on both the proposed change and the allocation of needed resources.

In the social work literature, tactics have been divided into three broad categories: collaboration, campaign, and contest (Brager & Holloway 1978; Brager et al. 1987). In this chapter, we use these terms to describe the relationship between the action and target systems. *Collaboration* implies a working relationship where the two systems agree that change must occur, whereas contest tactics indicate disagreement between the two systems. *Campaign* tactics are used when the target must be convinced of the importance of the change, but when communication is still possible between the two systems. The effectiveness of the "campaign" may determine whether collaboration or contest follows. *Contest* tactics are used when neither of the other two are possible any longer. Change efforts that begin with one set of tactics may progress to other sets, depending on the evolving relationship between the action and target systems. The continuum along which these tactical categories fall is as follows:

Collaboration↔Campaign↔Contest

Although we categorize these relationships, success may hinge on the change agent's ability to keep the action and target systems in a state of continual interaction. It is possible that what begins as a collaborative relationship will move to conflict when new issues arise during the change process. It is equally likely that the relationship will vascillate between various gradations of communication, with both systems uncertain about the other, even when compromise can be reached. In short, these relationships ebb and flow, sometimes unpredictably, given the political situation, and sometimes all too predictably, given the change agent's prior experience with the target system.

Our concern is that the social worker never take the relationship between the action and target system for granted. To assume that the target is immovable before communication has been attempted demonstrates poor use of professional judgment. To assume that the target will embrace the cause once the facts are known is naive. Assumptions have little place in assessing the relationship between the action and the target system. We believe that regardless of what types of tactics are used, communication should be maintained with the target system if at all possible. If communication ceases, it should be because the target system refuses to continue interaction.

Within each of the three categories are tactics that are typically used. The framework in Table 14.1 guides our discussion. Some of the following conceptualization is drawn from previous literature (Brager & Holloway 1978; Brager et al. 1987). In some areas, we offer slightly different perspectives and add new tactics. Throughout the following discussion, we attempt to provide an analytical framework to guide an action system in selecting the most appropriate mix of tactics.

## Collaboration

*Implementation.* Collaborative approaches include instances when the target and action system agree that change is needed. Under collaboration, we place (1) implementation and (2) capacity building tactics.

Implementation tactics are used when the action and target systems work together cooperatively. When these systems agree that change is needed and allocation of resources is supported by critical decision makers, the change simply needs to be implemented. Implementation will most likely involve some problem solving, but it is not expected that adversarial relationships will be a concern in these type of collaborative efforts.

*Capacity Building.* Capacity building includes the tactics of participation and em-

TABLE 14.1
Tactical Behaviors

| Relationship of Action and Target Systems | Tactics |
|---|---|
| *Collaboration* | |
| Target System agrees (or is easily convinced to agree) with action system that change is needed and supports allocation of resources | 1. Implementation<br>2. Capacity building |
| *Campaign* | a. Participation<br>b. Empowerment |
| Target system is willing to communicate with action system, but there is little consensus that change is needed: or target system supports change but not allocation of resources | 3. Education<br>4. Persuasion<br>a. Cooptation |
| *Contest* | b. Lobbying<br>5. Mass media appeal |
| Target system opposes change and/or allocation of resources and is not open to further communication about opposition | 6. Bargaining and negotiation<br>7. Large-group or community action<br>a. Legal (e.g., demonstrations)<br>b. Illegal (e.g., civil disobedience)<br>8. Class action lawsuit |

powerment. Participation refers to those activities that involve members of the client system in the change effort. Empowerment is the process of "helping a group or community to achieve political influence or relevant legal authority" (Barker 1987, p. 49).

For example, a problem may be defined as exclusion of a neighborhood from decisions that affect them. The focus of the intervention is on building a capacity for greater self-direction and self-control—that is, actually teaching people how to get involved in the decision-making processes in their communities and taking greater control over the decisions that affect their lives. This approach often emerges in situations where disenfranchised communities become targets for development, freeways, airport expansion, and other such encroachments.

Through professionally assisted change efforts, perhaps led by a neighborhood social service organization (change agent system), neighborhood resident (client system), and city council (controlling system and perhaps target system) agree that community citizens should have a greater voice in developments that affect their community. The focus of the change or intervention, however, is not on the target system (city council/planning commission) but on educating, training, and preparing community citizens for a fuller participation in decisions that affect their communities. Tactics would include education, training, and actual participation in civic organizations and activities.

Empowerment involves enabling people to become aware of their rights, and teaching them how to exercise those rights so that they become better able to take control over factors that affect their lives. Mobilizing the efforts of self-help groups and voluntary associations...as well as the client system's informal support structure may be used to assist in guiding the target system toward consensus with the change effort.

## Campaign

Campaign implies a group effort to convince target system members that a cause is just or a change is needed, and that resources should be allocated. Campaign tactics require a good deal of skill on the part of the change agent and action system. Lack of consensus rules out collaboration, yet a firm disagreement has not been established. Under this heading we include the use of education, persuasion, and mass media appeals designed to influence public opinion.

*Education.* Educational tactics can be an integral part of campaigns. Therefore, we use educational tactics to describe those interactions in which the action system presents perceptions, attitudes, opinions, data, and information about the proposed change with the intent of convincing the target system to think or to act differently. The objective is to inform. The assumption is that more and better information will lead to a change in behavior. It is a difficult tactic to use because opponents of the change can also be expected to inform decision makers armed with different sets of data and information, and there is seldom an absolute "truth" in dealing with complex organizational and community problems. In many cases where education fails to produce the desired result or falls short of having the desired impact, the change agent turns to persuasion.

*Persuasion.* Persuasion refers to the art of convincing others to accept and support one's point of view or perspective on an issue. Social workers must frequently use persuasive tactics in addition to collaboration because their causes are not always embraced by decision makers, who often must be convinced through persuasion that the change is worth pursuing. This means that the change agent must understand the motives and reasoning of the target system in order to identify what incentives can be used to negotiate an agreement.

Skillful communication requires that the action system must carefully select its leadership from those persons who have the ability to persuade. Persons who are seen as nonthreatening to the target system and who can articulate the reasoning behind the planned change are particularly useful. For example, in a change effort, particular actors may be perceived as unreasonable, as troublemakers, or as chronic complainers by members of the controlling system. It is not in the best interest of the client system for those persons to be the only spokespeople for the change. Clients themselves can also be powerful spokespersons, providing information and a viewpoint that persuades people of the need for change.

Framing the problem statement to make it more palatable to target system members is a persuasive technique. This requires the ability to think as the target thinks. For example, a social worker hired as a long-term care ombudsperson was working closely with a coalition of advocates for nursing-home reform to end abuse in long-term care facilities. Nursing-home administrators were very upset over the nursing-home reform coalition and perceived them as not understanding the difficulties with which they coped on a daily basis. They sincerely wanted to provide quality care, but were frustrated by staff who were not properly trained to work with geriatric populations. By framing the problem as a training problem designed to better prepare employees and reduce turnover, the ombudsperson was able to persuade administrators to cooperate with the action system. When the ombudsperson met with the local nursing home association, she acknowledged that she was aware that the administrators wanted to operate high-quality facilities. She also noted that recent studies revealed that high staff turnover rates often contributed to lack of continuity and lower patient care, sometimes leading to abuse. She explained that she and her colleagues would be willing to develop training for nurses aides because they interacted most intimately with patients, yet were most vulnerable to high turnover. Essentially, one of the contributing factors leading to abuse was being addressed, but it was framed as reducing an administrative nightmare—high staff turnover.

Cooptation is defined as minimizing anticipated opposition by absorbing or including members of the target system in the action system. Once target system members are part of the planned changed effort, it is likely that they will assume some ownership of the change process. Persuasion is used to coopt new persons into the action system. This is valuable to the success of the change effort because it is important to include persons who are viewed as powerful by the target system. These persons may be relatively neutral and may have little interest in obstructing the change effort. However, if they can be convinced to support the change effort (or even to allow their names to be used in publicity), their participation may sway others who respect their opinions. Cooptation is most effective as a tactic when opponents or neutral parties can be helped to recognize a self-interest in the proposed change.

Cooptation can be formal or informal. Coopting individuals is called informal cooptation, whereas coopting organized groups is referred to as formal cooptation. Formal cooptation means that an entire group agrees to support a cause. Because their governing structure agrees that the change effort is worthwhile, the group may issue a statement to that effect. This formalizes the commitment, even though there are always members of any group who may, as individuals, disagree with the proposed change.

Formal cooptation of a number of groups leads to coalition building. A coalition is a loosely woven, ad hoc association of constituent groups, each of whose primary identification is outside the coalition (Haynes & Mickelson 1986). For example, the purpose of the National Health Care Campaign is to provide health care coverage to all American citizens. This change effort brings together hundreds of organizations such as the National Association of Social Workers and the American Public Health Association. On a state by state basis, health care campaign chapters are forming. Interested change agents have encouraged local groups to join in the efforts—forming a coalition dedicated to the stated goal. The diversity of the coalition contributes to a powerful alliance of individuals and groups that vascillate between collaboration and campaign tactics as they attempt to address health care needs.

Lobbying is a form of persuasion that addresses policy change under the domain of the controlling system. The action system will have to determine if it is necessary to change agency policy, to amend current legislation or to develop new legislation in order to achieve their goal. Haynes and Mickelson (1986) delineate three essential concepts for social work/lobbyists to consider. First, one should always be factual and honest. Trying to second guess or stretching the facts to support one's position is devastating to one's professional reputation as well as to the change effort's credibility. Second, any presentation should be straightforward and supported by the available data. The problem identification and analysis process...will assist the change agent in organizing the rationale for change. Third, any discussion should include the two critical concerns of decision makers—cost and social impact of what is proposed. If the cost is high, the social worker is advised to calculate the costs of allowing the identified problem to remain unresolved.

*Mass Media Appeal.* Mass media appeal refers to the development and release of newsworthy stories to the print and electronic media for the purpose of influencing public opinion. This tactic is used to pressure decision makers into a favorable resolution to the identified problem. The expectation is that if the proposed change can be presented to the public in a positive way and decision makers' refusal to support the proposed change can be presented as obstructionist or somehow negative, then decision makers will feel pressured to change their position. Where decision makers are high-profile people like elected representatives who depend on a positive public perception, this can be an effective tactic. Use of mass media depends on news reporters' agreement that the proposed change is a newsworthy story, and assurance that one's cause will be presented accurately. Use of any media must always include consideration of clients' rights to privacy.

### Contest

Under the heading of contest we include the use of bargaining and negotiating, the use of large group or community action, or class action lawsuits. Large groups in community action can be further divided into legal and illegal tactics. Contest tactics are used in situations where: (1) the target system cannot be persuaded by the action system, (2) the target system refuses to communicate with the action system, or (3) it is perceived that only lipservice is being given to the proposed change. Contest tactics mean that the change effort becomes an open, public conflict as attempts are made to draw broad support and/or to pressure or even force the target system into supporting or at least accepting the change. Once this occurs, the action system must be prepared to face open confrontation and to escalate its coercive techniques.

Conflict is inevitable in social work practice. There will be times in the experience of every macro practitioner when incredible resistance is encountered in addressing the needs of oppressed population groups. Social work as a profession developed in response to a basic societal conflict—the persistent antagonism over individualism and the common good. Conflicts over the rights of various population groups have spawned violent confrontations rooted in basic value systems and beliefs. We believe that physical violence and terrorism cannot be condoned in any change efforts in a civilized society. Nonviolent confrontation, however, including civil disobedience, is an option when there is a communication stalemate between the target and action systems.

Contest tactics will require widespread commitment and possible participation from members of the support system. It is critical to the success of these tactics that the support system and its subsystems—initiator, client, and change agent—are comfortable with contest tactics because there are risks that are not present when using collaboration and campaign tactics. It is likely that the time and energy necessary for effective change will increase and relationships can become disrupted. When collaborative and campaign tactics are employed, tactics can move toward contest. However, once contest tactics are employed it is not likely that one can return to collaborative or campaign tactics. Without a clear understanding of what contest tactics involve and without full commitment from the support system, contest tactics are not advised.

*Bargaining and Negotiation.* Bargaining and negotiation refer to those situations in which the action and target system confront one another with the reasons for their opposition. Bargaining and negotiation occur when there is a recognized power differential between parties and a compromise needs to be made. These tactics are more formalized than persuasion, often involving a third-party mediator. Members of the target system will typically agree to negotiate when the following factors are in place: (1) there is some understanding of the intentions and preferred outcomes of the action system, (2) there is a degree of urgency, (3) the relative importance and scope of the proposed change is known, (4) there are resources that facilitate the exercise of power, and (5) they perceive the action system as having some legitimacy. In order to negotiate, both the action and the target systems must perceive that each has something the other wants, otherwise there is no reason to come together (Brager et al. 1987).

Bargaining and negotiation can result in a win-win situation, where both target and action systems are pleased with and fully support the outcome. The result can be a win-lose where one system is clearly the victor, or a lose-lose where both systems give something up and are disappointed in the results.

*Large Group or Community Action.* Large group or community action refers to the preparing, training, and organizing of large numbers of people who are willing to form a pressure group and advocate for change through various forms of such collective action as picketing, disruption of meetings, sit-ins, boycotting, and other pressure tactics. Peaceful demonstrations are legal activities, often used by both groups at either extreme of an issue, to express their views. Civil disobedience activities intentionally break the law. When action system members deliberately engage in illegal activities, they must be ready to accept the consequences of their actions. The change agent is responsible for making potential participants fully aware of these risks before the decision is made to proceed.

*Class Action Lawsuits.* Class action lawsuits refer to those instances where an entity is sued for a perceived violation of the law and it is expected that the finding of the court will apply to an entire class of people. These tactics are often used with highly vulnerable populations such as the chronically mentally ill, the homeless, or children, where it is unlikely that they have the capacity or the resources to protect their own rights. Public interest law organizations may be resources for the action system in developing class action tactics.

### Considerations in Selecting Tactics

A few salient considerations need to be weighed in selecting the best tactic or mix of tactics. These considerations include:

1. What are the current *objectives* of the change effort?
2. What is the perception (by those promoting change) of the *controlling and host systems*?
3. What is the perception (by those promoting change) of the role of the *client system*?
4. What *resources* are needed and available for each tactic?
5. What are the *ethical* dilemmas inherent in the range of tactical choices?

*Objectives.* Objectives often tend to evolve as the change process moves along,

TABLE 14.2
Relationship of Current Objectives to Tactics

| Current Objective | Relationship of Target and Action System | Possible Tactics |
|---|---|---|
| 1. Solving a substantive problem; providing a needed service | Collaborative | Implementation through joint action |
| 2. Self-direction; self-control | Collaborative | Capacity building through participation and empowerment |
| 3. Influencing decision makers | In disagreement but with open communication | Education, and persuasion through . cooptation, lobbying, etc |
| 4. Changing public opinion | In disagreement but with open communication | Education, persuasion, mass media appeal. |
| | Adversarial | Large group or community action |
| 5. Shifting power | Adversarial | Large group or community action |
| 6. Mandating action | Adversarial | Class action lawsuit |

and a reexamination prior to selection of tactics is in order. For example, with the problem of domestic violence, the condition may have been brought to public awareness by the perceived need for additional emergency shelter space for battered women. However, as the problem is analyzed and better understood, the objectives may shift toward consciousness raising for all women in the community who are perceived to be at risk of violence. Thus strategy and tactics would move from advocating for service provision to educating for empowerment. Since tactics can change as objectives change, it is worthwhile to make one last check to insure that all are clear and in agreement on current objectives. The following questions can be used to guide the action system's reexamination of the change objectives.

1. What are the stated objectives of this change effort?
2. Given what has been learned in the change process thus far, do the stated objectives need to be revised?
3. Which best describes the intent of the current objectives?
   a. to solve a substantive problem or provide a needed service
   b. to increase self-direction or self-control of the client system
   c. to influence decision makers
   d. to change public opinion
   e. to shift power
   f. to mandate action
4. Do members of the action system have any concerns about the intent of the current objectives that require further discussion?

The range of objectives and likely accompanying tactics are indicated in Table 14.2.

*Controlling and Host Systems.* The controlling and host systems can be perceived in a variety of ways. If they are seen as employers or sponsors of the change, then collaboration is likely. If they are seen as supporters of, but not participants in the change, capacity building (through participation and empowerment) may be the tactic of choice. If they are seen as neutral or indifferent, a campaign strategy may be in order. If, however, they are seen as oppres-

TABLE 14.3
Relationship of Controlling and Host System Roles to Tactics

| Perception of Role of Controlling and Host Systems | Relationship of Controlling, Host, and Action Systems | Possible Tactics |
|---|---|---|
| 1. Sponsors; supporters; co-participants; colleagues | Collaborative | Implementation through joint action |
| 2. Neutrality or indifference | Collaborative | Capacity building through participation and empowerment |
| 3. Uninformed barriers; not sure about change | In disagreement but with open communication | Education and persuasion |
| 4. Informed barriers; opponents to successful change | Adversarial | Bargaining; large-group or community action |
| 5. Oppressors | Adversarial | Large-group or community action |
| 6. Violators of rights | Adversarial | Class action lawsuit |

sive or unresponsive to their primary clientele, then some type of contest approach will likely be selected. Discussion of the following questions may assist the action system in assessing their relationship with the controlling and host system.

1. Who are the critical actors in the host and controlling system(s)?
2. What term(s) best describe(s) the action system members' perceptions of the host and controlling system actors?
   a. sponsors, supporters, co-participants, or colleagues
   b. neutral or indifferent actors
   c. uniformed barriers who are not sure about change
   d. informed barriers or opponents
   e. oppressors
   f. violators of rights
3. Are action system members' perceptions similar or dissimilar?
4. If they are dissimilar, what are the different perceptions and what are the implications of this divergence of opinion for the change effort?

Table 14.3 illustrates the various perceptions of roles that might be assigned to the controlling and host systems, and the logical tactic for each.

*Primary Client.* *The role of the primary client* can vary, and the way in which this role is perceived can affect selection of change tactics. Sometimes it may be difficult to determine who the primary client really is. For example, in addressing the needs of the elderly, the change agent may discover that caregivers are suffering from stress and fatigue. In this situation, one must ask if the primary beneficiaries of a change effort will be the older persons themselves or their caregivers?

If the primary client is seen as a consumer or recipient of service, then a collaborative change approach is the most likely tactic. If the primary role is as a resident of a community or potential participant in an effort to achieve self-direction and control, then a capacity building approach is, perhaps, more appropriate. If the primary client is seen as a person who needs a ser-

TABLE 14.4
Relationship of Client-System Role to Tactics

| Perception of Role of Client System | Relationship Client and Target Systems | Possible Tactics |
|---|---|---|
| 1. Consumer; recipient of service | Collaborative | Implementation through joint action |
| 2. Resident of the community in need of greater self-direction and self-control | Collaborative | Capacity building through participation and empowerment |
| 3. Citizen/taxpayer not permitted full full participation | In disagreement but with open communication | Education and persuasion |
| 4. Victim; underserved needy person | Adversarial | Mass media appeal |
| 5. Victim; emploited person | Adversarial | Large group or community action |
| 6. Person denied civil rights | Adversarial | Class action lawsuit |

vice (but this need is not acknowledged by the controlling system), as a victim, or as a voter or constituent with potential power to influence decision makers, then some type of contest approach is likely to be employed. The following questions guide the action system in assessing the role of the primary client.

1. Who is defined as the primary client?
2. How do members of the action system describe the primary client?
   a. consumer or recipient of service
   b. resident of the community in need of self-direction or self-control
   c. citizen taxpayer not permitted full participation
   d. victim, underserved needy person
   e. victim, exploited person
   f. person denied civil rights
3. Do action system members agree or disagree in their descriptions of the primary client? Do clients agree or disagree?
4. What role does the primary client play within the action system?
5. How much overlap is there between the client and the action systems?
6. What mechanisms does the action system use to obtain input from the client system?

Table 14.4 displays client roles, approaches, and tactics.

*Resources.* Finally, *resources available to the action system* should be examined in relation to each of the tactics being considered. If collaboration is the tactic of choice, then several resources are needed. These include technical expertise capable of understanding whether or not the change is being properly implemented, monitored, and evaluated. In order for a capacity building tactic to be used, grass roots organizing ability, together with some teaching and training expertise, must be available to the action system. If there is conflict, either skilled persuaders, media support, large numbers of people willing to do what is necessary to bring about change, or legal

TABLE 14.5
Resources Needed by Action Systems for Each Tactic

| Tactic | Resources Needed |
|---|---|
| 1. Collaboration—joint action or problem solving | Technical expertise; monitoring and evaluation capability |
| 2. Capacity building | Grass roots organizing ability; teaching/training expertise; opportunities for participation; some indigenous leadership; willing participants |
| 3. Persuasion | Informed people; data/information; skilled persuaders/ lobbyists |
| 4. Mass media appeal | Data/information; newsworthy issue or slant; access to news reporters; technical expertise to write news releases |
| 5. Large group or community action | Large numbers of committed people (support system); training and organizing expertise; informed leadership; bargaining and negotiating skills |
| 6. Class action lawsuits | Legal expertise; victims willing to bring action and provide information; at least enough money for court costs |

expertise must be available. The following questions may assist the action system in assessing resources.

1. What tactics are being considered at this point?
2. What resources will be needed to adequately use these tactics? (e.g., expertise, training, time, funding, equipment, etc.)
3. What members of the action system have access to the needed resources?
4. If additional resources are needed, should the boundaries of the action system be expanded to include persons/ groups who have access to additional resources?

Resource considerations are illustrated in Table 14.5.

*Professional Ethics.* ...Ethics are the behaviors that bring values into action. An ethical dilemma is defined as a situation in which a choice has to be made between equally important values. Tactical choices are no exception. Decisions regarding what tactics to use are based on the values held by action system members. It is often the clash of action and target system values that leads to the selection of contest tactics.

Three ethical principles [discussed in a previous chapter were] autonomy, beneficence, and justice. These principles are deeply enmeshed in macro-practice change. A clash between autonomy and beneficence occurs when the client system is not willing to risk the little they have, yet, when the action system wants to push for a quality of life change. The client system may have limited control over their lives, but their right to decide (self-determination) that they do not want to risk the little control they have must be respected by action system members if it is clear that client system opinion is being fairly represented. Alternately, the action system may be heavily composed of professionals who are acting on the principle of beneficence. They may sincerely believe that they know what is best for the client system. Rights of clients take precedence over the wishes of the action system when such a conflict emerges.

This clash was illustrated in a social work intern's first field experience. Working for a small community center in the southwest, she discovered that many of her Hispanic clients lived in a crowded apartment complex with faulty wiring and inadequate plumbing. With the backing of her agency, she began talking with clients to see if they would be willing to engage in a change process directed toward their living conditions. As she analyzed the situation, she realized that any change process would involve housing and public health personnel in the action system. Her clients begged her not to bring these concerns to the attention of local authorities. Many members of the client system were illegal aliens and they feared that their exposure to public authorities would assure their deportation. The client system was willing to accept poor housing conditions rather than risk the consequences of exposure. The client system's autonomy was in conflict with the change agent system's beneficence.

The clash between justice and autonomy is exemplified when the action system demands redistribution of resources and the target system believes that in giving up their control over valued resources they have less freedom. Macro change frequently appeals to the principle of justice, for it is usually through the redistribution of valued resources (e.g., power, money, status, etc.) that change occurs. Because justice is a basic ethical principle that raises emotions when it is violated, change agents can become so obsessed with injustice that any means is viewed as an appropriate tactic if it leads to a successful end. It is our contention that this type of thinking can lead to professional anarchy whereby tactics are perceived as weapons to punish the target system rather than as actions to enrich the client system. In these situations it may be too easy for the change to take on a life of its own and for the professional to assume a beneficent role. Righteous indignation may overtake sound judgment.

[Sometimes it is appropriate to consider] the use of covert tactics in certain situations where legitimate channels of communication have been tried and where clients agree that covert means may be their only chance for success. These considerations must be carefully weighed because the use of covert tactics usually raises ethical concerns.

To guide the action system in discussing professional ethics, we pose the following questions:

1. What are the value conflicts between the target and action systems?
2. What ethical principle(s) appear to be guiding the activities of the action system?
3. Is there the potential for a clash of ethical principles between the client and action systems?
4. If covert tactics are being considered, what conditions have led to this decision?
   a. The mission of the target agency or the community mandate is being ignored.
   b. The mission of the target agency or the community mandate is being denied for personal gain.
   c. Change efforts have been tried through legitimate channels but the

target system will not listen.

d. Client system members are fully aware of the risks involved, but are willing to take the risks.

e. Other ________________________

There are very few situations where there is clearly a right or wrong tactic. Berlin (1990) explains, "we are all vulnerable to oversimplified bipolarizations. We search for order, find meaning in contrasts, and learn by maintaining an 'essential tension' between divergent experiences, events, and possibilities. It is this allowance of contrasts that differentiates either-or, narrowing and excluding bipolarizations from those that are encompassing or transforming" (p. 54).

It is common to think dichotomously (e.g., win-lose, right-wrong, good-bad, consensus-conflict). In conflict situations, dichotomous thinking may assist the radical change agent in believing that the target system represents evil, whereas the action system represents good. This fuels the fire of confrontation and is appropriate in some situations. However, we believe that the professional social worker has a responsibility to carefully analyze what is happening before making assumptions that lead directly to the use of contest tactics. This means that the majority of change efforts will utilize collaboration and campaign tactics as the action and target systems attempt to communicate with one another. Although consensus-conflict is a dichotomy, we believe that the majority of interactions happen in the various gradations in-between—where varying degrees of communication occur.

If the action system attempts to collaborate or is willing to compromise but the target system remains unmoved, then contest tactics may have to be employed. What professionals must guard against, however, is action system members making assumptions about target system members without attempting to communicate with them. In short, decisions about what tactics to use depends on the situation, the proposed change, and the relationships among actors in the action, client, and target systems.

## FOCUS B: PREPARING A WRITTEN PLAN

When all the foregoing tasks have been completed, the proposed change should be written up in the form of a short, concise plan. This will include a few pages on the purpose, the problem, and the proposed change. A page on costs, and a few pages on expected benefits should make clear what resources will be requested, how they will be spent, and what benefits will be derived from implementation of the proposed change.

A few pages should be used to lay out the strategy and tactics, outlining roles, responsibilities and time lines in Gantt chart form. This will be helpful in insuring that the proposed strategy and tactics are well coordinated as they are implemented. Any documents from the data collection and problem analysis phases that are felt to be helpful and are clear and concise can be attached to the plan.

This brings the change effort up to the point where it is ready for action. A community or organizational problem affecting a target population has been identified and thoroughly thought out. A general approach to an intervention has been proposed, and a hypothesis developed proposing a relationship between problem, intervention, and outcomes. Alternative strategies have been carefully thought through, participants selected, issues weighed, and tactics selected.

Clearly there is more to be done prior to the full implementation of change. It is not the intent [here], however, to get into the details of project or program planning. The macro practitioner, as conceptualized here, could reasonably be expected to withdraw at the point of acceptance of the proposed change and turn responsibilities over to those who will provide leadership in implementation of the policy, program, or project experts.

**CONCLUSION**

...[As with all tactics, a] proposed plan of action is sketched out, including specification of key participants, activities, and time lines.

As with all professional practice, the approach is modified by the practitioner to fit the situation. If conditions dictate immediate action, some procedures will be shortened or streamlined. If time allows and the significance of the proposed change dictates, each task will be carried out with careful attention to detail.

In any case, it is our position that some changes will always be needed in the field of human services, both in organizations and in communities. These changes, we believe, require the professional assistance and consultation of social workers knowledgeable about macro-level change. They require informed, and sometimes scholarly participation and guidance in order to insure that what is achieved is what is most needed to address the social problem in the best interest of the target population.

We believe that social workers are well qualified to lead or coordinate the planning stages of such change efforts and to bring them to the point of action, and this book is intended to assist in that process. As the change effort moves into its next stages, we would expect that the necessary expertise—legal, media, organizing, planning, designing, managing, or whatever is needed—would be sought from additional available sources and from elsewhere in the social work literature.

**REFERENCES**

Barker, R. L. (1987) *The social work dictionary*. Silver Spring, MD: National Association of Social Workers.

Berlin, S. B. (1990) Dichotomous and complex thinking. *Social Service Review*, 64(1): 46-59.

Brager, G., and S. Holloway. (1978) *Changing human service organizations: Politics and practice*. New York: Free Press.

Brager, G., H. Specht, and J. L. Torczyner. (1987) *Community organizing*. New York: Columbia University Press.

Haynes, K. S., and J. S. Mickelson. (1986) *Affecting change: Social workers in the political arena*. New York: Longman.

**APPENDIX A: ACTION SYSTEM DISCUSSION IN CONSIDERATION TACTICS**

## Objectives

1. What are the stated objectives of this change effort?
2. Given what has been learned in the change process thus far, do the stated objectives need to be revised?
3. Which best describes the intent of the current objectives?
   a. to solve a substantive problem or provide a needed service
   b. to increase self-direction or self-control of the client system
   c. to influence decision makers
   d. to change public opinion
   e. to shift power
   f. to mandate action

4. Do members of the action system have any concerns about the intent of the current objectives that require further discussion?

**Controlling and Host Systems**

5. Who are the critical actors in the host and controlling system(s)?
6. What term(s) best describes the action system members' perceptions of the host and controlling system actors?
   a. sponsors, supporters, co-participants, or colleagues
   b. neutral or indifferent actors
   c. uninformed barriers who are not sure about change
   d. informed barriers or opponents
   e. oppressors
   f. violators of rights
7. Are action system members' perceptions similar or dissimilar?
8. If they are dissimilar, what are the different perceptions and what are the implications of this divergence of opinion for the change effort?

**Primary Client**

9. Who is defined as the primary client?
10. How do members of the action system describe the primary client?
    a. consumer or recipient of service
    b. resident of the community in need of self-direction or self-control
    c. citizen taxpayer not permitted full participation
    d. victim, underserved needy person
    e. victim, exploited person
    f. person denied civil rights
11. Do action system members agree or disagree in their descriptions of the primary client?
12. What role does the primary client play within the action system?
13. How much overlap is there between the client and the action systems?
14. What mechanisms does the action system use to obtain input from the client system?

15.

**Geoffrey Pawson and Terry Russell**

# SOCIAL PLANNING: A CHILD WELFARE EXEMPLAR

Ross suggests that the impetus for social planning is dissatisfaction within a community about a particular condition (1955:135). Gilbert and Specht (1977:1), however, contend that in most situations social plans are developed and implemented by experts who often rely on their own conception of community well-being.

In child welfare, the relationship between a child, the child's parents, and the community is a triad that requires support to maximize the potential of the relationship. This interdependency experiences stress when the types of support that society must offer are nontraditional since parents and communities are highly protective of the sanctity of the family. Community desires to preserve the traditional meaning of family present severe barriers to legislative reform, and few politicians are willing to challenge such opinions even if they are cognizant of problems that require attention.

Hibbard (1981:557-65) argues that a new social planning paradigm rests on cultural pluralism, and although there is a range of viewpoints as to how it should be applied, the common element is the displacement of authority for planning from experts and elites to those involved in social interactions. Social planning interventions must include the various individuals and groups that will be affected as well as the larger community that may be indirectly involved.

Boles (1980:344-59) traces the development of comprehensive day care legislation in the United States. Despite three separate bills introduced in the Congress and Senate, day care is still thought of as a program for the poor based on the assumption that it will facilitate their obtaining or maintaining employment. Boles concludes that legislation providing such care to a range of different people may be possible if programs are federally guaranteed under a specific funding formula, but the responsibility for program design and administration must rest with local providers and consumers. This allows for local differences within a pluralistic society; also, it strongly indicates that services for a range of families are likely to follow a path of incremental development.

The basic strategy of the social worker in community planning for children and families may be to support an incremental growth of services rather than fight for universal programs. As communities have opportunities to consider the benefits of programs available in other jurisdictions, citizens can be encouraged to initiate their own efforts to obtain such services. In order to minimize local resistance, practitioners should promote the establishment of quality programs that are not perceived as radical innovations. Further, efforts should be made to involve a range of potential consumer groups in planning forums that allow people involvement in de-

---

Geoffrey Pawson is executive director of Ranch Erlo Society, Regina, Saskatchewan; Terry Russell is director of Child and Youth Services, Regina Mental Health Region, Saskatchewan.

signing the types of programs they are ready to utilize.

The community practitioner needs to maintain a short- and a long-term perspective in social planning. For example, new ideas in child welfare and family services can be introduced through attempts to prompt agencies and community groups to establish new programs. Although these may be rejected in the short term, the ideas that are planted may germinate later.

The potential for planned change based upon empirical data, internally consistent approaches, and trial or pilot applications is clearly evident. However, the practitioner must encourage participants to include as part of the strategy a variety of contingency plans, since what seems a logical and rational case of action to planners based upon their knowledge and perceptions may not be perceived as valuable by constituents with limited information or different needs. This suggests that community education and public relations are vital factors in the planning process. Mechanisms to educate the public can include widely circulated factual documents, public forums, conferences, community advisory groups, and other forms of constituency involvement. These mechanisms inform citizens, clarify issues, and encourage inputs that can serve to revise proposed plans in order to increase their acceptability.

Local citizen groups and their representatives should be given opportunities to exchange ideas and express their attitudes. Even planning at regional and federal levels should offer the opportunity for communities to control what happens in their jurisdiction. This does not assume that local area management is most beneficial for clients; rather, it assumes that an incremental approach based on local control is most productive in the long run, and encourages development of a variety of programs that reflect local attitudes and customs.

## COMMUNITY DEVELOPMENT

The major emphasis in community development is the process of community building where the organizer creates an identification of common interests through stimulating and facilitating community awareness and involvement and the growth of citizen leadership (Brager and Specht 1973:27). Many of these concepts have evolved in rural areas or undeveloped countries, and they have been translated, with some difficulty, to urban areas within North America (Grosser 1973:204).

An example is the case of Sandy Bay, an isolated Indian village in northern Saskatchewan, Canada. In the past thirty years, the social fabric of this community has been devastated by change due to the village's location in a resource-rich area of the province. As a result of outside intrusions, traditional patterns of mutual help through extended families and neighborhood networks began to deteriorate, and children were particularly vulnerable. Previously, children were an accepted community responsibility; if parents could not care for their children, another family provided for them.

In the early 1960's, Sandy Bay was accessible only by air or overland through the bush. Local services were provided by an outpost nurse, a policeman, and a priest, all of whom were residents in the community. When children were neglected or temporarily abandoned, a provincial child welfare worker was contacted by radiophone to come up and investigate the problem. In many cases, children were temporarily removed from the village until parents returned or family disputes were resolved.

This system was extremely expensive and not particularly effective.

Because the village was identified as having some of the worst social problems in the area, a community development project was planned for Sandy Bay by the Department of Social Services. Social workers began flying into the village and staying for several days. Initially they slept in an abandoned building because of the lack of housing, but this inconvenience was necessary in order to meet the local people and become familiar with village customs. It became clear quite early in the process that the only formal group in the community was the local chapter of Alcoholics Anonymous (AA), whose members met nightly at the recreation center. Workers joined this group every evening and noted that both children and adults came to the recreation hall to talk with this group.

Gradually, the subject of protective services was introduced by the social worker, and the group was asked to consider alternatives to the present system of care. A child care committee was formed after extensive deliberations lasting several months, during which the expectations and responsibilities of the proposed committee were examined in great detail. Finally, the committee developed both an approach to the problem that included identification of children requiring protection within the village and a resource network utilizing extended family members and neighbors (Soiseth 1970:8-9).

The Minister of Social Services for Saskatchewan formally recognized the work of the group with a plaque that was hung in the local recreation hall. Further, one member of the committee was authorized to serve as a resident child welfare worker, under the authority of existing legislation, and he was provided with an identification that indicated his status and legal authority in child welfare matters. From this small beginning, Sandy Bay residents went on meeting and set up day care services, a group home for older adolescents, foster care, and an alcohol treatment unit. The University of Regina, through its School of Social Work, was an active participator and resource for the community and made a film, *We Can*, designed to show other communities how they might proceed to resolve problems based on the Sandy Bay experience.

This example indicates the importance of developing goal congruency and consensus in a problem area. Although the community social worker, sponsor, and community were highly committed to instituting workable programs for children, it can be argued that a range of other factors helped to stimulate this interest. For the community practitioner, the existing system of care was inadequate, and there were indications that its child welfare policies and services were contributing to family breakdown rather than strengthening family life in Sandy Bay.

With the Department of Social Services serving as sponsor, both political and financial benefits were apparent. The multitude of social problems in the village were well known, and these difficulties were adding fuel to an ongoing controversy about exploitation of rural natives living in resource-rich areas of the province. If changes could be facilitated, it was anticipated that both the village and the wider community would benefit and in time there could be increased support and public responsiveness to these concerns.

In terms of the community, the villagers were most anxious to keep their children at home, but there was a sense of powerlessness. The group of AA members who formed the first child care committee were committed not only to performing designated child care functions but also to aggressively attacking the alcohol problem within the village. The skills they learned about obtaining resources and collaborating to institute programs carried over to a range of other problem areas.

Part of the strategy used by the community worker was the use of symbols. These included the plaque from the Minister and an identification card for the villager designated as a child welfare worker. The importance of these symbols is evidenced by the fact that the original plaque still hangs in the recreation hall, and when the indigenous child welfare worker lost his wallet in a canoeing accident, he immediately informed the community worker that "his card had drowned." A new one was quickly issued.

One major strength of this model rests on the community identifying common concerns. Application of this practice approach in child welfare is particularly appealing due to the high priority most people accord to serving those who require special protection. Also, this approach stimulates the transfer of power to community members, which means that they experience a sense of regaining control of decisions regarding the welfare of their children. This can be a powerful motivating force.

## COMMUNITY LIAISON

The role of working with communities through direct involvement of agency staff, usually administrators, has been identified as a legitimate community practice function. Murphy (1954:308-9) listed a variety of community interorganizational activities, while Sieder (1960) expanded on this aspect of agency operations by focusing on mobilization of support for agencies and development of community resources.

Brager and Specht (1973:223-30) indicate that an executive can offer important resources for boards such as knowledge, reports on communication with staff and other agencies, and assistance in decision-making.

Although social agencies are capable of producing positive community relationships, it is inherent in the approach that there is a need to balance the needs of clients with the needs of organizations. If the equilibrium tips in either direction, programs can be seriously affected and jeopardize the credibility of an agency or have a deleterious affect on clients.

The development and growth of a residential treatment center in Saskatchewan, Canada, reflect one aspect of the community liaison approach. In 1964, a change of provincial governments resulted in the closing of the only residential treatment center in the province due to questions about its cost effectiveness. Within two years, a large number of emotionally disturbed children were being placed in treatment centers located outside the province. A newly appointed Director of Child Welfare was most interested in reestablishing residential treatment services. When this interest became known, a professional social worker moved to mobilize professionals and citizens so that a proposal was presented that was formally accepted by the Minister of Social Welfare within two weeks.

The strategy of the social worker in developing the original proposal evolved through discussion with a variety of people who were already familiar with the attitudes of government or who had worked in the residential care field. Key variables appeared that needed to be dealt with in the proposal. First, the Minister of Social Welfare was a Mennonite farmer who highly valued rural life for raising children. The previous center had been located within a city neighborhood whose residents had opposed the program. Second, the new government was suspicious of civil service staff based on its perception that these people did not support the government and therefore should not be entrusted with developing the program. Third, although the government was receptive to reestablishing residential treatment services, it wanted to maintain tight fiscal control in order to prevent spiraling costs. Based on this information gathered from knowledgeable people, an ad hoc group decided to locate the center in a small rural setting outside a major city. This met the requirements of the Minister while facilitating the program's ability to obtain needed professional services.

In developing community support, the community worker recruited a few respected community leaders who were well known to the government for their political support. This group also was a source for the agency's first board of directors, and their involvement alleviated the government's concern about funding a service that was in opposition to its political ideology. This type of board was not fully representative but was a rational response to the realities of the environment (Pfeffer 1972:226).

The proposed program was based on plans for a facility that would care for twelve children, and there was no attempt to conduct a survey of needs since it was already known that the demand clearly outstripped the allocated resources. By beginning small, it was hoped the program would grow over time as its worth and the need for its services were demonstrated.

Another strategy was careful timing of the project. The organizer submitted the proposal early enough to have special project money allocated by the beginning of the new budget year. Although the government agreed only to a per diem rate and monthly advance payments, this provided sufficent cash flow to arrange a mortgage on some property, refurbish the residence, and hire staff. All of this had to occur within three months, due to concern that prolonged delay or debate over the project, or other requests for programs, would jeopardize the new service.

The community worker operated as the center or linking agent of an informal system that was backed by a loosely organized board. Major interorganizational involvements focused on the public founder, and the Department of Social Welfare was kept constantly informed about developments in order to coordinate efforts.

From this small beginning, the population of the center expanded to eighty children in ten years, and a range of programs was established including group homes, specialized foster care, special education facilities, summer facilities, and wilderness programs. The first board of directors was highly committed to the program. Over time, the board became educated about the purposes of the center, and appropriate committees were appointed to set policies and oversee agency operations.

In analyzing this example within the context of the community liaison approach, the initial requirements of interorganizational involvements, mobilization of support from the community's leaders, and obtaining resources were all met. It is clear that the service was designed to suit the requirements of the government but in such a way that the integrity of the program was not violated and a needed service was initiated.

The strengths of the community liaison approach include rapid application of ideas for services based on predetermined goals. Since the goals are specific, citizen and consumer involvement can be selective, thereby creating the potential for a committed and cohesive organization. This in itself facilitates the effectiveness of the model in selected situations.

The basic weakness of this model is that it usually does not allow for a high degree of widespread community participation. By developing an organization of like-minded citizens the potential for constructive criticism may be thwarted, thereby creating the possibility that the program will not meet the needs of particular groups in the community. Further, organizational goals may become so parochial that they do not take into account other community needs or recognize the importance of collaborative action within the network of agencies. However, community liaison can produce change for community benefit as long as the weaknesses are recognized and safeguards such as advisory groups and interagency collaboration are maintained.

## PROGRAM DEVELOPMENT AND COORDINATION

Litwak and Hylton (1962:566) give three reasons for agencies to enter into formal linkages with other organizations: interdependence, information gathering, and monitoring the allocation of resources. Evan (1971:33-45) goes further, arguing that agencies use other groups as sources for new ideas, while Reid (1964:420) points out that sustained interorganizational relationships and cooperation lead to coordination.

Community practitioners can achieve coordination in a variety of ways. Two examples illustrate this point. In 1970, the Commission on Emotional and Learning Disorders in Children (CELDIC) completed a national study of Canadian children entitled *One Million Children.* Six national voluntary agencies and one international agency agreed to sponsor the study, and funding for this ambitious undertaking was provided through a combination of federal, provincial, and foundation grants, and contributions from the business community. Provincial and territorial organizations brought thousands of people together to consider the present state of children's services in Canada. Service agencies, advocacy groups, associations, and concerned citizens shared a variety of program information with each other in small gatherings that were conducted across the nation. This involvement provided a means of heightening public awareness, developing interorganizational linkages, and redefining the needs and programs required by children in various communities and regions. Also, the meetings provided a forum for informally evaluating existing service delivery systems.

From the work of CELDIC, local and national coalitions formed and pressed government for expanded resources based on their revised sense of what needs existed. This would not have occurred if there had been no opportunities to build relationships and share information. No national solutions were instituted, given the federal structure of Canada, but a variety of services strengthened, and new resources were made available through governmental and private sources. In fact, the report has provided a philosophical foundation for a decade of service development.

The second example involves the establishment of Mobile Family Services in Regina, Saskatchewan, an agency that was developed as a coordinated effort involving the city police, child welfare, family social services, and mental health agencies. The initial collaboration of these agencies was directed toward obtaining federal and provincial funding to launch innovative programs appropriate for the changing life style of youth during the 1960s. The project involved hiring young people to operate a twenty-four-hour crisis telephone program with appropriate follow-up services. Though it has been argued that the youth were co-opted, the service that resulted was beneficial to the children who were served and did help agencies to move toward more flexible modes of service and greater recognition of the need to coordinate their efforts. As the youth crisis subsided and the special funding was withdrawn, the original agencies agreed to continue the project in expanded form through existing agency budgets. The expanded services included child abuse, emergency child welfare and social assistance, social service participation in emergency police calls involving suicide and domestic disputes, and emergency services. To achieve these ends, further professionalization of the service resulted, and the original emphasis on youth participation ensured the move toward quality programs and fostered the coordination of efforts among the participating agencies.

Analysis of these two examples suggests that collaboration can lead to coordination and heightened interest in particular issues that are of common concern. In these instances, collaboration stimulated and encouraged agencies to review and adapt their policies and practices in order to provide services in a more effective way. The basic strategy of the community practice involved bringing in agencies together around specific issues and arranging various community forums to encourage the design of new resources, assessment of existing services, and collaboration with integrated service delivery systems.

Use of the model assumes that there is enough goal consensus to support mutual collaboration. This is an ideal that is seldom maintained over time since disequilibrium can occur if strong agencies become sources of power unto themselves. This can lead to organizational inflexibility, which is usually the condition which prompted the original coordination effort. Also, the coordination effort can be sabotaged in the initial stage if organizational domains are threatened or agency resources are usurped. Nevertheless, this model holds considerable potential for community social workers, providing that common objectives are self-evident or can be developed.

## POLITICAL EMPOWERMENT

Generally, political empowerment occurs through some recognized authority delegating power to a particular group for specific purposes or through groups assuming power based on interest, expertise, or other resources.

In the child welfare field, the use of political empowerment as a community practice strategy has been very limited. Children and youth do not usually have an organizational base on which to build, and society does not expect the young to act as an organizational force nor does it accept them when they behave as if they are a force. Children in need of protection, often by definition, do not have parents or a concerned community who are perceived as having power. Consequently, outsiders—concerned citizens and professionals in child welfare—have unwittingly contributed to this problem through projecting a sense of powerlessness upon these children, their families, and their immediate community. As a result, political empowerment as a community social work strategy in child welfare has received only minimal emphasis to date.

Political empowerment requires commitment to a common central ideal. This is usually accomplished by adopting values that provide the ideology underlying the organizational activity (Katz and Georgopoulos 1971:356-66). In child welfare the usual ideological focus is protection of children through the provision of the best possible services. Rather than work to empower the children and families who are most centrally concerned, social workers have tended to institutionalize programmatic solutions, and through professionalization, they lose sight of the political character of their activity (Corwin 1972: 472-75).

In children's services, the moral question is seen in the protective attitude of society toward children. Economically, child welfare services are highly dependent on public or private funding since it is not possible or socially desirable for children's programs to compete in an open-market system. Political problems are always in the background, and protective services, for example, are known to be politically volatile. Consequently, professional groups often are empowered to handle difficult child welfare matters. At no time are child welfare services autonomous from the environment in which they operate. Traditionally, the legitimacy of child welfare has been derived from the community at large that has expectations about the need to protect and care for children caught in situations that expose them to serious risks not of their own making.

Child welfare social service agencies must deal with environmental complexity, which is defined as risk, dependency, and interorganizational relationships (Osborne and Hunt 1974:231-46). In most communities attitudes toward child welfare are extremely conservative and services are dependent on public or charitable sources. Consequently, there has been extreme caution in developing approaches which are unusual or innovative. There are seldom any "risk" programs undertaken which are not first legitimized by strong endorsements from national associations. Thus, the majority of essential child welfare services are legitimized by the general community, but service providers do not often gain or even seek legitimacy from client populations or citizen groups.

Experimental programs which utilized community workers with gangs of youth have successfully transferred some power to client groups in some instances. However, this has usually been an exercise in short-term process rather than the basis of lasting change. Youth street organizations have a transitory membership which is not suited to continuing organizational responsibility or evolution. Nevertheless, the strategies of political empowerment can have an impact when they form the basis of youth work.

Probably the most significant uses of political empowerment in child welfare services to date have involved the empowerment of parents to act on behalf of their children. The parents of children with specific handicaps such as mental retardation, learning disability, and autism have become powerful forces over the last decade as child advocates, fund raisers, and service providers. Parent-dominant organizations have been especially powerful in the development of community-based alternatives to institutionalization.

These parent empowerment organizations are usually begun as parent-professional-community partnerships. The development of the political action approach usually passes through three stages. First, a group of concerned citizens take a collective action to develop an organization that will advance their interests. Second, funding problems are addressed. At this point, the political action model is often in jeopardy, since allocation of funds for specific projects often diverts the attention of the group away from more universal issues. Many groups stop at this point, and they place all of their energies into building a specific service, such as a school for retarded children. It can be argued that the provision of funds for projects is a conscious co-optation of the group by funders in order to divert the attention of the members away from more global issues.

The final phase emerges when the empowered group recognizes the range of needs that are not being met due to their involvement in providing direct services. At this point, members reassume the role of advocates. Many examples are evident, such as schools for retarded children that were operated by parents being turned over to public authorities. This frees the group to direct attention to new endeavors, often with the specific objective of starting services and then turning them over to others to operate. This form of the political empowerment model has great potential since members are usually highly committed advocates who are free to and willing to develop a strong power base.

Finally, political empowerment in child welfare is an important issue arising among certain racial and ethnic minorities, most notably blacks and the North American Indians (Cardinal 1977; Hudson and McKenzie 1981; Johnson 1981). Criticisms have been made of cross-racial adoption (Sanders 1975), the lack of appropriate foster care, and the need for provision of treatment services on reservations (Simon 1973). In Canada and the United States, ethnic and racial interest associations are extremely concerned about child welfare services which they describe as a form of cultural genocide. The disproportionate numbers of Indian children who are in the care of child welfare authorities is cause for concern (Canadian Council on Children and Youth 1978:130-5). There is little doubt that child welfare services will become an integral part of the Indian rights movement in the years to come. Community practice strategies which empower communities to care for their children will be an essential part of this movement.

## REFERENCES


Abbott, Grace. 1938. The Child and the State, vol. 11: *The Dependent and Delinquent Child, the Child of Unmarried Parents.* New York: Greenwood Press.

Axinn, June and Herman Levine. 1975. *Social Welfare: A History of the American Response to Needs.* New York: Harper and Row.

Bagnell, Kenneth. 1980. *The Little Immigrants: The Orphans Who Came to Canada.* Toronto: Macmillan of Canada.

Bartlett, Harriet M. 1958. "Toward Clarification and Improvement of Social Work Practice." *Social Work* (April), 3(2):3-9.

Betten, Neil. 1973. "American Attitudes Toward the Poor." *Current History* (July), 65(383):1-5.

Beveridge, Sir William. 1942. *Social Insurance and Allied Services.* New York: Macmillan.

Boles, Janet K. 1980. "The Politics of Child Care." *Social Service Review* (September), 54(3):344-62

Brager, George A. and Harry Specht. 1973. *Community Organizing.* New York: Columbia University Press.

Canadian Council on Children and Youth. 1978. *Admittance Restricted: The Child as Citizen in Canada.* Ottawa: M.O.M. Press.

Cardinal, Harold. 1977. *The Rebirth of Canada's Indians.* Edmonton: Hurtig.

Child Welfare League of America. 1981. *Child Welfare Planning Notes.*

_______. 1982. *Urgent Bulletin* (an open letter to member agencies).

Cohen, Nathan E., ed. 1960. *The Citizen Volunteer: His Responsibility, Role, and Opportunity in Modern Society.* New York: Harper and Row.

Corwin, Ronald G. 1972. "Strategies of Organizational Survival: The Case of a National Program of Educational Reform."*Journal of Applied Behavioral Science* (July/August), 8(4):451-80.

Costin, Lela B. 1979. *Child Welfare: Policies and Practice.* New York: McGraw-Hill.

Coughlin, Bernard J. 1979. "Deinstitutionalization: A Matter of Social Order and Deviance." *Child Welfare* (May), 61(5):293-301.

Etzioni, Amitai. 1961. *Complex Organizations: A Sociological Reader.* New York: Holt, Rinehart and Winston.

Evan, William M. 1971. "The Organization-Set: Toward a Theory of Interorganizational Relations." In Mauer, ed., *Readings in Organizational Theory: Open System Approaches*, pp. 31-45.

Geismar, L.L. and Beverly Ayres. 1959. *Patterns of Change in Problem Families.* St. Paul, Minn.: Greater St. Paul Community Chest and Councils.

Gilbert, Neil and Harry Specht. 1977. *Planning for Social Welfare.* Englewood Cliffs, N.J.: Prentice Hall.

Gill, David G. 1974. "Institutions for Children." In Schorr, ed., *Children and Decent People,* pp. 53-88.

Grosser, Charles F. 1973. *New Directions in Community Organization: From Enabling to Advocacy.* New York: Praeger.

Hasenfeld, Yeheskel and Richard A. English, eds. 1975. *Human Service Organizations.* Ann Arbor, Mich.: University of Michigan Press.

Herman, Paul, ed. 1970 *Delinquency and Social Policy.* New York: Praeger.

Hibbard, Michael. 1981. "The Crisis in Social Policy Planning." *Social Service Review* (December), 55(4):557-67.

Howe, Elizabeth. 1978. "Legislative Outcomes in Human Services." *Social Service Review* (June), 52(2):173-88.

Hudson, Pete and Brad McKenzie. 1981. "Child Welfare and Native People: The Extension of Colonialism." *The Social Worker* (Summer), 49(2):63-66.

Johnson, Patrick. 1981. "Indigenous Children at Risk." *Policy Options* (November-December), 2:47-50.

Kadushin, Alfred. 1969. *Child Welfare Services.* New York: Macmillan.

Kahn, Alfred J. 1979. "Child Welfare." In *Encyclopedia of Social Work,* pp. 100-114. 17th ed. Washington, D.C.: NASW.

Katz, Daniel and Basil S. Georgopoulos. 1971. "Organizations in a Changing World." *Journal of Applied Behavioral Science* (May-June), 7(3):342-70.

Kenniston, Kenneth and the Carnegie Council on Children. 1977. *All Our Children.* New York: Harcourt Brace Jovanovich.

Kramer, Ralph M. and Harry Specht, eds. 1969. *Readings in Community Organization Practice.* Englewood Cliffs, N.J.: Prentice-Hall.

Lansburgh, Terese W. 1977. "Child Welfare: Day Care of Children." In *Encyclopedia of Social Work,* pp. 134-46. 17th ed. Washington, D.C.: NASW.

Lerman, Paul. 1970. *Community Treatment and Social Control: A Critical Analysis of Juvenile Correctional Policy.* Chicago: University of Chicago Press.

Litwak, Eugene and Lydia F. Hylton. 1962. "Interorganizational Interdependence, Intraorganizational Structure." *Administrative Science Quarterly* (March), 6:395-420. Reprinted in Hasenfeld and English, eds., *Human Services Organizations: A Book of Readings.*

Marsh, L. C. 1943. *Report on Social Security for Canada.* Ottawa: Edmund Cloutier Printer.

Mauer, John H., ed. 1971. *Readings in Organizational Theory: Open-System Approaches.* New York: Random House.

Mayer, Morris Fritz, Leon H. Richman, and Edwin A. Balcerzak. 1977. *Group Care of Children: Crossroads and Transitions.* New York: Child Welfare League of America.

Meezan, William, Stanford Katz, and Eva Monoff Russo. 1978. *Adoptions without Agencies: A Study of Independent Adoptions.* New York: Child Welfare League of America.

Murphy, Campbell G. 1954. *Community Organization Practice.* Boston: Houghton Mifflin.

Osborne, Richard N. and James G. Hunt. 1974. "Environment and Organizational Effectiveness." *Administrative Science Quarterly* (June), 19(2):231-46.

Parker, Jacqueline K. and Edward M. Carpenter. 1981. "Julia Lathrop and the Children's Bureau: The Emergence of an Institution." *Social Service Review* (March), 55(1):60-77.

Pfeffer, Jeffery. 1972c. "Size and Composition of Corporate Board of Directors: The Organization and Its Environment." *Administrative Science Quarterly* (June), 17(2):218-28.

Piper, Edward and John R. Warner, Jr. 1980-81. "Group Homes for Problem Youth: Retrospect and Prospects." *Child and Youth Services,* 3(3/4):1-11.

Platt, Anthony M. 1970. "The Rise of the Child-Saving Movement." In Herman, ed., *Delinquency and Social Policy,* pp. 15-20.

Powers, Edwin. 1970. "Crime and Punishment in Early Massachusetts, 1620-1692." In Herman, ed., *Delinquency and Social Policy,* pp. 8-12.

Pumphrey, Muriel W. and Ralph E. Pumphrey. 1973. "Private Charity in the Twentieth Century."*Current History* (July), 65(383):29-32.

Rauch, Julia B. 1975. "Women in Social Work: Friendly Visitors in Philadelphia, 1880." *Social Service Review* (June), 49(2):241-59.

Reid, Joseph H. 1974a. "From the Executive Director." *Child Welfare League Newsletter* (Spring), 4(1):1.

_______. 1974b. "From the Executive Director." *Child Welfare League Newsletter* (Summer/Fall), 4(2):4.

Reid, William. 1964 "Interagency Coordination in Delinquency Prevention and Control." *Social Service Review* (December), 35:418-28.

Romig, Dennis A. 1978. *Justice for Our Children.* Lexington, Mass.: Lexington Books.

Rooke, Patricia T. and R. L. Schnell. 1981. "Child Welfare in English Canada, 1920-48." *Social Service Review* (September), 55(3):483-506.

Ross, Murray G. 1955. *Community Organization: Theory and Principles.* New York: Harper.

Rothman, David J. 1971. *The Discovery of the Asylum—Special Order and Disorder in the New Republic.* Boston: Little, Brown.

Ruderman, Florence A. 1968. *Child Care and Working Mothers: A Study of Arrangements for Daytime Care of Children.* New York: Child Welfare League of America.

Sanders, Douglas. 1975. "Family Law and Native People," p. 14. Unpublished background paper prepared for the Law Reform Commission of Canada.

Santiago, Letty. 1972. "From Settlement House to Antipoverty Program." *Social Work* (July), 17(4):73-78.

Schorr, Alvin L., ed. 1974. *Children and Decent People.* New York: Basic Books.

Sieder, Violet M. 1960. "The Citizen Volunteer in Historical Perspective." In Cohen, ed., *The Citizen Volunteer: His Responsibility, Role and Opportunity in Modern Society.* pp. 41-58.

Simon, Bill, Jr. 1973. "The Social Conditions of Indian Reserves in Eastern New Brunswick." Unpublished report prepared for the Union of New Brunswick Indians.

Siporin, Max. 1975, *Introduction to Social Work Practice.* New York: Macmillan.

Soiseth, Len. 1970. "A Community That Cares for Children." *Canadian Welfare* (May/June), 46(3):8-10.

Statistics Canada. 1976. *Social Security National Programs: A Review for the Period 1946 to 1975.* Ottawa: Statistics Canada.

Thompson, James D. and William J. McEwan. 1958, "Organizational Goals and Environment: Goal Setting and an Interaction Process." *American Sociological Review* (February), 23(1):23-36.

U.S. Department of Health and Human Services. 1982. *Quarterly Public Assistance Statistics: Jan.-Mar. 1981.* Washington, D.C.: U.S. GPO.

Wolins, Martin and Irving Piliavin. 1964. *Institutions or Foster Family: A Century of Debate.* New York: Child Welfare League of America.

Woodroofe, Kathleen. 1975. "The Irascible Reverend Henry Solly and His Contribution to Working Men's Clubs, Charity Organizations, and 'Industrial Villages' In Victorian England." *Social Service Review* (March), 49(1):15-32.

Young, Robert C. 1966. "Goals and Goal-Setting." *Journal of the American Institute of Planners* (March), 32(2):78-85.

Zald, Mayer N. 1963. Comparative Analysis and Measurement of Organizational Goals: The Case of Correctional Institutions for Delinquents." *Sociological Quarterly* (Summer), 4(3):206-30.

Zietz, Dorothy. 1969. *Child Welfare: Services and Perspectives.* New York: Wiley.

16.

Felix G. Rivera and John L. Erlich

# ORGANIZING WITH PEOPLE OF COLOR: A PERSPECTIVE*

*A new process of community organizing—one relying less on issue-based mobilization and more on community education, leadership development and support, and building sustainable local organizations—needs to be implemented.*
Bill Traynor, "Community Development and Community Organizing," *Shelterforce*, March-April 1993, p. 7.

## INTRODUCTION

Increasingly the anger, frustration, and pent up passions of poor people, especially poor people of color, have been directed at their own communities. Acts of many kinds of violence—from drive-by shootings to child abuse—have become such a commonplace occurrence that they generate little public reaction. The reasonable demands of neighborhood people for jobs, health care, education, decent housing, and social services are lost in the strident distress of middle-class and lower-middle-class residents who see the quality of their lives eroding and their children's prospects declining.

Across the country, renewed efforts are underway to attack and reverse the effects of neglect, decay, and abandonment. But if the recent past is a reasonable predictor of the near future, these efforts will go largely undocumented and unrewarded.

Indeed, there is very little written material available to guide such efforts among people of color. Extensive treatments of community organizing with people of color do not seem to exist. Anecdotal and brief narrative descriptions are inadequate to the task. The reasons for this deficiency are multiple, complex, and interwoven. Racism—political, economic, and social—is at the root of the problem.

At the same time, societal interest in the problems of the poor has sharply declined, especially in the 1980s. Despite all the research evidence to the contrary, the disenfranchised are again being forced to bear the major burden for their oppression. The problems of drug abuse, crime, inadequate housing, alcoholism, AIDS, teen pregnancy, and underemployment have had their most devastating impact on poor communities of color. The lack of resources to combat these problems falls most heavily on the same people. The growing national debt has served conservative forces well as an excuse for not meeting the urgent need to expand services in these areas.

As if these many problems and needs were not enough, the incredibly dramatic population increases are sobering testimony to the daunting challenges ahead for us all. Census Bureau preliminary reports show an increase in all populations of color. Out of a total of over 248 million people in the United States, almost 30 million are African American, representing 23 percent of the population and an increase of 64.6 percent over the 1980 Census figures. Native Americans, Eskimos, and Aleuts share

*An earlier version of this article appeared as Chapter 1 in Felix Rivera and John L. Erlich (eds.), *Community Organizing A Diverse Society* (Boston: Allyn and Bacon, 1992).

.08 percent of the population with almost two million people, representing an increase of 33.7 percent from the last census. Asian and Pacific Islanders, over seven million strong, represent an increase of 144.9 percent from 1980, with their 2.9 percent representation; Latinos share 8.9 percent of the population with over 22 million people, an increase of 87.3 percent from the 1980 census.[7,8]

These figures are far from being fixed. A heated debate is going on about the problems of undercounting, especially in communities of color. The Census Oversight Committee claims that over two million African Americans have not been counted. They state that the undercount is between 5.5 percent and 6.5 percent, compared to an undercount of 5.2 percent in 1980. Other critics of the Census claim that the undercount is as high as nine million people. Whatever the final count will be, these statistics are a reminder of the enormous amount of work that needs to be done by agents of social work. The challenge is unparalleled in this nation's history.[2]

The government's pro-Contra and anti-Salvadorian rebel role in Central America, the invasion of Grenada and Panama, and the vast commitment to the Persian Gulf, however justified they may have been, have contributed to a decline in our commitment to racial equality. In a curious twist of logic, the withdrawal of support for communities of color at home is partly justified by resources demanded abroad because peoples of color cannot manage their own affairs.

Our priorities in foreign affairs, along with a realignment of domestic preferences, has sharply reduced not only support for community-based human services but the resources necessary to provide training for people to work in these services as well. One result is decreased interest in and demand for trailing in community organization and community development. In many cases, the rhetoric of working along multicultural lines has been a smoke screen to avoid funding programs for desperately underserved ethnic enclaves. All too many joint police and community antidrug efforts, for example, make good copy for the six o'clock news while deflecting public attention away from underlying problems of poverty and racism.

The fact that community organization has been the most resistant of the social work methods to consistent definition has further exacerbated this situation. As Erlich and Rivera have noted, community organization has evolved from being the general rubric under which all social work practice beyond the level of individual, family, and small group was subsumed—including grassroots organizing, community development, planning, administration, and policy-making—to being the smallest sub-segment of macro level practice (where it exists at all). This definitional difficulty is well-illustrated by one of the better contemporary definitions of community organization:

> *Community Development* refers to efforts to mobilize people who are directly affected by a community condition (that is, the "victims," the unaffiliated, the unorganized, and the nonparticipating) into groups and organizations to enable them to take action on the social problems and issues that concern them. A typical feature of these efforts is the concern with building new organizations among people who have not been previously organized to take social action on a problem.[10,20]

However, by any definition, it was not until the 1960s that large numbers of schools of social work were willing to regard it as a legitimate concentration. Majors in community organization in graduate schools increased from 85 in 1960 to 1,125 in 1969, or from 1.5 percent to over 9 percent of full-time enrollments.[11]

By 1989, the number of students nationwide training to work as organizers had declined significantly. The Council on Social Work Education's most recent statistics demonstrate that there were 154 master's degree students (1.8%) in Community Organization and Planning, 417 (4.9%) in Administration and Management, and 101 (1.2%) in a combination of C.O. and Planning with Administration or Management. Given the fact that there are now many more schools of social work than in 1960, the trends do not augur well for community organizing. Despite growing acceptance as a legitimate area of study in social work, urban planning, and labor studies, community organization and planning has been held hostage by the political and social vagaries of a society that has never accepted its strategies as tactics, especially if methods like public demonstrations and boycotts caused disruptive embarrassment to those in positions of political authority and power.[24]

From an educational standpoint, the result has been a diminished community organization curriculum—few field placement opportunities, few courses, and sparse literature. This is particularly surprising in light of the important, documented successes of community organization and development during the 1960s and early 1970s.[12]

Community organizing and community development by people of color have been virtually ignored. Isolated electives and rare articles in the professional journals have done little to fill this void. Work of a multicultural nature has received only slightly more attention. No book is available which addresses a broad range of the organizing efforts currently going forward in diverse minority communities. This...is a first effort to remedy that situation.

What is the status of community organization practice this...attempts to address? The civil rights gains of the 1960s in voting rights, public accommodations, and job opportunities, for example, were tempered by the belief that the African-American community had gone too far, that its gains were based on unacceptable levels of violence. Quickly forgotten by the white community was the continuing history of violence experienced by African Americans and other communities of color. "What more do they want?" was more than mere inflammatory rhetoric. These gains seemed to threaten white job security, community housing patterns, and long-cherished social interaction networks. The bitter residue of racism remains, and the resentment experienced throughout much of the United States has been part of the conservative backlash we are witnessing (as everything from Skinheads and antiminority high school violence to English-only public school curricula poignantly illustrates).

Similarly, efforts toward enfranchisement of new voters, changes in immigration laws, and women's and gay rights have also suffered from the schism between methods deemed acceptable and resulting "reasonable" benefits. As long as "someone else" did the social protesting, and as long as it was far enough away from their homes and places of work, most white people did not complain actively, or publicly resist slow, nondisruptive changes.

A concomitant shift has marked that reluctant acceptance of the "worthy" among each ethnic minority (largely dependent on whose economic interests are being threatened) while at the same time rejecting those without education, job skills, or at high risk for drug problems and sexually transmitted diseases.

Not surprisingly, with the emergence of reverse discrimination as a legitimate response to the enfranchisement of people of color, a new consciousness permeated schools of social work whose espoused philosophy was that of commitment to aiding poor and oppressed populations. It was no longer in fashion to invite a Black Panther as a speaker for a seminar on social action, or a Young Lord from New York's Puerto Rican community to discuss how they initiated the movement against lead poisoning in New York's slum tenements, or have Angela Davis address the systematic exclusion of women of color by the women's movement in key policy and strategy sessions. Instead, the invited ethnic "leaders" tended to focus on issues like creatively funded drug education programs, multicultural day-care and preschool efforts, and the demographics of rapidly expanding minority populations around the country.

As funding sources evaporated, people of color began being relegated to the not-so-symbolic back of the bus once again. The rapacity with which affirmative action was attacked became trendy. Ethnic studies programs were closed or cut back at alarming rates throughout the country and many community-based agencies in ethnic areas were forced to close their doors. The Supreme Court's chipping away at civil rights legislation seemed to be a culmination of much of the backlash being experienced.

## PEOPLE OF COLOR AND ORGANIZING: A TROUBLED ALLIANCE

Why has community organization not been more successful in working with people of color? What happened to some of the cross-cultural efforts that appeared to be so productive in the 1960s and early 1970s? Traditionally, much of the writing on community organization attempts to be color blind. Organizers work with specific strategies and tactics applied to different situations, but the methods that combine them rarely—if ever— change.[5,13]

Alinsky's mobilization model is a good case in point.[19] Too often the level of analysis of a community's problems has been determined by an organizing strategy that identifies a particular strata of people or social problem for intervention. By doing so, the racial and cultural uniqueness of the community is ignored. These organizers are not conservative or even liberal community organizers but well-intentioned, progressive thinkers who have been victimized by what may be termed "organizers' myopia" because of their single-minded organizing ideology or preordained methodology.[19]

One thing that becomes readily apparent...is the absence of an easily identified "radical" or "progressive" ideology along class lines. That does not mean [this piece] is apolitical; far from it. What it does point out, however, is the fact that issues surrounding race, culture, and their attendant problems are often more urgent concerns than social class that has often been historically conceptualized by white theoreticians apart from the dynamics deemed more critical to the self-determination of communities of color by communities of color. Middle-class Asians, Latinos, or African Americans are still viewed as minorities because of a most easily identifiable characteristic: skin color. Good clothes and an elegant briefcase are not much help when you need a cab in the middle of the night in Chicago or Washington, D.C.

People of color have traditionally been caught between the polarized struggles of conservative and liberal theoretical forces. Too many liberal community organizers have emphasized class issues at the expense of racism and cultural chauvinism, relegating them to "logical" extensions of the political and economic structure. Much of the neo-Marxist literature has treated race from a reductive, negative posture: "super-exploitation," and the "divide and conquer" strategies of individual capitalist employers. On the other hand, many conservative thinkers have emphasized a kind of uniqueness of each community which divides it from other communities of color, as well as separating those who can "make it" from those who cannot.[3,21,26]

These perspectives largely disregarded many questions, including the fact that racism existed long before monopoly capitalism was institutionalized. The logic fortunes of race relations are not necessarily coterminous with those of capitalism, as the persistence of racial antagonism in postcapitalist societies (like Sweden) demonstrates. The structural analysis that leads to a unified ideological interpretation of racism is thus deficient.

What too many organizers fail to consider is that there appears to be little or no history or contemporary evidence to substantiate that relations established and legitimated on the basis of race were or are identical to those established and legitimated on the basis of class. For example, the increasing violence against students of color on our college campuses cannot be explained primarily as a class phenomenon, especially when one recognizes that many of these students of color are economically similar to the white students attacking them. By continuing to look at racism as a mostly broad structural issue, organizers are underestimating the roles played by schools, churches, social welfare agencies, and other institutions in negatively influencing and changing race relations.

How might we best define the equality and liberation struggles being waged by the African-American communities? The Native-American communities? The Chinese-American and Vietnamese communities? The communities of women of color? The immediate reaction of most oppressors is based on skin color and other physical characteristics, language, culture, and lastly, class. The oversimplification of the struggles of people of color has led to unwarranted generalizations about their economic, social, political, and cultural behaviors and attitudes as groups.

Writers criticize the tendency of mainstream and radical theorists to divide society into separate domains culturally and structurally. They argue that this arbitrary bifurcation promotes tendencies toward essentialism (single-cause explanations) in contemporary thinking about race. Race and culture cannot be separated as "things in themselves."[25] They have to be linked to other social processes and dynamics operating in a society that continues oppressing communities because of skin tone. At least three dynamics—race, class, and gender—are significant in understanding oppression and the roles played by social welfare institutions in that process. None are reducible to the others, and class is not necessarily paramount.[25,18]

The phenomenological day-to-day realities of race, language, class, gender, and age help to shape ideological perspectives and give force to the hostilities with which one lives (as well as the strengths that make survival possible). The resulting process is difficult to analyze because it manifests itself differently from one community to another across the country, thereby making the task of organizing against these attacks that much more difficult a challenge. These realities do not lend themselves easily to simply categorizations by agents of social change or schools teaching community organization practice. The need for a more integrated and receptive social change paradigm in working with communities of color must be a main goal of organizers.

The conservative tradition in community organizing—especially within social work education—has also had an impact on the way organizers of color and their communities view the political implications of the social change efforts in which they have been involved. The conventional perspective that education should be ideologically value-free and politically nonpartisan has been especially evident in community organizing. Typical textbooks on organizing have avoided clear political and moral positions on issues.[9,27] These books were guided by a "professional" and largely mechanistic value base.

Fisher[11] notes:

> The social work tradition views the community essentially as a social organism; it focuses on social issues such as building a sense of community, gather together social service organizations, or lobbying for and delivering social resources. It assumes that basically the community's problem is social disorganization. The organizer functions either as an "enabler" to help the community gather itself together or as an advocate to secure additional services for the community. The strategy is gradualist and consensual, which means that organizers assume a unity of interest between the power structure and the neighborhood and assume a willingness of at least some in power to meet community needs.

In contrast, Freire proposes:

> ...one cannot be a social worker and be like the educator who's a coldly neutral technician. To keep our options secret, to conceal them in the cobwebs of technique, or to disguise them by claiming neutrality does not constitute neutrality; quite the contrary, it helps maintain the status quo.[15]

Many professors of macro practice still resist the systematic inclusion of discussions on analyzing power and confrontational empowerment, the development of critical consciousness and racism as fundamental components of community organization. The lack of attention to critical consciousness—that is, how personal and political factors interact with each other and one's work, as well as how values, ideas, and practice skills are influenced by social forces and, in turn, influence them—is both particularly noteworthy and undermining. This neoconservative stance has had the net effect of leaving students of color (as well as white students) confused about their potential roles in their communities and how far they might go in fighting racism and social injustices.

While the rhetoric of self-determination implies that students are intended to be agents of social change, the reality clearly calls for modest improvements that do not seriously upset the status quo. The tools that might help lead to more fundamental change through a thorough questioning of what is happening and what it means to a community and a person working there are largely absent from the curriculum. Indeed, as a totality, the picture is not very promising.[14]

## A PARADIGM FOR ORGANIZING WITH PEOPLE OF COLOR

The different racial and cultural characteristics present in oppressed and disadvantaged communities represent an unprecedented challenge to organizers of the 1990s. We are defining culture as a collection of behaviors and beliefs that constitute "standards for deciding what is, standards for deciding what can be, standards for deciding how one feels about it, standards for deciding what to do about it, and standards for deciding how to go about doing it." A recent history of benign or belligerent neglect has required people of color to mobilize their skills and limited resources in creative ways that challenge prevailing community programs. Although they get little attention or help from mainstream society—indeed, in some areas, overt opposition is more typical—many of those communities are trying to tackle their problems with strategies unique to their situations.[17]

For example, the African-American community of West Oakland, California has attacked the drug problem head-on, with many community leaders making themselves visible enemies of major dealers. Also, nearby, an African-American first-grade teacher has promised to pay for the college education for her entire first-grade class if they maintain a "C" average and go on to college. The teacher annually saves $10,000 from her modest salary for this fund. In the rural mountains of Eastern Puerto Rico there is an exciting revitalization of the community through an energetic community development program. Southeast Asian communities in Boston, New York, Houston, and San Francisco have organized legal immigration and refugee task forces to help fight the arbitrary deportation of undocumented workers. Derelict neighborhoods in New York, Chicago, and Philadelphia are being revitalized through cooperatives and community development activities. Native-American tribes are attacking problems of alcoholism through indigenous healing rituals which utilize the sweat lodge ceremony as its core. Success rates are often dramatic. In the village of Akhiok, Alaska, 90 percent of its adults were chronically drunk. After Native treatments, at least 80 percent were able to sustain sobriety. The Latino community in Boston has a very successful grassroots health program called "Mujeres Latina en Action" which has successfully integrated Third World health models that include the concept of the extended family in health care delivery systems. A cultural- and gender-sensitive model of community organization is used to reach women in the barrios.

Traditionally, communities of color have not been involved in issues related to ecology and the protection of the environment. For many neighborhoods, these are among the last priorities when the many problems people face are listed. However, one example bears special attention, for it may well be a model for similar actions across the country. In California's East Los Angeles, which is predominantly Mexican American/Chicano, a group of Latina mothers was organized by a parish priest in the mid 1980s into militant urban ecologists. They call themselves Mothers of East Los Angeles. They have successfully mobilized against threats to their community, such as (1) the construction of a state prison in a residential area near neighborhood schools, (2) an above-ground oil pipeline that would have cut through their middle-to-low income barrio while avoiding much more affluent coastal towns, (3) the local use of dangerous and potentially polluting pesticides, and (4) local construction of a large incinerator. They believe in peaceful tactics and wear white kerchiefs as a symbol of their nonviolent philosophy. They are often seen pushing strollers during demonstrations, and they lobby the state capitol, engage in letter writing, and serve as pacesetters of a growing environmental movement in the Los Angeles area among people of color.

From the ethnic-sensitive practice perspective, organizing strategies in the Vietnamese or Laotian communities (and with different ethnic groups within these communities) cannot be the same as in the Puerto Rican, African-American, Native American or Japanese-American enclaves.

The experience of one of the editors illustrates this point. In the early 1970s he was organizing a Mexican-American barrio. One of the outcomes of the struggle was the establishment of a storefront information and referral center. In furnishing and decorating the center, several political and cultural posters were displayed—much to the anger of the viejitos (elders) in the neighborhood. One particular poster featured Emiliano Zapata, and the staff was told in no uncertain terms that the poster had to come down because Zapata was still perceived as an enemy. Several fathers of the viejitos had fought against Zapata during the Mexican Revolution! Although the editor is a Latino, he is not of Mexican descent. However, he does know the conflicting loyalties of Mexico's revolutionary history and should have checked with the community to be sure none of the posters would be offensive. This apparently innocuous mistake set the organizing effort back many months and required the staff to work doubly hard to regain the community's confidence.

Unfortunately, the history of organizing is replete with such examples. Certainly organizers of color must accept a share of the blame. However, the overwhelming majority of organizing writers and practitioners are white males, may of whom come from liberal or radical traditions, and who most often got their theoretical and practice feet wet in the social upheavals of the 1960s. Their apparent successes seemed destined to be color blind. From a community perspective, white radical groups were often more enamored of their political ideologies than they were committed to the needs of minority neighborhoods. The Detroit-based battles of African-Americans within the United Auto Workers is a prime example. Frequently hovering on the fringes were white radical groups looking to make the struggle their own. They were very critical of the efforts of people of color, accusing them of being culturally nationalistic and methodically not progressive enough. Too often we forget that experiencing racism, economic deprivation and social injustice are the key relevant politicizing forces in most urban areas. Indeed, it was this kind of elitist attitude that caused many minority organizers to shy away from predetermined ideological postures that seemed to define peoples *for* them. Even many liberal white groups seemed to disdain poor whites in favor of more visible organizing efforts in communities of color.

Thus, it is not sufficient to identify the three classic (and presumably "color blind") models of community practice—locality development, social planning, and social action—as being the foundation within which community organizing with people of color takes place. Factors that must be addressed are (1) the racial, ethnic, and cultural uniqueness of people of colors; (2) the implications of these unique qualities in relation to such variables as the roles played by kinship patterns, social systems, power and leadership networks, religion, the role of language (especially among sub-groups), and the economic and political configuration within each community; and (3) the process of empowerment and the development of critical consciousness. (This is in contrast to what Freire has called "naive consciousness," or a tendency to romanticize intense, satisfying past events and force the same experiences into the future without taking fully into account such multidimensional elements as those noted above.) In addition, the physical setting within which the community finds itself is an essential component for consideration as it plays a significant part in the way people view their situation. The need for a new, revised paradigm is clear and urgent.[22,15]

FIGURE 16.1
Organizer's Contact Intensity and Influence

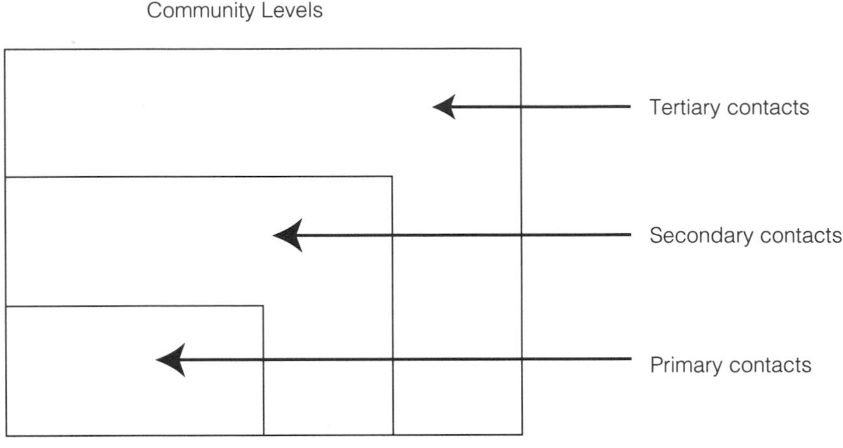


One of the most critical factors affecting organizing outcomes hinges on determining how strategies and tactics are played out based on the nature and intensity of contact and influence will help to determine the constraints placed on the organizers' (whether indigenous or an outsider) knowledge and identification with the community, and when and how technical skills may be brought into play. This "meta approach" will help organizers arrange their strategies and tactics within parameters that are goal, task, skill, and process specific. We suggest that the degree and nature of contacts is a three-tier process which—for the sake of simplicity—may be conceptualized as contact intensity and influence at the primary, secondary, and tertiary levels of community development (see Figure 16.1).

The primary level of involvement is most immediate and personal with the community. It is that level that requires racial, cultural, and linguistic identity. The primary level of contact intensity and influence is the most intimate level of community involvement where the only way of gaining entry into the community is to have full ethnic solidarity with the community. For example, this would not be possible for a Chinese American in a Vietnamese or African-American area.

The secondary level consists of contact and influence that is one step removed from personal identification with the community and its problems. Language—although a benefit and help—is not absolutely mandatory. Many of the functions are those of liaison with the outside community and institutions, and service as a resource with technical expertise based on the culturally unique situations experienced by the community. Examples of persons able to work at this level include a Puerto Rican in a Mexican American neighborhood or a person identified as Haitian in an African-American area.

The tertiary level is that of the outsider working for the common interests and concerns of the community. Cultural or racial similarity is not a requirement. The responsibilities of these organizers will see them involved primarily with the outside infrastructures as an advocate and broker for communities of color. However, their tasks are less that of liaison and more of a helpful technician approaching or confronting outside systems and structures. Clearly, whites and nonsimilar people of color may be particularly effective at this level.

The issue over whether or not organizers should be part of the racial and cultural group with whom they work has been given much attention within and outside communities of color. Alinsky and his Industrial Area Foundation organizers were often in the middle of this question. However, a careful review of these efforts suggests that in most cases, indigenous organizers played key roles in the success of their organizations. Thus, it seems imperative that if communities of color are going to empower themselves by giving more than symbolic recognition to the ideal of self-determination and community control, then we must search hard for the successful roles played by people within their own communities and the lessons they can teach outside organizers. Furthermore, many emerging communities of color are underrepresented in the society's infrastructure because their languages and customs make them especially difficult to approach. In the emerging Southeast Asian communities, there are nationalities, ethnic and subethnic groups whose cultures are quite different from one another and where there exists an assortment of languages, dialects, and idioms. An outside organizer simply does not stand a chance of gaining rapid access to such unique and insular community groups. Even the Native American nations, it should be remembered, speak over 200 different languages. Clearly, special care must be taken in recruiting people to work in widely varied Indian communities—on reservations and rancherias, in both rural and urban areas.[6,10,12,19]

The knowledge necessary to understand and appreciate customs and traditions in all communities is an incredible challenge. Organizing and social strategies are complex and stress-inducing enough without further exacerbating the community's problems by having organizers who have very limited (or no) awareness of the customs, traditions, and languages of these communities. That is not to say that persons without some of this knowledge cannot fulfill certain important functions; for indeed, they have served and should continue to serve effectively in secondary and tertiary roles. But we must emphasize that the most successful organizers are those individuals who know their culture intimately: its subtleties of language, mores, and folkways. A white outsider, however sensitive and knowledgeable, simply cannot appreciate all that needs to be considered about a fundamentally different nonwhite culture or subculture. Some newly emerging communities are so well defended that there would be little chance for an outsider to gain meaningful admission to them, not to mention becoming a successful organizer. However, it must be very clear that cultural and racial similarity—by themselves—are no guarantor of organizer effectiveness or community acceptance. Indeed, an arrogant, know-it-all insider may be viewed with more suspicion than a similarly styled outsider.[16]

Despite these difficulties, there are common practice elements that may be identified as prerequisite to successful organizing. These principles are not exhaustive, but if organizers take command of these elements, they can increase the likelihood of being effective change agents in their communities. Knowing when and how to mix and phase these strategies and skill areas is critical to the successful outcome of a struggle. Organizing has to be conceptualized as a process that is educational both for the community and the organizers.

### Organizer's Profile

What follows is a summary of those qualities—knowledge, skill, attributes, and values—that are most important in contributing to the success of organizers. It is recognized that the list is an idealized one in the sense that those few who have already fully attained the lofty heights described can probably also walk on water. Realistically, it is a set of goals to be used by organizers and communities together to help achieve desired changes. The careful reader will also note that many of these qualities are addressed by each contributor in describing a particular community...

1. Similar cultural and racial identification. The most successful organizers are those activists who can identify with their communities culturally, racially, and linguistically. There is no stronger identification with a community than truly being a part of it.

2. Familiarity with customs and traditions, social networks, and values. This dimension of organizing stresses the importance of having a thorough grounding in the customs and traditions of the community being organized. This is especially critical for those people who have cultural, racial, and linguistic identification, but who, for a variety of reasons, have been away from that community and are returning as organizers.

For example, how have the dynamics between organized religion and the community changed throughout the years? Ignored, its effect may imperil a whole organizing effort. Both the definition of the problems and the setting of goals to address them are involved. A number of Latino mental health and advocacy programs regularly consult with priests, ministers, and folk healers about the roles they all play (or might play) in advocating for mental health needs. These mental health activities are very clear about the importance of these other systems—formal and informal—in the community's spiritual life. The superstitions and religious archetypes are addressed by a variety of representatives, thereby making the advocacy work that much more relevant and effective. The Native American nations give deference to their medicine man, with no actions being taken until he has given approval. Similarly, the Vietnamese, Cambodian, and Laotian communities have strong religious leaders who help to define community commitments and directions.

All too often, there exists a cultural gap, as typified by younger, formally educated organizers working with community elders. The elders may be too conservative for the young organizers, or they disagree about tactics. Knowledge of and appreciation for the culture and traditions will help close the gap among key actors, or at least reduce the likelihood of unnecessary antagonisms.

3. An intimate knowledge of language and subgroup slang. We separate this dimension from the one just mentioned to emphasize its importance. Knowledge of a group's language style is indispensable when working with communities that are bi- or monolingual. Many embarrassing situations have arisen because of the organizer's ignorance of a community's language style. Approved idiomatic expressions in one area of the community may be totally unacceptable in another. Some expressions have sexual overtones in one

community while being inoffensive to other communities. Certain expressions may denote a class bias which may be offensive to one group of people or another. The literature on sociolinguistics has done an excellent job in alerting us to the importance of language subtleties and nuances. For a discussion on the role played by the same language in culturally different populations see Harrison.[18]

4. Leadership styles and development. Organizers must be leaders and lead organizers, but they must also work with existing community leaders and help in training emerging leadership. We recognize that there are significant differences in leadership styles from one community of color to another.... Indispensable to the composition of a successful leader is the individual's personality, how the individual's roles fit within the organizing task, and how personal values help to shape a world view. However achieved, a leader should have a sense of power that may be used in a respectful manner within the community.

5. An analytical framework for political and economic analysis. This is one dimension where the understanding of the dynamics of oppression through class analysis is paramount. A sophisticated knowledge of political systems with access and leverage points is very important. It must include an appraisal of who has authority within the ethnic community as well as who in it has power (often less formally acknowledged). The sources of mediating influence between the ethnic community and wider communities also must be understood. This knowledge fulfills two needs: (1) it helps to give the organizer the necessary analytical perspective in judging where the community fits in the hierarchy of economic analysis, and (2) it serves as a tool for educating the community, thereby increasing the community's consciousness of the roles and functions of the organizer within broader economic and social systems.[23]

6. Knowledge of past organizing strategies, their strengths, and limitations. It is imperative that organizers learn how to structure their organizing activities within an historical framework. This framework helps them to look at those strategies and tactics that have succeeded and failed in each community in the past. Since so little knowledge-building is evident in the field, it is critical that organizers develop and share an historical knowledge base that helps identify the many mistakes made to finally illuminate those techniques that appeared to have recently worked best in similar situations.

7. Skills in conscientization and empowerment. A major task of the organizer in disenfranchised communities is that of empowering people through the process of developing critical consciousness. How the personal and political influence each other, and the local environment in which they are played out, is a key to this process. It is not enough to succeed in ameliorating or even solving community problems if there is little or no empowerment of the community.

At the same time, power must be understood as both a tool and part of a process by the organizer. As Rubin and Rubin write "...community organizations need not focus exclusively on campaigns to achieve specific goals; they can make building their own power a long-term effort." Power may be destructive or productive in the sense of germinating ideas and concerns, and being integrative, or community-building. Of course, power is typically experienced in poor communities as both a negative and positive. The kind of power which is based on threats is often the most common in disenfranchised areas. When

FIGURE 16.2
Development of Critical Consciousness

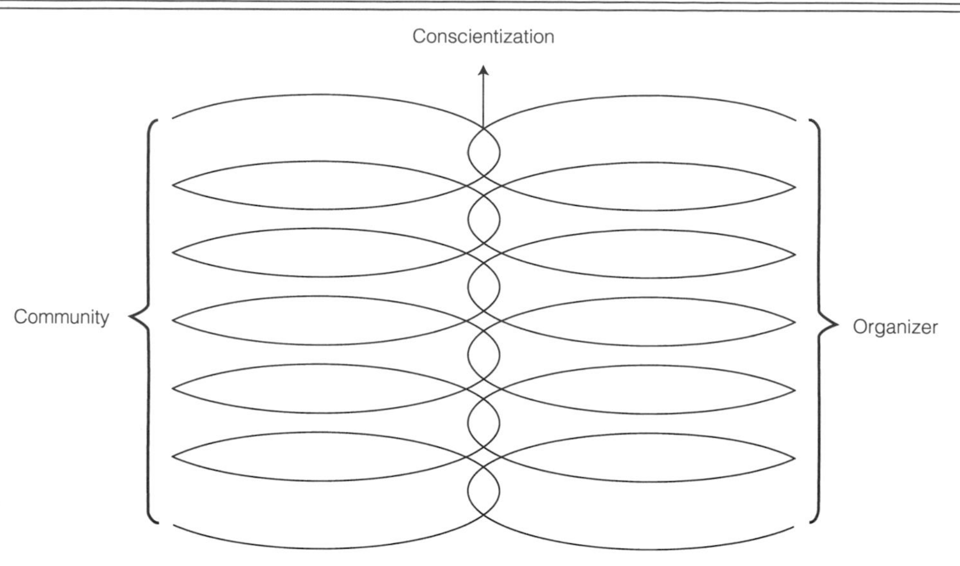


Organizer A makes the Target B act in ways it does not wish to act solely because of the sanctions A can levy against B, typically this becomes an imposed "win-lose" situation. A limited special hiring program usually takes this form.[23]

Power may also be a form of exchange, when Organizer A and Target B involve themselves in a reciprocal relationship or exchange because both parties have something to win from the process. Exchange is an integrative component of power because it involves some degree of trust, where the final outcome may be "win-win." Coalition building often takes this form. Power may also be defined as love—love for community, lifestyle, or family—which should motivate an organizer and the community.

Organizers and communities need to view each other as subjects rather than objects, as learners, and as equals. No organizer should enter a community with a sense that she or he has "the" answers for it. The development of critical consciousness through the process of conscientization may be visualized as a double spiraling helix, where both the organizer and community learn from each other the problems at hand and the strategies and tactics employed [Figure 16.2].[4]

The phenomenology of the experience is based on praxis, the melding of theory and experience, for both parties which in turn makes them stronger actors because their learning is mutual, supportive, and liberating of any preconceived notions one had about the other.

8. Skills in assessing community psychology. Organizers need to learn about the psychological makeup of their communities—free from stereotypes. Scant attention has been paid to this knowledge area by most community organizers. Methodologies without the understanding of the moti-

vations of the communities are a risky undertaking.

Organizers also need to understand what tends to keep a community allied and synergized. What is the life cycle of the community? Is it growing, mature, or declining? Are there new arrivals? Have they been in the community for generations? Does their language work as a cohesive force, or because of the multigenerational patterns, serve as a problem in getting people together? If the community has experienced a failure recently (like the loss of a valued school), what has it done to the shared psychological identification of the community? Does it feel frustrated and powerless? Or has it served to focus anger? If the latter is the case, what strategies may be employed to mobilize the community to action?

9. Knowledge of organizational behavior and decision making. Knowledge about organizational behavior and decision making are critical to the success of an organizer. The work of Bachrach and Baratz around decisionless decisions and nondecisions as decisions has demonstrated its worth in the field. Decisionless decisions are those decision-making strategies that "just happen" and "take off on a life of their own." Nondecisions as decisions are defined as:

> ...a means by which demands for change in the existing allocation of benefits and privileges in the community can be suffocated before they are even voiced or kept covert; or killed before they gain access to the relevant decision-making arena; or, fail all these things, maimed or destroyed in decisionimplementing stage of the policy process.[1]

An awareness of these dynamics is necessary both to be able to ascertain strategies being employed by the institutions targeted for change, but also, as a tactic that may also be employed by the community in its organizing.

10. Skills in evaluative and participatory research. One of the reasons communities of color have lost some of their political, economic, and legal victories is the increasing vacuum created by the lack of supportive information that has kept up with growing social problems experienced by most communities. Many communities are being victimized by data and demographics that have redefined their situations in manageable terms as far as the traditional systems are concerned. There needs to be an expanded role for organizers to include developing skills in demographic and population projections, and in social problem analysis. More organizers should develop theories about the declining social, economic, and political base of communities of color, and how people are still managing to survive in times of open hostility and encroachment on their civil rights and liberties. Crime, including drugs, is a major arena for these pressures.

Research continues to be an indispensable and very powerful tool for social change. Organizers should pay special attention to the use of participatory approaches, where both researchers and community people are involved as equal participants in securing knowledge to empower the community.*

Skill in evaluation research is another indispensable tool for organizers. The editors are not just suggesting that evaluative research be used only to assess program outcomes, but more to analyze the success and value of different organizing strategies and their relevance in disparate situations.

11. Skills in program planning and development and administration management. One of the bitter lessons learned

---

*For example, an entire issue of the *Community Development Journal* was devoted to participatory research and evaluation, thus stressing its international importance in working with disenfranchised and oppressed communities (1988).

from the War on Poverty had to do with the setup for failure nature of the administrative jobs offered to many people of color. Most had little or no administrative or managerial experience. One of the editors, then little-experienced, was offered a position that required him to administer a four-county migrant education and employment training program. With crash courses on organizational behavior, information processing, and budgeting, the challenge was met, but there were many mistakes along the way. Needless to say, the mistakes were widely reported by the program's detractors and administrator's enemies.

Many administrators of color have fallen by the wayside because they had not been given the opportunity to sharpen their managerial skills, and thus, a self-fulfilling prophecy of incompetence was validated in the eyes of people who desired to see these programs fail. Organizers must be aggressive in seeking out this knowledge base and not be deterred by the institutional barriers—financial, political, or otherwise—to attaining it.

12. An awareness of self and personal strengths and limitations. Reading through the list above may raise the question, "Does such a superorganizer possessing all the enumerated skills and knowledge exist?" The answer is both yes and no.

There are people throughout the country with these skills, and many who have most of them. We ask that organizers of color know their limitations and struggle to improve themselves. Organizers must know when to seek help, when to share responsibilities, and when to step aside to let others take over. Conversely, skilled and knowledgeable organizers must be open to sharing their expertise with communities and community leaders, especially when such sharing may mean their departure can be that much sooner.

A successful organizer is that individual who gains respect within the context of the actions being taken, not the individual who is (or appears to be) more knowledgeable than another. Honest intentions and abilities are worth more than degrees. Organizers also need to understand how to react to stresses. We all have our ways of coping with conflict. We need to know when our coping is no longer working for us, thereby jeopardizing the community. The danger of burnout is too well-documented to be ignored.

Finally, we would like to caution against "doing it for the community." Not only is this counter-productive, but also it increases the risk of feeling that one is being eaten alive by the people with whom one is working. All too often this results in another abandonment of a community whose experiences with social services have been much more of good rhetoric than serious social change.

## ENDNOTES

1. P. Bachrach and M.S. Baratz, *Power and Poverty: Theory and Practice* (New York: Oxford University Press, 1970), 42.
2. Felicity Barringer, "Two Million Blacks Not Counted Head of Census Panel Asserts," *New York Times,* March 12, 1991, p. A5-A6.
3. R. Blauner, *Racial Oppression in America* (New York: Harper & Row, 1972), 29-42.
4. Kenneth Boulding, *Three Faces of Power* (Beverly Hills: Sage Pubs., 1989), 25.
5. H. Boyte, *The Backyard Revolution: Understanding the New Citizen Movement* (Philadelphia: Temple, 1980).
6. S. Burghardt, *The Other Side of Organizing* (Cambridge, MA: Schenkman, 1982).
7. Census Bureau Press Release CB91-100, in *Census and You.* April, 1991, 3.
8. "Census Shows Profound Change in Racial Makeup of the Nation," by Felicity Barringer, *New York Times*, March 11th, 1991, A6-A9.

9. A. Dunham, *The New Community Organization* (New York: Crowell, 1970).

10. John L. Erlich and Felix G. Rivera, "Community Organization and Community Development," in N. Gilbert and H. Specht, *Handbook of the Social Services* (Englewood Cliffs, NJ: Prentice Hall, 1981), 472-489.

11. R. Fisher, "Community Organization in Historical Perspective: A Typology," *The Huston Review* (Summer 1984), 8.

12. R. Fisher, *Let the People Decide: Neighborhood Organizing in America* (Boston: Twayne, 1984).

13. G. Frederickson, *Neighborhood Control in the 1970s* (New York: Chandler, 1970).

14. P. Freire, *Education for Critical Consciousness* (New York: Seabury, 1973).

15. Paulo Freire, *The Politics of Education: Culture, Power and Liberation* (Granby, MA: Bergin & Garvey, Pubs., Inc., 1985), 29.

16. J. Gibbs, L. Huang and Associates, *Children of Color*: (San Francisco, CA: Jossey-Bass, 1989).

17. W. Goodenough, *Culture, Language, and Society* (Reading, MA: Addison-Wesley, 1971), 21-22.

18. Lawrence E. Harrison, "Underdevelopment Is a State of Mind." Cambridge: *Harvard Educational Review* (August 1988). Special Issue, "Race and Racism in American Education."

19. Sanford Horwitt, *Let Them Call Me Rebel: Saul Alinsky–His Life and Legacy* (New York: Knopf, 1989).

20. R. Kramer and H. Specht, *Readings in Community Organization Practice,* 3rd ed. (Englewood Cliffs, NJ: Prentice Hall, 1983), 15-16.

21. J. Roemer, Divide and Conquer: "Microfoundations of Marxian Theory of Wage Discrimination,"*Bell Journal of Economics,* 10 (Fall, 1979), 695-705.

22. J. Rothman and J. Tropman, Models of Community Organization and Macro Practice, in F. Cox et al. (eds.), *Strategies of Community Organization,* 4th ed. (Itasca, IL: Peacock, 1987), 3-26.

23. H.J. Rubin and I. Rubin, *Community Organizing and Development* (Columbus, OH: Merrill, 1986), 234.

24. E. Spaulding, *Statistics on Social Work Education in the United States: 1989* (Alexandria, VA: Council on Social Work Education, 1990), 6.

25. E.P. Thompson, *The Making of the English Working Class* (New York: Vintage Books, 1966).

26. W. Trattner, *From Poor Law to Welfare States,* 3rd ed. (New York: Free Press,1984).

27. R. Warren and D. Warren, *Neighborhood Organizer's Handbook* (Notre Dame, IN: Notre Dame Press, 1977).

28. Marc A. Zimmerman and Julian Rappaport, "Citizen Participation, Perceived Control, and Psychological Empowerment." *American Journal of Community Psychology* (16, 5, 1988), 725-750.

PART FOUR

# Administration, Management, and Policy

The human service field is made up of hundreds of thousands of organizations, big and little, in a not-for-profit sector. Additionally, much of government (for example, the departments of social services and health) and significant portions of the commercial sector (the human resources departments) are human service enterprises. The administration and management of these programs is the highest concern. Without effective and efficient management and administration, not only will the programs themselves falter, causing pain and disruption to clients and staff, but also, at another level, this same bumbling will erode confidence in the ability of the social service sector to deliver social service programs.

Historically the social service sector has been instructed by boards and the community at large "to become more businesslike." Our management practices of emphasizing greater degrees of concern for and involvement of the staff were labeled "bleeding heartism" and "silly" approaches to dealing with "the hard facts of administration." It is perhaps a sad comfort for us now to observe that many of the very businesses whose practices we were supposed to emulate have failed spectacularly. Indeed, the decline of American business has become a publicly accepted fact. The techniques that business had used in the past proved incapable of producing the quality and quantity of goods required for global competition. Perhaps even worse, a subset of those failures involved ethically questionable and possibly criminal behavior—the billions of dollars lost in the "thrift scandal," the organizations that bribe foreign governments, and so on. Suffice it to say that there is no magic management solution. Furthermore, the very practices that we were faulted for are now gaining favor, as the importance of employees as people is being recognized.

Thus, American professional practices have new prominence, but there are new responsibilities as well. Part Four will focus on several critical issues.

Supervision and management activities are crucial to successful community organizing, and to social and human service work in general. Jean Kruzich and Michael Austin, in a piece revised for this volume, provide some detailed considerations of what mangers and supervisors actually need to do.

Roslyn Chernesky and Marcia Bombyk focus on women administrators in social work and social welfare, a field with a predominance of women far exceeding those in management slots. They deal with some of the issues affecting the woman administrator.

Karen Feinstein's piece, "Innovative Management in Turbulent Times," suggest ways in which one can take advantage of the difficulties that these "turbulent times" now present to us. David Austin's piece on leadership and the human services executive uses a competing values scheme developed by Robert Quinn in his book *Beyond Rational Management* (San Francisco: Jossey-Bass, 1989).

Policy change in organizations and the introduction of change are difficult but necessary activities. The introduction of strategic change provides an overall prospective on some of the key requisites. "On-Site Analysis: A Practical Approach to Organizational Change," written by agency administrators Myers, Ufford, and Magill, makes some specific suggestions. The on site analysis technique has been developed and applied by human service professionals in literally hundreds of organizations in North America. It is the best technique we know for human service agencies.

In his discussion of an empirical study of administrators, Ric Hoefer suggests some of the necessary important skills and how they rank among beginning, middle, and top executives. There is much agreement in the ordering of skills and perspectives: The main difference among the levels is that several administrators are expected to *know* more in each of the categories.

Henry Havassy provides techniques to help the classic "middle manager" cope with being the locus of conflicting expectations, as well as in dealing with the issues arising from it.

Finally, there are questions about policy—organizational policy and agency policy. One can debate policy endlessly, but there are particular techniques that are useful in the provision of policy information, and a piece on the techniques of policy analysis concludes this section.

—John E. Tropman

17.

Jean M. Kruzich and Michael J. Austin

# LEADING AND MANAGING COMMUNITY ORGANIZATIONS IN THE '90s

The literature on social service management continues to grow, providing increased depth and breadth in its coverage of the knowledge and skills needed to successfully lead social service agencies. Case materials, texts, and professional journals provide conceptual frameworks and empirical research results that can serve to guide management staff in conducting program evaluations, staffing programs, developing an information system, and a host of other managerial topics. Yet, this literature tends to focus primarily on administration and supervision issues as they relate to direct-service agencies. While the management of both direct-service and community-organizing agencies share some similarities, there are some important differences that relate to the unique characteristics of community-organizing agencies that impact supervisory and management practices.

Community organization approaches encompass (1) locality development with its focus on neighborhood or community involvement, (2) social planning with its focus on interagency problem solving and planning, and (3) social action, with its emphasis on social movements and political strategies seeking a redistribution of power, resources, and community decision making (Rothman, 1979). It is not unusual to find a community organization agency that incorporates one or more of these approaches. Thus, a neighborhood development association may be involved in the development of block clubs (locality development), in collaborating with the city planning department on a long-term plan for neighborhood improvement (social planning), and in organizing a chapter of the Gray Panthers in an effort to make the needs of senior citizens more apparent to city officials (social action). Just as an organization may incorporate more than one approach to community organizing, so too an agency may be involved in providing primarily direct services and secondarily seek to carry out specified community organizing activities.

This article is designed to provide a general overview of the roles and functions of supervisors and executives of community organizing agencies. Such agencies include United Way Community Planning Councils, neighborhood associations, community-based, nonprofit development corporations, Associations for Battered Women, and community action councils. Special attention will be paid to tasks and issues involved in supervising individuals carrying out organizing activities and some of the unique characteristics of citizen involvement with a focus on executive-board relationships. Our analysis begins with a discussion of the role of community organizing technology and its focus on community change, the organizer's work, and the

Jean M. Kruzich is an associate professor at the School of Social Work, University of Washington; Michael J. Austin is at the University of California, Berkeley.

ideology of the organizer. Community organizing technology clearly impacts the roles of agency supervisors and directors in a manner that is different from the performance of management roles in direct service agencies.

## THE NATURE AND FOCUS OF THE SERVICE TECHNOLOGY

A major distinction between direct service to clients and community organizing is the technology used. Technology refers to techniques that are applied to some kind of raw material which the organization transforms into a product (Perrow, 1970). For the direct-service worker, techniques may include individual, family, or group counseling, case consultation, or skill training. Examples of such techniques include offering training in activities of daily living for a group of nursing home residents, providing group counseling for sexual abuse victims, delivering workshops on parent effectiveness training, and offering case consultation to paraprofessionals in a residential treatment center. On the other hand, the technology of community organizing is likely to include writing proposals, organizing block clubs, developing a survey of a community's assets and needs, negotiating interagency collaborative agreements, building coalitions to put pressure on a state legislature, or lobbying to get lower electricity rates for homeowners. While both caseworkers and community organizers work with individuals and groups (interactional tasks) and engage in problem solving (analytical tasks), these tasks are carried out through different methods.

One aspect of any technique is its visibility. Unlike the clinician, the bulk of whose work is often carried out in an agency's office, the organizer's work is carried out in neighborhoods, other agencies, community centers, and residents' homes. Consequently, not only is the organizer's work more visible; it is also performed in a wider range of settings. In addition, the organizer often works in groups so that he/she is likely to be involved with larger numbers of clients than the direct-service worker. In the same vein, the diversity of individuals that are part of the organizer's practice is likely to be greater.

Besides using different technology, the community organizer's focus of change is also different from the direct-service worker's. While direct-service worker's major focus is to help clients adjust to their environment by individual change, the organizer's focus involves changing environments in the community or in institutions such as prisons, schools, and welfare departments through mobilizing a group of community members in a way that reallocates resources. This focus may often involve confrontation or conflict with politicians and bureaucrats and, at times, other social service professionals. Requiring other groups or organizations to change may involve significant resistance and hostility, which is similar to that found in the counseling process. What is different is that the conflict may be with a societal institution that enjoys a good deal of community support and not a single client.

In addition, the fact that community organizing as a method often attracts individuals who are strongly committed to client groups may well result in conflicts between the worker and executive, with the organizer's focus on maximizing client empowerment and the administrator's emphasis on agency survival.

The following three sections examine different aspects of managing community organizations: first, supervision of community organizers: second, the roles of the executive; and third, citizen involvement.

## SUPERVISING COMMUNITY ORGANIZERS

In this section, supervision is discussed in the context of community organization agencies. The issues involved in the transition from organizer to supervisor are addressed. In addition, a framework is provided as an aid to the supervisor and worker engaged in articulating their understanding of community work. The importance of management by objectives and strategies as well as performance evaluation and staff development of organizer is discussed. The supervisory issues noted in this section are relevant for both the supervisor operating at the program level as well as the director of an agency devoted to community organizing activities.

### Transition from Organizer to Supervisor

The transition from organizer to supervisor is rarely a smooth or easy process. Many issues, including the use of authority, decision-making style, orientation to relationships, orientation to effectiveness, and colleague orientation, emerge as one shifts from one role to another.

The changes in one's use of authority can be quite confusing. As an organizer, one derives one's authority primarily from the client group in relationship to one's expertise, experience, and relationship-building capacities. The organizer's reputation is built primarily in the community. In contrast, the supervisor's authority is derived from expertise in working with subordinates and from the supervisor's middle management position. In this position, the reputation is built primarily within the agency as supervisors exercise authority in seeking the cooperation of subordinates and compliance with organization demands. The exercise of supervisory authority is also related to maintaining one's managerial credibility with supervisors. If you are unable to exercise authority in managing subordinates, your transition from organizer to supervisor may be incomplete.

The second transition issue involves decision-making styles. The primary decision-making style of the organizer is to be responsive to the client population and to optimize the client group's capacity to act in pursuit of its own interests. In essence, organizers move with the flow of decision making which emerges out of citizen involvement. In contrast, the supervisor seeks to guide organizational decision making, which emerges out of staff involvement, in order to identify compromises. Such compromising results when subordinates compete for the supervisor's time and attention, which must be rationed across a group of subordinates in a manner by which subordinate capacity building must be shared equally and thereby not necessarily meeting all of the unique needs of each organizer. This can be most unsettling to the new supervisor seeking to continue the optimizing approach to decision making acquired as an organizer.

The third issue includes relationship building. One of the critical skills of an organizer is the capacity to build effective relationships with a client population whether it is the process of developing neighborhood cohesiveness, the goal orientation of strategies designed to change public policies, or the task orientation of an interagency planning group seeking to develop new services. In contrast, the supervisor-subordinate relationship reflects a different orientation, with a concern for helping staff members develop their skills in order to become the best workers possible as well as building the organization through fundraising recruiting and developing volunteer leadership. The managerial relationship requires a special conserving of energy in order to maintain a balance of time and commitment to personnel supervision and program supervision tasks (Bobo, Kendall & Max, 1991).

The fourth issue in making the transition from organizer to supervisor involves one's orientation to effectiveness. The organizer usually defines his or her effectiveness in terms of the results gained, issues won, and capacity built by the client population. For example, if the organizer helped to get streetlights installed in the neighborhood, such an outcome could reflect on the organizer's effectiveness. In contrast, the supervisor tends to assess effectiveness in terms of a range of projects or programs that contribute to the goals of the agency. Effectiveness is more than the successes of one organizer. The viability and survival of the agency is frequently built upon the capacity of supervisors to document fully, assess, and interpret the combined effectiveness of staff across several projects or activities. One's orientation to effectiveness clearly differs in relation to one's position as an organizer or as a supervisor of organizers.

The last issue relates to one's colleague orientation. In most cases, organizers provide peer support to one another as they engage in the difficult processes of mobilizing people and resources. The collegiality among organizers, similar to that experienced by caseworkers, usually involves the sharing of successes and failures, the seeking of advice, and the sharing of personal life experiences. This orientation to colleagues clearly shifts into a new arena when one assumes the somewhat lonely position of supervisor. This middle management loneliness is based, in part, on the perception that it is difficult to share supervisory worries with subordinates, and it requires special effort to build a peer support group of supervisors inside and/or outside the agency. At times, peer support inside the agency is difficult to achieve if there is competition with other supervisors for office space, additional staff, additional financial resources, or the director's attention. In the case of smaller agencies where the executive assumes supervision of organizers, no peer support in the agency may be available. The changes in one's orientation to collegial relations can be one of the most personally distressing aspects of the transition from organizer to supervisor.

The five transition issues have been identified primarily to alert all supervisors of the need to recognize and work on the dilemmas inherent in making a shift from one role to another. Ignoring these issues or denying their importance simply means that they will need to be addressed in the future (that is, pay now or pay later).

### Understanding the Nature of Community Organizing Work

One's definition of community organizing will obviously vary according to the setting and the goals to be achieved. However, the major issue in this section is the recognition that supervisors must develop and articulate their own understanding of the nature of community organizing. This capacity is essential for assisting staff to understand their work, for teaching organizing skills to your staff, for advocating with staff the special needs of your unit, and for communicating with significant others in the community.

In an effort to demonstrate one approach

FIGURE 17.1
Framework for Conceptualizing Community Organizing Work

| Major Job Functions | Methods of Practice | | |
|---|---|---|---|
| | Social Action | Locality Development | Social Planning |
| 1. *Outreach* | | | |
| Case Finding/Problem Finding | Tasks | Tasks | Tasks |
| Constituency Building | Tasks | Tasks | Tasks |
| 2. *Resource Mobilizing* | | | |
| People and Influence | Tasks | Tasks | Tasks |
| Money and Materials | Tasks | Tasks | Tasks |
| 3. *Advocacy* | | | |
| Client and Group | Tasks | Tasks | Tasks |
| Systems and Legislature | Tasks | Tasks | Tasks |
| 4. *Administration* | | | |
| Intra-Agency/Organization | Tasks | Tasks | Tasks |
| Interagency/Organization | Tasks | Tasks | Tasks |

to conceptualizing community organizing work and to stimulate discussion and debate, a framework was developed and is highlighted in Figure 17.1. The framework is built on three assumptions: (1) that community organizing practice can be meaningfully divided into the three models: social action, locality development, and social planning; (2) that there are work functions common to all three methods involving outreach, resource mobilization, advocacy, and administration; and (3) within each work function there are essential tasks that are the major ingredients of a community organizer's job description.

Job functions or duties in Figure 17.1 refer to a constellation of essential activities carried out by an organizer. For example, outreach is defined in terms of case-finding and constituency-building tasks; resource mobilizing is defined in terms of mobilizing people and political influence as well as money and materials; advocacy is defined in terms of advocating for systems change related to either administrative or social policies; and the administrative role is defined in terms of intra-agency tasks (such as record keeping, performance evaluation, maintaining tax exempt status) and interagency tasks (like coalition maintenance, newsletters, planning and implementing conferences or rallies).

The tasks within each cell can be defined as action or action sequences grouped through time with specified outcomes. Task statements include specific action verbs and outcome statements, which define worker behavior in terms of the work to be done in relationship to the worker and the work organization (Austin, 1981). Such specificity is useful for clarifying the nature of the job for both the supervisor and the organizer and can be used in job descriptions, performance evaluations, and career-development activities related to upgrading the knowledge and skills of the organizer. A list of selected community organizer tasks is noted in Figure 17.2.

## Managing by Objectives and Strategies

Supervisors of community organizing staff need to expand the traditional administrative approaches of managing by objec-

FIGURE 17.2
Selected Tasks Relevant to the Job of a Community Organizer
(L.D. = Locality Development; S.P. = Social Planning; S.A. = Social Action)

I. *Outreach*
1. Develops information network with neighborhood residents in order to monitor unmet community needs. (L.D.)
2. Conducts community needs assessment surveys in order to develop interagency planning proposals. (S.P.)
3. Participates actively in local coalition of organizations in order to monitor violations of client rights. (S.A.)

II. *Resource Mobilizing*
1. Organizes campaign to recruit volunteers for developing a block watch anticrime program. (L.D.)
2. Develops grant proposal to submit to a local foundation in order to meet an emerging community need. (S.P.)
3. Meets with union representatives in order to secure political support and financial resources for a consumer boycott. (S.A.)

III. *Advocacy*
1. Confers with city hall representatives about neighborhood public housing resident in order to influence a favorable decision for resident. (L.D.)
2. Testifies before state legislature in order to influence legislation affecting community agencies. (S.P.)
3. Organizes picket of local companies in order to change policies unfair to disadvantaged consumers. (S.A.)

IV. *Administration*
1. Prepares report on neighborhood conditions in order to develop new agency program to address those conditions. (L.D.)
2. Organizes campaign to approach several local foundations in order to seek financing for new service program. (S.P.)
3. Develops a telephone tree or network in order to alert consumers quickly about the need to write to their legislative representatives. (S.A.)

tives to include managing by strategy. Since supervisors actively model behaviors for their subordinates, they need to help organizers specify their objectives in relationship to a client population or a set of organizations. These objectives usually relate to the mission of the agency or organization that employs the organizer. Organizational auspice is a critical component of everyday practice about which organizers need regular reminding and reinforcement of the agency's mission.

Managing by strategy represents a more future orientation to organizing practice, whereas managing by objectives tends to reflect the past and present. Managing by strategy seeks to focus on specifying future goals and mechanisms which the client population needs to consider. Managing by objectives tends to emerge from extrapolational planning, which uses past and present information to guide practice. Managing by strategy utilizes transformational planning by which the future is defined in terms of the ideal, and current practice is oriented toward reaching the ideal. Both perspectives are important components of the modeling done by supervisors for their subordinates. For example, a supervisor using management by objectives seeks to help the organizer carry out the agency's program goals and objectives as set out for the year and developed out of prior agency expertise. Still, the supervisor also needs to include managing by strategy by involving the organizer in thinking strategically about the future in such a way as to develop emerging goals and objectives related to client needs but not yet formalized through agency planning and decision making.

Management by strategy involves considerable creativity, risk taking, competence, and worker autonomy.

The day-to-day practice of organizers parallels the work of direct-service personnel. For example, case management processes are critical attributes of clinical personnel (Austin, 1981). Similarly, project or task group development and implementation are essential features of organizing work. Some community organizations consider part of their mission as increasing skills of organizational participants, including community members. In these cases the importance of hiring staff who share the racial, cultural, and linguistic identity of the community will be of crucial importance (Rivera and Erlich, 1992) and may involve hiring staff who will need a good deal of training. In these situations where developing participant skills is seen as a form of empowerment and a goal in itself, the supervisor is likely to have to play an even more active role in providing support. Three methods that can be used in supervising organizers are project consultation, process consultation, and program consultation. Project consultation, like case consultation, involves providing organizers with specific advice and assistance for conducting their day-to-day work. Process consultation can address the methods by which the organizer intervenes or works with a target population. Program consultation relates to the involvement of organizers in formulating programs relevant to the employing agency or organization which are then communicated across and up the organization. Program consultation relates back to managing by strategy, in which the supervisor and his or her unit of organizers can influence the future direction of the employing agency by spelling out new directions and programs for community organizing.

**Evaluation and Upgrading Staff**

The final dimension of supervision addressed in this section includes performance evaluation and staff development. The mechanisms of good personnel management are available for both supervisors and community organizers, and they require an understanding of the difference between a periodic career development conference and the annual performance review. The career development conference is usually an annual or semiannual supervisor-subordinate meeting designed as a supportive and educational event devoted to the future learning needs and experiences of the organizer. It is built upon the premises of increasing professionalization and lifelong learning.

In contrast, the annual performance review is usually an agency requirement reflected in agency personnel policies. Sound performance evaluations allow the supervisor and organizer to identify agency-related problems that need to be corrected by organizational change and worker-related performance difficulties that may involve training. The supervisor needs to be a good diagnostician in order to identify whether difficulties in job performance are due to organizational structural problems or a lack of aptitude, motivation, or training (Whelton & Cameron, 1991). Performance review tools include the graphic rating form, the management by objective (MBO) approach, and the essay or the combined essay/graphic approach (Austin, 1981). The graphic rating form includes specific criteria relevant to the community organizer's job, with rating categories ranging from excellent to poor. The criteria might include use of judgment, resourcefulness, self-control, planning capacities, and cost consciousness. The MBO approach is an outcome-oriented approach in which objectives are set at the beginning of the year and are assessed at the end of the year. The essay approach is simply a narrative report, which includes a description of the work performed, the strengths of the worker's performance, and the areas of work performance requiring continuing attention or improvement. The essay/graphic approach combines these two methods by encouraging both narrative comments and ratings ranging from excellent to poor in such areas as accomplishment of job requirements, knowledge of job, reliability, communication capacities, and personal relationship capacities.

Central to both periodic career development conferences and annual performance reviews are the supervisor's capabilities for giving and receiving feedback. These communication skills are essential in conducting such conferences and reviews. Besides the periodic reviews, staff also need regular feedback: Nothing on the formal evaluation should be a surprise. If supervisors are only critical or only laudatory of staff performance in their ongoing feedback and performance reviews, they are depriving staff of relevant information necessary for career planning and effective job performance.

Staff development is obviously related to performance evaluation. The data generated from career conferences and performance reviews need to be jointly converted, by the supervisor and organizer, into plans for updating and upgrading staff. Poorly performed tasks can be translated into learning objectives to be met on the job, through in-service training, or through continuing education programs. Acquiring the capacity to perform new tasks as a result of job enlargement or job enrichment can also be addressed through staff development planning. At times, the supervisor acts as a trainer by tutoring staff, formulating growth-enhancing questions, sharing power by exploring new areas of knowledge and skill together, and assessing community educational resources for the purpose of guiding the education of subordinates.

It is particularly important for supervisors to conceptualize the range of knowledge and skill relevant for the effective job performance of organizers. The knowledge and skills should be related to the functions and tasks noted in Figures 17.1 and 17.2. Since all staff are by definition different, each organizer probably has different educational needs. Some of the knowledge and skill areas relevant to community organizing practice might include: (1) written and oral communication, (2) community and leadership analysis, (3) program development, (4) citizen participation, (5) community and organizational change tactics, (6) assessment of community needs and assets, (7) grant writing and fund raising, (8) political and legislative lobbying, (9) using the media, (10) interorganizational relations, (11) community development techniques, (12) problem-solving and decision-making skills, (13) building and maintaining coalitions, and (14) task group management. Most organizers probably reflect different capacities to demonstrate excellence in these areas. An accurate and detailed job description can be an invaluable tool in ensuring a mutual understanding of the organizer's responsibilities and needs for supervision.

In the next section, we shall move from the perspective of the supervisor to the managerial roles of the agency or organization executive who is ultimately responsible for the job performance of all staff.

## THE ROLES OF THE EXECUTIVE

### Managerial Roles

The administrator or chief executive of a community agency is expected to wear

FIGURE 17.3
Mintzberg's Ten Managerial Roles

| | |
|---|---|
| *Interpersonal Roles* | |
| Figurehead: | Performs duties of a ceremonial nature. |
| Leader: | Carries out staffing duties including hiring, training, motivating, promoting, dismissing. |
| Liaison: | Develops and maintains relationships with individuals outside the agency. |
| *Informational Roles* | |
| Monitor: | Seeks information on internal operations and external events. |
| Disseminator: | Sends factual and value information to staff. |
| Spokesperson: | Transmits information to organization's environment. |
| *Decisional Roles* | |
| Entrepreneur (Innovator): | Initiates and designs controlled change in organization. |
| Disturbance Handler: | Responds to involuntary situations and change beyond his/her control. |
| Resource Allocator: | Oversees system by which organizational resources are allocated. |
| Negotiator: | Negotiates with other organizations or individuals. |

many hats. Since some community organizations have only two or three permanent staff persons in addition to volunteers and student interns, the agency director may also have direct supervisory authority over workers—a task usually performed by middle managers and first-line supervisors in larger social service agencies. One useful way of looking at the executive's position is by examining the ten different roles that represent organized sets of administrative behaviors. Mintzberg (1973) identified three role clusters and ten roles that are defined in Figure 17.3. These rolc clusters group activities into three broad groups: interpersonal, informational, and decisional. Together, these role clusters comprise the major dimensions of the executive's job.

These roles provide a framework for the executive to organize tasks and clarify the amount of time spent in carrying out each role. An executive's analysis of *current* activities, which delineates the amount of time currently spent in the different roles, together with *future* projections, offers useful information to the board members in developing performance evaluation criteria for the executive. In a similar vein, an executive's analysis of his or her performance on either a role cluster or an individual role can provide valuable information on potential areas of improvement. By using roles to conceptualize the position, executives can move toward a clearer specification of the activities that comprise their job descriptions, offer clear criteria to board members for performance evaluation purpose, and identify areas of need for an executive development plan.

Within interpersonal roles, as *figurehead*, an agency executive of a local organization may attend the opening of a neighborhood bank cooperative or an honors dinner for high school youth in the neighborhood. A community development agency executive might be called upon to perform the figurehead role more often than, for example, the director of a planning organization where the agency is not part of a particular neighborhood or serving a specific target population. Though the amount of time spent in the role will vary with different types of agencies, it is part of any executive position.

The *leader* role involves virtually all interpersonal relationships between the leader and the led wherein the administrator seeks to integrate the workers' and organization's goals by involving staff in decisions regarding goals and objectives. Two different ways to achieve this integration are the democratic and bureaucratic leadership styles. In the former, workers are involved in decisions regarding goals and objectives, and cooperation among staff, board, and executive is cultivated with a view toward the personal development of each of the workers. A bureaucratic approach follows a hierarchical chain of command with staff having limited input into decisions. Rules and guidelines are used to control behavior, with attempts to minimize the discretion of the staff person.

In general, a number of factors support community organizations operating at the democratic participatory end of this continuum rather than the bureaucratic end. Their size, which is generally smaller than other types of community organizations, together with the focus on empowering individuals, provides support for a more collaborative approach. In addition, boards of community organizations are likely to be composed of neighborhood residents or clients, whose position as consumer and regulator represents a major force in shaping policy and guidelines.

The administrator's *liaison* role includes interaction with other executive directors, membership on other community organizations' boards, and attendance at conferences and professional meetings. This role focuses attention on the task environment, which includes the agency's consumers, competitors, suppliers of resources, legitimators, and regulators (Lauffer, 1978). Performing the liaison function allows the manager to strengthen relationships with funders, foresee change in public policies that will impinge on the agency's mission, and find out how competitors and/or directors of similar agencies are responding to problems.

While these first three roles are primarily interpersonal in nature, the next three require skills in information processing. As *monitor*, the executive seeks information that helps detect changes in the environment, identifies problems, and builds up knowledge. The executive obtains information from four areas: (1) internal operations (for example, hearing that an employee is unhappy and planning to quit), (2) external events (for example, contacts with the city's office of Community Development result in finding out that there is some money left over from their allocations that the agency might be eligible for), (3) analyses/reports (such as demographic data on the changing composition of the agency's neighborhood), and (4) pressures (like individuals and groups that make demands on the executive for different organizational priorities, support for another organization's involvement with the agency's clientele, and the like).

Just as the agency head needs to gather information, he or she also plays the central role in the way information is disseminated in the organization, thus the role of *disseminator*. The amount and kind of information shared with staff will depend upon the administrative style of the executive, the staff's understanding of the agency's mission and goals, and the director's capacity to articulate the mission and goals. In addition to articulating the agency's philosophy, the administrator must provide factual information that he or she alone is able to gather as a result of the status and connections that come with the position.

As *spokesperson*, the executive is involved in educating relevant publics about the agency activities and programs by speaking at community forums, using a newsletter, appearing on television or radio, attracting coverage in local newspapers, or through other forms of communication. This role is particularly important because of the visibility of the organizer's work and agency involvement with many different elements in the environment. While all employees have a part in communicating the agency's purpose, the executive has primary responsibility for representing the organization. Only if the executive has been able to provide leadership that successfully combines worker and organizational interests is the agency able to present a coherent picture to the public. The messages the executive or staff communicate to the task environment may range from annual financial reports to funding agencies to newsletters that give special recognition to agency volunteers.

The last role cluster is decisional, and it includes roles that use strategy development—a planning process whereby a series of decisions are made in order to deal with a problem or issue.

The manager as *entrepreneur* or *innovator* is involved in activities such as assisting in developing a new board training program, computerizing agency records, or offering workshops on using the media to community leaders. The executive has a major responsibility in setting the organizational culture. Does the agency focus on the needs or deficits of the community or on its assets and competencies? While the administrator may initiate and design a plan to bring about the change, there are at least three ways the change process may be handled (Mintzberg, 1973): (1) delegate all responsibility for the different phases of the change effort, based on the size of the change or expertise; (2) authorize staff responsibility for working out the details of the plan; but control signoff or approval before the plan is operationalized; and (3) maintain control and responsibility for the planning and implementation phases.

In the role of innovator the manager initiates change voluntarily, whereas in the role of *disturbance handler* he or she deals with involuntary situations and changes that are partially beyond the manager's control. A rent strike by members of a cooperative housing association or growing factionalism in a coalition of organizations addressing racism in the police department might require the director to take action. Losing a major funding source or the lease on the agency's building are also events that require decisive action on the part of the executive. These disturbances can be grouped into three types : (1) conflicts between staff and/or board member, (2) resource losses or threats thereof, and (3) conflicts with other agencies regarding territory, responsibilities, or authority.

Organizational resources are money, time, material, equipment, person power, and agency reputation, and the executive as *resource allocator* plays a key part is this ongoing process— one usually characterized by conflict and bargaining. Everything from how the executive spends time to setting priorities for the use of staff time and travel monies is included. Once again, the degree of staff involvement in these decisions will depend on the executive leadership style.

The manager also plays a central role as *negotiator* because of his or her authority to commit resources. Negotiating a major contract with the Department of Housing and Urban Development (HUD) or participating in a collective bargaining session with an employees' union regarding staff compensation and benefits are both negotiating activities. In both instances it is the manager's ability to commit organizational resources that legitimizes this involvement.

A review of these ten roles describes the sets of behavior the executive needs to undertake if the organization is to succeed with its mission. By distinguishing between roles where the focus is the external environment (figurehead, liaison, spokesperson, negotiator) and roles primarily aimed at internal affairs (leader, monitor, disseminator, innovator, and resource allocator) the overview points up the major task of the executive—that is, constantly to operate on the boundaries, balancing the external demands of the environment with the internal needs of the agency and its staff.

While it is useful to discuss the ten managerial roles sequentially, they are interrelated—with effective performance in one role tied to ability to perform in another role. As understanding of the factors that influence resource allocations (Kins & Fawcett, 1987), community mobilization (Freudenberg, Lee & Silver, 1989) empowerment (Zimmerman & Rappaport, 1988) and service to diverse populations (Washington, 1987) grows, the executive, in his/her role as monitor, needs to keep abreast of the developing knowledge base and disseminate relevant findings to staff. Similarly the executive's liaison role that involves staying abreast of new tactics, sources of funding, and community resources provides the bases for supporting innovations in the agency.

## CITIZEN INVOLVEMENT

An agency's board of directors is usually responsible for establishing policy guidelines, reviewing and adopting budgets, evaluating major programs, establishing job classifications, and selecting and evaluating the agency's chief executive (Lauffer, 1978). These responsibilities are impacted by the directors' perception of the usefulness of citizen involvement and by board activities. If the board is seen as a time-consuming burden or as a rubber stamp for executive decisions, the executive will have little reason to ensure that information is fully shared, particularly when the data might raise questions. If, however, the board is seen as an asset, as a group of individuals who act as advocates for clients and agency as well as liaisons between the community, other agencies, community groups, and elected officials, the executive will promote board involvement.

A strong board is usually capable of recognizing and dealing with ideological differences that may lead to such potential conflicts as disagreements over the respective functions of the board and the executive or different views about the future direction of the agency. While policy determination is a board responsibility and policy execution is the responsibility of the executive and staff, these responsibilities are frequently shared—despite their different sources of authority and power. The board is the executive's employer, and yet the executive is generally held responsible for the results for the agency programs. Because of a sense of responsibility, the executive may see it in his or her best interest to avoid sharing information on agency problems that may reflect unfavorably on his or her abilities. This response limits how well the board can carry out its tasks. However, there are numerous mechanisms to help manage conflict and develop trust through cooperation. The following section on board development and training will highlight some methods of reducing conflicts that result from a lack of clearly defined roles and expectation.

A second area of potential ideological

differences may be reflected in the composition of the board. While the boards of most direct-service agencies include community members, the majority are professionals and community leaders who share similar educational and work experiences as well as a socioeconomic status that frequently matches the attributes of the agency's executive. In contrast, the boards of community organization agencies are usually dominated by consumers and activists keenly invested in the specific programs of the agency. Examples of such organizations might be neighborhood development agencies, housing cooperatives, tenants' unions, and citizens' action councils. The executive may well be faced with two unique issues when consumers of the service dominate the board. First, the board's concern for clients may be such an overriding factor that members fail to consider the value of staff expertise, the possibility of alternative funding sources, and program strategies that will win support from the larger community. A board with such a perspective may view the executive as conservative and unwilling to serve the real needs of people. From the executive's perspective, the board members lack the experience and expertise necessary to work with city officials and foundations; such a perspective may lead the executive to see the board as unrealistic and naive.

Board compositions that are primarily or totally consumers do not help create the same web of relationships. Thus, one would expect that the executive of a consumer-controlled board would need to spend more time performing the liaison role to ensure obtaining necessary information. In contrast, a board made up of professionals and other agencies' staff people plays a liaison role that is helpful in alerting the executive to changing political and economic realities. This kind of board also acts as a bridge to other agencies and their successes and failures with different strategies.

Just as a consumer-controlled board creates special challenges for the executive, different conflicts are likely to develop with a board composed primarily of professionals. While these individuals may help give the agency status and prestige, they could also be a conservative force that impedes the agency's choosing the most effective strategy or focus. Since most human service professionals operate on a collaborative or consensus approach, there may be little support for more activist strategies involving conflict. An executive who has had work experience as an organizer would recognize the importance of pressuring organizations to change at the risk of alienating some community institutions such as the police or schools. Board members unfamiliar with advocacy and social action strategies may be unwilling to support activist strategies.

Regardless of board composition, clarity about both the structure of the board/executive working relationship and the ideological focus of agency efforts is needed. Differences of perspective that are acknowledged, addressed, and worked through can result in a clear view and shared commitment to agency tasks and mission. In order to play a strong role in the agency, the board needs training. The next section discusses what is needed to help a board be effective and suggests ways in which staff and executives can assist in developing an effective board of directors.

## Board Training Issues

In order to be effective, a board must include an adequate and qualified membership, a firm philosophical and rational basis for existence, an organizational framework from which to work, an understanding of the functions they are expected to perform, and the knowledge, skills, and assistance to accomplish these functions (Peterfreund, 1980).

The most important element of an effective board is active, committed, and informed members. The best way to ensure the selection of such board members is strategic recruiting after locating individuals who meet the board's needs. Steps in the recruitment process include:

1. Assessing board membership needs, which includes:
   a. Examining the composition of the current board in terms of age, sex, income level, and racial-ethnic backgrounds; also, examining occupations, knowledge, skills, experience, and educational background to determine gaps in expertise. In addition, note future projects and directions and assess gaps in skills needed to deal with issues effectively.
   b. Recognizing any requirements concerning board composition in bylaws or federal regulations. Examine any problems regarding turnover or excess absenteeism in an attempt to understand them.
2. Advertising for prospective board members: Consider newspapers (especially local ones), flyers, posters, contacting community groups and individuals.
3. Screening, interviewing, and orienting prospective board members.

Once individuals are chosen, specially designed orientation programs can provide information vital to board member function by specifying roles and responsibilities. The following types of information are helpful (Peterfreund, 1980):

- History, purpose, philosophy of the agency
- An organizational chart, description of programs, client characteristics, agency finances
- Role and organization of the board, articles of incorporation, and major board and agency policies

While the board, the executive, and the staff should be involved in developing orientation materials, new board members should have the opportunity to meet with agency staff and the director, to participate in workshops or training sessions focusing on the role of the board, to ask questions after reading the orientation material, and to engage in a "buddy system" where each member is assigned to an experienced member for the first six months (Peterfreund, 1980).

In addition to recruitment and orientation activities, there needs to be a recognition of the value of ongoing board development as reflected by the commitment of the executive director. In organizing the planning group, board members, executive, and staff need to be involved in designing a board development program which includes:

1. Assessing board needs (compare actual performance with ideal performance).
2. Prioritizing areas identified by needs assessment (include consideration of time necessary from board and staff and other resources required).
3. Setting goals for accomplishment (make them clear, measurable, and acceptable to all involved).
4. Developing a plan of action for board development (include content areas and educational methods).

The content of development activities will vary according to type of agency and board composition. For a social planning organization composed primarily of professionals and lay leaders, board training may be aimed at increasing knowledge of advocacy and lobbying. If the board is composed primarily of low-income consumers with little experience in working on committees, the board development program might stress the knowledge and skills of working in task groups.

## SUMMARY

The purpose of this article was to provide an overview of supervisory and management functions in a community organization. We began by describing some characteristics of community organizations that seem to set them apart from direct-service organizations. The technology of the community organizer is usually more visible, is performed in a wide range of settings, includes a larger number of individuals, and is aimed at changes in institutions or social arrangements. The community organizing technology attracts persons with ideological perspectives that are often divergent from those of the supervisor. All of these factors seem to influence supervisory and administrative responsibilities.

The supervisor must clearly understand the organization's functions and the tasks that flow from them. Clearly defined tasks inform and facilitate cooperative planning strategies; they also provide a base for performance evaluation and staff development. Just as the supervisor needs to conceptualize the organizer's work, the executive needs to examine his or her job. Managerial roles for describing executive functions provide a framework for assessing the executive's current and future job activities. These roles also act as a classification scheme that executives and boards can use to evaluate and assess performance.

The last section focused on citizen involvement, particularly in relation to executive–board relations. The success of the administrator in implementing policy is in part dependent on the degree of support and involvement of a committed board. That section also identified potential sources of conflict in executive–board relations as well as possible methods to help develop and maintain an effective board.

## REFERENCES


Austin, Michael J. (1981). *Supervisory management for the human services.* Englewood Cliffs, NJ: Prentice-Hall.

Bobo, K. Kendall, J. & Max S. (1991). *Organizing for social change: A manual for activists in the 1990's.* Washington, DC: Seven Locks Press.

Freudenberg, N., Lee, J., & Silver, D. (1990). How black and latino community organizations respond to the AIDS epidemic: A case study in one New York City neighborhood. *AIDS Education and Prevention,* 1(1), 12-21.

Lauffer, A. (1978). *Social planning at the community level.* Englewood Cliffs, NJ: Prentice-Hall.

Mintzberg, H. (1973). *The nature of managerial work.* New York: Harper & Row.

Mondros, J.B., & Wilson, S.M. (1990). Career selection and sustenance of community organizers. *Administration in Social Work,* 14(2), 95-109.

Perrow, C. (1970). *Organizational analysis: A sociological view.* Monterey, CA: Brooks/Cole Publishing Company.

Peterfreund, N. (1980). *Community mental health center board development.* Washington, DC: U.S. Government Printing Office.

Rivera, F.G., & Erlich, J.L. (1992). *Community organizing in a diverse society.* Boston: Allyn & Bacon.

Rothman, J. (1979). Three models of community organization practice: Their mixing and phasing. In F.M. Cox, et al. (Eds.), *Strategies of community organization* (3rd ed.). Itasca, IL: F.E. Peacock Publishers, Inc.

Seekins, T., & Fawcett, S.B. (1987). Effects of a poverty client's agenda on resource allocations by community decision makers. *American Journal of Community Psychology,* 15(3), 305-320.

Washington, V. (1987). Community involvement in recruiting adaptive homes for black children. *Child Welfare,* LXVI(1), 57-68.

Whelton, D.A., & Cameron, K.S. (1991). Developing management skills (2nd ed.). New York: HarperCollins Publishers.

Zimmerman, M., & Rappaport, J. (1988). Citizen participation: Perceived control and psychological empowerment. *American Journal of Community Psychology,* 16(5), 725-750.

## 18.

**Roslyn H. Chernesky and Marcia J. Bombyk**

## WOMEN'S WAYS AND EFFECTIVE MANAGEMENT

It is no longer unusual to suggest that the managerial style of women may differ from that of men, that the qualities women bring to organizations may be strengths rather than weaknesses, or that today's organizations are in need of what women have to offer in order to thrive and be effective. As the debate in the recent *Harvard Business Review* reflects (Debate, 1991), these ideas are not universally accepted and are frequently regarded with skepticism; however, their possibility is at least being discussed and studied.

This article presents an overview of the qualities associated with women and links these qualities to the ways women manage. The authors describe their study of women managers and how they perceive of gender differences in their approach to management (Chernesky & Bombyk, 1988). The data offer empirical support for the idea that women bring a unique view and understanding of their experience of caring to their administrative positions. The study complements the growing literature in which selected women describe their gender-based management style (Cantor & Bernay, 1992; Hegelsen, 1991; Loden, 1985; Rosener, 1990). The article concludes with a discussion of the implications of women's unique management style as well as some of the risks inherent in conceiving of gender-based management styles.

When it was suggested more than ten years ago that women manage differently than men (Baird & Bradley, 1979; Hooyman, 1978; Rosener & Schwartz, 1980), such a possibility was largely ignored and denied. In a period of rapid increase in the number of women in executive, managerial, and administrative jobs, great strides had been made in convincing those who hire administrators that women were no different than men in the way they man-

---

The authors would like to thank the editor of AFFILIA and SAGE Publications, Inc., for permission to reprint this study originally published in Chernesky, R.H., & Bombyk, M.J. (1988, Spring), Women's Ways and Effective Management, *AFFILIA 3*(1), 48-61, © 1988 Women and Social Work, Inc.

Roslyn H. Chernesky and Marcia J. Bombyk are professors at the Graduate School of Social Services, Fordham University.

aged. The Women's Bureau (1985) reported that women holding managerial positions rose from 22 percent in 1975 to almost 40 percent in 1985. Between 1977 and 1985 the number of women managers increased by 102 percent, while the number of male managers increased only 4 percent (Women's Bureau, U.S. Department of Labor, 1985). Women learned how to be accepted and acquire the look of successful managers, especially by dressing "like one of the boys." They took seriously the warnings that to act "like women" would only confirm that they were unsuitable for executive leadership. The message was clear: Behavior associated with women, and especially behavior that was stereotypical of women, was undesirable, and a sign of weakness.

Not surprisingly, a number of studies during this period, from the mid-1970s to the mid-1980s, demonstrated that the way women and men managed was more similar than different (Chapman, 1975; Donnell & Hall, 1980; Harlan & Weiss, 1982). A more definitive analysis meta-analyzed seventeen studies of gender differences in leadership, concluding that it was not possible to claim that gender influenced leadership behavior in nonlaboratory settings (Dobbins & Platz, 1986). Determining that women and men managers do not differ bolstered the popular thesis during this period that management and leadership behaviors were gender-neutral.

## INTEREST IN NEW LEADERSHIP

Despite the effort of demonstrating that women managers were the same as men, the possibility that women's management style was different from that of men remained intriguing. It captured the imagination of many who saw a need for fundamental changes in American industry, corporations, and service organizations and those who looked toward Japanese management, Theory Z, quality circles, and total quality management. The lack of effective management was increasingly considered the major reason why American business was neither competitive nor productive.

The traditional style of management was rapidly losing favor. There was increasing evidence that workers preferred managers who supported worker participation and showed a high concern for interpersonal relationships (Hornstein, Heilman, Mone, Tartell, 1987). Controlling, autocratic leadership, and preoccupation with tasks and productivity at the expense of relationships were seen as less effective leadership approaches. A consensus was emerging that this style of management, which Rosener (1990) refers to as the command-and-control approach, was outdated and inappropriate for today's organizations (Bradford, 1991; Cohen, 1991).

The times were calling for a new kind of leadership and new kinds of organizations. Zaleznik (1989) claimed "business in America has lost its way, adrift in a sea of managerial mediocrity desperately needing leadership..." (p.11). He described how the overconcentration of the "dominating managerial mystique" guides today's mangers who impose structure and process to establish control, preserve order, and prevent chaos. Burns (1979) referred to the new management style as "transforming leadership" in which the leader "taps the needs and raises the aspirations and helps shape the values—and hence mobilizes the potential followers." Kanter (1983) identified "change master" skills needed for today's organizations, which include kaleidoscope thinking, the ability to articulate and communicate visions, the ability to build coalitions and teams to carry out ideas, and the sharing of credit so that everyone who works is rewarded.

The preferred leadership style became relationship-oriented, supportive, democratic, and participative. The most appropriate leader today is one who can "lead others to lead themselves" (Manz & Sims, 1991, p. 18). Referred to as an "interactive style" (Rosener, 1990), or "coaching" (Evered & Selman, 1989), the new style disdains beliefs about being in charge, controlling and commanding others, prescribing behaviors, and maintaining order and replaces them with beliefs about empowering people to contribute more fully and productively (Block, 1987). Effective managers build trust and commitment without relying on their hierarchical position, bring out the best thinking in work groups, help integrate different points of view, and encourage consensus problem solving and decision making.

## WOMEN'S WAYS

The connection between the newest kind of leadership desired in managers today and the qualities women are said to bring to management has become increasingly apparent. Rosener and Schwartz (1980) suggested that women's approach was based on synthesizing, intuition, and qualitative thinking. Loden (1985) noted that concern for people, interpersonal skills, intuitive management, and creative problem solving were qualities that women were encouraged to develop and rely on, and therefore bring to management.

Drawing upon psychological theories, Grant (1988) identified qualities unique to women. She suggests that women engage in cooperative communication, seeking a means of conciliation with others instead of getting involved in competition or confrontation. Women strongly value interpersonal ties, show concern for others and give importance to attachment and connectedness. They view power as a transforming force from within, equated with giving, caring, nurturance, and strength. Women's capacity for empathy with others and seeing themselves as connected to others leads them to value closeness and nurture intimacy. Thus, women are more able to express different emotions and feelings of vulnerability. Finally, women's biology, related to pregnancy and childbirth, grounds them in an earthly practicality and concreteness regarding day-to-day realities.

Women's management style therefore reflects their experience of caring, cooperating, and connectedness. Women bring to their positions sensitivity and empathy toward others, enabling them to foster a sense of belonging among workers, which in turn breeds loyalty and encourages people to do their best (Hughey & Gelman, 1986). Women dislike hierarchical structures that place the leader at the top of the ladder, alone and isolated. They prefer to be in the center of things so they can be "connected to all those around them as if by invisible strands or threads constructed around the central point" (Helgesen, 1990). Women encourage participation, share power and information, enhance other people's self-worth, and get others excited about their work (Rosener, 1990).

## WOMEN'S WAYS OF MANAGING

The study presented here is a first step toward understanding how women administrators actually implement their managerial responsibilities in ways that reflect and stem from their being women. Data were collected using a questionnaire mailed to all 381 women affiliated with the Executive Women in Human Services, a network of women in management positions in New York City that was founded in 1979. Of the 381, 92 responded, for a response rate of 24 percent.

The respondents ranged in age from 32 to 74, and the mean age was 47 years. They were all experienced administrators (the mean years of administrative experience were 12, and none had been administrators for fewer than 2 years). Furthermore, they were generally highly educated; two-thirds had master's degrees, and 45 percent held master's degrees in social work, and there were as many holders of doctorates as of bachelor's degrees (15 percent each). (Only 4 percent had only a high school diploma.) The majority (64 percent) had obtained some formal training in administration, irrespective of their terminal degree or discipline.

More than half the respondents (63 percent) held top-level executive positions, and 37 percent were in middle management. The majority of agencies in which they were employed, which varied widely in size, provided direct services. Twenty-nine percent of the respondents managed fewer than 10 staff members; 42 percent, 20–60 staff members; 28 percent, more than 60 staff members; and 16 percent, over 100 staff members. Forty-three percent were responsible for budgets of under $1 million; 39 percent, for budgets of $1–$5 million; 18 percent, for budgets of over $5 million, and 9 percent, for budgets of over $15 million.

## FINDINGS

The respondents overwhelmingly thought (78 percent) that they brought qualities, values, or perspectives to their administrative positions that were different from those of men. All those who believed in their unique qualities cited examples; the 178 examples that were given could be placed in nine relatively discrete categories, as shown in Table 18.1. Only a small proportion (8 percent) did not fit into the categories.

The nine categories are closely related to the areas that are considered characteristic of a woman's approach to administration, according to feminist theory. For example, the respondents stressed their sense of caring and their concern for people as well as the quality of the environment, sensitivity to the needs of women workers, investment in workers, a cooperative orientation, openness in communication, a global perspective, recognition of inequities, and intuition.

Nearly two-thirds (62 percent) of the respondents believed they were doing something that a typical male administrator in their position would probably not do. Only 15 percent thought they were not doing anything that was different, and 22 percent were not sure. The respondents cited eighty-nine examples to illustrate what they thought they were doing differently. Using content analysis, the authors determined that just over half were examples that demonstrated the respondents' sensitivity to workers and their problems. These women executives believed that they listened more to their workers' concerns, became more involved in their workers' lives, and did more to help their workers cope with the stress they faced than would male executives. They cited their use of such administrative prerogatives as establishing flextime, extending maternity leave, and allowing staff members to bring their children to work on days when school is closed.

How women administrators are more visible and available to workers was the

TABLE 18.1
Qualities That Women State They Bring to Administration That Are Different from Those of Men

| Quality | Percentage Cited ($N = 77$) |
|---|---|
| Concern for people; sensitivity, empathy, and compassion; a tendency to nurture or mother | 60 |
| Investment in workers, support of workers, attempt to give workers responsibilities, help workers get promoted, serve as mentors | 32 |
| Appreciate of dual roles and responsibilities of women workers in relation to family and career and of the skills as well as the problems they bring, given their socialization and experiences | 26 |
| Commitment to staff participation in decision making, to cooperation and collaboration among workers as opposed to hierarchical and competitive structures, and to process rather than product | 26 |
| Patience, intuition, concern with details, and a broader and more global perspective of life and the world | 21 |
| Communication that is open and honest, a willingness to admit doubt or error, comfort with giving compliments and with just listening | 18 |
| Recognition of sexism, discrimination, and inequities in the workplace; commitment to affirmative action | 13 |
| Sensitivity to programming for and the service needs of women and children | 9 |
| Concern with the quality of the work environment and improving the physical work conditions | 8 |

second most frequently cited example of differences by 18 percent. Many stressed their efforts to keep communication open and to keep staff informed about what was going on, especially with the board of directors. Illustrations included pitching in to get done on time, remembering the birthdays of workers with a token celebration, and helping out by handling clients when staff members were unavailable. The most frequently mentioned action was that of fixing up offices to make them more pleasant for working.

The respondents' identification of the kinds of tasks one would expect to be influenced by being a woman and their illustrations were consistent with the authors' expectations. Their comments on "handling conflict among workers," for example, emphasized the desire to resolve the conflict as quickly as possible through a process that brings the parties together. Their illustrations of "leadership style" emphasized cooperation, participation, and a nonhierarchical approach that includes, rather than excludes, as many people as possible. "Developing staff" reflected a transforming relationship style in which the respondents' concern for the growth and learning of staff were paramount. "Maintaining job satisfaction" and "motivating workers" also emphasized their concern for others and their attempts to make life easier for their workers. The examples they gave included altering work schedules and hours to accommodate workers, involving workers in decision making, and paying particular attention to opportunities to provide positive feedback, support, and appreciation.

In summary, the study demonstrated that women do believe that they bring special qualities, values, and perspectives to their administrative positions because they are women and that they believe that they act on their uniqueness, doing things and carrying out their administrative tasks differently from their male counterparts. How the respondents claimed they are different and what they claimed they are doing differently conformed to the authors' expectations about gender differences. The results thus provide strong support for the notion that women administrators bring to their positions women's experience of caring. Women anticipate, interpret, and respond to the needs of others and thereby are sensitive and empathic toward others as well as nurturing and cooperative.

## IMPLICATIONS FOR PRACTICE

While the debate continues as to whether men and women have different management styles and if any differences are indeed significant, several important issues have emerged and will influence management thinking for some time. First, it is no longer possible to believe that management or leadership styles are gender neutral. Second, there has been a clear shift in the preferred style from what had been the more traditional command-and-control approach to the heretofore less favored care-and-empower style. Third, women managers are likely to benefit most from this shift since women seem to be more comfortable with the requirements of the new leadership style than men.

In a climate that sought tough leaders and extolled the "leader as a striking figure on a rearing white horse, crying 'Follow me!'" (Manz & Sims, 1991), in which administrative man (Denhardt & Perkins, 1976) was taken at face value, women (as well as some men) were disadvantaged. Aware that their behavioral styles did not fit the ideal management model, women had three alternatives. They could accept that they were failures who could not prove themselves to be effective managers, no matter how hard they tried. Or, they could learn how to conform to the dominant style, thereby rejecting a more comfortable style, which may have come to them more naturally. Others could be among those who Gordon (1991) claims choose to abandon careers as managers, seeing that as the only alternative.

For years women managers experienced the kinds of frustration and rejection that outsiders, in general, experience. Not surprisingly, these incidents affected their performance and behavior (Chernesky, 1986), invariably confirming that they did not understand or appreciate the rules of the game and did not warrant being players. While the adjustment and coping patterns required of individual women mangers interfered with their ease in managing, organizations were simultaneously denied the unique contributions women could more easily make. Similarly, male managers were often constrained to use a traditional leadership style that was expected of them when they, too, may have preferred an alternative approach.

The current debate allows women managers a greater opportunity to use a style that they may prefer, one that is just as likely to be gender-related as the supposedly gender-neutral traditional style. Women managers will now be able to hold on to and be proud of their leadership style, and not feel defensive about it nor necessarily feel the need to adapt to the style their male colleagues choose. Men managers should be equally comforted in the knowledge that they, too, can make use of leadership styles that were previously considered signs of weakness.

## CAUTIONARY NOTE

Although we are excited about the growing support for this new leadership style as well as the current interest in gender-related management styles, we are reminded how easily such thinking reflects a backlash against women (Faludi, 1991). For example, this line of thinking supports the sex-stereotyping of women that has already worked to channel women into jobs and positions for which their qualities and skills were considered most suitable. We are likely to see women continue to predominate in positions where human relations or interpersonal skills are highly valued. These have traditionally been lower-level management jobs, such as supervision, where people skills are viewed as more essential than technical or conceptual skills (Katz, 1986).

If an organization's need for caring, participation, and empowerment is left to women and is not developed by men managers, neither men nor women will be fulfilling their managerial potential and performing optimally for the organization. A healthy organization, according to Sargent (1981), is an androgynous organization, one in which both masculine and feminine behaviors are valued and incorporated. Such an organization would free all individuals to behave in ways that can benefit them both personally and professionally.

## CONCLUSION

The pressure to conform to an ideal style will continue despite a shift in the image of the ideal. It is the very notion that there is a "best" leadership style that has dominated the history of management thinking and has created tensions, denied opportunities to differ, and cast some individuals as more desirable and valuable to an organization than others. We are concerned about this tendency.

There is sufficient data on leadership and effectiveness to remind us that just because a style is natural or comfortable does not mean that it is the best or even the correct style to use under the circumstances. Flexibility and adaptability are important indicators of effective leadership. Reliance on any one style is bound to be detrimental. Excessive emphasis on a care-and-empower style can create a variation on the management mystique that will result in its being as ineffective as the traditional approach. Perhaps future thinking about the elements of effective management will be directed at the balance and synthesis of these currently polarized approaches.

## REFERENCES

Baird, J.E., & Bradley, P.H. (1979). Styles of management and communication: A comparative study of men and women. *Communication Monographs, 46*, 101-111.

Block, P. (1987). *The empowered manager*. San Francisco: Jossey-Bass.

Bradford, D.L. (1991). Debate: Ways men and women lead. *Harvard Business Review*, 69, 158-159.

Burns, J.M. (1979). *Leadership*. New York: Harper and Row.

Cantor, D.W., & Bernay, T. (1992). *Women in power: The secrets of leadership*. New York: Houghton Mifflin Co.

Chapman, J.B. (1975). Comparison of male and female leadership styles. *Academy of Management Journal, 18,* 645-650.

Chernesky, R.H. (1986). A new model of supervision. In N. Van Den Bergh & L.B. Cooper (Eds.), *Feminist visions for social work* (pp. 163-186). Silver Spring, MD: National Association of Social Workers.

Chernesky, R.H., & Bombyk, M.J. (1988). Women's ways and effective management. *AFFILIA: Journal of Women and Social Work, 3*(1), 48-60.

Cohen, A.R. (1991). Debate: Ways men and women lead. *Harvard Business Review*, 69, 159.

Debate: Ways men and women lead (1991). *Harvard Business Review*, 69, 150-160.

Denhardt, R.H., and Perkins, J. (1976). The coming death of administrative man. *Public Administrative Review, 38,* 379-384.

Dobbins, G.H., & Platz, S. (1986). Sex differences in leadership: How real are they? *Academy of Management Review, 29,* 118-125.

Donnell, S.M., & Hall, J. (1980). Men and women managers: A significant case of no significant difference. *Organizational Dynamics, 8,* 60-77.

Evered, R.D., & Selman, J.C. (1989 August). Coaching and the art of management. *Organizational Dynamics, 18*(2), 16-32.

Faludi, S. (1991). *Backlash: The Undeclared War Against American Women.* New York: Crown.

Gordon, S. (1991). *Prisoners of Men's Dreams.* Boston: Little Brown & Co.

Grant, J. (1988). Women as managers: What they can offer to organizations. *Organizational Dynamics, 16*(3), 56-63.

Harlan, A., & Weiss, C.L. (1982). Sex differences in factors affecting managerial career advancement. In P.A. Wallace (ed.), *Women in the Workplace* (pp. 59-100). Boston: Auburn House.

Helgesen, S. (1990). *The Female Advantage: Women's Ways of Leadership.* New York: Doubleday.

Hooyman, N. (1976). Roots of administrative styles: Modes and models. In E. Wattenberg (Ed.), *Room at the Top* (pp. 15-19). Minneapolis: University of Minnesota Press.

Hornstein, H.A., Heilman, M.E., Mone, E., & Tartell, R. (1987). Responding to contingent leadership behavior. *Organizational Dynamics, 15*(4), 56-65.

Hughey, A. & Gelman, E. (1986, March 17). Managing the women's way. *Newsweek,* pp. 46-47.

Kanter, R.M. (1983). *The Change Masters.* New York: Simon & Schuster.

Katz, R.L. (1986). Skills of an effective administrator. *Harvard Business Review,* 52, 91-102.

Loden, M. (1985). *Feminine Leadership or How to Succeed Without Being One of the Boys.* New York: Times Books.

Manz, C.C., & Sims, H.P. (1991). Superleadership: Beyond the myth of heroic leadership. *Organizational Dynamics, 19*(4), 18-35.

Rosener, J.B. (1990). Ways women lead. *Harvard Business Review, 68,* 119-125.

Rosener, L., & Schwartz, P. (1980). Women, leadership and the 1980s: What kind of leaders do we need? *New Leadership in the Public Interest.* New York: NOW Legal Defense & Education Fund, 25-36.

Sargent, A.G. (1981). *The Androgynous Manager.* New York: AMACON.

Women's Bureau. (1985 July). *Facts on U.S. Working Women.* Washington, DC: U.S. Department of Labor.

Zaleznik, A. (1989). *The Managerial Mystique: Restoring Leadership in Business.* New York: Harper & Row.

19.

**Karen Wolk Feinstein**

# INNOVATIVE MANAGEMENT IN TURBULENT TIMES: LARGE-SCALE AGENCY CHANGE

## INTRODUCTION

Agencies wishing to survive and prosper... are faced with the challenge of becoming flexible, well-informed organizations able to respond to threats and challenges in an increasingly unpredictable environment. This requires that agencies have the capacity to envision and carry out large-scale change when indicated. Changes may involve the adoption of new programs, servicing of new consumers, development of new subunits and affiliates, and the hiring of new staff or creation of new staff functions.

Most importantly, agencies are being called upon to establish their own directions: public guidelines that determine what services are to be provided, in what manner, and to whom are increasingly rare. To respond, many nonprofit organizations have embraced strategic long-range planning.

The contention here is that strategic planning offers the potential for large-scale organizational change when it embraces organizational development strategies as an integral part of the planning process. As agencies analyze their current strengths and weaknesses and identify opportunities for growth, they must also build a willingness and capacity for change. Presented is a case study of how an organizational development approach can be built into the strategic planning process, ensuring the likelihood and effectiveness of large-scale change.

## STRATEGIC PLANNING AS A PROCESS

Increasingly popular with both private and public, for-profit and nonprofit organizations, strategic planning has become an accepted activity of every group that considers itself adaptive, flexible, and prescient. In essence, strategic planning is a systematic approach for adapting to change. By anticipating obstacles and maximizing opportunities, a strategic plan helps an organization direct future action; blueprints for action encourage a management style that is proactive, directed, and efficient. The assumption is that an organization which plans ahead uses its energies most productively, out-performs its competition and promotes cohesion among its different subsystems and constituents (Steiner, 1979; Lauenstein, 1983).

Strategic planning has become increasingly popular with nonprofit organizations over the past few years. With the cutback in public monies (federal budget-trimming in the human services and constitutional

---

Dr. Karen Wolk Feinstein is president of the Jewish Health Care Foundation of Pittsburgh, PA. This research was supported by grants from the Permanent Charity Fund, Inc., the Gillette Company, and the *Boston Globe*. This paper was prepared for the Symposium on Community Organization and Administration, Council on Social Work Education 30th Annual Program Meeting, Detroit, March 11–14, 1984.

amendments that delimit state spending), nonprofits face stiff competition for reduced government funds. Also, federal and state governments have chosen to withdraw from the practice of program design and the earmarking of funds, favoring instead local initiative, planning, and program development. Federal programs such as Title XX, Comprehensive Health Planning, CETA, and LEAA have been replaced with more open-ended block grants.

Additionally, the environment is increasingly unpredictable as the rate of change accelerates. "Trends" have shorter lifecycles than they did in earlier decades, and organizations must adapt rapidly to a fluid society.

Because of this, the pressure is great on individual nonprofit organizations to direct their own course, maximize their growth opportunities, and demonstrate their viability and purposefulness. National and regional offices of federations, such as the United Way and Boy Scouts of America, are urging their member affiliates to engage in long-range planning, and Boards and funding sources consider long-range plans to be an essential component of good management.

Strategic planning is much like standard planning practice, with some technical refinements. The basic elements of planning remain the same:

1. Assessing
   —External environment
   —Programs
   —Internal organization/operations
   —Organizational mission/aspirations
2. Defining
   —Threats
   —Opportunities
   —Alternatives
3. Selecting
   —An appropriate direction
      Programs
      Organizations
      Facilities
      Financial
   —Appropriate strategies
   —High-priority projects
4. Developing
   —Project implementation plans
   —Organization plan
   —Operating plans
      Program
      Financial
      Development
      Facility
5. Monitoring/updating
   —Planning assumptions
   —Progress against plan (United Way of America)

Obviously, the long-term prospective (usually three to five years) requires greater spacing of milestones, more intricate tactics, and both base and contingency plans. Also, strategic planners tend to display a very basic marketing orientation, i.e., environmental threats and opportunities, and internal strengths and weaknesses, are evaluated relative to their effect on:

—how the organization is perceived,
—what consumers need and want,
—characteristics of the competition,
—potentials for the development of new services and consumer groups (Kotler, 1982).

Finally, strategic planning employs a systems approach perspective to data gathering, analysis, and action. Interrelations among subparts of the organization, between the organization and its environment, and among critical constituencies, are articulated and analyzed. A primary goal of the whole process is minimization of the friction, inconsistencies, and antagonisms among subsystems that hinder the effectiveness of the unit as a whole (Steiner, 1979).

The product of a strategic planning effort is a comprehensive blueprint for action that can ensure the organization's survival and enable it to serve more people better. Once constructed, this blueprint eases individual decision making, provides clarity to all important constituents (board, staff, client, funding sources, etc.), and reaffirms the organization's social purpose.

## THE ORGANIZATIONAL DEVELOPMENT APPROACH

The author had an opportunity during the past year to test a particular strategy for long-range planning. She has termed this the "Organizational Development" or "Diagnostic" approach to strategic planning. Essentially, this approach stresses the broadest possible involvement of key stakeholders—with both horizontal and vertical linkages to the system—in the first (or diagnostic) phase of the planning process.

The author concluded that this initial diagnostic process, often referred to as the situation audit, current appraisal, data collection, environmental analysis, or, most commonly, the needs assessment, is the most critical part of the planning exercise. It is at this point that the organization collects data on the internal and external environment, strengths and weaknesses, and opportunities and threats. On the basis of this information, the long-range action plan is devised, after the information has been analyzed, weighed, and tested.

Figure 19.1 is a model of the strategic planning process. In the organizational development approach, efforts are concentrated in the early stages (the establishment of the data base, data analyses, and identification of opportunities, threats, strengths, and weaknesses). It is during these processes that key participants can provide their perspectives and preferences and that planners can build organizational commitment and enthusiasm for organizational change.

The basic assumptions on which the organizational development approach is premised are as follows: (1) the answer to many of these questions will differ depending on the perspective of different constituent groups; (2) clear and widespread consensus on these issues is rare within organizations; (3) the broader the information sources (horizontal and vertical) the nearer the conclusions are to reality; (4) the data gathering process itself offers a unique opportunity to build trust and clarity. Based on these premises, the role of the planner in this approach is to set up a wide communication loop, receiving information from and providing information to key constituent groups as the diagnostic process proceeds.

Clearly, planners who choose this approach are attempting to avoid certain common pitfalls of strategic planning. Too often, plans are shelved by organizations because persons within the organization have never developed a real commitment to the process, or because the final recommendations are not realistic or widely accepted, or because obstacles and resistance were not anticipated and accommodated. The organizational development approach attempts to build in legitimacy, acceptance, and accommodation from the first phase of the planning process—the diagnostic phase. In so doing, the planner adopts the role of facilitator and enabler, moving along a process of open-problem definition and clarification that involves the widest possible participation in information retrieval.

The planner, in a sense, becomes immersed in the organization which he/she

FIGURE 19.1
Strategic Planning Process

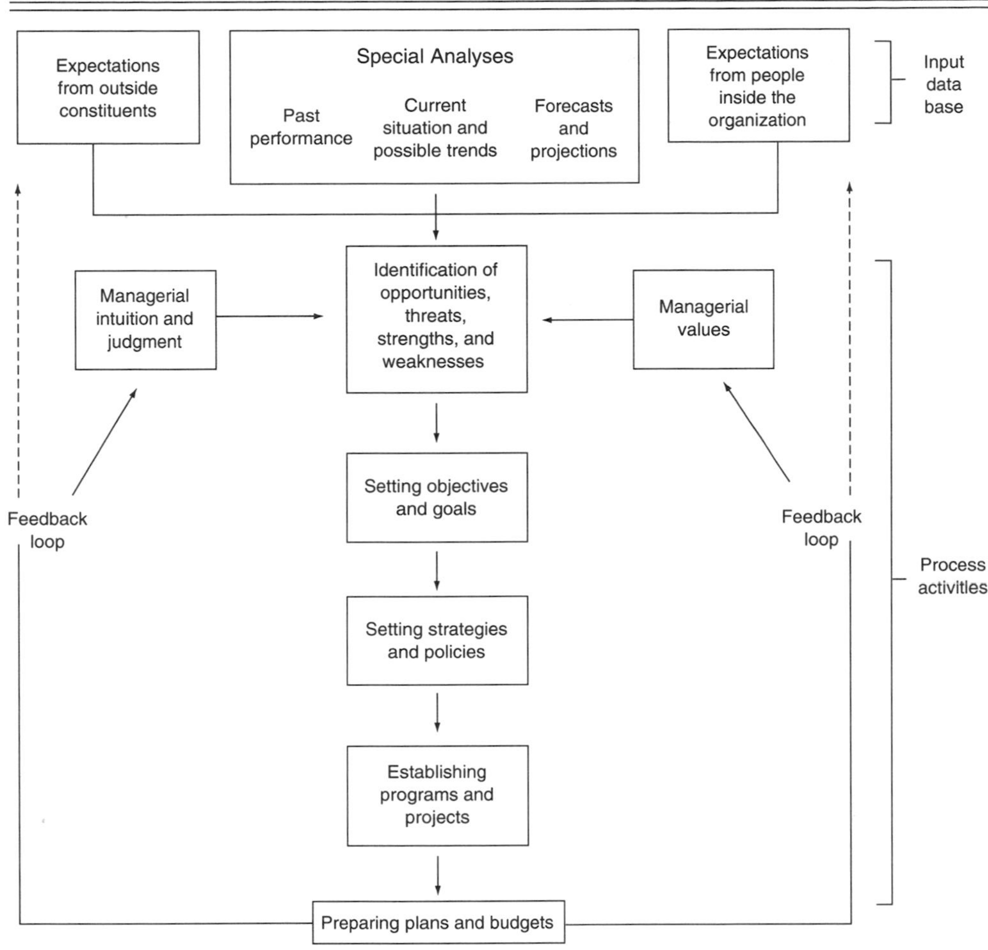


United Way of America, 1983.

studies and operates openly under the assumption that there will be different "realities" for different constituents. The planner is not a wizard, pulling ideas and recommendations from objective and measurable "facts"; rather, he/she is a neutral observer receiving and sharing information in a somewhat continuous flow, noting consistencies and inconsistencies where they occur, and highlighting recurrent themes that suggest salient problems and possibilities.

Obviously, the organizational development approach resembles what in traditional planning literature is often referred to as the locality development, educative, or collaborative approach (Rothman, 1979; Burke, 1975; Specht, 1975). Importantly though, the difference between this approach and a more technocratic method is

TABLE 19.1
Different Approaches to Strategic Long-Range Planning Needs Assessment Stage*

| | Technocratic | Diagnostic |
|---|---|---|
| Problem Definition | Problem is defined<br>Parameters known or suspected | Problem is defined as process unfolds<br>Research focus evolves with process |
| Role of Planner | Expert professional | Facilitator, educator |
| Data | Objective, quantifiable, measurable | Subjective, impressionistic, qualitative |
| Accountability | CEO and Board of Directors | The organization as a whole and key constituents |
| Focus of Study | Macroenvironment (trends: social, political, economic, demographic) | Microenvironment (programs, management, consumers, volunteers, funding) |
| Methods | Gathering and analysis of factual data | Communication with key constituents |
| Style of Data Collection | Minimal, efficient, summative | Broad, inclusive, formative |
| Data Analysis Style | Methodical, inductive | Creative, deductive |
| Attitude toward Organization | Distance; analytic | Immersion; participatory |
| Priority Setting | Technical: cost-benefit analysis, administrative action | Political/strategic: search for agreement and consensus compromise & accommodation |
| Distribution of Action Plan | Narrow (Board and Management) | Widespread—various constituents groups, funding sources, interested parties |

*It is important to note that the differences are those of emphasis, not exclusion. Planners performing strategic planning cannot afford to neglect either dimension (the technocratic or diagnostic) entirely or the plan would have narrow applicability.

one of degree; both technocratic and diagnostic planners must collect both objective and subjective information and solicit input from key constituents. However, it is suggested here that the two approaches differ in emphasis in many areas (see Table 19.1).

Of primary importance, however, are two overall objectives in this approach: the planner encourages the organization to regard the conclusions and recommendations of the needs assessment stage as its own, and the planner facilitates the broadest possible participation in the diagnostic effort. In this way, the planner is preparing key subparts of the organization to accept and understand recommendations for change that result from a strategic planning process.

## CASE MODEL: THE BOY SCOUT COUNCIL

### Background

The scout council of a large metropolitan region embarked on a long-range strategic planning project for a number of reasons: the national office of Boy Scouts of America encourages its affiliates to do so; the local United Way requires three-year plans now if agencies are to qualify for multi-year funding options; members of the council—both staff and Board—were concerned about decreasing participation rate among youth and volunteers as well as other financial and programmatic problems.

Conceptually, local scout councils are set up to be self-sustaining and to enjoy natural growth through the volunteer efforts of individual communities. This is dependent on the steady demand for the basic scouting program on the part of parents and youth, the continued interest and ability to serve well on the part of volunteer leaders, and the fulfillment by chartered community organizations of their mission as set forth in the charters.

Today, scout councils face stiff competition from other youth-serving organizations which are well-equipped organizationally for sophisticated marketing, information management, and fundraising. Additionally, changes in today's family—the prevalence of dual career and single-parent families—present obstacles to voluntarism, the key to scouting's historical success. The fact that there are fewer youth and that many children are bussed to schools outside their neighborhoods present different dilemmas.

A needs assessment project was developed to provide information necessary to the council Board in the preparation of a long-range plan. The planner chose to use a diagnostic strategy that would ensure maximum input from, and feed back to, key constituent groups. Because a clear and present concern of the council was the declining demand for participation on the part of youth and volunteers, the diagnostic process focused on obtaining information from four groups critical to participation:

—parents of scout-age youth
—volunteers
—chartered community organizations (sponsors)
—community leaders

Additionally, to assist in membership projections, assessment of successful recruitment efforts, targeting of underserved areas and groups, and reconsideration of current districting patterns, considerable demographic data were gathered on:

—characteristics of families and youth in the council region
—concentration of youth
—numbers currently served by scouting
—characteristics of individual communities and districts
—population projections
—refugee characteristics and distribution

## Research Methods

The planner had defined two general goals for this diagnostic phase: the collection of information essential to the growth of the scout council, including growth in scout and volunteer participation and in funding support; and organizational development in a system where morale appeared unusually low, and confusion and suspicion among critical subparts appeared high. The formative research strategy employed in this diagnostic approach was deemed ideal for accomplishing this dual mission, as it permits the ongoing and widespread exploration of critical issues and refinement of hypotheses and conclusions.

It was decided that a viable plan for future action would require informed recommendations related to the improvement of recruitment/public relations efforts, the understanding of natural market segments (and their tastes and preferences) occurring within the council region, responsiveness to trends in the funding environment, management quality and program satisfaction, and opportunity for growth and expansion.

Four different questionnaires were constructed and administered (one by telephone to 416 parents of youth, two by mail to 500 volunteers and 71 sponsoring organizations, and one by face-to-face interviews with over 30 community leaders). Additional information was obtained by meeting with council staff, Board members, funding sources, and with individual volunteers who felt that some of the issues they wished to raise were not covered in the questionnaire.

Also, researchers attended committee meetings in each district and at the staff and Board level to uncover salient issues and to assess the breadth and depth of feelings on these issues. Meeting attendance was also an important means of insuring that key constituent groups understood the objectives and format of this diagnostic process. All in all, it is estimated that members of the research team were able to make contact with all significant vertical and horizontal relationships of the council, including the regional and national offices of the international scout organization.

In general, information was sought in four different areas:

*The Demand for Scouting*

- perceive needs of youth in general
- boy scouting as a program (utility and enjoyment)
- school schedules/time conflicts
- transportation difficulties
- activity scheduling preferences
- reasons for joining scouts
- reasons for dropping out
- competing youth activities
- what scouts enjoy most about scouting
- expenses of scouting
- effective recruitment methods
- preferred volunteer qualifications and characteristics
- future participation plans
- obstacles to participation
- barriers to recruitment
- funding priorities (community leaders)

*Image Measurement*

- benefits of scouting (short and long-term)
- knowledge of scout program rescouting
- general communication linkages/networks
- trends (image modifications over time)

*Market Segmentation by*

- race
- district
- age
- occupational status
- household structure
- previous participation
- extent of participation
- other community commitments
- income
- number of children (adults)
- school affiliation (youth)
- sponsor affiliation

*Client Satisfaction*

- quality of local program
- quality of local management
- benefits of volunteering
- most important elements of scouting program
- reasonableness of expenses
- conditions necessary to increase participation
- elements of program needing improvement
- quality of sponsors
- internal communication: quality and quantity
- quality of volunteer

This information answered the following questions:

- How popular, relevant, and accessible are the organization's present services and programs (responsiveness)?
- Whom does the agency serve and how well (markets and market satisfaction)?
- What are the needs, wants and interests of key internal constituents (Board, management, staff, and volunteers)?
- What is the image of the organization in the community?
- Who are the competition; how well does the organization "compete"?
- What large-scale macroenvironmental social forces pose opportunities and threats?
- How do key stakeholders assess the quality of present management and staff?

**COMMENTS ON STRATEGY**

Obviously, a strategy such as this amasses large amounts of unstandardized data. However, the planning team was convinced that, although the process of interpreting the questionnaire results along with the large quantity of factual data (demographic statistics, population projections, service distribution ratios) was a cumbersome one, the final conclusions and recommendations were creative, multidimensional, and well-documented. One indication of this was the wide acceptance accorded the final report of the needs assessment; no significant constituent group questioned its conclusions, and the planning director was encouraged to play an active role in the development and implementation of the long-range plan. The diagnostic strategy, though time consuming and laborious, had paid off.

Several strategic considerations contributed to the overall acceptance of the final report and the success of the process. Planning team members had invested three-months' time in preparation of the planning effort. They had read numerous local, regional, and national reports relating to scouting in particular and youth activities in general. They had consulted many key community leaders and collected the bulk of the demographic data long before the first questionnaire was prepared. Because the planners were well-informed, the relevance and utility of research questions were not challenged, and respondents developed confidence in the process and the team.

Multiple-choice questions were balanced with many opportunities for open-ended response, clarification, and expansion. The value of these open comments was inestimable. Some respondents indicated that they wanted to meet personally with the Project Director, and these meetings were arranged.

Overall, the planning team members were visible and accessible, and they regarded it as their responsibility to share information and insight as well as to collect data. In particular, they spent a considerable amount of time informing people about the intent and utility of strategic long-range planning. This was important, because some people were initially hostile to a process which they did not understand, that was costly and time-consuming, and that was performed by "outsiders." Resistance to change was not infrequent, and, as one respondent put it, "every time scouting changes, things get worse" (Feinstein, 1983).

Previous efforts by the planning team to understand the council well before the four questionnaires were administered proved to be very useful. Often researchers were asked questions by respondents related to the mission, program, structure, and membership procedures of the council, and it would have been awkward, and often harmful, to plead ignorance. Overall, the researchers regarded these questions as opportunities to inform people about the organization and considered them as an ancillary benefit of this diagnostic approach.

Interestingly, the actual process of planning, not merely the outcome, proved to be valuable. Parents and community leaders reported that they were encouraged that the council had undertaken strategic planning and saw this as an indication of good management. Staff and volunteers became equally enthusiastic as the process progressed and overall they regarded it as an opportunity to improve their leadership rather than a threat to their job security.

## REFERENCES

Burke, E. Citizen participation strategies. In R. Kramer & H. Specht (Eds.), *Readings in community organization practice.* Englewood Cliffs, NJ: Prentice-Hall, Inc., 1975.

Feinstein, K.W. *Directions for scouting.* Prepared for the Greater Boston Council, Boy Scouts of America, 1983.

Kotler, P. *Marketing for nonprofit organizations.* Englewood Cliffs, NJ: Prentice-Hall, Inc., 1982.

Lauenstein, M. The strategy audit. *Journal of Business Strategy,* 1983.

Rothman, Jack. Introduction. In Cox et al. (Eds.), *Strategies of community organization.* Itasca, IL: F. E. Peacock Publishers, Inc., 1979.

Specht, H. Disruptive tactics. In R. Kramer & H. Specht (Eds.), *Readings in community organization practice.* Englewood Cliffs, NJ: Prentice-Hall, Inc., 1975.

Steiner, G. *Strategic planning: What every manager must know.* New York: Free Press, 1979.

United Way of America. *Strategic planning.* U.W.A., 1983.

## 20.

**David M. Austin**

# THE HUMAN SERVICE EXECUTIVE

Little systematic attention is given to the role of the executive in human service organizations in contemporary social work literature. When it does deal with the executive, the literature reflects a number of traditional attitudes. One is the suspicion held by practitioners in human service professions towards administrators in general as the source of fiscal constraints and intrusive rules and regulations. Another is the suspicion that social movement activists hold towards persons in positions of public authority, the "bosses," holding them personally accountable for the continued existence of social problems. Still another perspective regards with great suspicion the continued male domination of executive positions in service organizations largely staffed by women (Kravetz & Austin, 1984).

Current textbooks in social work administration focus on "management" as a

---

David M. Austin is a Bert Kruger Smith Centennial professor at the School of Social Work, The University of Texas at Austin.

generic process, or on "entry level" or "mid-management" positions. This analysis, however, deals specifically with the position of senior administrator, or chief executive officer, in human service organizations.

There are two highly visible and distinctive models of the organizational executive in the society-at-large. The most widely recognized model is that of the Chief Executive Officer (CEO) of the for-profit corporate firm. The corporate executive role combines policymaking—as a member of the corporation board of directors—and implementation—as the senior administrator. Conceptually, this is the simplest version of the chief executive officer role. There is ultimately a single yardstick to measure the effectiveness of executive performance—financial returns to the shareholders.

The second widely recognized executive model is that of the generalist public administrator, the federal department executive, the state agency administrator, the city manager (Gortner, Mahler & Nicholson, 1987). According to long-established principles of public administration (Wilson, 1978) the public administrator is responsible for policy implementation but is not a policymaker—elected legislative bodies make policy. This is, in fact, a more complex version of the CEO role. There are several different yardsticks to measure the effectiveness of public administrator performance: consistency of implementation with legislative intent; continuity of the governmental organization; and break-even financial management, that is, operating within the limits of available financial resources. In the instance of both the corporate CEO and the public administrator, however, the quality of the products actually produced by the organization, while important, is not the most critical yardstick for judging executive performance.

Analyses of the CEO role in voluntary nonprofit and governmental human service organizations often attempt to fit the characteristics of that position into one of these two widely recognized models. However, the role of the executive in human service organizations is, in many ways, a distinctive, and even more complicated, role (Austin, 1983). The characteristics of the position of human service executive are shaped not only by the organizational characteristics which voluntary nonprofit and governmental human service organizations share with other types of formal organizations, but also by the distinctive characteristics of human service organizations (Austin, 1988).

Similar to corporate executives, human service executives, particularly those who are also experienced professional specialists, are usually active participants in policy formation, as well as in implementation, even if the executive position is formally defined as not being a policymaking position. In fact, most policy issues come to the policy board as a recommendation of the executive. Similar to the public administrator, the human service executive is concerned with the congruence of implementation to policy, with organizational continuity, and with "break-even" financial performance. And, similar to the public administrator, the human service executive has no direct personal economic stake in the financial performance of the organization. Specifically, the executive salary does not increase in proportion to the size of the organizational budget.

But the role of human service executive is also distinctly different from either the corporate executive or the public administrator. One of the critical differences is that the most important yardstick for judging executive performance in a human service organization is the quality of the services actually produced by the organization (Patti, 1987). In turn, one of the important and distinctive characteristics of the position of human service executive is that it involves dealing with the interface between two distinctive social structures—the service production organization and the organized human service profession.

## THE EXECUTIVE POSITION

The characteristics of the executive position have been analyzed in a variety of ways. The approach used in this analysis is based on the concept that the executive position, and the preferred style of executive performance, involves an interactive, adaptive "contingency" process between an individual and a structural context. That process is shaped, in turn, by both the operational characteristics of a particular organization, and the situation of that organization in its environment.

The same organization may require different executive performance styles at different stages in the development of the organization. Human service organizations producing similar products, but in different environments, may require a different mix of elements in the executive position. Different individuals may shape the specific elements in the executive position in different ways. Moreover, effective executive performance may require that a particular individual uses different executive styles at different times during an executive career. There is no single universal definition of the characteristics of the executive role, or of the "best" style of executive performance. The following discussion examines an inclusive model which may be useful, however, in analyzing the mix of elements in the executive position in a given organization at a particular time.

### The "Competing Values" Model of Executive Functions

One inclusive framework for the analysis of the functions of service production organizations is the competing values approach presented by Robert E. Quinn in *Beyond Rational Management: Mastering the Paradoxes and Competing Demands of High Performance* (1988). (See Figure 20.1.) This analytic framework is built around two dimensions, representing competing orientations, or "values" in the organizational context—centralization-decentralization and internal-external.

The combination of these two dimensions distinguishes four sectors of organizational activity with very different and often antagonistic functional requirements: (1) human resources mobilization and motivation; (2) organization and control of production processes; (3) resource acquisition and adaptation to the task environment; and (4) goal-oriented strategic management. This competing-values analysis of organizational functions has been applied by Edwards, Faerman and McGrath (1986) to the assessment of performance effectiveness of human service organizations.

However, this analytic framework can also be used for examining the component elements of the executive position in human service organizations on the premise that the chief executive officer is ultimately responsible for all aspects of organizational performance. In combination these four sectors deal with the two major criteria for assessing organizational outcomes—quality of services produced and continuity of the organization.

No single executive position involves equal emphasis on all four of these sectors. In any given organization the senior administrator may be primarily involved in some sectors while other persons who are

FIGURE 20.1
Competing Values Framework: Effectiveness

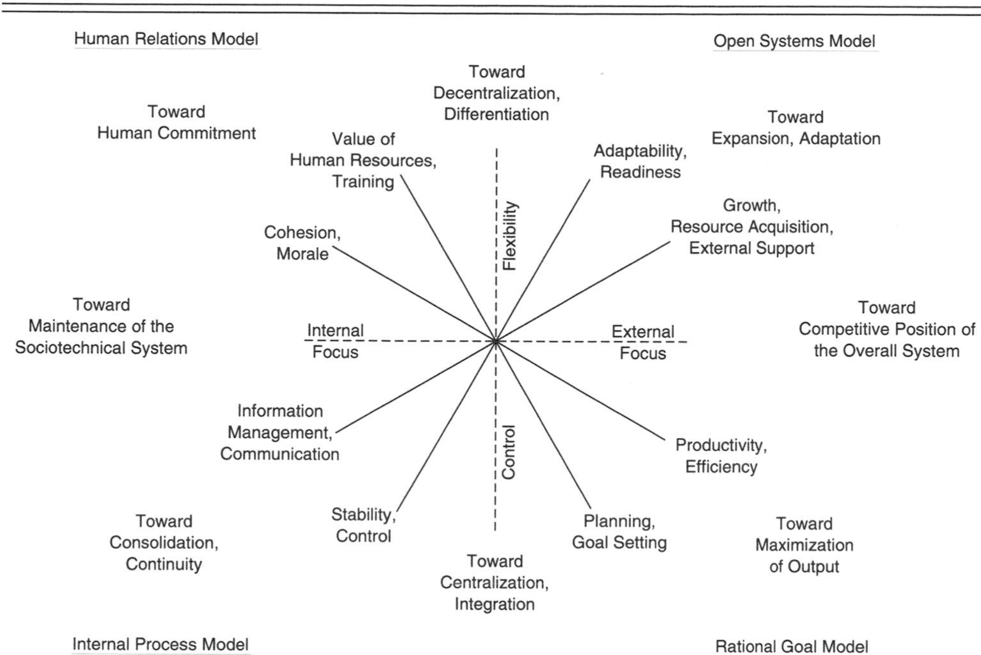


From: R.E. Quinn (1988) *Beyond Rational Management: Mastering the Paradoxes and Competing Demands of High Performance*, used with permission from Jossey-Bass Publishers, San Francisco.

part of the executive component may carry major responsibilities for activities in other sectors. Yet, the chief executive officer is ultimately responsible for the effectiveness or organizational performance in all four sectors. The following material summarizes some of the key concepts associated with each sector of organizational performance, including relevant executive roles. (See Figure 20.2.)

*1. Mobilization and Motivation of Human Resources.* One of the major sectors of executive responsibility involves the mobilization and motivation of the personnel who constitute the human resources of the organization. This sector is particularly critical in human service organizations, which are "labor-intensive," and in which most of the services are produced and delivered through person-to-person interactions. In the competing values model this sector is defined by the concepts of "internal" and "decentralized." The focus is on the role of the executive in dealing with those individuals who are "internal" to the organization, and who, as autonomous individuals with the skill competencies required in service production, represent decentralized centers of authority and influence which cannot be directly controlled by the executive. Quinn (1988) identifies two specific executive roles in this sector: *mentor* and *group facilitator*.

FIGURE 20.2
Competing Values Framework of Leadership Roles

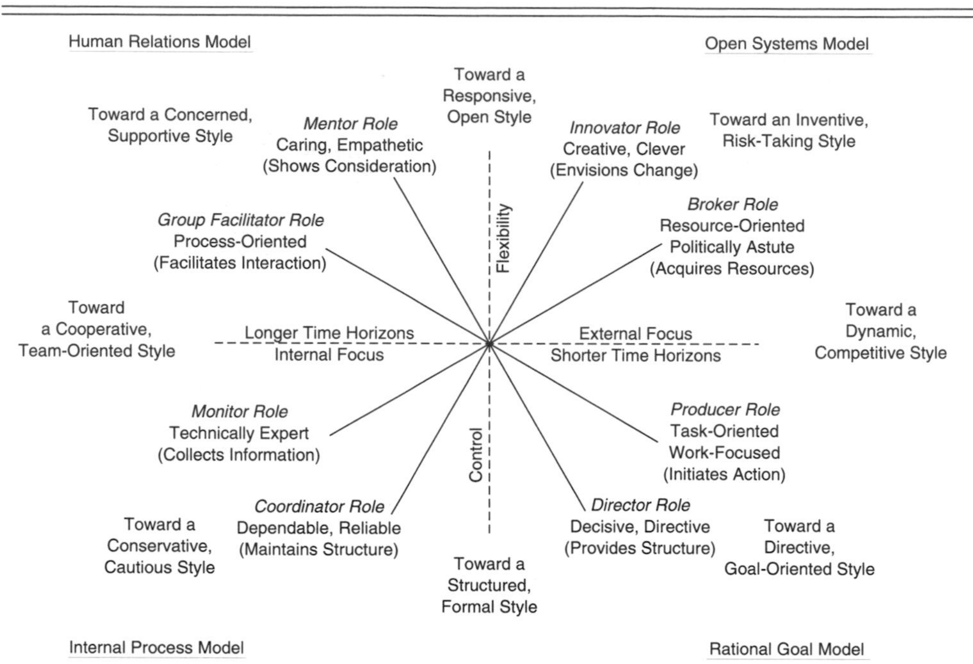


From: R.E. Quinn (1988) *Beyond Rational Management: Mastering the Paradoxes and Competing Demands of High Performance*, used with permission from Jossey-Bass Publishers, San Francisco.

In many human service organizations the employed staff includes members of one or more professional disciplines, an important factor in the decentralized pattern of interpersonal relationships which must be dealt with. The human resources of human service organizations also often include a wide variety of volunteer personnel, including both service volunteers and policymaking volunteers. Moreover, given the role of co-production in the service technologies of human service organizations, service users may be a critical element in human resource mobilization and motivation. Symbols and traditions, the use of special events, and the definition of organizational values are all elements of "organizational culture" which may be significant in motivation.

The processes of human resources mobilization and motivation are often identified, as they are in the Quinn framework, with a "human relations model" and "commitment," or with an emphasis on "cohesion/morale" as in the Blake and Mouton Managerial Grid (1964). The "human relations" model for human resource mobilization and motivation, emphasizing group processes, team-building and participatory decision making, has often been advocated as being particularly congruent with, and supportive of, the "humanistic" and "service" orientation of human service practitioners. The strong emphasis on the importance of morale, or "commitment," in such organizations may also be associated, in part, with the fact that few human service organizations are able, either for structural reasons or financial reasons, to use financial rewards, or rapid career advancement, as major methods of individual motivation.

Under the participatory "human relations" model the primary role of the executive may be viewed as being the ultimate "team leader." However, it is not clear that the "human relations" model, developed by management personnel primarily around efforts to improve work group performance in industrial production, using "T-groups," "management by objectives," "parallel organizations," and "quality circles," is the only relevant model for the mobilization and motivation of personnel in human service organizations. In the human service organization the quality of service often depends primarily on the competence and commitment of individual staff personnel interacting with individual service users in a co-production process, rather than on the work group. Indeed, decentralized individual responsibility, or "professional autonomy," may be more important in motivation than elaborate group participation processes in an organization in which ultimate authority is, in realty, highly centralized.

Moreover, to the extent that a model of internal participatory decision making, primarily involving employed personnel, becomes the controlling framework for decision making in all aspects of the organization, the interests of other stakeholders may be undervalued. Critical as it is, the mobilization and motivation of organizational human resources is only one of four functional sectors of executive performance.

*2. Internal Organization of Production Processes.* Given the labor-intensive, individualized nature of most human service production activities, the systematic organization of personnel activities and the monitoring of service production activities are also major elements in the executive position. In the competing values model this sector is defined by the concepts of "internal" and "centralization." It involves the technical areas commonly dealt with in discussions of management tasks (the organizing, staffing, directing, coordinating, reporting and budgeting functions of the "classical" model of public administration)—budgeting and fiscal controls, time control and scheduling procedures, information and communication systems, personnel administration systems, the structure of formal authority, reporting systems, technical training programs, evaluation and quality control, technical equipment and management of facilities. Quinn (1988) identifies two executive roles in this sector: *monitor* and *coordinator.*

In a small organization the chief executive officer may carry out many of these tasks directly. However, these are also the executive tasks which, in larger organizations, are most likely to involve technical staff specialists, and sometimes very large staff components, for example in financial management, or personnel administration. This is also an area in which "rational" and "systematic" procedures often have their widest application, and, indeed, "scientific management" focuses almost entirely on technologies applicable to this sector.

In the past decade, computerization has been a major feature in all of these technical areas, illustrating the fact that they, in many instances, involve structured decision-making choices among known alternatives—the available combinations of direct salary and fringe benefits for staff compensation, the possible variations in employee work schedules and user demand schedules which can be fitted together, using queuing theory, to design the most efficient work-load schedule for direct service personnel, the choice of a communication system or of computer software programs, the design of organizational facilities, the procedures for handling organizational funds.

There are also the areas in which consistent decisions, centrally controlled, appear to have a direct connection with efficiency, and effectiveness, and in which "command and control" techniques developed in goods production industries have most frequently been applied. However, the effectiveness of such approaches must also be judged by their impact on the equally important processes of motivation and commitment among the people involved in the organization. The development of the concept of "sociotechnical design" represents one effort to combine the objectives of efficiency and personnel motivation (Barko & Pasmore, 1986).

In human service organizations, in particular, this sector involves complex decisions about program organization, or the structure of production roles involving professional specialists, and professional technology. These program structure and technology issues include decisions about the most effective and efficient way for specialized professional personnel to participate in the implementation of "intensive" technology (Thompson, 1967), as well as decisions about the role of less specialized "generalists," and "paraprofessionals," clerical staff, volunteers, and service users.

Given the complexities and uncertainties of professional production activities, executive performance in this sector may be viewed as being based primarily on the experience of the executive with the "core" production technologies of the organization, rather than on knowledge of the more general management technologies. Executives in human service organizations are often selected primarily on the basis of professional education and previous professional experience. However, the quality of actual executive performance is often shaped by the requirements of the other three sectors in which the professional executive may have had limited experience.

*3. Resource Mobilization and Organizational Adaptation in the Task Environment.* Given the degree to which human service organizations, both voluntary nonprofit and governmental, are environmentally dependent, the executive is constantly involved in activities which cross the formal boundaries of the organization. These include, among others, financial resource procurement, personnel recruitment, the establishment and maintenance of organizational legitimation, making adaptations in organizational programs in response to environmental changes, managing external requirements for reporting and accountability, negotiation of informal and formal interorganizational agreements on user referral, cost-sharing in joint projects, and participation in action coalitions. In the competing values model this sector is defined by the concepts of "decentralization" and "external." That is, it involves dealing with individuals, and organizations, that are not under the direct control of the executive, and that are external to the formal boundaries of the organization. Quinn (1988) identifies two executive roles relevant to this sector: *innovator* and *broker.*

This sector involves, in particular, the political or "open systems" dimension of executive performance least subject to technical rationalization or computerization. The quality of executive performance may be viewed as involving "political" or "negotiating" skills, and an understanding of the nature of power relationships in the task environment. It is also the sector in which individual short-term "contingency" decision making by the executive may frequently be required, in contrast to the systematic and long-term participatory internal decision making processes which may be important in human resource mobilization and motivation. It is, perhaps, the sector of activity least likely to be fully delegated to other members of an executive component. However, it may also be the sector which policy makers, both volunteer and legislative, define as their particular area of activity, with explicit limits being placed on the scope of activities of the executive.

The effectiveness of the process of "contingency decision making," or "strategic adaptation," whether carried out by "policy makers," or the executive, or both, may be severely constrained by considerations involving other performance sectors. For example, successful "opportunity seizing" initiatives involving responses to short-term funding opportunities may be inconsistent with overall organizational goals, may require substantial expenditures for the development of new technical production procedures, and may disrupt the cohesiveness and morale of organizational participants.

*4. Strategic Management for Goal Accomplishment.* The fourth sector of executive performance is the goal-oriented process of improving both effectiveness and efficiency, and enhancing the relative position of the organization in its environment. In the competing values framework this sector is defined by the concepts of "centralization" and "external." This sector encompasses organization-centered activities identified as productivity improvement and goal setting in which the executive plays a central role. Again Quinn (1988) identifies two executive roles in this sector: *producer* and *director.*

Since human service organizations are established as "goal-achievement" organizations, that is, to accomplish particular societal objectives, goal definition is particularly important. For "externally dependent" human service organizations this involves efforts to estimate developments in the environment, including the user environment, as well as developments potentially affecting the availability of financial and personnel resources, technological developments, political and legislative developments. Moreover, in nonprofit and governmental human service organizations, organizational continuity takes on a high value, since the "sunk costs" involved in the original effort to create the organization, and the "good will" represented in the community legitimation of the organization, cannot be converted to a set of financial resources to be used for another purpose.

The range of task responsibilities of the executive in these four functional sectors thus includes the interpersonal processes of personnel motivation, the technical competencies involved in organizing and monitoring production, the political processes involved in dealing with the task environment, and the analytic and conceptual processes involved in productivity improvement and goal accomplishment. As Quinn emphasizes, these involve "competing values" and paradoxes, since the conceptual orientation and skills most needed in one sector may be the exact opposite of those required in another sector.

The distribution of time and energy among these four task sectors will vary from time to time within any one organization, and will vary among different organizations in different environments. Responsibilities may be divided up differently among the individuals who are part of what often must be a multi-person executive component. Individuals who are part of such a multi-persons executive component will bring different mixtures of skills. Fundamentally, however, it is the responsibility of the chief executive officer in the human service organization to have an overview of the pattern of activities in all four sectors and to determine the extent to which the requirements of effective performance are being met in all four sectors.

**EXECUTIVE STYLE**

Many textbooks on administration deal with administrative style through a description of two traditional theories identified as "scientific management," that is, the executive as a rational analyst and believer in "command and control," and "human relations management," the executive functioning primarily as an interactive process leader within a structure of participatory decision making groups. Both of these theories are rooted, fundamentally, in a United States model of industrial production in which there is an assumption of an almost total separation in the relationships between "management" and "workers." This separation involves not only differences in roles and responsibilities, but, in general, involved differences in socio-economic background, and often differences in ethnic/cultural background between the two groups of organizational participants. This pattern of separation is reinforced by a general lack of career mobility opportunities between industrial production roles and management roles with industrial managers being recruited largely from among college and university graduates without production experience (Reich, 1983).

Consistent with this model is the assumption of a fundamental conflict of interests between "workers" and "bosses" which must be systematically "managed" by executives in order to achieve efficiency and effectiveness in production. Scientific management (Theory X), and various forms of human relations management (Theory Y and Theory Z), are alternative approaches, designed by management, to deal with the "alienation" which develops out of this separation of interests.

"Successful" application of either of these management approaches in the industrial context means increased production of "goods" with increased efficiency. Both scientific management and human relations management have been promoted as "the solution" to issues of effective executive performance in human service organizations. Indeed, a great deal of attention has been devoted in the 1970s and 1980s to the executive application of the principles of "scientific management," often with a substantial sacrifice of motivation and commitment among staff personnel. Alternatively, application of "human relations" methods has been advocated as the solution to problems of motivation. However, both of these traditional models of administrative style have limited applicability to human service organizations because several of the underlying assumptions do not apply.

The basic assumption of a fundamental structural conflict of interests between administrators and direct service personnel does not apply (although the actual situation in some individual organizations may appear to support such an assumption). In most human service organizations executives and direct service personnel share some form of common professional identity. Executives, and other administrative personnel, in general, are recruited from among persons with at least some direct service, "front-line" experience. Systematic socio-economic and ethnic/cultural distinctions between administrators and direct service workers are less likely to be a major factor, although there are often very obvious gender differences between the majority of front-line workers and the majority of administrators (Alexander & Kerson, 1980).

The "intensive" or individualized nature of service production technology, whether it involves the handling of an individual child abuse family situation, teaching a classroom of elementary students, or providing nursing care for a terminally ill AIDS patient, works against the model of increasing efficiency solely through the application of standardized, scientifically tested production techniques. On the other hand, the motivations which support "committed" participation of both employed personnel and volunteers in service production activities are as likely to be individualistic as they are to be based on membership in a cohesive "work group."

Indeed, the level of "commitment" among both employed staff and volunteers, which is a major factor in the effectiveness (and efficiency) of human service production, is more likely to be connected with organizational goals and with personal concerns about the needs of service users than with other members of a "production work group." While "participatory" process among organizational members, including union organization, can be valuable for a number of reasons, any consistent connection between the intensity of such processes as a regular ongoing part of organizational life and increased service productivity or improved service effectiveness is difficult to establish.

Given the differences between large-scale industrial firms and human service organizations, models of executive style other than "scientific management" and "human relations" are essential for understanding the characteristics of effective executive performance in human service organizations.

*The Managerial Grid* by Blake and Mouton (1964) is one of the more widely recognized behavioral models of executive style which attempts to overcome the dichotomy between task-oriented scientific management and motivation-oriented human relations. The Grid combines two dimensions, one dealing with productivity/efficiency and the second dealing with morale/cohesion, in effect combining the scientific management emphasis on technology and the human relations emphasis on interpersonal processes and motivation. The preferred "9,9" executive maximizes both dimensions.

These two dimensions, however, deal only with the competencies required in the internal quadrants of the Quinn model, "internal processes" and "human relations." That is, they focus primarily on executive competencies and behavioral styles involved in *intra*organizational processes. The Grid does not deal directly with the behavioral styles which are effective in the external processes involved in maintaining the resource flow from the task environment, and in goal-oriented planning and development for the organization.

The resource dependency of human service organizations, both voluntary nonprofit and governmental, points to the importance of the "political" skills required for building and maintaining effective linkages with external sources of legitimation and funding. Similarly, the role of external factors in shaping the goal-oriented development of the organization highlight the importance of the cognitive skills involved in analyzing information about the environment which may guide the pattern of future development of the organization.

## Interactive Leadership as an Executive Style

The relevant behavioral model for the human service executive is that of *interactive leadership*. Leadership is a widely used by seldom defined concept. Indeed, most textbooks dealing with administrative theory tend to ignore the concept of executive leadership. A full discussion of interactive leadership as an executive style is beyond the scope of this article. But two key elements can be emphasized. One is the pattern of active, personal involvement of the executive in a continuous process of interaction with other organizational participants, both individually and in groups. The second is the inclusive focus of attention by the executive on the total organization and its context, that is, a "systems management" approach. Such an approach involves a balance between attention to effectiveness of service production, and attention to the continuity and development of the organization over time.

The model of an interactive style of executive leadership has been described in the writings of Sayles (1979) and Peters and Waterman (1982) among others. The emphasis is on the pattern of personal interaction between the executive and other people throughout the organization including service users. This includes interaction with individuals as well as being part of a variety of group processes.

It would appear that both to learn about social systems and to cope with them, the appropriate working level is the process level. This means that managers and researchers alike need to concentrate on the behavioral interaction that underpins organizational life (Sayles, 1979, p. 8).

Sayles suggests that the central concept of executive behavior is "action in time," that is, a never-ending series of contacts with other people which have as their focus two elements of systems management: *contingency responses* and *reduction of uncertainty* (1979). Peters and Waterman (1982) describe the core focus of executive activity as "managing ambiguity and paradox," while Quinn (1988) focuses on "managing the contradictions of organizational life." All three of these authors are critical of the rational "scientific management" model for executive behavior, focusing instead on an evolving, interactive, problem-solving approach, which includes the use of participatory groups but also includes a high level of individual one-to-one activity on the part of the executive.

A particularly critical element in the interactive pattern of leadership in human service organizations involves the relationship of the executive to professional specialists. Most textbooks on administration ignore the distinctive role of professional specialists as self-directed service producers. Indeed, some of the literature on administration in human service organizations argues for a "deprofessionalized" model of staffing (Epstein & Conrad, 1978). However, as in most human service organizations, when the executive comes from a professional background, the relationship between the executive role and the professional role can become particularly complex. In some settings the executive as professional may function as the senior practitioner, ultimate professional supervisor, and professional consultant (and even as part-time practitioner). However, a pattern of monopolizing both the role of senior administrator and senior professional may seriously limit the ability of other professional practitioners in the organization to function independently. Moreover, a preoccupation by executives with maintaining or enhancing their personal professional identity may mean that inadequate attention is given to organizational members who are not part of the same profession.

Other executives who are professionals may suppress their personal professional identity, and avoid personal relationships with professional practitioners in the organization, in favor of a technically oriented identity as an administrator, and a "command and control" approach to the organization of professional activities. Neither of these two models, the executive as professional practitioner, or as the "pure" administrator, is really consistent with the model of interactive executive leadership. The interactive human services executive who is also a professional can maintain a professional identity while allowing other members of the professional staff to carry major responsibility for professional leadership. Moreover, interactions with other professional staff members should be balanced by interactions with other organizational members.

A second element of the interactive executive leadership style is an inclusive focus on the full range of organizational functions as described earlier in the competing-values framework (Quinn, 1988). This involves the management of a complex process of interpersonal communication which emphasizes the unity of the organization within a decentralized structure in the face of the organizational forces which tend to fragment and divide. Sayles (1979) describes it as the "recombination of elements separated by the division of labor" (p. 26). This includes an emphasis on the purpose of the organization as a whole, including attention to the symbols and traditions which embody the social values and social goals which underlie the existence of the organization.

Particularly important for the interactive executive is an understanding of the tensions that can exist, for example, between maximizing participatory processes in order to reinforce motivation and commitment among staff personnel and being personally involved in the systematic analysis of financial, social and political forces which may shape the goals of the organization in ways that are not consistent with staff preferences (Quinn, 1988). Similar tensions exist between the carefully controlled application of technical knowledge about the most effective, and most efficient, production methodologies, and the highly interactive, and unpredictable, "political" support-building processes which go on with critical external constituencies (Quinn, 1988).

It is a critical function of interactive executive leadership to pay attention to the "whole" of the organization, as well as to the balance among the "parts." This includes attention to the future, as well as to the present, to organizational maintenance as well as to organizational effectiveness. While the production of effective and useful services for individuals in need of those services is the primary objective of organizational activity, the organization itself is a major tool for that production. It embodies past investments not only in facilities and equipment but also in the efforts involved in creating and maintaining the organization to the present. It is a critical resource for service production in the future in response to the "needs" of future service users. Executive attention to maintenance and development of the organization as a community resource is, therefore, of equal importance as a leadership function as the attention which is given to current production activities.

## MEMBERS OF ETHNIC MINORITY GROUPS AND WOMEN IN EXECUTIVE POSITIONS

Any analysis of the position of the human service chief executive officer needs to give specific attention to the dynamics affecting members of ethnic minority groups and women in such positions. In most human service industries, women are the largest group of organizational employees, and are often the largest group of service users. Similarly, members of ethnic minority groups are represented among both employees and service users in nonprofit and governmental human service organizations in larger proportions than in most other sectors of society. The number of women in general, and of men and women from ethnic minority backgrounds who are seeking executive positions, is steadily increasing. This means that during the rest of this century and into the 21st century there will be a steady, and probably turbulent, process of change in the ethnic and gender pattern of executives in human service organizations (Alexander & Kerson, 1980).

Currently, however, executive positions in human service organizations, as well as in much of the rest of society, are perceived as being embedded in a white, male culture (Chernesky, 1983). Ethnic minorities and women in executive positions are under pressure to adapt, in varying ways and to varying degrees, to the characteristics of this culture (Arguello, 1984).

There is an increasing body of journal literature which deals with particular aspects of the pressures facing women, both in gaining access to executive positions in human services and in functioning effectively in those positions. There is a much more limited body of published material dealing specifically with the experience of persons from ethnic minority backgrounds (Arguello, 1984). Again, however, it is striking that textbooks on administration give relatively little attention to these specific issues. Among all of the issues potentially involved in such situations two are touched on briefly here. One issue is that of the relationship of persons of ethnic minority background to the white male executive culture, and the personal problem of "marginality." The other issue involves the role of persons of ethnic minority background who are in executive positions in bringing about changes in their organizations, in particular, in implementing affirmative action employment objectives.

In the case of individuals of ethnic minority background there are many pressures to conform to the informal expectations of the white male executive culture, and to suppress culturally rooted patterns of personal behavior which are not viewed as consistent with that culture. One of the alternatives is to attempt to become wholly accepted within the dominant white male culture and to adopt the symbols, and values, of that culture, while curtailing any involvement in, or identification with, their own distinctive cultural background. While this may be viewed as the best option for personal career success, it may also have very high personal costs. It is, in general, never possible for individuals who are not inherently part of that culture to become a total participant in the informal aspects of that culture, regardless of the quality of individual performance in an executive position.

There is, therefore, always the potential risk of cultural "marginality," that is, of becoming an individual without a real personal definition of cultural identity. Marginality can also be intensified by the pressures of functioning constantly in a situation in which a different cultural group is dominant even if there are no overt expressions of discrimination or antagonism. In situations of serious organizational conflict "marginal" individuals may find themselves isolated without any systematic source of support, either personal or political. One of the factors in the resistance of many white/Anglo males, who are otherwise reasonable individuals, to the changes which are not taking place is anxiety over the possibility of having to function in organizational settings in which it is not taken for granted that the white male culture is dominant at the executive level.

One of the alternatives in handling the potential stresses of "marginality" may be the maintenance of a personalized support system, that is, being part of a group, or network, in which one is not a "marginal" person, but a support system which also does not make extensive demands on the time or resources of the individual, or embody values which are significantly in conflict with the executive culture.

Another alternative for executives of ethnic minority background, and women executives, is to make an explicit decision to maintain dual cultural identities, that is, to establish a place for oneself in the dominant white male executive culture by giving serious attention to the informal expectations within that culture, as well as to the formal requirements of role performance, while also investing substantial time and effort in maintaining an identity which is rooted in the culture of origin. Such a decision involves extra costs in time and money. Moreover, while this may provide an alternative base of personal identification, special psychological costs are involved when there are situations in which the cultural expectations or values of different groups are in direct conflict.

These issues of cultural identity and cultural linkages can be particularly acute when policy and/or administrative decisions represent conflicts between important values, for example, between individualized responses to individual service situations and consistency with established rules and procedures. When the participants in the white male executive culture identify with the concept of absolute choices between "right" and "wrong," that is, with clear-cut definitions of rules and regulations, support by executives of ethnic minority background of decisions affecting individual service users which conflict with those principles may be criticized as "biased," or "special-interest pleading," particularly when persons of ethnic minority background are those involved as service users. Support of across-the-board enforcement of rules, however, may be viewed by others as denial of one's own culture background, and a refusal to recognize the real problems of real people.

A second potential source of stress involves the relation of executives who are from ethnic minority backgrounds, as well as women executives in general, to processes of change going on within human service professions, such as the use of affirmative action initiatives to increase the number of women or of persons of ethnic minority background in administrative positions. Norms of administrative impartiality may argue against explicit support for efforts to bring such changes within the organization, while personal commitments to principles of social justice, together with the requirements of affirmative action policies, may argue for active executive support of such change efforts.

But such proactive action often involves extra personal costs, and may involve risks to the extent that affirmative action efforts conflict with the preferences of other persons in executive and policy-making positions. Again, such efforts may be attacked as "special interest" advocacy. However, the failure of persons with executive authority to play an active role in bringing about change may well be viewed by other persons from ethnic minority backgrounds as clear evidence of "institutional racism."

Leadership expectations, and stresses, for persons from ethnic minority backgrounds in executive positions, as well as for women, are likely to be more complicated and more intense than those for persons who are part of the dominant white male executive culture during the changes which may characterize the next twenty-five to fifty years in the United States. This requires simultaneous attention to structural sources of extra stress and to the development of personal supports that may help in coping with such stresses.

## SUMMARY

The position of chief executive officer in human service organizations is critically important for the development of effective services in education, health care, and social services. Within social work the particular requirements of this position have received little attention. The human service executive position involves comprehensive responsibility for systems management, that is, for dealing with the interrelated elements of personnel motivation, production technology, resource mobilization, and goal-oriented planning and organizational development. Models of scientific management and human relations management developed in for-profit industrial firms have been introduced with very little examination of their applicability to human service programs. A critical element in human service administration is the interaction between executive management and professional specialists. A model of interactive executive leadership is the most relevant to the requirements of human service organizations. However, any serious examination of the position of the executive in human service organizations must also give specific attention to the conditions facing individuals from ethnic minority backgrounds and women in such positions.

## REFERENCES


Alexander, L.B. & Kerson, T.S. Room at the top: Women in social administration. In F. Perlmutter & S. Slavin (Eds.), *Leadership in social administration.* Philadelphia: Temple University Press, 1980.

Arguello, D.F. Minorities in administration: A review of ethnicity's influence in management. *Administration in Social Work*, 1984, *8*(3), 17-28.

Austin, D.M. Administrative practice in human services: Future directions for curriculum development. *Journal of Applied Behavioral Science*, 1983, *19*(2), 141-151.

Austin, D.M. *The political economy of human service programs.* Greenwich, CT: JAI Press, 1988.

Barko, W. & Pasmore, W. Sociotechnical systems: Innovations in designing high-performing systems. *Journal of Applied Behavioral Science*, 1986, *22*(3).

Blake, R.R. & Mouton, J.S. *The managerial grid.* Houston: Gulf Publishing, 1964.

Chernesky, R.H. The sex dimension of organizational processes: Its impact on women mangers. *Administration in Social Work*, 1983, *7*(3/4), 133-141.

Edwards, R.L., Faerman, S.R. & McGrath, M.R. The competing values approach to organizational effectiveness: A tool for agency administrators. *Administration in Social Work*, 1986, *10*(4), 1-14.

Epstein, J. & Conrad, K. The empirical limits of social work professionalization. In R. Sarri & Y. Hasenfeld (Eds), *The management of human services.* New York: Columbia University Press, 1978.

Gortner, H.F., Mahler, J. & Nicholson, J.B. *Organization theory: A public perspective.* Chicago: Dorsey Press, 1987.

Kravetz, D. & Austin, C.D. Women's issues in social service administration: The views and experiences of women administrators. *Administration in Social Work*, 1984, *8*(4), 25-37.

Patti, R.J. Managing for service effectiveness in social welfare: Toward a performance model. *Administration in Social Work*, 1987, *11*(3/4), 7-22.

Patti, R.J. *Social welfare administration: Managing social programs in a developmental context.* Englewood Cliffs, NJ: Prentice-Hall, Inc., 1983.

Peters, T.J. & Waterman, R.H. *In search of excellence.* New York: Warner Books, 1982.

Quinn, R.E. *Beyond rational management: Mastering the paradoxes and competing demands of high performance.* San Francisco: Jossey-Bass, 1988.

Reich, R. B. *The next American frontier.* New York: Times Books, 1983.

Sayles, L.E. *Leadership.* New York: McGraw-Hill, 1979.

Thompson, J.D. *Organizations in action.* New York: McGraw-Hill, 1967.

Wilson, W. The study of administration. In J.M. Shafritz & A.C. Hyde (Eds.), *Classics of public administration.* Oak Park, IL: Moore Publishing Co., 1978.

## 21.

**Robert J. Myers, Peter Ufford, and Mary-Scot Magill**

# ON-SITE ANALYSIS: A PRACTICAL APPROACH TO ORGANIZATIONAL CHANGE

On-site analysis has now been used successfully to help people in organizations in a number of settings in Canada, Australia, and the United States. Host organizations of "on-sites" and "on-site follow-ups" have included voluntary agencies, private enterprise, educational institutions, international agencies, and a variety of government and nongovernment organizations.

From *On-Site Analysis: A Practical Approach to Organizational Change* by Robert J. Myers, Peter Ufford, and Mary-Scot Magill. OSCA Publishing, 94 Markland Dr., Etobicoke, ON M9C1N8.

Robert J. Myers is chairman, Greenshield of Canada, and president, On-Site Analysis; Peter Ufford is consultant to the president of External Affairs, University of British Columbia; Mary-Scot Magill is a consultant in Toronto.

## WHAT IS "ON-SITE ANALYSIS"?

On-site analysis is an organizational problem-solving and staff development process. It is also an intensive and challenging group evaluation and problem-solving process. People doing similar work in other organizations join with the staff of an organization to help them analyze their operations at the workplace, or "on-site." The process is facilitated by a leader who is trained and experienced in its specific analysis and problem-solving techniques. The entire analysis, including the writing and presentation of a final report, is completed in no longer than five and no fewer than three full days.

**On-site analysis helps an organization by using methods that will enhance not**

**only its operations but also its staff's development and capacities.** Together the group of "visiting" and "host" participants assess organizational strengths and weaknesses, identify and prioritize problems, and develop practical recommendations (action plans) to solve them. On-site analysis is a participative yet structured group process. The people working in the organization are involved in every step of the group assessment and problem-solving process guided by the on-site leader.

## FACT-BASED GROUP PROBLEM-SOLVING

On-site analysis follows a prescribed methodology which includes a trained team leader who facilitates and manages the entire process, ensuring that everything is "up for question and review." An on-site analysis, or "on-site," as it is commonly referred to, is not an "audit" performed by an "external" group. Nor is it an "external review" whereby problems are identified and solved "for" an organization by "outside experts."

Throughout the on-site process, current organizational realities and trends (often including environmental factors) are identified and taken into account by all participants. The goals of on-site analysis include identifying strengths and weaknesses, protecting and enhancing selected strengths, selecting problems to be solved, generating alternative solutions to them, and developing practical recommendations for change—*including practical first steps that can be acted on immediately.*

After dealing with perceptions, organizational strengths and weaknesses are identified from *facts* obtained through the questioning and probing that are part of every on-site analysis. The problems revealed by the analysis of facts, rather than those which may have been *perceived* to be most critical by members of the host organization at the outset, become the focus of the remaining analysis and group problem-solving steps. In some cases, the problems revealed through analysis are the same (or similar to) those already perceived by *some* members of the organization. Surprisingly often, they arc different.

## THE REPORT

The results of on-site analysis are prepared in a report that is written and finalized by all participants in the on-site (not just the visiting team) as part of the three-to-five day process itself. The report is never written or finalized by the "outsiders" to be sent back to the organization afterwards, as is often the case with other types of consultation. Its drafting and final production by the group is an integral part of the on-site analysis.

The content of the report includes summaries of the analysis, observations, conclusions, and concrete recommendations (action plans) developed by the group throughout the week. It is both a record of the most important discoveries of the group and a blueprint for action following the on-site if recommendations are accepted.

The report is *presented* to an appropriate group, such as the board of directors, on the final day of the on-site. In the case of an organization choosing on-site analysis as a practical staff development or training exercise only, this presentation may be made only to other staff—but such is rarely the case.

We would like to emphasize that although on-site analysis formally closes with the presentation of the report written and revised by all members of the group as part of the on-site, the report itself is not the "product." *The learning for participants* and *the change that results in the organization* are the products of the on-site process.

## THE GOALS AND METHODS OF ON-SITE ANALYSIS

The primary goal of on-site analysis is to bring about an environment in which change to improve organizational performance and effectiveness can occur. This includes an analysis of strengths and problems, and steps to enhance the strengths and solve the problems. It results in a staff team who clearly understand the current situation and are committed to do something to improve it. In many cases, it actually starts change to occur.

**These primary goals are achieved through a group problem-solving process which includes a rigorous, fact-based assessment of exactly what the organization is doing at the time of the analysis and what it has been doing over the previous three-to-five years.** Areas of greatest potential for improvement are identified by the group, and those agreed to be most important become the focus for the remaining steps of the process.

On-site analysis is specifically designed to ensure that facts about what is and has been happening in the organization are scrutinized and worked with by the group as a group. One result of this is the emergence of a common perception of organizational strengths and weaknesses—an understanding of the organization's performance now and over the past five years that is shared by all participants.

On-site analysis provides a unique organizational problem-solving opportunity that includes identifying strengths and problems (based on facts vs. perceptions) and reaching agreement about the problems and their solutions. It also contributes to staff development.

On-site analysis is designed to build *consensus* about both the strengths of the organization that need to be protected and might be further strengthened and the weaknesses that most need to be addressed. It is designed to produce *clarity* (about the facts), *consensus* (about what the facts reveal), and *commitment* (to action, that is, to what must be done to improve operations)—to use the "three C's" popularized by Warren Bennis years ago.

**The important secondary goal of on-site analysis is to encourage practical learning for all participants.** This includes the demonstration or modelling and experience of effective group analysis and problem-solving techniques that can be applied to many other situations and the conceptual and technical learning which often take place for both visiting and host participants as well as what is learned about the host organization itself.

## THE RESULTS OF OUR EXPERIENCE TO DATE

Since the beginning of the program, more than 500 "on-sites" and "on-site follow-ups" have been conducted in Canada and elsewhere. Over 250 of these have been part of United Way/Centraide Canada's service to its members. According to the staff and volunteers involved, these have been invaluable in helping communities improve local operations. The program has benefitted the national organization and individuals working with it in a number of other ways as well. Responses from other participating organizations, including those outside the voluntary sector, have been equally positive.

Regardless of the type of organization or enterprise, the majority of major on-site recommendations have been implemented and positive results evident within a year following completion of the analyses. The on-site process has therefore been successful to date in terms of resulting in implementation of major recommendations for change. This is the only "yardstick" which we feel adequately measures the impact and usefulness of on-site analysis.

We believe that the successful results of on-site analysis to date stem from both the assumptions about people and problem-solving on which the process is based and a methodology which applies proven theories about how people learn and when they institute change—both in themselves and in their organizations.

## COMMON ASSUMPTIONS—AND DIFFICULTIES—IN CONSULTATION OR MANAGEMENT

On-site analysis is designed to break through many of the barriers to effective help (help that does result in organizational change) that so easily arise from some of the more traditional assumptions about the role of consultants (or managers) and the appropriate involvement of members of the host organization (or of one's own staff) in evaluation and problem-solving.

### What We *Don't* Believe...

In many aspects of their lives, most people hold certain beliefs which influence their expectations, and their expectations, in turn, often influence their choices and behavior—their actions. This is also true of people either working in or trying to help organizations. While it is perhaps unintentional and would often be denied, we have observed that the traditional role of the consultant (and often of managers) is frequently consistent with at least some of the following assumptions:

- that people working in an organization (or "under" a manager) are by and large incapable of solving their own problems
- that the consultant or manager is the one who can or must come up with solutions (i.e., is expected to be the "expert")
- that "involving the staff" usually means "obtaining information from" them, either written or by interview, usually one at a time as opposed to any group discussion
- that it is the proper role of the consultant or manager to write reports, which may or may not include suggestions and ideas of some members of the staff
- that the people in the host organization whom it is most important to involve are those who will be evaluating the results
- that the evaluation of the consultant may be largely or even entirely based on the originality of the proposed solutions (content) and not on whether they are implemented; the same may occasionally be true of managers considered to be "ineffective, but brilliant nonetheless!"
- that it is not necessarily the responsibility of consultants to outline the practical "first steps" that must be taken immediately in order to implement the solution(s) they propose.

Many similar assumptions would be held by some managers, and would necessarily influence both the way they work and the way they feel they are *expected* to work with their colleagues.

## THE ON-SITE APPROACH (WHAT WE DO BELIEVE)

On-site analysis is based on very different assumptions about organizational problems and the role of the consultant or manager.

These include different assumptions about people's capabilities, the impact of perceptions, and the value of "number crunching" and open group processes in effecting change. We believe that:

- People working in organizations are usually capable of solving their own problems; most often the help that they need is with problem-solving methodology.
- People doing similar work in different organizations can offer invaluable (and seldom tapped) help to one another, especially when offered in a situation that does not require them to give "expert advice" or to "sell" solutions.
- For all of us, "facts" are not always what they appear to be; individual perceptions of facts and their significance are often based on individual history, attitudes, assumptions, and values; these can be natural barriers to effective organizational problem-solving.
- Because of the effect of varying perceptions, addressing only presented or perceived problems will not necessarily solve the most pressing problems, achieve consensus, or initiate change in an organization.
- Identifying problems accurately takes time; doing so as a group requires even more time, involving people in ways often entirely new to them, and in a more "open" process than many are accustomed to.

The process of "global analysis," a major step of the on-site process, helps find the facts that, with a trained leader skilled in group problem-solving, lead the group to identifying and agreeing on *what needs to be done to improve the situation(s) causing problems*. This then becomes the shared agenda for group problem-solving.

We also believe that:

- Separating the problem-solving process from any group (or staff) negatively affects their "ownership" of solutions; without involvement, people are less likely to be committed to implementing resulting recommendations for change.
- The host and visiting team members should write the report *together* as part of the problem-solving process for both the learning and additional ownership of results which this can and does create.

Perhaps most importantly, we feel strongly that:

- Evaluation of the problem-solving process should be based not on the ideas which are presented, but on *whether or not change occurs in the organization as a result*, and that
- Recommendations must begin with what can be done in the short run, including a number of obvious, practical steps that can be taken immediately. Only then can attention and planning be effectively focussed on longer term results.

## ON-SITE METHODOLOGY AND EXPERIENTIAL LEARNING

The methods of on-site analysis are based on the above assumptions and on well-researched and documented observations about the effectiveness of experiential learning compared with other methods. These include those which indicate that *people learn best by:*

- being involved in the (educational) process
- being challenged to think and to contribute

- having to share, interpret, generalize and summarize what they are learning as they learn it
- working in intensive, focussed groups—hand in hand with individual assignments
- learning by doing, and having to apply what is learned as it is learned
- working in settings which "deemphasize" status (levelling or "equalizing" processes can encourage participation)
- being involved in setting objectives
- having action plans and clear roles in those plans for meeting objectives they have been involved in setting
- having the opportunity to carry out plans and assume new roles
- pursuing any personal or professional goals that may be part of their motivation to learn.

On-site analysis is specifically designed to encourage and afford considerable learning for both visiting and host participants.

## CRITICAL TO METHODOLOGY: FULL PARTICIPATION

Almost all of us (consultants, managers, teachers, leaders of any sort) enjoy being considered experts at least some of the time. However, in on-site analysis it is the composition of the team (visiting and host) which ensures that most of the needed expertise (skills, knowledge, and abilities) is available in the group.

**In on-site analysis, the leader's role in bringing about participation and contributions from the entire group is as important as his or her own expertise, analytical skill, and problem-solving ability.**

An on-site analysis is completed in an intensive, focussed, and thorough review in which everything is questioned. Follow-up on-site assistance or other on-sites are similarly intensive and focussed.

**The on-site leader must assume the role of challenger: He or she must use *challenging techniques* as well as the usual facilitation skills.** The participation of the host and visiting team members through being challenged to think and to contribute to finding facts and making observations from them helps to build clarity and consensus about organizational strengths and weaknesses. It also helps establish group commitment to the resulting recommendations.

Experiential learning and full participation contribute to creating the "climate" that will be needed to implement recommended changes—and strengthen participants' commitment to doing so. Writing and presenting the report as a group becomes yet another vehicle of learning that can help to bring about change or the environment that is needed for change to occur.

## ORGANIZATIONAL GOALS: CLARITY AND NEW (OR RENEWED) COMMITMENT

Though we admit it may not be true of everyone, we have observed that many people want to do a better job, and want to achieve positive results for their organizations. Many also want to learn through new experiences, and are motivated by opportunities to develop new skills and competencies.

A process which gives birth to new ideas, new perceptions, new objectives, and plans of action can be stimulating and exciting for people who want to learn. On-site analysis is frequently such a process.

On-site analysis can result in a number of positive "by-products" for individuals working in an organization, such as clarification of (and new or renewed commitment to) organizational goals. While such benefits cannot be guaranteed for every participant, they can and often do result from on-site analysis.

Through consensus about the organization's current state, about the problems that most need to be solved, and about the solutions most likely to solve them, on-site analysis fosters *commitment to change* and is *specific and definite about how to begin to make that change happen.*

The clarity of the shared (and often new) perceptions of what the facts reveal about the organization which emerges through the analysis leads eventually to consensus about and ownership of identified strengths and problems, and to a shared commitment to finding solutions. Our experience has shown all three (clarity, consensus, and commitment) to be essential if consultation is to be effective in bringing about change in organizations.

. . .

## WHAT HAPPENS DURING ON-SITE ANALYSIS?

At first glance some elements of the on-site process may appear to be similar to those of other consultative techniques. Consider headings #1, 3, and 5 below for example. However, each step of on-site analysis serves a purpose often different from the traditional purpose of similar activities, and each is carried out in ways that differ considerably from more traditional approaches, as explained in the text below each heading. In on-site analysis:

1. **Facts are obtained and analyzed (clarity)** but only after *perceptions* have been identified and assessed. Usually wide-ranging perceptions of "the facts" are iden-

**Basic Elements: Steps in the On-Site Process**

While various adaptations of on-site analysis afford experienced leaders greater flexibility in using the process to help people identify and do what needs to be done to improve performance, a standard on-site analysis follows a prescribed format of thirteen basic steps:

Step 1 Preparing for the On-Site—Including the Background Questionnaire
2 Leader's Meeting with Visiting Team
3 On-Site Reception
4 On-Site Interviews
5 Opening Session and Report Back on Interviews
6 Perceptual Snapshot
7 Global Analysis
8 Group Identification of Strengths and Weaknesses, Problem Identification, and Next-Level Analysis
9 Problem Selection and Group Problem-Solving, including Enhancing Strengths and Solving Problems
10 Writing the On-Site Report
11 The Essential "Dry Run" Presentation
12 Presentation of the On-Site Report
13 The On-Site Follow-Up

tified, some of which become the basis of the review. In on-site analysis this preliminary stage is followed by a *deliberate switch of focus from perception* to facts. After facts (numerical data only) have been thoroughly analyzed by the group as a group, the subsequent assessment of organizational strengths and weaknesses is often different from perceptions initially held about the organization—including some thought to be based on facts.

2. **Strengths are identified and protected or enhanced.** After strengths and weaknesses have been identified, the first task of on-site analysis is to concentrate on protecting and enhancing strengths. In our experience, strengths are often taken for granted and are therefore not protected; also, because they are seen as strengths, they are seldom scrutinized for ways they can be improved to become even greater assets to the organization.

3. **Weaknesses (problems) are identified** from observations and conclusions *based only on the examined facts.* Again, the problems identified through the group's analysis are often quite different from those initially known or perceived to be problems.

Because it is a group process based on facts obtained by and displayed before the entire group, "global analysis" (analysis of facts about the organization as a whole) results in *a shared perception of, and agreement about, the problems that most need to be solved.*

Even where analysis reveals that strengths and weaknesses had already been accurately identified, the process of global analysis ensures that they are clearly understood and agreed to be so by *all* members of the group. All too often, only one or two members will have seen the problems clearly but have been unable to obtain general agreement about their analysis and therefore about the proposed solutions. Global analysis directly addresses this common difficulty.

The clarity and commitment for members of the organization that result from going through global analysis together can have tremendous benefits for the team's future effectiveness.

The consensus which results from global analysis can also be invaluable in creating enthusiasm and a willingness to "get on with" solving problems for all members of a group who now clearly understand the situation, and can communicate with one another from a common, factual basis rather than varying individual perceptions and opinions.

4. **Solutions are developed and selected** using specific *group* problem-solving techniques which often result in solutions that may have been "unthinkable" or not thought of at all prior to the on-site. We have found that solutions generated and selected by the group are seldom those perceived to be "obvious" ones beforehand; still, selected solutions often do seem obvious (even simple) by the time the group has developed and selected them as part of the on-site process.

5. **Recommendations are made.** In on-site analysis, final recommendations are made and agreed on *by the full group.* Most recommendations also include *practical first steps* that can be acted on immediately to initiate change in desired directions.

6. **On-site follow-up.** We recommend that all on-sites should be "followed up" at a mutually agreed upon time 3–8 months later. The usual follow-up is a day and a half long and repeats the basic on-site group process, i.e., analysis, identification of strengths and weaknesses, development and selection of solutions, etc. The follow-up on-site is not a review of the on-site report, but rather a fresh look at the situation a few months later.

## WHAT IS IT LIKE FOR PARTICIPANTS?

The on-site process is intensive and challenging. It is *intensive* because of the singular focus and need to work as a group for several long, consecutive days in ways that many people may not be accustomed to, even those used to "working in groups." It is *challenging* because it requires people to examine (and sometimes discard) their perceptions to make observations from facts, to develop conclusions, to identify problems, and to look beyond their "first answers" again and again for other possibly better ones.

Participating in on-site analysis can nonetheless be a very positive experience. It can be positive because of the sense of liberation (sometimes exhilaration!) that can come from finding *new ways of seeing and dealing with challenges.* This sense of positive excitement is often heightened because it is shared; these "breakthroughs" or "insights" are usually arrived at as a group.

On the other hand, people should be forewarned that the discomfort of participating in on-site analysis can also be heightened because:

(a) people do work together as a group through long, intensive days, and
(b) they are guided by a leader whose role is to maintain the challenging, probing, "never-say-die" atmosphere in search of "another and another" (possibly better) idea or answer.

. . .

## CHANGE IS THE BOTTOM LINE

Good ideas are seldom in short supply, but people in organizations are often without the means to implement them.

With help from the on-site process, ideas are developed and solutions selected on the basis of newly generated common perceptions of the organization's current achievement and areas of greatest potential for improvement. There is *a clear and common view of both the strengths that need to be enhanced or protected and the problems that need to be solved.* Finally, there is a common (and, in the end, public) commitment to plans of action most likely to protect identified strengths and solve identified problems.

We usually remind people at the opening reception of any on-site analysis that what the on-site will produce are some ideas and recommendations that will be developed by the host and visiting participants working together as a team throughout the next few days.

*What happens to those recommendations will be up to the organization to decide.* If nothing better than what they are already doing results from the process, they can always return to doing what they were doing before the on-site began. (As far as we know, *no one* has yet selected that option!)

A new way of looking at an organization's activity that is shared by the entire staff and includes a set of practical recommendations that everyone agrees are based on facts about the organization's current situation can be a potent incentive to begin to make things happen.

On-site analysis creates *the opportunity to arrive at that "new way of looking," and to do so as a group.* It is different—but (so far!) it *does* work—both for organizations and for the people working in them.

. . .

22.

Richard Hoefer

# DESIRED JOB SKILLS FOR HUMAN SERVICE ADMINISTRATORS

Two important practical questions face persons interested in managing human service programs. First, "What are the important skills needed to do the job?" and second, "Which degree program provides the best curriculum to learn those needed skills?"

Surprisingly, the first query is often overlooked as a research question. There are many books and countless articles related to it, but little in the way of empirical study is done to confirm or disconfirm opinions on the matter. This chapter addresses the issue as its main focus.

In a related issue, many potential students question which type of master's program best prepares graduates to work in an administrative position in a human service agency: the Master's in Social Work (M.S.W.), the Master's in Business Administration (M.B.A.), or the Master's in Public Administration (M.P.A.). Some might even believe that a master's degree is unnecessary or can be obtained after some years in the work force, after one has an administrative position.

The literature in social work devoted to this second question exists but is fairly unsophisticated and nonempirical. The general trend is to argue that an M.S.W. degree is superior to either an M.B.A. or an M.P.A. for human service administration due to the value system students are exposed to during their education (Cupaiuolo and Dowling, 1983; Cupaiuolo and Miringoff, 1988; Hart, 1988; Neugeboren, 1987). Some of these authors state that social work administrators can learn specific skills from other disciplines but that it is inappropriate for people trained in business management or public administration to actually be in charge of human service organizations.

Another group of authors takes the position that there are benefits to looking at the fields of business and public administration to improve administration in social work (Austin, 1983b; King and Correa, 1983; Mullen, 1983; Rimer, 1991).

In a rare empirical paper on the topic, Keys and Cupaiuolo (1987) report on a series of interviews they conducted with administrators to understand the relationship between the social work profession and government public welfare agencies. They found "almost unanimous opinion that schools of social work prepare their graduates poorly for management and administrative positions" in public welfare (Keys and Cupaiuolo, 1987:50). Respondents believed that social work managers are not the only appropriate administrators for such agencies, but "economists, public administrators, health analysts, etc." are also needed (Keys and Cupaiuolo, 1987:50).

This chapter adopts the viewpoint that

---

Richard Hoefer is an assistant professor at the School of Social Work, University of Texas at Arlington. The author gratefully acknowledges the research assistance of Guangzhi Zhao and the editorial and substantive comments of Regina M. Hoefer.

the most important thing in social administration is not the degree which managers hold but the skills, attitudes, and experiences the managers possess. It may be that one type of degree provides more of the necessary skills than another, in which case it should be preferred. Before addressing that issue, however, we must agree on the skills to be desired of human service managers. As noted above, this issue is seldom addressed.

The literature is already replete with the ideas of academics regarding which skills are important. This research answers the question "What skills do current administrators of nonprofit organizations think are important?"

## METHODS

The results of this study are based on responses to a mailed survey of current administrators of human service programs. Based on a search of social work administration texts and journal articles (for example: Anderson, *et al.,* 1977; Ginsberg, 1988a and 1988b; Hayden, 1988; Lewis, *et al.,* 1991; Weiner, 1990), thirty-seven skills and attitudes were selected as important for human service organization administrators. Respondents were asked to rank each item's importance, on a seven-point scale, for entry-level, middle-level, and top-level administrators in their agency.

The survey was sent to the agency directors of 100 randomly selected Chicago area human service agencies. Forty-one usable responses were received. It is not known exactly how closely this group of respondents matches the complete sample, as the responses were anonymous, nor is it clear if the results will automatically generalize to areas other than Chicago. Despite these qualifications, the results are suggestive of the needs of human service agencies and thus have strong importance for students and designers of curricula for human service administrators.

## RESULTS

The surveys returned were generally filled in by the top person in the agency (75 percent), but sometimes by the vice president or deputy/assistant director (10 percent) or personnel officer (15 percent).

The majority of the organizations were private nonprofit agencies (63 percent). Government agencies were also well represented (27 percent). Few private forprofits responded to the survey (7 percent). There were a few organizations in an "other" category (3 percent).

A number of fields of practice were included in the responses. Health and social service agencies were the largest categories (24 percent and 22 percent, respectively), while child welfare and mental health also were well represented (17 percent and 12 percent, respectively). Other fields of practice with some respondents were aging (7 percent), education (7 percent) and "other" (10 percent).

Table 22.1 shows the mean scores for each skill, by administrative level.

The items included in the survey are indeed important ones. No skill has an average value of less than 3.00 (on a seven-point scale, where 1.00 is "Not at all important" and 7.00 is "Most important"). Not all skills are equal, however; there is strong agreement on which are most important and which are the least important across the three levels.

A total of fifteen different skills place in the "top eleven" across the different levels: nine are common to each of the levels. These nine are commitment to clients, pro-

TABLE 22.1
Mean Scores for Each Skill, by Administrative Level

| Variable | Administrative Level | | |
|---|---|---|---|
| | Entry (n=26) | Middle (n=36) | Top (n=41) |
| Commitment to clients | 6.22 | 6.44 | 6.59 |
| Professionalism | 6.08 | 6.80 | 6.75 |
| Oral communication | 6.04 | 6.49 | 6.83 |
| Written communication | 5.81 | 6.27 | 6.78 |
| Identifying with agency | 5.74 | 6.08 | 6.63 |
| Leadership | 5.70 | 6.54 | 6.90 |
| Conflict resolution | 5.63 | 6.30 | 6.63 |
| Program planning | 5.61 | 6.00 | 6.25 |
| Service delivery technology | 5.50 | 5.60 | 5.92 |
| Decision-making | 5.46 | 6.19 | 6.85 |
| Group dynamics | 5.44 | 6.19 | 6.48 |
| Coordinating | 5.31 | 6.08 | 6.38 |
| Meeting management | 5.31 | 6.11 | 6.39 |
| Personnel management | 5.19 | 5.95 | 6.40 |
| Ambiguity tolerance | 5.11 | 5.86 | 6.10 |
| Agency policy area | 4.92 | 5.92 | 6.45 |
| Negotiation | 4.89 | 6.02 | 6.23 |
| Marketing | 4.61 | 4.97 | 5.56 |
| Strategic planning | 4.52 | 5.64 | 6.41 |
| Knowledge of community | 4.51 | 5.54 | 6.08 |
| Evaluation/research | 4.50 | 5.43 | 5.89 |
| Entrepreneurial attitude | 4.48 | 4.97 | 5.85 |
| General social policy | 4.42 | 5.39 | 5.77 |
| Experience in human services | 4.38 | 5.20 | 5.50 |
| Budgeting | 4.27 | 5.17 | 6.21 |
| Organization theory | 4.19 | 5.38 | 6.10 |
| Political process | 4.11 | 5.11 | 5.98 |
| Experience in agency | 3.96 | 4.58 | 5.10 |
| MIS | 3.88 | 4.81 | 5.49 |
| Statistics | 3.84 | 4.62 | 5.10 |
| Database | 3.77 | 4.37 | 4.77 |
| Spreadsheet | 3.67 | 4.27 | 5.03 |
| Word processing | 3.52 | 3.83 | 3.64 |
| Accounting | 3.50 | 3.97 | 5.00 |
| Fund-raising | 3.42 | 3.86 | 4.99 |
| Administrative law | 3.15 | 4.31 | 5.28 |
| Political connections | 3.04 | 4.11 | 4.65 |

1 = Not at all important, 7 = Most important.

fessionalism, oral communication, written communication, identifying with agency, leadership, conflict resolution, decision-making, and group dynamics.

Three elements on this list are attitudes (commitment to clients, professionalism, and identifying with agency) and the rest are learnable skills. The attitudes deemed important here have much to do with the values of social work. The skills are those which are necessary in any management position.

Even though all of the skills are valued at least to some extent, there is complete agreement on which of these 37 skills are least important. The same skills are the "ten least important" at each level. Half of these ten are computer-related skills such as MIS, statistics, spreadsheet, database, and word processing.

Despite this small variation in the types of skills considered most important and least important, there is generally an increase in the importance of each skill as one moves from entry-level to top-level administration. Thus, a person who wishes to climb in the hierarchy need not learn new skills as much as he or she should become more proficient in skills already possessed.

## CONCLUSION AND IMPLICATIONS

The importance of thirty-seven management-related skills and attitudes to current human service administrators was found to be quite consistent at the entry, middle, and top levels of management. While some of the most desired elements are specifically social-work oriented, most are skills which are important in any type of organization. The least important factors tend to be computer-related skills and other sorts of specialized knowledges such as administrative law and accounting, where it is possible to hire the expertise.

The implication of this research for persons in the field is to concentrate on improving communication and leadership skills while maintaining the most important attitudes, such as commitment to clients, if they wish to rise in the ranks. The question of which management degree is "best" to attain these skills and to strengthen important attitudes is not yet answered, but should be the focus of future empirical research.

## REFERENCES

Anderson, Wayne, Bernard Frieden, and Michael Murphey (Eds.). (1977). *Managing human services.* Washington, DC: International City Management Association.

Austin, David. (1983b). Reply to Professors McDonough, Mullen, King, and Correa. *Journal of Applied Behavioral Sciences, 19*(2), 159–161.

Capaiuolo, Anthony, and M. Dowling. (1983). Are corporate managers really better? *Public Welfare, 41,* 12–17.

Cupaiuolo, Anthony, and Marc Miringoff. (1988). Is there a degree of choice for human service management? In Paul Keys and Leon Ginsberg (Eds.), *New Management in Human Services.* Silver Springs, MD: National Association of Social Workers (pp. 44–57).

Ginsberg, Leon. (1988a). Applying modern management concepts to social work. In Paul Keys and Leon Ginsberg (Eds.), *New Management in Human Services.* Silver Spring, MD: National Association of Social Workers.

Ginsberg, Leon. (1988b). Data processing and social work management. In Paul Keys and Leon Ginsberg (Eds.), *New Management in Human Services.* Silver Spring, MD: National Association of Social Workers.

Hart, Aileen. (1988). Training social administrators for leadership in the coming decades, *Administration in Social Work, 12*(3), 1–11.

Hayden, Wilburn. (1988). A curriculum model for social work management. In Paul Keys and Leon Ginsberg (Eds.), *New Management in Human Services.* Silver Spring, MD: National Association of Social Workers.

Keys, Paul, and Anthony Cupaiuolo. (1987). "Rebuilding the relationship between social work and public welfare administration, *Administration in Social Work, 11*(1), 47–58.

King, Donald and Mary Correa. (1983). "Additional comments on administrative practice in human services: Future directions for curriculum development." *Journal of Applied Behavioral Science, 19*(2), 157–159.

Lewis, Judith, Michael Lewis, and Federico Souflée, Jr. (1991). *Management of Human Service Programs* (2nd ed.). Pacific Grove, CA: Brooks Cole.

Mullen, Edward. (1983). "Additional comments on administrative practice in human services: Future directions for curriculum development," *Journal of Applied Behavioral Science, 19*(2), 154–156.

Neugeboren, Bernard. (1987). Enhancing legitimacy of social work administration, *Administration in Social Work, 11*(2), 57–66.

Rimer, Edward. (1991). The impact of efficiency on social work administration education, *Administration in Social Work, 15*(1/2), 133–146.

Weiner, Myron. (1990). *Human Services Management: Analysis and Applications* (2nd ed.). Belmont, CA: Wadsworth.

## 23.

**Henry M. Havassy**

## EFFECTIVE SECOND-STORY BUREAUCRATS: MASTERING THE PARADOX OF DIVERSITY

Middle managers in human services are often seen as caught in the middle between the conflicting expectations and demands of superiors and subordinates (Feldman, 1980; Holloway, 1980; Perlmutter, 1983). In addition to conflicts within the organizational hierarchy, other sets of conflicting expectations and demands make the middle manager's challenge even more complex (Kahn, Wolfe, Quinn, Snoek, & Rosenthal, 1964; Mills, 1976, 1980; Whetten, 1978). Conventional wisdom tends to view middle managers as powerless and frustrated. However, research and experience show that their position can be one of critical importance and significant influence and that some individuals are exceptionally effective in this role (Kanter, 1982; Keller, Szylagyi, & Holland, 1976; Schuler, 1977; Whetten, 1978). Much can be learned from the way successful managers view and carry out their roles.

This article addresses three interrelated issues: (1) the multiple-role conflicts inherent in the position of middle managers, (2) empirical findings on how effective middle managers in human service organizations deal with these conflicts, and (3) practice implications for middle managers and organizations.

### MANAGERS IN THE MIDDLE

In this study, middle managers were defined by three conditions: (1) they report to organizational superiors who have little or no direct contact with the actual service-delivery context; (2) they manage line supervisors or direct-service providers who have contact with the client community but little or no direct contact with the higher levels of the vertical organization; and (3) their work site is located in the service-delivery community. Lipsky (1980) called direct-service providers "street-level bureaucrats"; thus, middle managers can be seen as "sec-

---

Henry M. Havassy is a lecturer at the School of Social Work, Haifa University, Mt. Carmel, Haifa, 31999 Israel. This article is based on a paper presented at the Annual Conference of the National Association of Social Workers, New Orleans, September 1987. The author is grateful to Irit Erera, Zvi Eisikovits, the anonymous reviewers, and the editorial staff for most helpful comments on an earlier draft, and to Robert Biller, Terry Cooper, Samuel Taylor, and Francine Rabinovitz for their help in developing this research.

ond-story bureaucrats." Although this term may seem pejorative, the opposite is intended. Second-story bureaucrats, although operating at neither the upper level nor the street level, make daily decisions that make the bureaucracy work and that strongly influence the quality of service provided. As such, they are key people whose potential and importance are often underestimated. Some examples of second-story bureaucrats include the director of a local welfare office, a family service agency, a neighborhood mental health clinic, or a community center; a hospital unit director; a school principal; and a head nurse.

Second-story bureaucrats are in a unique position linking social resources and human needs, that is, linking human-service intentions and delivery. They are at the nexus of many different groups and social systems—at the nerve center where those groups and systems connect and interact (Figure 23.1). Each group or system is a role-set for the middle manager, that is, a source of expectations and demands (Gross, Mason, & McEachern, 1958; Katz & Kahn, 1966; Merton, 1957). These multiple role-sets are often at odds with one another, causing intersender conflict and role overload: "Pressures from one role sender oppose pressures from one or more other senders...[and] various senders' expectations...[are] impossible to complete" (Kahn et al., 1964, p. 20; also see Kahn & Quinn, 1970; Merton, 1957). Organizationally, upper management expects middle managers to obtain worker compliance and implement policy; subordinates expect middle managers to represent their interests and accommodate their needs (Dalton, 1959; Holloway, 1980; Likert, 1961; Perlmutter, 1983). Similarly, middle managers work at the nexus between the norms and expectations of society in general and those of the local community, which includes clients, community organizations, local leaders, and other services. The expectations of the general society and those of the local community may conflict over basic values and specific issues related to the delivery of human services. Finally, the middle manager must respond to both the norms of the profession and the day-to-day reality of service delivery. Professional norms and standards reflect performance expectations that may conflict with day-to-day pressures of service delivery in specific cases.

Each of these constituencies has resources needed for, and plays a part in, effective service delivery. However, each constituency has a different perspective on its needs, the services to be provided, and the appropriate process of doing so. The diversity of perspectives is paradoxical: Different perspectives may conflict sharply with one another, yet *each is valid within its own framework of values and concepts.* Each captures a part of reality. Therefore, a critical role of the second-story bureaucrat is bridging the different perspectives to integrate the resources needed for effective service delivery (Abramszbk, 1980; Mintzberg, 1973; Pettes, 1979; Wexley & Yukl, 1977), Weick (1979) claimed that organizing is the negotiation of the meaning of situations. In these terms, the middle manager's role is to negotiate, among actors with different perspectives or constituencies, both a workable level of common meaning about the nature of a given situation, and a subsequent course of action acceptable to all parties.

## STUDY OF EFFECTIVE MIDDLE MANAGERS

The current study was conducted to explicate the role of second-story bureaucrats and the factors that contribute to effective

FIGURE 23.1
Position of Second-Story Bureaucrat Between Systems

performance of this role. Effective second-story bureaucrats were interviewed in depth to learn how they bridge the various vertical and horizontal systems. Management studies based on interviews of successful practitioners have been used often in recent years (Bennis & Nanus, 1985; Kanter, 1983; Klauss et al., 1981; Peters & Waterman, 1982). In-depth interviews enable access to managers' perceptions of the multiple meanings of situations and behavior, and can be used to explore the interplay between these varied interpretations in ways much more sensitive than are possible with a standardized questionnaire.

## Research Sample

Expert second-story bureaucrats were identified with the help of academics, senior executives, and middle managers in city and county bureaucracies and nonprofit organizations. The second-story bureaucrats ($n$ = 23) worked in diverse organizational settings and human-service fields. Nominators were asked to identify individuals who were exceptionally effective in the second-story bureaucrat role. The nominations were then validated by a questionnaire sent to the subject's immediate supervisor, a subordinate, a peer, and (when possible) a respondent from the community. Although there are no generally accepted criteria for professional effectiveness and different respondents surely used different criteria, there was almost complete consensus regarding the excellence of the managers in the sample (compare Kanter, 1983, p. 373).

A limitation of this design is that the

sample is not randomly selected from the population of second-story bureaucrats. The findings therefore relate directly only to those interviewed. The purpose of the study, however, was to develop a model grounded in effective practice; hence the sampling was not intended to represent the entire population of second-story bureaucrats. When such models are called for, representativeness of the sample may be sacrificed in favor of variety (Strauss, 1987). This purposive sample was meant to capture the widest available variety of organizational settings and human-service fields in a group of managers who are regarded as experts (Helmer & Rescher, 1960) rather than as a representative sample. The explanation of what enables them to be particularly effective is based on similarities identified across diverse action settings and on role and communication theory about multiple role-sets, role conflict, and boundary spanning. Independent validation of the findings by the interviewees, as well as reactions of other professionals in subsequent presentations made in various settings, gives a strong base of intersubject objectivity to support these findings (Helmer & Rescher, 1960).

### Data Collection and Analysis

The study data are the meanings and subjective interpretations that expert informants gave to social situations and behaviors related to their practice experience. These data were collected in an iterative process of individual and group interviews. Twenty-three effective second-story bureaucrats were interviewed in three rounds of in-depth individual and group interviews. The interviewees were asked to report several critical incidents in their work with different constituencies and to describe the roles they played in bridging the constituencies. Attention was focused on specific actions, the rationale or assumptions underlying the choice of these actions, and their perceived consequences. A content analysis of the interviews was conducted using such emergent categories as personal attributes and elements that contributed to effectiveness in horizontal systems, in vertical systems, and between systems (Strauss, 1987). The data were analyzed for similarities and common themes within and across interviews. After the first 10 interviews, the interviewees were invited to a group session to discuss the interim findings. The interviewees were asked to identify deficiencies in the synthesized material, items of greatest importance, and missing elements and to comment on whether the organization of the material reflected their experience. The group feedback also served to check the accuracy of the data recording and synthesis and the emergent content categories. The group interviews provided additional information and examples, sharpened the organization of material, and helped to revise the collective description developed from the first 10 interviews.

In the second round, 10 additional second-story bureaucrats were interviewed individually. These interviewees also were given part or all of the synthesis of findings from the first round and were asked to comment on it. The response of additional experts provided a further test of the intersubject objectivity of the findings. After the second round of individual interviews, the synthesis was expanded to include an initial attempt to interpret the data through unifying themes that could explain the particular effectiveness of these second-story bureaucrats. This synthesis was discussed in a second group interview to which all interviewees were invited.

In the third round, three additional

second-story bureaucrats were interviewed, and three who had been interviewed previously were reinterviewed. The purpose of this round was to further test the model developed in the first two rounds and to clarify the interpretation of the data. This round was followed by a final group session that focused on the explanatory model rather than on the details of the data.

## MODEL OF EFFECTIVE SECOND-STORY BUREAUCRAT BEHAVIOR

The study showed that although these 23 effective managers experienced all the conflicts and contradictions typical of middle management, they were able to master them. The interviews produced inventories of management behaviors and techniques commonly used by these individuals. These behaviors and techniques are generally recognized skills of good management and thus by themselves are not sufficient to explain why these managers are particularly effective. The explanation is to be found in qualitative differences in using the techniques. Effective second-story bureaucrats seem more like master artisans than superior technicians.

A good technician has the skills and knowledge to efficiently produce standardized, interchangeable products or outcomes. Only when the circumstances or needs tend to be uniform are the technician's products predictably effective. On the other hand, an artisan is sensitive to emerging needs and requirements and can apply requisite skill and knowledge contextually in situations that require idiosyncratic responses. The products of the artisan are individualized and unique (Bensman & Lilienfeld, 1973; Eisikovits & Beker, 1983).

The iterative interviewing and data synthesis process produced a model to explain the artisanship of these second-story bureaucrats. This composite model reflects the management behavior of the interviewees as a group but does not describe any one of them exactly. Through systematic interviewing and intersubject validation, the practice wisdom of these expert informants was captured, reconceptualized, and used as the basis for the model (Figure 23.2) (Argyris & Schon, 1974; Glaser & Strauss, 1967; Schon, 1983).

The composite model includes four elements: (1) the ability to engage diversity, (2) an orientation toward emergent social systems, (3) the commitment to efficacy, and (4) a mission-and-value orientation. The remainder of this article will elaborate the first element, the ability to engage diversity. (The entire model is elaborated in Havassy, 1986).

## ABILITY TO ENGAGE DIVERSITY

The model shows that effective second-story bureaucrats are able to deal with their multiple role-sets by virtue of their ability to engage diversity and to learn from the richness of different and even conflicting perceptions within a given situation. "Engaging diversity" is a complex process that includes interacting and meshing with different perspectives, accepting and dealing with the differences rather than trying to unify or gloss over them. It entails a commitment to maintain, master, and use the diversity of perspectives. Three interdependent factors jointly produce the ability to engage diversity: (1) considerable tolerance for ambiguity, (2) maintenance of multiple loyalties, and (3) cross-system translation.

FIGURE 23.2
Model of Effective Second-Story Bureaucrat Behavior

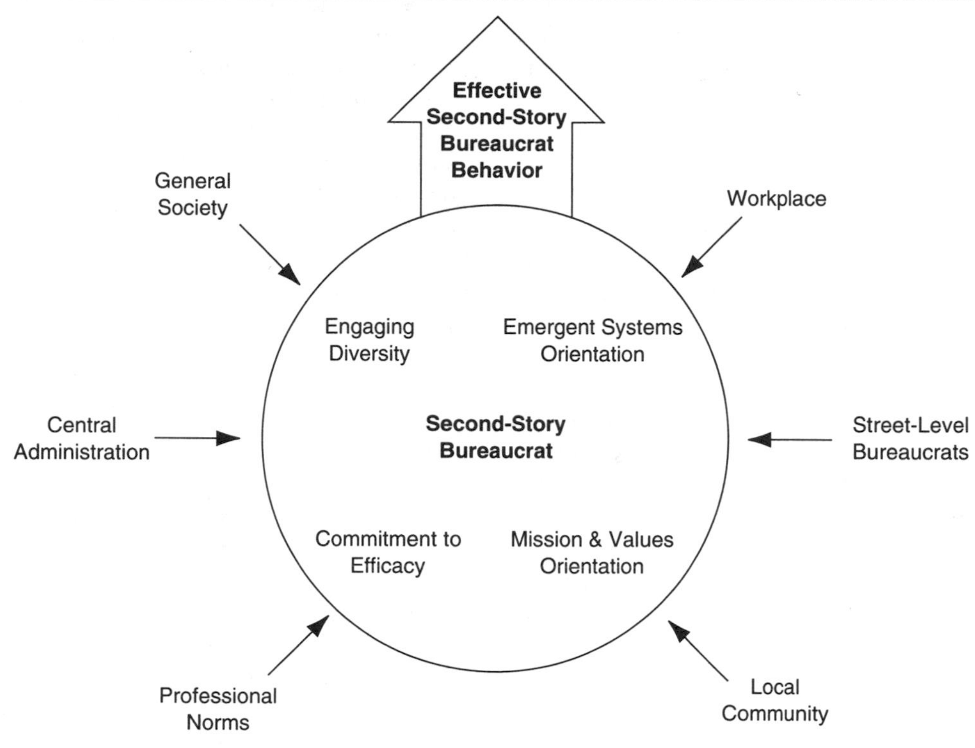


## Tolerance for Ambiguity

The capacity to simultaneously grasp the different and seemingly contradictory aspects of a situation at the nexus of multiple systems is at the core of the second-story bureaucrat's effectiveness. Rather than being paralyzed by diversity and apparent conflicts or inconsistencies, effective middle managers can see or create an underlying interconnectedness. As one manager said, "You need to see everything from six points of view simultaneously!" In accepting this diversity, they are able to develop a much richer understanding of a situation and its potentiality than would be possible by espousing one perspective at the expense of the others.

The managers did not like to view seemingly conflicting viewpoints as opposites. In their thinking, these managers naturally went to a level of analysis where the "opposites" were interrelated. One interviewee said, "I see a real polarization when I see opposites. It's either this or that, and I don't see [how you can then put them together]. When you say differences or divergent opinions, I can see ownership of that." Here is a wonderful example of perception creating reality. Conventional definitions of a situation may lead others to become immobilized or to access the potential of only one of several facets of a situation. The way that effective second-story bureaucrats define their situation provides a rich understanding and facilitates action that is flexible and appropriate to the context.

## Multiple Loyalties

The second-story bureaucrat is a boundary agent between various constituencies that present different demands and expectations, including that of loyalty to each. Boundary agents, by importing to their organization the views of its environment, are liable to have their own loyalty questioned (Adams, 1980; Mills, 1980; Mintzberg, 1973). When outside their organizations, boundary agents may be suspect because of assumed loyalty to their own organization. Second-story bureaucrats are able to effectively span the boundaries between various systems by maintaining loyalty to multiple groups. This maintenance of multiple loyalties is based on their ability to see beyond temporary or issue-specific contradictions and conflicts. In the words of one interviewee, "It's keeping a balance between the needs expressed from above...and what people bring to me as their problems and needs. Unless I feel there's a balance...I will not be satisfied with my work."

These multiple loyalties come together into a systemic loyalty, geared to general service values and goals rather than to a simple organizational or parochial loyalty. Second-story bureaucrats actively avoid creating or reinforcing a we-they view of the relations between different groups; they emphasize the underlying unity and try to help each party understand the larger picture that encompasses the needs and concerns of the different sides. Another interviewee said, "...we have to see that we [branch and central units] are one agency. It's not us versus them...."

The second-story bureaucrats in this study stressed that integrity is intertwined and strongly interdependent with the ability to maintain multiple loyalties. They repeatedly stated their belief that "you really can't trick people for very long. They find you out and then the trust, which is so important, is gone." Their credibility derives in large measure from their ability to internally maintain and externally display these loyalties.

## Transcending Diversity: Cross-System Translation

Effective action requires the second-story bureaucrat to mobilize and use resources from horizontal and vertical systems and to influence others to take action leading to desirable results. A key to the effectiveness of the managers interviewed is their ability to put their grasp of diversity and their multiple loyalties into action through cross-system translation.

"Cross-system translation" is expressing needs, expectations, and demands of one system in the terms and concepts of another system. The effective manager is able to share in the view of each group without being limited to it. He or she is thus able to translate or interpret the situation into each system's terms and concepts in a way that enables each group to act in a way that is appropriate and meaningful for that group. For example, in the hands of an effective second-story bureaucrat, "head office" reporting forms required of a caseworker may take on meaning as a professional review and evaluation tool.

At its best, this translation can go a step further and enable the different parties to interact directly, without the ongoing mediation of the manager in the middle. The process of cross-system translation does not necessarily bring the different parties to share the same view of the situation, nor should it. Instead, the process develops compatible views that enable the different parties to interact directly and constructively, enriching one another's understanding of the situation. A challenge of the role is to know when to translate and when to get out of the middle and enable direct communication. It can be as difficult to step out of the situation as it is to bring people together. Yet, if the second-story bureaucrat does not do so, she or he can become an impediment to communication:

> You've got to...go beyond just communicating in different ways [with different groups]. You need to come up with a common language and a common goal that's acceptable to the whole, to the two [so-called] opposites...The different groups do not need to share the same view, but [they need] to be able to communicate.

## Engaging Diversity in Practice

*Identifying with Diverse Constituencies.* When dealing with different constituencies, effective second-story bureaucrats can identify with each point of view and see it as containing a valid understanding of the situation, without necessarily agreeing with everything. For example, a community mental health clinic was called upon to run an extended-hours program. Even before this demand, the staff had been feeling overworked. The director fought to avoid the extended-hours program, but his superior insisted that the program was needed and that it was equitable, in the division of labor within the region, for this clinic to take on the program. The second-story bureaucrat was able to understand and accept the positions of both his superior and his staff. How did he reconcile the two?

> I came back to staff, and as enthusiastic as I can be, said, "Look, we have to do this extended-hours program, so let's do the best program that we can and be creative." As a middle manager, it was my job, once I lost that battle, to really make it an exciting, meaningful program. It did turn out to be a dynamite program. We did outreach and let the various agencies that open on the weekend know that we too were open....It turned out to be the model weekend program in the region....
>
> If I had told my staff. "We're ordered to do this thing. Let's do the minimum," people would drag in there and hate what they're doing. Morale problems would escalate....They would feel like they're spinning their wheels and getting no satisfaction out of it. In this case, not only did I abide by the regional decision, but in the interest of my own organization's health I had to make this as meaningful as possible for staff as well as for the people we serve.

The demand for extended hours came from higher levels of management in response to perceived political and service needs. However, in presenting the demand to his staff, the second-story bureaucrat translated it into terms of professional values and responsibility and of local-unit identity and pride. Thus, although the demand came down through the vertical system, the actual program was defined within the horizontal system. The result fully satisfied the superiors, provided much intrinsic satisfaction for the staff, and gave clients dedicated service at convenient hours.

*Creating Win–Win Situations.* In situations of conflict like the case above, effective second-story bureaucrats can see and absorb the perspectives of the different groups involved. They are not limited to taking one side or another or taking no side and seeking compromise through mutual concession. They fully engage conflicts, take both sides, and seek satisfaction of the real issues and demands of all parties (Follett, 1973). This method helps reframe the conflict situation for one or all sides in a way that enables satisfactory action and offers the possibility of creating win–win situations. Cross-system translation enriches the effective manager's understanding of the situation, and the interaction between perspectives creates action choices that could not come from within any one perspective. Interacting with the various parties in this positive way makes it possible to access more resources from the different systems and parties.

Obviously these managers are not always successful in resolving conflicts in this manner. But they perform at their best in conflict situations when they absorb and maintain diverse viewpoints and maintain multiple loyalties to create situations that are satisfactory for all. This process can be seen in the case of the extended-hours program and in the following case:

> Upper management issued a directive on how [preparation of child welfare court reports] was to be done. I read it and said it would not work. I feel that my job is to make things work. I knew that the goal was to get the kind of controls and supports workers needed so that the reports got to court on time. That was a given. I let upper management know that the directive was not workable, and why. I developed an alternative with my staff...and later it became a model for replication. I'm never one to say, "OK, you say implement, we implement." I just don't feel that's right. That's not fair to the clients, not fair to administration....But I analyze where and why it doesn't work and where there might be a better way. I try to get input from my staff, and see where they're at and what can be done and what can't be done....I'm not trying to be a maverick, just trying to be responsible and make things work.

*Embracing Independence and Conformity.* Understanding the paradox of diversity leads to an ability to think independently—to question what makes sense, what is right, and whether there is another way of thinking or acting.

> It's the ability to perceive and to know that things can be different and then to ask the right questions....My gift, if you want to call it that, is the ability to walk out and just ask questions of the organization, of how we handle clients, how staff does things, the whole process. What are we about? What can we do better?

Because second-story bureaucrats have contact with different groups and their perspectives, they are able both to conform to, and to see the limitations of, any one perspective. It would be easier to simplify such a situation by choosing one group and conforming to its expectations. However, these managers tend to take the more difficult but more rewarding route of embracing multiple perspectives, and with them, both conformity and independence.

Many of these observations may seem to be commonplace and even obvious. But we only need ask how many managers we know who exhibit the capacity to embrace multiple perspectives and to translate values and viewpoints from one system to another. Further, by rediscovering the obvious we highlight it and enhance our awareness of its relative significance.

## IMPLICATIONS

### Organizations and Managers

Middle managers can play an important role in bridging systems and groups in and around the organization. As organizations come to recognize this role, they can learn to take maximum advantage of it. Organizational structures and procedures can be developed to use second-story bureaucrats as translators, interpreters, and facilitators to communication across system boundaries, rather than as neutral conduits of information and instructions. An organizational climate of open communication and decentralized decision making helps to legitimize and facilitate the second-story bureaucrat's bridging of diversity. In addition to the organizational benefit of richer and more productive communication, the legitimation and appreciation of this role can ease some of the stress commonly associated with the middle manager position.

Individual second-story bureaucrats can evaluate their own ability to engage diversity. Some will find strengths in this area that they had taken for granted and, by "rediscovering" them, can make better use of themselves and their ability. Others will find that they need to improve their ability to embrace and mediate diversity. Understanding that this ability is composed of accepting the paradox of diversity, maintaining multiple loyalties, and translating across systems can focus such efforts.

## Selection and Training

The ability to engage diversity does not appear to be an ability that a person either has fully or does not have at all; rather, the ability seems to be present in degrees that differ from person to person. Accordingly, there are implications for both selecting and training second-story bureaucrats.

An important consideration in selecting candidates for second-story bureaucrat roles should be their ability to engage diversity. Using this criterion requires the development of appropriate assessment tools, such as role play and problem-solving simulations that reveal action choices in situations of conflicting demands and expectations.

Although it is unlikely that managerial training programs can radically change a person's ability to engage diversity, they may be able to effect significant improvement. Such training can be divided into conceptualization and skill-development components.

Training can help managers conceptualize the processes of linking various groups and social systems. It can sensitize individuals to the diversity of perspectives and to alternative approaches to dealing with a given situation; it can help them to understand, legitimize, and value different perspectives and approaches. This enhanced conceptualization can help in-service trainees to understand and interpret their experiences—both successes and failures—and to identify new action choices. It can help prepare preservice trainees for the diversity and complexity that await them and can provide a conceptual base to help them maximize their individual abilities to engage diversity.

Training can improve skills in translating situations, ideas, and needs into the perspectives of different groups; facilitating effective direct communication between such groups; moving fluently among various roles; and defining and expressing loyalties to different constituencies. The metaphor of the artisan suggests an important training consideration: Artisans learn by doing and modeling, by going through stages of apprenticeship. Likewise, second-story bureaucrats might profit most from experiential learning and mentorship to achieve the sensitivity and flexibility required for the contextual use of standard skills.

## Research

The value of expert informants has been recognized and demonstrated in other qualitative studies. However, further research comparing more and less effective second-story bureaucrats is likely to further clarify and elaborate the model, sharpening the identification of the characteristics of effective practitioners. Whereas this study used reputation as a criterion for effectiveness, other studies could use other criteria, such as normative performance expectations, and compare the modi operandi of more and less effective managers.

Another limitation of the study design is that it is based on a partial set of observations. The interviewees reported their interactions with other organizational actors, but the study did not have access to the observations of these others about the same events and behaviors. Studies encompassing other relevant actors in the role-sets could enhance understanding of effective second-story bureaucrat behavior and strengthen the findings of this study.

Qualitative methodologies such as the one used in this study have the advantage of both collecting in-depth information about the experience of organizational actors and giving such actors the opportunity and skills to practice reflectively. For instance, if second-story bureaucrats were taught to be participant observers of their own practice, they could simultaneously develop valuable knowledge and enhance their own performance. The "reflective practitioner" model developed by Schon (1983) comes closest to what is suggested here.

Whether a manager is caught between different systems or bridges them can be the difference between effectiveness and mediocrity for the services and between efficacy and powerlessness for the manager. The ability to engage diversity is a key element in the effective manager's success in bridging and linking. Understanding this key can help second-story bureaucrats take maximum advantage of their abilities, and it can help organizations to select and train those individuals best suited for such a role and to take maximum advantage of the contribution that middle managers can make to effective human services.

**REFERENCES**

Abramszbk, L. W. (1980). The new M.S.W. supervisor: Problems of role transition. *Social Casework, 61,* 83–87.

Adams, J. S. (1980). Interorganizational processes and organization boundary activities. In B. Staw & L. L. Cummings (Eds.), *Research in organizational behavior* (Vol. 2, pp. 321–355). Greenwich, CT: JAI Press.

Argyris, C., & Schon, D. (1974). *Theory in practice.* San Francisco: Jossey-Bass.

Bennis, W., & Nanus, B. (1985). *Leaders: The strategies for taking charge.* New York: Harper & Row.

Bensman, J., & Lilienfeld, R. (1973). *Craft consciousness.* New York: John Wiley & Sons.

Dalton, M. (1959). *Men who manage: Fusions of feeling and theory in administration.* New York: John Wiley & Sons.

Eisikovits, Z., & Beker, J. (1983). Beyond professionalism: The child and youth care worker as craftsman. *Child Care Quarterly, 12*(2), 93–112.

Feldman, S. (1980, Spring). The middle management muddle. *Administration in Mental Health, 8,* 3–11.

Follett, M. P. (1973). Constructive conflict. In E. M. Fox & L. Urwick (Eds.), *Dynamic administration: The collected papers of Mary Parker Follett.* New York: Hippocrene Books.

Glaser, B., & Strauss, R. (1967). *The discovery of grounded theory.* Chicago: Aldine.

Gross, N., Mason, W. L., & McEachern, A. W. (1958). *Explorations in role analysis.* New York: John Wiley & Sons.

Havassy, H. M. (1986). *Second-story bureacrats in human services: Middle managers as a critical link in effective policy formation and implementation.* Unpublished doctoral dissertation, University of Southern California, Los Angeles.

Helmer, O., & Rescher, N. (1960). *On the epistemology of the inexact sciences.* Santa Monica, CA: Rand Corporation.

Holloway, S. (1980, Winter). Up the hierarchy: From clinician to administration. *Administration in Social Work, 4,* 1–14.

Kahn, R., & Quinn, R. (1970). Role stress: A framework for analysis. In A. McLean (Ed.), *Mental health and work organizations.* Chicago: Rand McNally.

Kahn, R., Wolfe, D., Quinn, R., Snoek, D., & Rosenthal, R. (1964). *Organizational stress: Studies in role conflict and ambiguity.* New York: John Wiley & Sons.

Kanter, R. M. (1982, July–August). The middle manager as innovator. *Harvard Business Review, 60,* 95–105.

Kanter, R. M. (1983). *The change masters: Innovation and extrepreneurship in the American corporation.* New York: Simon & Schuster.

Katz, D., & Kahn, R. (1966). *The social psychology of organizations.* New York: John Wiley & Sons.

Keller, R. T., Szylagyi, A. D., & Holland, W. D. (1976). Boundary spanning activity and employee relations: An empirical study. *Human Relations, 29,* 699–710.

Klauss, R., Fisher, D., Flanders, L., Carlson, L., Griffith, M., & Hoyer, M. (1981). *Senior executive service competencies: A superior managers' model.* Washington, DC: U.S. Office of Personnel Management.

Likert, R. (1961). *New patterns of management.* New York: McGraw-Hill.

Lipsky, M. (1980). *Street-level bureaucracy.* New York: Russell Sage Foundation.

Merton, R. (1957). *Social theory and social structure.* Glencoe, IL: Free Press.

Mills, R. H. (1976). Role requirements as sources of organizational stress. *Journal of Applied Psychology, 61,* 171–179.

Mills, R. H. (1980). Organization boundary roles. In C. L. Cooper & R. Payne (Eds.), *Current concerns in occupational stress.* New York: John Wiley & Sons.

Mintzberg, H. (1973). *The nature of managerial work.* New York: Harper & Row.

Perlmutter, F.D. (1983, Fall/Winter). Caught in between: The middle management bind. *Administration in Social Work, 7,* 147–169.

Peters, T. J., & Waterman, R. H., Jr. (1982). *In search of excellence: Lessons from America's best run companies.* New York: Harper & Row.

Pettes, D. E. (1979). *Staff and student supervision.* London: George Allen & Unwin.

Schon, D. A. (1983). *The reflective practitioner: How professionals think in action.* New York: Basic Books.

Schuler, R. S. (1977). Role conflict and ambiguity as a function of the task-structure-technology interaction. *Organizational Behavior and Human Performance, 20,* 66–74.

Strauss, A. A. (1987). *Qualitative analysis for social scientists.* Cambridge: Cambridge University Press.

Weick, K. (1979). *The social psychology of organizing* (2nd ed.). Reading, MA: Addison-Wesley.

Wexley, K. N., & Yukl, G. A. (1977). *Organizational behavior and personnel psychology.* Homewood, IL: Richard D. Irwin.

Whetten, D. A. (1978). Coping with incompatible expectations: An integrated view of role conflict. *Administrative Science Quarterly, 23,* 254–280.

24.

John E. Tropman

# POLICY MANAGEMENT IN THE SOCIAL AGENCY

## INTRODUCTION

In this brief article we will focus on key elements of policy, from a methods perspective. In social work, the concept of "policy" is used in two senses—social policy and policy management.

Social policy focuses on the substance of policy, and is interested, through analysis and proposal, in advancing more humane, just, and inclusive laws, rules, and guidelines. Policy management refers to the central skills needed to bring these kinds of changes about. It is a social work method, like administration and community organization, and shares much with them. To make a distinction among them, one might say that policy managers mobilize and direct ideas, while administration mobilizes and directs workers, and community organization mobilizes and directs communities.

## THREE RESOURCES FOR AGENCIES

Basically, organizations are run on three kinds of resources—money, people, and ideas.

*Money* is the agency's financial resource; it buys the staff and equipment needed to develop and deliver programs. *People* are the human energy of the agency. As workers, they deliver the programs and make them work. *Ideas* provide the agency's conceptual energy—what to do, who to involve, how to influence. Ideas provide the vision and set the purpose for the organization. Ideas—as innovations—become the new programs of the organization. Ideas of justice, inclusion, and diversity become new social policies and then social programs.

In most organizations we spend a lot of time on the money resource; less, and often considerably less, on the people resource; and almost none on the idea resource. Many organizations have adequate money and adequate staff, but no ideas about how, really, to apply them efficiently and effectively.

## A DEFINITION OF POLICY

Ideas are the start of policy, and any discussion of policy needs to begin here. **Policy is an idea, which is a guide to action, is written, and has the approval of legitimate authority.**

Policy begins with an idea. That thought is then transformed into action guidelines. Those action guidelines are then written down, reviewed, discussed, changed, and finally approved by legitimate authority. The form of a policy can be a law, new governmental regulations, or personnel policy passed by the agency board of directors.

## THE WORK OF POLICY MANAGEMENT

Policy work involves paying some attention to each of the policy elements. The first task of the policy manager is to ensure that there is a **constant supply of new ideas** into the agency. In this sense, ideas are resources just like money and people. And, like money and people, they need to be organized, shaped, and applied to organization goals if they are to be of any use. Hence the policy manager—or worker playing the policy manager role—is continually seeking new ideas from staff, from other agencies, from the media, from anywhere, and circulating them around to see if there is anything there worth following up on. Seeking new ideas is a major task.

**Turning ideas into guidelines for action** is the second major policy management task. Ideas from elsewhere need to be tailored to the agency. Policy managers will involve others in this process—workers, community people, administrators, and so on. It is essential that appropriate, realistic applications of new ideas be developed. It is also essential that someone have the responsibility for orchestrating this process. We use the word "orchestrating" to indicate that the policy manager is not the person who "does it all." Rather, the policy manager is one who sees that it gets done, in a process that may involve many others.

**Writing it down** is the third major responsibility. Usually there are many, many drafts. Indeed, it is through the writing process that the guidelines for action are developed. Someone once said that "Writing is God's way of letting us know how sloppy our thinking really is!" An idea is suggested, and everyone agrees "it" would be good, but there is often much unclarity about what "it" actually is. Writing the guidelines down allows those involved to actually envision the steps of action. Many problems often surface at this phase, and consequently new drafts are written to take those concerns into account. Obviously, this often is a time-consuming process.

**Approval by legitimate authority** is the final step in the policy management process. Approval involves taking the proposal to some authoritative group—the agency's board, a city council, or a state legislature. Getting approval is a complex process in and of itself, often involving more modifications of the draft policy in question. But it is a crucial step in the policy management process, and requires much attention to exactly what happens during that process, who the influential persons might be, how they can be influenced, and so on.

## POLICY SKILLS

There are numerous specific policy skills which, for purposes here, can be grouped into two general areas—intellectual, referring to managing ideas, and interpersonal, referring to managing people.

**Intellectual skills** refer to abilities like writing, seeking, storing, and organizing new ideas for future use. They involve the ability to be critical of suggestions while not being hostile, to see both the "forest and the trees," to manage decision-making settings (see Article 35 on running effective meetings), as well as blending ideas from different sources. Intellectual skills also include a large element of the practical, which makes the policy manager different from the thinker. The policy manager's goal is to help ideas become practical. In some contexts, this part of the policy manager role is called the "policy technician" or "policy analyst."

**Interpersonal skills,** on the other hand, focus on working with people. Skills here involve persuading, listening, reinterpreting and rephrasing, brokering, and negotiating. The individual is the crucial component, and seeking to understand what the person really wants, and working to meet those needs through appropriate modifications in the policy proposal is an important part of the interpersonal skill repertoire. In addition, the interpersonal side of the policy manager is similar to aspects of the community organizer. In each role, there are building of networks and development of relationships with opinion leaders, as well as elements of "pressing the flesh" or "working the room," which are so necessary to building both the general and specific interpersonal relations required for success in policy development and enactment.

## THE STAGES OF POLICY

The policy process has well-recognized stages. At each, both intellectual and interpersonal skills are needed to accomplish the tasks and to progress to the next phase.

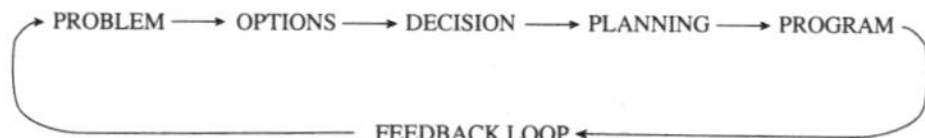


The **problem** phase involves developing ideas about what is wrong, and what different thinkers and interests judge the problem to be. Often, the policy manager will do research here to determine the scientific thinking on the subject, as well as to talk with any individuals affected by "the problem."

After the problem has been defined, developing policy **options**—different approaches to corrective action—must be considered. Frequently the policy manager will find out what other communities, agencies, and firms have done about a similar problem. The various solutions are organized into several options for consideration.

From this list of options, authoritative bodies select one (or several) **decisions,** which is hard, because it allocates goods and values in the system, and defines "winners and losers." Nonetheless, as the well-known saying goes, "not to decide is to decide." Policy managers must help decision groups come to closure.

**Planning** is the next step. It involves developing the more specific operating guidelines that will make the policy decision workable.

Running the **program** is next. Here, the policy is actually put into practice, and information from what happens is placed in the **feedback loop,** which is the process of evaluation. There is a continual monitoring—of the program and efforts made—to see what modifications must occur in the policy process. As the diagram suggests, modifications can take place throughout the process, and at any point during it. In its most extended form, the feedback loop reaches all the way back to the problem, so that the problem is redefined and the policy process once again is activated.

## POLICY, PRACTICE, AND THE POLICY/PRACTICE GAP

Sometimes, people think that policy is "the way we do things around here." That is practice. Almost all policies (and the plans and programs attached to them) have some variation in actual practice. In general, as long as such variation is small, it is fine. Variation often represents a way in which the actual situation is dealt with while respecting the essential sense of the policy. However, if the policy/practice gap begins to increase, it is time for a closer look. In most cases of this sort, the feedback loop has become inoperative, and there seems to be no way that policy can be changed. All too often, in situations like this, the policy is left alone, and the practice is changed! However, it is much better to keep any policy up-to-date, and monitoring the policy/practice gap is a good place to begin.

## VISION AND STRATEGIC POLICY MANAGEMENT

One of the most important policies for an agency is its strategic direction. Regretfully, many agencies have neither a strategic direction nor a strategic plan. The policy manager, or person designated to play policy-management functions, can help the agency in developing strategic planning.

One begins with a **SWOT** analysis as part of the problem definition phase. SWOT stands for strengths, weaknesses, opportunities, and threats. Teams are assigned to develop reports in each area, with respect to the agency. What are its strengths? What are its weaknesses? What opportunities are available for exploitation? What threats face it? Policy managers are useful in helping each of the groups work out their information and reports.

When data have been collected on these points, a conference is held to process the information. At this conference, a **vision** for and of the agency is developed (or redeveloped, improved, or reaffirmed) that provides direction, invokes opportunities, neutralizes threats, builds on strengths, and corrects weaknesses.

From this step—visioning—a strategic plan emerges. (Here, again, the policy manager might be a key draftsperson.) This plan lists several specific goals that will make the vision come to life. Then, operational goals are developed from the strategic plan, with timelines and responsible persons defined.

## CONCLUSION

This brief discussion of policy management provides an introduction to the policy-management process, and to some of the skills and actions it requires. It is intended as a first step in the development of policy competency and, through that, improving the documents that guide and direct our social agencies.

## REFERENCES

Tropman, John E. (1986). *Policy management in the human services.* New York: Columbia.

Tropman, John E. (1987). Policy analysis. In A. Minahan (Ed.), *The encyclopedia of social work.* Silver Spring, MD: NASW.

PART FIVE

# Evaluation

As mentioned in the Introduction to this volume, evaluation is perhaps that area where we have been most neglectful. The human services enterprise is not alone here, to be sure, and doubtless there are many reasons for our avoidance of evaluation. One, of course, is the difficulty of getting measures on some of the interventions that we seek to create. Secondly, there is every reason to believe that a considerable number of those measures don't make any difference, and the fact that negative evaluations make people feel bad often causes, or at least contributes to, avoidance. Furthermore, the fact that clients and client systems *are* our clients tends to diminish in the eyes of some the value of their feedback. Still in all, clients are customers, and we must attend to the views of those we serve more closely. Usually customers and clients will tell us if we are helping them or not, and it is important to ask.

How does one approach the whole matter of evaluation? There are four critical steps that should be kept in mind in designing a system of program development: monitoring, oversight, assessment, and appraisal. These four components are the necessary legs for a system of program evaluation; without each of them it is very difficult to be accurate, because it will turn out that key parts needed to complete the evaluation are missing.

Monitoring is simply the data-keeping or record-keeping aspect of the program evaluation system. Without basing data on who comes to the service, how many, how often, etc., it is very difficult to build toward the final overall appraisal. In a classroom situation, this stage would be analogous to the keeping of attendance records: A simple check whether a student was present or not provides the first step. Many organizations in the human service field (outside the human service field, too, for that matter) do not know the basic demographics of their programs and services. There is always considerable "lore" about who has been using the services, how these uses have changed, and whether anyone is being helped, and so on, but when pressed for the actual numbers, executives and program managers step away. The foundation of any system of program evaluation, then, is a basic set of numbers that outline the patterns of use.

The second step in program evaluation is oversight. This phase builds from phase number one, monitoring, but it is different in that it applies standards and expectations to the numbers as it looks for gaps, problems, and difficulties. Some investigations and comparisons allow for early midcourse corrections. In a classroom situation, oversight could occur when a professor applies the two-time absence rule. Thus, Jim, who is absent for three times, is invited in to discuss the issue. Alternatively a simple "pop quiz" allows the prof to have some sense of where the student is with respect to the course material. In an agency setting, an example would be the proportion of those clients who are staying longer than the twelve visits provided by policy. Oversight—which means "look over" rather than "overlook"—should be frequent, and not terribly fateful with respect to the "evaluatee"; it is that process of constant checking and comparing that allows for the correction to be made before problems in an agency or program become too severe.

The third level of the evaluation system is assessment. Assessment is potentially more fateful than oversight and involves the much more occasional review and judgment about a particular person's or organization's performance. In a classroom setting, an example would be the midterm or final exam. These are more fateful, but do not totally determine. Exams allow a fair amount of information to be put together and provide an opportunity to see whether this information can indeed be pulled together by the student in question. In a business setting, a number of criteria might be applied during an assessment process, such as the quality of the product, the price of the product, the efficiency of the program, and so on. Intercomponent ratings and judgments are made at this time. In an agency, an assessment may take into account the facts that a particular program is very popular and that people do seem to be helped by the particular mode of counseling given there, but assessment is extremely expensive and only a few people are being helped at any given time. It is important to understand in the assessment process that judgments are made about the relative weights and values of these different criteria. It is also important to understand that assessments are built on monitoring and oversight.

The fourth step in the system of program evaluation is appraisal. Appraisal represents a final, fateful judgment on a "go" or "no go," continue or not continue, fire or retain basis, concerning that which is being evaluated. In a school setting it is analogous to the final grade—all information from the other three steps is taken into account, but finally, a judgment is made. In real estate, where the term "appraisal" has common usage, a broker will look at a house offered for sale. The broker will inspect the physical property and also records of the past sale of the house, as well as of other houses in the area, will relate those factors to the current market, and will come up with a "market value," which can then be used in setting the asking price for the house. The word appraisal, as used there, contains the twin elements of factual research and judgment; each of these elements is important. In the case of the classroom, the professor may use the final and midterm grades, any quiz grades, attendance records, and other aspects of judgment (did the student try very hard or was the student apparently lackluster?) in deciding how the grade will finally be assigned.

In program evaluation it is important to stress the systemic and step-wise nature of the approach. All too often "program evaluators" are brought into a program that is in progress and are asked to employ criteria that were never part of the original "deal" anyway. This approach naturally is troubling to those being evaluated, who rightly feel that the evaluators do not understand the complexities and difficulties that the program faced. Thus, it is absolutely imperative that program evaluation as well as personnel evaluation be an ongoing and continuous part of the activities of the agency, not an episodic, occasional element.

The articles in this section pick up on various aspects of these concerns. Robert Washington's piece on alternative frameworks, revised for this volume, provides different ways in which one may approach the evaluation process. Peg McCartt Hess, Gail Folaron, and Ann Buschmann Jefferson present an evaluative model for family reunification services, which has broad application. William Birdsall's and Roger Manela's "The Nitty Gritty of Program Evaluation" provides some key technical tips and hints. It was prepared especially for this volume, and it aims at informing the practitioner about the very basic things that are helpful in evaluating a program. Elenore Chelimsky's piece, "The Politics of Program Evaluation," deals with one of the key aspects, the "political" or "emotional" component of program evaluation. While written some years ago, it still has an up-to-the-minute flavor, and Chelimsky has provided revisions that place these issues in a contemporary context.

—John E. Tropman

25.

**Robert O. Washington**

# ALTERNATIVE FRAMEWORKS FOR PROGRAM EVALUATION

Evaluation designs are always confronted with methodological issues which call attention to the debate around the question of rigor versus relevance. On the one hand, the evaluation must be rigorous enough to stand the test of replicability and deal with the problem of attribution and rival hypotheses; on the other, it must be adaptable enough to yield decision-relevant data. The complex task of the evaluator is to strike the delicate balance between this dichotomy; this is not an easy task. Williams and Evans (1969) observed.

> We have never seen a field evaluation of a social-action program that could not be faulted legitimately by good methodologists, and we may never see one. But, if we are willing to accept real-world imperfections, and to use evaluative analysis with prudence, then such analysis can provide a far better basis for decision making than we have had in the past.

If program evaluation is to inform policy formulation and program development then the minimum requisite of any efficient design is that it (1) measure change, i.e., demonstrate effect; (2) include procedures which rule out rival hypotheses which might alternatively explain the noted effect; and (3) describe how and why the change took place. On the other hand, there are factors over which the evaluator has no control which may affect a good evaluation. For example, almost all program evaluations in the human services are conducted in a political arena. The evaluator must therefore understand how political demands for certain types of evaluative data, or how efforts to protect programs performing below standards, may influence our choice of certain evaluation designs. Moreover, the political ethos that affects the decision environment in which evaluation takes place may also require the use of analytical and statistical procedures that attempt to correct defects resulting from the use of certain designs which are less rigorous than others, although they may be the most feasible design, given the nature of the decision environment.

Since the "politics" of evaluation is a reality with which the evaluator is constantly confronted, he needs to know what his options are with respect to designs and the analytical framework which informs such designs (Washington, 1987).

There are at least four conceptual models which are generally accepted as analytical frameworks from which to select an evaluation design.

The term "conceptual model" is used here to refer to an explanatory frame of reference within which certain social and behavioral science concepts are used as tools for circumscribing evaluative behavior. This explanatory system offers the evaluator a way of thinking which defines the means to be employed as well as the ends to be served in evaluative research. The term also suggests that there are precisely

---

Robert O. Washington is a professor at the Graduate School, University of New Orleans.

formulated concepts drawn from business, public administration and the social sciences which provide us with clues as to what it is about human service delivery systems that should be studied and evaluated. In other words, a conceptual model provides us with a "change" or "intervention" theory which forms the analytical framework within which the evaluation will be conducted.

Since outcomes from most services imply directed social change, it is useful to have a "change" or "intervention" theory. Such a theory tends to identify what constitutes the desired change to be measured as well as to provide clues as to how the change should be measured. Usually, the change or intervention theory developed by the evaluator will be couched in a particular discipline. For example, some evaluators use organizational theory as their analytical framework. Organizational theory uses the rigorous methods of economic analysis, but also incorporates findings of behavioral science research. Using organizational theory then, the evaluator is likely to conceive a human service program as a complex social system. This framework, for example, provides the foundation for the systems model evaluation.

## THE SYSTEMS MODEL

The systems model of evaluation is based upon efficiency and relates to questions of resource allocations to produce certain outputs.

The systems model assumes that human services organizations are essentially open systems in that (1) they exist in a highly interdependent relationship of exchange with their environment—a relationship that includes the utilization of a wide variety of inputs, (2) they have the ability to make improvements in service provision; and (3) they have the capability of modifying or changing provisions in order to adapt to client needs or demands. Although the systems model presumes an identifiable flow of interrelated events moving toward some goal, it assumes that certain resources must be devoted to essential nongoal activities as maintenance and preservation of the system. From this viewpoint, the central question in an evaluation of the effectiveness of an intervention should be: How close does the organization's allocation of resources approach an optimum distribution? Etzioni (1970), a central proponent of this model, suggests that what really is important is whether there exists a balanced distribution of resources among all organizational needs rather than the maximal satisfaction of any single organizational requirement.

The systems model of evaluation assumes that the evaluator must answer at least four questions: (1) how effective is the coordination of organizational subunits? (2) how adequate are the resources? (3) how adaptive is the organization to environment and internal demands? and (4) were the goals and subgoals met?

While the measurement of general organizational goals is central to the systems model, proponents of the systems model tend to minimize the need to measure how well a specific organizational goal is achieved. They contend that such a strategy is unproductive and often misleading since an organization constantly functions at a variety of levels with a variety of goals which are sometimes conflicting. Moreover, they contend, overattention to a specific goal will lead to underconcern for other programmatic functions. Systems protagonists also contend that allocating excessive resources (resulting in waste duplication and inefficiency) to achieve a particular goal is just as detrimental to system "steady state" as withholding such resources.

The systems model of evaluation tends to be more productive in decision making among organizations which employ program budgeting. The general idea of program budgeting is that budgetary decisions should be made by focusing upon overall goals. In other words, program budgeting is a goal-oriented program structure which presents data on all of the operations and activities of the program in categories which reflect the program's goals. Inputs, such as personnel, equipment, and maintenance, are considered only in relationship to program outcomes. Program budgeting, then, lays heavy emphasis upon relating costs to accomplishing the overall goal.

Program budgeting has two essential characteristics: (1) the budget is organized by programs rather than by objects of expenditure, and (2) the program shows not only current needs but also future needs for resources, as well as the financial implications of the programmed outputs.

From the perspective of the evaluator, program budgeting contains two important pieces of information. First is the organizational goals and objectives. The second is a statement of the financial resources required to achieve the goals and objectives.

Drawing from program budgeting procedures, the two most frequently used evaluation strategies employed in the systems model are cost-effectiveness analysis and cost-benefit analysis.

### Cost-Effectiveness Analysis

There are many and varied reasons why it may be of limited value to apply cost-benefit techniques to a particular human services program. However, such a program may be effectively evaluated with a slightly modified version of cost-benefit analysis known as cost-effectiveness analysis. Unlike cost-benefit analysis, which attempts to quantify benefits of a program in money terms, cost-effectiveness analysis utilizes output variables in nonmonetary forms to serve as indices for benefits of specific programs. The output variables are specified by various goals of a specific program, such as number of persons trained in a given skill, employment, or level of proficiency on a standardized test.

### Cost-Benefit Analysis

Cost-benefit analysis involves the use of economic theories and concepts. It is designed to tell us why a program or one of its components works in addition to how well it works. The concept of "cost-benefit" defines the relationship between the resources required (the cost) to attain certain goals and the benefits derived. One of its basic premises is that many decisions involving the location of limited resources are often made on the basis of how those resources can be most optimally used, avoiding waste, duplication, and inefficiency. Cost-benefit analysis is a tool for decision makers who need to make choices among viable competing programs designed to achieve certain goals. It is not designed to favor the "cheapest" nor the "costliest" program, but rather the optimal program in terms of the available resources and the explicit goals. Usually costs as well as benefits are given a dollar value over time, and benefit over cost ratios are computed. A ratio in excess of one indicates worthwhileness from an investment point of view. The higher the ratio, the greater the value and worth.

The cost-benefit calculus is not a wholly satisfactory tool for evaluating human services programs, because of its incapability to measure "psychic" or "social" benefits.

Psychic and social benefits are defined here to refer to the state, or well-being, of the recipient or the changes that take place in attitude and behavior as outcomes. Weisbrod (1969) argues that an evaluation design built around cost-benefit analysis is likely to reach negative conclusions about the effectiveness of any human services program, since only "economic" benefits and costs are taken into account. (Remember, an evaluation design built upon the systems model is concerned primarily with "allocative efficiency.")

One of the precautions in interpreting the cost-benefit data is, while a particular human services program may be judged inefficient, it may not necessarily be considered undesirable. It may, for example, have certain favorable income redistributional consequences which are socially preferable to other benefits. As an illustration, educational programs which focus upon socialization, social competence, and good citizenship do not produce the kinds of outcomes and changes which can be measured by the "payoff-rate" concept. Thomas (1967) noted:

> ...the social benefits of education, whose value is almost impossible to express in quantitative terms, are a major portion of education's output. Examples of these nonquantifiable benefits are reduction of civil strife, greater social harmony between persons of diverse ethnic and social backgrounds, less capacity for the political process to be seriously influenced by extremist groups, etc. The problem for the evaluator is that such benefits, while impossible to quantify, are nonetheless of crucial importance relative to the basic justification of a particular program.

There is general agreement that the utility of a cost-benefit model as an evaluative tool lies in its emphasis on a systematic examination of alternative courses of action and their implications. But it is important to note that data from such a model should be only one piece of evidence in the appraisal process and, from the vantage point of the evaluator who is concerned more with "social" than economic benefits, such data may not be the most significant piece of evidence. When programs have goals that go beyond simply maximizing the return on public investments irrespective of who receives the benefits, a simple cost-benefit ratio is an insufficient indicator of program effectiveness.

## THE GOAL-ATTAINMENT MODEL

Of the models to be presented, the goal-attainment model of evaluation is the most commonly used. This model, given prominence by Sherwood (1964) and expanded upon by Levinson (1966) stems from a conception of evaluation as the measurement of the degree of success or failure encountered by a program in reaching predetermined goals.

The goal-attainment model of evaluation relies heavily upon strategies which measure the degree of success in achieving specified goals. It assumes that specific goals can be assessed in isolation from other goals being sought by the program. The goal-attainment model is derived from theories and motivation (forces which energize and direct behavior) and Lewinian field theory. This model is very useful in measuring abstract goals and functions "to define the indefinable and to tangibilitate the intangible" (Mager, 1972, p. 10). A basic premise of the goal-attainment model of evaluation is that if the ultimate goal is met, then a series of prior accomplishments were fulfilled. This model emphasizes the measurement of outcomes rather than inputs, assuming that if the goal is met, then the appropriate combination of inputs was made.

The evaluator does not measure the phenomena he or she is studying directly. Rather, he or she observes and measures empirical manifestations or indices of these phenomena. It is not criteria themselves which are measured, but their equivalents-indicators. For all practical purposes, the goal-attainment model employs the ex post facto research design. Since the fundamental question asked by the model is *was the goal met?* empirical inquiry can take place only after manifestations of the independent variables have already occurred. Therefore, the focus of the model is upon the clarification of goals and program objectives, and the evaluation of their accomplishment. The evaluation of accomplishment is extended to test the hypothesis that a certain form of intervention has a beneficial outcome.

## Goal-Attainment Analysis

Analytically, measuring goal-attainment involves five steps. They are as follows:

1. *Specification of the goal to be measured.*

In using the goal-attainment model, the evaluator must make clear distinctions between goals and objectives. A goal for our purpose is a statement which represents in general terms an end to which a planned course of action is directed. A goal statement should also state, explicitly or otherwise, the outcome behavior of the consumer and/or a desired state or condition once the planned course of action is completed.

2. *Specification of the sequential set of performances that, if observed, would indicate that the goal has been achieved.*

A level of performance achieved within some temporal context which represents an approximation toward the goal is defined as an objective. An objective is operationally defined in terms of a beginning and an end point, so that either the existence or nonexistence of a desired state or the degree of achievement of that state can be established. It may be *qualitatively* or *quantitatively* defined. A qualitatively defined objective is one that is either obtained or not in terms of empirical observation. A quantitatively defined objective is one that is obtained and can be measured in terms of degrees.

For purposes of evaluation, then, goals should as far as possible be defined operationally. That is, they should be expressed as discrete objectives. In this way, the degree of achievement of the various objectives or level of performance of the target for change can be a direct measure of goal attainment. Conceived in this way, goal attainment can be measured in terms of achieving certain objectives. Therefore, the achievement of all of the objectives should represent 100 percent goal attainment.

3. *Identification of which performances are critical to the achievement of the goal.*

An evaluation process must identify proper criteria to be used in measuring program success. In the goal-attainment model, success criteria are stated in terms of benchmarks. The use of benchmarks presumes that certain levels of performance are more critical to goal attainment than others. These are treated as criterion tasks in that they constitute specific, necessary conditions of goal attainment. Precise measures of achievement are set up, and data on them are collected systematically. Since achievement of performance is expected to occur in a time sequence, achievement of data should be expressed in terms of changes.

One of the major characteristics of the goal attainment model of evaluation is that it does not require that input factors be individually defined. For example, if one were evaluating a counseling program, one need not be concerned about the number of counseling sessions; the amount of money spent for counseling; the amount of effort the counseling staff exerts toward the achievement of counseling goals; the nature and demands of the counseling components in relationship to other program components; the characteristics inherent in staff members which affect their ability to carry out the goals or the debilitating and facilitating features of the counseling environment. As already pointed out, the basic question is: Was the goal met? Consequently, the evaluator can identify what goals were achieved, but he may or may not be able to explain why they were achieved or why others were not.

4. *Description of what is the "indicator behavior" of each performance episode.*

For the most part, indications of goal attainment will be observed as measures of changes in performance, using some normative criteria. Moreover, since achievement of objectives is defined in terms of beginning and end points, the achievement of an objective may represent the conclusion of a "performance episode." Therefore, the "indicator behavior" of a performance episode is some measurable behavior which can be observed in kind or amount within some time frame. For example, let's say that the goal is to improve morale among workers. The "indicator behavior" may be characterized as absenteeism. Measures of absenteeism are selected as *frequency* and *length.* In this case, the objective may be to reduce absenteeism each month more than it was the previous month over a six-month period. Benchmarks for measurement may be established as a reduction of at least one absence per month over the previous one.

5. *Testing collectively whether each "indicator behavior" is associated with each other.*

In most cases, the indicator behavior should be the same for each performance episode. This facilitates standardization of measurement and makes it easier for outcomes to be compared from one episode to the other. Different evaluators studying the same phenomena may report different outcomes. Without standardization, there is a problem of determining whether the differences are in fact actual differences or differences in measures. When measures are standardized, one source of the differences—the measures used—is controlled and the likelihood is then increased that the differences observed reflect differences in the phenomena.

In some situations, the nature of the change being measured will dictate different indicator behaviors from one performance episode to the other. The evaluator, therefore, must be sure that he adheres to proper research methodology to insure this; multiple measures are preferred because they yield higher validity than single measures.

Measurements of goal-attainment yield, principally, information about outcomes. For program planning, the human services worker may also need a more detailed description of the social environment that produced outcomes. More often than not program administrators need information on what were the specific levels of input, what resources they require and how these levels of input relate to outcomes. In other words, did a particular level of input make a difference?

### Strengths and Limitations of the Goal-Attainment Model

One of the major limitations of the goal-attainment model is that in an ex post facto study, the evaluator cannot always attribute goal attainment to a specific set of input variables. Also, goal attainment may be the result of environment factors over which the human services worker has no control, or there may be factors which neither the worker nor the evaluator can account for.

A third limitation of the goal-attainment model centers around the fact that evaluators often ignore the distinction between ends and means, or output and input. As Terleckyj (1970) suggests, the mere expenditure of funds for a certain goal is often equated with the intended achievement.

A fourth limitation of this model is that it may be too narrow in its evaluation methodology and too formal in its consideration of goals. Also, it may not take into account sufficiently the informal goals that emerge or the unanticipated events that produce new goals and activity.

A strength of the model is that it assumes that individual goals in a program can be evaluated in isolation from other program goals. Another strength is that the model is considered an objective and reliable analytical tool because it omits the values of the evaluator in that he is not required to make any judgments about the appropriateness of the program goals.

A third and important use of the model is its capacity to measure abstract goals by operationalizing the goal into discrete measurable objectives. Finally, perhaps, one of the major strengths of the model is that the measurement of goal attainment need not be rigidly quantitative. For example, the achievement of an objective signifies that the goal has been met to some degree in terms of some defined event. When all the objectives have been achieved, the goal is said to have been met. This argument is based upon the assumption that the goal is met if a series of prior accomplishments are fulfilled.

### When to Use Goal-Attainment Model

Evaluations may be classified in a number of ways. They may be classified by *what* is being evaluated, by *who* conducts the evaluation, by the *decision* that is to be affected by the evaluation, and by the *method* used. The appropriate classification used depends upon the purpose of the evaluation.

Evaluations may also be classified in terms of their purpose. They may be conducted in order to make decisions about resource allocation, program changes, and capacity building and for measuring accountability.

The goal-attainment model of evaluation seems to be best suited for capacity building. In other words, it serves the purpose of developing a data base, improving in-house capacity to collect and assemble relevant outcome data and measures, and provides rapid feedback on problems requiring technical assistance.

The goal-attainment model of evaluation is relatively easy to carry out but the conclusions that may be drawn are necessarily limited. Therefore, this evaluation strategy can be justified only when the relationship between inputs (as independent variables) has already been demonstrated or will be tested in subsequent studies.

## THE IMPACT MODEL

The next mode of evaluation to be discussed is the *impact* model, which involves the formulation of hypotheses that are to be tested. It employs experimental designs in which hypotheses are stated in terms of the comparative effectiveness of certain program inputs. It begins with the premise that since human services programs are designed to improve the social position of recipients, the experimental hypotheses should be stated in a manner which predicts that the intervention will be more beneficial to the recipient than the usual social practice (control condition). As implied from the foregoing, an essential difference in the application of the impact model and the goal-attainment model is in the assumptions made in the use of the impact model. One assumption is that in order for the evaluator to estimate the effects of a particular human services program, it is necessary to compare the experiences of the recipients of services with those of some reference group. Comparisons of the outcomes of the reference group represent what would have happened to the clients in the absence of the program or intervention.

A second assumption is that the impact model is predicated upon the notion of cause and effect. It consists of (1) a set of theoretical concepts or ideas which trace the dynamics of how it is expected that the program will have the desired effects, and (2) a theory which logically interrelates a set of principles and procedures, which imply that certain decisions rather than others be made with respect to day-to-day program situations.

Since most program outcomes are influenced by multiple causal factors, a search for cause-effect relationships becomes largely one of testing for associations between some arbitrarily selected causes and the hypothesized effect. The question raised by the impact model is: *"What difference does the intervention make?"* In this sense, the impact model is more rigorous than the goal-attainment model. It assumes that in order to determine what differences the intervention makes, it is necessary to measure the relationship between the program goals (the dependent variables) and a variety of independent variables, including the personal characteristics of participants, the program components, and the conditions under which the program operates. The notion that most of the dependent variables with which the evaluator deals are functions of more than one independent variable is essential to the model. Therefore, the analysis should treat simultaneously all of the independent variables which are believed to be relevant. To omit some variables in the analysis may lead to distorted conclusions due to correlation or interaction among these variables and those independent variables which are included in the analysis.

This line of reasoning calls for the use of multivariate techniques. Proponents of the impact model often complain that the weakness in the goal-attainment model is that few investigators use regression analysis, for example, as a means of controlling for the effects of population in determining differences between programs.

To maximize the use of experimental techniques, Freeman and Sherwood (1970) suggest that the impact model should incorporate three kinds of hypotheses: (1) *Causal hypothesis*—A statement concerning relationship between the input and the outcome. "A statement about the influence of one of more characteristics or processes on the condition which is the object of the program. The hypothesis assumes a causal relationship between a phenomenon and the condition or behavior in which change is sought." (2) *Intervention hypothesis*—A statement about what changes the input will produce. "A statement which specifies the relationship between the program (what is going to be done) and the phenomenon regarded, in the causal hypothesis, as associated with the behavior or condition to be ameliorated or changed." (3) *Action hypothesis*—A statement about how that change will affect the behavior or condition the worker is seeking to modify. The action hypothesis is necessary in order to assess whether the intervention, even if it results in a desired change in the causal variable, is necessarily linked to the outcome variable, that is the behavioral condition that one is actually seeking to modify. This hypothesis is also necessary because although the chain of events may be true in a real-life situation, it may not necessarily hold true when it is brought about by intervention.

Impact evaluations should provide five essential sets of information. They should provide all of the data necessary: (1) to determine if a particular program should be continued; (2) to determine which of alternative programs achieve the greatest gains for a given cost; (3) to present information on the components of each program and the mixes of components which are most effective for a given expenditure so that maximum operating efficiency can be achieved; (4) to provide relevant information for determining which programs best serve individuals with particular demographic characteristics; and (5) to suggest new program thrusts.

The impact model uses an experimental design. Therefore, it insists upon random assignment of subjects to the experimental and comparison groups. Herein lies the limitation of the model. Developing designs based upon controlled experimentation in evaluative research has always been troublesome. While it is always desirable, it is not always essential nor possible.

One of the basic principles of controlled experimentation in evaluating human services programs is that treatment and control conditions must be held constant throughout the period of intervention. Under these circumstances, experimental designs prevent rather than promote changes in the intervention, because interventions cannot be altered once the program is in process if the data about differences engendered by intervention are to be unequivocal. In this sense, the application of experimental designs to evaluation conflicts with the concept that evaluation should facilitate the continual improvement of the program. Dyer (1966) makes the following observation:

> We evaluate, as best we can, each step of the program as we go along so that we can make needed changes if things are not turning out well. This view of evaluation may make some of the experimental design people uneasy because it seems to interfere with the textbook rules for running a controlled experiment. ...There is one kind of evaluation to be used when you are developing an educational procedure....I would call *concurrent* evaluation. And there is a second kind of evaluation...I would call *ex-post facto* evaluation; it is what the experimental design people are usually talking about when they use the word evaluation (p. 18).

The objective of the impact evaluations is to be able to say definitely that a particular intervention has led to a particular outcome that would not have occurred otherwise. In the absence of experimentation, this is not wholly possible. But the larger problem in conducting an experimental evaluation in the human services field is related to the ethical problem of denying services in order to have a truly experimental model.

In a true experimental design, random assignment of subjects is based upon the probability theory that each subject has an equal chance of being assigned either to the control or treatment group. In the regular course of service, clients are almost never assigned to programs on this basis.

## THE BEHAVIORAL MODEL

The behavioral model of evaluation (BME) is derived from behavioral constructs. It places a heavy emphasis upon measuring goal attainment, but regards goal statements as statements which define the dependent variable in terms of behavior(s) the client should be able to demonstrate at the end of the service intervention. It differs from the impact model in that it places little importance upon controlled experimentation on the ground that the selection of comparison groups which match up in all respects except for the intervention is rarely if ever possible.

The BME begins from the premise that the effectiveness of human services should be measured in terms of the extent to which desired changes take place in the behavior of individual clients. This model is grounded in three important behavioral science concepts which argue that: (1) the phenomenon with which the evaluator deals is behavior (dependent variable) and the independent variables which control behavior are elements of the environment (2); since behavior is a function of an environmental stimulus, then, the most effective way to change behavior is to change the environmental circumstances which influence it; and (3) since behavior is a function of the environment, the social function of human services programs is to provide the individual with the skills to cope with the environment.

The primary question raised by the behavioral model of evaluation is: *To what extent has the program intervention improved the client's ability to gain mastery over his/her environment?*

The BME conforms to what Penka and Kirk (1991) call *clinical evaluation* and often incorporates ideographic models which eschew group comparisons and experimental designs on the assumption that averages obtained from individual scores lend themselves to different interpretations from data derived from grouped means. For example, in evaluating forms of clinical practice, the basic evaluation question if often stated as: When, for whom and under what situations is the intervention most effective? Ideographic models also imply that individual-derived data differ from grouped-derived data in that, as Shontz (1976) noted, entirely different functional relations apply to group data than apply to data from individuals. He uses the following examples:

> ...Suppose that several members of a group perform the same task, and that the average remains stable because the performances of half the group improve from practice while the performance of the other half deteriorate from fatigue. The statement, that performance on this task remains stable and is therefore unaffected by either practice or fatigue, is clearly untrue, whether that statement is applied to the group or to the individuals who compose it.

An essential tenet of ideographic models is to use the individual or the "treatment" group as its own control by employing pre- and post-treatment measures. The assumption is that each "subject" is its own control and the behavior of the subject before treatment is a measure of the performance that would have occurred if there has been no treatment. The research design which has gained the most attention recently in ideographic outcome studies is the single organism design variously referred to as N=1, single-case design, or as Fischer refers to it, "single system design." Fischer uses the term *single system design* because it "rightly suggests that this form of research can be used with subjects other than individuals, including families, groups, organizations, and communities, all of which may be viewed as single systems for evaluation purposes." This paradigm relies heavily upon what Campbell and Stanley have called the interrupted time-series design in which two periods of observations are separated by application of the intervention. It may also be used with two equivalent samples in which treatment is used with one and is absent in the other. It may be depicted as follows:

| "One group time series": | Pre-Test | Treatment | Post-Test |
|---|---|---|---|
| | $T_1T_2T_3T_4$ | X | $T_5T_6T_7T_8T_9$ |
| "Control-group time series": | Pre-Test | Treatment | Post-Test |
| Experimental | $T_1T_2T_3T_4$ | X | $T_5T_6T_7T_8T_9$ |
| Controlled | $T_1T_2T_3T_4$ | | $T_5T_6T_7T_8T_9$ |

Wood (1978) encouraged the use of a combination of both the one-group time series and the control-group time series. In this case, one employs first the "N=1" model of an interrupted time-series in which two periods of observation are separated by application of the intervention. Then, the "N=2" paradigm, a time-lag control design, is employed, in which an intervention is applied to one subject after a base observation period but is withheld temporarily from another subject. After an experimental period, the intervention is applied to the second subject, and both subjects are monitored for a second experimental period.

As a strategy for collecting data that will lead to the discovery of individual changes in behavior, the single-organism approach has much to recommend it. Properly employed, it is at least as demanding as large sample methods, and it usually leaves less to chance.

## GOAL SPECIFICATION

Each of the four frameworks presented assume the presence of certain preconditions: (1) the program is clearly articulated; (2) the goals and/or expected effects are clearly specified; and (3) the causal assumptions linking the program to the goals and/or effects are plausible (Rutman, 1977).

Good evaluation designs also seek to determine the appropriateness of the goal and the feasibility and attaining it (Washington, 1982). The purpose of evaluation of human service programs is viewed as a system, including people and processes engaged in an interrelated flow of events and activities moving toward some goal, purpose, or end. The process of measuring the extent to which the goal has been met is not as simple as it may appear. One of the problems is that sometimes the goals of the program are not clearly defined. Goals may either be stated poorly, or the publicly stated goals may not be the ones by which the program's activities are guided. One of the spillover effects of program evaluation, then, may be that the process of evaluation assists the administrator in sharpening a definition of the organization's mission and goals. Specifying program goals may assist the administrator in operationalizing goals structurally as part of a strategic planning process. It may also help him/her to identify indicators of success.

It is the position of this author that, when feasible, the evaluator should be hired while the program is in its early planning stage. There are indeed several advantages to this initial involvement of the evaluator. Since many agencies seldom define program goals clearly, the evaluator can not only describe accurately those goals, but can actively help the program to identify and decide upon those goals. This dual role extends to the design and description of the relationship between input variables and goals. In order to help identify goals and key variables, however, the evaluator must also have complete information about the program to be evaluated. Here again, on-the-spot involvement early in the program's planning and development stages is clearly an advantage because the evaluator can assist in setting up a data collection mechanism which collects the kind of evidence required to determine whether the goal was met.

## REFERENCES


Campbell, Donald, and Stanley, Julian, *Experimental and Quasi-Experimental Design for Research* (Chicago; Rand McNally and Company, 1963).

Dyer, Henry S., "Overview of the Evaluation Process," *On Evaluating Title I Programs* (Princeton, NJ: Educational Testing Service, 1966).

Etzioni, Amitai, "Two Approaches to Organizational Analysis: A Critique and a Suggestion," In Herbert C. Schulberg, Alan Sheldon, and Frank Baker (Eds.), *Program Evaluation in the Health Fields* (Port Washington, NY: Human Sciences Press, 1970).

Fischer, Joel, "The Social Work Revolution," *Social Work* (May 1981), pp. 199–206.

Freeman, Howard E., and Sherwood, Clarence C., *Social Research and Social Policy* (Englewood Cliffs, NJ: Prentice-Hall, 1970).

Levinson, Perry, "Evaluation of Social Welfare Program," *Welfare Review, 5* (December 1966), pp. 5–12.

Mager, Robert F., *Goal Analysis* (Belmont, CA: Fearon Publishers, 1972).

Penka, Cindy E. and Kirk, Stuart A., "Practitioner Involvement In Clinical Evaluation," *Social Work* (November 1991), pp. 513–517.

Ribich, Thomas I., *Education and Poverty* (Washington, DC: The Brookings Institution, 1968).

Rutman, Leonard, *Evaluation Research Methods: A Basic Guide* (Beverly Hills, CA: Sage Publications, 1977).

Sherwood, Clarence C., "Methodological Measurement and Social Action Considerations Related to the Assessment of Large-Scale Demonstration Programs." Paper presented at the 12th Annual Meeting of the American Statistical Association (Chicago: The Association, 1964).

Shontz, Franklin C., "Single-Organism Designs," in Peter M. Bentler, et al. (Eds.) *Data Analysis Strategies and Designs for Substance Abuse Research.* Research Issue N. 13 (Rockville, MD: National Institute on Drug Abuse, 1976), p. 29.

Terleckyj, Nestor E., "Measuring Possibilities of Social Change," *Looking Ahead, 18* (6) (August 1970).

Thomas, Alan J., "Efficiency Criteria in the Urban School System." Paper presented to the AERA, New York City, February 18, 1967. Mimeographed.

Washington, R.O., "Evaluation: Design and Method" in Thomas Meenaghan, Robert O. Washington, and Robert M. Ryan, *Macro-Practice in the Human Services* (New York: The Free Press, 1982, Chap. 4).

_______, *Measuring Program Effectiveness In The Human Services* (Boston: The Social Policy Research Group, Inc., 1987).

Weisbrod, Burton A., "Benefits of Manpower Programs: Theoretical and Methodological Issues," in Somers and Wood, *Cost Benefit Analysis of Manpower Programs* (Kingston, Ontario: Queen's University, 1969).

Williams, Walter and Evans, John W., "The Policies of Evaluation: The Case of Head Start," *The Annals* (September 1969), pp. 385.

Wood, Katherine, "Casework Effectiveness a New Look at the Research Evidence," *Social Work, 23* (6) (November 1978), pp. 437–458.

26.

## Peg McCartt Hess, Gail Folaron, and Ann Buschmann Jefferson

# EFFECTIVENESS OF FAMILY REUNIFICATION SERVICES: AN INNOVATIVE EVALUATIVE MODEL

In 1987, the U.S. Department of Health and Human Services identified unsuccessful family reunification as a child welfare system outcome failure, citing national figures regarding the high proportion (29 to 33 percent) of children reentering the child welfare placement system (*Federal Register,* 1987). The agency asserted that when a former foster child "reappears at the agency the system has the responsibility to examine in sufficient detail not only the reason for deciding again to place the child in foster care but the factors that led to this traumatic repetition" (Gershenson, 1987, p. 1). To that end, the department funded a three-year project to pilot the Professional Review Action Group (PRAG) model for reviewing cases of disrupted family reunification in an eight-county area in Indiana. This service evaluation and corrective action model provides for case reviews, periodic reporting of review findings (a feedback mechanism for the agency and community), and recommendations for and documentation of corrective actions (Figure 26.1) (Hess & Folaron, 1992).

Peg McCartt Hess is an associate professor and formerly Professional Review Action Group (PRAG) project director at the School of Social Work, Indiana University; Gail Folaron is a lecturer at the School of Social Work, Indiana University, and formerly PRAG research coordinator; Ann Buschmann Jefferson is Child Welfare director, Marion County Division of Family and Children, Indianapolis.

## EXAMINING AND DEFINING PROBLEMS CONTRIBUTING TO PLACEMENT REENTRY

To examine unsuccessful reunifications, the case activities required for successful reunification were identified. The following case activities were defined by project staff as essential to achieving family reunification:

- accurately identifying and assessing, with the family, the problems and needs that required placement to protect the child
- developing a quality case plan that reflects accurate assessment, changes required for the child to be safe with the parents, agency and parent responsibilities, the permanency goal, and services to support achievement of the permanency goal
- engaging family members in appropriate services that specifically target identified problems and needs
- coordinating the multiple services provided to all family members, including foster family care and parent-child visiting
- monitoring and assessing the family's adherence to the service plan and the degree of actual change achieved
- assessing whether and at what time reunification should occur
- preparing all family members for the transition process of the child's return

FIGURE 26.1
Professional Review Action Group Model as Implemented to Review Cases of Placement Reentry

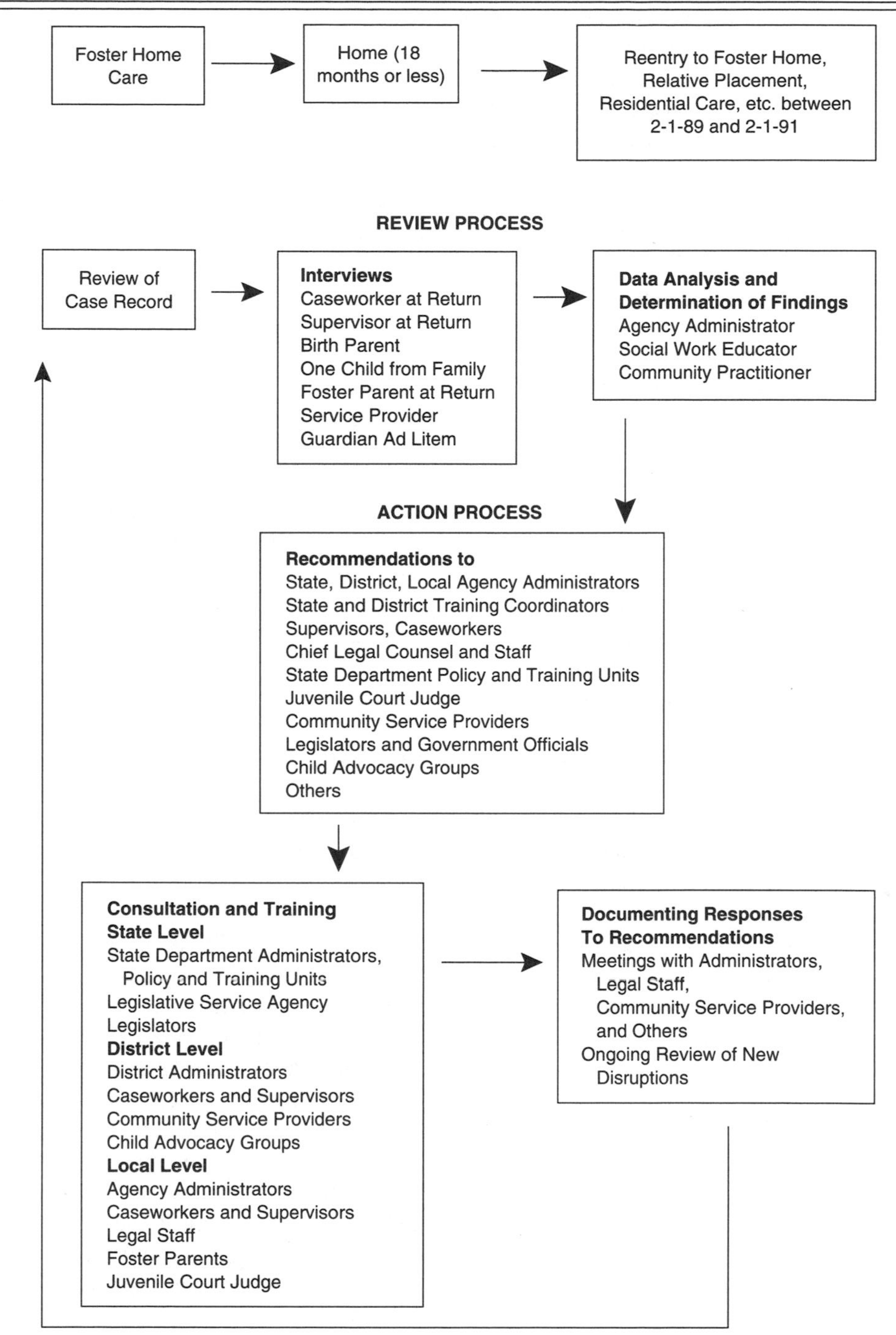

home, including the development of a specific plan for the child's protection
- coordinating the continuation of services to support family members following reunification
- closely monitoring the child's safety in the home until reunification has stabilized.

A screening tool was developed to identify problems that affected whether and how effectively essential case activities were completed. Family characteristics contributing to placement reentry were also included. Some of the 49 problems identified in the tool were caseload size and caseworker turnover, insufficient community resources, the number and severity of parents' problems, insufficient involvement of foster parents in decision making, the child's willingness and ability to adapt to return, and the parents' attitude about reunification. This instrument reflected discussions about reunification with agency staff, foster parents, and community practitioners and the literature regarding reunification (Barth & Berry, 1987; Block & Libowitz, 1983; Boyd, 1979; Claburn, Magura, & Chizeck, 1977; Fanshel & Shinn, 1978; Farmer & Parker, 1989; Fein, Maluccio, Hamilton, & Ward, 1983; Fein & Maluccio, 1984; Gruber, 1973; Hubbell, Hirsch, Barrett, Condelli, & Plantz, 1986; Jackson & Dunne, 1981; Lahti & Dvorak, 1981; Maas & Engler, 1959; Rzepnicki, 1987; Shapiro, 1976; Stuart, 1982; Turner, 1984a, 1984b; Wald, Carlsmith, & Leiderman, 1988).

## CASE STUDY METHOD

The PRAG model involves thorough case reviews conducted on all families who had children placed in foster homes for their protection by public child welfare agencies, who were reunified following services to improve family conditions, and who had children reenter placement on or after February 1, 1989, after having been home for 18 months or less. The 62 cases described in this article include all families known to have a child reentering placement between February 1, 1989, and February 1, 1991, and fitting these criteria. Fifty-six cases were served by a county department of public welfare in a metropolitan area, and six were served by rural county departments in an eight-county area defined by the state agency as a district. In 32 of the families, the child reviewed was the only child reentering placement. Among families with several children reentering placement, in nine cases the review process focused on the most victimized child, in 16 cases it focused on the only child old enough to be interviewed, and in five cases it focused on the only child meeting the project criteria.

The method for implementing this review model is consistent with qualitative case study research methodology, including the triangulation of data for validity and reliability (Denzin, 1989; Stake, 1978; U.S. General Accounting Office, Program Evaluation and Methodology Division, 1987). Family and case service data collected through the PRAG reviews were analyzed both quantitatively and qualitatively to contribute to the field's knowledge about effective reunification practice.

In each PRAG case review, the authors read the family's agency case record and interviewed the agency caseworker and supervisor at the time of the child's return home, the foster parents in the last placement before the return home, the primary contractual community service provider, the child's parents, and the child. Others were interviewed when essential information would otherwise be unavailable. Case record review and interview guides were developed specifically for the reviews and were designed to determine which problems included in the screening tool occurred in each case. Forty-six children, 44 parents, 52 foster parents, and 44 community service providers were interviewed. Sixty-four interviews were completed with caseworkers and 39 with supervisors. Reviews averaged 12 hours, including the review of the case record, interviews, and case staffings, and excluded travel time and time spent in locating case records and people for interviews.

Family and case service data generated through the case record review and interviews were analyzed by three experienced professionals: a social work educator, a community social work practitioner, and a child welfare public agency administrator. Subsequently, the problems that directly affected placement reentry in each case were identified.

Reviewers regularly shared their findings and recommendations for corrective action with agency administrators and with others who had the authority to address identified problems. This feedback mechanism is a critical aspect of the review model, allowing for problem solving concerning identified service delivery system problems.

## PROBLEMS CONTRIBUTING TO PLACEMENT REENTRY

A combination of family and service delivery system problems specifically and directly contributed to placement reentry.

### Parent Problems

The most frequent contributor to placement reentry was the nonresolution of parent problems that precipitated placement (Table 26.1). This contributor partially related to the number and severity of the parents' problems. Families were experiencing multiple, serious, and chronic problems (Table 26.2). The majority of families were headed by a single parent (52 percent; $n$ = 32). Sixty-five percent ($n$ = 40) of the mothers were Caucasian, and 35 percent ($n$ = 22) were African American. The mothers' mean age at birth of first child was 19.

Of particular interest is the finding that in 66.1 percent ($n$ = 41) of the cases, persistent ambivalence about the parental role and family reunification was identified as a characteristic of the custodial parents. Ambivalent parents were found to be more likely to have requested a child's placement both before the disrupted reunification and again at reentry; to refuse at least one service; and to be inconsistent in attendance in court, visits with their children, and participation in services (Hess & Folaron, 1991). In 35 cases (56 percent), the parents' ambivalence directly contributed to placement reentry.

The number and severity of most families' problems would have warranted immediate and extensive intervention on multiple fronts. Even with such a response, in the authors' opinion, some of the 62 families whose cases were reviewed would most likely not have successfully achieved reunification.

### Service Delivery System Problems

Several service delivery system problems appeared to substantially contribute to the lack of resolution of parents' problems. The case activities described earlier as essential to achieving family reunification occurred unevenly. For example, in 68 percent ($n$ = 42) of the cases, the public agency or community service provider's

TABLE 26.1
Problems Contributing to Reunification Disruption of Families ($N = 62$)

| Problem | $n$ | % |
|---|---|---|
| Service delivery system problems contributing to reentry | | |
| Preparation of family for reunification inadequate or insufficient | 50 | 80.6 |
| Agency case management services inappropriate or inadequate | 49 | 79.0 |
| Agency guidelines and policies insufficient or inhibited good practice | 46 | 74.2 |
| Poor assessment or decision making by caseworker or service provider | 42 | 67.7 |
| Large caseworker caseload or caseworker turnover | 42 | 67.7 |
| Visiting plan inadequate to prepare for reunification | 37 | 59.7 |
| Lack of clarity or insufficient or inappropriate expectation in case plans or service agreements | 36 | 58.1 |
| Gap in service by agency | 35 | 56.4 |
| Referrals to appropriate services inadequate | 32 | 51.6 |
| Parental involvement in service use insufficient | 29 | 46.8 |
| Coordination services or cooperation among agency or service providers insufficient | 28 | 45.2 |
| Case monitoring or contact by agency or service providers with parents insufficient, leading to lack of information for decision making | 27 | 43.5 |
| Caseworker training or experience insufficient or inadequate | 24 | 38.7 |
| Community resources inadequate | 22 | 35.5 |
| Case monitoring or contact by agency or service providers with child insufficient, leading to lack of information for decision making | 21 | 33.9 |
| Parent or family problems contributing to reentry | | |
| Parents' behaviors or problems that precipitated placement not resolved | 56 | 90.3 |
| Number and/or severity of parents' problems high | 51 | 82.3 |
| Parents placed child at risk to meet own needs | 43 | 69.4 |
| Parents' attitude about reunification negative | 35 | 56.4 |
| Family unable to adapt to child's return | 21 | 33.9 |

Note: "Agency" refers to public child welfare agency; "service provider" includes any community service provider.

TABLE 26.2
Parent or Family Problems of 62 Children Reentering Placement Between February 1, 1989, and February 1, 1991

| Problem | $n$ | % | Problem | $n$ | % |
|---|---|---|---|---|---|
| Neglect | 50 | 80.6 | Ambivalence | 41 | 66.1 |
| Physical abuse | 50 | 80.6 | Violence between adults | 35 | 56.4 |
| Dependency in relationships | 46 | 74.2 | Sexual abuse | 32 | 51.6 |
| Poverty | 44 | 71.0 | Diagnosed mental health problems | 29 | 46.8 |
| Substance abuse | 43 | 69.4 | Developmental disability | 19 | 30.6 |

assessment was incomplete or inadequate, leaving problems unidentified. In some instances, parents agreed to drug and alcohol or psychological evaluations, but some parents were never required to comply, resulting in a lack of information regarding risk for service planning. Frequently, the parent's partner was excluded from the assessment, case planning, and treatment. In cases where the parent's partner had abused the child, the court's typical intervention was to order no contact between the offender and family members. Despite this order, the offender often continued to function as a family member, thus placing the child at continued risk.

In the majority of cases, the parents' responsibilities in the case plan and requirements identified in court reports included completion of services (for example, completion of parenting classes) rather than expectations of specific behavioral change. Parents thus were able to comply with the case plan while demonstrating little or no change, creating a legal double-bind that contributed to premature reunification. In eight cases, because of parents' adherence to the case plan, the court returned the child home despite the agency's recommendation of continued placement.

*Agency Resources.* The current national crisis in child welfare staffing has been well documented (Kamerman & Kahn, 1989; National Association of Social Workers, Commission on Family and Primary Associations, 1989; National Commission on Child Welfare and Family Preservation, 1990; U.S. Advisory Board on Child Abuse and Neglect, 1990). In Indiana between 1978 and 1990, reports of child abuse and neglect increased 2,505 percent from 2,000 to 50,098. In addition, limited funding was available to increase child welfare staff, thus resulting in caseloads of between 55 and 80 children (Indiana Youth Institute, 1991). Although state law was amended in 1984 to incorporate the federal mandate that reasonable efforts be made to reunify children in placement with their families, high caseloads and high staff turnover have severely undermined the child welfare system's effectiveness in reunification and permanency planning efforts.

In the metropolitan county served by the PRAG Project, caseworker turnover had reached more than 80 percent per year by February 1, 1989. Because of high caseworker turnover, in this county 73 percent of the cases were served by five or more consecutive workers. Because of turnover, for weeks or months at a time, a number of cases had not been covered at all or were covered by an overloaded supervisor. This left children, families, and foster families with no or limited agency services for lengthy periods. In almost half (47 percent, $n = 29$) of the 62 cases reviewed, the decision to reunify the family was made by caseworkers who had six months' experience or less when they were assigned the case. In half ($n = 31$) of the cases, the caseworkers had one year or less experience.

Interview data confirmed that newly assigned caseworkers and community service providers optimistically gave families a "fresh start" or "another chance" to achieve reunification. Inexperienced workers were often either unfamiliar with the family's case record or unable to identify and interpret critical case information, such as indicators of violence between adults in the household and of substance abuse. This led to poor case decision making. Less-experienced caseworkers reported being discouraged by the lack of time to learn what they needed to know about family problems and community services. Supervisors described great difficulty in monitoring the large numbers of cases for which they were responsible (an average of 35) and in providing guidance to inexperienced and overwhelmed workers.

Both high caseloads and high turnover hindered the development of worker-family relationships within which families' problems and needs could be explored. High caseload size was found to directly result in the following:

- inadequate time for caseworkers to talk with children, children's parents, foster parents, and community service providers and inadequate time for reading case records and reports from service providers, leading to insufficient data for assessment and for case decision making

- inadequate time for caseworkers to prepare family members to cope with problems and stresses related to family reunification, contributing to recurrence of abuse and neglect following return home
- inadequate time for case staff (or conferences) regarding parents' progress and changes, leading to insufficient case coordination and cooperation among those providing services to families, thus resulting in gaps in services and recurrence of abuse or neglect
- inadequate time for both caseworkers and supervisors to engage in regular review of case activity, goals, and decision making
- an informal system of caseworker prioritization of cases for attention to cope with caseload size, resulting in a pattern of increased caseworker activity on cases before and after six-month reviews and little case activity during the interim periods, including the weeks immediately following family reunification; premature case closings; and insufficient contact, particularly when parents were not cooperative and aggressive outreach and casework services were required.

*Agency Policy and the Legal Process.* The reviewers were constantly confronted with the powerful influence of the expectations within the practice environment on case activities and outcomes. In each area of case activity, neither state nor local policy fully defined the minimum required of agency staff to accomplish reunification. Policy either was insufficient to support good practice or inhibited good practice, thus contributing to the overriding problem: Children were returned home without resolution of the family problems that precipitated their placement.

Agency staff decisions regarding reunification or the pursuit of other permanency goals were made without sufficient written regulations regarding the timetables for case decision making, the steps to be taken before reunification (such as the development of a plan for the child's protection), and the agency's response to parents' inconsistent participation in services. For example, in 60 percent ($n = 37$) of the cases, the agency visiting plan was insufficient to provide an opportunity for family members to learn and practice new behaviors and patterns of interaction and to provide the transition necessary for successful reunification. Visiting plans were also insufficient to allow the agency to assess family functioning and change. In 44 percent ($n = 27$) of the cases reviewed, children were returned home without unsupervised or overnight visits. Without overnight, weekend, or extended visits in the home, the actual change achieved and continuing risk to the child in the home could not be adequately assessed. No written standards addressed the minimum visit frequency or the sequence of visiting that should safely be completed before reunification could be recommended.

Further, caseworkers, supervisors, and community service providers tended to misinterpret current policy as mandating reunification as the only successful outcome of all placements. Relative placement, voluntary relinquishment, and other permanency options appeared rarely to have been explored with parents, even when their histories, statements, or behaviors indicated strong disinterest in reunification.

In interviews with PRAG reviewers, caseworkers, supervisors, and service providers frequently expressed their belief that according to policy, reunification was the only possible placement outcome. When asked about unsuccessful returns, caseworkers often explained to the PRAG interviewer, "We are required to return children home at least one time before we can consider any other plan," or "They have to go home sometime." In some instances, caseworkers serving parents who, for several six-month review periods, did not complete the requirements standing in the way of return home dropped the requirements to reunify the family.

## RECOMMENDED CORRECTIVE ACTIONS

Periodic written and verbal reports of PRAG case review findings and recommendations for changes within the service delivery system were provided to people with authority to address identified problems (Figure 26.1). Organizationally, feedback regarding corrective action was given to individuals and groups at the county, district, and state levels. The first feedback report was presented to district administrative staff in April 1989 after four case reviews had been completed. Subsequently, reports were made routinely to the district department of public welfare (DPW) director; county DPW directors; child welfare division administrative, supervisory, and casework staff; the district training coordinator; the agency's chief legal counsel and staff; the juvenile court judge; foster parents; the director and staff of the child welfare division of the state department of public welfare; legislators and government officials; administrative and direct service staff of community agencies; and child advocacy organizations. To enhance communication and problem solving within the system, whenever possible, recommendations for change were made to groups that included people who could work together in their various roles to resolve the problem.

Two unpublished interim reports were disseminated broadly. Each described in detail the resource and policy problems described earlier and outlined recommendations for change. The First Interim Report of the Professional Review Action Group Project, *The Impact of Caseload Size and Caseworker / Supervisor Turnover on Foster Care Reentry* (Hess, Foloran, & Jefferson, 1991), was presented as legislative testimony and to state agency policymakers. Information from the report was also reported to the public by the press (Haddix, 1991a, 1991b). This report was updated and disseminated as additional cases were reviewed. Whenever possible, PRAG project staff emphasized the critical nature of the impact of high caseloads and turnover on outcomes for individual children served by the system and asserted that without increased resources, the impact of implementing other recommended corrective actions was limited. The following recommendations were offered for resolving problems related to caseload size and turnover:

- State caseload standards should be changed to reflect current national child welfare standards with an increase in caseworkers, supervisors, and support staff consistent with these standards.
- Child welfare caseworker and supervisory positions need to be reclassified to reflect the specialized responsibilities.
- Immediate attention should be given to decreasing turnover, retaining staff, and maintaining reasonable salaries.

- Recruitment efforts need to be developed to attract people with education and experience relevant to child welfare services.
- Cases should be assigned to new staff only after they have completed extensive mandatory training.

Legislation was introduced to the state assembly in 1990 and again in 1991 to address child welfare caseload size, caseworker-supervisor ratio, and staffing resources. Although this legislation was ultimately defeated, Indiana Public Law 154, establishing a commission on abused and neglected children, was enacted in the 1992 legislative session. The commission's responsibilities include reviewing current state and national workload standards and qualifications and training of public service providers.

The Second Interim Report of the Professional Review Action Group Project, *The Impact of Policy on Foster Care Reentry,* described the policy and procedural problems identified in the first 25 cases reviewed through the PRAG Project (Hess, Folaron, & Jefferson, 1989). The 23 policy recommendations made in this report were reviewed by state department of public welfare administrators and policy consultants. Recommended changes in risk assessment; the minimum required caseworker contact with families, children, and foster parents; the format used to record case plans; requirements for supervisory involvement and approval of case decisions; and the visiting sequence required before reunifying families were subsequently incorporated into the state agency's policy manual.

At the district level, recommendations for corrective action addressed the process for making critical case decisions; the need for improved communication and information sharing at decision points; court and legal issues; supervisor and caseworker training needs; issues related to community services, including service gaps, program design, and training needs; and issues related to case information recording and transfer.

With regard to the process for making critical case decisions and the court and legal issues, the recommended changes were initiated and are in varying stages of completion. An example is the establishment of a policy directive that staffings be held for all cases moving toward reunification before recommending reunification to the court. To ensure that the staffing addresses all critical issues and that all relevant sources of information, including foster parents, have been consulted, a reunification checklist and guidelines for developing safety plans were developed for use by casework and supervisory staff. Recommended changes in the content of court reports were also implemented, as were changes in the timing and nature of the agency's response to parents' lack of adherence to agreements regarding evaluation and treatment. As recommended, cases are being provided with services following reunification for a longer period than the six months previously used. This change reflects the review finding that placement reentry occurred on average eight months following family reunification, suggesting the need for supportive services for a longer period than had been believed to be necessary. As recommended, greater attention is now being given to considering permanency options other than reunification following placement reentry, particularly when placements have been voluntary and parents have demonstrated ambivalence about caring for an individual child.

A number of problems identified through PRAG reviews were addressed through supervisory and caseworker training. The identified need for knowledge and skill in accurately identifying family problems resulted in additional training in risk assessment and case planning surrounding substance abuse, sexual abuse, and domestic violence and assessment of deeply felt or consistent parental ambivalence. In several instances, PRAG reviewers assisted in training development and delivery. Selected agency staff participated in PRAG case review staffings as an additional training mechanism.

The majority of services provided to families with children in placement are offered by community service agencies. Therefore, recommendations for change addressed insufficient coordination of services, difficulties in ensuring the timely flow of case information between the public agency and other agencies, confusion in role expectations when community agencies are monitoring the safety of children in their own homes following reunification, and insufficient community resources for impoverished families, particularly those with problems of substance abuse and domestic violence. Recommendations resulted in the development of clearer contractual agreements between the public agency and its contractual providers and in the development and funding of new community programs. Overall, presentation of PRAG findings and recommendations heightened community awareness of the service needs of families with children in placement.

As noted, PRAG reviewers provided consultation and training to individuals and groups as they moved to implement recommended changes. Through involvement in agency and community meetings and through continued reviews of new disruptions, the PRAG staff tracked whether and how recommended changes were implemented and documented the impact changes appeared to have.

## DISCUSSION

The implementation of the PRAG model in an eight-county area demonstrated the model's effectiveness in identifying problems contributing to foster care reentry. Perhaps more importantly, however, because of the thorough nature of the reviews and the familiarity of the reviewers with both the service delivery system and reunification practice, the review findings provided a credible source of program evaluation data and of recommendations for change. Finally, the ongoing, rather than time-limited, nature of the review-recommendation process and the mutual access of the reviewers and service delivery system personnel to each other created a neutral forum for problem solving and a collaborative, rather than adversarial, approach to program evaluation and change.

The feedback loop inherent in the model's design increases the likelihood that the positive qualities of case study program evaluation connect with ongoing program development. The model not only allows for but requires that the presentation of findings regarding service delivery system problems becomes an intervention for change. The changes already prompted through the implementation of the PRAG model strongly suggest that the model provides an effective tool for understanding and addressing unwanted policy, program, and practice outcomes.

From a broader perspective, the findings strongly suggest that continued refinement and clarity are needed in the policy that shapes permanency planning for children. In many of the cases reviewed, the degree of parents' ambivalence about parenting, a history of two or more unsuccessful reunifications, and the length of time the child had been in placement should have strongly suggested that reunification was not an appropriate case goal. In a few cases, reunification may have been an inappropriate goal initially. The singular definition of reunification as *the* rather than *a* successful placement outcome reflects a potentially dangerous implementation of family preservation and appears to undermine practitioners' ability to achieve permanency for children. To counter misinterpretation of current mandates and to support differential assessment and planning, agency policy and practice guidelines should clarify under what conditions and within what time frames permanency goals may and should be pursued and who should be involved in making or changing case goals. Policy should address the following questions:

- In which types of cases might reunification be an inappropriate initial case goal?
- When parents do not adhere to service agreements, what steps should be taken to ensure progress toward the child's permanency?
- At what point should the permanency goal be changed when parents are not complying?
- Within what period of time or after how many failed reunifications should another case goal be established?
- What should be required in terms of planning for a child before involuntary termination of parental rights is pursued?

Inevitably, the problems of insufficient resources to support effective practice must be addressed at both the state and national levels. The authors are unaware of any reported successful permanency planning program that has high caseloads as a program component. The resolution of the multiple family problems identified in the cases reviewed can only be explored in the context of the practitioner-client relationship. Worker-family relationships cannot develop when high caseloads and frequent caseworker turnover prevent continuous and frequent contact with parents and children. High turnover ensures that caseworkers are not sufficiently familiar with case histories to detect patterns of risk to children; caseworkers' limited training and experience further handicap their ability to do so. The lack of resources, particularly sufficient staff, directly and negatively affects a public agency's reunification services.

The PRAG model provides an effective method for identifying problems contributing to system outcome failures. Many of the problems identified by implementing the model in Indiana have been or are being rectified. Others, however, call for a massive state and national commitment of resources to families and children at risk. Each of the 62 cases reviewed has documented the painful cost to at least one child of our not having committed these resources sooner.

## REFERENCES

Barth, R. P., & Berry, M. (1987). Outcomes of child welfare services under permanency planning. *Social Service Review, 61,* 71–90.

Block, N. M., & Libowitz, A. S. (1983). *Recidivism in foster care.* New York: Child Welfare League of America.

Boyd, P. E. (1979). They can go home again! *Child Welfare, 58,* 609–615.

Claburn, W. E., Magura, S., & Chizeck, S. P. (1977). Case reopening: An emerging issue in child welfare services. *Child Welfare, 56,* 655–663.

Denzin, N. K. (1989). *The research act* (3rd ed.). Englewood Cliffs, NJ: Prentice Hall.

Fanshel, D., & Shinn, E. (1978). *Children in foster care: A longitudinal investigation.* New York: Columbia University Press.

Farmer, E., & Parker, R. (1989). *Trials and tribulations: A study of children home on trial in four local authorities.* Bristol, England: University of Bristol, Department of Social Administration.

Fein, E., & Maluccio, A. (1984). Children leaving foster care: Outcomes of permanency planning. *Child Abuse and Neglect, 8,* 425–431.

Fein, E., Maluccio, A. N., Hamilton, V. J., & Ward, D. (1983). After foster care: Outcomes of permanency planning for children. *Child Welfare, 62,* 485–558.

Gershenson, C. (1987). *Professional Review Action Group (PRAG).* Washington, DC: U.S. Department of Health and Human Services, Administration for Children, Youth, and Families.

Gruber, A. R. (1973). *Foster home care in Massachusetts.* Boston: Governor's Commission on Adoption and Foster Care.

Haddix, M. (1991a, January 15). Welfare system may be keeping families apart. *Indianapolis News,* pp. A1, A5.

Haddix, M. (1991b, January 21). Child welfare: A poor parent. *Indianapolis News,* p. A6.

Hess, P., & Folaron, G. (1991). Ambivalence: A challenge to permanency for children. *Child Welfare, 70,* 403–424.

Hess, P., & Folaron, G. (1992). *Focused program evaluation and development: A guide to implementing the Professional Review Action Group Model (PRAG).* Indianapolis: Indiana University School of Social Work and the Indiana State Department of Public Welfare.

Hess, P., Folaron, G., & Jefferson, A. (1989). *The impact of policy on foster care reentry* (Second Interim Report of the Professional Review Action Group Project). Indianapolis: Indiana University School of Social Work and Indiana State Department of Public Welfare.

Hess, P., Folaron, G., & Jefferson, A. (1991). *The impact of caseload size and caseworker/supervisor turnover on foster care reentry* (First Interim Report of the Professional Review Action Group Project). Indianapolis: Indiana University School of Social Work and Indiana State Department of Public Welfare.

Hubbell, R., Hirsch, G., Barrett, B., Condelli, L., & Plantz, M. (1986). *Evaluation of reunification for minority children* (Executive summary). Washington, DC: CSR Incorporated.

Indiana Public Law 154, Commission on Abused and Neglected Children, 1992.

Indiana Youth Institute. (1991, January). *A crisis in child welfare: The high cost of neglecting a system.* Indianapolis: Author.

Jackson, A. D., & Dunne, M. J. (1981). Permanency planning in foster care with the ambivalent parent. In A. N. Maluccio & P. A. Sinanoglu (Eds.), *The challenge of partnership: Working with parents of children in foster care* (pp. 151–164). New York: Child Welfare League of America.

Kamerman, S., & Kahn, A. (1989). *Social services for children, youth, and families in the United States.* New York: Columbia University School of Social Work and the Annie E. Casey Foundation.

Lahti, J., & Dvorak, J. (1981). Coming home from foster care. In A. N. Maluccio & P. A. Sinanoglu (Eds.), *The challenge of partnership: Working with parents of children in foster care* (pp. 52–66). New York: Child Welfare League of America.

Maas, H., & Engler, R. (1959). *Children in need of parents.* New York: Columbia University Press.

Maximizing reunification in foster care with minimum re-entry rates. (1987). *Federal Register, 52,* 49279–49280.

National Association of Social Workers, Commission on Family and Primary Associations. (1989). *The staffing crisis in child welfare.* Silver Spring, MD: National Association of Social Workers.

National Commission on Child Welfare and Family Preservation. (1990). *Factbook on public child welfare services and staff.* Washington, DC: American Public Welfare Association.

Rzepnicki, T. (1987). Recidivism of foster children returned to their own homes: A review and new directions for research. *Social Service Review, 61,* 56–70.

Shapiro, D. (1976). *Agencies and foster children.* New York: Columbia University Press.

Stake, R. E. (1978). The case study method in social inquiry. *Educational Researcher, 7,* 5–8.

Stuart, M. (1982). *Reunification.* Denver: University of Denver Graduate School of Social Work.

Turner, J. (1984a). Reuniting children in foster care with their biological parents. *Social Work, 29,* 501–505.

Turner, J. (1984b). Predictors of recidivism in foster care: Exploratory models. *Social Work Research & Abstracts, 20*(2), 15–20.

U.S. Advisory Board on Child Abuse and Neglect. (1990). *Child abuse and neglect: Critical first steps in response to a national emergency.* Washington, DC: U.S. Department of Health and Human Services.

U.S. General Accounting Office, Program Evaluation and Methodology Division. (1987, April). *Case study evaluations* (Transfer Paper 9). Washington, DC: U.S. General Accounting Office.

Wald, M., Carlsmith, J., & Leiderman, P. (1988). *Protecting abused and neglected children.* Stanford, CA: Stanford University Press.

## 27.

**William C. Birdsall and Roger W. Manela**

# THE NITTY GRITTY OF PROGRAM EVALUATION: A PRACTICAL GUIDE

## INTRODUCTION

Program evaluation carried out at the agency level must be responsive to the fact that the agency's central focus is the delivery of service. A major goal for the agency is to help its program staff and administrators improve their decisions about the operation of the agency. Some of these decisions focus on the internal operation of the agency. For example, should the agency stop an ongoing activity or start a new one? Should it hire more people, lay some people off, or reassign some of its staff? Should it try to expand its service to a new group of clients or should it narrow its focus and concentrate on a subset of the clients it now serves? Other decisions focus on external factors, such as the availability of funds or the impact of what other agencies are doing.[1]

While the issues that program evaluation addresses are important ones, the activity of program evaluation itself may be neglected or even ignored in the normal functioning of a busy agency. Unless it proves its worth, program evaluation is bound to be a low priority for an overworked agency administrator and her/his staff. Given the pressure to provide services to the agency's clients, agency staff are likely to see evalu-

William C. Birdsall is a professor at the School of Social Work, The University of Michigan; Roger W. Manela is a social worker for the Detroit Public Schools.

ation as justified only if it can improve the provision of service. If program evaluation is to get the attention it deserves and the resources it requires, the evaluation must become an integral part of agency operations, taking the pulse of the agency's programs and helping ensure their health. If it is seen as simply bureaucratic red tape, program evaluation will always be a low priority, guaranteed to have little impact on agency operations. But, if program evaluation is geared to inform both the long- and short-term decisions the agency must make, it is likely to flourish.

The fact that human service agencies gather and store data on the clients they serve, record the amount and type of services they provide, and keep relatively complete records on revenue by source and expenditures by type of means that, at a minimum, modern human service agencies usually have important data on how they spend their money, whom they serve, and what services they provide. Careful analysis of these data can help an agency catch administrative problems, assess the impact of its interventions on clients, and determine the costs and possibly the benefits of its activities. Such an analysis can establish the extent to which the agency's programs conform to standards of accountability and justify the current allocation of redirection of funds.

Another focus of program evaluation is on patterns of service to at-risk populations. This kind of analysis can show who is served by what activities and who gets left out. It can highlight the effects of eligibility rules and outreach programs, the ways staff interact with potential clients, and patterns of client self-selection. It can inform decisions about coordinating, consolidating or expanding a program, and it can reveal whether a program actually helps people, without causing undesirable side effects. The information from the evaluation can be used to improve current services and create new and better service programs. Over time, data collected by this kind of evaluation can be used to highlight changes in an agency's clients, the services it has provided to them, and the consequences of those services.

## EVALUATION PROCESSES

Program evaluation is a process that follows a logical sequence of steps. It begins with needs assessment and proceeds to the design or choice of an intervention. The next phase is the monitoring of the intervention process, followed by the analysis of its immediate impact on the agency's clients. The evaluation process concludes by considering the long-run consequences of the program for clients and other affected parties. Careful measurement and analysis are necessary at every stage of this process. Thorough needs assessment and careful monitoring of agency activities are essential to ensure that the program being evaluated did in fact provide appropriate interventions to the proper clients. If one does not understand or correctly identify client needs, the agency may not implement potentially effective interventions, and the services it implements may not provide what the client needs. With this kind of mismatch between client needs and agency services, an impact analysis may erroneously conclude that an intervention is ineffective when, in fact, it was inappropriately applied. Without careful monitoring, an evaluator can easily draw the wrong conclusions. Good needs assessments usually are based on an understanding of what interventions are feasible, how well they are likely to work, and what consequences they are likely to produce. Proper monitoring also is grounded in an understanding of the client's perspective on her/his needs and desired outcomes. This sensitivity to the client's perspective ensures that an evaluator can have confidence that appropriate interventions have been applied to the proper persons.

## Needs Assessment

Whatever the nature of the client, be it a community, a group of people, or an individual, the client's needs must be identified and assessed before the agency can proceed. In almost all human services agencies, needs-assessment data in its most elementary form are collected on intake forms filled out for every new client. Such forms are typically used to record information on a concrete presenting problem, which could be as simple as a needed resource, an item of information, or a referral, or it could be as complex as a family collapsing in the face of long-term unemployment or parental substance abuse.

Usually the agency has some standard against which to measure need. Viewing client problems in terms of such a standard gives the agency a basis for determining who is at risk and who is not, who is eligible for service and who is not, who the program should try to reach and who it should not, who will be the clients of the program and who will not. This kind of evaluation is likely to use data from a variety of sources and develop baseline measures for the specific populations the agency serves. The focus at this stage is on identifying the populations at risk for the problems the agency addresses.

The scope of the needs assessment is important. A wider assessment can delineate the extent of a problem and help the agency mobilize support for programs that address that problem, but it is unlikely to help the agency identify specific clients. On the other hand, a needs assessment that focuses on a particular neighborhood or subpopulation will help the agency match its services with the needs of specific potential clients.

## Monitoring Ongoing Programs

Once needs have been assessed, the agency must design interventions to fit the needs, then begin to route specific clients to the appropriate intervention. If the intervention is new, it is a good idea to try the services with selected subpopulations and refine them in light of the results of these initial tests. At this stage, the goal of program evaluation is to make a fairly rapid appraisal of the agency's ability to deliver its new services. If there are any apparent problems with the new services, the evaluation should help the agency identify and correct them.

Once the agency has tested and refined its services to the point that they can be delivered on a regular basis, the focus of the evaluation should shift to monitoring whether the delivery of those services is proceeding as planned. Appropriate questions at this stage include: Are there services actually getting to the people who need them? Are there important segments of the population at risk that are not being served? How can the agency improve the ways it delivers its services?

## Impact Assessment

Monitoring how an agency delivers its services is a necessary condition for improving the way the agency operates, but it does not specifically assess the effectiveness of the services the agency provides. To do this, one must measure the direct impact of the agency's services on its clients to determine whether the clients or their situations have changed due to the agency's interventions. At this stage, the focus of program evaluation shifts to comparing the client's profile after he/she has received the agency's services with the client's profile at entry. While it is usually difficult to trace the causal linkages between the postintervention profile of the client and the particular services the agency has provided, a simple description of what has happened to the client since contacting the agency can go a long way toward helping determine whether or not the agency is accomplishing its mandate.

Ideally the evaluation should determine not just the immediate impact of a given intervention on the client, but the more ultimate outcome for the client's life. However, it is rare for an ordinary agency to have the expertise, let alone the time and resources necessary to carry out such a formal evaluation of the outcomes of its interventions. In most agencies it is a giant step just to evaluate the immediate impact of services on specific clients.

### Cost Analysis of Services

Evaluating the costs of the agency's services in order to improve those services and control their costs is another aspect of program evaluation.[2] Human service agencies keep data on their expenditures to satisfy the interests of funders and others outside of the agency. Careful analysis of the data on an agency's expenditures can help agency administrators adjust the focus of current programs as well as plan for the future. If one knows the number of clients the agency has served and the cost of serving them, one can calculate the average cost of service per client. However, this kind of gross cost data is not enough. Agencies also need to know the cost of each different intervention and which types of clients or classes of problems cost the most to serve. While such cost data do not directly imply any specific actions, they are a first step toward deciding whether some activities cost too much for the impact they produce.

## EVALUATION PRINCIPLES

The preceding section has described the stages of the evaluation process in human service agencies. The following section describes some practical principles to keep in mind when designing and carrying out program evaluation.

### 1. Perspective: Keep in Mind What Is Important

In designing and carrying out an evaluation it is essential to maintain perspective and keep the evaluation relevant to the mandate of the organization you are evaluating. To stay relevant, the evaluation should focus on analyses that the agency can use to improve its operations and the decisions it makes about its future course of action. This means that the evaluation has to focus on issues such as: (1) Who needs what services within the scope and mandate of the agency? (2) What services are being delivered, by whom, to whom? (3) Is the process of service delivery proceeding as planned, and if not, do deviations improve or hamper service delivery? (4) Are the services effective? For example, are the expected changes in clients or their situations occurring? (5) What are the short-term and long-term positive and negative consequences of the agency's interventions on its clients, their relatives, and others in the community? (6) How efficiently are services being delivered? Are they being delivered within budget? If there are deviations from budget, are they in accord with the needs of the client and the mandate of the agency? (7) Could funds be reallocated in ways that would improve service delivery and lower cost without diminishing the effectiveness of services?

### 2. Evaluation As an Iterative Process: Return to the Important Questions

A good general pattern to follow in designing an evaluation and in analyzing data is to work back and forth across the range of questions just posed. Program evaluation is not a linear activity. It unfolds more like a spiral on which relatively narrow and focused questions are juxtaposed with larger, more general issues. One may begin by trying to focus on the analysis of a set of variables about a particular service, only to find that the analysis spirals to a larger policy issue and its implications. Analysis of the impact of the agency's programs may suggest that the needs of clients are not well addressed or even well understood. Trying to set a standard for an assessment of need may suggest a method for measuring the impact of an intervention. Monitoring an activity may raise questions about the level of understanding which personnel have of the goals of the agency. This in turn may highlight the fact that the agency's goals need clarification in all sorts of ways and for all sorts of reasons.

During the design of the intervention and again during the data analysis, one's thinking may make a number of such jumps as one's focus shifts from one level to another. This kind of serendipitous exploration of ideas and issues is inherent in the process of design and analysis, but in program evaluation it tends to be exaggerated by the range of purposes that the evaluation serves.

### 3. Readily Available Data Are Often the Best Data: Use Them

One way to simplify the design of an evaluation and reduce the effort it requires is to use available data wherever possible, such as client records or personnel records. All human service agencies routinely collect a variety of important data on clients, program activities, staff, and costs. Most of these data are gathered to satisfy demands from external sources, funders, regulators, etc., and this dictates the format of the data. Usually these data get only the most cursory analysis, and the analysis seldom relates one category of information to another, such as cost data and impact data. But, for an evaluator who can see the link between these data and analyze and present them in ways that help the agency improve its operations, they can be pure gold. For example, human service agencies routinely collect background information on their clients. If an evaluator uses these data to prepare profiles of an agency's client populations, possibly comparing the clients the agency serves with the characteristics of the broader population, these data take on new relevance for agency administrators and policy planners.

Agencies are likely to have a great deal of data on the services they provide: logs of staff activities, notes on specific interventions used with different kinds of clients, even measures of change in clients. Some of this information will be available in centralized records, but much is hidden in case reports and client files. A good program evaluator should be able to root it out and use it in an evaluation, without having to start a whole new data collection effort. Sampling extant records and analyzing what they can tell us is an excellent beginning, and it is often sufficient in itself to provide the key to improving an agency's service delivery.

Another advantage to using available data is that intake and service delivery information is collected routinely and periodically as a normal part of agency operations. If you initiate a special data collection effort for an evaluation, you must establish special procedures, use considerable staff time or hire additional staff, and disrupt established agency routines—a good way to make evaluation unpopular. Also, by using data that the agency routinely collects, you have a built-in capability for analyzing changes over time. You can look backwards over the past, and you can build in analytic procedures that will enable the agency to continue to repeat the evaluation in the future.

### 4. Know Your Audience: Present Results for a Busy, Intelligent, Decision Maker

In so far as it is feasible, choose a simple presentation over a complex one, and use graphic instead of numeric presentations wherever possible.[3] The adage "A picture is worth a thousand words" translates in the computer age into "A graphic is worth a thousand numbers." Busy administrators and tired board members are bound to be pleased when, instead of having to struggle to understand relationships presented in tabular form, they can see those relationships at a glance when the same data are presented in simple bar or pie charts. Today there are powerful programs available on inexpensive PCs that make it easy to display statistics in a variety of graphic formats.[4] The use of such graphics not only makes it easy to interpret the data, it adds punch and professionalism to your presentations.

Combine graphic presentation with textual analysis. A graphic representation of data, no matter how clear and concise it is, cannot by itself make all the points you want to make in your analysis. It certainly cannot spell out the implications of the data. While the discovery of relationships in the data may require formal statistical analysis, pointing out those relationships to an interested audience may only require a simple explanation, such as: "Notice that referrals to our agency dropped off last winter, probably because that's when the Salvation Army began its program."

Even though a graphic is more lively than a table, it cannot make the data and the program come alive as well as anecdotes and stories about actual clients and events. This means that the data need to be complemented by text in a written report and by a script in an oral report. Until this is done, the evaluation is not complete. All too often, evaluation reports begin with a short introduction and then present nothing but statistical charts and tables, with no text to lead the reader through the analysis, point out the insights of the evaluator, and translate a sterile array of statistics into an interesting story that has a theme, presents a point of view, and draws some conclusions.

## AN EXTENDED EXAMPLE

In the preceding sections we described program evaluation in human services agencies, presented some principles to follow when doing program evaluation, and suggested some useful techniques. In this section we give examples of how to use some of these techniques. The examples are based on the case of a small mental health program that is aimed at improving the

GRAPH 27.1
Family Situation

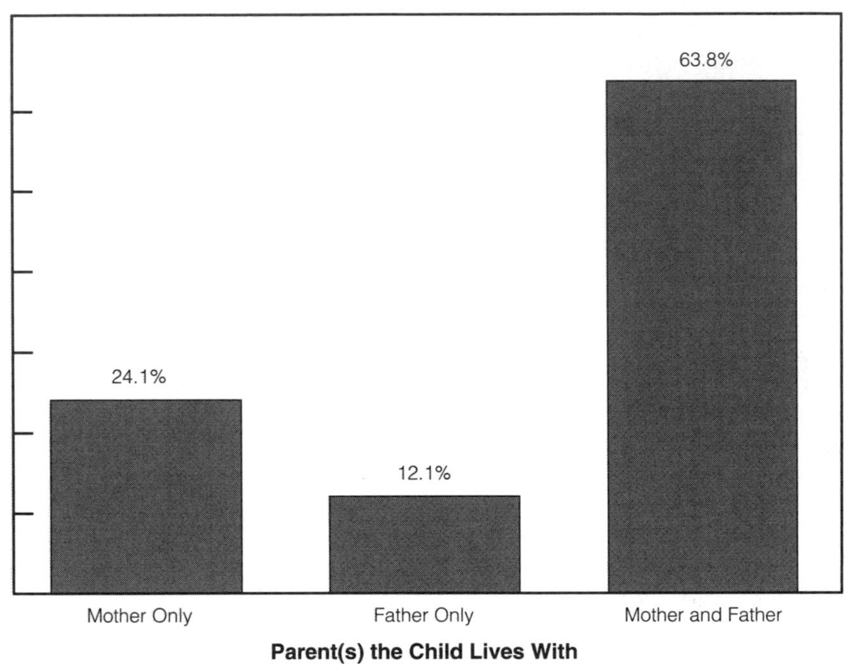


school attendance of young children at risk of serious educational difficulties because of severe family problems. Spotty attendance in the early grades is seen as an indicator of the beginning of such difficulties. The data are based on the actual operation of the program, with some changes to prevent disclosure. Our focus is on ways to present data on client needs and client outcomes. We will comment on the strengths and limitations of these particular data for evaluation purposes, and suggest what kinds of additional information would be useful.

Virtually all human service agencies gather sufficient data to profile their clients and the problem(s) that brought them into the agency. It is important for various constituents, particularly the public and potential funders, that the agency present this information in a clear and concise form. The principle we follow in presenting such data is to use graphic presentations whenever possible. We have already noted that for persons not accustomed to analyzing data, graphs are generally much better than tables. Graphs are such a powerful presentation technique that even sophisticated audiences absorb and retain more information from a graphic presentation than from data tables.

Graph 27.1 presents the "Family Situation" of the children served by the program in the form of a bar chart. The text at the

GRAPH 27.2
Family Situation

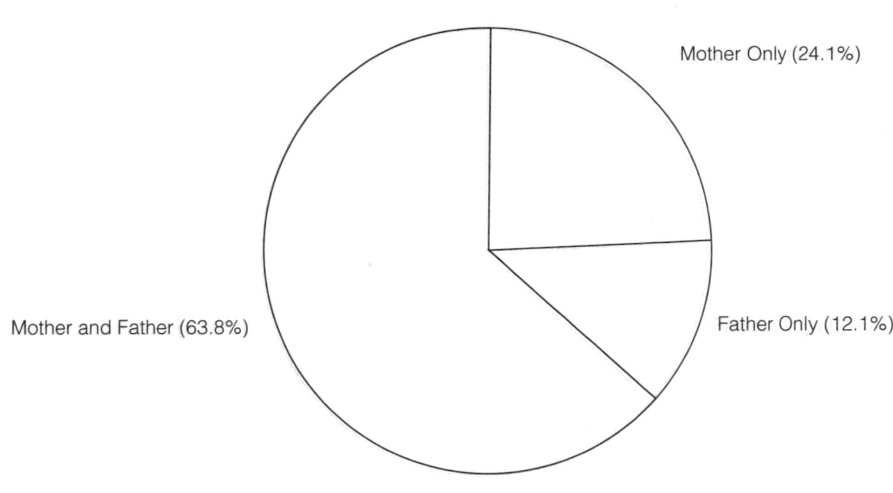


bottom and the relative size of the bars immediately tell the audience that two thirds of the children lived with both parents, about one quarter lived with their mother only and the rest lived with their father only. The percentages above the three bars serve two purposes. First, they are there for the people who want to see the actual numbers, whether for detail or for reassurance. Second, it is easy to make errors in producing a graph, and linking numbers to the bars coordinates the graphic picture with the data and its meaning.

The same information in Graph 27.1 is presented in the form of a pie chart in Graph 27.2. While bar charts are commonly used and easy to interpret, other useful graphic formats may be more appropriate for presenting certain kinds of data. For example, when the goal is to describe the composition of a group, particularly if the categories of the data are mutually exclusive, as they are in this case, a pie chart is as good or better than a bar chart.

Graph 27.3 profiles several different dimensions of the client's gender, family income, presence of parent(s), and age of children. Seeing the profile in this form, one is much more apt to remember that the children are nearly evenly divided by gender, and that the majority (nearly four fifths) are from families with incomes well below the poverty threshold of $13,360 for a four-person family. Higher incomes are absent because only children with a family income below $20,000 are eligible for this program. This kind of sociodemographic information, or data very similar to it, is almost always gathered on clients. Furthermore, it is relatively easy to compare these kinds of data on the program's clients over time. Such a comparison highlights

GRAPH 27.3
Client Profile

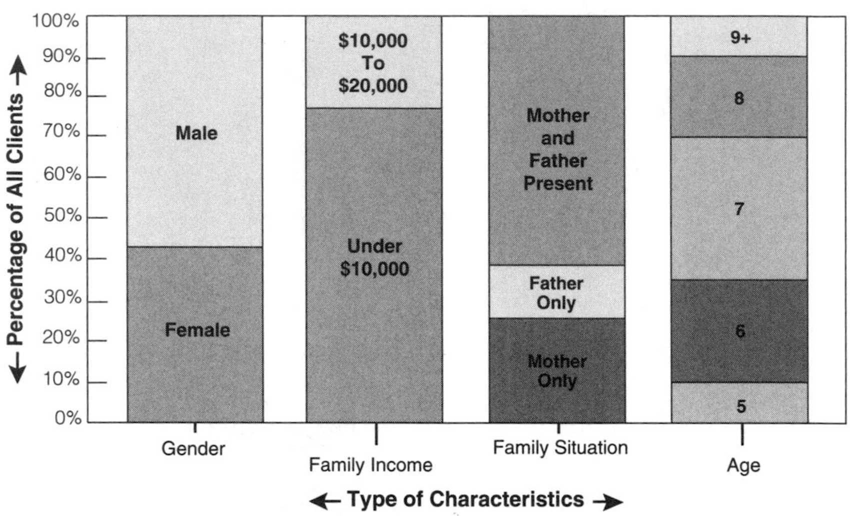


changes that may occur so gradually that they would otherwise go unnoticed by those who carry out the agency's day-to-day activities. By making comparisons, over months and over years, one is able to see the extent to which an agency's clients have changed and to seek the reasons for those changes. This kind of analysis also helps one rethink the fit between the interventions the agency provides and the needs and characteristics of its clients.

So far, we have focused on the analysis and presentation of simple demographic data on the agency's clients. A more challenging task is the analysis and presentation of information about the problems that these clients experience. Data on client problems can highlight whether the interventions the agency undertakes focus directly on client problems (e.g., protective services aiming at stopping abuse or neglect) or are incidental to them, as is true for many of the problems faced by families of the children in the program we are examining here. Establishing what clients need also is an important step toward meeting the agency's requirement for accountability, and it helps convince various persons and organizations to become stakeholders in the agency and its programs.

The problems of the children's families in the program we are examining are portrayed in Graph 27.4. (Note that any given family may have more than one type of problem. When this is the case, a pie diagram ordinarily is not appropriate.) The viewer immediately sees that substance abuse is the most prevalent problem among these families, while physical abuse and neglect also are quite prevalent.

Data such as those presented in Graph 27.4 can be very important for eliciting the support of funders, stakeholders, and the

GRAPH 27.4
Prevalence of Problems in the Home

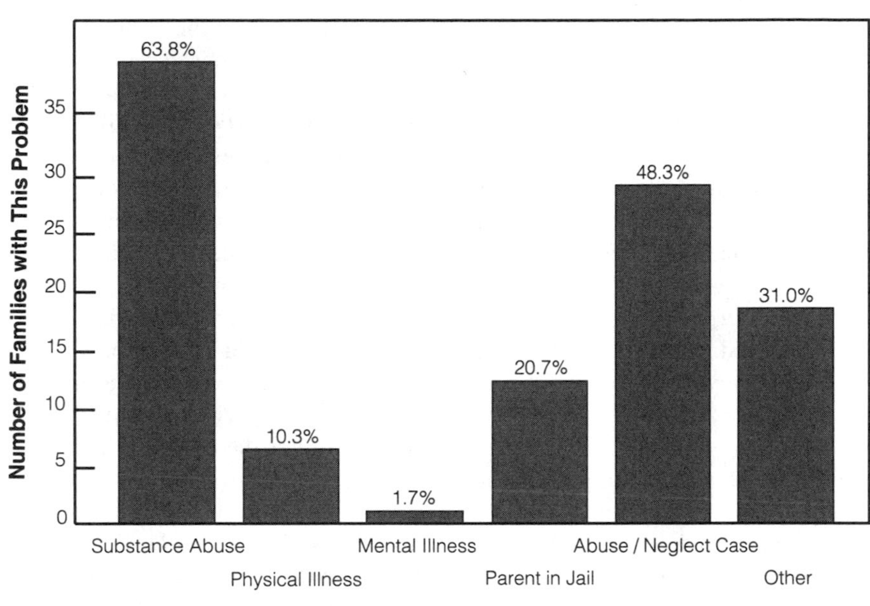


general public. The graph may tell the whole story to some viewers, but it is still important to add in either written or oral form such statements as: "Notice that nearly half of the children we serve are abused or neglected."

Virtually all agencies have records that link clients with service delivery activities, although in smaller agencies, these data may be in case files or in daily, often handwritten, time logs. It will probably require considerable effort to render these data useful. Most agencies also compile summaries of their activities with clients. These can help one assess the number and frequency of an agency's contacts with a client and what transpired during those contacts. In addition to the data presented here, the program we are considering records data on its on-going activities: the frequency of contacts with individual children, contacts with their parents, etc. For brevity, these are not portrayed, but they are crucial data for the purpose of monitoring program activities.

We turn now to data on the program's impact that help us determine the effectiveness of the program's interventions. If we find that the program has been effective, we can try to focus on how and why its effects have been achieved. If we find that the program has not been effective, we can try to identify some of the reasons and what can be done about them. The analysis and presentation of impact data is one of the more challenging aspects of program evaluation. The challenge comes from having to deal with the tentative nature of the causal connection between a program's interventions and any changes that occur in the clients or their situations. Even in the best of cases, it is difficult to conclude that any changes, positive, negative, or neutral, are "caused" by a given intervention. Probably, the best we can do is build a strong case, based on a well-reasoned argument, supported by a variety of data, that the intervention contributed to the changes. Data on impact on clients, when presented in a clear, concise manner can help agency administrators show what their programs have accomplished. Impact data also can help service delivery staff improve the effectiveness of their interventions with clients.

The goal of the program that we are considering here is to reduce attendance problems in the early grades among students who may be at risk of serious educational difficulties owing to severe family situations. (Poor attendance is an indicator of such difficulties.) The program has collected data on the absences and on the tardiness of its clients during three periods: in the semester before they entered the program, in the semester in which the program intervened to prevent absences, and in the following semester. We will focus on the data on absences and, for the sake of brevity, ignore the data on tardiness.

The distributions of absences for these three semesters are presented in Graphs 27.5, 27.6, and 27.7. We have presented these three graphs on the same page with the identical scale so that we can see precisely any shifts in the distribution of absences. By comparing the three graphs, we see that the distribution of absences shifts to the left. This indicates that absences become less frequent; there is a shift downward in the average level of absences. In fact, the average number of days absent fell from 12.7 days per term before the intervention to 11.0 days absent during the term in which the children were enrolled in this special program, to 10.0 days in the term immediately after the program. This decline in absences of 2.7 days per term that occurred between pretreatment and posttreatment is statistically significant.

The data on absences portrayed in the previous graphs are the only data available for this program that can help us determine whether it is a success or a failure.[5] But, if we were designing the evaluation from scratch, what other supporting data could we use? It would strengthen the case for the effectiveness of the program if we had supplementary data to reinforce our confidence that it is the program that is influencing the behavior of the children and their families in a way that helps improve school attendance. For example, if we knew that these students' grades improved after the intervention, it would lend considerable support to the case for the effectiveness of the program. In addition, it would help to have a record of absences and average grades of the children from the same school who were not in the program. We would expect the average absences of the children not in the program to be below 12.7 days per term (the average of our client group). After all, an important criterion for admission to the program was excessive absences. It would make a great deal of difference to our analysis if the average for the not-in-program children is 10, in which case the clients improved to the class average. On the other hand, if the class average is 2 or 3, it means that our clients made only marginal gains, whatever the statistical significance of those gains.

The final example is Graph 27.8 which is a scatter diagram portraying the relationship between each child's level of absence

GRAPH 27.5
Preprogram Absences

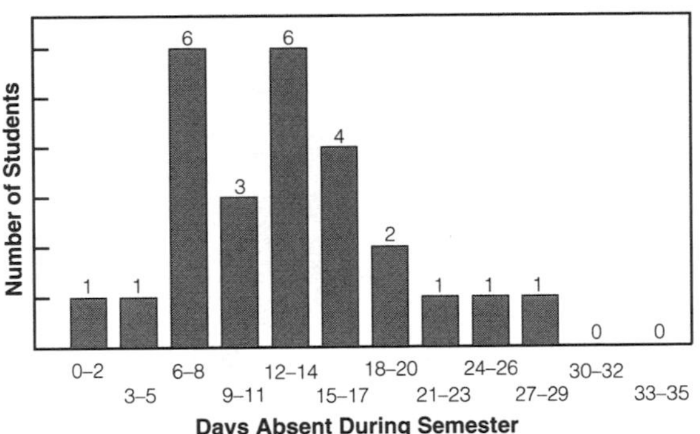


GRAPH 27.6
During-Program Absences

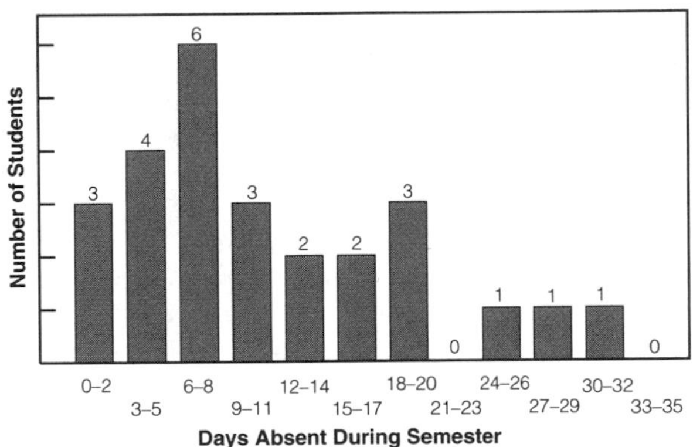


GRAPH 27.7
Postprogram Absences

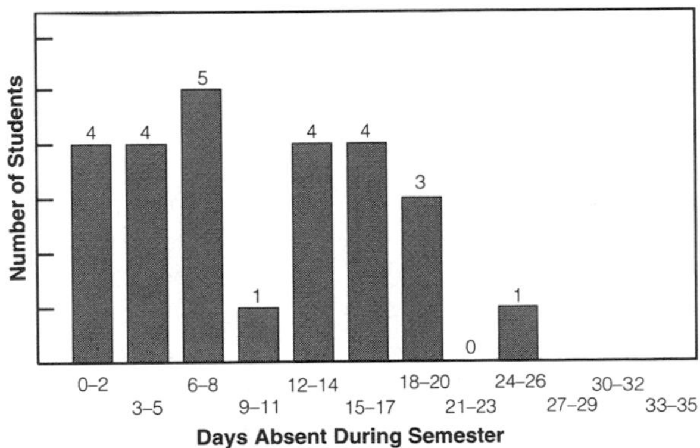

GRAPH 27.8
Absences Before and After Program

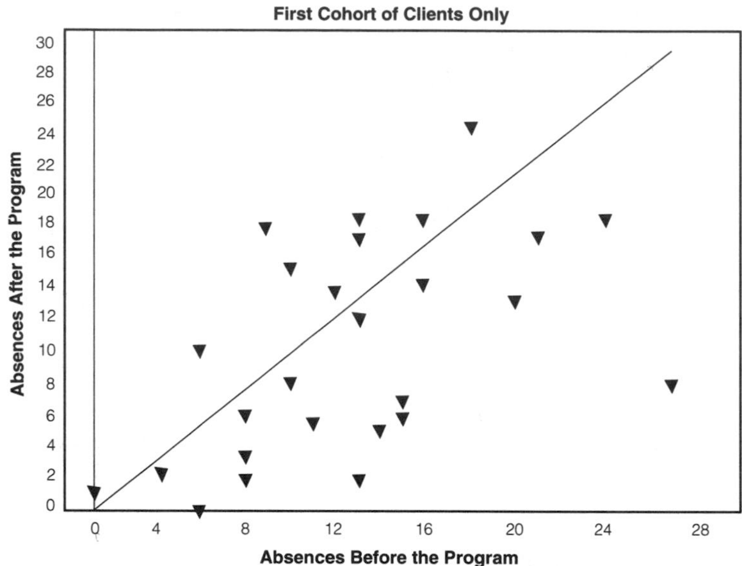


before the intervention on the horizontal or x-axis and after the intervention, on the vertical or y-axis. This graph can be used to show audiences the improvement in attendance. The after-program absences of the students who are below the diagonal line (19 of the 27 students) are lower than their absences before the program; those above the diagonal have more absences; anyone on the diagonal would have an equal number of absences before and after the intervention.

## More Data That Could Help Assess Impact

Another type of data that could help establish whether the program is succeeding or not is health data on the children. Presumably, a major determinant of absences for ordinary children in the early grades is their health. These children (and at least an equivalent number of nonclient children) or their parents could be asked the frequency of visits to physicians in each of the school terms being studied. With such data, one could begin to model absences as a function of the program, taking into consideration the health of the child.

We have attempted to show that effective program evaluation need not be complicated. In fact, if there is an overriding principle in the discussion presented here, it is that keeping the evaluation simple and straightforward ensures that it will be useful to those who can benefit from it most: the agencies, their staff who deliver the services, their constituents who fund and support the delivery of those services, and ultimately the clients who receive those services.

## NOTES

1. An excellent and very practical overview of program evaluation for the potential practitioner is Posavac and Carey (1989). Another good text is Rossi and Freeman (1982). For a more detailed treatment of some topics, see Grinnell (1988). Austin et al. (1982) is a good handbook. Pietrzak et al. (1990) is a good example of the techniques applied to a particular problem—in this instance, child abuse.

2. Levin (1983) is an excellent source for all sorts of cost-based evaluation techniques. It is clear and accurate in its conceptualizations and very useful for ordinary situations. Weisbrod (1983) applies a benefit cost analysis to a mental health intervention and explains the sequence of actual decisions and judgments that must be made in a realistic context. Even if the evaluator is not intending to actually do a benefit cost analysis, Weisbrod's exposition is helpful for anyone trying to understand and apply economics to human service programs.

3. Tufte (1983) stands by itself as the source for both the principles and good practice of displaying quantitative information. Tufte (1990) builds on his earlier book, but is also an independent treatise on how we understand by seeing.

4. The graphics initially prepared for this paper were produced using Lotus 123, the most widely used spreadsheet computer program.

5. Although our data may seem limited, we have considerably more responses to the questions we are asking than many programs either collect or report.

## BIBLIOGRAPHY


Austin, M. J., Gary Cox, Naomi Gottlieb, J. David Hawkins, Jean M. Kruzich, and Ronald Rauch. (1982). *Evaluating your agency's programs.* Beverly Hills, CA: Sage Publications.

Grinnell, R. M., Jr. (Ed.). (1988). *Social work research and evaluation.* Itasca, IL: F. E. Peacock Publishers, Inc.

Levin, H. M. (1983). *Cost effectiveness: a primer.* Beverly Hills, CA: Sage Publications.

Pietrzak, J., Malia Ramler, Tanya Renner, Lucy Ford, and Neil Gilbert. (1990). Number 9 of Sage Source Books for the Human Services. *Practical program evaluation: Examples from child abuse prevention.* Beverly Hills, CA: Sage Publications.

Posavac, E. J., and Raymond G. Carey. (1989). *Program evaluation: Methods and case studies.* Englewood Cliffs, NJ: Prentice-Hall, Inc.

Rossi, P. H., and Howard E. Freeman. (1982). *Evaluation: A systematic approach.* Beverly Hills, CA: Sage Publications.

Tufte, E. R. (1983). *The visual display of quantitative information.* Cheshire, CT: Graphics Press.

Tufte, E. R. (1990). *Envisioning information.* Cheshire, CT: Graphics Press.

Weisbrod, B. A. (1983). An experiment in treating the mentally ill: A guide to benefit-cost analysis. Chapter 6 of *Economics and medical research.* Washington, DC: American Enterprise Institute.

28.

**Eleanor Chelimsky**

# THE POLITICS OF PROGRAM EVALUATION

What do we mean when we talk about the politics of program evaluation? David Easton wrote thirty-seven years ago in *World Politics* that "the study of politics is concerned with understanding how authoritative decisions are made and executed for a society" and that "the output of a political system is a political decision or policy." Public policy, then, is the product of politics. Evaluation, with its purpose of providing high-quality information to decision makers, automatically claims a role for itself in the political process. It is based on the idea that the best information, made available to decision makers, would surely be useful to them in making and executing public policy. Unfortunately, in the very early seventies, rumors began to be heard in the land (later, alas, confirmed by studies) to the effect that evaluations were not often used in decision making.

At first we tried to come to grips with the problem by looking for ways out of the difficulty that would not require too many major changes in our paradigm or too many shifts in our work-style. We said that if our work was not used, this was because some evaluations simply were not good enough, forgetting—or not yet realizing—that policymakers typically use any data at hand and that some mediocre evaluation work has in fact been well used. Or we said that maybe evaluation was used, but we could not trace that use because evaluation was just one of many factors influencing decision making. We said that "use in decision making" might be too narrow a goal for evaluation, that there were many meanings—at least seven—attributable to the term "research utilization." We said that we needed to develop information supporting negotiation rather than information supporting decision making. What we were doing was turning the question of "why isn't evaluation used?" into the question "what, in fact, is reasonable use?" This in turn led to the idea that expectations for the use of evaluations were unrealistically high.

There had also been a 1973 paper in *Evaluation* by Carol Weiss, "Where Politics and Evaluation Meet," in which she made two crucial points: (1) that "as a matter of record, relatively few evaluation studies have had a noticeable effect on the making and remaking of public policy," and (2) that "only with sensitivity to the politics of evaluation research can the evaluator be as strategically useful as he should be." Thus, the lack of evaluation use was beginning to be recognized as such and to be seen not so much as a problem that could be whisked away without major changes in the evaluation paradigm, but

---

Eleanor Chelimsky is director of the U.S. General Accounting Office's (GAO) Program Evaluation and Methodology Division, which conducts studies of individual government programs for Congress; the opinions expressed in this article are her own and not the policy or position of the GAO. She previously directed the MITRE Corporation's work in program evaluation, policy analysis, and research management. She has been a Fulbright scholar in Paris, president of the Evaluation Research Society, and the recipient of the 1982 Myrdal Award for Government and the GAO Distinguished and Meritorious Service Awards for 1985 and 1991. She was elected president of the American Evaluation Association, 1994–1996.

rather as the newly perceived and difficult problem of integrating the disparate worlds of politics and evaluation research.

After the appearance of Weiss's article, and between about 1975 and 1980, a spate of articles and studies were published that sought to relate evaluations generally to the larger political and policy context within which they operate. One of the most important of these was the 1980 book by Lee Cronbach and Associates, *Toward Reform of Program Evaluation.* Looking back today at many of these studies, we can get the best sense not only of what we have learned about politics and evaluation but also how we have changed our outlook and practice.

It was typical in those studies to read statements attesting to the importance of politics to evaluation, statements such as Cronbach's: "a theory of evaluation must be as much a theory of political interaction as it is a theory of how to determine facts" or "the evaluators' professional conclusions cannot substitute for the political process." Nevertheless, there were not many cogent, action-oriented, systematic, and specific discussions of how the integration of evaluator and politics should or could take place. We did hear suggestions for the introduction of "research brokerage" or of "a bridging function," both of which sought to solve the integration problem by interposing some person or unit between the evaluation and the political user. This suggestion required a whole new breed of "interface analysis," and it never bore fruit, as James Sundquist predicted when he broached the idea in 1978 in *Knowledge and Policy: The Uncertain Connection.*

One reason that concrete suggestions were so hard to come by may have been that the political domain with which evaluation had to interact was so little understood by evaluators. In 1975, when I was organizing the MITRE Corporation's symposium on the use of evaluation, it was considered unusual to have evaluators from many different evaluative disciplines (such as psychology, sociology, economics, political science, or operations research) and from many different substantive program areas (not only the usual health, education, and welfare; but also, for example, energy and the environment). It was a novelty for these evaluators not only to sit down together, but to sit down with their policy-making and program managing sponsors and users in different federal agencies. What came out of that symposium was a set of concrete dissatisfactions that users had with evaluation's performance, many of which were political and many of which were shocking to the evaluators present.

We heard that evaluation often cannot be used because of bureaucratic relationships and conflicts, that some program managers really prefer to be ignorant, and that evaluations will only be used if management really wants them. We heard that evaluation seemed to its users to be an ivory-tower process, and that when it emerged from that tower, it was too late to be useful, too full of jargon to be understood, too lengthy for the reading time available to users, and too likely to be answering a question quite different from the policy question originally posed. All of this was important to hear, not only because it was a kind of beginning excursion into the agency politics of evaluation, but also because the information had a chance of being assimilated or internalized by evaluators, given that most evaluations at that time had been developed for agencies of the executive branch.

When Cronbach's book on evaluation reform came out in 1980, many of the lessons of agency politics learned at the MITRE symposium had been learned by at least some evaluators. We were still far from having a political framework comprehensive enough to plan our integration work against, because, for the most part, legislative politics had remained unexamined. While Cronbach properly reproached us in 1980 for taking a too narrow view of the political arena in which agency decisions are made and evaluation use occurs, this view, in turn, seems narrow to us today because it failed to include legislative politics.

This was not just a matter of leaving something out. First, many of the points made, which are right on target about agency politics, are notably inappropriate with regard to legislative politics. For example, after considering what we have learned in six years of working with Congress, we need to rethink premises such as "a social agenda almost never calls for a choice between fixed alternatives"; or "only rarely are 'go/no go' decisions made"; or "timeliness is a much-overrated concern." Congress continually makes choices between fixed alternatives and votes on go/no go decisions; and an evaluator who did not understand the critical importance of the timing of congressional policy cycles—involving program authorization, reauthorization, appropriations, and budget—would be spinning his or her wheels and wasting a lot of money. The importance of timeliness with regard to legislative politics, at least, cannot be overstated. Second, without an understanding of legislative politics, we cannot understand—or worse, we actively misunderstand—the dynamnics of cross-branch politics; that is, the reciprocal process of legislative/executive agency interactions. I caution against overgeneralizing from agency evaluations politics to all evaluation politics.

Another result of failing to include legislative politics in our thinking is the continuing restriction of evaluation's application to social issues only. Over and over, we read of evaluation's preoccupation with social programs, with social reform, with social concerns; but legislative politics means that evaluation must broaden its focus to be optimally useful. Working for Congress, evaluators are expected to exercise their skills in all policy areas, social or not. Because I had included a single legislative perspective on evaluation in the MITRE symposium, I recognized the need to also include energy and the environment—two largely nonsocial, technological areas that were and are of great concern to Congress—in the 1976 symposium agenda.

To characterize the politics of evaluation today, we are dealing with a process of continuous translation for which the evaluator must assume a major share of responsibility. I represent the process as a five-part continuum, or framework, which involves, first, the development of a policy question. (I do not exclude program questions or imply that all questions for evaluation are policy questions, but, rather, I include all types of questions under this rubric insofar as they are asked by policy actors and emerge from the political process.) The policy question is then translated into an evaluation question which typically alters the policy question so that it becomes researchable. In the third part of the continuum, the evaluation question is translated into the evaluation proper: its design, its performance, and the reporting of its findings. The fourth part is the translation back into policy language of the results of the evaluation: that is, it is the policy answer to the original policy question. The fifth part entails the use of the evaluation findings somewhere in the cross-branch political process and the return, completing the continuum, to the formulation of new policy questions.

## DEVELOPING POLICY QUESTIONS

Evaluation can no longer be seen as completely a creature of the evaluator's choosing—with the evaluator being entirely free to select the program he or she wants to evaluate and to determine alone the questions to be asked about the program. Instead, insofar as we are dealing with evaluations that have been sponsored and are intended to be used in the political environment, the choice of the program to evaluate emerges in real terms from the political process. The determination of the types of policy questions to be asked are a function of the decision makers, whether legislative or executive or both. It occasionally happens that both congressional and agency policymakers are in accord about what the important questions are, as in the recent emphasis on teenage pregnancy, for example, or the earlier issue of cost containment in health care services.

My framework involves both an empowering of the decision maker with regard to the evaluation product and a shift in the role of the evaluators from the political one of seeking to reform society or, as Weiss put it, improving "the way that society copes with social problems," to the scientific one of bringing the best possible information to bear on a wide variety of policy questions. Such a change squares well with definitions of evaluation that see it as "the application of scientific research methods to the assessment of program concepts, implementation, and effectiveness" or as the provision of "careful and umbiased data" about programs, or as "a process by which society learns about itself." It does not square well with the notion that "an evaluator should not undertake to serve an agency unless he is in sympathy with its general mission," or with program advocacy or partisan definitions of evaluation in which evaluators seek to be a voice for the program, or a voice for the underdog or for some other special group. Similarly, it cannot accommodate precepts such as "it is unwise for evaluation to focus on whether a project has 'attained its goals.'" Such a precept assumes that the evaluator chooses the questions. Actually, the politics of the legislative oversight function may require that evaluators focus on the question of goal attainment.

The primary purpose of having the policy question be one that is of major concern to politicians is to maximize the use of the findings. When the user generates the questions, and when the purpose of the evaluation is to produce the highest quality information for policy or program use, this has the effect of eliminating any congressional suspicions that "the questions set for discovery (by the evaluators) have predetermined answers" or that "the assumed posture of objectivity among program evaluators masks subtle but important biases and hidden agendas."

In legislative politics, the most credible evaluations are those whose use will be maximized. This may seem paradoxical, given that high methodological quality may not ensure use, and we have seen that adversaries in the political process will often use any data that support their case. Some people believe that the best way to achieve policy use is through partisan evaluation that supports either the policymaker's ideology or the evaluator's own, but credibility involves more than methodological quality: it involves responsiveness to the specific policy question and information need. Partisan use by policymakers is not helpful for the credibility of an evaluation. On the contrary, partisanship is, at best, a short-term strategy that is not well adapted to legislative politics. In Congress, partisan work that is well received by one committee would be quickly discredited by another, and worse, the reputation for partisanship would remain with the evaluator over the longer term. Independent analysis that is strong methodologically and seeks to be as objective as humanly possible, serves a much wider legislative audience and can be the focus of cross-committee or even House- and Senate-wide debate. (We have seen this happen on three separate occasions in our work on chemical warfare.)

An evaluation that is read and whose findings are used in the policy process will have a political influence; such an influence is inherent in the fundamental interaction of evaluation with politics. Evaluation's main value to policy in the long run is not its capacity for political influence but its contribution of systematic, scholarly, independent, critical thinking to the decision making process.

Decision makers may fail to ask certain kinds of questions because either they do not want to, they do not think of them, or there is not time to get answers. In exploring some of the questions decision makers at different levels and positions in both branches of government tend to ask, I recently pointed out that there are some areas in which evaluators are not often asked questions, even though they could probably contribute powerfully to useful answers. An example of this is the rarity with which decision makers pose relevant evaluative questions prior to the introduction of a new program. As a result, there is habitually a serious dearth of evaluative information entering the area of policy formulation in time to influence the proposal.

Many of us spend much of our time doing retrospective studies: these are and will continue to be the meat and potatoes of evaluation research. Congress asks us for them and asks the executive branch to do them, and they are needed; but these studies are not the easiest ones to insert into the political process, and they may well be the least propitious from the viewpoint of use. When we at the U.S. General Accounting Office (GAO) do one of them, we always try to focus hard on what it will be possible to accomplish uniquely through legislative means. We know how hard it will be to change much of anything in a long-established, well-entrenched agency program.

By contrast, before a program has started, evaluators can have an enormous effect in improving the reasoning behind program purposes or goals, in identifying the problems to be addressed, and in selecting the best point of intervention and the type of intervention most likely to succeed. The tempo at which new programs are sometimes introduced presents some difficulty. Recently, Senator Moynihan complained that the provisions of the Gramm-Rudman-Hollings bill were still being tinkered with while he was being asked to vote on it. The pace often becomes so frantic that the lead time necessary to gear up for evaluative work is simply impossible to obtain if results are to be ready soon enough to be useful.

At the GAO we have developed a method I call the Prospective Evaluation Synthesis which is specifically intended to be useful in the formulation of new programs. We have used this method a number of times, including a study of a proposed program focusing on teenage pregnancy. Essentially, the method seeks to gather information on what is known about past, similar programs and apply the experience to the architecture of the new one. In the case of teenage pregnancy, Senator Chafee asked us to look at the bill he was introducing; we managed to secure four good months to do the work, and it has been a major success both from the legislative point of view and our own. From a more general, political perspective, providing understanding ahead of time of how a program might work can render a valuable public service—either by helping to shore up a poorly thought-out program or by validating the basic soundness of what is to be undertaken. True, there are questions that decision makers do not pose to evaluators that could usefully be posed, which seems a priori to be a problem for the framework; however, even when evaluators have been free to choose the questions, this particular type of question has not often been asked. Also, evaluators can always influence the next round of policy questions through their products.

## TRANSLATING POLICY QUESTIONS

The second part of the continuum is the translation of the policy question into an evaluation question. We have found in working with Congress that this is one of the most sensitive and important political interactions in the entire process, and it has to be given a great deal of thought, care, and attention. This is the point at which the sponsor is going to learn if the policy question being asked is researchable. If the evaluator concludes that it is not researchable, this may be because the issue or program is immature; for example, it may be impossible to answer cause-and-effect questions if there has been little or no prior conceptual development in the field to guide the execution of such work. In this case, it would be wise to try to transform the question from the cause-and-effect type to another type that could be answered, if in fact such an answer would also be useful to the decision maker. We could move, say, from asking what the factors are that cause high quality and productivity in an organization, to asking either what is known about high quality in an organization and how it is defined or what the characteristics are of people and work processes in a number of selected organizations whose high quality and productivity are recognized. This eminently rational process of transforming a cause-and-effect question into a descriptive question based on evidence of researchability is fraught with risks.

Sponsors do not like to have their questions modified; to them, this smacks of the researcher substituting his or her wisdom for that of the policymaker. So a change needs to be carefully and persuasively explained and negotiated. In Congress, there is often a real need for findings that are generalizable to the nation, whether or not a national study is feasible in terms of time, costs, and the type or locus of the program. In programs heavily dependent on state variation, for example, there is a continuing problem of how to obtain in-depth knowledge that can help illuminate that variation and at the same time develop more superficial but politically needed knowledge about what the situation is nationwide. The translation is not always an obvious or easy one.

In thinking of the fourth part of the framework continuum—when evaluation findings will have to be translated back into policy findings—it is critical for both the evaluator and the sponsor to remember the importance that a powerful methodology will have at that time for being persuasive if the evaluation deals with a controversial policy area. That is, it is rarely prudent to enter a burning political debate armed only with a case study, even if that case study were the most rational approach to the original policy question.

The movement from policy question to evaluation question must be carefully prepared, with a lot of thought given to the sponsor's time requirements, the cost, the relation of the type of findings expected for the particular policy need, the kind of program and its locus, the prior research done, and the likely controversiality of the issues.

The evaluator also needs to think beyond the sponsor, in this part of the continuum, to the entire federal context of the program. The question may have been raised by legislative policy actors, but in order for any evaluation recommendations to have an effect, the evaluator knows it will be necessary for executive branch policy actors to think those recommendations are right and to act on them. This entails another subcomplex of questions for the evaluator who wants the evaluation to be useful, including such issues as: "Have we got the right problem from the agency viewpoint?" If they do not think so, is that because it is unimportant or because they just do not want to think about it? Is the question symptomatic of a deeper problem that should be addressed? Who is in a position to do something about the problem? What if a power change occurred during the conduct of the evaluation—a new administration might come in or control of the Senate change hands—what effect would that have on the usefulness of the findings? The evaluators cannot necessarily do something about all of these issues, but they and others may have a great impact on the eventual use of the findings. At the minimum, legislative evaluators have a major interest in maintaining good relations with executive branch agency evaluators if those agencies must implement the recommendations and ultimately resolve the problem being treated by the evaluation.

A related consideration in conducting negotiations on the change from policy to evaluation question is that policymakers and their staffs are impatient with the typically equivocal nature of findings. For them, what is uppermost is their political need to take unequivocal policy positions. This reemphasizes the importance for evaluators working within a policy context to be aware of the type of political debate into which their finished evaluation will likely enter, and to structure the evaluation design—once the evaluation question is settled—not so as to deal with every conceivable issue, but to produce strong, well-focused information which will be usable in that particular debate.

## DOING THE EVALUATION

The third part of the continuum involves doing the evaluation. Although the evaluator now begins a phase of the work in which he or she is in at least relative control, both the evaluation design and the writing of the report need to be understood with the political context in mind. A sixth point about the changes in evaluation practice that are brought about by the use of this framework has to do with the narrow limits of policymakers' interest in past experience. Decision makers look forward; evaluators look back. Although it is often the case that policy actors are genuinely interested in knowing what effects a program had, their interest almost never stops there. Almost invariably the evaluator will be asked to say what the evaluation findings mean in prescriptive terms: if it is a descriptive study, there will usually be a normative question posed and, nearly always, an invitation to say what the findings signify for future programs. In the GAO's Program Evaluation and Methodology Division

(PEMD) we have come to understand that we must expect these kinds of questions; even in an exploratory study, if it is for Congress, we try to build in a panel of experts, carefully chosen to reflect the widest possible spectrum of political opinion as well as both substantive and methodological expertise. We bring these experts in early in the study to help us develop the criteria we know we will need to make use of in answering the normative questions that will be asked. For example, in a descriptive management study, how will we decide what degree of communication in an organization is adequate and what degree is inadequate? In a medical study, what counts as "progress" and what counts as "lack of progress" in treatment or patient management techniques? In a study of research utilization, how many omissions or distortions of the findings does it take to constitute misuse? Cronbach wrote in 1980: "An evaluation of a particular project has its greatest implications for projects that will be put in place in the future." What we have now learned is how to build features into a design that will allow us to speak a little more strongly about the significance of our findings for those future projects.

Another point of change implied by the framework for the execution of the evaluation design involves the need for a wide range of approaches and methods, often used in combination so that the strengths of one can palliate the weaknesses of another. Responsiveness to a policy question does not allow the luxury of, as Cronbach expressed it, "chapels dedicated to the glorification of particular styles." The political environment has its exigencies even here. National data are nearly always wanted. Again, there is a similar kind of mystique surrounding heavily quantitative impact evaluations; for congressional staff generally, they are the most considered studies (a 1979 survey reported by Florio, Behrmann, and Goltz in *Educational Evaluation and Policy Analysis* showed that "information on the impact of legislative policy and authorized programs is significantly greater in importance" than other types of information, such as demographic information on populations served and affected, opinions and reactions of interested population groups, or program-descriptive information.) When the evaluation is situated within the confines of a really emotional debate, a quantitative, generalizable impact study can offer protection for the evaluator, but such a study may be neither feasible nor appropriate for the question. Even when it is the right study to do, if legislative policy staff are given a choice between timeliness and the kind of powerful methodology that could be persuasive, staff will generally choose timeliness, so great are the political pressures of deadlines on Capitol Hill. Thus, the translation from an evaluation question to a design that is appropriate (both methodologically and politically) is not always easy.

An additional point concerns getting the agreement of the sponsor on the evaluation design once it is completed. While this generally goes without saying in the executive branch, discussion of evaluation designs with legislative staff has been much less frequent. We have adopted this as a formal procedure in PEMD evaluations, using the discussions in several ways. First, the design will include some conclusions about how long the evaluation will take, what methods will be used, how likely we are to get answers to the questions posed, how unequivocal those answers are likely to be, how credible the study will be (especially if it is on a controversial subject), and what types and numbers of reports will be produced. The design meeting with the sponsor involves a staff briefing, discussion of any changes the sponsor wants, and agreement on how the evaluation will be conducted and reported. The issue of reporting relates once again to the problem of timeliness in Congress: the design will choose among various types of products—statement of fact, briefing report, testimony, full-length report—based on the sponsor's timing needs.

We have also used the design discussions to help initiate legislative staff into some technical aspects of evaluation. The necessity for this is dictated by misunderstandings that have arisen when congressional staff have not been carefully briefed on exactly what work is being pursued. The two biggest problems we have had are overly grand expectations about what can be accomplished in a short time and lack of awareness of what the immaturity of a subject area can mean for the evaluation's ability to produce strong information. In one case, we were given only twelve months to produce a study that needed twice as much time. In another, we were expected to produce a methodology in a field in which the paucity of research indicated that we could, at best, produce guidelines.

The design meeting is also useful because congressional staff will typically explain to us how they expect to use our work, and this may well lead to a modification in the design or in the planned products. It also exposes us to important cumulative insights into the legislative process and into congressional relationships with the executive branch.

It is prodigiously important for evaluation use that the overall credibility of the evaluation be assured, and that we become aware of the kinds of efforts that have to be made to achieve that credibility during the conduct of the evaluation.

The use of the framework conflicts once again with former evaluation practice. One of Cronbach's theses advised evaluators "to release findings piecemeal and informally to the audiences that need them" because "the impotence that comes with delay may be a greater risk than the possibility that early returns will be misread." A worse and much more dangerous possibility is not that those early returns will be misread but that they will be wrong—because they are early and have not been systematically checked. The rules at the GAO about indexing, referencing, and quality assurance stand us in good stead on this. Staff who have not been a part of the evaluation team are the ones who do this work, and during the sometimes incredibly detailed shakedown sessions about the support for a figure or the appropriateness of some data analysis, the cries and whimpers of maddened researchers can be heard throughout the division. Disagreeable though the quality control process usually is, nearly everyone is glad we have it. We tend not to release information until we are sure it has satisfied the quality control process because we have learned that a loss of credibility takes a long time to recover from and can in fact prove fatal. While we recognize the extreme importance of early information on Capitol Hill, credibility is even more important: it is the critical prerequisite for use over the long term. Whether the issue is fairness, balance, methodological quality, or just plain old accuracy, no effort to establish credibility is ever wasted.

## ANSWERING POLICY QUESTIONS

In the fourth part of the continuum, the evaluation results are translated into policy answers to the original policy question. Here we are trying to communicate evaluation findings to a political audience in such a way that the findings will be both well understood and persuasive. This implies changes to typical evaluation practice. Another point speaks to the difficulty of establishing priorities among the findings. In politics, priorities are the heart of the matter—not ideology, not even consistency or persistency, but putting first things first at the right time. In evaluation, on the other hand, this is not only one of the most difficult things to achieve, it is rarely thought about at all. We evaluators have the habit of laying out all our results in the same careful, neutral phrases, leaving it to the scientifically trained audience to perceive the areas of success, of promise, of no result, of failure. We document everything, usually in the same neutral tone, with what has been described by Cronbach as "self-defeating thoroughness." The problem is that all of the evaluation's findings seem important to its author. It is painfully difficult to order them in a policy context, to trim surgically what is not relevant, to condense, to rank, to decide not only which finding is the most important but which is the most important that policy can do something about.

Once again we hear the cries and laments of unhappy evaluators. From the viewpoint of use, it is crucial to discriminate in communicating results between what is important and what is not and to be clear about how the findings should or could be acted on. Some findings are difficult to be clear about, except to say bluntly that they are not clear. In other cases, we simply do not know the answer to the policy question. It is important, from a political viewpoint, for us to become comfortable with the idea of saying that a conclusive answer is not available when in fact it is not. In our work, we have found that the knowledge that no knowledge exists is important policy information that decision makers do not necessarily have. In many cases, for example, Congress will be told by an executive agency that there is no evidence of certain unfavorable results in some program. What that often means is that the agency has not looked for such evidence. This is different from being able to say, "We have looked seriously and systematically, and there is no evidence one way or the other." If there is no evidence and this can be shown, then the way is cleared to get support for research that will, if possible, develop the needed information.

In trying to make findings clear, useful, and effectively available to policymakers, communication techniques need to be developed that may depart greatly from typical evaluation practice. A first effort has to do with banishing evaluation jargon. This is important not just because policymakers do not understand it but because it seems to them to hint at some private club, some special understanding, some incomprehensible ritual from which they are excluded. This gives rise not just to impatience but to irritation with the evaluator which carries over to the evaluation. It is the kind of irritation that H. L. Mencken expressed when he said a metaphysician was one who, when you remark that twice two makes four, demands to know what you mean by twice, what by two, what by makes, and what by four. The intelligibility of an evaluation report is critical for the use of its findings.

A second effort has to do with varying the written products so that the information can be presented briefly and succinctly but is backed up with all the supporting data needed by a variety of audiences. A third effort involves paralleling the delivery of reports with as much oral communication as possible. This is the style of reporting that is most natural to policymakers, especially those on Capitol Hill. Congressional staff and members of Congress are used to listening to constituents and lobbyists; they gather ideas and form judgments not only by reading but especially by talking with staff and colleagues, by holding committee hearings, by interacting personally with a wide variety of people. In this environment, oral briefings are crucial; testimony can be more useful than a major report. We now see video apparatus being pressed into service to help reconcile the tension between the need to document and the need for easy expression and understanding.

In general, when we think about the entire process, starting with the original policy question, of doing evaluation, we see that we have moved purposefully away from the anecdote or war story as a credible answer to a policy question. As evaluators, we are typically trying to get a sense of the size of a problem, of its range, its frequency, its direction, its average characteristics. After having determined the evaluation results, when we must move back into the political forum the policy question emerged from originally, we find that one of the most effective ways to present findings is to rediscover the anecdote, to illustrate the general findings via specific cases and analogies that graphically focus attention on and explain the larger points. When used in this manner, anecdotes are not expected to stand alone as answers to policy questions; instead, they are used as representative of the broader evaluative evidence—to explain the findings, to increase the political understanding and comfort level, and, above all, to improve the likelihood that the evaluation findings will be used.

## USING THE FINDINGS/GENERATING NEW QUESTIONS

The fifth and last part of the continuum involves use and the generation of new questions. In traditional agency focused evaluation practice, it has often been difficult to trace the use of evaluation findings. This is less true with legislative evaluation, where use can be measured in a number of ways. We have seen our own evaluations figure in program reauthorization. One example is our assessment of homeless and runaway youth centers which was a major factor in the doubling of the centers' reauthorization funds; another example is the change in the law—based on our findings about the situation of working mothers in the Aid to Families with Dependent Children (AFDC) program—that was enacted to allow a prolonged period of health insurance for earner families. Hearings are often organized around our findings. Examples are recent hearings on such issues as the Medicare Prospective Payment System, the defense industrial base, student aid, educational research, hazardous waste, poverty indicators, drinking age laws, and many others. Our findings and recommendations are incorporated in legislative direction to the executive branch. An example is our finding in the science and math teachers' study of the need for evaluation in the National Science Foundation (NSF) teacher-training programs, which NSF was then directed to perform by the Senate Appropriations Committee. We can measure the use of our findings in legislative debates that directly affect up-or-down congressional votes. Here I would cite our work on chemical warfare which, year after year, figured notably in the national argument about whether or not to produce binary chemical weapons. In legislative evaluation, use occurs—indeed, use is the rule, not the exception—and it is measurable.

We achieve a further use of evaluation findings through the synthesis method we have developed which brings together previous evaluations in a topic area, analyzes and compares them—reuses them—with the intent of developing a general finding about knowledge in that area. We engage in the same process of reuse in conducting the prospective evaluation synthesis.

The evaluator has the ability to influence successive rounds of policy questions that need to be asked but that, for one reason or another, may not be generated by policy actors. I see two types of questions that we must try to influence. The first type is descriptive: It is truly amazing how difficult it is to persuade policymakers of the importance of descriptive information. Our work on hazardous waste found that we simply do not know how many million metric tons of it are being generated every year in this country. Questions asking what is the size of a problem, how many people are involved in a program, what characteristics they have, what services they receive and how they feel about them, or, in a technological communications program, say, how many messages are sent, who sends them, and who receives them—these types of questions do not get asked in some agencies. As a result, more sophisticated questions about program benefits or effects cannot be adequately answered when Congress needs those answers.

A political factor contributing to the lack of strong program description is that, as Ernest W. Stromsdorfer noted, "the more political support there is for a program, the more limited will be the available systematic information on that program." Defense programs are a good example of this, and the fact that much of the information involved is classified, nonpublic information does not help. Rarely is there archiving of test and evaluation findings, even on a need-to-know basis; every effort to evaluate every weapon system has to start from scratch. Congress is beginning to look a little more carefully at the evaluative basis for moving into production with some weapon systems, so this may change.

On the other hand, relatively unpopular programs tend to produce more information and to be evaluated more often. Herman Leonard, in *Checks Unbalanced: The Quiet Side of Public Spending,* looks at some popular and unpopular programs and their ability to spend money without drawing attention to themselves. He points out, among other things, that social security has been able to commit over $100 billion annually for the last forty years without much discussion, while political controversy surrounds AFDC's budget of $10 billion or so. A large amount of systematic descriptive information is available on AFDC while a host of other more popular programs (such as defense and social security) have been largely able to avoid much public scrutiny.

The second type of question that is not asked much in executive agencies (it most definitely is asked in Congress) is the question of impact. Here the impediment remains twofold: the threat to decision makers and the paucity of incentives for accountability. Whereas, over the years, we have seen quite a few of these studies done in the executive branch despite the threat they unquestionably pose, over the past five years we have seen a marked reduction in results-oriented evaluations. Sometimes, the only way for these evaluations to be done in the executive branch is to have Congress mandate them, as has often happened in the past.

While it is true we have given up, for policy studies, some of our traditional freedom to choose programs and questions, leaving these now to emerge from the political arena, it is not clear that we would have been successful in any case in getting agency policymakers to ask many impact or descriptive questions. Where sponsored policy studies are concerned, the evaluator's freedom to ask certain questions may have always been more nominal than real. On the other hand, by noting the absence of answers to these questions in our findings and by recommending to Congress that these questions be asked, it is possible that we can get more attention paid to their importance the second time around.

**WHAT HAVE WE LEARNED?**

What have we learned about the politics of program evaluation? I can point to a number of lessons. First, we have learned that, to be successful, we must be useful to others, not ourselves. That means understanding the political system in which evaluation operates and understanding the information needs of those policy actors who are the users of evaluations.

We have also learned to conceptualize the political system a little more broadly, to include all sectors that make the kinds of policy decisions into which evaluation feeds—that is, not just executive but also legislative branch policymaking. Indeed, if the judicial branch continues to increase its use of cost-benefit and risk analysis, we will need to study and include the judiciary as well. Such study would certainly include evaluative ramifications on the kinds of evidence that need to be produced, and political ramifications of judicial use on decision making in the executive and legislative branches. This is important because evaluation's interactions with legislative and executive branch policy actors can be profoundly modified by the inclusion of a new set of policy actors from a different branch of government. Policy is never made in isolation: Legislative policy affects executive branch policy integrally, and the converse is equally true. Evaluators need to understand political interactions—no matter which branch they are working for.

We have learned that evaluators working for the legislative branch will be pressed to go beyond earlier horizons of social programs. The congressional functions require evaluative skills in such areas as defense; the environment; energy and natural resources; as well as, for example, in health, education, and welfare.

Planning for use involves understanding the political conditions under which evaluation findings will be used. We have learned that two of these conditions are that (1) the policy question posed must be of fundamental interest to the intended user, and (2) the eventual evaluation findings must answer that question. Both of these conditions empower the decision maker at the expense of a certain amount of the evaluators' discretion.

We have learned that a third political condition for use is credibility. If the evaluation is assailable on grounds of poor methodological quality or on grounds of partisanship, this will reduce the use made of its findings in Congress. The high quality and acknowledged objectivity of a study cannot ensure use if the policy question is not of interest; but poor quality and subjectivity will weaken use, no matter what the question is.

A fourth condition for use is timeliness. Evaluators working for the legislative branch must be concerned about the timing of the final product and how it dovetails with congressional policy cycles and plans for use. We have learned that what is most important sometimes is not having the best design, but having an adequate design that will bring the findings in at the time they were promised.

Overall, we have learned that there is no perfect evaluation design but that, rather, evaluators must try to achieve a balance involving timing, methodological strength, and cost. Often it is a matter of degree: A methodology that doubles the time necessary for performing an evaluation will be unacceptable no matter what its advantages. One which moderately increases the time while strengthening the conclusiveness of the information to be obtained may be enthusiastically accepted under some political circumstances.

Planning for use always incorporates the question, "who will implement the study recommendations?" We have learned that good relations with the implementing executive agency may be the sine qua non of that ultimate use.

Evaluators have not conducted many prospective studies. But we have learned that one of the most felicitous times for the introduction of evaluative thinking into the policy forum is before a new bill is proposed. New techniques need to be developed to enable the doing of this work on a very short time schedule.

Panels of experts can serve an important legitimizing function. We have learned that carefully chosen panels are a powerful aid in strengthening the political credibility of an evaluation's findings, especially when the study is of a controversial subject.

It is important for an evaluator to have mastered a wide variety of evaluation approaches. No single design or method can be counted on to address the diversity of policy questions that political debates engender.

The transition from policy question to evaluative question to evaluation design is not a straightforward process, and it usually involves several iterations. We have learned that, no matter how many negotiations there have been, it is wise to be sure the user agrees with the finished design and understands both how the study will be conducted and what kind of information will be available at its conclusion.

We have learned that indexing, referencing, and general checking of draft reports are activities that are worth their weight in gold: Although time is important, and all this checking does have to be planned for, there is enormous risk attached to any weakening of credibility.

Prioritization of the evaluation findings is also a condition for use. We have learned that telling all is tantamount to telling nothing. The important thing is to answer the policy question as clearly and simply as possible, to emphasize a few critical and striking numbers, and to do all that in such a way as to highlight those findings that give rise to policy action. Much time needs to be devoted to thinking out how we will present our findings so that they can be intelligible to our several audiences.

In the legislative branch, the use of evaluation findings is the rule, not the exception. In the past six years of working with Congress, we have learned that evaluations are a demonstrably important adjunct of policymaking, that they do figure in go/no go decisions, and that they often set the agenda for national debates.

A further use of evaluations can be achieved via studies employing metaanalysis or evaluation synthesis. Such secondary evaluation is a major tool in helping decision makers to make sense out of conflicting findings and to improve the quality of information available to them.

Descriptive questions are not typically raised by policymakers, which means that systematic information about some programs is often missing. We have learned that emphasizing in an evaluation report that such information is both missing and needed can help to get it provided at a later date.

Questions of impact seem to be asked less and less by executive branch agencies, more and more by legislative policymakers. We have learned that a legislative user can have strong leverage on programs, through the authorization and appropriations process or through oversight.

Finally, the fact of taking political processes into account when doing an evaluation transforms the way in which time is allocated. We have learned to devote much more time than we used to to negotiation, discussion, briefing, checking accuracy, prioritizing, and presentation.

I sum up all of these political lessons by saying that things have changed with respect to evaluation use. Beyond any doubt, the use in policymaking by Congress that we are seeing now is real, measurable, and growing dramatically. But if we are making progress, we owe a large debt of gratitude to those who cried failure in the past. They focused our attention on the political environment in which we expected our work to be useful but about which we knew little. This was important because use does not happen by itself. It requires some major modifications of traditional evaluation practice.

This is not to say that it is time to cry victory. We cannot do that until executive agencies realize there is growing risk in failing to evaluate their programs: If they do not, legislative agencies will. On the other hand, we have dispelled the notion that evaluation is not useful in policymaking. There is every reason to be hopeful about the future of evaluation research and practice, given the important role it is playing in improving the quality of information available to decision makers.

PART SIX

# Dilemmas of Practice

The field of human service delivery—and community organizations specifically—is full of conflicts, which occur at many levels, including the ideological. Some believe that the distribution of resources in a community (the *economic* "haves" vs. the "have nots") is the central conflict, which is essentially a "Marxian" perspective. Adherents feel very strongly that access to and control over resources is where action should be directed, and they are often among those pressing for a redistribution of those very resources (radically or not) and talking of pressing for economic justice.

Others believe that the distribution of power resources is most important (the *power* "haves" vs. the power "have nots"). Proponents of this approach often argue that, once an equality of influence is achieved, equality in other aspects will follow, since all inequalities stem from inequity of power. While some are certain of the rightness of their support of one or the other of these perspectives—economic or power—in the main they represent, for most community organization workers, a dilemma of practice.

On the one hand, there are some times and situations where economic power seems to be the key, where economic inequality is the most important problem to consider and rectify. On the other hand, there are also situations where inequalities of power seem to be the key, and their rectification the most important goal. The dilemma is ideological because at one level it is the dilemma of belief. What is right and how should one be guided? It is a practical dilemma as well, because beliefs often seek just actions. Should one pay more attention to the distribution of economic resources in a particular community or the distribution of political power? Sometimes these overlap, but often the economic and political centers are different.

These dilemmas are not the only ones that affect the community organization worker. Do the ends in a particular situation justify the means? This question applies to all professionals, but it has special meaning and is especially difficult when dealing with economic or political injustice. In an injustice situation, are illegitimate means permissible in order to make the situation right? And if one uses such illegitimate means, might one be, at least theoretically, on the same level as one's adversaries?

Community organization workers are also members of different groups having different interests, both in the local community and in the society at large. Sometimes, the agendas of a particular group are different from the particular beliefs or commitments that might be appropriate in a given situation, or that the worker personally feels. For example, on a religious ground, a Catholic social community organizer may feel pulled between the church's position on abortion and birth control and her or his own personal belief that "pro-choice" is the appropriate stance to take. Further, this issue may remain a personal one until the community erupts over a United Way allocation to a Planned Parenthood organization. At that point, some of the worker's co-religionists may invite him or her to join with them in opposing that allocation or even demand that he or she does so. Other co-professionals, however, may appeal to the worker on other grounds, and it is unlikely that any code of ethics will be helpful in this particular situation. Similarly, minority workers may have dual or multiple identifications as community members or members of a particular racial or ethnic group, and dilemmas of identification in action may flow from these commitments as well.

But dilemmas of practice stem not only from ideological or ethnic identifications. American culture has competing values at its very core. For example, we are taught to believe in and value achievement; getting ahead is an important goal. On the other hand, we also are committed to values of equality. Seymour Lipsit, in *The First New Nation,* analyzes the entire history of the United States as a playing out of the conflicts between values of achievement on the one hand and values of equality on the other. Similarly, we in this country value individualism, but we also value the community. Until they come up against each other, both values are perfectly reasonable; but there are times when they conflict.

Questions like these are among those addressed by the "Code of Ethics of the National Association of Social Workers," with comentary by Robert Cohen. When one has ethical dilemmas about what is right and wrong in practice, one can use this code as a point of reference. However, individuals may be members of several organizations having several codes of ethics, and sometimes these codes do not agree.

The pieces by Lew Rudolph ("Framework for Ethical Decision Making in Philanthropy") and Frank Loewenberg and Ralph Dolgoff ("Guides to Making Ethical Decisions") deal with dilemmas of decision making and provide specific guides for action.

The last two articles in this part deal with dilemmas relating to race and gender. Mylon Winn's piece on "Black Public Administrators" raises key questions about the opposing expectations that affect these professionals. Cheryl Hyde's treatment of the "Experiences of Women Activists" deals with the day-to-day perspectives of women in community organization.

—John E. Tropman

29.

# CODE OF ETHICS OF THE NATIONAL ASSOCIATION OF SOCIAL WORKERS; COMMENTARY

CONTENTS



## PREAMBLE

This code is intended to serve as a guide to the everyday conduct of members of the social work profession and as a basis for the adjudication of issues in ethics when the conduct of social workers is alleged to deviate from the standards expressed or implied in this code. It represents standards of ethical behavior for social workers in professional relationships with those served, with colleagues, with employers, with other individuals and professions, and with the community and society as a whole. It also embodies standards of ethical behavior governing individual conduct to the extent that such conduct is associated with an individual's status and identity as a social worker.

This code is based on the fundamental values of the social work profession that include the worth, dignity, and uniqueness of all persons as well as their rights and opportunities. It is also based on the nature of social work, which fosters conditions that promote these values.

In subscribing to and abiding by this code, the social worker is expected to view ethical responsibility in as inclusive a context as each situation demands and within which ethical judgement is required. The social worker is expected to take into consideration all the principles in this code that have a bearing upon any situation in which ethical judgement is to be exercised and professional intervention or conduct is planned. The course of action that the social worker chooses is expected to be consistent with the spirit as well as the letter of this code.

In itself, this code does not represent a set of rules that will prescribe all the behaviors of social workers in all the complexities of professional life. Rather, it of-

Reproduced by permission of the publisher and the author. Commentary by Robert H. Cohen is from the April, May, and June 1980 issues of the *NASW News*.

fers general principles to guide conduct, and the judicious appraisal of conduct, in situations that have ethical implications. It provides the basis for making judgements about ethical actions before and after they occur. Frequently, the particular situation determines the ethical principles that apply and the manner of their application. In such cases, not only the particular ethical principles are taken into immediate consideration, but also the entire code and its spirit. Specific applications of ethical principles must be judged within the context in which they are being considered. Ethical behavior in a given situation must satisfy not only the judgement of the individual social worker, but also the judgement of an unbiased jury of professional peers.

This code should not be used as an instrument to deprive any social worker of the opportunity or freedom to practice with complete professional integrity; nor should any disciplinary action be taken on the basis of this code without maximum provision for safeguarding the rights of the social worker affected.

The ethical behavior of social workers results not from edict, but from a personal commitment of the individual. This code is offered to affirm the will and zeal of all social workers to be ethical and to act ethically in all that they do as social workers.

The following codified ethical principles should guide social workers in the various roles and relationships and at the various levels of responsibility in which they function professionally. These principles also serve as a basis for the adjudication by the National Association of Social Workers of issues in ethics.

In subscribing to this code, social workers are required to cooperate in its implementation and abide by any disciplinary rulings based on it. They should also take adequate measures to discourage, prevent, expose, and correct the unethical conduct of colleagues. Finally, social workers should be equally ready to defend and assist colleagues unjustly charged with unethical conduct.

## SUMMARY OF MAJOR PRINCIPLES

### I. The Social Worker's Conduct and Comportment as a Social Worker

A. **Propriety.** The social worker should maintain high standards of personal conduct in the capacity or identity as social worker.

B. **Competence and Professional Development.** The social worker should strive to become and remain proficient in professional practice and the performance of professional functions.

C. **Service.** The social worker should regard as primary the service obligation of the social work profession.

D. **Integrity.** The social worker should act in accordance with the highest standards of professional integrity.

E. **Scholarship and Research.** The social worker engaged in study and research should be guided by the conventions of scholarly inquiry.

### II. The Social Worker's Ethical Responsibility to Clients

F. **Primacy of Clients' Interests.** The social worker's primary responsibility is to clients.

G. **Rights and Prerogatives of Clients.** The social worker should make every effort to foster maximum self-determination on the part of clients.

H. **Confidentiality and Privacy.** The social worker should respect the privacy of clients and hold in confidence all information obtained in the course of professional service.

I. **Fees.** When setting fees, the social worker should ensure that they are fair, reasonable, considerate, and commensurate with the service performed and with due regard for the clients' ability to pay.

### III. The Social Worker's Ethical Responsibility to Colleagues

J. **Respect, Fairness, and Courtesy.** The social worker should treat colleagues with respect, courtesy, fairness, and good faith.

K. **Dealing with Colleagues' Clients.** The social worker has the responsibility to relate to the clients of colleagues with full professional consideration.

### IV. The Social Worker's Ethical Responsibility to Employers and Employing Organizations

L. **Commitments to Employing Organizations.** The social worker should adhere to commitments made to the employing organizations.

### V. The Social Worker's Ethical Responsibility to the Social Work Profession

M. **Maintaining the Integrity of the Profession.** The social worker should uphold and advance the values, ethics, knowledge, and mission of the profession.

N. **Community Service.** The social worker should assist the profession in making social services available to the general public.

O. **Development of Knowledge.** The social worker should take responsibility for identifying, developing, and fully utilizing knowledge for professional practice.

### VI. The Social Worker's Ethical Responsibility to Society

P. **Promoting the General Welfare.** The social worker should promote the general welfare of society.

## THE NASW CODE OF ETHICS*

### I. The Social Worker's Conduct and Comportment as a Social Worker

**A. Propriety—The social worker should maintain high standards of personal conduct in the capacity or identity as social worker.**

1. The private conduct of the social worker is a personal matter to the same degree as is any other person's, except when such conduct compromises the fulfillment of professional responsibilities.
2. The social worker should not participate in, condone, or be associated with dishonesty, fraud, deceit, or misrepresentation.
3. The social worker should distinguish clearly between statements and actions made as a private individual and as a representative of the social work profession or an organization or group.

**B. Competence and Professional Development—The social worker should strive to become and remain proficient in professional practice and the performance of professional functions.**

---

*Code of Ethics as adopted by the 1979 NASW Delegate Assembly, effective July 1, 1980.

1. The social worker should accept responsibility or employment only on the basis of existing competence or the intention to acquire the necessary competence.

2. The social worker should not misrepresent professional qualifications, education, experience, or affiliations.

**C. Service—The social worker should regard as primary the service obligation of the social work profession.**

1. The social worker should retain ultimate responsibility for the quality and extent of the service that individual assumes, assigns, or performs.

2. The social worker should act to prevent practices that are inhumane or discriminatory against any person or group of persons.

**D. Integrity—The social worker should act in accordance with the highest standards of professional integrity and impartiality.**

1. The social worker should be alert to and resist the influences and pressures that interfere with the exercise of professional discretion and impartial judgement required for the performance of professional functions.

2. The social worker should not exploit professional relationships for personal gain.

**E. Scholarship and Research—The social worker engaged in study and research should be guided by the conventions of scholarly inquiry.**

1. The social worker engaged in research should consider carefully its possible consequences for human beings.

2. The social worker engaged in research should ascertain that the consent of participants in the research is voluntary and informed, without any implied deprivation or penalty for refusal to participate, and with due regard for participants' privacy and dignity.

3. The social worker engaged in research should protect participants from unwarranted physical or mental discomfort, distress, harm, danger, or deprivation.

4. The social worker who engages in the evaluation of services or cases should discuss them only for professional purposes and only with persons directly and professionally concerned with them.

5. Information obtained about participants in research should be treated as confidential.

6. The social worker should take credit only for work actually done in connection with scholarly and research endeavors and credit contributions made by others.

## II. The Social Worker's Ethical Responsibility to Clients

**F. Primacy of Clients' Interests—The social worker's primary responsibility is to clients.**

1. The social worker should serve clients with devotion, loyalty, determination, and the maximum application of professional skill and competence.

2. The social worker should not exploit relationships with clients for personal advantage, or solicit the clients of one's agency for private practice.

3. The social worker should not practice, condone, facilitate or collaborate with any form of discrimination on the basis of race, color, sex, sexual orientation, age, religion, national origin, marital status, political belief, mental or physical handicap, or

any other preference or personal characteristic, condition or status.

4. The social worker should avoid relationships or commitments that conflict with the interests of clients.

5. The social worker should under no circumstances engage in sexual activities with clients.

6. The social worker should provide clients with accurate and complete information regarding the extent and nature of the services available to them.

7. The social worker should apprise clients of their risks, rights, opportunities, and obligations associated with social service to them.

8. The social worker should seek advice and counsel of colleagues and supervisors whenever such consultation is in the best interest of clients.

9. The social worker should terminate service to clients, and professional relationships with them, when such service and relationships are no longer required or no longer serve the clients' needs or interests.

10. The social worker should withdraw services precipitously only under unusual circumstances, giving careful consideration to all factors in the situation and taking care to minimize possible adverse effects.

11. The social worker who anticipates the termination or interruption of service to clients should notify clients promptly and seek the transfer, referral, or continuation of service in relation to the clients' needs and preferences.

**G. Rights and Prerogatives of Clients—The social worker should make every effort to foster maximum self-determination on the part of clients.**

1. When the social worker must act on behalf of a client who has been adjudged legally incompetent, the social worker should safeguard the interests and rights of that client.

2. When another individual has been legally authorized to act in behalf of a client, the social worker should deal with that person always with the client's best interest in mind.

3. The social worker should not engage in any action that violates or diminishes the civil or legal rights of clients.

**H. Confidentiality and Privacy—The social worker should respect the privacy of clients and hold in confidence all information obtained in the course of professional service.**

1. The social worker should share with others confidences revealed by clients, without their consent, only for compelling professional reasons.

2. The social worker should inform clients fully about the limits of confidentiality in a given situation, the purposes for which information is obtained, and how it may be used.

3. The social worker should afford clients reasonable access to any official social work records concerning them.

4. When providing clients with access to records, the social worker should take due care to protect the confidences of others contained in those records.

5. The social worker should obtain informed consent of clients before taping, recording, or permitting third party observation of their activities.

**I. Fees—When setting fees, the social worker should ensure that they are fair, reasonable, considerate, and commensurate with the service performed**

**and with due regard for the clients' ability to pay.**

1. The social worker should not divide a fee or accept or give anything of value for receiving or making a referral.

## III. The Social Worker's Ethical Responsibility to Colleagues

### J. Respect, Fairness, and Courtesy—The social worker should treat colleagues with respect, courtesy, fairness, and good faith.

1. The social worker should cooperate with colleagues to promote professional interests and concerns.
2. The social worker should respect confidences shared by colleagues in the course of their professional relationships and transactions.
3. The social worker should create and maintain conditions of practice that facilitate ethical and competent professional performance by colleagues.
4. The social worker should treat with respect, and represent accurately and fairly, the qualifications, views, and findings of colleagues and use appropriate channels to express judgements on these matters.
5. The social worker who replaces or is replaced by a colleague in professional practice should act with consideration for the interest, character, and reputation of that colleague.
6. The social worker should not exploit a dispute between a colleague and employers to obtain a position or otherwise advance the social worker's interest.
7. The social worker should seek arbitration or mediation when conflicts with colleagues require resolution for compelling professional reasons.
8. The social worker should extend to colleagues of other professions the same respect and cooperation that is extended to social work colleagues.
9. The social worker who serves as an employer, supervisor, or mentor to colleagues should make orderly and explicit arrangements regarding the conditions of their continuing professional relationship.
10. The social worker who has the responsibility for employing and evaluating the performance of other staff members, should fulfill such responsibility in a fair, considerate, and equitable manner, on the basis of clearly enunciated criteria.
11. The social worker who has the responsibility for evaluating the performance of employees, supervisees, or students should share evaluations with them.

### K. Dealing with Colleagues' Clients—The social worker has the responsibility to relate to the clients of colleagues with full professional consideration.

1. The social worker should not solicit the clients of colleagues.
2. The social worker should not assume professional responsibility for the clients of another agency or a colleague without appropriate communication with that agency or colleague.
3. The social worker who serves the clients of colleagues, during a temporary absence or emergency, should serve those clients with the same consideration as that afforded any client.

## IV. The Social Worker's Ethical Responsibility to Employers and Employing Organizations

### L. Commitments to Employing Organization—The social worker should adhere to commitments made to the employing organization.

1. The social worker should work to improve the employing agency's policies and procedures, and the efficiency and effectiveness of its services.

2. The social worker should not accept employment or arrange student field placements in an organization which is currently under public sanction by NASW for violating personnel standards, or imposing limitations on or penalties for professional actions on behalf of clients.

3. The social worker should act to prevent and eliminate discrimination in the employing organization's work assignments and in its employment policies and practices.

4. The social worker should use with scrupulous regard, and only for the purpose for which they are intended, the resources of the employing organization.

## V. The Social Worker's Ethical Responsibility to the Social Work Profession

### M. Maintaining the Integrity of the Profession—The social worker should uphold and advance the values, ethics, knowledge, and mission of the profession.

1. The social worker should protect and enhance the dignity and integrity of the profession and should be responsible and vigorous in discussion and criticism of the profession.

2. The social worker should take action through appropriate channels against unethical conduct by any other member of the profession.

3. The social worker should act to prevent the unauthorized and unqualified practice of social work.

4. The social worker should make no misrepresentation in advertising as to qualifications, competence, service, or results to be achieved.

### N. Community Service—The social worker should assist the profession in making social services available to the general public.

1. The social worker should contribute time and professional expertise to activities that promote respect for the utility, the integrity, and the competence of the social work profession.

2. The social worker should support the formulation, development, enactment and implementation of social policies of concern to the profession.

### O. Development of Knowledge—The social worker should take responsibility for identifying, developing, and fully utilizing knowledge for professional practice.

1. The social worker should base practice upon recognized knowledge relevant to social work.

2. The social worker should critically examine, and keep current with emerging knowledge relevant to social work.

3. The social worker should contribute to the knowledge base of social work and share research knowledge and practice wisdom with colleagues.

## VI. The Social Worker's Ethical Responsibility to Society

### P. Promoting the General Welfare—The social worker should promote the general welfare of society.

1. The social worker should act to prevent and eliminate discrimination against any person or group on the basis of race,

color, sex, sexual orientation, age, religion, national origin, marital status, political belief, mental or physical handicap, or any other preference or personal characteristic, condition, or status.

2. The social worker should act to ensure that all persons have access to the resources, services, and opportunities which they require.

3. The social worker should act to expand choice and opportunity for all persons, with special regard for disadvantaged or oppressed groups and persons.

4. The social worker should promote conditions that encourage respect for the diversity of cultures which constitute American society.

5. The social worker should provide appropriate professional services in public emergencies.

6. The social worker should advocate changes in policy and legislation to improve social conditions and to promote social justice.

7. The social worker should encourage informed participation by the public in shaping social policies and institutions.

## A COMMENTARY

With the adoption of a revised Code of Ethics, NASW's Delegate Assembly took a noteworthy step in the continuing process of developing and extending standards for the social work profession.

Five years after the formation of NASW, the Delegate Assembly in 1960 adopted the association's first Code of Ethics. A principle enjoining discrimination was added in 1967, following which the code remained unaltered for more than a decade. During this period, however, a number of forces militated for revision, including:

- Changes in the profession, including growth in number of independent practitioners; new fields of practice; legal regulation; and expansion of the profession in diversity and size.
- The social and civil rights movements of the 60s and 70s and recognition of "the dissonance which may occur between professional values, agency imperatives and consumer demands."
- Shortcomings in the 1960/67 version, which failed to adequately address the issues such as confidentiality, personal behavior, research, fees, advertising, accountability, collegial obligations, advocacy, and others.
- Difficulties experienced by chapter and national committees on inquiry in adjudicating ethical issues.

In 1975, a task force was authorized and charged with recommending revisions in the NASW Code of Ethics and presenting them to the 1977 Delegate Assembly.

The task force noted that, although the language of the code needed updating, other areas demanded greater attention. For example, it recommended:

- A comprehensive study of all past complaints of unethical behavior which have come before the Committee on Inquiry.
- Establishment of a clearinghouse to act as an ongoing resource to the association, its units and its members in considering ethical questions.
- Development of a chapter action guide to promote action at the state and local levels.
- Appointment of a task force to initiate, direct, and review the above processes, and allocation of sufficient staff and other resources to support its work.

Although the 1977 Delegate Assembly did not adopt the specific proposals of the task force, it recognized its contribution toward code revision and authorized creation of a successor task force to continue the work and report back to the 1979 Delegate Assembly.

In October 1977, a seven-member task force was appointed by President Arthur Katz. Katz wanted to muster "an experienced, scholarly group that would be diverse, representative, and closely enough linked to other parts of the organizational structure to ensure continuity and relevance to association problems and needs."

The task force, led by Charles S. Levy, began by delineating the scope of its efforts and determining to develop a revised code which could serve both as a guide to ethical practice and to the adjudication of ethical issues. The focus was to be on the ethical conduct of social workers in their various roles, responsibilities, and professional relationships. Such considerations as implementation, education, and enforcement—as important as these were regarded to be—would not be addressed, but would be left for subsequent consideration and action by others in the NASW leadership structure.

From the outset, attempts were made to involve members and chapter committees in the process of code construction, via the *NASW NEWS* and via direct invitations by task force members and staff. The experience of several other professional organizations, e.g., American Psychological Association, International Federation of Social Workers, American Bar Association, was also taken into consideration.

Approximately three dozen ethical codes of other professions and organizations were identified and subjected to computer-aided scrutiny. Members of the task force identified principles which appeared to have relevance for social workers and grouped these under categories of ethical obligations owed by the social worker (e.g., to clients, colleagues, society, etc.). Data from all of the codes analyzed were fed into a computer and aggregated by category. Eventually, nonrelevant items were discarded (or moved to a more appropriate category); duplicative principles were deleted and only one or two of the best formulated ones retained.

A number of criteria guided task force deliberations. Included were the following:

- Ethical principles should be formulated at a level of generality/specificity which would be sufficiently inclusive and precise to provide guidance (to practitioners and adjudicating bodies), yet not attempt to cover every situation and variation thereof.
- The proposed code should not attempt to sort out "inspirational" principles from adjudicatory ones, but should include a mixture of proscribed and preferred behaviors. (This approach was in line with the dual purpose to be served; i.e., as a guide, as well as a basis for adjudication).
- The code should not attempt to formulate principles in a hierarchical arrangement, but should recognize that principles may, and often do, conflict with one another although each may be valid. As stated in the preamble to the proposed code: "Frequently the particular situation determines the ethical principles that apply and the manner of their application. In such cases, not only the particular ethical principles are taken into immediate consideration, but also the entire code and its spirit...."

The code should not be a credo; it should attempt insofar as possible to state principles affirmatively rather than as proscriptions. Sexist language, pejorative terms, and jargon should be avoided. Principles should be stated as a series of single declarative sentences and as clearly and concisely as possible.

## SECTION I. THE SOCIAL WORKER'S CONDUCT AND COMPORTMENT AS A SOCIAL WORKER

### Principle A.1:

**The private conduct of the social worker is a personal matter to the same degree as is any other person's except when such conduct compromises the fulfillment of professional responsibilities.**

*Discussion.* One viewpoint on private behavior is that, regardless of its nature, it should be considered entirely beyond the reach or coverage of an ethics code—"We shouldn't get into the question of personal conduct or morality."

An opposing view holds that certain behaviors might be so antiethical to social work values (e.g., financial contributions to the Ku Klux Klan), or might reflect such "moral turpitude" that, as professionals, we would be obliged to take action against the member.

In its resolution of these views, the task force agreed that the private or personal behavior of a social worker should be regarded as exactly that (i.e., not subject to the code), except insofar as such conduct might impinge on fulfillment of professional responsibilities. In a situation in which a member would be charged with breach of ethics stemming from private conduct, the critical question would be whether this interfered with carrying out professional responsibility. A jury of peers would have to decide that question, based on the facts of the particular situation.

### Principle B.1:

**The social worker should accept responsibility or employment only on the basis of existing competence or the intention to acquire the necessary competence.**

*Discussion.* Is it unethical per se to assume professional responsibilities or employment for which one is not equipped by training and experience?

For some, this issue goes to the heart of efforts to establish, promulgate, and enforce standards of professional competence and to provide assurance to clients and to the public that the quality of services offered can be relied upon and is commensurate with the task to be performed.

Although none of the task force members disagreed with the vital importance of promoting high standards of professional competence, others contended that the code must provide for those who aspire to more complex and professionally demanding roles; those still in training, in transition, etc. If the principles governing competence and professional development were formulated too stringently, aspirations might be inhibited and professional mobility impaired.

The resulting formulation of the task force attempts to combine the theme of responsibility for one's own undertakings and competency with recognition that latitude must be afforded to those who reach beyond their present capabilities, so long as they intend to acquire the requisite competence.

### Principle B.2:

**The social worker should not misrepresent professional qualifications, education, experience or affiliations.**

*Discussion.* This provision (along with another later in the code, V. M. 4.) addresses, in part, the issue of "advertising." V. M. 4. emphasizes the product—"The social worker should make no misrepresentations in advertising as to qualifications, competence, service or results to be achieved." I.B.2. deals solely with the person. The way in which the individual holds her/himself out, the accuracy of representation regarding qualifications, background and affiliations, is key here. Advertising, personal or otherwise, thus, is not defined as "good" or "bad," permissible or proscribed. The emphasis is on candor in presenting one's professional credentials properly, and in representing the nature, expectations and limitations of the service to be rendered.

### Principle E:

**Scholarship and Research. The social worker engaged in study and research should be guided by the conventions of scholarly inquiry.**

*Discussion.* Section 1.E., Scholarship and Research, is entirely new and was developed in response to the need of many social workers, especially researchers, academicians and evaluators, who were troubled by the absence of ethical guidelines in an area of practice often affecting the most vulnerable groups.

Although several of the principles set forth in I.E. might have been inferred from provisions in the old code, new concepts were introduced and others that before were implicit at best, have now been spelled out. The whole area of protection of human subjects—brought bluntly to our attention in recent years by revelations of disregard of basic human rights and callous use of unwitting individuals under the banner of scientific research—is addressed. The concept of informed consent and the emphasis on respect for privacy, which extends beyond merely "the people I serve" of the old code, also characterize section E.1.

## SECTION II. THE SOCIAL WORKER'S ETHICAL RESPONSIBILITY TO CLIENTS

### Principle F.3:

**The social worker should not practice, condone, facilitate or collaborate with any form of discrimination on the basis of race, color, sex, sexual orientation, age, religion, national origin, marital status, political belief, mental or physical handicap, or any other preference or personal characteristic, condition or status.**

*Discussion.* This principle, although similar to that contained in the old code, is more extensive in terms both of the nature of the social worker's obligation and the specific bases of proscribed discrimination. Practicing, facilitating or collaborating with *any form of discrimination,* is prohibited. Moreover, in addition to "race, color, religion, age, sex, or national ancestry" (the new code uses the term "national *origin*"), the revised code specifies "sexual orientation," "marital status," "political belief," "mental or physical handicap," or "any other preference or personal characteristic, condition or status."

The singular importance accorded to nondiscrimination in the new code is reflected by the reiteration of the principle later, in VI. P. 1., wherein the social worker is called upon, not merely to refrain from "practicing, condoning" discrimination against clients, but also to "act to prevent and eliminate discrimination against any person or group…"

**Principle F.5:**

**The social worker should under no circumstances engage in sexual activities with clients.**

*Discussion.* Members of the task force were in agreement that the issue of indulging in sex with clients needed to be addressed. Great damage has been done to clients who have been exploited by trusted physicians, therapists and other "helping" persons, and to the professions (especially in the mental health field) which have seen public confidence in their motives, competence, and integrity steadily eroded.

Thus the task force deliberately used the strongest language of absolute prohibition, "under no circumstances," found any place in the code. However, it was recognized that that which is to be prohibited is not easy to define. Certainly sexual intercourse is intended. But is that all? If the Principle referred to "sexual intercourse," rather than "sexual activities," it might be inferred that other sexual acts might be permissible. An attempt to list proscribed sexual behavior between social workers and clients would be unwieldy, as well as ludicrous.

In using the general term "sexual activities," the task force was aware of its imprecision. Might not a reassuring hug, a pat on the arm, holding a youngster on one's lap, kissing a child, etc., be viewed by some as a "sexual activity"? The task force concluded that the principle as stated would provide guidance where, in essence, there had been none, and that if a situation were brought to adjudication, a jury of peers would be able to determine whether the alleged "sexual activities" were of the sort covered by the prohibition.

**Principle H.1:**

**The social worker should share with others confidences revealed by clients, without their consent, only for compelling professional reasons.**

*Discussion.* If a client refuses to grant permission to the social worker to share confidential communications with others, should this constitute an absolute bar to disclosure by that worker? Some say that confidentiality within the professional helping relationship is of such transcendent importance that it should never be breached without the client's express consent. Others argue that a host of factors—ranging from the need for "case consultation" to the fear of being held legally liable for failure to disclose certain information (e.g., client's suicidal/homicidal tendencies)—militate against the "purist" approach. They contend that allowance for professional discretion should be made.

The formulation hammered out by task force members and delegates at the 1979 Delegate Assembly stresses the general principle—no disclosure without client consent—but allows for some latitude, i.e., "*compelling* (emphasis supplied) professional reasons."

The burden is placed on the worker to justify any breach of confidentiality. The mere assertion that a violation was warranted based on professional judgment would not suffice. The reason must indeed be compelling.

## SECTION III. THE SOCIAL WORKER'S ETHICAL RESPONSIBILITY TO COLLEAGUES

Members of the task force struggled to capture the essence of the ethical obligation owed one's colleagues. "Respect," "courtesy," "fairness," and "good faith" imply a good number of behaviors ranging from regard for social amenities and conventions to more formal notions of fair play, procedural clarity and orderliness. Notions of candor, consideration, and tolerance are also at the heart of the social worker's ethical responsibility to colleagues.

Several of the specific principles adopted extend well beyond the single tenet in the old code, i.e., "I treat with respect the findings, views and actions of colleagues and use appropriate channels to express judgment on these matters." For example, the concept of confidentiality is viewed in a broader context. The revised code requires that the worker "respect confidences shared by colleagues in the course of their professional relationships and transactions." Clearly this goes beyond merely, "treating with respect the findings, views and actions of colleagues." It carries into the sphere of collegial relationships the regard for privacy/confidentiality contained in the old code: "I respect the privacy of the people I serve." The new code also makes explicit the obligation to extend "to colleagues of other professions the same respect and cooperation" that one is expected to extend to social work colleagues.

Another concept not included in the old code is one which proscribes exploitation of a dispute between a colleague and employer for personal advantage. In part, this principle speaks to troublesome issues which sometime emerge as by-products of labor-management controversies, e.g., "scabbing." The use of the term "exploit" was carefully selected by the task force to provide guidance in the case of a colleague-employer dispute in which employment, promotion or other opportunity may arise. The mere fact that one may directly or indirectly derive some gain as a result of a colleague's misfortune, is not unethical per se. The element of *exploitation* must be present.

Finally, a basic component of sound practice/supervision/administration is reflected in the principle which calls for the worker to share evaluations with those evaluated or supervised. The notion of mutuality and openness with colleagues parallels that incorporated in the "client" section of the code: "The social worker should afford clients reasonable access to any official social work records concerning them."

## SECTION IV. THE SOCIAL WORKER'S ETHICAL RESPONSIBILITY TO EMPLOYERS AND EMPLOYING ORGANIZATIONS

The issue of "loyalty" to one's employing organization was particularly vexing. The frequency with which advocacy responsibilities, obligations to clients, and duties owed to colleagues conflict with agency practice or policy was noted.

One view presented was that social workers should avoid bureaucratic adherence to organizational rules and policies whenever these conflict with other professional obligations and values. "Loyalty" to one's employer too often provides a convenient excuse for failure to act, i.e., to "blow the whistle," to "go public," to confront. Social workers are obliged to be agents of change.

One could also argue that the concept of "loyalty" is not a mere abstraction but a basic value upon which trust, mutuality and joint efforts must rest. If one differs so strongly with an agency's policy, practices, and expectations, one should not work there in the first place. Accepting employment and the conditions thereof while harboring serious mental reservations about abiding by them could be viewed as disingenuous if not downright dishonest.

The task force sought to make a distinction between pre-employment knowledge and understandings ("commitments") and subsequent situations. In the first instance, the social worker should be bound by promises, agreements, and prior understandings. This is a matter of basic integrity and presents a different issue from situations which subsequently arise when agency policy, practices and conditions change.

## SECTION V. THE SOCIAL WORKER'S ETHICAL RESPONSIBILITY TO THE SOCIAL WORK PROFESSION

The social worker's ethical responsibility to the profession is made more explicit in the revised code. While the old code, for example, imposed an obligation "to *help* (our emphasis) protect the community against unethical practice by any individuals or organizations engaged in social welfare activities," the new code calls upon the social worker to "take *action* through appropriate channels against unethical conduct..." The worker is also expected to "*act* to prevent the unauthorized and unqualified practice of social work."

## SECTION VI. THE SOCIAL WORKER'S ETHICAL RESPONSIBILITY TO SOCIETY

The principles contained in this section, taken as a whole, are the broadest and the least susceptible to adjudication of any in the code. But despite their almost purely "inspirational" quality, they are vitally important to the total integrity of the code and to our professional posture.

Indeed, the principles included in Section VI are unique reflections of our values, our heritage and our obligations as a profession. The duties to "act to prevent and eliminate discrimination"; "to ensure that all persons have access to the resources, services, and opportunities which they require"; "to expand choice and opportunity for all persons {especially} disadvantaged or oppressed groups and persons"; "to promote conditions that encourage respect for...diversity of cultures"; "to advocate changes in policy and legislation to improve social conditions and to promote social justice"; and to "encourage informed participation by the public," are lofty principles toward which we set our sights as a profession. They are the essence of our social conscience and the most direct expression of the underlying values upon which our ethical code is grounded.

30.

**Lewis C. Rudolph**

# FRAMEWORK FOR ETHICAL DECISION MAKING IN PHILANTHROPY: A MATRIX OF RELATIONSHIPS

## USER'S GUIDE

This ethical framework is for students, professionals, and volunteers in the nonprofit human services field. As an outline, it can help to identify the major types of ethical dilemmas encountered in philanthropy—from fund raising and fund distribution to service delivery. As an organizational development tool, this list of questions may be used by students, professionals, and volunteers to stimulate ethical discussions and decision making about common practices. Used as an assessment instrument, it is a conceptual mirror to reflect upon standard operating procedures and policies in an ethical context.

I. Introduction
   A. Definition of "Ethical Framework"
      1. A conceptual starting point for thinking about choices in relation to commonly accepted moral principles such as:
         a. truthfulness
         b. fairness
         c. equality
         d. accountability
         e. nondiscrimination
         f. autonomy
         g. confidentiality
         h. justice
      2. A map for identifying issues that may create or bury conflicts
      3. A checklist to clarify and to promote ethical decision making
   B. Definitions of "Philanthropy"
      1. From the Greek root, *philanthropia,* "love to mankind"[1]
      2. "Dispensing or receiving aid from funds set aside for humanitarian purposes"[2]

II. A Matrix of Relationships
   A. Philanthropic organizations
   B. Contributors
   C. Service agencies
   D. Service recipients
   E. Professionals
   F. Volunteers

III. Gauging the Relationship Between Ends and Means
   A. To what extent does the "mission" of the organization clarify and define specific end results?
   B. To what degree does the organization document the need for contributing public dollars to the specific end results embodied in the mission?
   C. By what means does the organization raise money from the public?
   D. By what means does the organization distribute money?
   E. To what degree does the organization evaluate and communicate how the results of fund raising and distribution relate to the ultimate ends of the mission?

Lewis C. Rudolph is executive director of United Way of Androscoggin County, Lewiston, Maine.

IV. Towards What Ends Are Funds Raised?
   A. How are these ends identified?
   B. Is a formal needs assessment conducted?
   C. Were problems and services identified by:
      1. A survey of the general population?
      2. Key informant interviews?
      3. Clients/recipients of services?
      4. Quantifiable social indicators and other demographics?
   D. How is sampling error controlled?
   E. How is bias factored in or out of data collection and interpretation?
   F. How reliable are the data?
   G. How valid are the data?
V. By What Means Are Funds Raised?
   A. To what extent does the organization communicate honestly to contributors about how funds will be utilized?
   B. To what degree does the organization disclose to contributors its total financial picture?
      1. What is the percentage of administrative overhead and how is this calculated?
      2. What is the percentage that goes to direct services and how is this calculated?
      3. To what degree are the salaries of professionals (especially the chief professional officer and other top officials) excessive?
         a. How do they compare with salaries of professionals in other similar organizations with comparable budgets?
         b. Are they in line with community expectations?
      4. Is there full disclosure of all assets and liabilities, compiled by an independent certified public accountant?
      5. Is there full disclosure of all spin-off corporations, complete with an identification of their respective profit or not-for-profit status?
         a. What is the relationship between the spin-off organizations and the ends of the philanthropic organization?
         b. On what basis is any profit status justified?
         c. To what extent are all inter-business transactions disclosed?
   C. To what degree are the morals and values of contributors compromised and/or violated by fund raising methods?
      1. To what degree are contributors allowed the freedom to contribute or not to contribute?
         a. What is the range of choice available to contributors at the time of solicitation?
         b. To what degree does spoken or written communication involve coercion, deception, and/or violations of privacy?
      2. To what extent does the fund raising method place contributors at risk of violating the law or other acceptable codes of conduct?
      3. To what extent are contributors informed as to how their donations will be utilized?
   D. To what extent do contributors utilize illegal or immoral methods to make money for charitable donations?
      1. On what basis ought a philanthropic organization accept or refuse these funds?
      2. If a contributing organization

or individual makes money in a business whose aims or byproducts are contrary to the philanthropic organization's, on what basis should the donation be accepted or rejected?

E. To what extent ought a philanthropic organization allow itself to be utilized by another individual or corporate entity to promote or enhance public image?

F. If service recipients are featured in promotional appeals, to what degree do they freely choose to be involved?
   1. What is the extent of involvement by direct-service professionals to ensure that only appropriate clients are invited to take part?
   2. If minors or mentally impaired adults take part, do parents or guardians sign consent forms?
   3. To what degree are the rules of confidentiality applied or violated?
   4. Is the decision to publicly acknowledge clients therapeutically sound?

VI. On What Basis Are Funds Distributed?

A. How does the pattern of distribution conform to the defined ends of the philanthropic organization?
   1. How does it correspond to the goals and expectations of the contributors?
   2. How does it correspond to documented needs?

B. To what extent are distribution outcomes influenced by the perceived impacts on future fund raising?
   1. To what degree are relationships with major contributors factored into the process?
   2. To what extent are historical relationships with service agencies factored into the process?

C. To what degree is controversy over certain issues avoided in the decision-making process?
   1. On what basis is this practice justified?
   2. Does avoiding the conflict serve a greater good?
   3. Would facing the conflict serve a greater good?

D. How representative of the total community are the groups of contributors, staff, and volunteers who are responsible for fund distribution, with regard to:
   1. Age?
   2. Race and ethnicity?
   3. Gender/sexual preference?
   4. Occupation/retirement status?
   5. Geography?
   6. Income?
   7. Disability?
   8. Education?

E. To what extent are there conflicts of interest, both legal and perceived?
   1. Is someone involved in fund distribution benefitting directly or indirectly from the decision making?
   2. Is there a familial relationship entwined in the distribution process that could constitute nepotism?

F. If two or more agencies are competing for funds, is the decision-making process conducted fairly?
   1. Are funding guidelines and criteria communicated to competing agencies in advance of the decision-making process?

2. Are those guidelines and criteria applied consistently by fund distribution staff and volunteers?

VII. How Are Philanthropic Funds Utilized By Service Organizations?

A. To what extent do service agencies expend funds in a manner consistent with the purposes for which they were allocated?
1. Is funding restricted or unrestricted?
2. Is funding for core administrative support or support program funding?
3. Are there donor designations?
4. Are there board restrictions?
5. What does an audit analysis show?

B. What is the manner by which service agencies determine eligibility for programs subsidized by philanthropic funds?
1. To what degree are individuals subsidized who could afford to pay the full cost of services? Is a means test applied?
2. To what extent does the application of eligibility standards stigmatize or limit access to services for those who are unable to pay the full cost?
3. To what extent are the elgibility standards discriminatory in terms of age, gender, sexual preference, race, religion, or nationality?
4. Beyond any legal implications in a particular form of discrimination, how appropriate or inappropriate are these eligibility standards with respect to a particular field of service and/or population served? On what basis is discrimination justified?

C. To what degree does the service agency ensure an accurate accounting of the number of people served and/or units of service provided?

VIII. To What Extent Ought Service Agencies Be Entitled to Receive Funding From Philanthropic Sources?

A. To what degree is there full disclosure of all available assets and liabilities, including but not limited to audited financial statements from the service agency, as well as real estate and holding companies with which it conducts substantial business activities?
1. Is the agency managing its resources efficiently and effectively to justify a request from philanthropic sources?
2. Does the agency have access to other assets that it chooses not to utilize for the programs it wishes to run? On what basis is this justified?

B. How does the ratio of total dollars received from public sources to individuals served compare with ratios from other similar organizations in the community, for a particular field of service?
1. If there is an inequity, what is the justification for continuing this practice? On what basis ought the practice change?
2. To what degree is there funding parity for similar programs that serve different genders, races, religions, and/or nationalities in the community? What is the basis for justifying any disparity?

C. Is the agency pricing its services at a level appropriate for the local marketplace?

1. Does it charge full cost to those who can afford it?
2. If not, what is the justification for not doing so?

D. To what degree does a service agency demonstrate excessive profitability, beyond the limits of merely sound management? If so, on what basis ought it receive funds from a philanthropic organization?

E. To what degree does the content of an agency's programs provoke significant controversy within the community, sufficient enough that establishing or continuing a funding relationship may endanger the funding base of the philanthropic organization?
1. What would justify defunding or not funding such an organization?
2. On what basis ought the philanthropic organization go ahead and risk the loss of future dollars that might have been otherwise available to fund other services?

F. To what degree do a service agency's programs promote self-sufficiency or dependency, with respect to clients?

G. To what extent do the programs offered by the service agency constitute a duplication of effort, with respect to similar programs in the community serving the same populations?

H. To what degree is the service agency able to substantiate claims of a program's effectiveness in treating and/or preventing particular problems?

IX. Conclusions

A. The concept of philanthropy is consonant with ethical decision making.
1. In what ways does Immanuel Kant's practical imperative, "Act so as to treat man, in your own person as well as in that of anyone else, always as an end, never merely as a means,"[3] apply to a given issue?
2. Does John Stuart Mill's greatest happiness principle apply: "...actions are right in proportion as they tend to promote happiness, wrong as they tend to produce the reverse of happiness?"[4]
3. Are individual benefits subsumed by organizational needs?
4. Are ends differentiated from means?
5. Do professionals and volunteers recognize value-based decisions?
6. Is the organization able to make difficult choices among competing values?

B. Intensified competition for scarce resources will create more ethical dilemmas for philanthropy.
1. Professionals and volunteers need to become more fluent in ethical decision making.
2. Ethical decision making should be positioned as a key element of quality performance.
3. There is a need for accelerated organizational education in how ethical decision making applies to the following philanthropic activities:
   a. Defining missions
   b. Assessing needs
   c. Raising funds
   d. Distributing funds

e. Contributing funds
f. Utilizing funds
g. Accounting for funds
h. Providing services
i. Receiving services
j. Evaluating programs
k. Setting salaries

## NOTES

1. *Oxford English Dictionary,* 1971.
2. *Webster's Ninth New Collegiate Dictionary,* 1989.
3. Friedrich, Carl J. (ed.), *The Philosophy of Kant: Immanuel Kant's Moral and Political Writings* (New York: The Modern Library, 1949), p. 178.
4. Burtt, Edwin A. (ed.), *The English Philosophers from Bacon to Mill* (New York: The Modern Library, 1939), p. 900.

**31.**

**Frank Loewenberg and Ralph Dolgoff**

# GUIDES TO MAKING ETHICAL DECISIONS

Social workers must learn how to analyze both the problem situation and their own relation to it. [Previously] we examined various ethical issues that social workers face in their practice. In this chapter we will present a number of ideas which have aided social workers in their search for procedures that will aid them in making more effective ethical decisions. Philosophers have argued for centuries whether there is one and only one correct ethical decision for any given situation. Certainly, at the present time, we do not have enough knowledge to identify one and only one correct ethical decision for every professional practice situation. However, we do have considerable knowledge about the correct *way* for reaching ethical decisions.

## HOW *NOT* TO MAKE ETHICAL DECISIONS

There are a number of decision-making patterns that are not relevant for ethical decision making. Among these are:

### Personal Preferences

The decision to choose a pencil rather than a pen for writing a case record does not involve a question of ethics. Writing with pen or pencil is a question of personal preference. My choosing a pencil does not indicate that I think another worker's choice of a pen is unethical. However, if I choose to do nothing while my client commits suicide, another worker might be justified to consider my behavior unethical.

Frank Loewenberg is a professor emeritus at Bar Ilan University in Israel; Ralph Dolgoff is a professor at the University of Maryland at Baltimore.

### Feelings

Feelings are important and influence behavioral choices. However, having a strong feeling does not make something ethical. I may feel like having sex with a client, but does this make it an ethical professional behavior?

### Statistics

If most social workers think that something is right, does that make it ethical? If most social workers in your agency use sick leave for vacation purposes, does that make it ethical behavior? There may be strength in numbers, but statistics do not always reveal what is ethical.

## DECISION-MAKING MODEL

Decision making in social work practice takes place within a value context. Professional ethics are based on "the fundamental values of the social work profession that include the worth, dignity, and uniqueness of all persons as well as their rights and opportunities...(to) conditions that promote these values" (NASW Code of Ethics, Preamble). Essentially, the social work value system reflects a democratic ethic that provides for individual and group fulfillment and for respect of individuals and their differences, while at the same time recognizing the need for mutual aid and societal supports so that all persons can attain their maximum potential. Finding the proper balance between the opportunities and responsibilities of the individual and those of the community is a challenge that is not unique to social work. But within this balance, ethical decisions clearly follow a democratic ethos.

The subject of ethical decision making is far too complex to permit the development of a simple "how to" problem-solving model. Yet some model is necessary if we are to understand what decision making is all about. Making decisions is seldom a split-second act. Typically it is a process or series of thoughts and activities that occur over time and that result in a person or group acting (or not acting) in a particular manner. Every decision is approached step by step, so that one moves gradually through a series of stages until, at the end of the process, one makes "the" decision. To think that only one person, the decision maker, participates in this process is erroneous. Many different persons present information, react to assessments, introduce additional options, or make changes in the environment, which in turn change the nature of the decision or of the data on which the decision is based.

In real life it is almost impossible to identify any one discrete decision. Decision making is like an ever-continuing network or decision tree. Choices are influenced by previous decisions, which in turn lead to new directions. A simpler model of decision making may help social workers understand what is involved in ethical decision making. Such a model, like all models in science, will simplify reality by focusing on only one decision. A model is a permissible didactic device as long as it is understood that in real life every decision is preceded and followed by other decisions, many of which have a direct bearing on the matter under consideration. In Figure 31.1, we present one such general model for decision making.

The model of the decision-making process presented in Figure 31.1 is a general model applicable to many situations and is not necessarily limited to ethical decisions. In Figure 31.2 is a series of questions

FIGURE 31.1
General Model of Decision-Making Process

STEP 1
Identify the problem and the factors that contribute to its maintenance.

STEP 2
Identify the persons and institutions involved in this problem, such as clients, victims, support systems, other professionals, and others.

STEP 3
Identify the values relevant to this problem, held by the several participants identified in Step 2, including societal values, professional values, worker's personal values, and others.

STEP 4
Identify the goals and objectives whose attainment is believed to resolve (or at least reduce) the problem.

STEP 5
Identify alternate intervention strategies and targets.

STEP 6
Assess the effectiveness and efficiency of each alternate in terms of identified goals.

STEP 7
Determine who should be involved in decision making.

STEP 8
Select the most appropriate alternative strategy.

STEP 9
Implement the selected strategy.

STEP 10
Monitor the implementation, paying particular attention to unanticipated consequences.

STEP 11
Evaluate the results and identify additional problems.

FIGURE 31.2
The Ethical Aspects of Decision Making

For each step the social worker should consider the following:

A. What are the ethical issues involved? What are the principles, rights, and obligations that have an impact on the ethical question?

B. What additional information is needed to properly identify the ethical implications?

C. What are the relevant ethical rules that can be applied? Which ethical criteria are relevant in this situation?

D. If there is a conflict of interest, who should be the principal beneficiary?

E. How would you rank-order the ethical issues and ethical rules you have identified?

F. What are the possible consequences that result from utilizing different ethical rules?

G. When is it justified to shift the ethical decision obligations to another person (not the social worker)? To whom should it be shifted in this case?

that can help social workers further clarify and integrate the ethical aspects of their decision making in social work practice.

An ethical aspect is part and parcel of every step. This model is based on the assumption that social workers can plan rationally what is needed for intervention in human situations and that they want to minimize the irrational, impulsive, and the unplanned consequences of purposeful actions.

Several of the steps of the decision-making model, especially those that deal specifically with the ethical aspects of decision making, deserve further consideration and will now be discussed in greater detail.

## Clarifying Societal Values

Societal values usually, but not always, provide guidelines for professional ethical behavior. But there may be situations when a social worker is justified, even obligated, to act in ways that are contrary to societal norms. However, in every instance the worker has an obligation to clarify the relevant societal values. Radical changes in societal values have occurred within the lifetime of many social workers. Values that our parents or grandparents considered sacred have been swept away or have been altered so much that they are no longer recognizable. Though changes in values around life-styles and sexual mores gain headline attention, the most fundamental changes have taken place with respect to inequality and equality. Not too long ago it was self-understood that all people were not equal. An aged person did not enjoy the same rights as a working person. Women were considered inferior to men. Whites were thought to be better than everybody else. These views were held openly, even by the "best" people in society. Public policy was designed to reflect and support these values. It does not require any lengthy discussion here to point out that major changes have occurred with respect to these values. While racism, sexism, and ageism still exist in our society, these are no longer accorded the general respect and wide recognition that they once enjoyed.

The equality value is not the only value that has changed dramatically in our lifetime. Similar changes can be observed with respect to many other values. To the extent that ethical behavior in general reflects what society values, a social worker must have accurate knowledge of the current societal value stance. "Knowing" does not mean that a social worker must follow these values blindly, but she [or he] must take them into consideration when assessing a problem situation and when making her [or his] decisions. The application of societal norms may become problematic when a society accepts values which previously were disvalued, especially when the adoption of the new value occurs unevenly among different groups within society. For example, today the value to choose one's lifestyle freely, whether it be heterosexual, bisexual, or homosexual, is accepted by many but not all Americans. Gay rights, derived from this value, is an issue which still divides Americans because the adoption of this new value has not been uniform across American society. Social workers may find it difficult to identify the relevant societal value around this issue and thus not be certain which professional ethical principle applies.

## Clarifying Personal Values

Shakespeare had Polonius advise Laertes, "To thine own self be true...Thou canst not then be false to any man" (*Hamlet,* act I, scene III, lines 78–80). This same advice may also help social workers as they consider the ethical aspects of decision making. Before one can be true to oneself, one must know accurately what one really believes in. It is not enough to speak in generalities. Instead a social worker must carefully scrutinize and define her values. For example, today all reasonable persons value equality and abhor discrimination and exploitation on the basis of race, sex, or age. But how pervasive is the social worker's commitment to the equality value? Does it extend to persons with different sexual preferences? To persons who prefer "unconventional" life-styles?

Values can influence behavior only if they are unambiguous and specific. It is not enough for a social worker to say that she favors abortions. She must be able to define her values clearly. Until when does she favor abortions? If she holds that abortions are permissible in the first two trimesters, she needs to consider the ethical problems that arise when a defective baby is born prematurely at the beginning of the sixth month. Does it make an ethical difference whether such a defective body is inside or outside of the womb? These questions are raised here to emphasize that social workers must first clarify their own value stance if they want to be true to themselves.

Clarification of one's own values, though important, does not automatically resolve every value dilemma. Deciding on the ethical aspects of a practice situation becomes especially difficult whenever a social worker holds two values which provide conflicting directives. For example, a social worker may hold the following two values:

1. A woman has a right to decide whether or not she wants to become pregnant and, if pregnant, whether she wants to give birth to a live infant or to abort the fetus.
2. A social worker who has accepted employment in a social agency is obligated to act in accordance with the policies of that agency.

A social worker who endorses both of these values faces an ethical dilemma if she is employed by an agency which as a matter of policy opposes abortion and does not permit its workers to assist clients to obtain an abortion. How should such a social worker resolve her ethical dilemma? Should she ignore agency directives? Would it be better to refer a client who has requested an abortion to another agency which does offer such services? Or must an ethical social worker refuse to accept employment in an agency that has such a policy?

Unless a worker can clarify her own value positions, ethical decision making will reflect whatever value positions happen to be in fashion at the time. There will be those who will argue that this is not undesirable because it puts social work practice in the mainstream and because it makes for congruence between problems, environment, and solutions. However, in such a situation the practitioner's own values may get lost and it becomes increasingly difficult to be true to one's own self.

## ETHICAL ELEMENTS IN ASSESSING ALTERNATIVES

The social worker who is alert to the ethical aspects of practice will examine and assess the available options and alternatives somewhat differently than a colleague who is not as concerned with the ethical aspects of practice. This becomes clear when we consider various assessment criteria:

### Efficiency and Effectiveness

The efficiency criterion is concerned with the relative cost (including budget, staff time, agency and community resources) of achieving a stated objective. Whenever two options will lead to the same results, the one that requires less budget, less staff, and less time is the more efficient one. The effectiveness criterion, on the other hand, relates to the degree to which the desired outcome is achieved. When the implementation of one option results in halving the number of poor people in a country, while the second option reduces the poverty population by 80 percent, the latter option is the more effective one.

Difficult choices arise when the more efficient option is the less effective one or vice versa. But ethical questions about an option may reduce the relevance of the efficiency and effectiveness criteria. The most efficient or the most effective option may be rejected because of ethical implications. For example, killing poor people may be the most effective and the most efficient way of eliminating poverty—so long as no one is concerned with the ethical implications of the proposed plan. Everyone will agree that this strategy is unethical and totally unacceptable, no matter how efficient or how effective. More often the ethical assessment of an option is not as clear as in this example, so that a social worker will find it more difficult to make a decision. For example, what are the ethical implications of forcing poor people to work? Work is a desirable activity, highly valued in our society, but "force" means limiting a person's freedom, another important value in our society. The ethical assessment, in this case, demands that we assess "work" and "independence" against the loss of "freedom." Though social work ideology for some time rejected out-of-hand the various "workfare" programs that force poor people to work, some social workers have provided a more positive assessment of "workfare," which may indicate a change in the social work ideology regarding this type of program (Ginsberg, 1983). However, currently there are no widely accepted assessment procedures that can help a social worker weigh the ethical aspects of each option.

Another kind of ethical quandary was raised in recent years in connection with the efforts to deinstitutionalize patients of mental hospitals. The policymakers in some states tried to implement these programs less out of concern for improving the lot of hospitalized patients and more for the purpose of publicizing the need for additional community resources. In some instances, the option of releasing mentally ill patients from hospitals was adopted even though it was known that most communities lacked adequate resources for caring for these people. The state governments were unlikely to help communities with this problem since welfare budgets were about to be reduced. Was it ethical to institute a strategy that might result in some long-range improvements, but which in the short run would harm many fragile people?

### Protection of Clients' Rights and Welfare

The definition of rights and privileges changes over time. What is thought to be a right at one time may not be so defined in another era. These changes may create ethical problems. Journalists, for example, were once expected to get the news, no matter what the obstacles. Nowadays, when there is a greater concern for the privacy rights of individuals and families, journalists face an ethical dilemma—whether to pursue the news even if this means disregarding a person's privacy.

The changing definitions of what constitutes rights may also create ethical problems for social workers. Consider the ethical problems faced by social workers in the field of adoption as the right of adopted persons to information about their natural parents is becoming recognized in more and more jurisdictions. At one time the natural parents as well as adoptive parents were assured that such information would remain confidential and would never be shared with the adoptee. But when court decisions or legislative enactments in some states support the right of adopted persons to this information, social workers are placed in a difficult ethical position. They may have little choice when ordered by a court to reveal this information, but is it ethical for them to continue to tell natural and adoptive parents in other jurisdictions that this information will remain confidential?

### Protection of Society's Interest

Sometimes it is difficult to balance society's interests with a client's interests. If a client tells a social worker that he has committed a bank robbery, the social worker must weigh her obligations to the client against her obligations to society. Social control is a function of every social worker, but so is the maintenance of a helping relationship. If the practitioner cannot pursue both at the same time, to which should she or he give priority? Would the same ethical consideration apply if the client were a part-time prostitute in a town where prostitution violated the local law? Can law-breaking be overlooked when a client makes progress toward attaining identified goals? Does it matter whether or not the law violation physically harms another person? Keep these questions in mind as you assess dilemmas posed in the following exemplar:

---

**Security or Protection?**

John Newton was a likeable chap—twenty-two years old, not steadily employed, but always willing to help. Even before Ray Dunkirk, the community worker, had arrived on the scene, Newton had organized a number of young adults into a club. This club was well known in the neighborhood for the many helpful services it provided. The community's elderly population was especially appreciative of the security services this group gave them. Thefts, holdups, and even murder of older people had ceased ever since this club began to operate in the community.

But Dunkirk also became aware that Newton intimidated local store owners and obtained small payoffs from them in return for promising them "protection."

---

What was Ray to do? He considered various options, including the following:

1. To overlook Newton's protection racket in view of the many positive things he was doing that were benefiting the community.
2. To report Newton's protection racket to the police, since illegal activities should never be condoned.
3. To strengthen his relations with Newton with the view of helping to guide him away from the illegal activity, but in the meantime not to report the law violation to the police.

There are a number of ethical aspects to choosing the best option. One of these is the dilemma of how to balance the best interest of the various publics involved: oldsters, storekeepers, community, larger society, and others. But the major question is whether it is ethical to do something that might result in the return of violence against older people.

### The "Least Harm" Principle

Sometimes social workers are confronted by problems which permit only harmful options. Regardless of the option chosen by the client and/or the worker, some harm will come to one person or another, perhaps even to the client or the social worker. What is the ethical thing to do in such situations? The "least harm" rule suggests to choose the option that will result in the least harm, the least permanent harm, or the most easily reversible harm. Lest anyone think that the use of this rule will always avoid ethical problems, consider the ethical aspects of the following exemplar.

---

**Five Young Orphans**

Nancy Reisner, social worker in the local welfare department, had been assigned to work with five young children between the ages of three months and eight years whose parents were killed recently in an airplane accident. The children are temporarily placed in an emergency shelter, since they have no relatives who can take care of them. Long-term arrangements for their care must be made quickly.

The following options are under consideration: (1) a children's institution which can accommodate all five children or (2) foster homes pending adoption, but no foster home is prepared to take in more than two children.

The case was discussed at the weekly case conference. The social work staff was of the opinion that a foster home placement is better than an institutional placement, especially for younger children. On the other hand, the staff was aware that once the brothers and sisters were placed in separate foster homes, it would be most unlikely that they would ever again live together as a family unit.

---

One of the dilemmas facing Nancy Reisner was how to choose between two conflicting criteria: the best-interest-of-the-child principle and the family maintenance value. What is the most ethical way of solving this practice problem? Should short-term or long-term considerations be the deciding factor? Does the "least harm" principle offer guidance in this case? How?

Some have suggested that an intervention is ethical when the projected benefits exceed the projected risks (Diener and Crandall, 1978:24). But when the consequences of an intervention are the only consideration, ethics and values tend to be ignored altogether. This appears to be a modern version of the old maxim, "The ends justify the means"—a maxim that is hardly a helpful guide for ethical decision making. Such a guide does not specify whose cost or whose benefit are to determine the decision, nor does it tell the social worker how to predict future costs and benefits. This formulation also may ignore the rights a client has to control his own life.

How does a social worker decide what option to choose in any given situation? In the preceding pages we have discussed a number of criteria which may be helpful in the decision-making process. It may be helpful to summarize these principles here. Whenever considering two or more options, the social worker will choose (all other considerations being equal) the option which:

1. Is more efficient (relative cost to achieve the stated objective)
2. Is more effective (the degree to which the desired outcome is achieved)
3. Protects the worth, dignity, and opportunities of all persons
4. Protects society's interests and/or furthers the welfare of society as a whole, rather than that of any one segment
5. Protects the client's rights and furthers his welfare
6. Causes the least harm, the least permanent harm, and/or the most easily reversible harm

These principles are not arranged in any order of priority. Each principle applies *unless the ethical implications of an option contraindicate its adoption.*

## RANK-ORDERING ETHICAL PRINCIPLES

Whenever two or more ethical principles apply and point toward differing options, more specific guidelines are necessary. We need to remember that such guidelines are not meant to be magical formulas that can be applied blindly, but are offered here as guides to ethical decision making.

How should a social worker decide when one option is assessed to be the more efficient and another, more effective? Should Ray Dunkirk...give priority to the "welfare of society" principle or to the "least harm" principle?

When questions such as these are considered at all, they usually receive only the most generalized answers, or the rules are presented on such a highly abstract level that practitioners have not found them useful. Some guides to ethical decision making miss the point because their authors misunderstand how social workers make practice decisions. Social workers rarely make direct use of theoretical knowledge or philosophical principles when making practice decisions. Instead, knowledge and values are integrated in a series of practice principles—and these are what social workers use at the critical points of making practice decisions.

In the past few years a number of social work authors, including Lewis (1984), Reamer (1983), and Siporin (1983), have prepared guides for ethical decision making, but few social workers have used them in practice for the reasons stated earlier. We have used these and other sources in preparing our version of a guide that we believe will better help social workers in making ethical practice decisions.

A guide for rank-ordering ethical principles and ethical obligations must clearly indicate an order of priority. Once such a priority list has been established, the operating rule is that the satisfaction of a higher order obligation takes precedence over the satisfaction of a lower order obligation. Even though there is not yet any general agreement on the rank order of professional ethical obligations, we have developed our guide on the basis of our perception of what might be the consensus among social workers. In our guide, the first professional obligation, located on the uppermost rung of the priority ladder (Figure 31.3) is the strongest and takes precedence over all subsequent obligations. In a situation where two ethical obligations apply, the one on a higher rung on the priority ladder has priority. Thus, if both "confidentiality" (Obligation 5) and "full-disclosure" (Obligation 6) apply, the ethical obligation of confidentiality should receive prior consideration.

1. A social worker should make professional decisions that guarantee the basic survival needs of individuals and/or of society. The protection of human life (whether the life of a client or of someone else) takes precedence over every other obligation. The means for protecting human life might include health services, food, shelter, income, and so on as appropriate in each situation.
2. A social worker should make practice decisions that foster a person's autonomy, independence, and freedom. Freedom, though highly important, does not override the right to life or survival of the person himself or of anyone else. A person does not have the right to decide to harm himself or herself or anyone else on the grounds that the right to make such a decision is her or his autonomous right. When a person is about to make such a decision, the social worker is obligated to intervene, since Obligation 1 takes precedence.

FIGURE 31.3
Priority Ladder of Ethical Obligations

| | |
|---|---|
| Rung 1 | Life protection—basic survival needs of individuals and/or society |
| Rung 2 | Autonomy<br>Independence<br>Freedom |
| Rung 3 | Foster quality of opportunity and equality of access |
| Rung 4 | Promote a better quality of life |
| Rung 5 | Strengthen every person's right to privacy/confidentiality |
| Rung 6 | Speak the truth and fully disclose all relevant information |
| Rung 7 | Practice in accord with rules and regulations voluntarily accepted |

Text explaining each rung is below.

3. A social worker should make practice decisions that foster equality of opportunity and equality of access for all people.
4. A social worker should make practice decisions that promote a better quality of life for all people.
5. A social worker should make practice decisions that strengthen every person's right to privacy. Keeping confidential information inviolate is a direct derivative of this obligation.
6. A social worker should make practice decisions that permit her to speak the truth and to fully disclose all relevant information.
7. A social worker should make practice decisions that are in accord with the rules and regulations which she [or he] has voluntarily accepted.

Let us try to apply this scheme of rank-ordering ethical principles to one of the ethical dilemmas that the social worker of Debbie Roberts faced. This social worker... had to decide whether or not to contact the parents of twelve-year-old Debbie even though she had stated specifically that she did not want her parents to know that she was pregnant. Ethical Obligation 5 indicates that a social worker should not invade a person's privacy by involving others without the person's consent. Similarly, Ethical Obligation 2 stresses the ethical requirement to foster a person's autonomy. But Ethical Obligation 1 requires decisions that guarantee a person's survival. Since the social worker felt that Debbie's pregnancy involved danger to her health and welfare, she decided that she must involve Debbie's parents. She based this decision on the priority of Ethical Obligation 1.

## ORGANIZATIONAL BASE FOR PROFESSIONAL ETHICS

Ethical decision making is often presented as if the social worker who must make a decision is alone and lonely, cut off from every support system that might [provide] guidance, support, and recognition. Many have questioned this view. Frankena cites the philosopher W. D. Walsh, who wrote that "morality is first and foremost a social institution, performing a social role, and only secondarily, if at all, a field for individual self-expression." Frankena himself also argued in favor of a social morality (1980:33). While we do not deny the worker's responsibility for her [or his] ethical decisions, we note that she [or he] is a participant in a number of networks and social systems which support or which should support her [or his] ethical decision making. All decision making occurs within a social setting which influences, rewards, or guides certain behaviors and which limits, sanctions, and disapproves others. The social agency which employs the social worker is one such setting, the service delivery team or office is another, the professional association a third, and so on. Any discussion of steps designed to facilitate and strengthen ethical decision making that does not take these systems into consideration is not complete (Joseph, 1983).

Over the years these systems have developed various mechanisms that attempt to provide guidance and support. Here we want to discuss a number of those that are particularly promising for further development.

## Peer Review

Peer review permits a social worker to test her [or his] ethical decision making against that of her [or his] colleagues. In the past social workers have used informal groupings to review their professional practice decisions. Such groupings can also be useful for reviewing ethical decisions. However, informal groups, valuable as they may be, are no substitute for formal disciplined review groups. In this age of consumerism and accountability, formal review mechanisms are a necessity for every professional group that wants to survive.

Private practice raises additional considerations with regard to ethical decision making. The social worker in private practice is more isolated than her [or his] colleagues in agency-based practice and has less opportunity for interaction with peers. Controls and accountability of private practice social workers depend almost entirely upon the sensitivity and knowledge of the individual practitioner. Peer pressures which are so influential in agency practice are much less in evidence among private practice practitioners. Because of these considerations, social workers in private practice may want to organize peer review systems specifically geared to review their ethical decision making in order to ensure that their decisions will be of the highest ethical quality.

## Accountability Systems

Social agencies are accountable for what they do. So are the social workers who work in these agencies. Social agencies that want to implement this responsibility in a positive way must develop and operate accountability systems. These systems are characterized by the following features:

1. A sensing or monitoring system
2. A method for sampling activities or decisions
3. Clear indicators of the desired quality
4. Clear indicators or criteria of the desired quantity
5. Feedback systems that permit an early alert to problem situations

These accountability system features, as described by Hoshino (1978), relate primarily to practice performance, but there is no reason why such systems could not incorporate additional indicators that are also concerned with the ethical aspects of practice.

## In-Service Training and Consultation

Most agencies make a heavy investment in providing in-service training and consultation for their staff. These services can also be geared to educating staff members to the intricacies of the ethical aspects of decision making, to sensitizing them to the ethical implications of practice, and in general to strengthening the ethical level of practice.

### Appeals Procedures

Many agencies have appeals procedures, but often clients are not aware of them. "Forgetting" to inform clients about them may simplify the life of practitioners and administrators, but doing so does not help to raise the level of ethical practice. Appeals procedures do more than correct mistakes that social workers have made. One of their most valuable functions is to sensitize social workers to the ethical aspects of practice. An ombudsman or another type of appeals procedure should be readily available to clients and should function without stigma. Ethical social workers will welcome such strategies. Administrative review procedures also have a place in the support system, but they do not take the place of appeals procedures freely available to clients.

### Committee on the Ethics of Social Work Practice

Each agency should establish a Committee on the Ethics of Social Work Practice, analogous to Committees on the Rights of Human Subjects that exist in every research organization. Practitioners who have an ethical problem may bring it to the committee for consultation. Such a committee can serve as a forum where social workers can think through thorny ethical questions that occur in their everyday practice. Most important, this committee can be the locus for the routine monitoring of ethical practice within the agency.

### National Association of Social Workers

The National Association of Social Workers (NASW) must continue to encourage the strengthening of ethical decision making within the profession. The following are some of the ways in which this can be done:

1. Continue to revise and refine the Code of Ethics.
2. Encourage the formation of groups to study and review critical ethical decisions that arise out of actual practice experiences.
3. Develop a data bank of precedents with ethical implications.
4. Schedule activities that focus on the ethical aspects of practice, both at professional conferences and as part of continuing education programs.

With respect to the third item, it is desirable that social workers begin to collect data on ethical decision making. Such a data bank should not be limited to "success stories" but should also include errors, unanswerable questions, and embarrassing situations. The collection of this type of data will be helpful to practitioners as well as to students. This information will explicate the ethical quandaries which social workers have experienced, the preferred solutions, and the results achieved. Such a data base will also be helpful in the creation of case materials so necessary for the systematic development of needed social work knowledge.

## SUMMARY

In this chapter we have presented ideas that may help social workers in their search for more effective ethical practice. The values of the social work profession form the background for ethical decision making. Ethical decision making is the cornerstone for ethical practice.

Ethical decision making begins with the clarification of one's own values. Knowledge of what one really believes in is an inescapable basic step for social workers who seek to strengthen their ethical practice. Beyond this, it becomes important that social workers clarify the values of society and of the various groups with which they work. Clarification of these values permits social workers to become more sensitive and more aware of the values of others and of the possible conflicts between different value systems.

The individual practitioner carries a major responsibility for practicing in an ethical way. But social agencies and the professional organizations also have a responsibility for activating review mechanisms and support systems that foster ethical decision making and ethical practice. These provide the setting within which individual practitioners function. They are the support systems and social networks that tend to encourage or discourage ethical practice.

In this chapter we have presented our guide, which was designed to assist social workers in making ethical decisions. We believe that this guide is a realistic tool and thus represents a useful contribution in the development of social work professional ethics.

Finally, we have urged the creation of a data bank on ethical decision making and the creation of a case literature to encourage the development of systematic knowledge. By using the everyday experiences of social work practitioners, it may be possible to arrive at a better understanding of what is required for ethical decision making.

## EXERCISES

1. From your own professional or student experience identify two problem situations that have ethical implications. Try to use the guide that we have presented in this chapter to help you resolve these problem situations.
2. List several professional activities of social workers that you believe to be clearly outstanding examples of ethical behavior.

## BIBLIOGRAPHY

This bibliography lists the books and articles cited..., as well as additional literature on ethical problems in professional practice that may be of interest to the reader.


Abramson, Marcia. 1981. "Ethical Dilemmas for Social Workers in Discharge Planning." *Social Work in Health* 6 (4): 33–42.

Amnesty International. 1984. *Codes of Professional Ethics.* London: Amnesty International.

Bahm, Archie. 1982. "Teaching Ethics Without Ethics to Teach." *Journal of Business Ethics* 1: 43–47.

Bartlett, Harriett M. 1970. *The Common Base of Social Work Practice.* New York: National Association of Social Workers.

Bayles, Michael D. 1981. *Professional Ethics.* Belmont, Calif.: Wadsworth.

Bergin, Allen E. 1980a. "Behavior Therapy and Ethical Relativism: Time for Clarity." *Journal of Consulting and Clinical Psychology* 48: 11–13.

———. 1980b. "Psychotherapy and Religious Values." *Journal of Consulting and Clinical Psychology* 48: 95–105.

Bermant, Gordon; Herbert C. Kelman; and Donald P. Warwick (eds.). 1978. *The Ethics of Social Intervention.* New York: John Wiley and Sons.

Bernstein, Saul. 1960. "Self-Determination: King or Citizen in the Realm of Values." *Social Work* 5 (1): 3–8.

Bok, Sissela. 1978. *Lying: Moral Choice in Public and Private Life.* New York: Pantheon Books.

———. 1982. *Secrets: On the Ethics of Concealment and Revelation.* New York: Pantheon Books.

Brennan, Joseph G. 1983. "The Stockdale Course." In *Teaching Values and Ethics in College,* Michael J. Collins (ed.), pp. 69–80. San Francisco: Jossey-Bass.

Brown, Bertram S. 1968. "Social Change: A Professional Challenge." (unpublished paper.)

Buber, Martin. 1952. *Eclipse of God.* New York: Harper and Row.

Callahan, Daniel. 1980. "Contemporary Biomedical Ethics." *New England Journal of Medicine* 302: 1228–33.

Camus, Albert. 1942. *The Stranger.* New York: Knopf.

Carlton, Wendy. 1978. *In Our Professional Opinion: The Primacy of Clinical Judgment Over Moral Choice.* Notre Dame, Ind.: University of Notre Dame Press.

Cohen, Robert. 1980a. "The (revised) NASW Code of Ethics." *NASW News* 25 (4, April): 19.

———. 1980b. "Ethics—Responsibility to More Than Profession's Clients." *NAWS News* 25 (6, June): 10.

Constable, Robert T. 1983. "Values, Religion and Social Work Practice." *Social Thought* 9 (Fall): 29–41.

Corey, Gerald; Corey, Marianne; and Patrick Callana. 1984. *Issues and Ethics in the Helping Professions.* Monterey, Calif.: Brooks and Cole.

Council on Social Work Education. 1982. *Curriculum Policy Statement.* New York: CSWE.

DeFelice, Judith. 1982. "The Impact of Professional Social Work Education on the Development of a Non-Judgmental Attitude." Unpublished doctoral dissertation, Adelphi University School of Social Work.

Diener, Edward, and Rick Crandall. 1978. *Ethics in Social and Behavioral Research.* Chicago: University of Chicago Press.

Diggs, Bernard J. 1970. "Rules and Utilitarianism." In *Readings in Contemporary Ethical Theory,* Kenneth Pahel and Martin Schiller (eds.), pp. 260–82. Englewood Cliffs, N.J.: Prentice-Hall.

Dillick, Sidney (ed.). 1984. *Value Foundations of Social Work: Ethical Basis for a Human Service Profession.* Detroit, Mich.: Wayne State University Press.

Drane, James F. 1978. "Making Concrete Ethical Judgments." *Bulletin of the Menninger Clinic* 42 (2): 156–59.

Edel, Abraham. 1955. *Ethical Judgment: The Use of Science in Ethics.* New York: Free Press.

Elliott, Martha W. 1984. *Ethical Issues in Social Work, An Annotated Bibliography.* New York: CSWE.

Felkenes, Sandra. 1980. "The Social Work Professional and His Ethics." Unpublished doctoral dissertation, University of Alabama.

Fishkin, James S. 1982. *The Limits of Obligation.* New Haven: Yale University Press.

Fletcher, Joseph F. 1966. *Situation Ethics, The New Morality.* Philadelphia: Westminster Press.

Flexner, Abraham. 1915. "Is Social Work a Profession?" *Proceedings of National Conference of Charities and Corrections.* Chicago: Hindman, pp. 576–590.

Frankena, William K. 1973. *Ethics,* 2nd ed. Englewood Cliffs, N.J.: Prentice-Hall.

———. 1980. *Thinking About Morality.* Ann Arbor: University of Michigan Press.

Gewirth, Alan. 1978. *Reason and Morality.* Chicago: University of Chicago Press.

Ginsberg, Leon. 1983. "Workfare Is Working in West Virginia." *NASW News* (April): 3–4.

Goffman, Erving. 1959. *The Presentation of Self in Everyday Life.* Garden City, N.Y.: Doubleday Anchor Books.

Goldman, Alan H. 1980. *Moral Foundations of Professional Ethics.* Totawa, N.J.: Rowman and Littlefield.

Goldstein, Howard. 1973. *Social Work: A Unitary Approach.* Columbia, S.C.: University of South Carolina Press.

Greenwood, Ernest. 1957. "Attributes of a Profession." *Social Work* 2 (3, July): 45–55.

Halleck, Seymour L. 1963. "The Impact of Professional Dishonesty on Behavior of Disturbed Adolescents." *Social Work* 8 (2): 48–56.

———. 1971. *The Politics of Therapy.* New York: Science House.

Halmos, Paul. 1965. *Faith of the Counselors.* London: Constable.

Haney, Craig; Curtis Banks; and Philip Zimbardo. 1973. "Interpersonal Dynamics in a Simulated Prison." *International Journal of Criminology and Penology* 1:69–97.

Harrod, Howard. 1980. *The Human Center: Moral Agency in the Social World.* Philadelphia: Fortress.

Hazard, Geoffrey, Jr. 1978. *Ethics in the Practice of Law,* New Haven, Conn.: Yale University Press.

Hoshino, George. 1978. "Social Services: The Problem of Accountability." In *Social Administration,* Simon Slavin (ed.), pp. 299–309. New York: Haworth Press.

Howe, Elizabeth. 1980. "Public Professions and the Private Model of Professionalism." *Social Work* 25: 179–91.

Hughes, Everett C. 1965. "Professions." In *The Professions in America,* Kenneth S. Lynn (ed.). Boston: Beacon.

Jordan, Bill. 1974. *Poor Parents.* London: Routledge and Kegan Paul.

Joseph, M. Vincentia. 1983. "The Ethics of Organizations: Shifting Values and Ethical Dilemmas." *Administration in Social Work* 7 (3/4): 47–57.

Joseph, M. Vincentia. 1985. "A Model for Ethical Decision Making in Clinical Practice." *Advances in Clinical Social Work Practice.* Carel Germain (ed.). Silver Spring: NASW, pp. 207–217.

Karpel, M. A. 1980. "Family Secrets." *Family Process* 19: 295–306.

Keith-Lucas, Alan. 1977. "Ethics in Social Work." *Encyclopedia of Social Work.* Washington: National Association of Social Workers, pp. 350–55.

Kluckhohn, Clyde. 1951. "Values and Value-Orientations in the Theory of Action: An Exploration in Definition and Clarification." In *Toward a General Theory of Action.* Talcott Parsons and Edward A. Shils (eds.), pp. 388–433. Cambridge, Mass.: Harvard University Press.

Kohlberg, Lawrence. 1976. "Moral Stages and Moralization: The Cognitive-Developmental Approach." In *Moral Development and Behavior: Theory, Research and Social Issues,* Thomas Lickona (ed.), pp. 31–53. New York: Holt, Rinehart and Winston.

Kurzweil, Zvi. 1980. "Why Heteronomous Ethics?" In *Ethics in an Age of Pervasive Technology,* Melvin Kranzberg (ed.), pp. 68–71. Boulder, Colo.: Westview Press.

LeGrand, Julian. 1982. *The Strategy of Equality: Redistribution and the Social Services.* London: George Allen and Unwin.

Levenstein, Phyllis. 1979. "Ethical Considerations in Home-Based Programs." Paper presented at National Symposium on Home-Based Programs for Children and Families. Iowa City, Iowa. ERIC Document ED 181997.

Levy, Charles. 1976. *Social Work Ethics.* New York: Human Sciences Press.

———. 1982. *Guide to Ethical Decisions and Actions for Social Service Administrators.* New York: Haworth Press.

Lewis, Harold. 1973. "Morality and the Politics of Practice." *Social Casework* 53 (7): 404–17.

———. 1982. *The Intellectual Base of Social Work Practice: Tools for Thought in a Helping Profession.* New York: Haworth Press.

———. 1984. "Ethical Assessment." *Social Casework* 65: 203–11.

Lickona, Thomas (ed.). 1976. *Moral Development and Behavior: Theory, Research, and Social Issues.* New York: Holt, Rinehart and Winston.

Loewenberg, Frank M. 1978. "Professional Values and Professional Ethics in Social Work Education." In *Educating the Baccalaureate Social Worker,* Betty L. Baer and Ron Federico (eds.), pp. 115–29. Cambridge, Mass.: Ballinger.

———. 1983. *Fundamentals of Social Intervention,* 2nd ed. New York: Columbia University Press.

Loewenberg, Frank M., and Ralph Dolgoff, eds. 1972. *The Practice of Social Intervention.* Itasca, Ill.: F. E. Peacock Publishers.

McCann, Charles W. 1977. "The Codes of Ethics of the NASW: An Inquiry into Its Problems and Perspectives." In *Values in Social Work Education,* Boyd E. Oviatt (ed.), pp. 10–19. Salt Lake City: University of Utah Graduate School of Social Work.

McCann, Charles W., and Jane Park Cutler, 1979. "Ethics and the Alleged Unethical." *Social Work* 24: 5–8.

McDermott, F. E. (ed.). 1975. *Self-Determination in Social Work.* London: Routledge and Kegan Paul.

Maritain, Jacques. 1932. *An Introduction to Philosophy.* London: Sheed and Ward.

Martin, Mike W. 1982. "Organizational Authority and Professional Responsibility." *Clinical Sociology* 1 (1): 14–17.

Maslow, Abraham H. 1962. *The Farther Reaches of Human Nature.* New York: Penguin Books.

May, William F. 1980. "Professional Ethics: Setting, Terrain, and Teacher." In *Ethics Teaching in Higher Education,* Daniel Callahan and Sissela Bok (eds.), pp. 205–41. New York: Plenum Press.

Miller, Henry. 1968. "Value Dilemmas in Social Casework." *Social Casework* 13: 27–33.

Miller, Mary Susan, and A. Edward Miller. 1976. "It's Too Late for Ethics in Business Schools." *Business and Society Review* 17 (Spring): 39–42.

Moody, H.R. 1982. "Ethical Dilemmas in Long-term Care." *Journal of Gerontological Social Work* 5: 97–111.

Moser, Charles. 1980. Letter. *NASW News* 25 (9): 6.

Nader, Ralph; Peter J. Petkas; and Kate Blackwell. 1972. *Whistle Blowing*. New York: Grossman Publishers.

National Institute of Mental Health. 1981. *Ethical Issues in Mental Health Policy and Administration.* Washington D.C.: U.S. Department of Health and Human Servies, Publication No. ADM-81-1116.

Nietzsche, Friedrich. 1923. *Beyond Good and Evil.* Trans. Helen Zimmern. London: George Allen and Unwin.

Novak, Dennis H., et al. 1979. "Change in Physicians' Attitudes Toward Telling the Cancer Patient." *Journal of the AMA* 241: 537–42.

Pedersen, Paul B., and Anthony J. Marsella. 1982. "The Ethical Crisis for Cross-Cultural Counseling and Therapy." *Professional Psychologist* 13, 4: 492–500.

Perlman, Helen H. 1965. "Self-Determination: Reality or Illusion?" *Social Service Review* 39: 410–22.

———. 1976. "Believing and Doing: Values in Social Work Education." *Social Casework* 57: 381–90.

Pilseker, Carlton. 1978. "Values: A Problem for Everyone." *Social Work* 23: 54–57.

Pumphrey, Muriel. 1959. *The Teaching of Values and Ethics in Social Work Education.* New York: Council on Social Work Education.

Rawls, John. 1971. *A Theory of Justice.* Cambridge, Mass.: Harvard University Press.

Reamer, Frederic G. 1979. "Fundamental Ethical Issues in Social Work." *Social Service Review* 53: 229–43.

———. 1980. "Ethical Content in Social Work." *Social Casework* 61: 531–40.

———. 1982. *Ethical Dilemmas in Social Service.* New York: Columbia University Press.

———. 1983. "Ethical Dilemmas in Social Work Practice." *Social Work* 28: 31–35.

Reamer, Frederic G. 1983. "The Concept of Paternalism in Social Work." *Social Service Review* 57:2, 254–271.

Reamer, Frederic G. 1987. "Values and Ethics." *Encyclopedia of Social Work.* Silver Spring, Md.: National Association of Social Workers, Vol. 2, pp. 801–809.

Rees, Stuart. 1978. *Social Work Face to Face.* London: Edward Arnold.

Rehr, Helen. 1979. "Ethical Dilemmas in Health Care Delivery." K.L.M. Pray Memorial Lecture, University of Pennsylvania (mimeographed).

Reid, William J., and Patricia Hanrahan. 1982. "Recent Evaluations of Social Work: Ground for Optimism." *Social Work* 27: 328–40.

Reisch, Michael, and Chris L. Taylor. 1983. "Ethical Guidelines for Cutback Management: A Preliminary Approach." *Administration in Social Work* 7 (3/4): 59–72.

Rogers, Carl R. 1977. *Carl Rogers on Personal Power.* New York: Delacorte.

Ross, Judith W. 1982. "Ethical Conflicts in Medical Social Work: Pediatric Cancer Care as a Prototype." *Health and Social Work* 7(2): 92–102.

Rubin, Allen. 1985. "Practice Effectiveness: More Grounds for Optimism." *Social Work* 30: 469–476.

Salzberger, Ronald Paul. 1979. "Casework and a Client's Right to Self-Determination." *Social Work* 24: 398–400.

Sammons, Catherine C. 1978. "Ethical Issues in Genetic Intervention." *Social Work* 23: 237–42.

Schild, Sylvia, and Rita Beck Black. 1984. *Social Work and Genetic Counseling: A Guide to Practice.* New York: Haworth Press.

Schultz, Leroy G. 1975. "Ethical Issues in Treating Sexual Dysfunction." *Social Work* 20: 126–28.

Schutz, William C. 1967. *Joy.* New York: Grove Press.

Shirk, Evelyn. 1965. *The Ethical Dimension.* New York: Appleton-Century-Crofts.

Simon, Sidney B.; Leland W. Howe; and Howard Kirschenbaum. 1978. *Values Clarification: A Handbook of Practical Strategies for Teachers and Students.* New York: Hart Publishing Company.

Siporin, Max. 1975. *Introduction to Social Work Practice.* New York: Macmillan Publishing Company.

———. 1982. "Moral Philosophy in Social Work Today." *Social Service Review* 56: 516–38.

———. 1983. "Morality and Immorality in

Working with Clients." *Social Thought* 9(Fall): 10–28.
Smith, Huston. 1982. *Beyond the Post-Modern Mind.* New York: Crossroad.
Smith, William H. 1978. "Ethical, Social, and Professional Issues in Patient's Access to Psychological Test Reports." *Bulletin of the Menninger Clinic* 42 (2): 150–55.
Startz, Morton R., and Helen F. Cohen. 1980. "The Impact of Social Change on the Practitioner." *Social Coasework* 61: 400–06.
Tancredi, Laurence R., and Andrew E. Slaby. 1977. *Ethical Policy in Mental Health Care.* New York: Prodist.
*Tarasoff v. Regents of the University of California,* 17 Cal 3d 425, 551 P. 2d 334, 131 Cal. Rptr. 14.
Thomlison, Ray J. 1984. "Something Works: Evidence from Practice Effectiveness Studies." *Social Work* 29: 51–56.
Timms, Noel. 1983. *Social Work Values: An Enquiry.* London: Routledge and Kegan Paul.
Towle, Charlotte. 1965. *Common Human Needs.* New York: National Association of Social Workers.
Tymchuk, Alexander J. 1981. "Ethical Decision Making and Psychological Treatment." *Journal of Psychiatric Treatment and Evaluation* 3: 507–513.
Veatch, Robert M. 1981. *A Theory of Medical Ethics.* New York: Basic Books.
Vigilante, Joseph. 1974. "Between Values and Science: Education for the Profession During a Moral Crisis or Is Proof Truth?" *Journal of Education for Social Work* 10(Fall): 107–15.
Well, Marie, and Ernest Sanchez. 1983. "The Impact of the *Tarasoff* Decision on Clinical Social Work Practice." *Social Service Review* 57: 112–124.
Williams, Robin M., Jr. 1967. "Individual and Group Values." *Annals of the American Academy of Political and Social Science* 371: 20–37.
Wilson, Suanna J. 1978. *Confidentiality in Social Work.* New York: Free Press.
Wispe, Lauren. 1978. *Altruism, Sympathy, and Helping.* New York: Academic Press.
Yelaja, Shankar A. 1982. *Ethical Issues in Social Work.* Springfield, Ill.: Charles C Thomas.

## 32.

**Mylon Winn**

# BLACK PUBLIC ADMINISTRATORS AND OPPOSING EXPECTATIONS

## INTRODUCTION

A law student once stated that most of the significant issues in civil rights had been resolved by the courts. This conclusion may be correct if it means there is a legal basis for addressing various civil rights issues, but the same conclusion cannot be made about the experiences of black public administrators in the administrative arm of government. Lawrence Howard suggests that black administrators are expected to buffer white-controlled organizations against demands from the black community.[1]* Whether one agrees or disagrees with Howard, he implies that black administra-

Mylon Winn is an associate professor at the School of Public and Environmental Affairs, Indiana University–Purdue at Indianapolis.

*The "black community" is defined as blacks who live in a specific area in the community as well as blacks who are employed by an agency.

tors find themselves in a difficult position. Many would agree that most black administrators make significant contributions to organizations, that is, that they do more than serve as buffers. However, the administrative experiences of blacks do include having to deal with different expectations from members of the organization and the black community.[2]

Frederick Mosher believes that resolving different expectations is the most difficult moral problem faced by public administrators.[3] This situation is further complicated when one group pursuing their interest needs government services to help alleviate the effects of racial discrimination.

This chapter will focus on how black public administrators can address the different expectations they may encounter by discussing the bases of expectations from blacks and from members of the organization. The chapter will then suggest that by minimizing different expectations black public administrators can concentrate on responding to the public need for government service through policy-making and program management.

## THE BASIS OF BLACK EXPECTATIONS FOR THE PUBLIC SECTOR

One objective of black politics is to influence political decisions about the delivery of public benefits. Charles Hamilton points out that because black influence is limited it is necessary to resort to "demand making tactics" in order to eliminate barriers caused by a lack of political power.[4] Limited success, according to Hamilton, has led blacks to redefine the criteria for participation in the political process. Redefining the criteria for participation is important because it means (1) that blacks can claim a share of public benefits without posing a threat to other groups feeding at the public trough and (2) that blacks can alter their ability to influence government and increase their numbers in decision-making positions. The outcome is that government benefits are increased and the status of blacks is improved. Altering the relationship between blacks and the political system has one other important benefit, which Milton Morris points out in his discussion of the influence of blacks on public policy. Morris believes that blacks occupy the "untenable position of being almost entirely dependent on the beneficence of a political system that has been so clearly unsympathetic over time."[5] Changing their untenable position is a goal that seemed to have been a possibility during the 1960s and 1970s. The possibility that surfaced during those decades can be linked to several developments. Jewel Prestage points out that since 1900 blacks have been in an "uphill battle to achieve full participation in the political process."[6] Significant legal victories, such as the outlawing of white primaries in 1944 and the passage of the civil rights acts in 1957, 1960 and 1964, the anti-poll tax amendment in 1963 and the federal Voting Rights Act of 1965 are all a part of the uphill battle. This progress was accomplished through government and therefore enhances the importance of public institutions in the fight against racial discrimination. Success encourages hope that government will deliver, which is translated into expectations for public administrators who are charged with implementing as well as enforcing antidiscrimination laws.

During the 1960s and 1970s the preference for controlling institutions within the black community meant that self-government was viewed as a means of limiting, if not eliminating, the effects of racial discrimination. Even in this instance the need is for sympathetic public administrators who are supportive of the goals of black self-government. Perhaps more important than sympathetic administrators is having black public administrators who have experienced the negativeness of racism. The point is that while sympathetic white administrators can be helpful, having experienced racism provides an insight that makes the black public administrator more understanding, perceptive and willing to oppose racism.

The belief that black public administrators will be more responsive becomes the basis of accountability. When black public administrators fail to satisfy the standards of accountability, they may be reprimanded, for instance, by being accused of selling out their brothers and sisters. Such pressure can be a heavy burden for the black person who is sensitive to this kind of accusation. Adam Herbert believes that the ability of nonwhite administrators to fulfill their responsibilities will become increasingly difficult if there is a "collective perception" that minority administrators have exclusive understanding of the problems faced by people experiencing the effects of discrimination.[7]

## JUDGING TACTICS USED BY BLACKS: A CULTURAL FACTOR

Michael Lipsky observes that powerless groups must operate in the political arena with little to use for bargaining.[8] Because they do not have conventional political resources, they must rely on unconventional methods when dealing with organizations. Blacks may use tactics they consider legitimate which are inconsistent with ideas of professionalism favored by public administrators. Tactics such as office demonstrations, verbal outbursts during meetings and nonverbal behavior used to intimidate administrators are viewed as "disruptive behavior characteristic of a lower-class cultural way of life."[9] Judgment of this kind suggests that different cultural values are being used to reject the validity of tactics used by blacks. The judgmental values being used can be traced to Woodrow Wilson, who advised that European public administrators should be Americanized in language, thought, principles and objectives.[10] This means simply that public administration should be compatible with American cultural values.

Individualism is an important value in American culture which has been translated into organizational responses. Deryl Hunt argues that "conventional public administration tends to execute public policies as if the clientele were composed of discrete individuals."[11] This approach contributes to an orderly process of administration which provides a basis for administrative control. Subculture values that challenge the preference for orderliness and control are judged rigidly and, if perceived as a threat, rejected.

The different perceptions about the legitimacy of tactics used by blacks brings to mind Edward Hall's conclusion that culture determines what makes sense and depends on the context where the evaluation is made. The result, according to Hall, is that "people in culture-contact situations frequently fail to really understand each other."[12] The lack of understanding may be called racism, but the labeling does not get at the purpose of this kind of behavior. To the extent that public administration reflects the dominant culture (which is significant), the purpose is to support and maintain the belief that will ensure the survival of dominant culture and professional values.

Blacks educated in public administration programs or who progressed through the ranks are familiar with professional values that may influence their organizational roles. Herbert discusses several role determinants which he believes influence minority administrators' perception of their responsibility to their employing agency and their community. Two of Herbert's role determinants most relevant to the discussion here are system demands and colleague pressure. System demands refer to organizational performance expectations that are manipulated through various rewards and sanctions. The objective is to get administrators to follow orders without questioning their validity and to conform to organizational standards of acceptable behavior. Herbert suggests that there is a pronounced effort to find suitable minorities. However, prospective candidates are subject bo being weeded out if they are judged to be non-team players.

Colleague pressure involves judging whether a worker's job performance is acceptable to his or her colleagues. Herbert gives several examples of the extremes some minorities will go to in order to be accepted by their peers. For instance, minority police officers may be more forceful in order to gain the attention of their peers and get promoted; minority welfare workers will apply the rules rigidly to clients in order to be perceived as competent; and minority teachers will blame the students rather than the quality of the academic experience in order to be accepted by colleagues.[13] These examples demonstrate that blacks are subject to pressures to assume traditional roles that are compatible with dominant group organizational behavior. Resisting the pressures to conform means not responding to the dominant culture values that are the bases of organizational practices and behaviors. Carried a step further, practices and behaviors become professional standards that administrators are expected to incorporate into their value systems.

The discussion thus far has argued that black administrators may experience pressures from their colleagues and the employing organization. The pressure is to choose one or the other, which the black administrator may be unable to do without being labeled a "sellout" by blacks and a "non-team player" by the organization. This dilemma is an example of expectations that create an ethical problem for black public administrators. There is an option available which can help minimize, if not eliminate, the dilemma.

## ETHICS: A DEFINITION WITH EXPLANATION

One problem in discussing ethics is first to find a suitable definition. The definition of ethics used here borrows heavily from the work of Jeremy Plant. According to Plant, ethics is " 'right conduct,' which is appropriate to particular situations."[14] It is difficult to argue against situational ethics as long as the administrator making ethical decisions realizes that ethical relativism cannot be extended into the realm of the unreasonable. Frederick Mosher's argument that "standards of ethical behavior that are applicable and sufficient to a private citizen in his private social relationships are not in themselves adequate for the public decisions of an administrator" suggests that, regardless of the situation, what is reasonable for public administrators should exceed ethical standards for private citizens.[15]

## ETHICS: AN APPROACH TO RESOLVING OPPOSITE EXPECTATIONS

Resolving opposite expectations should be based on standards reflecting ethical values. Stephen Bailey's memorial essay to

Paul Appleby is a starting point for a partial discussion of ethical standards. Bailey's essentials of moral behavior—mental attitudes and moral qualities—are prerequisites for ethical conduct as well as necessary qualities for all public administrators. According to Bailey, mental attitudes involve an awareness on the part of public servants of the problems caused by personal and private goals versus the public interest; of the morally ambivalent effect of public policies; of the shifting of context and values priorities, which create administrative dilemmas; of the increasing difficulty of making ethical choices as administrators progress upward in an organization's hierarchy; of the need for flexibility in resolving administrative uncertainties that involve moral choices; and of the effect of using procedure, rules and standards nonproductively and the advantages of using them to promote fair and open administration. Bailey views these qualities as part of the essentials and turns his discussion to the moral qualities needed to practice ethical public administration.[16]

The essential moral qualities are optimism, courage and fairness, tempered by charity. Optimism is the ability to face uncertain and contradictory situations without becoming dysfunctional. Optimism is the basis for creativity in response to political conflicts that require risky solutions. Courage involves not retreating from unpopular, contradictory, and unclear situations when withdrawing is an easy solution. Administrators must not be afraid to make decisions and avoid passing the buck. Fairness tempered by charity means relying on standards of justice which encourage the exercising of power fairly and compassionately. Charity is the good quality that compensates for limited information and helps restrain the inclination for personal gain in favor of the public interest.[17]

Bailey's essentials cannot be ignored, because they emphasize moral ambiguities as well as propose prerequisites for ethical conduct. However, Bailey does ignore what he calls the obvious virtues—honesty, patience, sensitivity, etc.—and concentrates on his essentials. In a culture-contact situation, administrators cannot ignore the obvious, because by doing so they will find themselves between groups with opposing perspectives that may seem unresolvable.

## ETHICS AS OBVIOUS VIRTUES AND THE BLACK ADMINISTRATOR

The obvious virtues that black administrators can rely on are responsiveness and administrative integrity. To be responsive, black administrators must be accessible, able to communicate and, within reason, willing to share information. Responsiveness is accomplished through formal and informal interaction with members of the black community and white collegues. For instance, through responsiveness black administrators are able to share information with members of the black community. In situations where a policy is being made, black administrators can help members of the black community understand issues and their effects. This information can be used to formulate a response. The implication here is that when members of the black community fail to act, black administrators can argue that they have been supportive and thus have lived up to their responsibility.

Responsiveness to white colleagues includes being a competent administrator who does not resort to excessive actions in order to gain a colleague's acceptance. Administrative competence is a factor that lends itself to the accomplishing side of the obvious virtues. While being an ethical person is essential, an initial requirement for being competent is that black administrators must have the knowledge and the managerial skills as well as the ability to practice these skills successfully.

Among reasonable people, administrative competence should be viewed as a basis for limiting doubts about the ability of black administrators to perform their job responsibilities. It is more important, however, that competent black administrators be perceived as having some commitment to professional standards that many administrators find acceptable. Yet black administrators must keep in mind that, while professionalism is a desirable quality, responsiveness through professionalism may adversely affect problem identification, limits decision-making and policy-making and inhibits their ability to deal with routine and nonroutine situations creatively.[18]

In situations where black administrators find they are between their colleagues and the black community, they can turn to the obvious virtue—responsiveness. Equal responsiveness to colleagues and the black community can help minimize differences. Further, being equally responsive communicates a sense of fairness, which means that one of Bailey's essential moral qualities is to be utilized. Responsiveness is an important avenue for dealing with both the black community and colleagues, but it must be accompanied by administrative integrity. Administrative integrity includes honesty, being trusted and having moral convictions. In practice, administrative integrity involves black administrators' being honest in their dealings with colleagues and members of the black community. Honesty is the basis for developing trust, which is necessary if pressure on black administrators is to be minimized.

When people experience moral conflict because they disagree with an organizational policy or practice, they must be prepared to take an ethically based position opposing the policy or practice. In order to take an ethical position, individuals must "know they possess the moral beliefs and integrity of conviction to endure and fight for their position."[19] Where black public administrators are concerned, they must have ethical convictions that are applied fairly and consistently when dealing with colleagues and the black community. This is difficult, but blacks, as well as all other public administrators, do not have the luxury of being selectively ethical.[20] Honesty, trust, and moral convictions are worthwhile qualities that black public administrators must use, qualities that provide a basis for interacting with all others. Through interaction, black public administrators can identify a basis that can be used to eliminate cultural differences that serve as barriers. By eliminating barriers, black administrators can remove the need to serve as mediators and avoid being accused of serving as buffers to protect white administrators from demands of the black community.

## CONCLUSION AND IMPLICATIONS FOR POLICY-MAKING

It can be argued that all administrators experience the push and pull of interest groups and professional standards. This is true, but the race element is an additional factor that affects black administrators uniquely. The effect, as previously argued, is that black administrators find themselves having to respond to demands from white colleagues and from the black community. To respond to these demands, black administrators must become mediators.

Black administrators must realize that mediation involves devising alternatives to perceptions that their white colleagues and members of the black community have about how they should conduct themselves as administrators. It is argued that their conduct should be based on ethical administration, which means practicing the obvious virtues discussed previously. Black administrators should realize that mediation involves devising proposals that exceed the constraints imposed by demands made by members of the black community and organizational colleagues. Proposals should introduce conditions that both sides can accept and use as a basis for additional discussion. The effect is that instead of being in the middle, black administrators can assume an active role in shifting, to some degree, the focus of their activities from responding to interest-based demands to administration and policy-making. To shift from interest-based demands, black administrators must have credibility with colleagues and with members of the black community. Credibility is based on responsiveness to issues and concerns held by each side. It is the basis for each side's inclination to accept proposals as well as their willingness to engage in discussions intended to develop ideas that both groups can accept. In this sense the limitation of cultural logic is transcended and the focus can shift to problem resolution, decision-making and policy development.

In conclusion, the discussion of ethical administration—the obvious virtues—is intended to introduce a degree of consistency that protects an administrator's credibility. Ethical administration is no panacea for the conflict that can emerge in situations where there is culture based on conflict, but it does offer a dimension that is consistent with the legacy left by Martin Luther King, Jr.[21] Adam Herbert believes that minority administrators have "life experiences which give them an appreciation for certain social, economic, and political realities which they can often articulate more effectively than others."[22] Thus, if black administrators are not hampered by limitations imposed by their colleagues and the black community, they can focus on articulating these experiences in the policy process.

## NOTES

I am indebted to Nancy J. Winn, John Hodges and T. McN. Simpson for their helpful and insightful comments on an earlier draft of this chapter.

1. Lawrence C. Howard, "Black Praxis of Governance: Toward an Alternative Paradigm for Public Administration," *Journal of Afro-American Issues* 3 (Spring 1975): 145.

2. On this point, see Adam W. Herbert, "The Minority Public Administrator: Problems, Prospects and Challenges." *Public Administration Review* 34 (November/December 1974): 556–563.

3. Frederick C. Mosher, *Democracy and the Public Service,* 2d ed. (New York: Oxford University Press, 1982), p. 230.

4. Charles V. Hamilton, "Racial, Ethnic and Social Class Politics and Administration," *Public Administration Review* 32 (October 1972): 638–645.

5. Milton D. Morris, *The Politics of Black America* (New York: Harper & Row, 1975), p. 281.

6. See Jewel L. Prestage, "Black Political Participation," in Bryan T. Downes (ed.), *Cities and Suburbs* (Belmont, Calif.: Wadsworth, 1971), p. 195.

7. Herbert, "The Minority Public Administrator," p. 559.

8. Michael Lipsky, "Protest as a Political Resource," in Downes, *Cities and Suburbs.*

9. For a more detailed discussion on this point, see Hamilton, "Racial, Ethnic and Social Class Politics and Administration," p. 646.

10. Woodrow Wilson, "The Study of Administration," *Political Science Quarterly* 2 (June 1887): 197–222.

11. Deryl G. Hunt, "The Black Perspective on Management," *Public Administration Review* 34 (November/December 1974): 521.

12. Edward T. Hall, *Beyond Culture* (Garden City, N.Y.: Anchor, 1976), p. 188.

13. Herbert, "The Minority Public Administrator," pp. 560–561.

14. Jeremy F. Plant, "Ethics and Public Personnel Administration," In Steven W. Hays and Richard C. Kearney (eds.), *Public Personnel Administration* (Englewood Cliffs, N.J.: Prentice-Hall, 1983), pp. 290–296.

15. Mosher, *Democracy and the Public Service,* p. 230.

16. Stephen K. Bailey, "Ethics and the Public Service," in Roscoe C. Martin (ed.), *Public Administration and Democracy* (Syracuse, N.Y.: Syracuse University Press, 1965), p. 292.

17. Ibid., pp. 293–297.

18. Mosher, *Democracy and the Public Service,* chap. 5.

19. J. Patrick Dobel, "Doing Good by Staying In," *Public Personnel Management* 2 (Summer 1982): 126–139.

20. For further discussion on this point, see Melbourne S. Cumming, "Andrew Young: A Profile in Politico-Religious Activism," *Western Journal of Black Studies* 3 (Winter 1979): 228–232.

21. Peter A. French, *Ethics in Government* (Englewood Cliffs, N.J.: Prentice-Hall, 1983), p. 10.

22. Adam W. Herbert, "The Evolving Challenges of Black Urban Administration," *Journal of Afro-American Issues* 3 (Spring 1975): 177.

## 33.

**Cheryl Hyde**

# EXPERIENCES OF WOMEN ACTIVISTS: IMPLICATIONS FOR COMMUNITY ORGANIZING THEORY AND PRACTICE

*I long to hear that you have declared an independency—and by the way in the new Code of Laws which I suppose it will be necessary for you to make I desire you would Remember the Ladies, and be more generous and favourable to them than your ancestors....If perticuliar care and attention is not paid to the Ladies we are determined to foment a Rebelion, and will not hold ourselves bound by any Laws in which we have no voice, or Representation.*

—Abigail Adams to John Adams
March 31, 1776

The field of community organizing would be wise to heed the words of Abigail Adams to her revolutionary husband, John. Contributions of women activists have been virtually ignored by the field of social work. Consequently, social work has a diminished knowledge base and has alienated large numbers of talented women. Ironically, both the past and the future of community organizing are tied intimately with the action of women. Foremothers include Jane Addams, Dorothea Dix, and Lillian Wald. Current trends suggest that "women's issues," such as poverty, the family, and reproductive rights, will be on national, state, and local agendas for years to come. In order to prepare for the future, we

Cheryl Hyde is a professor at the School of Social Work, Boston University.

need to understand the talents of the past and present.

This paper explores the experiences of women activists, primarily in the labor, peace, and feminist movements. A number of salient themes, generated in interviews with and presentations by women activists, are identified. Suggestions are made as to how and why these themes should be integrated into community organizing practice. Given that a personal research goal of the author is to generate a community organizing theory based on the experiences of women, the discussion of themes is preceded by a newly developed analytical framework for collective practice. This project also represents a preliminary attempt to weave qualitative research methods, feminist thought, and women's experiences into an understandable and meaningful whole.

Such an approach is a departure from traditional community organizing theory and practice for a number of reasons. First, critical attention is paid to the impact of gender. Second, women's experiences are considered legitimate and credible, an important factor given that the needs, thoughts, and actions of women organizers are rarely addressed in the literature and in training. Third, the benefits of cross-fertilization are illustrated, since none of the women interviewed considered themselves "community organizers," yet their actions are quite applicable to the field. Finally, the analysis is from neither a community organizing model perspective (Rothman, 1979) nor a "how-to" approach (Alinsky, 1969, 1972; Kahn, 1982; Speeter, 1978; Staples, 1984). Rather a wholistic approach is presented that focuses on the "how" or process of organizing instead of the "what" or product of organizing. Important work along this line has been done by Brandwein (1981), Burghardt (1982), Freire (1974), Galper (1980), and Galper and Mondros (1980).

## BACKGROUND AND CONTEXT

This project reflects much of the author's thoughts and experiences as a feminist activist. This experience includes legal advocacy for women, labor education, and, currently, consciousness-raising workshops on unlearning or confronting the "Isms"—racism, sexism, heterosexism, classism, ageism, and handicapism. Much feminist analysis has been brought to bear on this project. A complete discussion on feminist scholarship, however, is beyond the scope of this paper. Nonetheless, the women's movement is a rich, yet uncultivated area for community organizing. The reference section of this paper includes a number of sources that ought to be incorporated into community organizing curricula. For the purposes of this paper, many basic tenets of feminist thought are seen in the identification of salient themes.

A nonpositivist, qualitative research approach was selected because this methodology seemed best suited for women to define their reality, rather than it being imposed upon them. The analysis is based primarily on interviews with and presentations by women activists (listed at the end of the paper). The interviews were open-ended, and much of the richness in the material results from "chasing tangents." Five issues, however, were raised in all of the interviews: (1) Reasons for becoming an activist; (2) How organizing is accomplished; (3) Structure of the organization; (4) Gender dynamics within the organization; and (5) Type of training. Additional interviews and relevant material published in a variety of social-change oriented journals supplement the analysis.

Although this paper focuses on the experiences of women activists, its application should not be limited to a female audience. The purpose of this project is defeated if the results are not considered in an integrative fashion. For a variety of reasons, including sex-role sterotyping and "either-or" analytical frameworks, there exists the temptation to dichotomize the findings. By way of a warning, two dichotomies should be mentioned: male versus female styles, and process versus product orientations. Each shall be considered briefly.

There is a growing body of literature, particularly in the area of group development, on male and female styles of leadership, power, and authority. Within this literature there is general agreement that masculine and feminine styles do exist. Furthermore, masculine styles are typified by aggressive, task-focused, and competitive traits, and feminine styles are typified by passive, interpersonal-focused, and cooperative traits (Bokemeier & Tate, 1980; Brandwein, 1981; Gilligan, 1982; Hyde, 1983; Johnson, 1976; Reed, 1981; Van Wagner & Swanson, 1979). The community organizing field needs to be attentive to these different styles, for in varying degrees they have implications for the recruitment and training of both practitioners and constituents. Reed (1981) suggests three areas in which gender differences influence the training of group leaders: assumptions about gender-related behaviors, gender composition of groups, and a group's reaction to female leaders. It is her contention, shared by others, that these issues surrounding gender need to be brought to the forefront of a training experience. Failure to acknowledge or plan for them could undermine the overall goal of the group.

The existence of masculine and feminine styles, however, does not mean that they are intrinsic traits (Brandwein, 1981:189). Many feminine traits, however, do emerge in the themes presented below. Therefore, they receive what may appear to be a lopsided emphasis, especially given that the community organizing field is seen as having a masculine orientation. This study does not conclude, however, that women are the only people capable of nurturance, emotions, and other feminine actions, nor that their behavior is limited to these traits. Such conclusions limit both women and men. As one woman involved in the peace movement states:

> The notion that women are more nurturing and, therefore, should participate to save the earth is usually sexist. That's our sex role stereotype. The fact is that everyone has the capacity to nurture. That women have been socialized to do so is a reality, and it's an asset we have going for us. But at the same time we recognize it as a strength, we must deplore it as a mandate. If that's done, then I think we're talking feminism. (Popkin & Delgado, 1982:40)

Community organizing would be enhanced if a greater integration of masculine and feminine characteristics occurred. For this to happen, organizers need to be aware of these different traits, to stop dismissing feminine traits as weak and ineffective, and to encourage both men and women to acquire a more integrative style in their organizing.

A second dichotomy, often viewed as a component of the male-female split, is between process and task (or process and product). Crow (1978) and Riddle (1978) provide thoughtful discussions on the damaging impact that this dichotomization has on organizing and social change efforts. A process orientation focuses on *how* things are accomplished and attention is paid to the development of trust, sensitivity, empathy, and support among group members. A product orientation focuses on *what* things get accomplished and attention is paid to the efficiency, action, rational order, and task completion. There are strengths and weaknesses in both approaches and a savvy organizer needs to determine a balance. There is a distinct bias, however, in this paper toward a process orientation. This is partly due to the emphasis placed on process by the women activists. It is also a reaction to the lopsided product/task orientation found within community organizing. Here again, the ideal would be an integration of process and product.

FIGURE 33.1
Wholistic Collective Practice Paradigm

Strategic

Structural

Subjective

Relational

## EMERGING PARADIGM

As stated above, one goal of this project was to develop a paradigm that would prove useful for future analysis. This paradigm would emerge from and reflect the experiences of women activists, suggest a wholistic approach to community organizing, and relate all components to one another rather than force a linear or causal ordering. The result is referred to as a Wholistic Collective Practice Paradigm, illustrated in Figure 33.1.

The four dimensions, subjective, relational, strategic, and structural, represent different concerns or levels within collective practice. Briefly, definitions for these dimensions are:

*Structural:* Focuses on the organization, its purpose, development, apparatus, and positions. Also focuses on connections between organizations.

*Strategic:* Action aspects of practice, with emphasis placed on the strategy as a process. Tactical steps are considered a subunit of this dimension.

*Relational:* Focuses on the relationships between people-people and people-organization. Stresses the collectivity, its origin, maintenance, and growth. Also focuses on the process of others engaging in strategies.

*Subjective:* Introspective or reflexive statements by the individual (such as the organizer). Captures the assessments, interpretations, and opinions of the individual. This transcends all dimensions.

Collective practice, such as mobilizing or organizing, is the process of connecting these four dimensions toward the goal of some form of intervention or social change. All of these dimensions are connected to or interdependent upon one another. No dimension is more important to the process than another, although at a given point in time one may have greater emphasis placed upon it. This paradigm can be envisioned as a mobile trying to balance its parts.

Within each of these dimensions are themes that specifically relate to the experiences of women organizers. There is considerable overlap, in that a theme is not constrained to one dimension. In fact, the power of this paradigm is that it forces us to consider that an act has implications on a variety of levels. For example, when an organizer considers a fundraising effort, she/he needs to consider the organizational structure, pre and post effort, the steps involved, the opinions, desires, and skills of the collective and individual concerns. While the development of this paradigm is in its preliminary stage, it may provide a new frame of reference or a way of thinking about or analyzing community organizing efforts. It conveys the importance of considering a variety of dimensions simultaneously (a difficult notion to grasp, see Boulet, 1981). Furthermore, it suggests that the practitioner needs to allow the group to define its own reality, rather than imposing a predetermined, ordered plan upon it.

A number of themes appear consistently and without prompting in the descriptions of the experiences of the women interviewed. At the very least, these themes should be seriously considered in relation to current community organizing practice. A process by which these themes can be integrated into practice is important. Hopefully, these themes, and the dimensions, will serve as a foundation for the generation of a new community organizing theory.

**THEMES**

*(1) The Wholistic Organizer.* Many of the women activists stated that to be an organizer meant to involve oneself fully. One woman stated it quite eloquently: "What is my view of social change? It is a wholistic approach. It involves all, the spiritual, actions and intellect. It is engagement" (KL). This notion of total engagement or investment was echoed by others. Considerable attention was paid to personal investment and to the alienation felt when emotions were denied. Thus, an organizing effort should not focus solely on what is being done. It also needs to incorporate the intellectual and emotional needs of individuals and the collective.

The wholistic organizer should not be equated with the organizer who does everything. Alinsky believed that an organizer needs to be adept at all phases, yet this creates a power dynamic between organizer and group that many of the women felt unnecessary and detrimental. First, it places too much emphasis on the organizer as expert, a pressure that often leads to burnout and disinvestment. It also suggests that the group becomes too dependent on the organizer's expertise and will be unable to function once the organizer leaves the setting. Second, it closes a door for the organizer in terms of her or his own learning. There was overwhelming sentiment that while an organizer can offer something to the organizing effort, the effort serves as an educational experience for the organizer.

When one woman said, "...overall, the whole thing has been very enlightening" (TN), she was referring to the skills and insights she gained while being the facilitator to a self-help group. She, and others, also acknowledged that they do not know everything. Rather than limiting the group's development, this can free up the group to explore the skills and strengths of others. Thus, delegation, support, interdependence and the acknowledgment that everyone can contribute something, become focal points for the organizing process.

*(2) Fulfillment Through Organizing.* Closely tied to the wholistic organizer is the notion that organizing, aside from reaching a goal, can be a fulfilling process in and of itself. The learning and support gained while organizing became as meaningful as achieving the product. One woman described organizing as a "natural high" (KG), despite the struggles and setbacks. In fact, one way of overcoming disappointments was with support for others. The encouragement of bonding and the development of support networks were considered of primary importance by the women.

*(3) Personal as Political: The Indigenous Organizer.* A common image of a community organizer is the person who goes into the community, helps people organize around an issue, and then leaves. There is little sense as to the actual investment of the organizer into the issue. This image did

not apply to these women activists. Their reasons for becoming activists varied, but the common theme was that they became involved because the problem or issue was personally experienced. Reasons include:

"It started with my own health. I was misdiagnosed" (TN)

"I think I initially became involved because of self-interest. The neighborhood was going down and nobody was doing anything about it" (Hayes, p. 24).

"Whatever it (project) is, it will have a lot of personal investment. Like Braun Court, this is important. It's our home (scheduled for rezoning). I am guided by personal issues, I need that kind of investment to organize" (FS).

"Listening to the (women's) music is like being on dope without drugs. I had a lot of friends who were musicians and we would get together. It filled a need, it was something very personal. And, I can't sing or anything, but I know how to organize and thought, why not organize an event that would feature women performers" (KG).

"I feel strongly that what I'm doing is for them (her children)" (TL).

These personal reasons for being an activist stem from two main sources. One is the need to gain knowledge. Perhaps the best or, at least, most recognized example of this is the book *Our Bodies, Ourselves.* This book began with a group of women who gathered to discuss their health needs and how they were not being met by the current medical establishment. The outcome was the Boston Women's Health Collective and the publication of one of the most influential books regarding health care and self-help. Often, the need to obtain knowledge is accompanied by the need to disseminate any information so that it could help others. The women believed it was important that others have access to information and to demystify previously denied information so that it could be understood and used.

Another reason stems from a reaction to unmet needs and hostility found within male-dominated organizations. Both Freeman and Evans (1980) argue that early participants in the women's movement had endured degrading and humiliating treatment within the leftist and student movements of the 1960s. These women obtained important skills while working in the movements, yet were not given credit for their contributions and were not treated seriously. Demands for equality were scoffed at and ignored. Women caucuses began to be formed and experiences were shared, thus creating an environment that provided a springboard for the feminist movement. This analysis suggests, again, the importance of personal fulfillment and investment.

*(4) Use of Emotions.* In many of the organizing efforts, emotions provided the cornerstone. The Women's Pentagon Action (Linton & Whitham, 1982; Popkin & Delgado, 1982) was mobilized around mourning, rage, empowerment, and defiance. Every activity was tied into expressing these emotions. (In my own work, I use an equation Awareness = Pain = Healing = Growth, as a way of emotionally contextualizing an antiracism [or other ism] workshop. Exercises help participants pass through these stages.)

Women stressed the importance of bonding, of people getting to know each other so that they could work together in a way that was mutually fulfilling and rewarding. Attention to emotional or personal needs improves the overall organizing effort: "I learned that if a person feels important, they will help and get involved" (EK). Not only does the acknowledgment of emotions and bonding help people become invested, it also serves as a source of reserve energy in the face of opposition.

Knowing that others care often comforts an individual when confronted with derogatory comments, hecklers, etc. Fears and concerns can be addressed within a supportive environment. This sounds obvious, yet it is often overlooked because accomplishing the task has assumed a disproportionate emphasis, to the detriment of the group. Rather than denying emotions, they should be used as a way of building personal ties and as a context for mobilizing. When emotions are used as a focus of organizing or as a source of strength, attention must be paid to the building of support networks (they won't happen spontaneously) and to the allowance of time so that people can sufficiently express their feelings.

*(5) Attention to the Environment.* The themes identified thus far have stressed the importance of support, emotional bonding, and personal investment. Women stressed that a "safe" environment was essential to developing these interpersonal sides of organizing. A safe environment is one in which trust, respect, equality, and validation of an individual's experiences takes place. It was viewed as a high priority among most of the women: "I want a good, open working environment, where people are safe. A safe environment is definitely one of my interests and needs. It's a place where people trust one another" (FS). Most of the women said that a safe environment was all-female, although all-female environments are not necessarily safe. One women suggested: "That with all women staffs you have differences in power and control. You don't have the male/female battles. It is a support and sanctuary that you can invest in" (QZ).

A safe environment, however, is not an environment that is conflict free. The creation of a safe environment allows for the airing of problems, for the exchange of diverse ideas in a direct manner. In building a safe environment, attention is paid to the creation of a process through which information, grievances, and thoughts can be heard. For one woman, consensus decision making was the key. Her experience of being an organizer/participant in a local women's peace camp proved rewarding, in part because the planning group had taken considerable time in determining a consensus style that was accessible and available to all participants: "...(P)ositive stuff [was] that a lot of feelings got heard and a lot of subtle adjustments were made in the actual plan, that, because people were heard, ideas came forward and... it was very rich, very diverse...and that doesn't happen when you have an uncomfortable environment, when it's not a safe environment to talk" (MB). Taking the time to address the environment can pay off in the long run with increased commitment, greater group ownership for the project and organization, and different, creative ideas.

*(6) Gender Dynamics.* In connection with discussion on a safe environment were comments regarding gender dynamics. Most of the women saw clear differences between male and female styles of organizing that were in line with the stereotypes outlined above. These differences were particularly apparent in comments on power/control and communication:

> Regarding Affinity Groups for a peace action and the lack of recognition given to a facilitator: "so they don't acknowledge what a facilitator is and it's the men that don't, I'm sure it is, that disrupt it because they don't have a sense of what collective work is and they're not trained...but they're not comfortable with having somebody who is the person, who is trying to help everyone manage their feelings and their conflict" (MB).

> "Men and women are different as organizers. One of my major complaints is with men. Orga-

nizationally, they are always dealing with power issues. Women are more trusting, more sensitive, able to communicate and relate to others.... Women intuitively use group process and interpersonal skills. Where men are rational and intellectual.... very un-intimate, real 'heady.' Can't listen to others." (FS)

"What I have noticed is that where men are involved, they end up being power hungry. Not cooperative." (TN)

"I was taught the Alinsky model. Charging white knight saving the day. I knew that I couldn't do that." (TL)

In order to break down the walls that exist between men and women, it is important that women's experiences and concerns are respected and treated seriously. It is also important that men become trained in other methods of decision making, leadership, and control, given the opinions against hierarchical, male-dominated, aggressive, individualistic settings.

*(7) Bridging Differences.* A common concern among these women was closing gaps that exist along racial, sexual preference, class, age and handicap lines. Consequently, confronting one's own biases, rather than ignoring them, was seen as central to individual and group development. Before, or in conjunction with an organizing effort, internal group prejudices are addressed. Rather than hide these problems so that an illusion of solidarity is created, these women stress the importance of raising these issues directly as a way of furthering growth and opportunities. Failure to do so will lead to divisiveness, anger, frustration, and, ultimately, disintegration.

*(8) Women's Culture and History.* Virtually every woman had a female role model who served as a source of inspiration and courage. These were not necessarily famous women, but they were women who helped make a struggle understandable and workable through their actions. Some of these role models were known personally as they were bosses, friends, or other activists. Others served a symbolic purpose, such as in the Women's Pentagon Action, in which women who died from the violent acts of men were remembered in ceremonies. Still others represent feminist culture (music and arts) and are viewed as a source of sustenance and connection: "I turn on 'Sweet Honey in the Rock' and understand Bernice Reagan's meanings of social actions, consciousness raising. Need this global meaning. You need emotional support" (KL).

Community organizing needs to rediscover the female organizers of its past. It should also consider the life histories of women in a variety of movements for they will suggest a different way of mobilizing.

*(9) Training.* There was no consistent view of the best training. Many of these women received their training through experience and not through any formal educational process. Some took advantage of available training opportunities presented by organizations, such as settlement houses, the Midwest Academy, and labor schools. Of concern to the field of community organizing should be the resentment felt toward the increased professionalization of the field. One woman, when asked why she went back to school, said: "It's time for the credentials" (KG); another said: "All I'm getting is a piece of paper that says I'm qualified" (FS). These women have demonstrated that grassroots experience, particularly if one is open to learning from others, is a valuable means of gaining an education of organizing. Community organizing needs to determine ways of tapping this knowledge and creating learning situations that are meaingful to women.

**CONCLUSION**

This paper has explored some common threads among women activists with the hope that these findings can be incorporated into community organizing practice. It presented an analytical paradigm that stresses a wholistic approach to collective practice. The paradigm's four dimensions—subjective, relational, strategic, and structural—comprise an integrated, interdependent whole—much like a balanced mobile. Within these dimensions are themes, nine of which were presented. Most of these themes focused on the emotional and interpersonal aspects of organizing, a view often overlooked or ignored in current community organizing theory and practice. I hope that serious consideration of these themes occurs and that community organizing, from training through the execution of efforts, changes in ways that accept and integrate the experiences of women activists. In the words of Abigail Adams, "Remember the Ladies," and the future will be stronger and more vital.

**REFERENCES**

## Primary Sources

Some identifying factors have been eliminated and the initials recorded in order to ensure confidentality.


EK. Interview, May 1984. Involvement in labor education, minority women.

FS. Interview, October 1984. Involvement in tenant rights, housing reform, youth issues, economic/poverty issues.

KG. Interview, June 1984. Involvement in consumer services, the arts, feminist networking.

KL. Presentation, October 1984. Involvement in peace work, civil rights, labor education.

LD. Presentation, October 1984. Involvement in labor organizing.

MB. Interview, May 1984. Involvement in peace work, environmental issues.

QZ. Interview, October 1984. Involvement in reproductive rights, labor organizing, neighborhood organizing.

SA. Presentation, October 1984. Involvement in desegregation, student rights, peace work.

TL. Presentation, October 1984. Involvement in women's economic rights, peace work.

TN. Interview, October 1984. Involvement in health issues.


## Secondary Sources: Interviews/Diaries


Fahey, Maureen. "Block by Block: Women in Community Organizing (an interview with Betty Deacon)," *Women: A Journal of Liberation,* 6 (1):24–28, 1978.

Hayes, Lois. "Separatism and Disobedience: The Seneca Peace Encampment," *Radical America,* 17 (4):55–64, 1983.

Linton, Rhoda, and Michele Whitham. "With Mourning, Rage, Empowerment and Defiance: The 1981 Women's Pentagon Action," *Socialist Review,* No. 63–63, 12 (3–4):11–36, May–August 1982.

Omi, Michael, and Ilene Philipson. "Misterhood Is Powerful: Interview with Ladies Against Women," *Socialist Review,* No. 68, 13 (2):9–27, March/April 1983.

Plotke, David. "Women Clerical Workers and Trade Unions: Interview with Karen Nussbaum," *Socialist Review,* No. 49, 10 (1):151–159, January–February 1980.

Popkin, Annie, and Gary Delgado. "Mobilizing Emotions: Organizing the Women's Pentagon Action, Interview with Donna Warnock," *Socialist Review,* No. 63–63, 12 (3–4):37–48, May–August 1982.


## Secondary Sources: References


Adams, Abigail. "Letter to John Adams, March 31, 1776," in *The Feminist Papers,* Alice Rossi (ed). New York: Bantam, 1973, pp. 10–11.

Alinsky, Saul D. *Reveille for Radicals,* New York: Vintage Books, 1969 (1946).

Alinsky, Saul D. *Rules for Radicals: A Pragmatic Primer for Realistic Radicals,* New York: Vintage Books, 1972.

Bokemeier, J.L., and J.L. Tate. "Women as Power Actors: A Comparative Study of Rural

Communities," *Rural Sociology,* 45:238–55, Summer 1980.

Boston Women's Health Book Collective. *Our Bodies, Ourselves: A Book by and for Women,* New York: Simon and Schuster, 1973.

Boulet, Jacques. "Complementary Epistemological Foundations of Community Organization: Societal and Action Theories," *Social Development Issues,* 5 (2 & 3):121–125, Summer/Fall 1981.

Brandwein, Ruth A. "Toward the Feminization of Community and Organizational Practice," *Social Development Issues,* 5 (2 & 3):180–193, Summer/Fall 1981.

Burghardt, Steve. *The Other Side of Organizing,* Cambridge, MA: Schenkman, 1982.

Campbell, Dolores Delgado. "Shattering the Stereotypes: Chicanas as Labor Union Organizers," *Women of Color/Women Organizing,* 11:20–24, Summer 1983.

Cantarow, Ellen. *Moving the Mountain: Women Working for Social Change,* Old Westbury, NY: The Feminist Press, 1980.

Ecklein, Joan (ed). *Community Organizers,* New York: John Wiley & Sons, 1984, 2nd ed.

Cook, Blanche. "Female Support Networks and Political Activism," *Chrysalis,* 3:43–61, 1977.

Crow, Ginny. "The Process/Product Split," *Quest,* IV (4):15–23, Fall 1978.

Deckard, Barbara Sinclair. *The Women's Movement: Political, Socioeconomic and Psychological Issues,* New York: Harper & Row, 1983, 3rd ed.

Evans, Sara. *Personal Politics: The Roots of Women's Liberation in the Civil Rights Movement and the New Left,* New York: Vintage Books, 1980.

Fisher, Berenice. "Who Needs Woman Heroes?" *Heresies,* 3 (1):10–13, 1980.

Freeman, Jo. "The Origins of the Women's Liberation Movement," *American Journal of Sociology,* 78 (4):792–811.

Freire, Paulo. *Pedagogy of the Oppressed,* New York: Seabury Press, 1974.

Galper, Jeffry. *Social Work Practice: A Radical Perspective,* Englewood Cliffs, NJ: Prentice-Hall, Inc., 1980.

Galper, Jeffry, and Jacqueline Mondros. "Community Organization in Social Work in the 1980s: Fact or Fiction?" *Journal of Education for Social Work,* 16 (1):41–48, Winter 1980.

Gilligan, Carol. *In a Different Voice: Psychological Theory and Women's Development,* Cambridge, MA: Harvard University Press, 1982.

Gittell, M., and N. Naples. "Activist Women: Conflicting Ideologies," *Social Policy,* 13:25–27, Summer 1982.

Gregory, Carole E. "Black Women Activists," *Heresies,* 3 (1):14–17, 1980.

Hyde, Cheryl. "Toward a Model of Gender Sensitive Community Organizing: A Synthesis of Current Research," unpublished seminar paper, December 1983.

Johnson, A.D. "Women and Power: Toward a Theory of Effectiveness," *Journal of Social Issues,* 32 (3):99–110, 1976.

Kahn, Si. *Organizing: Guide to Grassroots Leaders,* New York: McGraw-Hill Book Company, 1982.

Lawson, Ronald, and Stephen E. Barton. "Sex Roles in Social Movements: A Case Study of the Tenant Movement in New York City," *Signs: Journal of Women in Culture and Society,* 6 (2):230–247, Winter 1980.

Masi, Dale A. *Organizing for Women: Issues Strategies, and Services,* Lexington, MA: D.C. Heath and Company, 1981.

Mayo, Marjorie (ed). *Women in the Community,* Boston: Routledge & Kegan Paul, 1977.

McAllister, Pam (ed). *Reweaving the Web of Life: Feminism and Nonviolence,* Philadelphia: New Society Publishers, 1982.

Morgan, Robin (ed). *Sisterhood Is Powerful: An Anthology of Writings from the Women's Liberation Movement,* New York: Vintage Books, 1970.

Morgan, Robin. *Going Too Far: The Personal Chronicle of a Feminist,* New York: Vintage Books, 1978.

Przestwor, Joy Chrisi. *Connecting Women in the Community: A Handbook for Programs,* Cambridge, MA: The Arthur and Elizabeth Schlesinger Library, Radcliffe College, 1984.

Reed, Beth Glover. "Gender Issues in Training Group Leaders," *Journal for Specialists in Group Work,* 161–169, August 1981.

Riddle, Dorothy. "Integrating Process and Product," *Quest,* IV (4): 23–32, Fall 1978.

Rothman, Jack. *Planning and Organizing for Social Change: Action Principles from Social Science Research,* New York: Columbia University Press, 1974.

Rothman, Jack. "Three Models of Community Organization Practice, Their Mixing and

Phasing," *Strategies of Community Organization,* Fred M. Cox, John L. Erlich, Jack Rothman and John E. Tropman (eds). Itasca, IL: F.E. Peacock Publishers, Inc., 1979, 25–45.

Speeter, Greg. *Power: A Repossession Manual—Organizing Strategies for Citizens,* Amherst, MA: University of Massachusetts, Citizen Involvement Training Project, 1978.

Staples, Lee. *Roots to Power: A Manual for Grassroots Organizing,* New York: Praeger Publishers, 1984.

Steinem, Gloria. "The Politics of Talking in Groups," *MS.,* May 1981, pp. 43–45, 84–89.

Stonehall, Linda. "Cognitive Mapping: Gender Differences in the Perception of Community," *Sociological Inquiry,* 51 (2):121–128, 1981.

Van Wagner, Karen, and Cheryl Swanson. "From Machiavelli to Ms: Differences in Male-Female Power Styles," *Public Administration Review,* 39: 66–72, January 1979.

West, Guida. *The National Welfare Rights Movement: The Social Protest of Poor Women,* New York: Praeger Publishers, 1981.

Women's Crisis Center, Ann Arbor. "Organizing a Women's Crisis-Service Center," *Strategies of Community Organization,* Fred M. Cox, John L. Erlich, Jack Rothman and John E. Tropman (eds). Itasca, IL: F. E. Peacock Publishers, Inc., 1979, pp. 478–483.

PART SEVEN

# Work Guides

This volume has emphasized the practical and usable; however, there are some special areas that require additional focused attention.

Community organizers have much need for skills and tips regarding human resources. To address this, we have asked John Martin, an agency administrator, to prepare a piece on the job description as the "bare bones" of human resources concerns. There are points here that all community organizers will find helpful, and the point of view is from the practioner's perspective.

Meetings are a staple of the community organization professional's work. Effective meetings are needed, but almost never happen. The article on "The Effective Meeting," by John Tropman and Gersh Morningstar, details a number of techniques that can be used to achieve the three key elements: the decisions get made; the decisions are of high quality; and people have fun!

The use of data is a crucial element in community organization practice. But many of the "guides" for using community data are too complicated to be helpful. The work of Richard Douglass is masterful in this regard, and he has revised his popular piece for this volume. It helps community organizers understand and present community data.

Should one be unclear on a term, phrase, or calculation, Gottman and Clasen's "Troubleshooting Guide" will help. As an example, the worker can look up terms like "regression" and get a simple explanation of what is involved.

The use of numbers arises again in creating the budget, which is often presented as complex and only for the "expert." Marilyn Flynn has developed a series of key points that will assist the community organization professional in understanding and modifying budgets.

Finally, there are strategic considerations. Strategic planning was discussed briefly in the piece on policy management: Specific details will assist the process.

Here, the "Index of Dissimilarity (ID) and the Professional Unit Method of Analysis (PUMA)," by Tropman and Tropman, are presented. These are simple but powerful, easy-to-use techniques for comparing the present situation with the desired state, and for learning how much it costs to make the transition.

—John E. Tropman

34.

John Martin

# THE BARE BONES OF PERSONNEL MANAGEMENT: THE JOB DESCRIPTION

## INTRODUCTION

This article delineates the use of the job description as a central tactical tool in personnel management. The job description is a core element that flows from the agency mission and incorporates numerous components. It is the axis upon which hang essential personnel procedures necessary to the satisfactory performance of the job.

Job descriptions, combined with performance standards, drive the agency toward its mission in a steady, manageable manner. Job descriptions are important key elements in managing human service organizations. They are also underutilized and therefore underappreciated. I will attempt in this article to draw attention to the job description, not only as a basic tool for identifying, clarifying, and grouping tasks, but also as a basis for recruiting, screening, and employing staff; establishing expectations for performance; developing, evaluating, and compensating staff; and for budgeting.

## WRITING JOB DESCRIPTIONS

Job descriptions are developed from an analysis of tasks. According to a University of Minnesota Continuing Education and Extension Task Force report, there are five (5) steps to developing job descriptions. First, write a brief overview of the job. Second, list all activities that are performed on a regular basis. If the job currently exists and someone currently performs the job, it may facilitate this step to ask the individual to make a daily log of activities for a week or two. Then, identify those activities that occur monthly, quarterly, or annually. If this is a new position, you will not have the benefit of a daily log and will need to revise your beginning job descriptions according to the reality of functioning after several months' experience. The third step is to group related activities into categories. For instance, the activities: (1) answer telephone, (2) take messages, and (3) route calls, can be summarized into the category, "Act as Receptionist." The fourth task is to assign a percentage weight for each category. The weight should indicate the relative importance as a percentage of the job. You should end up with three to five categories that include all of the activities you have listed. The fifth step is to review your work to see if you've missed any significant aspects of the job.

Following these steps you will have a description that encompasses three to five categories. Each one will have listed all of the activities that comprise it. By weighting each category as a percentage of the job, you will have allocated 100 percent of the job's importance and time. You may then attach any educational requirements or special training or skills required to implement

John Martin is president of Catholic Social Services of Washtenaw County and visiting professor of Social Work, The University of Michigan.

this job description successfully. You may also identify the salary for this position (determining salary ranges will be discussed later in this article). Finally, you may add a statement that the employee is expected to carry out these activities in a positive, constructive manner.

Job descriptions give employees and supervisors accurate definitions of the work to be performed. They also fulfill other functions. Good job descriptions provide consistency from employee to employee. They standardize the work. They can, as you will see later in this article, lead to predictable outcomes, in terms of quantity, quality, and timeliness of work performed. Well-developed job descriptions also ensure conformity between the work performed and the mission of the agency: They serve to integrate performance with mission and purpose. Additionally, they ensure compliance with contractual obligations for those positions whose funding is largely dependent upon a contract from some external entity such as a governmental unit.

## PERFORMANCE STANDARDS

Once your job description has been developed, you may go about the task of writing performance standards—the specification of employee expectations. The standard or expectation should identify the type of performance with which the supervisor would be completely satisfied. This is a high but achievable level of performance. Standards should apply to the position, not to the person currently in the position, and they may express the quantity, timeliness, as well as the quality of work expected. Every category should have three or four standards. Standards also establish the baseline for future procedures such as evaluation and merit pay determination. While the process of writing job descriptions can best be done mutually between employee and supervisor, determining performance standards is the responsibility of the supervisor. In addition to listing the quantity, quality, and timeliness expected in your performance standards, you may also identify ongoing training or staff development expectations. As an example, the category, "Provide Counseling," has six job activities and four performance standards:

The job activities are:

1. Conduct assessments.
2. Establish goals.
3. Develop treatment plans.
4. Evaluate progress.
5. Assess client satisfaction with service outcomes.
6. Record each session in client records.

The performance standards are:

1. Perform five billable client interviews per day.
2. Seventy percent of clients will report satisfaction with outcomes.
3. Eighty percent of counseling will be short term—between 8 and 12 total sessions.
4. Worker will be expected to review two articles on short-term treatment and attend one external workshop on client satisfaction surveys.

## RECRUITING, INTERVIEWING, AND SELECTING

We now have a powerful tool called a job description, with its corresponding performance standards. It is a relatively simple task to use these documents to develop a structured interview guide, to be utilized to interview applicants for a position. You know the educational requirements for the position, along with any specialized training or skills it requires. You can take the job description and its corresponding performance standards and develop a few questions from each of the major duties, enabling you to ascertain the interest, potential, and ability of applicants to perform the job satisfactorily. You or your interviewing team (which is becoming more and more common in practice) can rank each applicant according to their responses to questions in each of the major job duty categories. Your ranking system can be as simple as very favorable, favorable, or unfavorable. These rankings can be compiled and used as one indicator in your screening process. If your agency has affirmative action plans, your ranked interview guides can demonstrate compliance or noncompliance with those plans, as they relate to the applicants. The goal of employing staff is to make the best possible match between the specific job requirements and the interest and abilities of the applicants. You increase the odds of reaching this goal through structured interview guides that are based on job descriptions and performance standards. If each candidate is given a copy of the job description and performance standards, she or he has a clear understanding of the requirements and has a good basis upon which to decide whether or not it is a good fit.

## JOB POSTINGS

The art of recruiting applicants for a position is simplified by a well-developed job description with concise performance standards. From these documents you can create position descriptions or job postings that can be disseminated through professional journals, newspapers, employee bulletin boards, and schools of social work. These job postings can summarize the major duties of the job description and simply but clearly communicate the essence of the job.

## EVALUATION

Evaluation is a mutual and continuous process between the employee and the supervisor. Evaluation should be goal oriented and growth oriented. Formal evaluation conferences should be held at least twice a year, using the performance standards identified in the job descriptions. The standards themselves should be reviewed for validity, completeness, and accuracy. If they continue to be acceptable, they may be used to evaluate performance. When standards are indicative of acceptable performance, the employee and supervisor individually and independently may rank the employee's performance as "below standard," "acceptable," or "above expectation," for each standard. The rankings may be compared in a joint session. The supervisor will then complete a final ranking. Any ranking that is below expectation or above the standard should state the reason for the deviation from the standard. Having performance standards, such as five billable interviews per day, lets you identify systemic problems, as well as individual problems. If the counseling staff members are unable to achieve a particular standard consistently, you can determine if this indicates an individual or a systemic problem. Perhaps the standard is too high, your marketing is ineffective, the community need is low, the agency reputation as a provider of counseling services is poor, or you have too many F.T.E. (Full-Time Equivalent) counselors for the volume of work. Good performance standards allow for clarity of problem identification.

## TERMINATION

If an employee's performance is below the standard, and you have ruled out systemic problems, that individual should be given time (say three months), support, additional training, and/or supervision, in order to either bring performance up to the standard, or face demotion, transfer, or termination.

## COMPENSATION

A simple method of determining competitive compensation is to survey the market to determine the average salary paid someone performing the duties in a particular job description. With sufficient data, you can arrive at an average salary. That average salary becomes the midpoint. Your salary scale for that position could range from 20 percent below the midpoint to 20 percent above the midpoint. Your hiring range extends from the beginning to the midpoint. If the average salary in your market for a comparable position is $30,000 annually, your midpoint is $30,000 and your scale for that position is $24,000 to $36,000 annually. Your entry level becomes $24,000 to $30,000.

## MERIT PAY

Merit pay decisions can be based on the comparison of actual performance against predetermined expectations. Social service systems need to consider various forms of financial incentive plans in order to reward superior performance. Merit pay, based on "meritorious performance"—that is, performance that is above and beyond the standard or the expectations for the job—is one way of increasing compensation and/or rewarding individual achievement.

## PROMOTION

If an employee is being considered for promotion to a managerial position, it is very useful to compare the employee's current job description with the job description for the managerial position. If similarity exists between the categories or performance standards of the two job descriptions, you have comparable functions, and comparisons can give you some basis for predicting success at the managerial level. This analysis can be very useful in promotion or transfer decisions.

## STAFF DEVELOPMENT

Performance standards may contain professional training or staff development activities that are expected of the employee in order to keep skills current. Staff development, driven by performance standards, will promote the accomplishment of an agency's mission and goals, as it upgrades staff functioning. Incorporating staff development expectations into the performance standards does not leave this vital function solely to the individual interest or needs of staff, but rather ties interest and needs to the job to be performed. When performance falls below standards, the need for staff development activities may be indicated.

## BUDGETING

If we use the category example, "Provide Counseling," and the performance standard of "five billable client interviews per day," and we know we can project that the average billable counseling session generates $30.00 in revenue, and that each full-time staff person works 230 days per year (260 days minus 30 days' paid time off), we can project each full-time staff counselor will generate $34,500 (230 days × 5 billable sessions × $30.00 average fee). Using these assumptions, based on job description and performance standards, building an annual budget becomes an objective activity. Similarly, the professional growth standard lets you determine your annual expense for staff development (e.g., a library journal, books, etc., plus workshops and conferences). This approach allows building the budget from the "bottom up." Sometimes job descriptions overlap programs, and a worker's time has to be allocated to more than one service. Job descriptions that indicate the percentage of time spent in each service can be a helpful tool in functional budgeting.

## INNOVATION

Organizations need to be open and flexible as they implement their mission in our constantly changing environment. To develop this adaptive ability, the system needs innovative personnel—personnel who can identify new opportunities and devise creative tactics and procedures. One way to augment the development of an environment in which innovation is encouraged and rewarded is to build the expectation to be innovative into the job description and performance standard. Then you can monitor, evaluate, and reward innovation.

## SUMMARY

This article has dealt with the development of job descriptions and their corresponding performance standards as well as the manner in which these tools can serve as a basis for both job postings and structured interview guides to be used in recruiting, interviewing, and selecting staff. Job descriptions and performance standards should also guide evaluation, compensation, merit pay, promotion, and termination decisions. The article has explored the use of job descriptions and performance standards in staff development planning, budgeting, and encouragement of innovation. It has been demonstrated that this one tactical tool becomes a basis for the development and use of other administrative techniques in managing personnel in a human service agency.

## REFERENCES

Austin, Michael J. *Supervisory Management for the Human Services*. Englewood Cliffs, NJ: Prentice-Hall, 1981.

*Conducting Performance Appraisals for CEE Civil Service Employees*. A Handbook for Supervisors. University of Minnesota. Continuing Education and Extension. June 1988.

Dessler, Gary. *Personnel/Human Resource Management*. 5th ed. Englewood Cliffs, NJ: Prentice-Hall, 1991.

Kaplan, Judith S. *Guidelines for Conducting Effective Performance Appraisals*. St. Paul: University of Minnesota, 1990.

Lauffer, Armand. *Assessment Tools*. Beverly Hills: Sage, 1982.

Mondy, R. Wayne, and Robert M. Noe. *Human Resources Management*. 4th ed. Needham Heights, MA: Allyn & Bacon, 1990.

Pecora, Peter J. and Michael J. Austin. *Managing Human Services Personnel*. Newbury Park, CA: Sage Publications, 1989.

35.

John E. Tropman and Gersh Morningstar

# THE EFFECTIVE MEETING: HOW TO ACHIEVE HIGH-QUALITY DECISIONS

## EXECUTIVE SUMMARY

Antony Jay's piece, "How to Run a Meeting That Gets Things Done," appeared in the March-April 1976 issue of *Harvard Business Review*. It was reprinted in the previous editon of *Tactics and Techniques of Community Practice*. Though the structure and dynamics of meetings have attracted much attention since the publication of that classic, meetings are still widely regarded as some sort of resented, necessary evil of organizational life. This article reviews some of the reasons why things go wrong in meetings, presents seven important principles that underly the meeting process, and proposes twelve "rules" for making meetings go right. A thorough understanding of these principles and diligent application of these rules will lead inevitably to more effective meetings with higher quality group decisions. Experience with these principles demonstrates that higher quality decisions will come even in the face of recurring problems of personality in meetings.

## INTRODUCTION

Meetings and committees are crucial to the American way of business. In spite of the fact that we have many negative attitudes and orientations toward them, meetings remain THE primary mechanism through which American business decision making is accomplished. Rarely are those decisions made in isolation. Almost always, in fact, those decisions are the direct or indirect product of some group meeting in committee.

We do love our myths about business leadership and the captains of industry. We can all recount endless apocryphal tales of the hard-headed CEO, closeted alone for days while wrestling with some potentially cataclysmic decision, emerging, finally with a directive. The fact that it seldom happens this way doesn't seem to bother us particularly.

Some business myths are not harmless. Some can lead, in fact, to real catastrophe for a company or an organization that refuses to shed them in spite of strong evidence to the contrary. Among the more dangerous are those we perpetuate about committees and the meeting process: "A committee is a group that takes minutes to waste hours"; "A camel is a horse designed by a committee"; and "If you want to be certain nothing gets done about a problem, turn it over to a committee." Reality is quite different.

Almost no important business decision is made entirely outside the meeting context, without some shaping by the meeting process, without some review by other committees. Meetings and group decisions are powerful and essential elements in any organizational enterprise. Successful business cannot function without them.

---

Gersh Morningstar is a consultant, editor, and writer in Florida.

In the abstract, meetings don't deserve their bad press. Theoretically, a meeting is like an elegant, cleverly structured, intricate, action game. In our society, it is a game everyone must play at one time or another: in business, it is a game played without end. The problem is that almost everyone plays it badly. Unlike baseball (another game the elegance of which is axiomatic), for meetings there is no organized learning system that begins in grade school, continues through high school, moves to the sand lots, then on to the minor leagues, and finally to the majors. Chris Schenkel does not broadcast the World Series of Meetings, so very few of us ever get to see the game played well. While there are a handful of meeting "major leaguers," most of us have never seen them perform. If by chance we do run across one, we view him or her as a "Natural" with inborn skills we think cannot be learned. We are, nevertheless, thrown into the game without proper training, without a knowledge of the rules, with little concept of effective game strategy and tactics, and without a clear understanding of which position (role) we are being expected to play. Our only role models for the game are poor players ourselves. So, we condemn the game when our real problem is the ineptitude of the players.

The experience of most of us with meetings leaves us wanting to get back to something that at least has the appearance of being productive. While meetings, ideally, may be places where decisions should be made, all too frequently they are exercises in inefficiency.

Cohen, March, and Olsen address this point in their famous paper, "The Garbage Can Model of Decision Making." They argue that all organizations have four forces running through them: (1) people who know the organization's problems; (2) people who know the solutions to the organization's problems but may not, themselves, know the problems; (3) people who control organizational resources; and, (4) "decision makers looking for work." Individuals representing these organizational segments need to be assembled in one place if organizational goals are to be achieved. Too frequently it doesn't happen. In some meetings people get together who know the problems but have no solutions or resources. In others, decision makers get together to take action, which may be (often is) irrelevant.

For most organizations, then, worries about the inefficiencies of group decision making are appropriate and well targeted. The solution, however—avoiding meetings, reducing their number, getting rid of committees—is the wrong approach. This solution must inevitably lessen the quality of decisions presently being made, for it truncates the base of wisdom, knowledge, and experience available for decision making.

The best solution lies in learning to play the meetings game with skill. The first step in that learning process is understanding why things go wrong.

## WHY THINGS GO WRONG

To prescribe a suitable remedy, we must first have a proper diagnosis. We begin with a series of questions: Why are meetings generally viewed with such negativity? Why don't meetings accomplish what they should accomplish? Why do so many view meetings as a waste of time? In short, why *do* things go wrong? There are many answers.

### Values

Group decision making—most group activity, in fact—runs counter to the popular view most Americans hold of themselves as fierce individualists. We believe that things run better if we do them ourselves, on our own, without having to rely on others. "I can't get any work done if I have to be in meetings all the time." The implicit assumption here is that meetings are the antithesis of work, that work is something we do alone in our offices. Not only is work viewed as best done while alone, but credit for work is seen as an individual reward. In our arts as in our industry we glorify the individual and deprecate the group. Every day must be a replay of *High Noon*. Things go wrong in meetings because, too often, the committee room is a coliseum of conflict instead of a center of cooperation.

### Hidden Functions

Meetings and committees perform a number of hidden functions on behalf of society, which can confound and confuse decision making. Social purpose, for example, is embedded in the meeting process that is related to American traditions of representative democracy and pluralism. In our society we recognize that individuals have both a need and a right to have their say on important issues. This has extended itself into the political system of American business, where the committee has become a way in which diverse factions are allowed to argue their various points of view. It gives those who would lose out in a simple majority vote a chance to be heard.

### Lack of Training

Playing the meetings game effectively requires a certain amount of skill that can only be achieved through expert training. While we provide ample opportunities for practice (everyone participates in meetings), such practice is without guidance and focus. As important as the group decision-making process is to every aspect of business life, our society devotes little time and almost none of its resources to teaching the rules of the meetings game and training individuals in the application of those rules. Things go wrong in meetings because the participants simply have no idea how to make them go right.

### The Self-fulfilling Prophecy

Because we have no "good meeting" referent, much of our experience with meetings is negative. Out of that experience base have come strong negative expectations about meetings and the effectiveness of the group decision-making process. We expect meetings to be time wasters, and we engage in behavior that causes them to turn out that way. Things go wrong in meetings because we expect them to go wrong.

## HOW TO MAKE THINGS GO RIGHT

### Seven General Principles of the Meetings Game

Meetings and group decision making can be improved. Learning and then applying a few simple rules (prescriptions, if you will, for curing the ailing meeting process) will quickly yield dramatic improvements in both the quality of meetings and the quality of the decisions that emerge from them. Seven broad principles form the basis for these rules, and examining those principles will help to place the twelve rules I will present in proper perspective.

An important caveat must precede that examination. Principles and rules go only part of the way toward improving business meetings and the decision that come from them. People are people. Potential conflict between us and among us exists whenever two or more of us gather. Yet, there are places—a courtroom, a ballgame, a play, an orchestra performance—where the very existence of rules makes for better performance possibilities. Still, rules (and the principles that underlie them) do not of themselves guarantee outstanding performance in meetings. (Neither do they guarantee it in courts, ballgames, plays, and orchestra performances.) What they do accomplish is to give groups more of a fighting chance by preventing some bad things from happening.

There are many principles involved in the meetings game. The list that follows is not exhaustive, but these seven are seen by meetings professionals as among the most important.

*1. The Role Principle.* Just as there are roles in a play that various actors fit into, there are various meeting roles; and these are as well defined as the parts in a play. At the very least these include the role of Chair and the role of Member. There is usually a Recorder role, as well, and often a Staffer role. Sometimes, too, there are specialized roles—Advisor, for example. Everyone connected with a meeting casts himself or herself (or is cast by someone else) into one of those roles. As long as each participant plays the assigned role, speaking lines and presenting behaviors appropriate to that role, meetings run as smoothly as a well-oiled machine. Problems arise when the actors attempt to expand their parts in a conscious or unconscious effort to usurp the role of someone else (usually the Chair, but all too frequently Chairs have been known to take on the Member role.)

One of the reasons most frequently reported to me for why things go wrong is "mental illness," i.e., "All the people on my committee but me are crazy." While that may be overstating the case a bit, many observers see aberrant or inappropriate behavior on the part of committee members as the root cause of some major meeting problems. These are common occurrences: a committee member voices constant anger, making other members uncomfortable, and the Chair seems incapable of firm control; one member dominates discussion to such a degree that other members get up and leave; one member gets so involved in minutia (harping on minutes, for example) that the productive work of the committee goes unaccomplished. Such disruptive behavior causes us to focus on personalities. But the real problems have very little to do with personalities. Rather, the problems arise when individuals depart from their assigned and defined roles within the meeting context.

Once we recognize that our focus should be upon the roles that participants must play in the meeting and *not* upon the personalities they bring to their parts, we move away from the negative effect that inevitably accompanies a focus on individual personalities. We can begin to consider the dynamics of the group more rationally and with more reason.

*2. The Orchestra Principle.* In considering the dynamics of the group, I have found it especially instructive to relate the meeting process to an orchestra performance. The orchestra has a score to perform (something like an agenda). There are the rehearsals before the performance (as there is some degree of preparation for any well-planned meeting.) There is a conductor to lead the orchestra through the performance (as there is a Chair to guide the meeting.) The musicians, each with his or her own contribution to make to the totality, come together as a body on a preplanned basis to make music (just as meeting participants should always be brought together on a preplanned basis to make decisions.)

We would find it surpassingly odd if we attended an orchestra concert, at the outset of which the oboe player stepped forward and played all of his notes in a Beethoven symphony and then left with the explanation, "I'm feeling a little pressed, and I've got to duck out early." That this kind of behavior happens routinely in meetings sheds still further light on why the meeting experience is so frequently unsatisfying.

*3. The Content Principle.* This principle is closely related to the Orchestra Principle. Meetings *should* be organized by content, but they are *usually* structured by person. Individual participants are allowed (encouraged, required) to present all of the material specifically related to them, all at one time, without regard to the possibility that this material might be of many different kinds and relate to many different items with which the meeting is concerned. Thus, we have "the treasurer's report," which is generally parallel to our oboe player giving us all of his notes at once. At best, meetings organized by person result in a great deal of repetition that fosters inefficiency and lengthens meetings unnecessarily. At worst, such organization reinforces the focus on personalities and generally works to the detriment of good meetings.

*4. The Three-Character Principle.* Matters before decision groups have one of three characters: they are informational, decisional, or discussional. Each is distinctly different. In the well-played meetings game, these are separated before the meeting begins and organized together so that the group can deal with all the information items at once, all of the decision items at once, and all of the discussion items at once. This is what I mean when I say meetings should be organized by content. This kind of organization leads to dramatic increases in the efficient use of meeting time and resources and leads to better decision making by the group.

Such organization may (and usually does) require some individuals to appear more than once on the agenda. This is no more odd than our peripatetic player doing his or her thing as the score requires throughout the symphony.

*5. The No-More-Reports Principle.* Reports are a major enemy of meetings for two reasons. First, they involve one individual heavily and all the others passively, which is not the reason the group was brought together. Second, they tend to be organized by persons rather than by topics (again, the ever popular "treasurer's report" or any other "reports" where individuals get up and report on all matters pertaining to their departments, regardless of the character of the information presented.)

Reports make it difficult for groups to cope with their expected tasks because they generally require the participants to move rapidly back and forth among items of different character that have differing requisites and make differing demands. The informational content of the usual treasurer's report should, in fact, be allocated across the agenda items and presented whenever, wherever, and only to the extent that it is relevant. The information contained in any individual's "report" should emerge as a natural part of the decision or discussion processes.

*6. The No-New-Business Principle.* The introduction and discussion of new business is a meeting enemy even more formidable than reports. It achieves this status not because there is no need for new business but, rather, because introducing it at the meeting disrupts the orderly flow of the meeting process. New business is, by definition, that about which little is known. The ability of the group to process the new business is severely limited. Neither the quality of any discussion about it nor any decisions made concerning it are likely to be of high quality. Injecting new business in a meeting is roughly equivalent to a football coach introducing a new play into a critical situation of a football game, a play that not only has never been practiced but is one the players are not even familiar with. In the well-played meetings game, what might be called "new business" is introduced at the end of the meeting, without discussion and as a kind of preview of some subsequent meeting.

*7. The Proactivity Principle.* Most groups spend most of their time reacting to issues. This fosters the appearance of items on an agenda that are already at some crisis point. The reactive position is always structurally weaker than the proactive one. It is therefore in the interests of good meeting process to reach out for issues, to garner them before they require crisis management. Small problems are easier to solve than big ones. Small decisions requiring minimal discomfort are easier to make than large decisions involving great pain.

## High-Quality Decisions

The goal of the meetings game is high-quality decisions. Well-played meetings games have nothing to do with making people happier in groups (although that will happen because some of the problematic activities will have been removed or changed.) For the most part, the feelings of the players are of only minimal concern. The real focus of the game is on the output of the group over time. That output needs to be assessed on a constant basis to provide effective feedback to the players on how well they are playing the game. I am about to present twelve rules for making things go right in meetings. The last of these rules provides one possible mechanism for conducting this ongoing assessment.

## Twelve Practical Rules to Make Things Go Right

Following are twelve rules that, if applied, will help things go right in meetings. These rules focus on both the substantive and procedural structure of information. They are concerned both with meeting items and with the kinds of considerations that are desired from those items. This latter is particularly important because it is the source from which individuals come to know the kinds of things that are expected of them.

Some of these rules deal with the meeting, itself. Others deal with the preplanning and preparation that go into the meetings.

*1. The Rule of Halves.* Identify the halfway point that lies between the end of the last meeting and the beginning of the next. During the first half of that period gather information about the kinds of items that are to be considered at the upcoming meeting.

End the item gathering at the halfway point. At that point examine all of the items that have been gathered. Remove all of those that can be handled on a one-to-one basis in people's offices. If something does not need group attention (and fully 40 percent of all items that generally come before meetings don't and should never be there), don't put it on the agenda. Removing such nongroup items permits more intensive focus upon the remaining items.

For each potential meeting item, assess what people, information, and/or resources are needed in connection with each and arrange for their presence at the upcoming session. If the appropriate information, individuals, or resources are not available, eliminate the item from the meeting. It makes very little sense to waste the group's valuable time discussing them.

Sort the candidate items into three groups: information items, decision items, and discussion items. Meeting participants not only want substantive information about what they are discussing, they want that information given to them in a procedural context. ("Are we just hearing about this? Are we deciding it? Or are we just noodling around?")

Information that once would have been presented in a single report (such as the treasurer's report) should be examined for each of its informational, decisional, and discussional components and scheduled appropriately.

*2. The Rule of Sixths.* As the final agenda is taking form, inspect the meeting items and seek to find those that flow in about the following proportions: (1) About one sixth should be items from the past, historical items that have not yet been completed. (2) About four sixths should be, relatively speaking, here-and-now type items. (3) About one sixth should be future oriented, "blue sky" items about which the meeting participants can do some proactive, plan-ahead type thinking.

The virtue of this system is not only that good ideas are generated, but that a certain amount of affect, especially around controversial items, is allowed to be expressed in a nonthreatening situation. Individuals are allowed to express their creativity in a context in which creativity may be expected to have some impact. This becomes a "psychic income" that meeting planners can provide for the group. It is more likely to keep individuals pleased, happy, and eager to return. This is a side benefit of proactivity that reaps great rewards.

*3. The Two-Meeting Rule.* As this system gets under way, in the meeting planning phase, look for controversial items and seek to schedule them according to the Rule of Sixths. At the very least, controversial items should be discussed at least twice, i.e., in at least two different meetings. The first discussion should be just that: a discussion. This process allows for affect to be expressed and for new ideas to be introduced about how difficult items might be approached. The next time such as issue comes up it can be for decision.

For very controversial items, two and even three iterations of discussion may be appropriate before a decision is taken. All too frequently our hesitancy to deal with controversial matters encourages us to delay them, taking them up only at the last possible moment under severe constraints of pressure and time.

*4. The Rule of Three Fourths.* By the three-fourths point in the time period between meetings, the agenda should be in its final form. Send it to the individuals attending the meeting so that they have time to review it and to read any accompanying materials. Usually the meeting packet contains three items: the agenda, minutes of the last meeting, and reports of various kinds. Each of these requires some specific attention.

*5. The Rule of the Agenda.* An agenda should look like a menu. Most agendas, unfortunately, are simply lists of topics that regularly pass up opportunities for structuring the decision-making context in a helpful fashion. With a menu-type agenda, items are segregated into their information, decision, and discussion groups. Instead of simply "the PDQ report," for example, the agenda might say something like "Information about the PDQ report" or "Decisions concerning the PDQ report" or "Discuss the PDQ report."

Below each agenda item, the "main dish" on the menu, provide a one-or two-sentence summary of the key elements of the item so that individuals scanning the agenda can have a full sense of what is involved.

As part of the item itself or in parentheses next to it use one of the three key words ("informational," "decision," or "discussion"). This allows the meeting participants to understand the context of the item.

Finally, on the right-hand side of the agenda, where price might be on a menu, put a running clock with differential amounts of time allocated to the different items. This tells the meeting participants when the meeting will start, when it will end, and how much time in the meeting is being allocated for each item.

*6. The Minutes Rule.* Provide content-focused minutes that give brief summaries of the main points of discussion. Skip a line and, in capital letters, put in the decision or action. It is here that names are mentioned, times are mentioned, and responsibilities are assigned. This cures the frequent problem of meeting attendees being unable to remember from one meeting to the next precisely what was decided. It also tends to prevent descriptions of decisions that are so vague no one later knows what they meant: "Take appropriate action."

Meeting minutes are almost always written in the wrong way—as descriptions of the meeting process, with long litanies of "he said" and "she said." Process minutes not only fail to convey fully the extent of the meeting work that went on, but they focus on individuals. Where such individuals perceive the minutes placing them in a bad light, it is not uncommon to engage in protracted discussions in order to improve their respective positions. Content minutes also tend to cure this problem.

*7. The Rule of Reports.* Use the executive summary technique and the options memo technique, as described below, for all reports to be presented at a meeting.

Most meeting planners send out too much information, sometimes so much that it becomes disinformation. Too often, a potential meeting participant will look at the huge packet of material sent to her or him as preparation for the next meeting, and put it aside "until I can really devote the appropriate amount of time to it." That time never comes, so the preparatory work becomes useless.

With the executive summary technique, all reports are reduced to no more than two pages. If an attendee wants or needs further information, it is available on request.

Options memos are designed to enhance discussion and to prevent it from becoming malfocused, one of the most common problems in groups. The technique presents all reports, written or oral, in three steps: a problem statement, a set of options that reasonable people might consider to handle the problem, and a set of recommendations for action based upon a selection from the options set.

Options memos encourage the work of the group and discourage rubber stamping of the work of a single individual or subcommittee (the "O.K., here's the problem, and here's what I think should be done about it" presentation). Options memos virtually eliminate the problem of the group focusing on whether to accept or reject a proffered solution rather than looking at the proposal, itself, as a basis for discussion and improvement.

Options memos present information that the group wants and needs. They answer latent questions and stimulate the beginning of the process of discussion. The act of discussing options often leads to the discovery of still further alternatives and may also uncover hidden difficulties. The final result is a decision on which the full force of the group has been focused. That decision is almost always an improved one with difficulties removed or diminished and positive features added.

*8. The Rule of Two Thirds.* All meetings are divided into three parts: a "git-go" part at the beginning, a heavy work part in the middle, and a decompression part at the end. Allocate information items and simple decisions to the first third of the meeting. Process difficult items in the middle third. Deal with discussion items in the last third.

Groups need a little time to get going, so key items don't belong at the beginning of a meeting. Toward the middle of the session, maximum attendance has been achieved, and energy, both physical and psychological, is at its high point. This is the time to handle the toughest items.

The decision making that occurs in the group under this model *does* tear at the fabric of group cohesion. This cohesion needs to be rebuilt whether the group is a gathering of strangers or is made up of people who work together on a daily basis. Discussion provides a way to continue group work, on the one hand, while allowing for group rebonding on the other.

*9. The Rule of the Agenda Bell.* Orchestrate meetings so that the emotional component follows a bell-shaped curve, as in Figure 35.1. Item 1 should always be minutes. If there are not enough people there to approve the minutes, they can be reapproved at a later point.

Item 2 is always made up of announcement items. These should take no more than about 10 percent of the total meeting time, which will prevent the meeting from becoming simply an oral newsletter.

Item 3 (a,b,c, etc.) contains decision items of only modest difficulty. Short, easy decision items allow the group to get going.

Item 4 (a,b,c, etc.) matters are the more difficult decision items.

Item 5 is always the single most difficult item on the agenda for that particular meeting. It should occupy space between the 40 percent and 60 percent points, allowing for optimum group attention and energy. Because of its difficulty, this item will almost always follow the Two-Meeting Rule; thus, this will be at least the second time in the history of the group that this item is being considered.

By the completion of Item 5, with one minor exception, all of the decision items have been handled. Item 6 (a,b,c, etc.) is composed of discussion items. There are items where thought is needed but where final resolution is not yet appropriate or is not yet in the purview of this particular group.

Item 7 is a short, easy decision item on which all can agree. Usually this will be an item that appears to be substantially trivial in content. It is not at all trivial, however, in its importance to the meetings game. Such an item allows the meeting to end on time and on a psychological note of agreement and accomplishment. ("Well, at least we got *something* done.")

*10. The Rule of Temporal Integrity.* Start on time. End on time. Keep to the rough in-

FIGURE 35.1
The Rule of the Agenda Bell

Remember that once you set the time frame, people adjust their internal expectations to that announcement. It's sort of an agreement.

Organize your agenda according to the agenda bell. If you cannot hand it out in advance, take a few minutes with the whole team and do it right there.

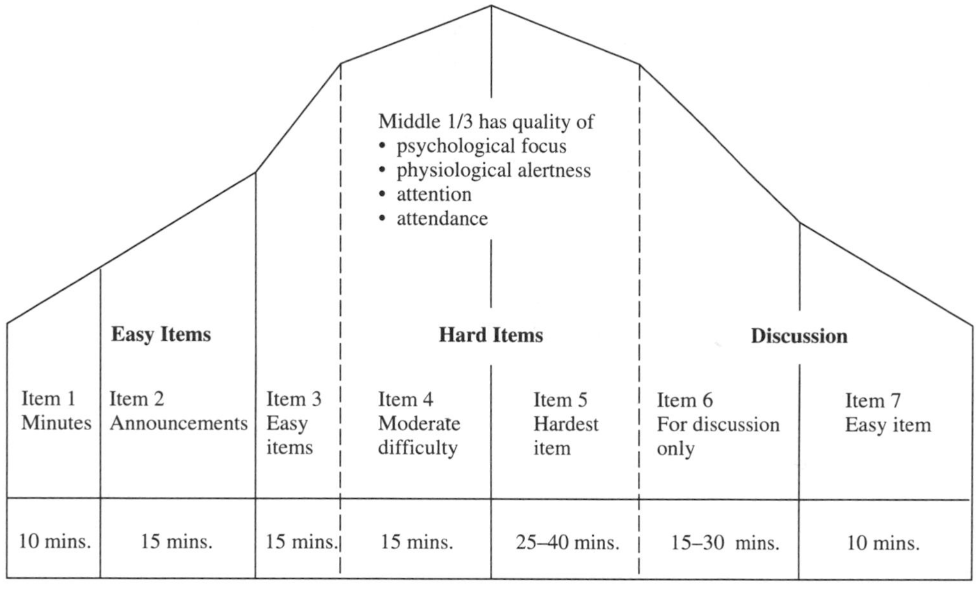


ternal time order. Carefully planned meetings held by properly prepared meeting attendees should almost never require more than an hour and a half.

*11. The Rule of Agenda Integrity.* Deal with all of the items on the agenda. Do *not* deal with any items not on the agenda. Individuals make attendance decisions based in part upon what they are informed will be covered. They invest time in reviewing meeting materials. Maintaining the integrity of the agenda reinforces the decisions to attend and provides a substantial return on the time investment. Nothing short of an act of God justifies changing the agenda at the last moment or wandering from the agenda during the meeting.

*12. The Rule of Decision Audit and Decision Autopsy.* For important groups, go back on a year- to a year-and-a-half basis and look at some of the key decisions made by the groups. Any evaluation can be used. Here is one I have found effective.

Take a sample of past decisions. For each decision, rate it "A" if it was an all-win situation—i.e., everyone benefitted though not necessarily equally. Rate it "B" if the decision had some winners and some losers but on balance had a positive result. Give it a "C" if a decision was made but nothing happened. A "D" rating is the inverse of "B": There were both winners and losers but on balance the result was negative. An "F," also known as the "nuclear war decision," is an all-lose decision.

Calculate a grade point average for the sample and feed it back to the groups. Whatever rating mechanism is used is purely a matter of choice. What is crucial is going back and looking at decisions in an effort to assess the strengths and weaknesses in the decision-making process.

This assessment leads to the autopsy. In any such review, take the very best decisions and the very worst ones, and take them apart. Answer, to the extent possible, the questions, "What went right and why?" "What went wrong and why?" It is imperative that both good and bad decisions be lined together in the autopsy process. Using only bad decisions in the autopsy generates group defensiveness and fault-avoidance behavior.

## CONCLUSION

Meetings can be improved. Therefore, meetings should be improved. Improvement means that the output of meetings—decisions—should be of the highest possible quality. In moving toward high-quality decisions, I have presented procedures that shorten time, focus discussion, and generally make meetings less painful. However, I wish to underscore that it is *not* removing pain from the meeting that is my goal. Rather, it is making the pain pay off.

As individuals experience meetings that are productive, that invite and involve their participation, a process of reinforcement will begin that can both reverse the negative aspects of the self-fulfilling prophecy as well as use that mechanism for improvement and achievement.

## SIDEBAR

### Effective Role Playing Helps Things Go Right

In the game of football it is not enough to know the rules to play the game well. It is also important to understand what is required of each position on the team—what the quarterback does, what the center does, what the linebacker does, and so on. The same is true of the meetings game. To play it well, it is important to understand what is required of the various positions on the meeting team because, over the course of time, we will each play all of the positions.

*The Chair Role.* The Chair is one of the key roles, and most of us have never learned to chair a meeting. Often, the decision to accept the responsibilities of a meeting Chair is a fairly casual matter, made without regard to much more than whether one has the extra time available that is always assumed to go with chairing a committee. There are, however, several things that a potential Chair ought to look into.

First, does the group have enough resources to do the kinds of things that it is being asked to do? Does it have the necessary money and/or people to accomplish its task?

Second, what are the politics of the group? Are they something that can be worked with, and, if so, how? A careful political assessment done in advance can save many future problems.

Third, employ self-assessment: "What does it mean for me to be Chair of the group? What kinds of signals does my reputation in the business convey? How will others react?" It is not possible to change some of these things, of course, but knowledge allows for behavioral alterations that can lead to productive results that might never have been possible without it.

Fourth, what is the purpose of the group? If the Chair is to be the custodian of this purpose, it should be written down and provided to the other members. This is true even for "simple staff meetings" held on a frequent, regular basis. If someone else is the custodian of the mandate, then that individual should be asked for it in writing. During the crafting period, negotiations about the nature of mandate, the scope, and the resources can be undertaken.

Fifth, and most importantly, the Chair needs to inquire of himself or herself whether it is possible to move from the role of partisan to the role of statesman. Many Chairs feel that once they assume the Chair, they will be able to get their own way. Unfortunately, as Antony Jay has pointed out, self-indulgence is one of the great problems groups face. It is necessary to assume the posture of a statesman if the meeting process is to be successful, facilitating the product of the group rather than promoting ones' own wishes and desires.

The role of the Chair falls, basically, into two parts: intellectual and interpersonal. Intellectually, the Chair needs to *blend* the ideas of those in the meeting. At key points, often after a round of discussion when everyone has had the opportunity to contribute, the Chair should summarize, suggesting to the group where it is at that moment, bracketing those areas of agreement and setting them aside, and refocusing the discussion on those items that remain. The process is really the decision process with individuals (often the Chair but not always)—summarizing, building, refocusing—until the entire decision stands before the group in a way that no individual would have anticipated.

In this process the Chair uses interrogative rather than declarative. Instead of saying, "That's a dumb idea," or "That's a terrific idea," the Chair raises questions of a "what if" nature. This is especially true of weak or bad ideas. The individual who offers a poor concept might well be the genius who provides the key to the solution of the next problem. Squelching that individual may cause him or her to retreat and contribute no further. The idea is to guide the contributing process in a way that invites the individual to confront some of the problems of the poor idea but, at the same time, receive support for the basic effort of suggesting and trying.

Jay points out that there is a sequence to the discussion process that facilitates that process if it is followed. First there is the discussion of the problem. Second, there is discussion of evidence and points of view about the problem. Third, there is an agreement about what the evidence and perspectives mean. Fourth, there is a decision. Fifth, there is action.

Insofar as possible, the Chair's job is to keep the discussion moving through these stages, seeing that each one is resolved before the next one is begun. Throughout, the Chair maintains equality for persons but equity for issues; i.e., people are all treated equally but issues are not. More attention is lavished on some issues than on others in order to achieve the appropriate and necessary group results.

With respect to interpersonal activities, the Chair must try to protect the weak participants and temper the strong in order to allow for an evenness of group participation. Those individuals who do not participate need to be invited to share their views. (They are often the ones who will protest most vocally in the restaurant after the meeting.) Feelings and affect need to be diffused. This is best accomplished by direct recognition: "Jim, you seem to feel strongly about this." We deal with the Jims directly instead of watching them glower in the corner.

The Chair supports the clash and conflict of ideas and, at the same time, seeks to find aspects of different types of suggestions that may become part of a general solution.

Throughout, the Chair has overall responsibility for the group product, not for getting her or his own way. The Chair exercises influences by asking questions and directing the discussion and by structuring and shaping the agenda and through the preparation and supervision of options memos.

The Chair's influence, then, is more indirect than direct. But this is appropriate. After all, if an issue is so clear cut that the Chair can decide it, it shouldn't be before the group in the first place.

*The Member Role.* The popular view is that the member's role is a passive one with nothing to do and nothing special to know. ("There's nothing to it. All I have to do is show up and doze off.") Like so many popular views, this one is also wrong.

To begin with, there is the matter of preparation. No procedural problems loom larger in poor meeting practice than those caused by the unprepared member. Without proper preparation, discussion becomes prattle, and the unprepared participant presents the worst of all possible role models for the other members. It is almost a truism that the unprepared members of a group will attempt to cover their lack of preparation with bluster, rancor, sarcasm, and general negativity. So, preparation is the first responsibility of the member.

Knowledge of how the meetings game is played is a second member responsibility. This means not only a thorough understanding of good meeting procedures in general (such as the meeting rules presented here), but a complete knowledge of the specific rules of the committee upon which the member sits. (While the rules of some groups are more formal than for others, all group decision-making bodies have specific rules of their own.) It is the member's responsibility throughout the life of the group to cooperate in the enforcement of committee rules. At the very least this includes such things as coming on time, coming prepared, and requiring the meeting planners to provide a straightforward agenda.

Third, the member needs constantly to monitor his or her level of participation in the meeting, contributing at a level that is appropriate for this particular group decision-making activity. Some groups are high-participation groups; others, low participation. Within either context it is the member's responsibility both to contribute at the appropriate level and to aid the Chair in seeing to it that all other members likewise contribute appropriately.

Fourth, while issue crystalization and decision focus are generally the Chair's responsibility, it does not always have to be the Chair's actions that accomplish them. The Member should be constantly alert for opportunities to provide summative reflections at various points and to assist in the crystalization of ideas.

The member should be equally alert to other members who have a tendency to dump on the group; i.e., raising problems, then sitting back with arms folded as if to defy the group to provide solutions. It is both correct and useful when one has a problem with a particular proposal or line of thinking to share that perspective, provided such sharing is accompanied by good-faith attempts to seek solutions. It is incorrect, unfair, and harmful for a member to raise an issue without making it clear to the other members what one's position is with respect to that issue. It forces the group to shift its focus away from the issue and into a mode where it must probe to see what makes the recalcitrant member happy.

Finally, members owe loyalty to the group outside the group. This means supporting group decisions that one opposed. It also means not knocking the group, its members, or its Chair in other meetings, at cocktail parties, or anywhere else.

*The Recorder Role.* The individual who is taking the meeting record (using the Rule of Minutes, of course) is in a unique position to facilitate and focus the group discussion. As the new meeting format involves not only a summarizing of discussion but also a brief statement of the actual resolution, the Recorder should use both of these to assist group functioning. As discussion is beginning to come to a close, for example, a Recorder can say something like, "Well, for the record, let me see if I understand the various points we have been discussing." A skilled Recorder can actually craft a summary on the spot and, in doing so, may uncover more or fewer areas of agreement than hitherto thought. In either case, it is to the advantage of the group. Similarly, the Recorder can shape the summative statement, itself. "As I understand it, here is what we have concluded." This helps focus and crystalize group activity and builds support for group decisions.

*The Staffer Role.* A Staffer is an individual who is paid or assigned to assist a group in carrying out its functions. This individual is different from other participants because the Staffer is *not* a member of the group—an extremely important point. All groups know who are and who are not members, even if everyone is well acquainted with one another, as is the case for most businesses.

The Staffer performs four kinds of functions for most committees. First, the Staffer is a researcher, providing various types of information for the group (political, historical, economic, scientific, items of program history, and so on).

Second, the Staffer is a knowledge synthesizer. It is not enough simply to present a range of information to a group (though some use it as a procedure for dumping on the group). Rather, the information should be organized, synthesized, integrated. This function is an important one for the Staffer to perform. For a committee considering executive compensation, for example, the Staffer might say something like, "Here is a list of other companies and the compensation packages they provide their executives. They seem to fall into the following groups, based on what appear to me to be the following kinds of criteria, linked in the following ways to corporate income, etc."

Third, the Staffer is a writer and a documentor. The role may involve taking minutes and recording. It usually involves the preparation of reports, preparing executive summaries, and generally doing the "legwork" of the committee.

Fourth, the Staffer is an aide to the Chair. In meetings, this usually involves sitting close by the Chair in a kind of dead zone that diminishes the physical position of the Staffer and emphasizes her or his "assisting" rather than "membering" function. The Staffer does not participate directly in discussions or decision making in the sense of giving an opinion on this matter or that.

Fifth, the Staffer is an administrator. In part, this relates to the function of aiding the Chair, and it may involve many things. The staffer may get out the minutes, may assist in preparing the agenda, may review meeting strategy with the Chair, may arrange for the meeting room, and so on. This "stage manager" activity is not especially dramatic, but it needs to be done if the setting for the meeting is to facilitate rather than hamper the meeting process.

**REFERENCES**

Avery, Michael, et al., *Building United Judgment: A Handbook for Consensus Decision-making* (Madison, WI: The Center for Conflict Resolution, 1981).

Bell, Arthur, *Mastering the Meeting Maze* (Reading, MA: Addison-Wesley, 1990).

Clifton, Robert, and Alan Dahms, *Grassroots Administration: A Handbook for Staff and Directors of Small, Community-Based Social Service Agencies* (Prospect Heights, IL: Waveland Press, 1987).

Cohen, M., J. March, and J. Olsen, "A Garbage Can Model of Organizational Choice," *Administrative Science Quarterly* 17 (1) (March 1972): 1–25.

Frank, Milo, *How to Run a Successful Meeting in Half the Time* (New York: Simon and Schuster, 1989).

Hackman, J. Richard, *Groups That Work (And Those That Don't); Creating Conditions for Effective Teamwork* (San Francisco: Jossey-Bass, 1990).

Jay, Antony, "How to Run a Meeting That Gets Things Done," *Harvard Business Review* (March-April, 1976).

Jay, Antony, "How to Run a Meeting," in F.M. Cox, J. Erlich, J. Rothman and J.E. Tropman, *Tactics and Techniques of Community Practice*, 2nd ed. (Itasca, IL: F.E. Peacock, 1984).

Kahneman, Daniel, Paul Slovic, and Amos Tversky, *Judgment Under Uncertainty: Heuristics and Biases* (New York: Cambridge University Press, 1986).

Kieffer, George, *The Strategy of Meetings* (New York: Warner, 1988).

Kleindorfer, Paul, Howard Kunreuther, and Paul Schoemaker, *Decision Sciences* (New York: Cambridge University Press, 1993).

Mosvick, Roger, and Robert B. Nelson, *We've Got To Start Meeting Like This* (Glenview, IL: Scott, Foresman, 1987).

Schwartzman, Helen B., *The Meeting: Gatherings in Organizations and Communities* (New York: Plenum, 1989).

Thomsett, Michael C., *The Little Black Book of Business Meetings* (New York: AMACOM, 1989).

Tropman, John E., Harold Johnson, and Elmer J. Tropman, *Committee Management in the Human Services,* 2nd ed. (Chicago: Nelson-Hall, 1991).

Tropman, John E., Meetings: *How to Make Them Work For You* (New York: Van Nostrand, 1984).

36.

**Richard L. Douglass**

# HOW TO USE AND PRESENT COMMUNITY DATA

The demand for quantitative demonstrations of service needs, measurements of change in target populations, effectiveness of programs, and other aspects of accountability for health and human services increases constantly. All levels of government private foundations and organizations that reimburse service providers expect clear and reliable estimates of service demand, as well as justification for program activities and outcomes. Health and human service workers and administrators must accommodate this emphasis on data-based planning and evaluation and learn to do it well as a regular aspect of professional life. The future will be more quantitatively oriented as our ability to deal with data accompanies the ubiquitous computer terminals on most professional desks.

## REASONS FOR INCREASING EMPHASIS ON QUANTIFICATION

The reasons for increasing emphasis on detailed data analysis in planning and evaluation are related to the ability and interest of service providers to find out more precisely what services should be offered and the extent to which services are effective. At the administrative level, the relative effectiveness of different approaches to similar problems can be determined only with sufficient and appropriate data.

For almost twenty years, health and human services financing has been in direct competition with other national priorities and political philosophies, forcing service providers to become more precise in terms of resource allocation and accountability. Sponsors of services use data to determine priority services and target populations. Routine outcome and process data are also used to select recipients of competitive grant support for continuation of programs and the initiation of new projects. Regulatory and accreditation obligations are similarly focused on quantification of all aspects of service delivery and management.

An immediate by-product of the increased expectation for quantification of service needs, activities, and outcomes is that successful administrators have discovered that improved information helps them to plan and provide better programs. Thus the external demand for increased quantification has generated a demand within the service delivery system itself for more precise and adequate measurement.

The remarkable evolution of new technologies to supply inexpensive measurement, data storage, and sophisticated analysis has accelerated the ability of services to provide meaningful data and to respond to both internal and external data analysis expectations. Community data sources, like state, county, and national statistical information are more accurate, current, and available for utilization than ever before. Professional boundaries are becoming ambiguous, with integrated service systems and interdisciplinary approaches to

---

Richard L. Douglass is an associate professor and director for the Program in Health Administration, Eastern Michigan University.

community problems. Social services and mental health and public health professionals now recognize the interactive nature of their activities and that economic problems—housing and transportation, for instance—have fundamentally important implications for services that have been offered only within strict departmental boundaries in the past. Dealing with complicated human problems is difficult without meaningful data to identify priorities, change, and resource needs.

To summarize, the competition among human services for scarce resources, the demand for accountability, professional recognition of the value of accurate measurement for planning and administering services, and an influx of quantitatively skilled personnel and technologies have interacted to produce an emphasis on quantification in the human services. This trend has been long in coming. Most other fields have developed quantitative methods earlier. However, many human service professionals have misgivings about translating the human condition into numerical abstractions and often are quite threatened by the trend toward quantification. Hopefully the information presented here will serve to reduce the anxiety.

## WHAT ARE COMMUNITY DATA?

Practitioners in health and human services frequently are unaware of many useful data sources bearing on community dynamics, population movements and changes, economic conditions, housing characteristics, etc. Such collections of community data are not often recognized because of a hesitation to use them and, in some cases, a reluctance to make them available.

Community data are compilations of periodic measures of the status of the community, activities of specific organizations and services, and other descriptive information including health, vital statistics, housing, and economic conditions. Community data consist of records, often collected routinely for purposes of documentation for regulatory accounting purposes.

Any specific analysis of such information with the intent of identifying changes or trends, or of making inferences about social conditions, is secondary to the purposes for which the data are collected. Thus, they are called "secondary data." In contrast, measurements specifically intended to be used for a particular analysis are referred to as "primary data." The utility of primary and secondary data for the community practitioner is largely determined by their characteristics. These will be discussed below.

## PRIMARY AND SECONDARY DATA

As indicated above, primary data are those sets of measurements collected by investigators for a specific purpose. Primary data include specially designed surveys of community residents, organization representatives, or service recipients. Primary data can take the form of special data collected during intake, termination, or follow-up interviews with the clients of social services. However, the overriding distinction between primary and secondary data is that primary data are collected only for a specific analytic purpose at hand, while secondary data are routinely collected for various purposes including documentation and subsequent use by others.[1]

Primary data, unlike case records, are not prepared routinely by community service organizations. Special-purpose measurements, however, frequently are routinized.

The difference between routine and routinized is subtle, but significant. Routinely collected data, such as client records, often are characterized by considerable missing information, less than optimum quality controls, and little or no understanding on the part of personnel recording the measurements of why the data are being collected. Frequently, there is no perceived need for the data, and the recording process is a burden to staff members.

Routinized data collection procedures are most common to primary data. The value and immediate utility of the measurements are usually well understood by the personnel involved in data collection. For these reasons, primary data tend to be specific and precise. Secondary data collection can be well supervised and the recording process routinized with adequate quality control. However, with the exception of secondary data generally collected by the Bureau of the Census and other highly skilled organizations, it would be folly to assume that secondary data generally approach the level of standardization and accuracy achieved with primary data collection.

Operational consistency of the data is the primary issue raised in routinizing or changing data collection methods. Operational consistency is defined as the comparability of measurements of a variable between groups or jurisdictions, or for single groups or jurisdictions over a period of time. Data collection is often poorly controlled. Routine data frequently have errors of recording, missing measurements, inconsistently defined meanings, and other shortcomings. Such negative characteristics reduce their utility for human service professionals. With the exceptions noted, primary data are more likely to be operationally consistent than are secondary data.

However, primary data are expensive to gather. Because the measurements are uniquely defined, designed, and collected, primary data collection requires the allocation of new resources that can substantially exceed the budget allocation for expected planning and evaluation activities. In addition to being expensive, primary data cannot be collected to measure events or characteristics from the past. Furthermore, the collection of primary data may present problems of confidentiality and practicality.

Thus, secondary data are often the only realistic source of community information. The likelihood of errors and operational inconsistencies in secondary data must be identified and understood clearly before a reasoned analysis can be made. Secondary data are available to community services from a variety of sources, discussed below. These and other sources of secondary data contain a wealth of information that is potentially useful for those who plan, manage, offer services, and evaluate community programs.

Major uses of secondary data in human service programs are: (1) to describe a community statistically; (2) to identify human service needs in the community; (3) to test hypotheses of change in a social condition after a change in services or the introduction of a new program; and (4) to anticipate changes in the profiles of need, service delivery, and program priorities in the future.

Accurate and useful description of change depends upon the operational consistency (or reliability) and the correspondence of the measurement used to the concept or idea being measured (or validity). While primary data often are more valid and reliable, secondary data may well be the only practical source of data because of constraints on staff, time, and budget. Fortunately, a careful search for secondary data often results in data that are adequate for the needs of the investigator at a minimal cost.

## SOURCES OF COMMUNITY DATA

A practitioner should undertake a thorough search to identify sources of information available locally and their usefulness before considering the collection of primary data. Because special-purpose investigations are often costly, there is a considerable payoff if existing data are uncovered. Possible sources of information include:

1. Federal and state government agencies, e.g., the Departments of Labor, Commerce and its Bureau of the Census, Housing and Urban Development, Health and Human Services, and Education, as well as comparable state agencies;
2. City and county planning departments and regional councils of governments;
3. State and local health departments and specialized units such as the Public Health Service Center for Disease Control and the National Center for Health Statistics;
4. Federations of social, health, and recreation agencies such as community welfare councils and united community services;
5. Comprehensive regional health-planning councils;
6. Medical health associations and community mental health agencies;
7. Funding agencies, both public (see 1 and 3 above) and private, such as the United Way, religious charities, and community chests;
8. Clearinghouses in many problem areas; for instance the Alcohol, Drug Abuse, and Mental Health Administration maintains clearinghouses that administer data banks and publish summary data on drug abuse, alcohol abuse, and mental health; its Biometry Branch publishes a useful "Statistical Note" series;
9. Universities, including departments, schools, libraries, research institutes, and individual faculty members with relevant research interests;
10. Libraries and local newspaper archives;
11. Annual reports and documents provided by hospitals and third-party payors for medical, mental health, and health care services and resource allocations.

## PRESENTATION OF COMMUNITY DATA

The statistical analysis of community data is beyond the scope of this article. However, the utilization of data eventually depends upon the clarity and accuracy of printed presentation. By this I mean the tables, charts, graphs, and other displays of numerical information that any data analysis ultimately requires. This section will describe the construction and variety of ways that numerical information can be presented.

### Tables: Numbers, Titles, Columns, Rows, and Cells

A table is an orderly arrangement of numerical information in columns and rows. There are few hard and fast rules for table construction. Perhaps the wisest are those given by a former director of the Bureau of the Census who wrote in the foreword of a manual on tabular presentation.

> In the final analysis, there are only two rules in tabular presentation that should be applied rigidly: first, the use of common sense when planning a table, and second, the viewing of the

TABLE 36.1
Demographic Characteristics of Homeless Black Men*
(Community Homeless Assistance Plan, Dade County, Florida, August 1991)

| Characteristic | No. | (%) |
|---|---|---|
| Age | | |
| 18–24 | 10 | ( 9) |
| 25–34 | 47 | (42) |
| 35–44 | 45 | (40) |
| ≥45 | 11 | (10) |
| Marital status | | |
| Never married | 62 | (55) |
| Married | 3 | ( 3) |
| Common-law spouse | 4 | ( 4) |
| Separated | 27 | (24) |
| Divorced | 15 | (13) |
| Other | 2 | ( 2) |
| Education | | |
| Less than high school diploma | 39 | (35) |
| High school diploma/General educational development certificate | 43 | (38) |
| Some college/Technical school | 26 | (23) |
| College degree | 5 | ( 4) |

*Sample size = 113.

SOURCE: Centers for Disease Control, Morbidity and Mortality Report, December 20, 1992.[3]

proposed table from the standpoint of the user. The details of mechanical arrangement must be governed by a single objective; that is, to make the statistical table as easy to read and to understand as the nature of the material will permit.[2]

*Numbers.* If more than one table is used in a report, each table should be numbered to indicate its place in the series. It is also easier to refer in the text to a specific table by use of its number.

*Titles.* Each table should have a title to indicate the *what, where,* and *when* of the contents of the table. Table 36.1 is used to illustrate these points. *What* the table contains indicates whether absolute numbers, computed numbers, or both are used; the title indicates how the contents of the table have been defined. For example, the title for Table 36.1 states that homeless black men are described by demographic characteristics. The *where* indicates the geographic area to which the information applies, as signified by "Dade County, Florida." The *when* is the time for which the data apply, August 1991.

The title should be as brief as possible; however, the content of the table should be absolutely clear from reading it. Titles of more than two lines are usually avoided. Further information needed for the understanding of the contents of the table can be placed in a headnote. The headnote follows the title and may be printed in smaller type and enclosed in brackets or parentheses. The information in the headnote should apply to many if not all items in the table. Such information may also be given in a note to the table.

In Table 36.1 the headnote indicates that the homeless men included in that table are those occurring within Dade County, Florida, and do not refer to homeless black men elsewhere. It also indicates that the data refer only to men who participated in the homeless assistance program.

TABLE 36.2
Prior Institutionalization of Elderly Homeless Persons in Detroit, Percentage Estimates by Race, Population Estimate of Homeless Persons over Age 59, Detroit, Michigan, July 1989

| Institutional Category | White n(est)% | | Black n(est)% | | Total n(est)% | |
|---|---|---|---|---|---|---|
| Alcohol or drug abuse inpatient treatment | 149 | 9% | 281 | 71% | 430 | 26% |
| Mental hospital inpatient | 373 | 23% | 132 | 8% | 505 | 31% |
| State or federal prison | 118 | 7% | 362 | 22% | 480 | 29% |
| Total by race | 640 White Estimates | 86% | 695 Black Estimates | 77% | 1415 Total Estimates | 86% |

SOURCE: Detroit Area Agency on Aging, Detroit, Michigan, 1992.[4]

*Columns.* Each column has a heading to state what is referred to in that column. In Table 36.2, one heading is "Institutional Category." The other headings refer to racial categories and total percentages.

In column headings, capitalization is headline style—important words are capitalized. (In published tables, this often depends on the style of the publisher.) In order to save space, there is a temptation to use abbreviations. These should be avoided unless the abbreviations will be readily understood, as those for the names of states, or days of the week. (In published tables, vertical rules dividing columns are usually omitted in the interest of economy.

*Rows.* The left-hand column of the table is called the stub; it contains row headings, which serve the same purpose as column headings, indicating what is contained in a particular row. The stub indicates the variable that is classified in the row headings, as shown in Table 36.2.

If data are stratified by more than one variable, for example, by age and sex, ethnicity, or cause of death, the variable that is stratified, or classified, in the stub is mentioned first in the title of the table. In Table 36.2, the stub column contains the various strata of institutional category, so institutional classifications are mentioned. Unlike column headings, only the initial words and proper nouns are capitalized in the row headings (or stubs), and abbreviations are used only when they are readily understood.

If stratification of items in a table is by two variables, as in Table 36.1, common sense suggests that the one having the greater number of categories will appear in the stub column. If classification is by age and sex or age and ethnicity, there will be more age groups than categories for sex and ethnicity, so the age groups will appear as row headings in the stub column. If deaths are stratified by age and by all causes of death (as in a table appearing in an annual report of a health department), there would be many more causes of death than age groups, so the causes of death would appear as row headings in the stub column while the age groups would be used for column captions.

The order in which row headings or column headings are arranged depends largely on whether or not there is progression. In a table presenting an age distribution, the youngest age group would appear as the first row followed by the other age groups in ascending order of magnitude. If the information in the table represents a time series, that is, information for different years, months, or days, the proper chronological order would be followed in the stub column or in the column headings.

If there is no progression from one group or another, as is usually the case with qualitative information, the order in presentation of row headings (or column headings) is determined by the size of the frequencies to which they apply. The category with the largest numbers should appear first, followed by other categories in descending order of magnitude of their frequencies.

*Cells.* Below the column headings, to the right of the row headings in the stub column, is the so-called "field" of the table, made up of cells. A cell is a space representing an interaction of a column and a row and containing a number or a symbol. The number may be an absolute number (as the number of homeless white former prisoners) or it may be relative number (a percentage of all former prisoners who are elderly, homeless persons in Table 36.2).

If the table contains computed values, such as percentages or rates, they should be expressed with the same number of decimal places. One would not record such values as:

| | | |
|---|---|---|
| 25.485 | but as | 25.5 |
| 12 | | 12.0 |
| 3.61 | | 3.6 |
| .7149 | | 0.7 |
| 11.6 | | 11.6 |

Percentages and rates are usually expressed with one decimal place to show that they are computed values, not absolute numbers. If rounding to the nearest tenth gives a whole number, this is written with a zero in the tenths position, as the 12.0 above. If the value is less than 1, this is written with a zero in the units position, as 0.7.

If computed values are included in the table, the reader should be informed as to what they represent. If they are rates, are they rates per 100, per 1,000, or per 100,000? If the computed values are rates per 1,000 this information may sometimes be included in the title, in a headnote, in a column caption, or in a spanner caption. Occasionally, the information may be given in a footnote.

In some tables both column and row totals will be given, while in others only one set of totals will be given. Occasionally, no totals will be given in a table, as in one that might give the number of births and deaths in Michigan for each year from 1900 to 1986. In such a table, neither row nor column totals would have any meaning.

If the totals are considered to be important, of more importance than individual items in the table, column totals will appear at the top of the columns and row totals will appear on the left, in the first column following the stub column. If the totals are of less importance than other items in the table, however, the column totals will appear at the bottom of the columns and the row totals in the column on the extreme right.

### Graphs: Bar Chart, Histogram, Frequency Polygon, Time-Series

A graph presents numerical information in pictorial, visual form. The graph does not present the information more accurately than does a table, but presents it in such a form so that contrasts and comparisons are more readily seen than in a table.

Graphs are most meaningfully used in combination with tabular presentations of the same information.

*Bar Chart.* Such a chart or graph consists of a series of rectangles, equal in width, equally spaced, but varying in length, the length of each rectangle or bar being dependent upon the amount that it represents.

Bar charts are usually used with qualitative variables or categorical measures (such as type of housing, type of treatment) when measurements have been grouped into categories (such as age groups divided into under 15 years, 15-64 years, and 65 years and over), or an unlimited array of other stratifications (race, geography, economic status, disease categories, etc.). Bar charts are also useful for chronological data when there is a wide gap between years, such as 1920, 1960, 1970, and 1990.

The bars may be horizontal or they may be vertical. While it is by no means a rule, there is a tendency to use vertical rather than horizontal bars when the information is for time periods.

To construct a bar chart, a scale is first drawn or computed. If bars are to be horizontal, the scale appears at the top of the graph; if vertical bars are to be used, the scale will appear at the left. The scale must start at zero and extend to some value beyond the highest amount represented by any of the bars. The scale is divided into equal intervals, with the intervals usually being 2, 5, 10, 20, 25, 100, etc., depending upon the quantities represented by the bars. If the scale is to be a part of the completed graph, the scale should have a caption indicating what the numbers represent—population in thousands, rate per 100,000 population, etc. If the scale is eliminated in the final graph, this information must be conveyed to the reader in the title or in a footnote, as illustrated in Figure 36.1.

All bars are equal in thickness and equally spaced, the space between bars usually being approximately one-half the thickness of the bars and the first bar being placed this same distance from the scales. The length of each bar is determined by the scale, although it is often necessary to approximate its length.

If there is progression, bars would be arranged in order of that progression. In Figure 36.1, each category of drug abuse appears in order, regardless of the bar lengths. However, with most qualitative variables there is no such progression, and bars are arranged in order of length, with the longest horizontal bar appearing at the top or, if vertical bars are used, at the left.

Each bar should be labeled to indicate what and how much it represents. If all bars are quite long and if the labels are short the information may appear on the bar itself. It is also possible to label the bars on the right, but a better practice is to put the part of the label indicating what the bar represents on the left, the amount on the bar itself.

In order to show more contrast the bars should be colored or crosshatched. Generally, the same color or the same crosshatching pattern will be used rather than using a different color or a different pattern for each bar.

Like a table, a graph should have a title telling the *what, where,* and *when* of the information portrayed. If the graph is for display purposes only, the title may appear at either the top of the graph or below it. For graphs included in reports or publications, it is common to find the title below the graph. If more than one graph appears in the series, they are numbered and are referred to as "Figure 36.1," "Figure 36.2," and so on.

*Histogram.* This form of graph is used to show a frequency distribution, preferably a

FIGURE 36.1
Percentage of Drug Use Among Homeless Black Men*
(Community Homeless Assistance Plan, Dade County, Florida, August 1991)

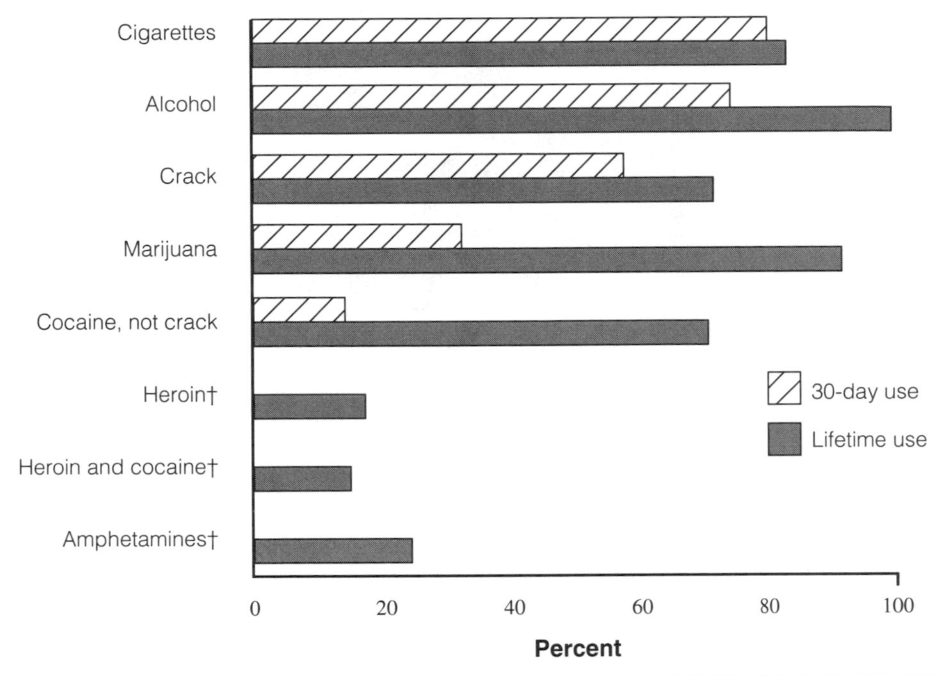


*Sample size = 113.

†No use was reported during the 30 days preceding the interview.

SOURCE: Centers for Disease Control, Morbidity and Mortality Report, December 20, 1991.

distribution with groups of equal intervals. A histogram has two scales, one on the vertical axis, and one on the horizontal axis. The vertical scale usually presents the frequency (size) of the concept or variable. The horizontal scale is used for some set of characteristics of the population or subject of the graph. This is the principal difference between a bar chart and a histogram. The horizontal axis of a histogram is always an ordinal or interval measure, progressing from left to right. These conventions are illustrated in Figure 36.2.

The scale on the vertical axis should start at 0, as the picture will be distorted if the scale starts at some value other than 0. (If there is another logical starting point—Zero should be represented, as in Figure 36.2.) The scale on the vertical axis would be divided into equal intervals, the intervals being 2, 5, 10, 20, 25, 100, or even higher values, depending upon the highest frequency in the distribution. If the highest frequency were 79 the scale would be set up in intervals of 10, going up to 80; if the highest frequency were 790 the scale would be set up in intervals of 100, going up to 800. For Figure 36.2 the maximum frequency is 41.

FIGURE 36.2
Age Distribution of Prisoners Aged 60 and Older in the Custody of the Michigan Department of Corrections, July 1991*

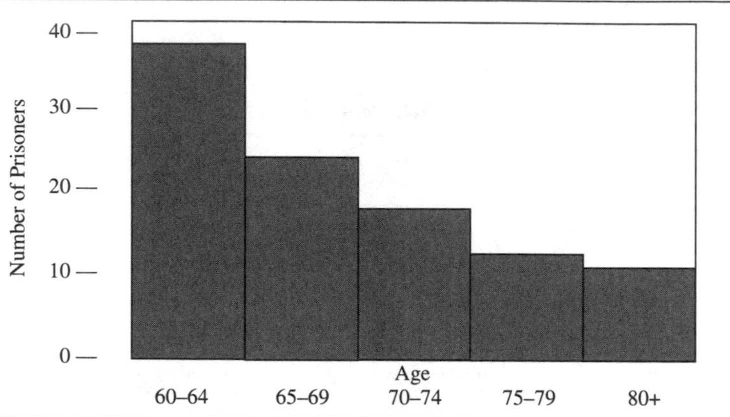


*20% Probability sample.

SOURCE: Michigan Department of Corrections, Lansing, Michigan, 1991.[5]

The horizontal scale starts at the lower boundary of the lowest measurement group. For example, in Figure 36.2 the first age category is 60-64. The scale proceeds to 65-69, 70-74, 75-79 and 80 plus.

Each scale should have an identification indicating what the measurement is (on the horizontal scale) and what the frequency represents (on the vertical scale). When very large frequencies are involved, the scale on the vertical axis might have a caption "Number in thousands" or "Number in millions," thus reducing the number of figures used on the scale itself.

In Figure 36.2, for the first measurement group, prisoners aged 60-64, a line is drawn parallel to the horizontal axis from the lower boundary to the upper boundary at a height determined by the number of prisoners included in that age group. Vertical lines then connect this line to the horizontal axis forming a rectangle. The procedure is repeated for each measurement group so that the resulting graph consists of a series of rectangles, similar in appearance to the bar chart in Figure 36.1, but differing from it in that there is *no space between the rectangles*. A histogram's horizontal axis is always a continuous dimension.

*Frequency Polygon.* The same type of information that was used for the histogram could also have been used for making one form of line graph known as the frequency polygon (Figure 36.3). The scales on the horizontal and vertical axes would be set up in the same way as for the histogram.

Instead of drawing a line between the upper and lower boundaries of a measurement group, a point is plotted at the height determined by the frequency of the group, at the midpoint class mark or median of the measurement group. The class mark is the average frequency for the group, as defined by units of the horizontal axis. When the frequencies for each measurement group have been plotted, the points are joined by straight lines. The frequency polygon has an advantage over the histogram in that more than one frequency distribution can

FIGURE 36.3
Percentage of General Assistance Recipients Who Were Also Homeless, Including the Initial Six Months Subsequent to Elimination of the General Assistance Program in 1992, by Year, Wayne County, Michigan, 1985–91

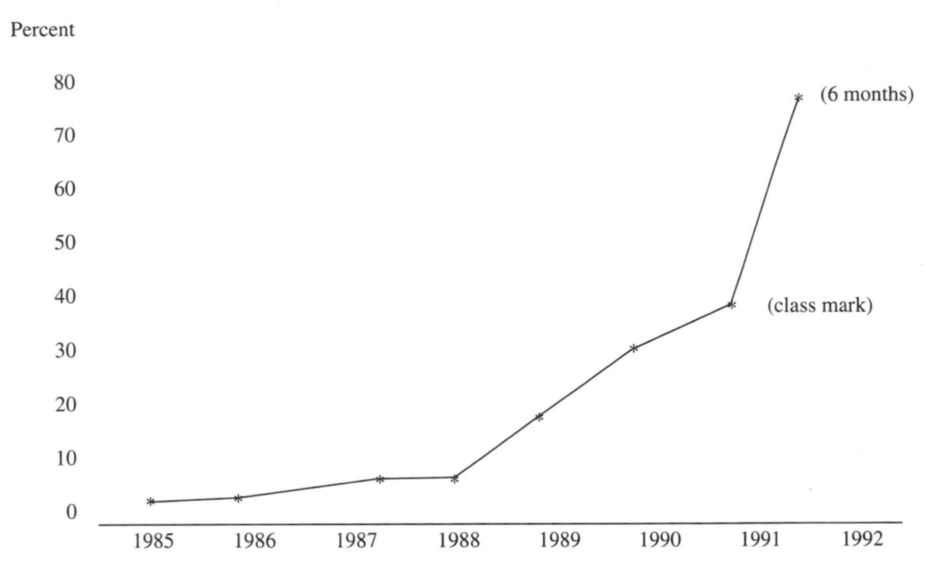


SOURCE: Wayne County Board of Commissioners, Detroit, Michigan, 1992.

be shown on the same graph. A special-purpose frequency polygon is a time-series.

*Time-Series.* If a graph is to illustrate a time-series, points are plotted at a height, according to the scale on the vertical axis, corresponding to the amount that is represented. If the quantity to be plotted is an average, the point is plotted midway between two points on the scale on the horizontal (time) axis. In a time-series graph, the horizontal (time) axis is always presented with equal units of time.

With respect to changes taking place over time, there are two techniques to be considered related to the amount of change that has taken place and the rate at which change has taken place. For example, we might wish to draw a graph to show the changes in the new-home purchase rate from 1960 to 1990. If we were interested in the amount of change, the graph would be drawn with the scale on the vertical axis being an arithmetic scale; if we were concerned with the rate of change, then the scale on the vertical axis would be a logarithmic one (both are shown below).

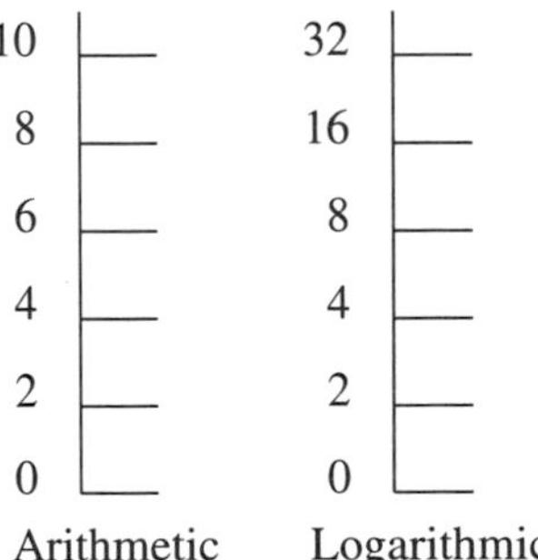

Note that in the scale on the left, equal distances on the scale represent the same amount of increase, in this instance, an increase of 2. On the scale on the right, equal distances do not represent the same amount of increase but they do indicate the same rate of increase, with each increment representing an increase of 100 percent or doubling of the value.

Most graphs used to show the rate of change will be made on a semilogarithmic grid; that is, one on which one scale (the scale on the horizontal axis) will be divided arithmetically, equal lengths of the scale representing the same number of years, while the vertical scale, against which the frequencies are to be plotted, will be scaled logarithmically.

## SUMMING UP

This brief introduction to the area of data utilization should complement the realization that in a more competitive world, health and human service delivery systems will be obligated to become highly quantitative for the justification, planning, and evaluation of services. Those who would administer and manage such services will recognize that accreditation, licensure, certification for reimbursement, and acquisition of new resources cannot proceed without a basic sophistication concerning data collection, analysis, and presentation. We can expect that improved and more universal quantification of services will stimulate comparative assessment and the design of improved services with greater levels of efficiency—objectives that should be agreeable to all of us who recognize that the problems we confront usually exceed our capacity to respond.

## NOTES

1. It should be noted that data collected for a specific purpose may subsequently be used for other purposes, taking on the character of "secondary data." The principal examples are survey data collected by universities and private polling organizations which are stored in libraries and made available to investigators for purposes other than those for which they were originally collected.

2. U.S. Bureau of the Census. *Bureau of the Census Manual of Tabular Presentation*, by Bruce L. Jenkinson (Washington, DC: U.S. Government Printing Office, 1949), p. iii.

3. Centers for Disease Control, USDHHS PHS. *Morbidity and Mortality Weekly Report*, 40 (50), December 20, 1992, pp. 866-867.

4. Douglass, R.L., et al. *Aging, Adrift, and Alone: Detroit's Elderly Homeless* (Detroit: Detroit Area Agency on Aging, 1988).

5. Douglass, R.L. *Oldtimers: Michigan's Elderly Prisoners* (Lansing, MI: Michigan Department of Corrections, 1991).

37.

John Gottman and Robert Clasen

# TROUBLESHOOTING GUIDE FOR RESEARCH AND EVALUATION

## INDEX TO THE TROUBLESHOOTING GUIDE

## WHY A TROUBLESHOOTING GUIDE?

The idea of this guide is to give you an intuitive feel for what kinds of techniques are available for research and evaluation so that you can be an intelligent seeker of these tools.

## I. DESCRIPTIVE STATISTICS

### Purpose:

To describe a population from a variable by describing the distribution of that variable in the population.

### Example:

Distribution of Income per Month in the Pokohaches Swamp School District. It presents a table of incomes and the percent of the population earning that income.

### Useful Concepts:

The *Mean* is a measure of central tendency of the distribution (the arithmetic average).

The *Standard Deviation* is a measure of the amount of variability of a given variable around the average. If most people have values of the variable close to the average, the standard deviation will be small.

*Probability* is the likelihood of an event's occurrence, or the relative frequency of a value or set of values of the variable. For example if 80% of the people earn between 4 and 6 thousand dollars a year, the probability if 0.80 that an individual chosen at random from the population will earn between 4 and 6 thousand.

## II. INFERENTIAL STATISTICS

### Purpose:

To make inferences about a population from knowledge about a random sample or random samples from that population.
*Example:*
Gallup Poll of opinions.

### Useful Concepts:

*Random Sampling* is a procedure for selecting a group to study which insures that each member of the population will have an equal chance of being selected to be in the sample.

The *Central Limit Theorem* establishes the importance of the normal distribution because the distribution of all sample means of a certain size is normally distributed regardless of the original distribution's shape.

*Statistical Significance* gives the maximum risk of generalizing from a sample to the population. Risk is the probability of error. "Statistically significant at *p* 0.05" means that there is less than a 5% risk in generalizing from sample to population.

The *Null Hypothesis* is a hypothesis that the population mean equals a fixed constant = $_0$, or that two samples come from the same population $_1 = _2$.

*A Statistically Significant Result at the 0.05 level* means that there is less than a 5% risk in rejecting the null hypothesis that = $_0$ (or that $_1 = _2$).

The *Variance Accounted for* is an index of correlation between two variables. If you account for variance in weight by the variable height, it means that height and weight are correlated. (The square root of the variance accounted for is the correlation coefficient, e.g., 49% variance accounted for is equivalent to a correlation coefficient of 0.70.)

*t-Tests* are tests for comparing the means of two samples to test the hypothesis that they really came from the same population and the observed difference is not larger than sampling error.

The *Chi-Square Test* is a test for comparing two samples when the measurement operation is counting. This test compares observed to expected frequencies. In the table below, we can see that in the sample in question, the males were predominantly brown-eyed and the females blue-eyed whereas we would have expected the color of eyes not to be sexlinked.

| | Males | Females |
|---|---|---|
| Brown Eyes | 15 | 6 |
| Blue Eyes | 7 | 16 |

## III. EXPERIMENTAL DESIGN

### Purpose:

To eliminate plausible rival hypotheses that account for observed differences.

### Example:

We know that the tested reading comprehension of girls is better than that of boys. One hypothesis is that the observed difference is due to the interest of the material read in school. A "design" is the detailing of the strategy to be employed in eliminating the rival hypotheses. Designs depend upon many factors including sample size, observation intervals, number of variables, and kind of data.

| | Fashion Story | Baseball Story | Total |
|---|---|---|---|
| Boys | 25 | 43 | 68 |
| Girls | 55 | 20 | 75 |
| Totals | 80 | 63 | |

Note that the number in the top, left-hand box is the average score of boys on the fashion story (25). Here we can see that overall girls read better (75 as opposed to 68) but that boys do better on the baseball story than girls.

Someone suggests a plausible rival hypothesis: "How do you know boys don't do better on the baseball story just because they have previous knowledge on the subject and the girls don't? It may not be interest at all." We would then have to control for that variable in our design.

### Useful Concepts:

*Dependent Variable*—This is the variable we are studying. For our example, it's reading comprehension.

*Independent Variable*—This is the variable we're trying to use to explain the observed variation in the dependent variable. For example, we might hope to explain differences in reading comprehension by the variable of the masculinity or femininity of the story.

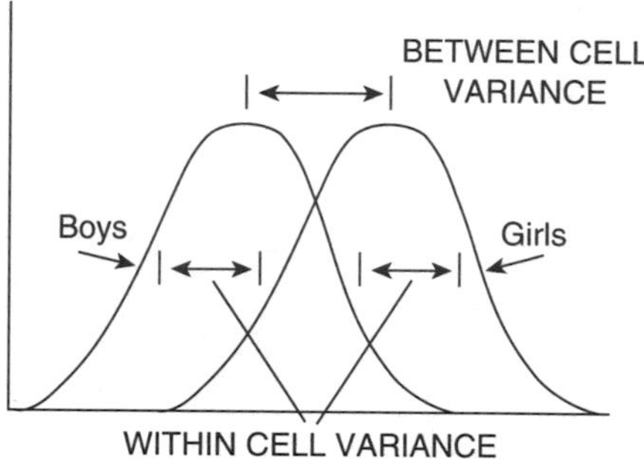


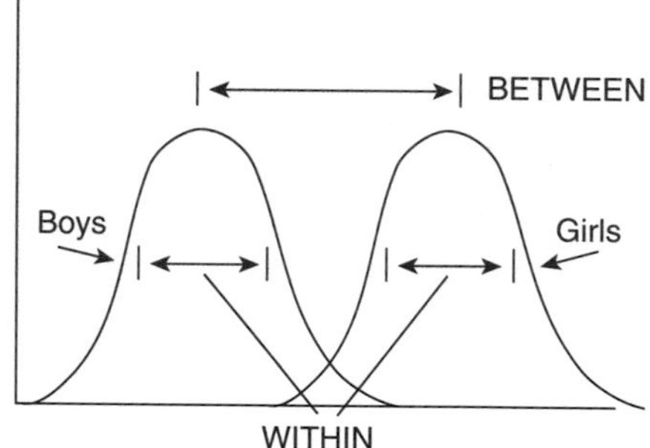


Total Variance in Reading Comprehension = Variance due to Sex Differences + Variance due to Interest Differences in Story Material + An Interaction of Sex and Material + Sampling Error.

*F-Test*—This test may be used to compare variances after the total variance is partitioned. For example, does the variance due to sex seem large in relation to sampling error?

The *F*-Test is mainly a ratio of between-cell variance to within-cell variance. In the curves in the figure on the top, the within cell variance is large compared to the between cell variance. In the figure on the bottom, the within-cell variance is small compared to the between-cell variance.

*Partitioning Variance*—The central idea of this procedure is to partition the total variance into independent parts, each of which represents a different variable's effect.

*Interaction*—In the design given in the example above, we can plot the cell means.

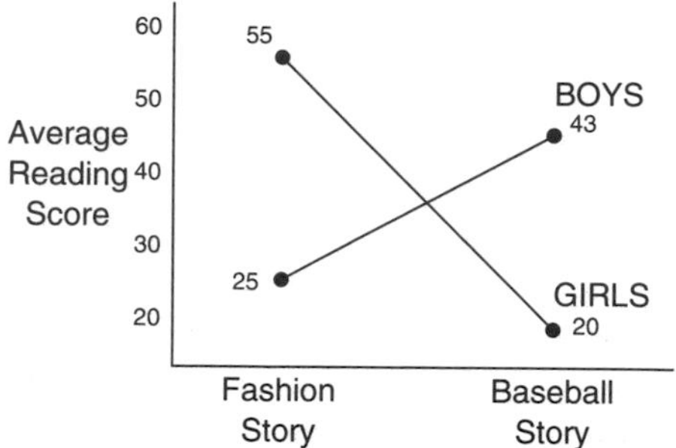


This is an example of interaction. Interaction is zero if the lines are parallel. In this case an interaction of zero would mean that boys (or girls) read better on all stories.

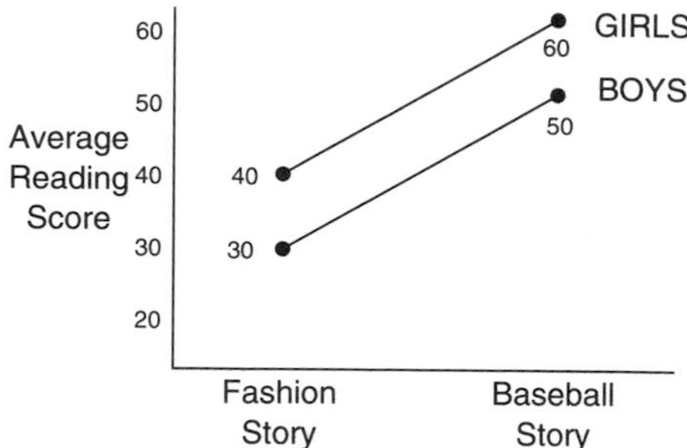


Interactions can cross (be "transverse") or just diverge (be "divergent").

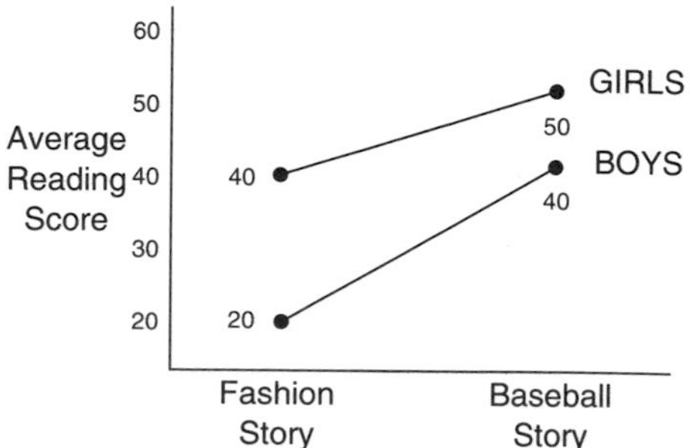

In this case, while girls are still reading better than boys, the difference is reduced in the baseball story.

*Analysis of Variance*—The analysis of variance is an experimental design for studying differences between cell means or combinations of cell means. The means are compared with respect to a common variance unit.

*Blocking*—Sometimes we want to split our design by blocking on a variable. For example, we may want to look at that reading data for high and low socioeconomic status children. Then our design would be:

| | | Fashion Story | Baseball Story |
|---|---|---|---|
| BOYS | High Socioeconomic Status | | |
| | Low Socioeconomic Status | | |
| GIRLS | High Socioeconomic Status | | |
| | Low Socioeconomic Status | | |

We do this hoping to reduce the within-cell variability by introducing a new variable. We also may wish to contend with the plausible rival hypothesis that we have not accounted for socioeconomic status and that perhaps that variable would explain our results.

*Analysis of Covariance* is a way of trying to control statistically for a variable which we are not able to control experimentally.

For example, two groups may differ in IQ. We could block by IQ, or we could use an analysis of covariance.

Here's how an analysis of covariance works. The dependent variable is related to a *covariate.* (Reading is related to IQ.) We use this relationship to try to predict reading score from IQ. Then we subtract the predicted score from the actual score and analyze the residual. We still hope to reduce the within-cell variability.

[Generally analysis of covariance is inferior to blocking unless the correlation between dependent variable and covariate is greater than 0.60 (Myers, 1966).]

*Internal and External Validity*—Campbell and Stanley (1963) list sources of plausible rival hypotheses which may jeopardize the conclusions of any experimental design. Please read their excellent article for an elaboration of these and examples of commonly used designs compared on these factors.

*Internal Validity*—factors representing extraneous variables which will confound the experimental variable if not controlled.

1. *History*—specific events occurring between the first and second measurement in addition to the experimental variable.
2. *Maturation*—processes within the subjects operating as a function of the passage of time, per se (growing older, hungrier, fatigued, or less attentive).
3. *Testing*—the effects of testing upon the scores of a subsequent testing.
4. *Instrumentation*—changes in obtained measurement due to changes in instrument calibration or changes in the observers or judges.
5. *Statistical Regression*—a phenomenon occurring when groups have been selected on the basis of extreme scores.
6. *Selection*—biases resulting from the differential selection of subjects for the comparison groups.
7. *Experimental Mortality*—the differential loss of subjects from the comparison groups.
8. *Selection-Maturation Interaction, etc.*—interaction effects between the aforementioned variables which can be mistaken for the effects of the experimental variable.

*External Validity*—factors which jeopardize the representativeness or one's ability to generalize.

1. *Interaction Effects*—effects of selection biases and the experimental variable.
2. *Reactive or Interaction Effect of Pretesting*—The pretesting modifies the subject in such a way that he responds to the experimental treatment differently than will unpretested persons in the same population.
3. *Reactive Effects of Experimental Procedures*—effects arising from the experimental setting which will not occur in nonexperimental settings.
4. *Multiple-Treatment Interference*—effects due to multiple treatments applied to the same subjects where prior treatments influence subsequent treatments in the series because their effects are not erasable.

**Samples of Common Designs**

1. One-Shot Case Study
(lousy design)

| X | $T_2$ |
|---|---|
| Intervention | Posttest |

2. One-Group Pretest-Posttest

| $T_1$ | X | $T_2$ |
|---|---|---|
| Pretest | Int. | Posttest |

3. Randomized Control Group

| | | | |
|---|---|---|---|
| Group 1 (R) | $T_1$ | X | $T_2$ |
| Group 2 (R) | $T_1$ | | $T_2$ |
| | Pretest | Int. | Posttest |

(R) = Subjects are randomly assigned to groups. Group 2 gets everything but the intervention, X.

4. Posttest-Only Design

| | | |
|---|---|---|
| Group 1 (R) | X | $T_2$ |
| Group 2 (R) | | $T_2$ |
| | Int. | Posttest |

Group 2 gets the posttest only.

5. Solomon Four-Group Design

| | | | |
|---|---|---|---|
| Group 1 (R) | $T_1$ | X | $T_2$ |
| Group 2 (R) | $T_1$ | | $T_2$ |
| Group 3 (R) | | X | $T_2$ |
| Group 4 (R) | | | $T_2$ |
| | Pretest | Int. | Posttest |

This design is equivalent to a two-by-two (2 × 2) *factorial design.*

| | | |
|---|---|---|
| Intervention | Group 1 | Group 3 |
| No Intervention | Group 2 | Group 4 |

(Every group gets
a posttest)

This design is recommended as a good experimental design by Campbell and Stanley (1963).

6. Interrupted Time-Series Design

| $T_1$ $T_2$ | $T_N$ x $T_{N+1}$ $T_{N+2}$ | $T_{N+M}$ |
|---|---|---|

7. Time-Lagged Time-Series Design

| | | | | |
|---|---|---|---|---|
| Group 1 | $T_1T_2$ | $T_N x T_{N+1} T_{N+2}$ | $T_{N+M}$ | $T_{N+M+1}$ |
| Group 2 | $T_1T_2$ | $T_N$ $T_{N+1} T_{N+2}$ | $T_{N+M} x T_{N+M+1}$ | |

8. Time-Series Flip-Flop Design

| | | | |
|---|---|---|---|
| Group 1 | $T_1T_2$ | $T_N X_Z T_{N+1}$ | $T_{N+M} S_B T_{N+M+1}$ |
| Group 2 | $T_1T_2$ | $T_N X_B T_{N+1}$ | $T_{N+M} X_A T_{N+M+1}$ |

The time-series designs are recommended...as excellent quasiexperimental designs. They can also be used to monitor and assess change in one person (doesn't have to be groups).

## IV. MEASUREMENT

### Purpose:

We often wish to make the assumption that we are measuring one variable on one continuum. Some techniques in measurement design allow us to test these assumptions.

### Example:

Designing an opinionnaire to measure students' attitudes toward school, peers, teachers, studies, and teaching methods. A student is asked to register the extent of his agreement with statements such as

| | Disagree | | | Neutral | | | Agree |
|---|---|---|---|---|---|---|---|
| School is fun | 1 | 2 | 3 | 4 | 5 | 6 | 7 |

by circling the number which best represents his opinion. Certain items are clustered as belonging to one scale or another.

### Useful Concepts:

*Reliability*—the extent to which the measurement procedure gives similar results under similar conditions. Methods of assessing:

1. *Stability (test-retest)* correlation between two successive measurements with the same test or inventory must assume times of testing are "similar conditions."
2. *Alternate forms*—two forms are constructed by randomly sampling items from a domain and a correlation is computed between "equivalent forms."
3. *Split-half*—a procedure used in place of alternate forms by dividing the items in half, hopefully into "equivalent halves."
4. *KR-20 and KR-21* are formulas used to assess an alternate form reliability. Formula 21 is given here (less accurate than formula 20, but easier to compute) where the items are scored 1 if "right,"

$$r = \frac{K}{K-1}\left(1 - \frac{M\,(\mathrm{K-M})}{KS^2}\right)$$

0 if "wrong," K is number of items, S is standard deviation, and M is the mean of the scale.

*Validity* is the extent to which a measurement procedure measures what it claims to measure. Methods of assessing:

1. *Content Validity* (snapshot). How well does the individual's performance in this situation correlate with his performance in other similar situations?
2. *Criterion-Related Validity* (motion picture). How well does this individual's performance on this measurement predict his performance in future related situations (how well do achievement test scores predict grades in college?)?
3. *Construct Validity.* Does the measurement procedure make sense as measuring what it claims to? Do the items which are supposed to be on one scale "hang together"? This can be assessed empirically by relating the extent to which presumably related constructs explain variation on the instrument in question. Here is an example where this kind of validity is crucial. Suppose you show that 92% of all high school seniors cannot read election ballots with comprehension. The instrument is *face valid.* It

has construct validity and you don't need to show content or criterion validity.

*Convergent Operations.* Different measurement procedures have different weaknesses. More confidence is obtained in a result when several different measurement procedures point to (or converge to) the same result.

*Scales* are attempts at quantifying a construct and converting it into a continuum.

1. Likert Scale. A scale composed of items each of which the subject rates on a scale. Examples:

a. School is fun. *SA A N D SD* (*SA* = strongly agree, *A* =agree, *N* = Neutral, *D* = disagree, *SD* = strongly disagree)
b. School is (check the blank):
Fun: – : – : – : – : – : – : – : Dull

Item *b* is sometimes called a *semantic differential* item. In this kind of item we can put any two words on either side of the line, for example,

Strong: – : – : – : – : – : – : – : Weak

2. *Thurstone type* or *equal-appearing interval* scales. These scales scale the items themselves. Items are first sorted by judges into three categories, then each category is broken down into three others along a continuum (hostility, favorableness, disruptiveness, assertiveness). Items are eliminated if there is large disagreement between judges. Items are selected to have mean values (across judges) spread across the continuum from 1 to 9, preferably equally spaced. The individual taking the inventory checks those times with which he agrees (or finds hostile or disruptive). He is given the score which is the sum of the mean judges' ratings for items checked. We might scale situations for the degree of assertiveness required and ask the subject to check the situations which are problems for him. The items not checked could be used to give an assertiveness score for him by adding the average of judged ratings. This places the individual along an assertiveness continuum.
3. *Guttman-Type* scales have items which vary along an attribute. Items can be ordered in difficulty, complexity, or value-loading so that answers to the last item will imply success or approval to all those preceding. Examples:

*Difficulty:*
I can add two numbers.
I can multiply two numbers.
I can divide two numbers.
I can compute a mean.
I can compute the standard deviation.

*Favorableness:*
1. Would you object to a retarded person living in your community?
2. Would you object to a retarded person working where you work?
3. Would you object to having lunch with a retarded person at work?
4. Would you object to a retarded person coming to your home for dinner?
5. Would you object to a retarded person marrying a member of your family?

*Item Analysis* is a procedure for selecting only items which discriminate in the same way the overall instrument is intended to discriminate.

A correlation is computed between each item and the total score on the instrument. For *dichotomous items* (yes, no; pass, fail) a two-by-two chi-square table is constructed.

For a multiple-choice test we wish there to be a strong relationship between choosing the correct alternative and high total score; also we want there to be a weak relationship between choosing distractors and high total score.

*Factor Analysis in Measurement Design* is a method for analyzing the extent to which items cluster by studying their intercorrelations. We have confidence in the conclusion that our test has four independent scales if the items within scales correlate highly but items across scales do not correlate very highly (see analysis of data).

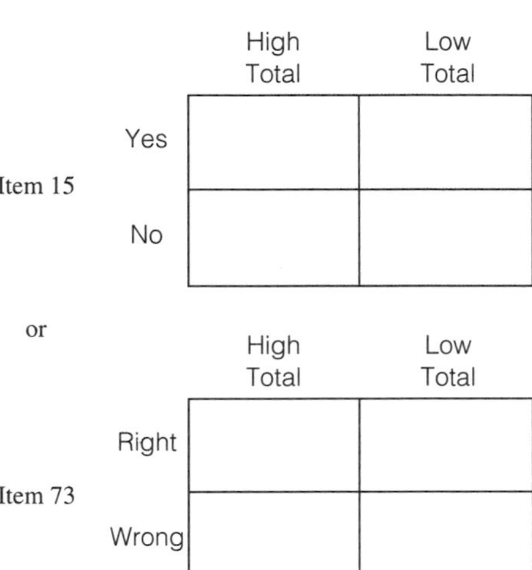


## V. ANALYSIS OF DATA

### Purpose:

To study the nature of relationships between variables.

### Example:

We wish to determine which variables will predict whether a citizen will vote Republican (or Democratic) in the forthcoming election.

### Useful Concepts:

*Correlation* measures the degree of relationship between two variables. Usually a

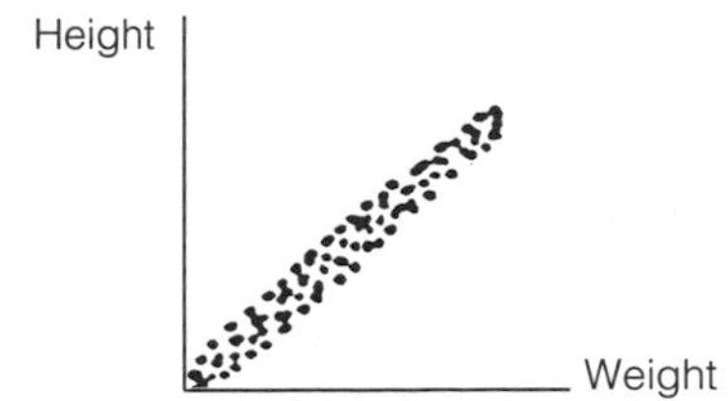

Strong *positive correlation.*

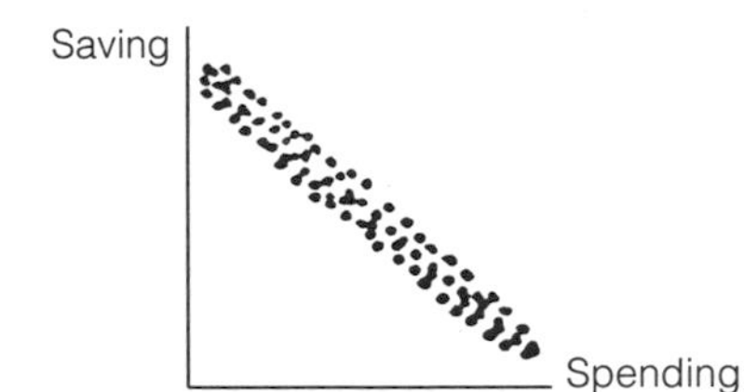

Strong *negative correlation.*

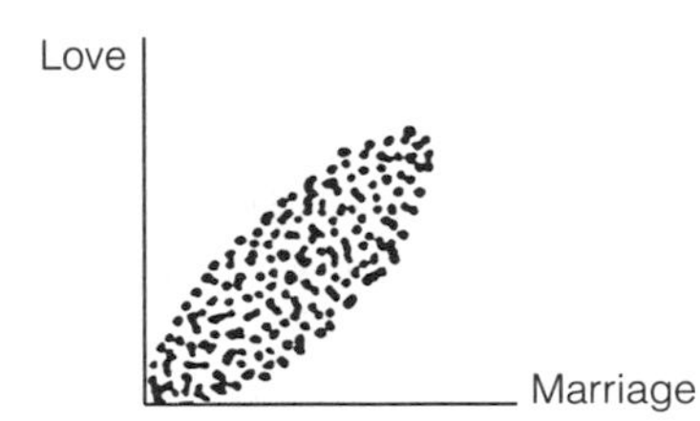

Weak *positive correlation.*

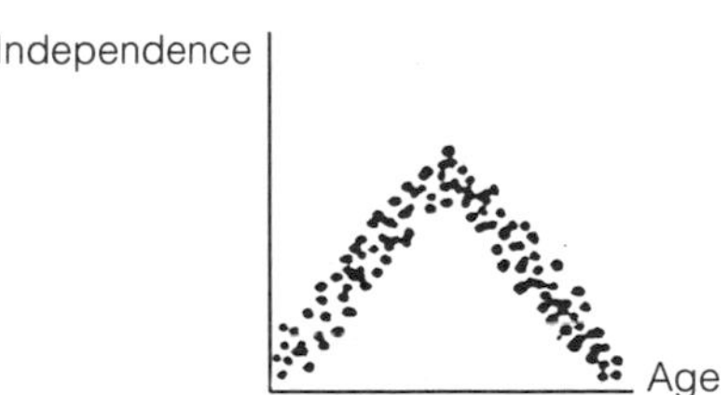

Curvilinear correlation (*positive sometimes, negative others)*

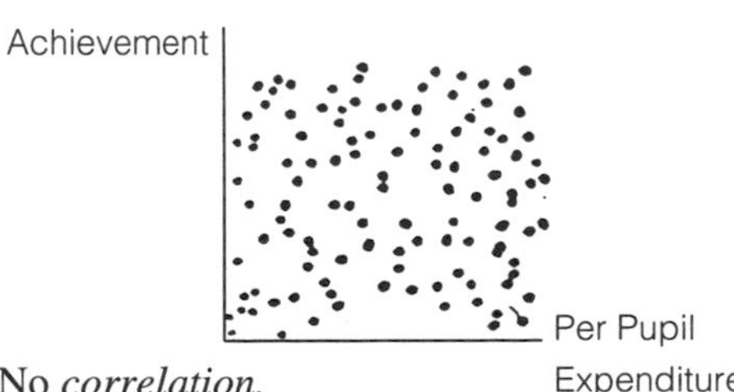

No *correlation.*

scatter diagram will provide an index for the eyeball.

The *Correlation Coefficient* gives an index of the degree of association (linear). 0 is no correlation, -1 is strongest negative, 1 is strongest positive correlation.

*Partial Correlations* involve calculating the correlation coefficient between two variables while statistically holding another variable constant. For example, ice cream sales may correlate with crime rates but not if the average daily temperature were controlled. Since we cannot control average daily temperature experimentally, we do it statistically. The correlation between ice cream sales and crime rate may be high but the partial correlation, controlling average daily temperature, may be quite low. Blaylock (1961) uses this technique to argue from correlation to causation.

*Regression* is a statistical procedure which is like a recipe for converting from one variable to another using the best (least-squares) equation.

*Multiple Regression* is a statistical procedure like a recipe relating one variable to a set of other variables. For example, if we relate high school dropout rates to school expenditures, teacher experience, and the average number of library books in the classroom, we will have a recipe that says, "our best guess from the multiple regression is that if we spend $3 more per pupil, dropout rates may decline by 2%. We could spend $1 per pupil by buying some books, and the other $2 by hiring more experienced teachers."

The multiple regression gives you a mathematical equation of the relationships between one variable and a set of variables.

It's like a recipe in the sense that how good a cake turns out is related to a host of variables (how much sugar, salt, flour, etc., you add). It differs from a recipe in that you can improve the product by adding more of anything, except that some variables are more important than others.

*Factor Analysis* is a technique for data reduction. It analyzes the statistical dependencies between a set of variables by looking at the way variables correlate. For example, it may reduce a set of 50 variables into 3 basic variables. Each of the three will be statistically independent (zero correlation if the variables are normally distributed) of the other two. Each of the three will be linear combinations of the original set of fifty. Some of the fifty will "load" more highly on one factor, others will load on other factors. Each factor is a weighted sum of the original fifty.

The three factors should try to account for as much of the variance in the original fifty as possible.

The problem comes in *naming* the factors, i.e., giving them some physical interpretation in the real world. This is where the procedure becomes subjective.

No one has really derived the sampling distributions of factor loading coefficients, so it's not clear how *stable* factors are. (See Principal Components Analysis.)

*Principal Components Analysis* tries to reduce data by a geometrical transformation of the original variables. An example is a scatterplot in three dimensions which gives a swarm of points in the shape of a football.

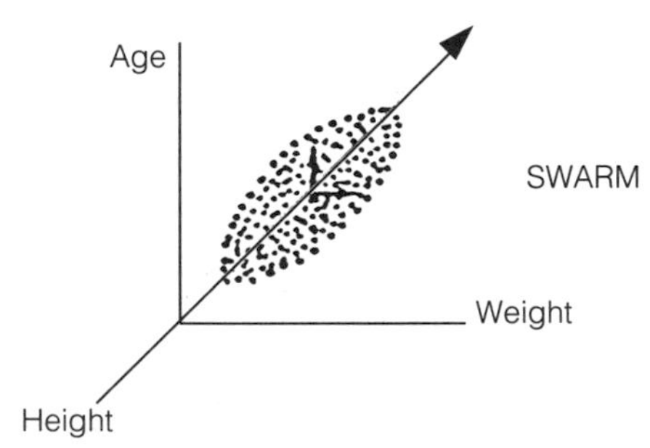

The new axes are those emanating from the swarm. The principal component is the main axis of the football. If most variance in the swarm is along one principal component (which will be a combination of the first three variables), we have reduced our data from three variables (which were correlated) to one variable. In general, we will reduce a large set of variables into a smaller set. Each variable in the smaller set is a linear combination (a weighted sum) of the original variables, and the new smaller set of variables are independent of one another.

The problem comes with interpretations—it's usually worse with principal components than factor analysis although the geometrical meaning is clearer.

*Canonical Correlations* are a procedure for factor analyzing two batteries of tests simultaneously to extract factors which are uncorrelated within their batteries but which provide high correlation of pairs of factors across batteries. For example, a researcher may have one battery of interest measures and another battery of skill or ability measures and he wants to know the overlap in measurement variance between the two systems of measures.

*Multiple Correlation* finds the optimal weighting to maximize the correlation between several variables (predictors) and another variable (the criterion).

*Multivariate Analysis of Variance* is a generalization of the analysis of variance to the situation where several variables are measured and these variables are statistically related.

The research issue behind the generalized tests is whether two or more sample groups should be thought of as arising from a single multivariate population or from two or more multivariate populations.

*Discriminant Function Analysis* is a procedure for predicting group membership of an individual on the basis of a set of other variables.

For example, if we can take medical measurements of various kinds, can we find the best way to combine these (weight them) to predict whether or not a person has cancer?

*Discriminant function analysis* is used extensively in theory construction finding *which* variables in *what* combination predict political party membership or any other group membership.

*Time-Series Analysis* is a procedure for analyzing observations over time for predicting trends, understanding the basis for fluctuations, and assessing the effects of interventions.

## REFERENCES

Blaylock, H.M. *Evaluating State and Local Programs at the State and Local Level.* Kalamazoo, MI: W.E. Upjohn, 1990.

Dowdy, G., & S. Wearden. *Statistics for Research* (2nd ed.). New York: Wiley Interscience, 1991.

Rutter, Michael. *Studies of Psychosocial Risk: The Power of Longitudinal Data.* New York: Cambridge University Press, 1988.

True, June A. *Finding Out: Conducting and Evaluating Social Research.* Belmont, CA: Wadsworth, 1989.

38.

**Marilyn L. Flynn**

# BUDGETING IN COMMUNITY ORGANIZATIONS: PRINCIPLES FOR THE '90s

## I. THE PURPOSE OF AGENCY BUDGETS

Budgeting in the 1990s is a key to agency survival, development of effective programs, and reconciliation of contending political interests in the human services. Knowledgeable budget planning and implementation can powerfully affect social policy at the local level and improve the quality of investment in human welfare. The acceptability of any budget should be judged from three perspectives: Does it promote management control or accountability? Does it successfully mediate between conflicting political interests? And does it invest in the best among competing programs?

*Budgets as a Tool for Management Control.* In most people's minds, budgeting is a method for increasing responsible management of an agency's fiscal resources. The budget makes explicit anticipated revenues and expenditures over a 12-month fiscal cycle. Administrative review and control are then exercised through regular comparison of actual income and expenditures with outlays and commitments in the original budget plan.

*Budgets as a Tool for Resolving Political Conflicts.* In addition to supporting the management function, budgets also play a powerful role in mediating among political forces in a community. The American system of government has fostered special interest group activity at the state and local level. These contending groups represent many stakeholders in the health and human services such as taxpayers, service providers, and service consumers (older persons, minorities, and others.) They vie with each other for attention and a larger share of public and private funds. Within organizations, programs, staff, management, contributors, and others wage similar battles. The clashes that take place are "political" to the extent that power and influence are at stake, and winners or losers will emerge from the debate. An effective budgeting process acts as a means of mediating political claims to scarce resources. When the budgeting process is successful, social disaffection among important interest groups is reduced, and community consensus enhanced.

*Budgets as a Tool for Investing in Productive Programs.* Budgets also represent investment decisions. Since the 1960s, budgets for social programs have been defined as investments with different "rates of return." Economists argue that the cost of an activity or service cannot be considered as "too much" or "too little" until measured against gains in productivity and other outcomes. In other words, a budget should support most those programs that require

---

Marilyn Flynn is a director at the School of Social Work, Michigan State University.

the lowest net investment to reach agency goals. To assess whether any program represents a good investment, modern budgeting techniques such as performance-based budgeting a zero-based budgeting can be used. These systems are described later in this article.

## II. PUBLIC- AND PRIVATE-SECTOR BUDGETING—SIMILARITIES AND DIFFERENCES

It may appear at first glance that budgets are essentially the same for all types of organizations. Revenues and expenditures are planned, reviewed, and reported, with revisions as necessary over the fiscal year. However, not-for-profit organizations have distinctive characteristics that fundamentally distinguish their budgeting and reporting process from for-profit firms. These differences include auspices or nature of corporate status, revenue sources, accounting methods, concern with "return on investment," need for political consensus in budget-making, and definition of corporate ownership.

### A. Differences Between Public, Private Not-for-Profit, and For-Profit Agencies: Legal Authority

*Legal Authority for Public Agencies.* Not-for-profit agencies can operate under public or private auspices. Public agencies are supported principally by tax revenues, staffed by civil servants, accountable to elected officials, and created by public law. Examples include public schools, departments of city or state government, and special tax district programs for parks. Public organizations are not incorporated, they do not pay taxes, and while they often set up advisory boards, they are not governed by the decisions of such groups.

*Legal Authority for Private Not-for-Profit Agencies.* Private not-for-profit agencies are established through articles of incorporation in a state and governed by a board of directors, which sets policy in keeping with the by-laws and private purposes of the organization. Not-for-profit status must be granted by the Internal Revenue Service under IRS Code 501(c)(3), which requires that the organization operate in the public interest and not for the gain of private individuals. Many private agencies act as contractors for public organizations, with as much as 90 to 95 percent of their annual budget derived from governmental sources. Such private organizations take on a "quasi-public" character, with lines of accountability tugging between public funders and their own boards of directors. This type of agency is increasingly common. Not-for-profit organizations do not pay taxes on revenues.

*No Individual Ownership of Assets in Not-for-Profit Agencies.* In their oversight of revenues and expenditures, officials of not-for-profit organizations exercise trusteeship for the community, but there is no individual ownership of agency assets. If revenues exceed expectations, this cannot be called a "profit," only a surplus. In the event of shortfall, a not-for-profit may fall into receivership, but not bankruptcy.

*Legal Authority in For-Profit Organizations.* Private business firms may operate under many legal statuses, with the most complex being that a for-profit corporation. For-profit corporations are legal entities entitled to tax rates that differ from those paid by individuals. Assets of the corporation are owned by the stockholders and bondholders, and the first obligation of the firm is to these individuals, not to the public at large.

## B. Difference in Revenue Sources Between For-Profit and Not-for-Profit Organizations

*The Cost-Revenue Relationship Between For-Profit Firms and Their Customers.* Business firms earn revenues through charging a price for goods or services that exceeds the cost of production. Charges are paid directly to the business by a purchaser or consumer. This one-to-one relationship is rarely completely unfettered. Taxes, social legislation, environmental laws, monopolies, discrimination, and other factors always cloud the signals sent by consumers and the response by producers. In general, however, there is a rough approximation to free-market conditions. The direct relation between supply and demand, price and volume produced, and customer and firm drives all exchanges.

*The Three-Party Cost-Revenue Relationship in Not-for-Profit Agencies.* Exchanges in the not-for-profit sector are complicated by the presence of three parties, not two. These parties include the client (customer), the service provider, and the third-party revenue source. These third parties may be individual or corporate contributors, foundations, legislative bodies, United Ways, or other independent sources. It is true that not-for-profits increasingly charge fees for service. Nonetheless, most service remains at least partially subsidized—especially in organizations seeking to maintain access for low-income and disadvantaged clients.

*The Central Role of Transfer Payments in Not-for-Profit Revenues.* Gifts, governmental grants and other revenues of this type are examples of "transfer payments." Transfer income is money shifted from one party to another to achieve purposes important to individuals or society. Parents give money to their children for college costs; the federal government pays old age benefits under Social Security; the United Way gives grants to member agencies for services. In the case of transfer income, dollars are "earned" by recipient organizations only in a relatively more general way. The modern notion of accountability is predicted on the idea that agencies must do what they promise and offer documentation that work has been performed. Nonetheless, it is much harder to establish a connection between production and outcome in the human services. It cannot be said, for example, that three hours of counseling will yield four units of happiness.

*The Central Role of Fund Accounting in Not-for-Profit Agencies.* One way in which third party funders influence outcomes of transfer income is to set broad constraints on how funds may be used. For instance, if the legislature authorizes income tax revenues to be spent for general operation of government, then the government cannot use these same funds to set up an economic development corporation for the state. A bequest to a private agency may require that only the interest may be expended and the principal left intact.

As a consequence, "fund accounts" are established by most public and private not-for-profit organizations to ensure that expenditures are consistent with funder or donor mandates. Fund accounting is the cornerstone of not-for-profit financial management and differs significantly from commercial account practices. Typically, a general operating fund is created, with additional accounts dedicated to restricted uses—e.g., building and grounds, endowments. Fund accounting means that options for program development or even the adequacy of budget to meet basic support costs may be much less flexible than total revenues to the agency might suggest. For example, one agency with a dilapidated structure was unable to use any of is multi-million dollar endowment for modernization. Terms of the gift severely restricted how funds from that account could be spent.

### C. The Concept of "Return on Investment" and Productivity in the For-Profit and Not-for-Profit Sectors

*Profit, Loss, and Cost Control in the For-Profit Firm.* The appealing side of private enterprise is of course the potential for substantial individual profit. Less attractive—but often equally probable—is possibility of substantial personal loss. And loss in the private sector can come abruptly and end in bankruptcy. As a consequence, efficiency and cost control are usually matters of close concern to most firms (with the exception, perhaps, of monopolies.) In fact, some industries have pooled information from individual firms to arrive at industry cost standards at varying levels of output or service. To use an example from the nursing home industry, there are widely accepted standards for the minimum number of nurse's aides per shift per day based on expected patient census. Facilities that operate with this number and charge average per diem rates per patient per day can expect to be profitable and still meet minimum licensing requirements.

*Survival, Financial Loss, and Need for Political Consensus in the Not-for-Profit Agency.* On the other hand, most public and private not-for-profits experience somewhat different pressures in setting expenditure levels relative to revenues. While real and threatened funding reductions have sporadically swept through the human services since 1980, few organizations have been completely defunded. The usual pattern is one of more gradual, extended, multi-year reductions. Furthermore, when organizations do succeed in accumulating a surplus at the end of their fiscal year, there is little reward—at least for those receiving public funds. A surplus usually reverts back to the public purse and cannot be carried over into the next year. Not-for-profits have thus been less preoccupied with productivity measures or "return on investment" than have private firms. Outside the hospital and nursing care industries, not-for-profits have developed virtually no industry standards for performance. With few agreed-upon standards and deep value conflicts underlying the budget process, it is not surprising that not-for-profits are far more driven to achieve political consensus than efficiency.

For those private agencies that rely extensively on more than one public funding source, the result is multiple sources of control and unprecedented complexities in defining a fiscal cycle. All agencies define for themselves a uniform period of time—generally one year—for planning and implementing their budget. This fiscal year may begin at any time selected by the board of directors or elected officials. The federal government begins its fiscal year in October; some state and municipal agencies start their cycle in July; and many private organizations are bound to the calendar year, with January as the lead month. As private agencies have grown to depend more on federal and state contracts, scrambled, multi-cycle multi-year funding patterns have followed. Budget planning is no longer a simple process of projecting anticipated expenditures based on revenue from one source during a single fiscal year. New computer-based techniques for tracking and managing budgets are likely to offer some relief.

### D. Fading Distinctions Between Public, Private Not-for-Profit, and Private For-Profit Organizations

*Users Fees.* The distinction between commercial and not-for-profit organizations still remains comparatively well-defined, although not-for-profits have increasingly adopted the language of the marketplace in personnel policies, strategic planning, and public relations. Since the first wave of retrenchment in the mid-1970s, public and private not-for-profit agencies alike have looked more closely at the business practice of fees-for-service. User fees as a revenue source have proliferated throughout museums, libraries, social service agencies, jails, and other nontraditional settings. Several issues have surfaced, including the impact of user fees on demand for service, particularly in programs targeted at the poor. At the same time, it is now more widely accepted that user fees have a place in the revenue structure of government and private agencies.

*The Emergence of Quasi-Public and Quasi-Private Organizations.* The most confusing blurring of distinctions seems to have occurred between public and private not-for-profit organizations. Beginning in the early 1970s, organizations have been created by public law—such as area agencies on aging and private industry councils—which are wholly supported by tax funds while governed by locally incorporated, private boards of directors. Other traditional private agencies that historically relied on individual gifts or United Way grants have shifted to major reliance on grant and contracts from government. Government requirements have acquired great influence over agency planning and budgeting practices—so much so that many private organizations are now virtually quasi-public.

## III. STAGES IN BUDGETING PROCESS

There are four stages in the budget process. These include (1) defining a problem to be solved, goals and intervention methods to be used, and target population(s); (2) planning future revenues and expenditures to support implementation of the program concept(s); (3) monitoring expenditures and revenues for variance from plan; and (4) making necessary revisions based on cost projections and program experience. Negotiation occurs at every stage, particularly in the case of public agencies.

### A. Defining Problem to Be Solved, Goals, Targeted Groups, and Program Interventions

*Clarifying the Problem to Be Solved and Assumptions about Causation.* Budgets are a means of solving community problems. They give force to certain programmatic visions of an improved future. Therefore, budgeting begins with a definition of the problem conditions about which agency is more concerned. Service organizations are formed in response to perceived problems such as ill health among older people, poverty, illiteracy, or other issues. Programs within organizations are really hypotheses about how a problem can be redressed, given the agency's beliefs about causation.

For example, if poverty among urban children were an agency's main concern, numerous solutions readily come to mind. Transfer more money through gifts or higher public assistance payments. Find employment for parents. Improve temporary shelter to allow parents to mobilize their own resources. Help family members complete their education. Recruit mentors to function as role models for the youngest. Present petitions to the city council. Con-

FIGURE 38.1
Illustration of Alternative Problem Solutions to Child and Family Poverty, Based on Alternative Definitions of Problem Cause

| *Definition of Problem Cause* | *Possible Problem Solution* |
|---|---|
| Poverty is caused by lack of parents in adequate jobs | Place long-term unemployed in jobs to secure income from work |
| Poverty is caused by lack of access to existing jobs | Set up program to transport urban workers to suburbs |
| Poverty is cause by leaving school without a degree | Train parents to teach their children study habits |
| Poverty is caused by teenage pregnancy | Set up teenage pregnancy prevention program |
| Poverty is caused by low self-esteem and social alienation | Set up group counseling in neighborhood churches to increase participation in positive peer culture |

duct research to document the pervasiveness of the problem. Coordinate existing services. And so on.

Which of these solutions should be adopted? This depends upon which underlying explanation for problem causes is most important to the agency and related funding sources. Outcomes goals then follow. Figure 38.1 shows how each idea about problem causation influences solutions or outcome goals in the case of an agency focus on child poverty.

*Selecting Outcome Goals Based on Problem Definition.* Clarity about the problem to be solved and agreement on the most important problem causes leads to a statement of goals or program outcomes to be achieved. Outcome goals are usually stated as increases in a desired status or decreases in a problem condition. Process goals only spell out how many units will be affected by the intervention itself: 20 families will be given shelter, 10 children will be fed, 15 parents will be counseled. Process goals are useful for monitoring implementation of a program; outcome goals are basic to measurement of change.

*Choosing Target Population(s).* Programs must have a target population. The target population can be described as the group which the program, with its limited resources, commits itself to serve. This population should be highly vulnerable to the problem condition in which the agency is interested and possess characteristics closely associated with agency mission or values. For example, assume the agency concerned with child poverty has decided that the most important cause of persistent low family incomes in the area is lack of transportation to available jobs in the suburbs. The agency might establish an outcome goal of increasing permanent placement of inner city jobless family heads in suburban employment, with an increase of 5 percent expected in the first program year. A 38-block city neighborhood is selected, in which 400 unemployed families reside. If the agency's mission and values emphasize help for minorities and maintaining intact family units, then neighborhood services would be further targeted on this group. Intact, minority families might constitute only 50 percent of those unemployed, or 200 homes. The agency would give this group highest priority in the use of its resources.

The target population is not the same as the client population. Many people in the target population go elsewhere for help, decide not to seek assistance, leave the community, or simply eliminate their problem in other ways than through the intervention offered by the agency.

*Conceptualizing a Program of Service.* Once problem conditions, goals, and target population(s) have been agreed upon, the problem of service must be conceptualized. This includes staff requirements, physical facilities, equipment, supplies, and other resources necessary to accomplish program goals, given the method or the type of intervention that the program will employ. The intervention should logically correlate with underlying theories about problem cause which the agency has considered as part of its problem statement. For example, in the case of the agency seeking to reduce family poverty through access of inner city unemployment to suburban jobs, transportation is one possible logical intervention. Another alternative is a job club that would teach people how to make "cold calls" or sell themselves more effectively to suburban employers. Still another option is a coordinated attack on discriminatory housing practices in the suburbs that prevent people from moving closer to available work. The choice of program concept depends on agency philosophy, disciplinary orientation, experience, funding options, and other variables.

The steps of defining a problem to be solved, the goals and intervention methods to be used, and a target population create the framework for budget preparation. In times of budgetary restraint, social inertia, and/or political turbulence, organizations sometimes retreat from the work of rethinking program foundations for the budget process. This undermines the most basic premise of budgeting in social organizations. Expenditures in not-for-profit organizations are investments in future productivity, cohesion, and well-being of a community. When budgeting becomes a tool for across-the-board cost reduction or enforcement of a no-growth policy independent of decisions about program it is as likely to waste resources as conserve them in the long run.

### B. Estimating Revenues and Expenditures to Support Program Plans

Once program goals and intervention methods are agreed upon, all other aspects of program operations can be fleshed out—facilities needed, personnel, supporting office and data processing systems, public relations strategies, and ideal dollar requirements. In the case of private agencies, other resources such as support for the board of directors, volunteer recruitment, and membership in allied organizational or professional groups should also be considered in the budget. The mission and values of the agency should be reviewed and reaffirmed as a backdrop to all deliberations, guiding choices between various budget alternatives.

*The Staffing Plan.* Agency budgets in the human services are labor intensive. Personnel costs usually range between 50 to 70 percent of total operations and should be considered carefully. A staffing plan must be created that shows the number of direct service employees, professional and paraprofessional, and support staff for each program by shift (where appropriate.) Staff should be shown as FTEs—of full-time-equivalents—in relation to the number of hours to be worked during the fiscal year, salary/wage rates, and fringe benefits. Staff functions should be reflected in an organization chart. This chart summarizes visually the main centers of responsibility in an agency and serves as another key element in clarifying where costs and revenues are produced in the course of an agency's work.

*Planning Units of Service to Be Produced.* In for-profit agencies, annual projects are made regarding the number of units to be produced, whether automobiles, cans of soup, premanufactured homes, or insurance contracts. In not-for-profit organizations, a similar estimate must be made, but there is more room for debate about how the product should be defined. Programs vary greatly in their concept of the production unit—e.g., number of clients served, hours of staff time, number of interviews or classroom sessions held, days of care, number of procedures completed. However these units are defined, they will have both cost and revenue implications. For example, an hour or therapy costs the agency $50.00 in staff salary, fringe benefits, insurance, and rental space; it may also generate $50.00 in insurance income.

*Estimating All Other Direct Operating Costs.* Once the staffing plan and units of service have been forecasted for every program, all other direct operating costs must be estimated. These usually include costs of space per square foot, utilities, communications (telephone, postage or postal meter), travel, vehicle repair, supplies, equipment, and printing/photocopying. Other examples of direct costs often incurred by organizations are assistance to clients, consultant fees, insurance, membership charges in professional associations, conference and staff development expenses, books, computer processing time, software and audit.

*Allocating Administrative Costs.* The allocation of administrative support costs across programs is a matter of continuing controversy, and no method is above criticism. Some expenses clearly can be charged to an individual program. For example, in a nursing home the activity director's salary would probably be charged to the rehabilitation division, while the secretary to the facility director would be shown as a cost in the administrative division. However, in one sense the director of any agency is related to all units of the organization, just as the photocopy machine is often utilized by most—if not all—programs. The most prevalent practice is to minimize those administrative costs that are most removed from direct program services and to spread the remaining overhead by an equal percentage across all programs.

*Deciding Among Alternatives for Line-Item Expenditures.* As revenues and expenditures for each program and support unit are being project by line item, it will inevitably become clear that many alternative budgetary strategies are possible. As a case in point, the amount of time and level of expertise for staff in a program can always be varied. The square footage allotted to each worker can be generous [perhaps]—if client confidentiality is an issue—or minimal. The amount of mailing and quality of the stationery, number of long distance calls allowed, size and frequency of luncheons provided to visitors, sophistication of computer equipment, and number of photocopies might all be powerfully affected by different assumptions about the number of community relations envisioned by individual agency programs. These alternatives should be documented, impacts on costs or revenues noted, and the most desirable choice selected in light of organizational objectives.

*The Revenue Budget.* Costs of operation are balanced by revenues. Revenues may be generated through user fees, interest, or income transfers—grants, gifts, public funds. Estimated revenues should be determined for each program and related to the number of service units.

*Budget Negotiation and Revision.* An approved budget represents policy decisions about diverse interests both internal and external to the organization. Elected officials, funding agencies boards of directors, contributors, clients, staff, management, public interest groups, unions, agency trade associations, and others often have a stake in the resolution of budgetary issues. The budget is thus an evolving document that will be modified many times during the planning and implementation phases. The most important factor in budget revision is the extent to which the core of direct client contacts is preserved.

*Need for Careful Planning.* Careful budget planning has become a necessity for any agency relying on federal or state revenues and third-party payments. The concept of "prospective reimbursement" has gained foothold in the health care field and is likely to spread to other human service sectors. Unlike previous years, in which agencies were reimbursed after service was provided, "prospective reimbursement" procedures require that payment in full be made at the point of diagnosis or intake. To remain viable, agencies will have to be much more proficient in projecting costs and selecting efficient alternatives for service delivery.

## C. Budget Implementation and Control

Once the budget has received final approval from the board of directors or the appropriate body of elected officials, the ensuing flow of expenditures and revenues must be closely monitored for variance from plan. The information and accounting systems which the agency has developed to record income and expenditures by program and support units is critical to control.

*Responsibilities for Budget Implementation.* Responsibilities for budget implementation are shared by the board of directors or local elected officials, agency administrator, business office, and program directors in an organization. The board approves the initial budget and the goals to be achieved; it subsequently must regularly review expenditures and revenues through its finance committee and submit reports to the board as a whole. These financial reports have traditionally been difficult for volunteers to interpret. However, elected officials and board members have public trusteeship for funds and are obligated to ask questions, no matter how elementary. Actually, sometimes the most elementary questions are the most discerning ones. Although specific tasks may be delegated to an agency executive, elected officials and board members have ultimate responsibility for ensuring that there are sufficient revenues to meet the financial needs of the organizations over which they hold oversight.

*Budget Variation and Correction.* Two of the most important elements of budget implementation are revision and future cost estimation. It is one thing to plan expenditures; actual experience may be another matter. These "variances" by line item, program, or division can strike in several places such as the rate at which funds are expended, unplanned fluctuations in costs or reimbursements, and changes in the nature of demands presented by the target population.

Corrections must be made as rapidly as possible when variances emerge. To a certain extent, funds can be transferred between budget categories or even between units in an organization. However, when these transfers exceed ten percent of plan, it is reasonable to assume that the ability of a program to meet its goals may be adversely affected. For this reason funding organizations often place a cap on the amount of allowable variance within any budget category and require formal application for a budget exception when proposed expenditures exceed that level.

*Forecasting Costs.* As agencies gain experience in budgeting, they can begin to anticipate future costs more accurately by using cost accounting methods. Cost accounting reveals how financial resources are used in relation to stated program purposes. Common in large, for-profit firms, cost accounting techniques often use complicated procedures for tracking costs for each unit of production. "Cost centers" are established, usually organized around departments, divisions, or other functional units of the firm. Data are collected daily on productivity, revenues, cash flow, payables, and staffing. Financial officers then prepare monthly cost reports, allowing management to make crucial comparisons between types of service, types of customers, and average costs. For example, out-patient clinic-based therapy might be compared with in-home counseling by hours of staff time required and/or square feet of office space required. Average salary and wage rates for all persons involved in delivering service for each type of program can be computed or limited to estimated costs of highly paid professionals.

Relatively few not-for-profits are large or sophisticated enough to afford a full-blown cost account system. Nonetheless, analysis of costs can still be carried out during budget implementation in a way that promotes good management and reduces variance from plan.

## IV. BASIC ELEMENTS OF ALL BUDGETS

*The Role of Accounting Systems.* All modern budgets in not-for-profit organizations are controlled through generally accepted accounting principles. These principles prescribe what information should be collected and how revenues and expenditures should be recorded as an agency carries out its business. Bookkeeping is the actual writing down of financial transactions as they take place, in keeping with the accounting method selected by an organization. Accounting systems generate periodic financial reports which show the financial status of an agency at a given point in the fiscal cycle. Accounting systems are essential for monitoring the amount and rate of expenditures in relation to revenues. Sophisticated systems can be used to estimate and track costs of operation so that appropriate charges can be made to funders or clients.

*The Chart of Accounts.* Accounting systems use code numbers to classify all financial activities. For examples, each digit of an accounting code structure for expenditures of an agency might typically identify the fund account to be charged, the department or program involved, and activity or commodity purchased. The United Way of America has a code structure that has been widely used by private organizations. Federal, state and local governments have statutorily defined codes. A private organization is free to create any classification scheme it chooses, as long as there is sufficient detail for tracking and oversight of financial status. The accounting code numbers are organized in sequence by revenue and expenditure accounts on a document called a "chart of accounts." Figure 38.2 gives a hypothetical example of the general form for a chart of accounts in a not-for-profit agency that uses a line-item budget. (For more discussion of line-item and functional budgets, see below.)

The chart of accounts is a creative document. For example, in this example the agency is tracking revenues from the Coke machine. Is this a trivial subcategory? It could easily be eliminated or combined with cafeteria income. However, the agency administrator has decided that revenue potential from the Coke machine is large enough to bear watching. In fact, the agency and its board can now play with the idea of adding more vending machines—or taking them out altogether.

Information is always costly to acquire, process, and report. The choice of whether to include a new line item or add subcategories depends on the overall value of the

FIGURE 38.2
Coordinated Services of Adams County Chart of Accounts

*Revenue Classification*

Government Contracts
- 110 Department of Social Services—Juvenile Division
- 120 Department of Mental Health
- 130 Department of Corrections
- 140 Other

Private Gifts and Grants
- 210 Individual Gifts—Annual Direct Mail
- 220 United Way of Adams County
- 230 Unrestricted Foundation Grants
- 240 Restricted Foundation Grants
- 250 Endowments

Client Fees
- 310 Fees for Service to Individuals—Private Pay
- 320 Fees for Service to Individuals—Insurance
- 330 Fees for Service to Families—Private Pay
- 340 Fees for Consultation to Other Organizations
- 350 Fees for Public Appearances

Services to Employees
- 410 Cafeteria
- 420 Coke Machine

Special Events
- 510 Annual Hullabalo Party
- 520 Annual Mudbath Contest
- 530 Garage Sales and Cookie/Cake Sales
- 540 Other

*Expenditure Classification*

Personnel
- 110 Full-Time Employees, Permanent
- 120 Part-Time Employees, Permanent
- 130 Contractual Employees, Full-Time
- 140 Contractual Employees, Part-Time
- 150 Overtime
- 160 Bonuses

Fringe Benefits
- 210 Pensions
- 220 Health/Hospital Benefits
- 230 Dental Care
- 240 Day Care
- 250 Educational Leave
- 260 FICA
- 270 Workmen's Compensation
- 280 Unemployment Compensation

Communications
- 310 Telephone
- 320 Facsimile Transmission, Telegram
- 330 Stamps, Postal Meter, Express Mail
- 340 Printing and Distribution Services
- 350 Photocopying
- 360 Newsletter, Brochures, and Annual Report

Travel and Transportation
- 410 Local Travel—Staff
- 420 Local Travel—Client Transportation
- 430 Out-of-Town Travel—Staff
- 440 Out-of-Town Travel—Client Transportation
- 450 Services to Agency Vans
- 460 Vehicle Purchase

Occupancy
- 510 Utilities: Gas, Electric, Water, Oil
- 520 Building Maintenance
- 530 Building Repair

financial data in monitoring income and outgo. But most important, the chart of accounts should serve as a mirror image of an agency's self concept—its definition of program groups, relevant functions, critical services. In effect, if properly conceptualized, the chart of account carries agency mission and roles into the realm of budget and finance. It is the basic building block for budgeting.

*Direct and Indirect Costs.* Whether shown in the accounting code structure or not, all agencies have direct and indirect sources of cost in the provision of service. Direct costs are those resources such as labor, floor space, equipment, or supplies that are used up in the process of giving assistance to agency clients. Indirect costs are those goods and services, tangible or intangible, that enable the agency to carry out program activities. For example, the grass must be mowed, auditors paid, a positive agency image maintained, staff development plan implemented to build future capacity, and effective board recruited. None of these actions is immediately connected to direct services such as teaching, counseling, coaching, consulting, inspecting, or other common agency program activities involving clients. However, if the grass and weeds cover building steps or poor agency relations leave the community with a sordid impression of client services, few clients may appear and donors may fade away.

## V. BUDGET FORMATTING AND REPORTING

### A. Line-Item Budgets

*Line-Item Budgeting to Emphasize Cost Control.* The way in which expenditures and revenues are shown in a budget profoundly affects the kinds of decisions that managers, policy makers, funders, and other concerned groups are likely to make. Public budgeting began in this country during the Progressive Movement at the turn of the century in New York City. The purpose was to build public trust in the ability of officials to control public expenditures in a responsible way. Gradually, private agencies imitated public practice. Line-item budget formats were standard for both public and private sectors. The primary orientation was cost control and reduction of expenditures—still a popular theme.

*Previous Expenditures As Basis for Traditional Line-Item Budgets.* Traditional line-item budgeting has always focused attention on the history of agency expenditures as a basis for making current decisions. The amount to be spent for salaries or other commodities used by the organization is reviewed against such factors as inflation and union demands. Increases or decreases are then calculated from the baseline set by the previous year's experience. Managers, funders, and policy makers are thus preoccupied with the total amount of revenue or expenditure necessary to maintain agency operations.

*Object Categories in Line-Item Budgets.* The line-item budget is constructed around objects or classes of items, with subcategories that vary among organizations, depending on the general character of the work performed. Figure 38.3 shows an abbreviated line-item budget for one hypothetical organization.

*Importance of Alternative Budget Formats Other Than Line-Item Budgets.* Since World War II, the potential of the budgeting process for contributing to policy and human service investment decisions has

FIGURE 38.3
Community Coordination Services, Inc.
Line-Item Budget
October 1, 1990–September 30, 1991

| | |
|---|---|
| Personnel | |
| 1. Executive Director, 1 FTE $30,000, 12 months | $30,000 |
| 2. Secretary, 1 FTE 14,500, 12 months | 14,500 |
| 3. Program Coordinator, 1 FTE $24,000, 12 months | 24,000 |
| Fringe Benefits | |
| 25% of total salaries | 17,125 |
| Occupancy | |
| Space rental, 3500 sq. ft. | 15,000 |
| Utilities | 7,500 |
| Travel 3000 miles @ .24/mile; | 720 |
| Two air fares @ $500.00 each | 1,000 |
| Equipment | |
| Major equipment purchase | 4,000 |
| Equipment repair | 1,000 |
| Equipment rental | 800 |
| Supplies | |
| Office | 1,200 |
| Communications | |
| Photocopying | 3,500 |
| Postal meter | 800 |
| Telephone | 4,500 |
| Newsletter, annual report | 5,000 |
| Other Overhead | |
| Consultants | 4,000 |
| Insurance | 6,000 |
| Audit | 2,000 |
| TOTAL: | $142,645 |

been more widely recognized. In particular, the way in which budget information is presented—the budget format—seems to influence how choices are made about allocation of funds. Four alternative approaches to budget formatting have received considerable attention, although none has achieved universal acceptance: zero-based budgeting (ZBB), performance-based budgeting (PerB), the planning/programming/budgeting system (PPBS), and program or functional budgeting (ProB). These formats are important, because they all reveal much more about productivity, performance, and cost control in relation to organizational purposes. They direct attention to the question of whether the best results for each major area of activity are being obtained for the level of investment made—and whether other options might yield better outcomes in light of state organizational goals.

*Performance-Based Budgeting.* Performance-based budgeting (PerB) constituted the first major break with traditional line-item budgeting. Proposed by a governmental commission under President Truman in 1949, this format was advocated as a way of clarifying the actual activities and functions supported by the federal budget. Performance-based budgeting uses measurable work units such as home visits or licensing inspectors to establish unit costs for each area of activity. For example, a child welfare protective services program might cost $2,000,000 per year to operate, with 20,000 visits to answer abuse and neglect complaints, or a unit cost of $100.00 per visit. In budget format, the presentation might be as shown in Figure 38.4.

In line-item budgets, managers and board members would be preoccupied with the total budget or with costs of commodities. In the performance-based perspective, interest shifts to output and cost. Unit costs can be compared between programs, across years, or within programs. At the present time, although the utility of unit cost comparisons is acknowledged, applications are limited because of the complex accounting support necessary. Moreover, work loads or work units must be measurable, which is not always the case in human service interventions.

*Lowest Unit Costs Not Necessarily the Objective.* Note that in Figure 38.4, it is pos-

FIGURE 38.4
Community Coordination Services, Inc.
Performance-Based Budget
October 1, 1990–September 30, 1991

| *Cost Center* | *Cost* | *Output* | *Unit Cost* |
|---|---|---|---|
| **Protective Services** | | | |
| Telephone screening | $200,000 | 40,000 calls | $ 5.00 |
| Home Investigations | 400,000 | 20,000 visits | 20.00 |
| Referrals | 100,000 | 5,000 calls | 20.00 |
| Status reporting | 300,000 | 40,000 records | 7.50 |
| **Family Treatment** | | | |
| Diagnostic assessments | 300,000 | 8,000 profiles | 37.50 |
| In-home counseling | 500,000 | 16,000 visits | 31.25 |
| Group treatment-clinic | 300,000 | 500 sessions | 600.00 |

sible to compare costs across programs. For example, home investigations under the Protective Services Program can be examined against in-home counseling for the Family Treatment Program. This is a distinct advantage of performance-based formats. Factors in service production that cause this differential can be looked at more closely for the current fiscal year or across years. It should be emphasized that driving for low unit costs is not necessarily the budget objective, however. The quality of services must never be disregarded, and excellence sometimes carries a higher price tag in terms of administration or service intensity.

*Using Budget Formats to Highlight "Opportunity Costs."* While performance-based formats highlight the relative cost of things to be done (performance), zero-based budgets, program/planning/budgeting systems, and program or functional budgets are directed toward an even more critical issue. If all funds are spent on Program A, they cannot be allocated to Program B. In theory, each extra dollar spent on Program A should bring about more benefit than if the dollar were used for any other purpose, including Program B. This is the "opportunity cost" of investment decisions. Budget formats such as ZBB and PPBS can dramatize the costs and benefits of alternative programs in relations to desired goals.

*Zero-Based and Program/Planning/Budget System Formats.* Zero-based budget formats require that once the budget has been set at 100 percent of available revenues, all expenditures should be rebudgeted at 80 percent, 90 percent, 110 percent, and 120 percent of the base amount. This method serves to highlight the value of each additional dollar added or subtracted to the budget base and gives a clearer picture of program priorities at successive funding levels. Through "service decision packages," zero-based budgets also demand that each program be evaluated by its rate of return on investment compared to other proposed programs. The PPBS format also emphasizes comparison of costs and alternatives in relation to goals. Milestones and performance criteria must be set for programs, with budget reporting by programs or cost centers and cost/benefit analysis performed across centers.

*Program or Functional Budget Formats.* Perhaps the most extensively used variant of PPBS is program budgeting. Program budgeting formats require that agency expenses and revenues be separated by responsibility center or program. The definition of "programs" unfortunately remains murky, since the term is often applied in an honorific way or to increase the visibility of a service activity. In theory, programs involve more than activities or services. They have a distinct target population and intervention technology and are linked to some concept of problem and problem causation. Programs prevent problem conditions from worsening or help clients to achieve positive changes.

In program budgeting, the functions necessary to achieve program goals become cost centers. In *Budgeting for Not-for-Profit Organizations*, Robert Vinter and Rhea Kish (1984) nicely capture the idea behind cost centers:

> Because every function represents a collection of costs, each is called a cost center. CCs represent clusters of distinguishable activities that accrue costs, to which expenditures can be assigned and for which ratios of resources to activities can be calculated and compared.[1]

Within each cost center, activities are budgeting by line item. Figure 38.5 gives an example for a hypothetical agency.

Program budgeting is superior to line-item budgeting alone, because it permits administrators and others to separate the relative contribution of each program to total agency costs. Is a program "too costly?" In Figure 38.5 above, should the Family Treatment Program be radically reduced? The answer depends in part on the mission of the agency, but it also should be evaluated in terms of consequences for families identified in the agency's other program—Child Protective Services. Perhaps increased costs of referral would outweigh benefits of cutting back on the agency's own staff of therapists. It is also useful to contrast the information obtained from a performance budget (Figure 38.4).

*The Future of Alternative Budget Formats.* Experience in the public and private sector over the second half of the 20th century discloses a mixed pattern in adoption of goal-oriented budget formats like zero-based and program budgeting. Some organizations have moved slowly toward more creative and complex budget formats, especially in the health care industry. However, the majority of not-for-profits and public agencies are still struggling with the break from traditional line-item formats. In order to make this transition, agencies will have to master techniques for coordination and control of everyday budget matters. This is still a formidable challenge in a period of massive deindustrialization, governmental budget crunches, and unpredictable policy shifts at the state, national, and international level. Goal-oriented formats thus remain largely a future vision, still to be attained.

## VI. BUDGET ISSUES IN THE 1990s

*Decremental Budgeting.* The normative experience in the not-for-profit sector until the mid-1970s was growth and revenue expansion. With the maturation of the social security system, acceleration of defense outlays, reduction in national productivity, and other trends, the competition for a shrinking economic pie has intensified. Social services have suffered proportionately larger reductions in rate of growth than any other health and human service sector, but virtually all have been affected.

Retrenchment, or permanent organizational restructuring due to revenue reduc-

---

[1]Robert D. Vinter and Rhea Kish, *Budgeting for Not-for-Profit Organizations* (New York: The Free Press, 1984).

FIGURE 38.5
Community Coordination Services, Inc.
Program Budget
October 1, 1990–September 30, 1991

***Program: Child Protective Services***

| | |
|---|---|
| **Personnel** (salaries and wages) | |
| Program Coordinator, 1 FTE | |
| 12 months @ $35,000 | $ 35,000 |
| Intake/screening workers, 2 FTE | |
| 12 months @ $18,000 | 36,000 |
| Caseworkers, 2 FTE | |
| 12 months @ $28,000 | 56,000 |
| Secretarial assistance, 2 FTE | |
| 12 months @ $14,000 | 28,000 |
| **Subtotal Personnel** | 155,000 |
| **Fringe Benefits** | |
| @ 25% of total salary and wages | $38,750 |
| **Occupancy** | |
| 200 sq. ft/worker = | |
| 1400 sq. ft. @ $8.00 sq. ft. | 11,200 |
| **Travel** | |
| 5000 miles @ .24/mi. | |
| **Supplies** | |
| Standard office | 1,500 |
| **Equipment** | |
| Copier | 5,000 |
| Beepers | 800 |
| Office | 4,000 |
| Computer rental and repair | 6,500 |
| **Other** | |
| Telephones | 6,000 |
| Consultants | 8,000 |
| Liability insurance | 2,000 |
| Administration | 2,000 |
| Total Child Protective Services Program | $240,750 |

***Program: Family Treatment***

| | |
|---|---|
| **Personnel** (salaries and wages) | |
| Program Coordinator, 1 FTE | |
| 12 months @ $45,000 | $ 45,000 |
| Psychologist, 1 FTE | |
| 12 months @ $45,000 | 45,000 |
| Family therapists, 4 FTE | |
| 12 months @ $45,000 | 180,000 |
| Group workers, 3 FTE | |
| 12 months @ $33,000 | 99,000 |
| Secretarial assistance, 2 FTE | |
| 12 months @ $14,000 | 28,000 |
| **Subtotal personnel** | $397,000 |
| **Fringe Benefits** | |
| @ 25% of total wages and salaries | 99,250 |
| **Occupancy** | |
| 300 sq. ft. per worker = | |
| 3,300 sq. ft. @ $8.00/sq. ft. | 26,400 |
| **Travel** | |
| 8000 mi @ .25/mile | 2,000 |
| **Supplies** | |
| Standard office | 1,200 |
| **Equipment** | |
| Video equipment | 1,200 |
| Copier | 3,000 |
| Computers—purchase and repair | 4,000 |
| **Other Direct Costs** | |
| Telephone, FAX | 6,000 |
| Total, Family Treatment Program | $540,050 |

tion, has reappeared as a phenomenon in many local organizations. A planned response to sustained budgetary contraction—"decremental budgeting"—can allow organizations under financial siege to emerge with core values preserved and a sense of continued accomplishment.

The main principles in managing retrenchment are (1) creating an early warning system for detection of adverse trends; (2) seizing the initiative in reacting to impending changes; and (3) implementing a fiscal strategy designed to maintain organizational robustness. Positive leadership under conditions of reduced resources is extremely difficult. The budget process under these circumstances inevitably produces unpleasant outcomes for those who lose priority. Continuous public interpretation of the basis for choice is essential in order to build a basis for cooperation. Opportunity costs must be clearly defined: If funds are not invested in preventive health care, for example, what will be the alternative costs for the community? The goals of program expenditures must be reaffirmed repeatedly so that those who will gain from the process can be mobilized as a coalition to support proposed actions. Retrenchment can bring revitalization or a sense of impoverishment, depending upon the manner in which program planning and budgeting is approached. Organizations that deny or try to cover up the fact of resource decline inevitably face lowered morale, deterioration in the quality of their services, increased long-run expenditures, and ultimately a cessation of capacity for planning or innovation.

Successful budgeting during retrenchment must be predicated on a clear and reasonable, accurate diagnosis of the reasons for decline in resources and an honest estimate of whether the slump is likely to be permanent. Rather than deferring expenditures on maintenance or salary, the impact of cutbacks can be softened by a search for means to raise productivity. The ability of the organization to change and experiment should be protected by allowance for at least some budgetary slack no matter how pressing the circumstances.

Budget preparation under conditions of political turbulence or economic upheaval should permit policymakers and community to compare costs and impacts of reductions at several funding levels. Beginning with the cost of a model program, the impact of reductions can be shown weighted against program increases to enhance efficiency, or simply the current budget base can reflect estimates for inflation. For each decrement of 5 percent below the current budget base, suggested changes in service should be proposed, with the impacts on clients, community at large, and financial status of the organization summarized. This procedure closely resembles an ABB format. The crucial governing principle is avoidance of across-the-board cuts either within programs or between units of an organization. Targeting of reductions based on priorities and full consideration of consequences for clients, agency, and community are the key.

*Automation.* The expansion of computer-based financial information and accounting systems in not-for-profit organizations of all sizes has accelerated with the introduction of personal computers. Expanded memory and storage capability, improved spreadsheet, graphics, and printing software, and methods for networking standalone computer systems have revolutionized both speed and accuracy of output. Technology has been modified continuously to increase acceptability and usefulness to individuals in agencies at all levels of technical skill.

There are now fresh opportunities to maintain, sort, and retrieve financial information in ways that permit improved critical analysis. The challenge now is not so much acquisition and operation of these systems as thoughtful determination of information objectives in a financial system and the relationship to client databases. Multi-year comparison are possible, which previously would have absorbed prohibitive amounts of time in preparation. The potential for evolution toward goal-oriented budget formats is greater than at any other time in this century. Whether this promise is fulfilled depends in part on whether agencies and communities are in fact prepared to engage in real policy debates about the alternative uses of resources for health and human welfare.

39.

**John E. Tropman and Elmer J. Tropman**

# INDEX OF DISSIMILARITY AND THE PROFESSIONAL UNIT METHOD OF ANALYSIS

## INTRODUCTION

Community organizers, planners, administrators, and policy professionals often seek easy ways to understand themselves and the processes in which they are engaged—and to find ways to communicate these processes to others. Two techniques—the Index of Dissimilarity (ID) and the Professional Unit Method of Analysis (PUMA)—can help accomplish these goals.

ID is a method for making ideal/real comparisons: What does the organizer want to do compared with what the agency want to do? What does the strategic plan propose compared with what is actually being done on a day-to-day basis?

PUMA allows a quick and easy conversion of organizational human resources (employees doing work) into financial resources (dollars) and back again. This method is excellent in the office, and works well with boards when applying for grants and contracts. For best results, ID and PUMA can be used together.

## THE INDEX OF DISSIMILARITY

The Index of Dissimilarity is useful in making ideal–actual assessments. It provides a numerical value that differentiates the organizer's or agency's actual activities from desires activities. ID is a relatively quick, yet sophisticated, measure that provides lots of information for minimum effort. It works in the following way:

Construct a small, simple questionnaire. It is simply a list of the major organizational activities or programs, plus some empty lines.

| Program Area | Should Be [A] | Actually Is [B] |
|---|---|---|
| Goal/Activity 1 | ____ | ____ |
| Goal/Activity 2 | ____ | ____ |
| Goal/Activity 3 | ____ | ____ |
| Goal/Activity 4 | ____ | ____ |
| Innovation | 15% | ____ |
| Goal/Activity *i* *(individual item)* | ____ | ____ |
| *Total* | *100%* | *100%* |

Organizers are asked to allocate the percentage of organizational time they feel *should* go to each activity, across from the activity (see above). In order for the index to work, calculations must not exceed 100%! Since workers may wish to propose allocating time to activities that are not currently undertaken for the organization, they can do so by filling in the name of the activity in the Goal/Activity *i* line (in the above chart). Note that we have added an item for "innovation"—doing new things, and undertaking new tasks. We have set

The late Elmer J. Tropman was director of the Forbes Fund of the Pittsburgh Foundation, Pittsburgh, PA.

this proportion at 15% in terms of ideal. "Real" is often 0%!

In the next column, the worker places the percentage of time that he or she feels *is* spent in the same activities. (In most instances, there are important ideal/real differences.) Then do up the worksheet.

Column C is the subtraction of column B from column A. Then the percentage differences in column C are summed, disregarding sign, and divided by two. The resulting number is called the Index of Dissimilarity, and it shows how different the organization's current activity is from that which it wants to be doing. This kind of information is excellent material that the worker can then use to refocus, redirect, and reinspirit himself or herself or the organization.

The important thing about the use of percentage allocations is that they clarify the choice process. Often, workers and agencies do not really know where their energies are going, but they do know that they are rushed in some areas, and things are not being done in others. By forcing the choice through the use of the 100% mechanism, differences in approach and emphasis are pinpointed.

Executives, for example, may wish to review with the staff whether their sense of agency effort—measured in worker weeks divided by program—makes sense in term of the priorities and values of the agency. It is common in human service agencies to experience organizational "drift" in which agency allocation, personnel and resources, moves slowly away from desired goals and objectives to other ones.

A variety of informal and historical mechanisms cause this process to occur, and it is frequently unnoticed. Actually, it

Index of Dissimilarity Worksheet

| | (A) "Should" % | (B) Actual % | (C) A-B% (ignore sign) |
|---|---|---|---|
| 1. Goal 1 | ___ | ___ | ___ |
| 2. Goal 2 | ___ | ___ | ___ |
| 3. Goal 3 | ___ | ___ | ___ |
| 4. Goal 4 | ___ | ___ | ___ |
| 5. Innovation | 15% | ___ | ___ |
| 6. Individual Items | ___ | ___ | ___ |
| 7. Individual Items | ___ | ___ | ___ |
| | 100% | 100% | $\Sigma\frac{\|A-B\|}{2}$ |

Index of Dissimilarity $\Sigma\left(\frac{|A-B|}{Z}\right)$

is the rule rather than the exception that this process occurs. A strategic assessment would note such a reallocation, at which time corrective or redirective activities could begin. It may also be the case that the agency is doing exactly what it is supposed to be doing in terms of its goals and objectives. But upon review, it turns out that the agency's goals and objectives should change. There again, the Professional Unit System will allow the overall allocation of effort to be seen more clearly, both in terms of personnel on the one hand, and in terms of dollars on the other.

One point should be stressed. The fact that there are differences does not make next steps immediately clear. Sometimes there needs to be a revision of activities to bring them more in line with goals. Sometimes more realistic goals need to be established. But the fact that one is analyzing the process will make the difference.

The Index of Dissimilarity is extremely flexible. Community organizers may want to use it to look at themselves, as well as their own allocation of time during the day or week in relationship to their own career and professional development interests.[1] Agency executives may wish to use it with staff, comparing the executives' assignment of workload and the staff's own percentage allocations. The fact that there are differences only points out what has already been known. What the index begins to show is the amount and scope of these differences and their location. As the beginning of a strategic process, either at the board level or within the organization, this technique provides a good start. Executives may also want to use it with community groups, or with the board of directors. The point is that there can be a broad range of applications. These uses are strengthened when they are combined, at the organizational level, with the Professional Unit Method of Analysis (PUMA).

## PROFESSIONAL UNIT METHOD OF ANALYSIS: PUMA

One key question posed by workers and agency directors relates to establishing a common, easy-to-understand basis for assessing exactly the extent of resources, in terms of personnel/money, available to do all organizational tasks. With that as a base, it is possible to begin looking at how those resources are allocated.

The first step is developing a professional unit that is simple enough to allow workers and directors to have an intuitive understanding of the process. However, this "unit" must be complete enough to be useful. Such a system is the Professional Unit Method of Analysis. When developed, it will work well for the worker, agency, board, and strategic planning effort. It will also work well for the executive, in terms of developing material and assignments with staff. Here's how to do it:

1. The worker (or executive director, or perhaps a small committee staff) calculates the number of direct service workers available to the agency. In this case, consider only individuals who perform the actual work of the agency, not those who do administration, supervision, janitorial work, secretarial work, and so on. In a community organization agency, it would be the number of organizers (FTE, or Full Time Equivalent workers); in a clinical agency, it would be the number of clinicians, up to

[1] One important application involves looking at four "life sectors" (time on self, time on job, time on family, time on civic involvement) with the ID. Ideal/real comparisons often reveal lots of time spent on the job, and little time on self and family and civic activities.

and including fractional amounts. In a planning agency, it would be the number of junior and senior planners, and so on. These are called direct service workers; the other workers are "support staff" for purposes here. Even the executive, unless she or he happens to see a client or spend some time actually reviewing some particular planning reports or policy documents, would be considered support staff. Let's assume it is known for purposes of these examples that an agency has ten direct service staff.

2. The next step is to calculate the number of weeks of work that are available to the direct service staff to do the agency work. In calculations that we have done in a number of trials, the approximate number turns out to be around 45 or 46 weeks out of the total 52 in a year. (Individuals have time off for vacation, sick leave, and things of that kind). But for purposes of ease of multiplication in this example, let us assume that the agency executive and board have 50 weeks of staff time per worker available for assignment to whatever tasks the agency chooses to undertake. This number is very important; it represents the total resource of the agency to actually do agency tasks, whether these tasks are community organization, clinical work, planning, or whatever.

3. The third step is to multiply the total number of workers by the total number of weeks available for work. In the example selected, there are a total of 500 worker weeks available for all agency programs and activities.

4. Divide the number of worker weeks into the total budget of the agency. This calculation gives the total dollar amount per worker week. In the example selected, let us further assume that the agency's budget is $500,000. What this would mean is that the total amount of money per worker week is equal to $1,000.

What the executive can now begin to do with this material is to engage in a process of analysis. PUMA fuses dollars and people into a single, easily comprehensible unit. Much of our planning and decision making is often done in terms of money (or disembodies monetary units), which removes it from the reality of human service organization activity. Therefore, the PUMA allows a crisper, cleaner approach to strategic thinking. After all, once organizational objectives have been determined, one has to begin to allocate staff and budget to them, along with ample support staff. PUMA provides the kind of overall broad picture and factual basis that allows organizations to look at both what they are doing and what they might be doing, and to try to see whether or not the actual activities correspond with the desired ones.

Once the number of PUMA units have been established, it is possible to translate them into the index of dissimilarity. In all cases, the total number of PUMA units equals 100%, and the resulting fractions can be used to look at organizational allocation overall (total number of PUMA units) or fractions of efforts with one's employees (her or his PUMA units).

## CONCLUSION

Community organization workers are also in need of tips and hints that will help make their job easier. Especially in the rough and tumble world of human service, the problem of strategic analysis of resources is often overlooked. These two techniques can be most helpful.

# Name Index

# Subject Index

TACTICS AND TECHNIQUES OF COMMUNITY INTERVENTION
Edited by John Beasley
Production supervision by Kim Vander Steen
Cover design by Lesiak/Crampton Design, Park Ridge, Illinois
Composition by Point West, Inc., Carol Stream, Illinois
Paper, Finch Opaque
Printed and bound by Edwards Brothers, Ann Arbor, Michigan